The Routledge Handbook of Critical Public Relations

T0382959

Critical theory has a long history, but a relatively recent intersection with public relations. This ground-breaking collection engages with commonalities and differences in the traditions, whilst encouraging plural perspectives in the contemporary public relations field.

Compiled by a high-profile and widely respected team of academics and bringing together other key scholars from this field and beyond, this unique international collection marks a major stage in the evolution of critical public relations. It will increasingly influence how critical theory informs public relations and communication.

The collection takes stock of the emergence of critical public relations alongside diverse theoretical traditions, critiques and actions, methodologies and future implications. This makes it an essential reference for public relations researchers, educators and students around a world that is becoming more critical in the face of growing inequality and environmental challenges. The volume is also of interest to scholars in advertising, branding, communication, consumer studies, cultural studies, marketing, media studies, political communication and sociology.

Jacquie L'Etang is Professor of Public Relations and Applied Communication at Queen Margaret University, Scotland.

David McKie is Professor of Management Communication at the University of Waikato, New Zealand.

Nancy Snow is Professor Emeritus in the College of Communications at California State University, Fullerton, USA.

Jordi Xifra is Professor of Public Relations Strategies and Tactics at Pompeu Fabra University, Spain.

Routledge Companions in Business, Management and Accounting

Routledge Companions in Business, Management and Accounting are prestige reference works providing an overview of a whole subject area or sub-discipline. These books survey the state of the discipline including emerging and cutting edge areas. Providing a comprehensive, up to date, definitive work of reference, *Routledge Companions* can be cited as an authoritative source on the subject.

A key aspect of these *Routledge Companions* is their international scope and relevance. Edited by an array of highly regarded scholars, these volumes also benefit from teams of contributors which reflect an international range of perspectives.

Individually, *Routledge Companions in Business, Management and Accounting* provide an impactful one-stop-shop resource for each theme covered. Collectively, they represent a comprehensive learning and research resource for researchers, postgraduate students and practitioners.

Published titles in this series include:

The Routledge Handbook of Critical Public Relations

Edited by Jacquie L'Etang, David McKie,
Nancy Snow and Jordi Xifra

LONDON AND NEW YORK

First published in paperback 2017
First published 2016
by Routledge
2 Park Square, Milton Park, Abingdon, Oxon OX14 4RN

And by Routledge
711 Third Avenue, New York, NY 10017

Routledge is an imprint of the Taylor & Francis Group, an informa business

British Library Cataloguing in Publication Data
A catalogue record for this book is available from the British Library

Library of Congress Cataloguing in Publication Data
  The Routledge handbook of critical public relations / edited by
Jacquie L'Etang, David McKie, Nancy Snow and Jordi Xifra.
      pages   cm. – (Routledge companions in business, management
and accounting)
Includes bibliographical references and index.
 1. Public relations–Handbooks, manuals, etc.   I. L'Etang, Jacquie.
 HM1221.R68 2015
 659.2–dc23
 2015003902

ISBN: 978-0-415-72733-4 (hbk)
ISBN: 978-1-138-21207-7 (pbk)
ISBN: 978-1-315-85249-2 (ebk)

Typeset in Bembo
by Out of House Publishing

Contents

Contents

Contents

Illustrations

Figures

Table

Contributors

Clea D. Bourne, PhD, is a lecturer and convenor of the MA in Promotional Media (Public Relations, Advertising & Marketing) at Goldsmiths, University of London. Her teaching brings together an array of critical literatures examining public relations, advertising and marketing as separate fields. Prior to this, she spent more than 20 years as a practitioner in various roles spanning advertising, marketing and public relations work in Jamaica and the UK. Her research explores the part that communicators play in shaping power relations in the dominant global discourses of our time, including financialisation, globalisation and climate change. She is also interested in discourses connected with individual, professional and national identity. Clea completed her doctoral work in public relations on a Centenary Scholarship from Leeds Metropolitan University (now Leeds Beckett) in 2011. She has since published articles in the *Journal of Public Relations Research* (forthcoming), *Public Relations Inquiry* and *Culture & Organization* (with Lee Edwards), and has contributed chapters to several edited collections. Her forthcoming book, *Trust, Power and Public Relations in Financial Markets*, will be published by Routledge in 2015.

Erica Ciszek, PhD, is Assistant Professor of Integrated Strategic Communication at the University of Houston's Jack J. Valenti School of Communication. Her work, which focuses on activism, critical-cultural public relations theory and LGBTQ issues, appears in several journals, including *Public Relations Review*, the *Public Relations Journal* and the *Journal of Communication Inquiry*. She has a book chapter in the first book on LGBTQ issues in strategic communications, *Coming out of the Closet: Exploring LGBT Issues in Strategic Communication with Theory and Research*. Ciszek earned her PhD in media and society from the University of Oregon, where she was a Park Doctoral Fellow and outstanding graduating PhD student. She has an MS in Mass Communication and Applied Research from Boston University, and a BA in Sociology/English from Colby College. Ciszek has worked in strategic communication and market research, and has contributed to LGBTQ publications.

Simon Collister is a senior lecturer at the London College of Communication, University of the Arts London in the UK, where he teaches strategic communication, social media and critical approaches to public relations. He is currently completing doctoral research into strategic political communication and digital media at Royal Holloway, University of London's New Political Communication Unit. His current research interests include: strategic communication; big data; computational aspects of communication; algorithms; the mediation of power; twenty-first century organisational models; and the future of the public relations industry. Simon has recently authored/co-authored articles in leading journals, including *Ephemera: Theory & Politics in Organization* and the *International Journal of Communication*; as well as authored/

co-authored book chapters on public relations and big data in *Share This Too* (2013) and on social media and text-mining in *Innovations in Digital Research Methods* (2015). He is co-founder of the research hub, The Network for Public Relations and Society, and also a founder member of the UK Chartered Institute of Public Relation's (CIPR) Social Media Advisory Panel. Before academia Simon worked with some of the world's leading public relations consultancies, including We Are Social, Edelman and Weber Shandwick.

Patricia A. Curtin, PhD, is Professor and SOJC Endowed Chair in Public Relations at the University of Oregon, Eugene. Her 23 years of professional communication experience include public relations work for small start-ups and agencies, with a specialty in employee relations. She received her MA (1991) and PhD (1996) from The University of Georgia and taught for ten years at the University of North Carolina at Chapel Hill, where she directed graduate programmes within the School of Journalism and Mass Communication. She joined the faculty of the University of Oregon in 2006, serving as public relations sequence coordinator for almost eight years. Her research encompasses agenda-building, international public relations and the development of critical/postmodern approaches to public relations theory, particularly the cultural-economic model. She is the author of approximately 75 refereed research studies and has won research awards from the Association for Education in Journalism and Mass Communication, the International Communication Association and the International Public Relations Conference. Within AEJMC, she has served as head of the public relations division, as chair of the elected Standing Committee on Research and as a member of the elected Standing Committee on Publications.

Kristin Demetrious, PhD, is an Associate Professor at Deakin University in Australia. Her research in public relations focuses on its power relations within different social, political and historical contexts, most particularly in relation to activism, civil society and gender. In 2013 she published her first monograph, *Public Relations, Activism and Social Change: Speaking Up*, which was awarded the 2014 PRIDE Book Award for Outstanding Innovation, Development, and Educational Achievement in Public Relations by the National Communication Association, USA. An edited collection with co-author Christine Daymon, entitled *Gender and Public Relations: Critical Perspectives on Voice, Image and Identity*, received the 2013 PRIDE Book Award in the same category.

Alina Dolea, PhD, is Associate Lecturer within the Department of Communication Sciences, Faculty of Letters, at the University of Bucharest. She received her PhD in Communication Sciences at the National School of Political Studies and Public Administration (Bucharest, Romania). Her research themes include international communication and promotion of countries (public relations, nation branding and public diplomacy), political and public communication, the construction of public issues and the role of media. She co-authored "Branding Romania: Cum (ne) promovam imaginea de tara / How (we) promote our country image" and published articles in the *Romanian Journal of Communication and Public Relations* and *Public Relations Review*. Her latest research on a social constructivist and interdisciplinary approach to country promotion was ranked second in the competition for "Best Faculty Papers in Public Relations" within the PR Division at the 64th Annual Conference of the International Communication Association (Seattle, May 2014). Dr Dolea is author of *Twenty Years of (Re) Branding Post-Communist Romania: Actors, Discourses, Perspectives 1990–2010* (Institutul European Publishing House, 2015). That draws a longitudinal analysis on the emergence of country promotion as a public issue in post-communist Romania, establishing a historicity of promotional practices, communication campaigns and public debates over a period of 20 years. She is a member of the Editorial Board of Sage's *Public Relations Inquiry*.

Mohan J. Dutta, PhD, is Provost Chair Professor and Head of the Department of Communications and New Media at the National University of Singapore (NUS) and Courtesy Professor of Communication at Purdue University. At NUS, he is the Founding Director of the Center for Culture-Centered Approach to Research and Evaluation (CARE), directing research on culturally centered, community-based projects of social change. He teaches and conducts research in international health communication, critical cultural theory, poverty in healthcare, health activism in globalisation politics, indigenous cosmologies of health, subaltern studies and dialogue, and public policy and social change. Currently, he serves as editor of the "Critical Cultural Studies in Global Health Communication Book Series" with Left Coast Press and sits on the editorial board of seven journals.

Lee Edwards, PhD, is Associate Professor in Communication and PR at the University of Leeds. She teaches and researches PR from a socio-cultural perspective. A critical scholar, her primary focus is on the operation of power through PR both within the occupational field and in wider society. As well as making theoretical contributions to the understanding of PR, she has published her empirical work on the exercise of power through PR as a cultural intermediary, and on diversity in PR. She is the author of *Power, Diversity and Public Relations* (Routledge, 2014); and *Understanding Copyright* (with Dr Bethany Klein and Dr Giles Moss, Sage, forthcoming). She is editor, with Dr Caroline Hodges, of *Public Relations, Society and Culture: Theoretical and Empirical Explorations* (Routledge, 2011). Dr Edwards is Secretary of the International Communication Association PR Division (2014–16) and won an ICA Communication Policy Division Top Paper award in 2013 (with co-authors Giles Moss, Bethany Klein, Fiona Philip and David Lee) for the paper "Justifying Copyright: Discourse, Legitimation and Critique". She is a regional editor for the *Journal of Communication*, and a co-editor of *PR Inquiry*. She is on the editorial board of the *Journal of Public Relations Research*, and is a reviewer for a wide range of journals including *Management Communication Quarterly*; *Consumption, Markets and Culture*; *Media, Culture and Society*; *Journal of Professions and Organisations* and *New Media and Society*.

Jesper Falkheimer, PhD, is Professor in Strategic Communication at Lund University, Sweden. For several years he has combined research with university management positions and has served as Rector for Campus Helsingborg at Lund University since 2011. His research interests are within the fields of strategic communication, public relations and media studies. Falkheimer is author and editor of 11 books and anthologies, and a number of international articles and chapters in *The Routledge Handbook of Strategic Communication* (2014), *The Handbook of Crisis Communication* (2010) and *Public Relations and Social Theory* (2009). Falkheimer is co-editor (together with Timothy Coombs, Mats Heide and Philip Young) of *Strategic Communication, Social Media and Democracy: The Challenge of the Digital Naturals* (Routledge, 2015). He is also an executive board member of the Swedish Public Relations Association, the public relations agency Gullers Group AB and the media cluster Media Evolution AB; a member of the advisory boards of European Communication Monitor (Bruxelles) and CCI International (New York); and Programme Director for the Communication Executive Programme at IFL, Stockholm School of Economics.

Kate Fitch, PhD, is a senior lecturer and Academic Chair at Murdoch University in Perth, Australia, where she has taught since 2001. She has published extensively on diverse public relations topics, including gender, culture, pedagogy, and its history in Australia and Southeast

Asia. Recent publications focus on the historical development of the Australian public relations industry; the role of tertiary education in the professionalisation of public relations; and the significance of gender for constitutions of public relations knowledge. Her current research investigates representations of female practitioners in Australia in the twentieth century. Kate is on the editorial boards of *Public Relations Review*, *Public Relations Inquiry* and *PRism*. She received a national teaching award in 2011 for her development of the public relations curriculum and its focus on work-integrated learning. She served on the Public Relations Institute of Australia's state council (2005–08) and national education committee (2008–11), and is now on the public relations expert advisory group for the Hunter Institute of Mental Health's Mindframe programme, which develops resources to promote socially responsible communication around suicide and mental health. Prior to joining the Murdoch University Kate worked in public relations roles in the arts, government and community sectors in the UK and Australia.

T. Kenn Gaither, PhD, is Associate Professor and Associate Dean of Communications at Elon University in North Carolina. His work, which focuses on international public relations theory and practice, appears in numerous journals, including the *Journal of Public Relations Research* and *Public Relations Review*. He has written or co-authored three books, including *International Public Relations: Negotiating Culture, Identity, and Power*. He is also series editor for the Cambria Press Communication Collection. During his nine years of professional public relations agency experience, he was a member of a public relations team that won a Hyundai MicroElectronics of America Excellence in Service Award. Gaither earned his PhD in Mass Communication from the University of North Carolina at Chapel Hill, where he was a Park Doctoral Fellow and outstanding graduating PhD student. He has an MFA in Literary Journalism and a BA in English Writing/Latin American Studies from the University of Pittsburgh. He is on leave from Elon to serve as President of the Institute for Shipboard Education, which runs the Semester at Sea programme. He has sailed on nine voyages in positions ranging from student to Executive Dean.

Robert L. Heath, PhD, is Professor Emeritus, University of Houston, recently edited the *Sage Handbook of Public Relations*, several other edited books and the second edition of the *Encyclopedia of Public Relations* (Sage). He has served as an area editor for, and contributed to, the *International Encyclopedia of Communication*. He recently published an edited *Master Work on Public Relations* for Routledge and an edited *Master Work on Strategic Communication* for Sage (with Anne Gregory). These master works are compendiums of previously published articles and chapters. He has contributed original chapters to numerous edited books and handbooks. He has written entries for various encyclopedias, including those mentioned above. Other encyclopedia contributions appear in the *Encyclopedia of Science and Technology Communication* (Sage), *Wiley Encyclopedia of Operations Research and Management Science* (John Wiley & Sons) and *21st Century Communication: A Reference Handbook* (Sage). He has published 20 books and more than 100 chapters and articles, and serves on the editorial and reviewer panels of several premier academic journals. He has received many honours from public relations professionals and academic associations and has lectured nationally and internationally on a wide array of topics.

Mats Heide, PhD, is Professor in Strategic Communication at Lund University. His research interests are within the fields of strategic communication and organisational communication, and he has especially focused on change communication and crisis communication. Heide is author and co-author of 12 books (in Swedish) and several articles and edited chapters in anthologies such as *The Routledge Handbook of Strategic Communication* (2014), the *Encyclopedia of Public Relations II* (2014), *The Handbook of Crisis Management* (2013) and *The Handbook of Crisis Communication* (2010). Heide is co-editor of *Strategic Communication, Social Media and Democracy: The Challenge of the Digital Naturals* (Routledge, 2015) together with Timothy Coombs, Jesper Falkheimer and Philip Young.

Manuel E. Hernández Toro is a senior lecturer at the University of Wolverhampton (UK), where he is the course leader of the MA in Public Relations and Corporate Communication. He holds an MSc in Public Relations from the University of Stirling and his research interest lies in examining the impact of processes and structure on collaborative configurations or regimes. Prior to joining the university in 2006, he worked as a journalist for Reuters. He also held posts in internal communication and marketing for organisations including Unilever and Brahma (now Anheuser-Busch InBev) in South America.

Øyvind Ihlen, PhD, is Professor at the Department of Media and Communication at the University of Oslo. He was previously Professor of Communication and Management at the Norwegian School of Management and at Hedmark University College. Ihlen has edited, written and co-written eight books, among them *Public Relations and Social Theory* (Routledge, 2009) and the *Handbook of Communication and Corporate Social Responsibility* (Wiley Blackwell, 2011). His award-winning research has appeared in numerous anthologies and in journals such as the *Journal of Public Relations Research*, *Public Relations Review*, the *Journal of Public Affairs*, the *International Journal of Strategic Communication*, the *Journal of Communication Management*, *Corporate Communications*, *Management Communication Quarterly*, the *International Journal of Organizational Analysis*, *Environmental Communication*, *Sustainable Development*, *Business Strategy and the Environment* and the *European Journal of Communication*. He is on the editorial board of nine journals and has reviewed for an additional 21 journals and publishing houses. Ihlen is President Elect of The European Public Relations Education and Research Association (EUPRERA) and has been Vice Chair of the Public Relations Division of the International Communication Association (ICA). His research focuses on strategic communication and journalism, using theories of rhetoric and sociology on issues such as the environment, immigration and corporate social responsibility.

Jane Johnston, PhD, is Associate Professor of Public Relations and Journalism at Bond University, Australia. Her research covers a diverse cross-section of these two fields. In 2000, with Clara Zawawi, she co-edited *Public Relations: Theory and Practice*, which is now in its fourth edition (the latest co-edited with Mark Sheehan in 2014). This was followed by *Media Relations: Issues and Strategies* (published in two editions). Johnston has published more than 50 journal articles, conference papers and book chapters – her research includes courts' communication practice, critical and narrative theory, and media diversity and change. Much of her research has been undertaken collaboratively with colleagues from public relations, journalism, criminology and the law. Her chapter in this book begins her ongoing interest in postcolonial theory and features an examination of recent government discourse about, and the counter-narratives surrounding, asylum seekers in Australia. Johnston is currently writing a book entitled *Public Relations and the Public Interest* (also for Routledge, forthcoming).

Priya Kurian is Professor of Political Science and Public Policy at the University of Waikato, New Zealand. Her research interests span the areas of environmental politics and policy, sustainability studies, science and technology studies, and development studies. She is the author of *Engendering the Environment: Gender in the World Bank's Environmental Policies*; co-editor of *International Organizations and Environmental Policy*, *On the Edges of Development: Cultural Interventions* and *Feminist Futures: Re-imagining Women, Culture, and Development*. Her interdisciplinary work has been published in major journals including *Sustainable Development*, *Public Understanding of Science*, *Public Relations Review*, *Citizenship Studies*, *Futures*, *Third World Quarterly* and *Journalism: Theory, Practice, and Criticism*. She was co-principal investigator (with Debashish Munshi) of a project on sustainable citizenship funded by a Marsden Grant of the Royal Society of New Zealand.

Ryszard Ławniczak, PhD, is Full Professor at Warsaw University of Technology. Until the end of 2012 he was Head of the Department of Economic Journalism and Public Relations at the University of Economics, Poznan (Poland). He has also served as Visiting Professor at the University of Melbourne (1991) and at the California State University, Fresno (1984, 1991). Additionally, Ławniczak has served as the economic advisor to the President of the Republic of Poland (1997–2005), and as a consultant to the Polish Premier (1994–97). In 2003 he was awarded the The Royal Norwegian Order of Merit by King Harald V of Norway. His research interest includes international public relations, foreign economic policies and comparative economics. He coined the concept of *transitional public relations* and promotes *the econo-centric approach in public relations*. Ławniczak published the first two Polish public relations books to be written in English: *Public Relations Contribution to Transition in Central and Eastern Europe: Research and Practice* (2001) and *Introducing Market Economy Institutions and Instruments: The Role of Public Relations in Transition Economies* (2005). A third book was published in 2011: *Challenges for Communication Management and Public Relations in International Mergers and Acquisitions*. In 2007 Lawniczak was listed among the 50 leading academic experts in the field of communication in Europe.

Shirley Leitch, PhD, is Dean and Professor of Communication at the College of Business and Economics, Australian National University, Canberra. Her research is focused on public discourse and change, including engagement and communication in relation to controversial science and technology. Recent work has included an analysis of the changing discourses of science policy and the implications for funded research. Her current projects include a book on social media with Judy Motion and Robert Heath, which will also be published by Routledge. During her career, Shirley has held over $5 million in National Competitive Grants and published more than 100 peer-reviewed papers. Shirley has also been named by the UK's *Guardian* newspaper as one of the top ten social media influencers in Australian higher education for her blog and Twitter-based communication.

Jacquie L'Etang, PhD, is Chair of Public Relations and Applied Communication at Queen Margaret University, Edinburgh, Scotland. Jacquie has been exploring public relations from a critical perspective since the late 1980s, initially publishing in *New Consumer*, the *Journal of Business Ethics* and the *European Journal of Business Ethics*. She co-edited (with Magda Pieczka) *Critical Perspectives in Public Relations* (1996) and *Public Relations: Critical Debates and Contemporary Practice* (2006). She is the author of two texts, *Public Relations: Concepts, Practice and Critique* (2008) and *Sports Public Relations* (2013). She has written on a range of themes – including diplomacy, rhetoric, anthropology, ethnography, gender and LGBT (with Lee Edwards) – but her long-standing interest is in public relations history and the role of public relations in society. She has been presenting papers and publishing on historical and historiographical themes since 1995 – including many articles and the monograph *Public Relations in Britain: A History of*

Professional Practice in the Twentieth Century (2004), and an edited collection with Meg Lamme and Burton St John III: *Pathways to Public Relations: Histories of Practice and Profession* (2014).

Stephen Linstead, PhD, DLitt, is Professor of Critical Management and Director of Postgraduate Research at the York Management School, University of York. A graduate of the Universities of Keele, Leeds and Sheffield Hallam, he is an elected Fellow of the Academy of the Social Sciences. In 2004 he was awarded a higher doctorate (D.Litt – Doctor of Letters) by Durham University for a substantial career contribution to the "humanitisation" of the field of Organisation Studies. His research interests encompass organisation theory and philosophy; aesthetics and organisations; language-based approaches to organising; gender and sexuality in organisations; qualitative methods, ethnography and culture. As a former semi-professional vocalist, he has an interest in the use of music and song as a form of ethnographic representation, and recently trained as an ethnographic film-maker. His publications include articles in *Organization Studies, Human Relations, Organization, Sociological Review*, the *Asia-Pacific Journal of Management, Management Learning* and *Gender Work and Organization*, as well as a best-selling critical textbook, 14 monographs and 16 special issues. These include two recent contributions: "The Territorial Organization" (in *Culture and Organization*, 2013, with Garance Maréchal and Ian Munro) and "The Dark Side of Organization" (in *Organization Studies*, 2014, with Garance Maréchal and Ricky W. Griffin).

Jairo Lugo-Ocando, PhD (Sussex), is Associate Professor at the University of Sheffield (UK), where he teaches public opinion and journalism and development. His books include: *The Media in Latin America* (2008), *ICTs, Democracy and Development: A Critical Perspective on Network Theory and the Politics of Neo-Modernity* (2007) and, more recently, *Blaming the Victim: How Global Journalism Fails Those in Poverty* (2015). His research looks at the intersection between poverty, development and media in relation to journalism and public relations. Before becoming an academic he worked as a journalist, correspondent and news editor for several media outlets in South America and the United States.

Jim Macnamara PhD, FPRIA, FAMI, CPM, FAMEC, is Professor of Public Communication at the University of Technology, Sydney, a position he took up in 2007 after a 30-year professional career in journalism, public relations and media research. He is the author of 15 books, including: *Public Relations Theories, Practices, Critiques* (Pearson Australia, 2012), *The 21st Century Media (R)evolution: Emergent Communication Practices* (Peter Lang, New York, 2010, 2nd edition 2014) and *Journalism and PR: Unpacking 'Spin', Stereotypes and Media Myths* (Peter Lang, New York, 2014).

David McKie, PhD, lectures in Strategic Communication and Leadership at Waikato Management School in New Zealand. Previously, he taught business communication in Libya in the 1970s, set up the first communication degree in Scotland in the 1980s and chaired a department of media and new technologies in Australia in the 1990s. McKie has authored/co-authored five books, including: *PR and Nation Building: Influencing Israel* (2013), *Please Don't Stop the Music: An Ensemble Leadership Repertoire* (2009) and *Reconfiguring Public Relations: Ecology, Equity, and Enterprise* (2007, an NCA PRIDE award winner). He has also published more than 35 book chapters, 60 refereed journal articles and/or spoken widely on the following areas: action learning and action research; change and leadership; creativity and innovation; emotional intelligence; futures; historiography; social marketing; and strategic communication. As CEO of RAM

(Results by Action Management) International Consultancy, McKie has also engaged in leadership and communication consultancy and run groups for individuals and organisations in Asia, Australasia, Europe and the USA. A Scot by birth, an Australian by naturalisation, a resident of New Zealand by choice and a citizen of the world by inclination, McKie tries to balance a sense of justice with a sense of humour.

Kevin Moloney, PhD, Senior Research Fellow at Bournemouth University in the UK, has spent the first half of his career *doing* public relations for business and higher education (Open University) and the second half teaching and researching the subject. His main focus is the intersection of public relations with political economy, especially with regard to the symmetry/ propaganda debate and the role of lobbying. He is the author of *Rethinking Public Relations: PR Propaganda and Democracy* (2006) and series editor of the Routledge New Directions in PR Research. Moloney is active in the UK's University and College Union and in the Dorset campaign for a Living Wage.

Judy Motion, PhD, is Professor of Communication and Convenor of Environmental Humanities in the School of Humanities and Languages, University of New South Wales, Australia. Her current research concentrates on the governance of science–society relations; the environmental dimensions of public policy; and the engagement dynamics of public controversy, advocacy and activism. Key research projects include the leadership of a five-year, New Zealand government-funded, research project entitled "Socially and Culturally Sustainable Biotechnology"; membership of a three-year, New Zealand government-funded research project entitled "Building Our Productivity: Understanding Sustainable Collective Productivity"; and most recently, a three-year, Australian government-funded research project investigating water governance issues entitled "National Development, Education and Engagement". Professor Motion is currently completing a book on social media with Bob Heath and Shirley Leitch, entitled *Public Relations: Fake Friends and Powerful Publics*, commissioned by Routledge. She has published in numerous journals including *Public Understanding of Science*, *Political Communication*, *Science and Public Policy*, *Media, Culture & Society*, *Organization Studies*, the *Journal of Business Research*, the *European Journal of Marketing*, *Public Relations Review* and the *Journal of Public Relations Research*.

Debashish Munshi, PhD, is Professor of Management Communication at the University of Waikato, New Zealand. His research interests lie at the intersections of communication, diversity, sustainability and citizenship. He is co-author of *Reconfiguring Public Relations: Ecology, Equity, and Enterprise* and co-editor of the *Handbook of Communication Ethics* and *On the Edges of Development: Cultural Interventions*. In addition, Munshi has written numerous articles for top journals such as *Public Relations Review*, the *Journal of Public Relations Research*, *Management Communication Quarterly*, *Public Understanding of Science*, *Citizenship Studies*, *Futures*, *New Media & Society*, *Business Communication Quarterly* and *Journalism: Theory, Practice, and Criticism*. He was co-principal investigator (with Priya Kurian) of a project on sustainable citizenship funded by a Marsden Grant of the Royal Society of New Zealand.

Magda Pieczka, PhD, is Reader and Co-ordinator of the Centre for Dialogue at Queen Margaret University, Edinburgh, Scotland. Magda has been exploring critical perspectives in public relations since the early 1990s and co-edited (with Jacquie L'Etang) *Critical Perspectives in Public Relations* (1996) and *Public Relations: Critical Debates and Contemporary Practice* (2006). Her 1996 chapter "Paradigms, systems theory and public relations" was one of the earliest critiques of Excellence and her argument that systems theory had become an ideology was a key intervention in the politics of the discipline. Her interests are focused on the professionalisation of communication in various industries, occupations and contexts and the study of communication in public engagement and policy-making. She has published articles and chapters on topics such as public opinion, public affairs, public engagement (including public understanding of science), dialogue and the professionalisation of public relations. She has twice won a Top Paper Award at the ICA (Division of Public Relations): in 2008 for her work on public relations consultancy and in 2013 for her work (with QMU colleague, Emma Wood) employing dialogue techniques in an action research context focused on young people's thinking about alcohol. The project was based around interventions designed collaboratively with school pupils and will have involved 3,500 teenagers by December 2015. This three-year project has been funded by the Robertson Trust (an independent Scottish grant-making body).

Katie R. Place, PhD (University of Maryland, 2010) is an Assistant Professor in the School of Communications and Department of Public Relations at Quinnipiac University in Hamden, Connecticut, where she teaches courses in public relations. Dr Place's research examines the nexus of gender, power and ethics in public relations. She has authored book chapters and peer-reviewed articles in the *Journal of Public Relations Research*, *PRism*, the *Journal of Mass Media Ethics* and *Public Relations Inquiry*. Prior to returning to academia, Dr Place worked in the public affairs and not-for-profit communications industries in the Washington, DC area.

Oliver Raaz, PhD, is a scientific assistant at the Department of Political and Communication Science (Chair of Organizational Communication) at the University of Greifswald, Germany. He studied communication science, political science and philosophy at the universities of Münster, Leipzig and Prague. Recently (2014–15), he spent five months as a Visiting Scholar at the School of Communication, Journalism and Marketing at Massey University (New Zealand). His PhD project combines a theoretically informed critique of transparency with a difference-oriented understanding of public relations within the framework of the CCO perspective. Therefore, he draws on autopoietic systems theory, post-structuralist discourse theory and actor-network theory. His main areas of research also focus on public relations history, non-standardised methodology and communication theory. Publications include "La normativité et la transparence – une combinaison problématique dans le processus scientifique" [Normativity and transparency: a problematic combination in scientific analysis] in A. Catellani, C. Hambursin and T. Libaert (eds), *La communication transparente: Communication, organisations et transparence* (2015); and Raaz, O. and Wehmeier, St. (2011) "Histories of Public Relations: Comparing the Historiography of British, German and US Public Relations" in the *Journal of Communication Management*, 15 (3), pp. 256–75. Since 2015, Raaz has served as a member of the editorial board of *Public Relations Inquiry*.

Phil Ramsey, PhD, is Assistant Professor in Digital and Creative Media in the School of International Communications, University of Nottingham Ningbo China. His teaching at Nottingham Ningbo has focused on political communication and arts and cultural policy. He previously taught at the University of Ulster on subjects that included public relations. Ramsey's research has addressed the political communication policies of New Labour in government, public sphere theory, media and cultural policy, and public service media. He has previously published on public relations and politics with Ian Somerville in *The Public Relations Handbook* (4th edition, Theaker, 2012), and on government communication in the UK in the *Journal of Public*

Affairs. Ramsey has also published on other topics in journals including the *International Journal of Cultural Policy, Cultural Trends* and *Media, Culture and Society*.

Mark Sheehan is Course Director of undergraduate Public Relations in the School of Communication & Creative Arts (SCCA) at Deakin University, Australia. He was the founding Postgraduate Course Director of the Master of Arts (Professional Communication) and from 2009 to 2011 Associate Head of School – Regional and Development. Since 2006 he has edited the *Asia Pacific Public Relations Journal* and has published widely on public relations history in Australia and in the areas of lobbying, crisis management and risk communication. He is the author and editor of over 30 publications on public relations including books, book chapters, articles and conference papers.

Nancy Snow, PhD, is an international scholar in Public Diplomacy and Propaganda Studies, based in Tokyo, Japan and Syracuse, New York. She co-edited the *Routledge Handbook of Public Diplomacy* with leading propaganda scholar Philip M. Taylor. Snow is Professor Emeritus of Communications at California State University, Fullerton, and has held several Adjunct Professor positions, including at the University of Southern California Annenberg School for Communication and Journalism, where she was the Principal Faculty involved in the establishment of the Center on Public Diplomacy. She has taught graduate-level marketing foreign policy as a Senior Adjunct Faculty with the Interdisciplinary Center (IDC) Lauder School of Government, Diplomacy and Strategy in Herzliya, Israel. Snow held a two-year Visiting Professor appointment at Syracuse University's Newhouse and Maxwell Schools, where she worked with the public relations faculty to expand a dual degree masters in public diplomacy. She held Visiting Professor appointments at Tsinghua University in China, Sophia University in Japan and UiTM in Malaysia. Author or editor of nine books, Snow is the two-time recipient of a Fulbright award (Germany, Japan). She was most recently a Social Science Research Council Abe Fellow and Visiting Professor at Keio University, where she completed a book about nation brand Japan since 3/11 (forthcoming).

Anne Surma, PhD, is an Associate Professor in the School of Arts at Murdoch University, Western Australia. She teaches literary studies and professional writing to undergraduates and supervises several doctoral students in the areas of literature, ethics, gender and writing At various stages in her career, Surma has also worked in private industry as an editor, writer and communications consultant. She has published on a range of writing-related topics, including the monograph *Public and Professional Writing: Ethics, Imagination and Rhetoric* (Palgrave, 2005). More recently she has explored cosmopolitan approaches to writing and has published her reflections in the book *Imagining the Cosmopolitan in Public and Professional Writing* (Palgrave, 2013).

Jennifer Vardeman-Winter (PhD, University of Maryland, 2008) is an Assistant Professor in the Jack J. Valenti School of Communication and an affiliate faculty member in the Women's, Gender, & Sexuality Studies programme at the University of Houston. Dr Vardeman-Winter teaches courses in public relations theory and management; critical/cultural public relations, issues and crisis management, and entrepreneurial communication in a practicum setting. Her studies concentrate on how gender, race and class affect public relations campaigns, particularly in public health/healthcare public relations. Dr Vardeman-Winter has published more than 20 articles and chapters related to public relations, gender and health. She recently served as the principal investigator for several grants totalling more than $150,000 from groups including the Texas Department of Housing and Community Affairs and Baylor Teen Health Clinics. As a former public relations practitioner in the high-tech field, Dr Vardeman-Winter continues to practice by working with groups like the Women's Health Initiative of Texas, the American Lung Association and local community health providers. She also serves in taskforce and officer positions for the Commission on the Status of Women and the public relations division of the Association for Education in Journalism and Mass Communications.

Damion Waymer (PhD, Purdue University) is Associate Provost for Special Initiatives at the University of Cincinnati. His programme of research centres on organisational rhetoric, particularly with regard to public relations, issues management, corporate social responsibility and strategic communication. His research projects address fundamental concerns about issues of diversity in general – and issues of race, class and gender, specifically – and how these social constructions shape and influence the ways that various audiences receive, react and respond to certain messages. He is the editor of the (2012) book, *Culture, Social Class, and Race in Public Relations: Perspectives and Applications* and is co-editor of *Rhetorical and Critical Approaches to Public Relations II*. Additionally, he has published more than 40 refereed articles and book chapters. His research appears in publications such as *Management Communication Quarterly*, the *Journal of Applied Communication Research, Public Relations Review, Public Relations Inquiry*, the *Journal of Public Relations Research, Journalism and Mass Communication Educator*, the *Journal of Communication Inquiry, Communication Quarterly, Qualitative Inquiry, The Qualitative Report* and elsewhere.

C. Kay Weaver (PhD, Stirling) is the Pro Vice-Chancellor of Postgraduate Research and a Professor in the Department of Management Communication at the University of Waikato, New Zealand. She has published many journal articles and book chapters advocating critical approaches to the study of public relations and strategic communication theory and practice. She also researches and writes about activist communication, gender, new technologies and representations of violence. She is co-editor of *Public Relations in Global Contexts* (2011) and *Critical Readings: Violence and the Media* (2006); and co-author of *Violence and the Media* (2003), *Women Viewing Violence* (1992) and *Cameras in the Commons* (1990). Weaver has taught across the fields of public relations, communication, media and film studies in both the UK and New Zealand.

Stefan Wehmeier, PhD, studied Communication Science, History and Economic Policy at Westfaelische Wilhelms-University Muenster, Germany. Since then he has been a business-to-business journalist (1998) and a public relations practitioner (Bertelsmann Subsidary, 1999). Between 2000 and 2006 Wehmeier was an Assistant Professor at the Department of Public Relations, University of Leipzig. In 2007 he became a Junior Professor at the Department of Communication at the University of Greifswald, Germany; and in 2008 he became Interim Chair of Communication Studies at the same institution. Since September 2008 Wehmeier has been Adjunct Professor at the Department of Marketing and Management at the University of Southern Denmark. His research areas are public relations, CSR, online communication, media systems and international media.

Paul Willis held leadership and board level positions in the public relations consultancy sector before joining Leeds Business School as Director of the Centre for Public Relations Studies in 2008. He has worked for private, public and non-profit organisations including BMW, Proctor & Gamble, The Cabinet Office and The Football Association. He began his career in the UK Parliament, before taking on an in-house public affairs role in The City of London, and then worked as a political consultant in Westminster. Willis is co-author of *Strategic Public Relations Leadership*. Other published research can be found in *Public Relations Review*, *The Journal of Public Affairs* and *Ethical Space*. He has also contributed chapters to *Exploring Public Relations* and *Strategic Communication*. In addition to co-creating a range of innovative Masters programmes with senior public relations practitioners, Willis has taught at the National School of Government. He is a Visiting Fellow at The University of Waikato, New Zealand, a Visiting Lecturer at Quadriga University, Germany and a member of the editorial advisory board of the *Journal of Communication Management*. He was the joint recipient in 2012 of the National Communication Association PRIDE Award for outstanding contribution to education.

Jordi Xifra, PhD, is Professor at Pompeu Fabra University, Barcelona, Spain, where he is the Director of the Master of Science in Strategic Communication and Public Relations, a jointly awarded degree with the University of Stirling (Scotland). His research interests are within the fields of the history of public relations, public relations sociology, public affairs and public diplomacy. He also leads a research group on thinktanks' communication management. Xifra is author and editor of more than 15 books on public relations and public affairs in Spain and South America, including: *Lobbying: Cómo influir eficazmente en las decisiones de los poderes públicos* (1998); *Teoría y estructura de las relaciones públicas* (2003), *Planificación estratégica de las relaciones públicas* (2005); *Los think tanks* (2008); *Manual de relaciones públicas e institucionales* (2011). His articles have been accepted for publication in *Public Relations Review*, the *Journal of Public Relations Research*, *American Behavioral Scientist*, the *Journal of Political Marketing*, *Comunicar*, *Historia y Comunicación Social*, among others. In 2004 he founded AIRRPP, the Spanish Public Relations Research Association. He is the co-editor of *Public Relations Inquiry* (Sage).

Part I
Origins and overviews

Introduction

Jacquie L'Etang, David McKie, Nancy Snow and Jordi Xifra

In our call for chapters for this *Handbook of Critical Public Relations*, we set the context as follows: "Critical theory has a long and fluctuating history – critical public relations is relatively recent. In the editors' view a critical mass has been reached and this handbook is a way to mark it." With our colours nailed to the mast for the *Handbook* as a potential tipping point, it is now up to you, the readers, and your responses over time, to decide if that has been achieved. In the same paragraph, we asked for "connections to – and differences from – critical theory, the current state of play of critical public relations across different areas, and its possible future directions". While no book could be comprehensive, we think the *Handbook* addresses these.

In the call, our "overall aim" was "to take stock of how, and where, critical public relations has emerged, its connections to – and differences from – critical theory, the current state of play of critical public relations across different areas, and its possible future directions". Although the book's final content and shape was more the result of vigorous debate among the editors than a comfortable consensus, we hope these chapters address each of those aspects, and that they do so in diverse ways. Certainly, the editorial call also welcomed "committed, argumentative, contentious, controversial" chapters. In equating *The Future of Excellence* (Toth, 2006) with the future of public relations, many authors in that collection assumed that the Excellence project was a terminal destination for the field. This *Handbook* set out to be more of a way-station, assisting diverse travellers in journeys towards a more egalitarian world. We feel confident that, while this is the first *Handbook of Critical Public Relations*, it will not be the last. The call for chapters concluded by inviting interested parties to "please let us know anything else you feel we have wrongly omitted" and, even though this book is finished, that invitation remains. We look forward to partnering with others taking critical PR forward and know that will involve critiquing our chapters, our choices, our content and our editing.

This *Handbook of Critical Public Relations* was, in its genesis, abbreviated to *CPR* in our communications with each other. Mainly for convenience, the abbreviation had an edge of black humour because CPR also stands for Cardio Pulmonary Resuscitation and it is not easy to reinvigorate a socially critical movement at this point in time. We lag behind in the Critical Handbook publishing stakes since Alvesson, Bridgman and Willmott's (2009) *The Oxford Handbook of Critical Management Studies* was published eight years before the first real *Handbook of Public Relations* (Heath, 2001). Yet in other ways it is hard to believe, if not a minor miracle, that *CPR* has not only appeared in print but has done so before the publication of a *Handbook of Critical Marketing*. This is despite marketing's substantially larger publication opportunities.

In contrast to the near miracle view of publication, it is also hard to believe that the field has taken so long to get to this stage. This is evidenced by the longer history, the number of authors, and the sheer range and volume of publications in critical management studies (see Linstead, this volume) – and critical marketing – (see Bourne, this volume; Brownlie, Hewer & Tadajewski (2013); Brownlie, Saren, Wensely & Whittington (1999); and Saren, Maclaren, Goulding, Elliott, Shanker & Caterall (2007)). Nevertheless, let us celebrate reaching this stage: 40 authors from around the world with 32 chapters covering a diverse range of themes as the world around us continues to change. One of the most relevant shifts has been in connotations of the word "critical" itself. Influenced by the growth of TripAdviser and other popular online reviews, Tancer's (2014) book title claims that, through social media, *Everyone's a Critic* in the contemporary world.

In the less anonymous academic PR world, the move to "own" the label "critical" has not, to date, been a popular one. Given the early struggles of critical PR scholars (see personal reflections below), we were surprised by the range of authors actively wanting to write chapters for a critical PR handbook. Partly, on reflection, we attributed this to the low bar for the term "critical" in the field. Almost anyone who disapproved, even mildly, of "the symmetrists" (Brown, 2006, p. 207), could see themselves as being "critical" in PR terms. Certainly, the demand from self-confessed non-critical authors (e.g., Macnamara, this volume; Willis, this volume) while unexpected, was strong and led us to include such chapters as adding value to the area. To those who did not make the cut, we apologise for the lack of justification for exclusion, and for the absence of further guidance. We underestimated how long the process would take and were simply running out of time from early in the project. As a result, we made the decision to spend what time we had on the work of the accepted authors, confident that there will be future *Handbooks of Critical Public Relations*.

One thing we did avoid was creating a kind of critical PR 101 to allow students to access summaries of main issues and main points, akin in part to Chris Hackley's (2009) *Marketing: A Critical Introduction*. This is not to dismiss such approaches. In fact, there exists a place for one in public relations because so few PR textbooks allocate much, if any, space to critical perspectives. Moreover, Hackley's (2009) introduction provides a useful synthesis of critical marketing that allows for comparisons with CPR. In this summary, marketing needs critical marketing because of:

- a perceived lack of real intellectual engagement with other disciplines
- complicity in environmental issues such as waste and destruction of resources
- intellectual shallowness, emphasising naïve instrumentalism over critical reflexivity
- a lack of moderation and a tendency to universalise North American neo-liberal values
- an overemphasis on quantitative modelling in a positive-empiricist social science.

(p. 4)

However, while agreeing with these points – and indeed many of the chapters that follow engage with them – what we had in mind was a range of broader and deeper individual reflections that an introduction can encompass. The chapters were not to bear the weight of one author speaking for, or attempting to synthesise, the whole of critical PR – especially a critical PR that is on the move. But even more than the contents are the movements of the people behind them, so we co-opt Burrell's (2009) afterword to the *Oxford Handbook of Critical Management Studies*: "Handbooks of whatever kind are built on trust, and therefore, we should be grateful that the authors and editors have worked together thus far to make such an *en masse* movement around Critical Management Studies possible" (p. 560). We extend that trust to the most important other stakeholders – our readers – in advance, and hope that, like Burrell's (2009) "runaway object" (p. 560) of CMS, the runaway object of CPR attracts more followers and more actions towards greater equality, freedom, and transparency. On the last of these we draw from our earlier writings to justify our ongoing practice:

> Oscar Wilde is reputed to have answered the standard customs officer question about anything to declare by stating "I have nothing to declare but my genius." Authors in public relations tend to imply that they have nothing to declare but their objectivity. This book doesn't. Instead, it is more informed than most by L'Etang's (2008) insight that "the position of the researcher is central to the nature of the story-telling and that requires more reflexivity than is common or conventional in much academic writing" (p. 324).
>
> *(Toledano & McKie, 2013, p. vi)*

From different standpoints, the feminist view that the personal is the political overlaps with the quantum physicist's view that there is no objective researcher. Barad (2007) is one of the rare theorists to hold a professorial position in both feminism and physics. She draws from quantum physics to confirm "how observations and 'agencies of observation' cannot be independent" (Barad, 2007, p. 31). We make no claim to (impossible) objectivity, and, accordingly, each editor offers a brief personal account of the shaping of themselves as "agencies of observation" (ibid., p. 31) with baggage from upbringing, education and life experiences that may bear on their contributions to this project.

Jacquie L'Etang: memories, experiences, reflections on becoming a critical PR academic

It may now be hard to believe just how difficult it was to articulate critical perspectives about public relations in the UK and Europe in the late 1980s and early 1990s. Some topics appeared to be off-limits. For example, as a lowly master's student in 1988 I was advised that my proposed dissertation on "PR and propaganda" was not suitable as it would "open a can of worms". The choice to tackle critical work in a field may be driven by a combination of curiosity and challenge, but at this time it was not an easy path. This was risky work.

Coming from a humanities background (BA American & English History and MA Commonwealth History), I simply remember being shocked that an academic discipline could be quite as narrowly focused as public relations was at this time, when it seemed there were so many interesting alternative ways of exploring the concept. My early interests (inspired by an applied philosophy MPhil on social justice) focused on CSR, ethics and propaganda. Little did I realise that this would entail challenging a paradigm and what this implied in terms of emotional cost (and possibly career development).

The pressures at this time came not only from the prevailing culture and values of established public relations academics, but also from more conventional peers (many of whom were former practitioners and possibly struggling with their own identity crises); from some senior practitioners and representatives of professional bodies who clearly regarded the articulation of critical perspectives as disloyal; and from some students. At the same time, some journalists, having spent a number of years criticising journalism and media degrees, found in public relations qualifications a new subject for ridicule. Only a few months into my first academic job I made the mistake of allowing a journalist to accompany myself and students on a field trip to the Glasgow School of

Art – a double-page spread followed, in which was articulated the view that no academics could be trusted to speak plainly and the worst type of all was the public relations academic. I was not too disappointed when that newspaper went out of business.

The first article I published (in 1989) aroused the ire of one practitioner who wrote a long letter of complaint to my senior colleague. The publication of *Critical Perspectives in Public Relations* (1996) resulted in letters of complaint to the University Principal. While some opposition was quite overt, there were also other, more subtle pressures, for example, being taken to one side by an established US academic and reminded that "we should all be working together and on the same side". On another occasion it was suggested that edited volumes "should cover the field" and that even critical volumes should include a token from the instrumentalists. Other incidents were more public, such as the occasion at the plenary session of a conference where a senior figure informed the whole audience that none of my students would ever work in public relations. Essentially, there was no space or place for public relations scholarship outside the mainstream. It was useful experience in being "Othered".

Working in a mainstream functional marketing department was also a challenge (among other things I was advised that if I was interested in communications I should give up public relations and try and get a psychology lectureship – something for which I was uniquely unqualified), and after several years a move to a media department provided a more supportive environment. Nevertheless, the experience of working in two very different academic disciplines (marketing and media studies) brought home the distinctiveness of a critical public relations approach that seeks to explore the wider societal implications of this practice without necessarily starting from a point of ideological opposition and overt hostility. Necessarily, in the wider university context one became aware of disciplinary snobberies, some of which still pertain. I recall a lecturer in politics who, in the course of a conversation about political communication that was taught on his degree, informed me somewhat piously that his students "wanted to save the world", leaving hanging in the air the implication that public relations students wished to destroy it. Then there was the history lecturer to whom I gave my book on the development of public relations in the UK saying that I would be interested in an historian's view and fondly imagining he might comment on my methodology or how my work connected with other historical work in the period under review. The book was returned to me with the acerbic comment that he could confirm that journalists in the 1950s and 1960s were moral and were not influenced by public relations practices. These sorts of experiences were probably shared by public relations academics of all persuasions, but seem more difficult to navigate from a critical position, not least because it may appear that those in the wider academy with whom one might wish to align may simply refuse to engage with any academic identified as being involved in the public relations field. And inevitably, as one of the first generation of public relations academics in the UK, there were no disciplinary mentors, and lacking the big practice CV and legitimacy that most PR academics had at that time (I'd spent ten years working at The British Council), pursuing the critical public relations agenda was always going to be a somewhat isolated experience.

It was hard in the late 1980s and early 1990s to publish critical work and I concentrated my efforts on business ethics journals and conferences. I recall being tremendously excited at getting hold of Toth and Heath's *Rhetorical and Critical Approaches to Public Relations* at the end of 1992 and waving it at a media studies colleague, announcing triumphantly: "Now you'll have to take the subject seriously!" However, as Kay Weaver points out in her chapter in this volume, mutual respect between the two disciplines remains elusive (and as indicated above there may be issues with those from other close disciplines such as politics and cultural studies).

As late as 1996, Magda Pieczka and myself noted our reasons for publishing our first book, *Critical Perspectives in Public Relations*:

At present there is no obvious outlet for publishing such material. One of [us] has already had the experience of having an article rejected from one of the public relations journals on the grounds it was too radical (the article was subsequently published by another refereed journal outside the field). Yet, as the history of almost any discipline can prove, development needs challenge as much as it needs consensus. In public relations, consensus seems currently quite strong; therefore, we feel we should set out to challenge….Some of the material has, along with some of our other critical work, been presented at conferences – with varying responses, some of which have been quite hostile. While this has not always been a pleasant experience, we firmly believe, journalistically, that if people appear not to want you to say something, then there is all the more reason to say it.

(L'Etang & Pieczka, 1996, p. xi)

Interestingly, there has been some strange mythologising about critical PR. I was amazed to discover that it was a not uncommon belief that Magda Pieczka and myself had such trouble getting *Critical Perspectives in Public Relations* published in 1996 that we had self-published the volume. This was not true as we had originally gained a contract from Routledge in 1993 or 1994, but were subsequently sold to International Thomson Business Press (ITBP) when the business list was sold. PR was not terribly well understood by publishers at that time and generally seen as business rather than communications. During the 1990s our other book proposals failed to be accepted by publishers, including a book on research methods for public relations and a book on PR and CSR.

Although *Critical Perspectives* had some airing in the UK and Australasia, it did not appear to make any impact in the US. Of course, in a pre-digital environment ideas flowed more slowly and we had always thought of the book as being a "slow burn". Despite this, the book did enable us to meet others such as Judy Motion, Anne Surma and Oyvind Ihlen who visited Scotland shortly after its publication; as did Liz Yeomans and Jo Fawkes. We already knew Kay Weaver (who had worked at Stirling) and it became increasingly clear that there were sympathetic others in Europe.

On reflection I can see that some of my writing was provocative at the time – for example claiming at a conference in 1994 that the notion of symmetrical public relations was like "going to heaven"; or arguing in relation to the politics of the discipline that

> What could be described as the *"pax symmetrica"* is itself based on the imposition and acceptance of a particular world view of commonsense, and is thus intrinsically hegemonic in that one overall framework maybe applied and the potential for disagreement may be restricted…Because there is so little content to the concept of "symmetry", the term appears to have become a euphemism for "good". "Symmetry" appears to offer liberation and free expression simultaneously, but it is also a potentially totalitarian ideology.

(L'Etang, 1996, p. 34)

Likewise, from 1995 onwards I challenged *the* four models partly because of their historical progressivism and underlying positivism. A more profound methodological issue was raised by the fact that the normative model was primarily used as a deductive tool to test scientific hypotheses, and then subsequently imposed as historical periods (colligation) onto the past. At this time I argued that

> I agree with L. Grunig that "public relations needs its own history" (Grunig, 1992: 78) but I think that we need a far wider range of history (sociological history and historical

sociology) than the case histories she recommends and which may simply be more grist to the theoretical mill of the dominant paradigm of public relations history. Real revisionist history will abandon the existing models and theories and develop new interpretations from cultural and sociological perspectives in a variety of national, ethnic and political contexts.

(L'Etang, 1995, p. 26)

This position remained a theme throughout a continuing and ongoing range of historical empirical and historiographical work, likewise challenging "the assumption in much of the literature that public relations was first developed in the United States and was then exported elsewhere" (L'Etang, 2004, pp. 5, 10).

Because of my personal career experiences it is quite hard for me to understand critical PR other than as a necessarily lonely position on the margins. While adversity facilitates some independence of mind, it probably also impacted upon the way I work in terms of keeping my head down and writing rather than circuiting conferences. I was, of course, uniquely fortunate that early in my career Magda Pieczka and I were colleagues and worked together for about 16 years. From my own perspective, things would have been very different without Magda. And although I have recounted some rather tricky critical incidents from my early experiences, I have benefited from numerous connections as a groundswell of critically focused work has emerged. But I continue to feel a tremendous sympathy for those PR scholars who work pretty much on their own, delivering largely functional degrees while their souls cry out to engage with central critical issues.

The scale and diversity of this volume amply demonstrate that there now exists a substantial body of scholars who self-identify as "critical" – some of whom unpack, deconstruct and critique that term. Now that there is a real community of non-functional scholars there is the opportunity to build multicultural critically inspired theoretical and empirical projects of societal relevance.

Jacquie L'Etang, PhD
2015

Nancy Snow: living the questions

As a Girl Raised In The South (GRITS) who now lives part-time in Tokyo, I've been on a journey of cultural identity and communication for as long as I can remember. Unlike the other editors who grace this volume, I do not come from a professional or academic grounding in public relations – critical or functional. My academic pursuits were associated with politics (BA in Political Science), with its focus on power relations and policy influence, as well as international relations (PhD, School of International Service, The American University), the realm of diplomacy, and threats or use of forceful persuasion. Little did I know that my life was on a quasi-parallel track with that of Jacquie L'Etang, whose graduate research proposal on PR and propaganda was deemed unsuitable by her advisor. Her work was too radical – too agitating – as the opening up of any can of worms might be. My own research post-dissertation took on the same sheen when I published my first book, *Propaganda, Inc.: Selling America's Culture to the World*, a short tract based on my experience working as a newly minted PhD at America's independent agency of propaganda – the euphemistically named United States Information Agency (USIA), better known as USIS overseas. Herbert Schiller, author of *Mass Communications and American Empire* (1969) and *Communication and Cultural Domination* (1976), wrote the Foreword to *Propaganda, Inc.* (2010); and Michael Parenti (*Against Empire* (1995), *Inventing Reality* (1992)) wrote the Introduction. The title of my first book is a nod to Schiller's *Culture, Inc.: The Corporate*

Takeover of Public Expression (1989). Herb Schiller warned me at the time of writing his Foreword that I would forever be seen as an academic iconoclast for associating with such radical company, but I recall thanking him: "I could not be in better radical company." From that moment, as a very junior scholar who was but a little sapling among the tall oaks, I continued to value critical analysis, despite the risks to one's promotion in the academy. What was our purpose as scholars if not to promote living the questions of our professional and personal lives? If not the academy to push societal buttons, then who else?

The questioning stance I took in my research and writing is grounded in living overseas where one is forced to continually confront one's standing in an unfamiliar surrounding. Living in societies where I may not speak the native language at all, or well enough, forces me to heighten my other senses. I become more attuned to social stratifications as I live the life of a cultural questioner. It is within this setting that I return to those critical analysts like Schiller, who wrote (in 1976):

> The struggles to overcome domination – external, where the power resides outside the national community; internal, where the power is exercised by a domestic ruling stratum – is the central, if not always recognized, issue in contemporary communications policy making. Internationally, nationally, and individually, the struggle, though often obscured, is between the forces of domination and those that resist and challenge that domination. All basic issues in communications today relate to this fundamental and increasingly intense confrontation.
>
> *(p. 70)*

I am part of this team of editors because, despite personal inhibitions about whether or not I truly belong in public relations, I know that I belong in a critical communications studies field that my academic mentors – Schiller, Parenti and another giant in the field, George Gerbner – modelled for me. Gerbner, the 25-year Dean of the Annenberg School at the University of Pennsylvania, founded the Cultural Environment Movement in 1996 when he was in his late 70s. He asked me to work with him to help communicate a message that media reform – and the environment of Schiller's (1973) book *The Mind Managers* – were as central a concern to our lives as the natural environment movement. While he focused a lot on television violence, his main theme was that cultural decision-making was "drifting dangerously out of democratic reach". It was in the hands of the marketers and salespeople who used content to bring eyeballs to advertisers. They had something to sell more than they were concerned about the stories we tell. I'd like to think that my experience with CEM and Gerbner pushed me further along in developing a questioning stance on communications and a commitment to public scholarship.

In 2008 I became Associate Professor of Public Diplomacy in the Newhouse School of Public Communications, Syracuse University. The Newhouse School is one of the best communications and journalism schools in the United States. I was on leave as tenured Associate Professor of Communications at California State University, Fullerton, and Adjunct Professor in the USC Annenberg School for Communication and Journalism. At SU I was affiliated with the public relations department since my task was to help build the dual degree masters in public diplomacy that combined an MA in Public Relations from Newhouse with an MS degree in International Relations from the Maxwell School. Many of these graduates go on to top positions in industry and government. I was never satisfied with just teaching core curriculum classes that prepared students for these top positions. At Newhouse, I wanted to teach classes that weren't about bringing the industry perspective to make public relations students profession-ready; rather, I wanted them to ask questions of the industry, its norms and ethics. With considerable prodding from me and interested students, I was given the green light to teach a course in propaganda and another course on Obama's first 100 days in office – but these special topics electives were seen as going against the grain of preparing young people to be future professionals. My academic life there was like a canary in a coalmine, not unlike the way I felt at times when I worked at the US Information Agency. Now as I witness the rise of ultra-nationalism and government public relations efforts to clean up the image of Japan in World War Two, I still feel like that little bird. It's my hope that this *Handbook* will serve as not so much a warning of danger but rather a wake-up call for more diversity and inclusiveness of perspectives in public relations.

Nancy Snow, PhD
Tokyo, Japan
2015

David McKie: the personal and the critical

My pathway to Critical PR is more like crazy paving than a direct route, but it began at birth. My parents started it off by calling me David, and a Scottish Presbyterian Sunday School teacher then clarified it with the Biblical story of David overcoming the giant Goliath. In other words, I was positioned from early on, regardless of how unequal the odds, to fight the good fight on the side of the underdog. I grew up in the 1960s when hope for radical change, an end to injustice, a liveable planet, and an outstanding sex life, all seemed to be as attainable as putting a human on the moon (and at least the last one happened).

So I was critical long before I was PR. After leaving school and delivering milk, cleaning offices, and working as a Tote clerk at the greyhound racing track, my career morphed from work as a statistician and systems analyst through to a 1970s doctoral love affair with Scottish Literature – with a side career in setting up the radical Scottish Labour Party (SLP) standing on a platform of greater socialism, greater devolution (en route to full independence), and greater integration into Europe – both Eastern and Western – and the rest of the world (especially the non-capitalist parts such as Africa, Cuba and South America). Suffice to say, our fight to make Scottish oil belong to the Scottish people (rather than Margaret Thatcher's government), failed.

I left Scotland disappointed, but returned in the 1980s to help set up the first Communication Studies degree in Scotland before moving on to supervise PhDs in Media Studies in Australia, where I co-published a book called *Eco-Impacts and the Greening of Postmodernity: New Maps for Communication Studies, Cultural Studies and Sociology* (Jagtenberg & McKie, 1997) and my first PR article (Synnott & McKie, 1997). In the previously unknown editorial intersections that these personal accounts have sparked, my frustration at not being able to initiate and participate in bringing about large-scale ecological and social change led to a (failed) attempt to join in with George Gerbner's environmental movement that Nancy Snow describes.

Instead, I moved to New Zealand and joined the amazing Management Communication Department at Waikato Management School. I don't use the word "amazing" lightly, as we tend to punch above our weight – for example, although we're a small department, six of the authors in this book work there, or once worked there; and seven of the others have joined us temporarily at various points as visiting academics. One Polish visitor, Professor Ryszard Ławniczak, deserves special mention as the originator of the idea for this *Handbook*.

On entering the PR field with the move to New Zealand, in 1997, I was shocked by a colleague's story of presenting a PR paper – which was critical and qualitative – to a large communication conference in the US. She described how she was attacked by a leading US academic as unscholarly (because she didn't use statistics), and as a communist (because she criticised Excellence theory). Living up to my biblical namesake's reputation, I responded by fashioning a slingshot to deliver to the same conference in the following year, entitled

"UnAmerican Public Relations". Organised as a ten-step programme along the lines of Alcoholics Anonymous, and to assist in moving away from the field's addiction to mainstream US PR, it proposed other approaches. These included abandoning Excellence – as a communication scholar it just puzzled me how such a simple notion as two-way symmetry could ever dominate a field when no other communication disciple seemed to consider it worth considering – and moving methods beyond narrow quantitative approaches as in my article entitled "Beyond Rats and Stats" (1997). Although I didn't know it at the time, it led to my first solo PR article (McKie, 1997) and marked the beginning of a personal campaign – now in its nineteenth year – to make PR less intellectually insular and raise consciousness of how it could play a vital positive role in ecology and social equity as well as business enterprise (see McKie & Munshi, 2007) – although in my role as CEO of a small consulting company I do use PR and PR skills openly.

Without negating the environmental and social damage that PR interventions can, and do, create, I also came to see PR, as an academic discipline, as an underdog among other disciplines. I also grew to appreciate PR as a field that includes corporate PR, but only as a subset of much larger social concerns. Indeed I'd argue – admittedly from observation rather than research – that across the globe, from amateur PR and activist PR through local government and non-profit organisations and a host of cause PR groups, corporate PR employs considerably less than 50 per cent of the people actually doing PR. That said, the corporate and government sectors almost certainly have a much higher average income level and many people equate PR with corporate PR – which is also the main subject of most PR textbooks. Even with this in mind it may still seem odd to look at PR rather than looking to a more conventionally critical discipline as Steven Seidman (2013), who looked "to sociology as a discipline that would help make sense of my individual and collective world" (p. vii). Yet Seidman (2013, p. vii) also goes on to recall,

> the disillusionment of my first few years as a sociologist. I expected my colleagues to share my moral vision of sociology. The reality was sobering. My colleagues, whom I admired for their research skills and their accomplishment, hardly read outside of their specialty areas; few of them deliberately linked their scholarship to public debates and controversies; much of the culture of sociology in the 1980s and 1990s seemed parochial – a world where "scientific" talk and status anxieties produced an insulated expert culture. I was distraught at the wreckage of professionalization: smart, well-intentioned individuals with good values, whose intellect was disciplined by a culture that often ignored history, non-American and non-"Western" cultures, and that lacked strong ties to a public world of moral and political debate.

Despite the more radical reputation of sociology, Seidman's experiences did not feel too far away from accounts of experiences in academic PR. Yet, in the latter, many participate with pride – rather than Seidman's guilt and disappointment – in a similar "professionalization". To adapt Seidman (2013), I believe that critical PR in this *Handbook* is not a discipline that ignores "history, non-American and non-'Western' cultures" and I hope that it helps to forge stronger "ties to a public world of moral and political debate" (p. vi). So, from my critical perspective, the key themes of current debate are: (1) economic rationalism deteriorating further into economic fundamentalism; (2) the dangerous stretching of the environmental, financial and social fabric; and (3) the massively asymmetric distribution of wealth in the contemporary world continuing to tilt even further in favour of the mega-rich at the expense of the rest. The Goliaths are clear, but, to go back to Frankfurt School Critical Theory, what's needed is Horkheimer's

(1947, p. 132) "denunciation of everything that mutilates mankind and impedes its free development" augmented by what Reynolds' (2006) book calls *An Army of Davids*, who have names from non-Western cultures and commitments to an equitable emancipation for the whole globe.

David McKie
Hamilton, New Zealand

Jordi Xifra: a personal journey – coming to PR from Catalonia

I am Catalan. And that, in Spain, today, is very critical, even radical. I was born and educated under Franco, in a conservative society whose only distinguishing feature was that we spoke the Catalan language that was banned by the regime. My father pioneered the teaching of public relations in Spain at a time when the few Spanish public relations professionals who were in practice were mainly engaged in propaganda, since they were responsible for communication in Franco's administration.

My father was not a public relations practitioner. He was Professor of Political Science and a lawyer (a good foundation for being interested in public relations, maybe even one of the best). I never knew why he was interested in public relations. In fact, because he founded the first public relations college, public relations were part of the family environment; but I never knew what public relations meant and I was never interested in this strange field. At that time, I was studying my Bacchalauréat at the Lycée Français (the greatest gift my parents gave me). After failing in my attempt to study film-making in Paris, I ended up studying law – following in the family tradition: my great-grandparents, my grandparents and my father were all lawyers.

As I said, my father introduced the teaching of public relations in Spain, and he founded the PR Higher Education College in 1968 – it still exists today as a University of Barcelona college. So when I finished my law studies, he offered me the opportunity to teach a course on freedom of speech. That was in 1984, but I still was not interested in public relations: my classes focused on the rights of journalists and people, rights that were just being recognised in Spain post-Francoism. For me, the law and the political dimension were more important than their consequences for the role of public relations practice. There was, at that time, and for a number of reasons, a scarcity of practice in Spain. Then, in 1987, my father asked me to assume the directorship of the public relations school in Girona. This was not favouritism: nobody wanted to take the risk of managing a public relations degree in a city of no more than 70,000 people and located near to Barcelona – where universities were offering public relations at undergraduate level.

But it was a challenge, and I like challenges. So I accepted. The immediate challenge was that if I had to manage a school of public relations, I also had to understand what public relations was about. So I started reading about public relations. For someone like me, who had studied law, it was not complicated. This all happened in the late 1980s, and my father died in March 1990. In other words, I had had a public relations pioneer at home who could not then share his knowledge with me. This fact, today, when my interest in the history of the discipline grows as each year passes, remains a source of regret. But life deals such blows, and I hope my father would have been proud of his son.

Once I began managing the Girona delegation of the PR Higher Education College, I was worried because there were no public relations books or handbooks in Spanish. When I started reading about the discipline, all the books were in English. It was also very difficult to buy any of these books – this being before the boom in online sales – and to make matters worse I did not speak English. And so I negotiated with Spanish publishers to publish the main English handbooks on public relations: Cutlip, Center and Broom (1985); Grunig and Hunt (1984); Pavlik (1987); Seitel (2001); Wilcox and Cameron (2005); and even Bernays' *Crystallizing Public Opinion* (1923). Casting modesty aside, these efforts enabled students and future lecturers to access the American body of knowledge of public relations. I think that the growth of interest in public relations as a discipline in Spain connects directly to the translations (and adaptations) of these handbooks and books. Translation of such works was not without its risks, especially in that it promoted an American-centered perspective of the field. But I preferred to deal with this danger in preference to living without public relations books. The danger had consequences for me. I did my PhD on public relations and political communication in 2001, applying Grunigian models to the electoral strategies of Spanish political parties during the first campaign that featured online communication. Today I think that we cannot apply such models without taking into account the cultural idiosyncrasies of the different countries. But in those days, this level of critical thinking hadn't come alive in me.

It is evident, therefore, that I was a victim of the dominant paradigm of public relations. But as the years passed I began to read UK authors, especially the contributions of Jacquie L'Etang and Magda Pieczka. They were like a breath of fresh air to me, and called into question the almighty Excellence paradigm. When I met Jacquie L'Etang in Girona – when the University of Girona awarded her the Jorge Xifra Heras award (an award set up in honour of my father) – we shared a lot of views on the theory of the discipline. In particular we saw the need to overcome the dominant paradigm, and to found a new journal to bring these concerns together – those discussion eventually turned into today's *Public Relations Inquiry*. She invited me to join the Radical PR Roundtable held in Stirling in July 2008 and there I had the honour and good fortune to meet David McKie, with whom I share a great friendship and with whom I serve on the organising committee that runs the annual Open University of Catalonia's Barcelona PR conference. Since 2011, that conference has brought the best scholars in the field to my country and through the participation of Bob Heath has opened up communal and diverse reflections on the field that auger well for its future. Meeting Bob has been another milestone in my public relations career. I have found in him the exact expression of wisdom: knowledge, an open mind, tolerance with divergence, a critical soul and a sense of humour.

I realised I needed to find ways to go beyond any dominant paradigm, and that the path opened up by David, Magda, Jacquie and others was related to what my thesis supervisor, Manuel Parés, had always said: "Public relations is not a managerial function, is a way of understanding life." Since then I have found new perspectives on which to focus my research, and to observe how public relations is a discipline "sponge" (i.e., a discipline that perfectly accepts an interdisciplinary perspective and, simultaneously, is enriched by this perspective). There still remains a danger, however: that the critical paradigm becomes the dominant one. If this happens, those who have criticised an academic caste will end up forging a new one. I hope this *Handbook* will serve to provide a critical approach to public relations from many different perspectives; and that it will also set out what critical PR means (or might mean), even if the journey is a radical one that cuts through to the roots of the field. There should be no sacred cows, or bulls; rather, there should be an approach characterised by its tolerance to, if not agreement with, many different perspectives in our discipline.

Jordi Xifra
Barcelona, Catalonia
2015

References

Alvesson, M., Bridgman, T., & Willmott, H. (Eds). (2009). *The Oxford handbook of critical management studies.* Oxford, UK: Oxford University Press.

Barad, K. (2007). *Meeting the universe halfway: Quantum physics and the entanglement of matter and meaning.* Durham, NC: Duke University Press.

Bernays, E. (1923). *Crystallizing public opinion.* New York, NY: Boni and Liveright.

Brown, R. (2006). Myth of symmetry: Public relations as cultural styles. *Public Relations Review,* 32(3), pp. 206–12.

Brownlie, D., Hewer, P. & Tadajewski (Eds). (2013). *Expanding disciplinary space: On the potential of critical marketing.* London, UK: Routledge.

Brownlie, D., Saren, M., Wensely, R. & Whittington, R. (Eds). (1999). *Rethinking marketing: Towards critical marketing accountings.* London, UK: Sage.

Burrell, G. (2009). Handbooks, swarms, and living dangerously. In M. Alvesson, T. Bridgman, & H. Willmott (Eds), *The Oxford handbook of critical management* studies, pp. 551–61). Oxford, UK: Oxford University Press.

Cutlip, S. M., Center, A. H., & Broom, G. M. (1985). *Effective public* relations, 6th edition. New York, NY: Prentice Hall.

Grunig, J. E., & Hunt, T. (1984). *Managing public relations.* New York, NY: Holt, Rinehart & Winston.

Hackley, C. (2009). *Marketing: A critical introduction.* London, UK, Sage.

Heath, R. (Ed.). (2001). *Handbook of public relations.* Thousand Oaks, CA: Sage.

Horkheimer, M. (1947). *Eclipse of reason.* New York, NY: Oxford University Press.

Jagtenberg, T., & McKie, D. (1997). *Eco-impacts and the greening of postmodernity: New maps for communication studies, cultural studies and sociology.* Thousand Oaks: CA: Sage.

L'Etang, J. (1990). Doing good, being good or looking good. *New consumer,* June

L'Etang, J. (1995). Clio among the patriarchs? Historical and social scientific approaches to public relations: A methodological critique. International Public Relations Conference, Lake Bled, Slovenia, 8–12 July.

L'Etang, J. (1996). Public relations and diplomacy. In J. L'Etang, & M. Pieczka (Eds), *Critical perspectives in public relations, 3* pp. 14–35. London, UK: International Thomson Business Press.

L'Etang, J. (2004). *Public relations in Britain: A history of professional practice in the twentieth century.* Mahwah, NJ: Lawrence Erlbaum Associates.

L'Etang, J., & Pieczka, M. (1996). Introduction. In J. L'Etang, & M. Pieczka (Eds), *Critical perspectives in public relations,* pp. xi–xv. London, UK: International Thomson Business Press.

McKie, D. (1997). Shifting paradigms: Public relations beyond rats, stats and 1950s science. *Australian Journal of Communication,* 24(2), pp. 81–96.

McKie, D., & Munshi, D. (2007). *Reconfiguring public relations: Ecology, equity and enterprise.* London, UK: Routledge.

Parenti, M. (1992). *Inventing reality: The politics of news media,* 2nd edition. Boston, MA: Cengage Learning.

Parenti, M. (1995). *Against empire.* San Francisco, CA: City Lights Publishers.

Pavlik, J. V. (1987). *Public relations: What research tells us.* New York, NY: Sage.

Reynolds, G. (2006). *An army of Davids: How markets and technology empower ordinary people to beat big media, big government, and other Goliaths.* Nashville, TN: Thomas Nelson.

Saren, M., Wensely, R., & Whittington, R. (Eds). (1999). *Rethinking marketing: Towards critical marketing accountings.* London, UK: Sage.

Saren, M., Maclaren, P., Goulding, C., Elliott, R., Shanker, A. & Catterall, M. (Eds). (2007). *Critical marketing: Defining the field.* Burlington, MA: Butterworth-Heinemann.

Schiller, H. I. (1969). *Mass communications and American empire.* New York, NY: Augustus M. Keeley Publishers.

Schiller, H. I. (1973). *The mind managers.* Boston, MA: Beacon Press.

Schiller, H. I. (1976). *Communication and cultural domination.* White Plains, NY: M. E. Sharpe.

Schiller, H. I. (1989). *Culture, Inc: The corporate takeover of public expression.* New York, NY: Oxford University Press.

Seidman, S. (2013). *Contested knowledge: Social theory* today, 5th edition. Chichester, UK: John Wiley.

Seitel, F. P. (2001). *The practice of public relations,* 8th edition. New York, NY: Prentice Hall.

Snow, N. (2010). *Propaganda, Inc: Selling America's culture to the* world, 3rd edition. New York, NY: Seven Stories Press.

Synnott, G., & McKie, D. (1997). International issues in public relations: Researching research and prioritizing priorities. *Journal of Public Relations Research*, 9(4), pp. 259–82.

Tancer, W. (2014). *Everyone's a critic: Winning customers in a review driven world.* New York, NY: Portfolio.

Toledano, M., & McKie, D. (2013). *Public relations and nation building: Influencing Israel.* London, UK: Routledge.

Toth, E. (Ed.). (2006). *The future of excellence in public relations and communication management.* Mahwah, NJ: Lawrence Erlbaum Associates.

Toth, E., & Heath, R. (Eds). (1992). *Rhetorical and critical approaches to public relations.* Hillsdale, NJ: Lawrence Erlbaum Associates.

Wilcox, D. L., & Cameron, G. T. (2005). *Public relations: Strategies and tactics*, 6th edition. Boston, MA: Pearson.

An historical overview of the emergence of critical thinking in PR

Lee Edwards

The history of critical thinking in PR is like any other in that it is a history of people and their relationships, institutions and their parameters, and personal dedication to change and development. In this chapter, I try to weave together these threads to contribute to the story of how critical thinking about PR has emerged over the past three decades.

As a critical scholar myself, I participated in this history, since I have benefited from the work of critical thinkers and have tried to open up new directions for scholarship through my own work. However, I am a relative latecomer; others have been pushing the boundaries of critical work far longer. In the process of writing this chapter, I benefited from conversations with many of these scholars; I am indebted to them, as well as to more recently arrived academics in the field, for their time and insight. In addition, it is important to note that what follows is an English-speaking history of critical thinking in PR. Language barriers mean that important work done in Europe and Scandinavia, presented at conferences such as Nordicom and published in German and Scandinavian language journals, remains somewhat hidden from the wider scholarly community, but in omitting them I do not mean to imply they have been unimportant in the field.

Context: foundations of the 'field' of critical PR scholarship

The first, and perhaps obvious point to make about critical PR scholarship is that its development has not been uniform. It has been shaped by the institutional parameters of the different geographies in which critical scholars work: the US, New Zealand and Australia, the UK and Europe. These four academic "worlds" have things in common, but also diverge from each other in important ways. The divergence helps to explain the ways in which critical thinking about PR has evolved differently, depending on where scholars reside.

Across all geographies, PR began as a functional discipline. It emerged in the 1980s and 1990s as a programme of study to train students for work in the burgeoning industry. In universities, the requirement was for staff who could teach practice, rather than challenge it; and in many cases, practitioners were actively invited to engage with the development of PR programmes as well as provide placements for students. Many early teachers of public relations themselves came from practice, and retained a loyalty to the profession that limited critical engagement with its effects.

PR degree programmes followed the need to provide students with skills rather than tools for critique (Fitch, 2014; L'Etang & Piezcka, 1996; Weaver, 2014). In competitive education markets, industry accreditation became a benchmark for quality, a means for students to distinguish "good" PR degrees from bad ones and establish which adhered to professional standards (Kruckeberg, 1998) – but it also tied academics to the functional, organisational paradigm in the classroom (J. Grunig & L. Grunig, 2002). Alongside the need for a "seal of approval" from industry, university programmes frequently depended on positive relationships with PR companies and departments for their supply of placements – and in the US and the UK at least, this made academics cautious about introducing a critical voice into their programmes, as well as into their research. Still today, undergraduate programmes in PR tend to be led by teaching skills-based learning rather than intellectual development.

Such tendencies were exacerbated in the US in particular, by the fact that research funding also came from industry, most notably from the International Association of Business Communicators (IABC), which funded not only the Excellence project (J. Grunig, 1992), but also the Velvet Ghetto report into women's position in the industry (Cline, Toth, Turk, Walters, Johnson, & Smith, 1986). While such support was valuable, it did little to encourage critical approaches. The result was research that complemented teaching curricula and fed into industry, focused primarily on organisational benefits and "best practice", and frequently explicitly supporting the Excellence paradigm. The Velvet Ghetto report, an early exploration of the position of women in PR, did provide evidence that discrimination was prevalent across the occupation, but the potential for using the results as a platform for critique remained dormant until the 2000s, when radical feminist scholarship became more widespread (see below). The larger, international Excellence project itself, underpinned by Grunig's earlier work on patterns of PR practice in industry, led to the emergence of two-way symmetry as a central tenet of PR theorising. A substantial number of scholars connected to Grunig pursued the development of the idea. The resulting dominance of two-way symmetry in the US academy, combined with the focus on organisationally driven analyses of PR that flowed logically from it, proved a very powerful underpinning for the majority of PR teaching across the world. In the early phase of PR education, US textbooks were the only ones available for teaching PR and even when new, region-specific books emerged, they diverged little from the functional approach.

The focus on practice and the development of two-way symmetry and Excellence as a paradigmatic focus for PR were central to establishing PR as an independent discipline within the academy as well as an important function in industry. By setting up PR as a specific business function (for most early research was focused on corporations rather than government or non-profit organisations) with clear processes, practices and benefits, many scholars in the US and elsewhere hoped that practitioners and indeed, researchers, would be recognised as authorities in an increasingly important area. Arguably, the strategy saw some success: the number of PR degree programmes mushroomed, more scholars came into the area, and over time more organisations began to recognise the value of PR as a means of establishing better relationships with audiences.

However, the mix of practice and education was not without its tensions. There has always been a divergence of views between those who feel that the purpose of PR education and research is to serve practice, and those who feel academics should deconstruct and challenge it. No matter where PR has been taught, this divide has emerged to a greater or lesser extent, and has marked the ways in which scholars have both collaborated and competed for the power to shape the field. The Public Relations Educators' Forum (PREF) in the UK, for example, was comprised of academics teaching PR (although it was initiated by a practitioner, Tim Traverse-Healey), but also provided an occasional channel to discuss specific issues relating the relationship between practice and education (e.g., criteria for recognition, curriculum content) with the industry association, the Institute of Public Relations (Bournemouth University, 2013). And while PR became more visible in teaching and industry environments because of its focus on delivering well-trained young professionals, as an intellectual domain it retained a limited reputation. The US academy was the main locus of PR-specific research during the 1980s, with almost all research published in JPRR and PRR coming from this region, and the vast majority of articles focused on functional work (Sallot, Lyon, Acosta-Alzuru, & Jones, 2003). The reliance on one main body of theory alongside the focus on building a core of identifiable knowledge, meant that PR researchers rarely published beyond core PR and communication journals. As a result, PR scholarship failed to connect with some of the grand theoretical work going on in other disciplines or connect with scholars working outside PR, despite obvious links to sociology, political communication, media studies and organisational theory.[1]

Compounding PR's isolation was the emphasis on quantitative research methods as a respected means of building knowledge. Early PR work was focused on proving the value of two-way symmetry and Excellence as an approach to PR that had practical application, and positivist epistemology underpinned this mission. As a result, quantitative studies dominated in published research (although in *Public Relations Review* in particular there was a greater openness to theory development and new ideas (Sallot et al., 2003)). The tendency was exacerbated by the fact that, in the US academy in particular, quantitative work tended to be (and still is – see, e.g., Watson & Riffe, 2014) easier to publish, more likely to be funded, and, therefore, was more important for academics trying to build their careers. Unfortunately, while positivist epistemologies have their place in any academy, they have limited power to develop exploratory ideas; interpretivist ontologies and epistemologies are much more productive in this respect. Their absence in the early years of PR meant that rich avenues for theorising PR beyond Excellence were left unexplored, increasing its tendency to intellectual isolation.

Nonetheless, as PR programmes grew and more people became involved in teaching and researching PR, an increasing number began to critique the assumptions of Excellence and promote alternative perspectives, generating more critical debates within the classroom as well as among scholars themselves. In the US, the potential for critique emerged as part of a focus on feminist analyses of PR, beginning with the Velvet Ghetto report in 1986 and continuing with the edited collection, *Beyond the Velvet Ghetto*, three years later (Toth & Cline, 1989). A small but important body of work also built up, focused on the profiles and experiences of Black PR practitioners in the field, revealing their motivations and successes as well as the discrimination they dealt with as part of their roles (Kern-Foxworth, 1989; Kern-Foxworth, Gandy, Hines, & Miller, 1994; Zerbinos & Clanton, 1993). While this early work was not strictly critical, and tended towards liberal rather than radical solutions to both gender and racial discrimination, the themes were picked up again in a more critical fashion over the following years (see below).

The edited collection *PR Theory* (Botan & Hazelton, 1989) included two important chapters from Pearson (on ethics, dialogue and PR) and Cheney and Dionisopoulos (proposing different ways of envisaging publics in PR theory) that started to move away from Excellence theory and explore new directions for PR scholarship in their respective areas. At the same time, scholars from the field of organisational rhetoric, led by Robert Heath, were trying to extend the relevance of rhetorical theory to PR. The edited collection *Rhetorical and Critical Perspectives of Public Relations* (Toth & Heath, 1992) created an important space for US scholars interested in widening the boundaries of PR to publish their work. The book made visible the desire of some academics to exercise and integrate more critical voices and different theoretical ideas into PR scholarship; chapters focused on critical readings of PR history, PR's role in public policy and corporate dominance, as well as specific analyses of PR's role in the nuclear, tobacco and oil industries.

Outside the US, critical thinking about PR emerged as part of attempts by academics to treat PR as an intellectual discipline worthy of study, rather than simply a form of professional training. In the UK, PREF brought PR academics together, and while there was a tendency towards a 'dual identity' among many members (serving practice as well as scholarship), the forum did play a part in ensuring that insights from other disciplines (sociology, political economy, media studies) informed discussions about how PR should be taught. L'Etang and Piezcka were particularly important in driving critical thinking forward in the UK during this period, and their book *Critical Perspectives in Public Relations* (L'Etang & Piezcka, 1996) delivered innovative analyses of PR from perspectives that were not available in other, more standard PR textbooks, including a forensic deconstruction of systems theory (Pieczka, 1996). The volume remains an early milestone in the development of PR perspectives beyond Excellence, and while its circulation was not wide at the time, it made its mark over the coming years among academics in the UK and Europe in particular.

Crossing continents: critical connections

Because of the institutional norms that prevailed in US teaching and publishing, the number of scholars developing a critical approach there remained limited, and most of the early energy around critical scholarship accumulated elsewhere, with the 1990s a particularly important decade for nascent thinking beyond Excellence. Part of the reason for the growth of critical thinking during this decade was the gradual maturation of PR as an academic discipline. Increasing numbers of scholars were awarded doctorates in PR, some of whom were to be among the most prolific critical thinkers in the field. Jacquie L'Etang, Magda Piezcka and Kay Weaver all completed their doctorates at the University of Stirling; Ian Somerville graduated from Queens University, Belfast; while on the other side of the world, Juliet Roper, Judy Motion and Debashish Munshi completed their doctorates at the University of Waikato. David McKie also moved to Waikato at this time and Weaver migrated there from Stirling. Thus, the two universities were becoming important centres for critical thinking about PR. In the US, Donnalyn Pompper, one of the most consistently critical scholars of PR for over a decade, also completed her doctorate at Temple University; while Linda Aldoory, who was to drive forward the field's feminist scholarship, graduated in 1998 from Syracuse University.

In addition, scholars from different areas of the world began to meet, developing connections that both assured these rather marginalised thinkers that they were not alone, and provided impetus for collaborative projects that came to fruition in forthcoming years. The University of Stirling and the University of Waikato both constituted important locations for such meetings: Heath, McKie, Motion and Weaver were among those most travelled. Some connections were also made at conferences; the panel at the 1997 ICA annual conference, "UnAmerican public relations: Global differences in theory and practice", brought together UK and Australasian scholars to present new ways of understanding PR, and was followed by a special issue of the *Australian Journal of Communication* with the same focus (see Weaver, 2014). In Europe the Bled conference and EUPRERA also provided a platform for academics to test out new ideas about PR.

All these scholars began publishing articles that theorised PR in new ways. However, it was still difficult to place critical scholarship in the two main PR journals, which remained dominated by the organisational paradigm and various aspects of Excellence theory. Nonetheless, Ray Hiebert in particular wanted to foster a range of perspectives of PR in his role as editor of *Public Relations Review*, and did publish some critical work (Leitch & Roper, 1998; Len-Rios, 1998;

Mickey, 1997), including Motion and Leitch's (1996) foundational article that put Foucauldian discursive analyses of PR firmly on the map for critical scholars. It was more difficult to publish in *Journal of Public Relations Research*, and the rather limiting situation of only having one special-ist PR journal where one might publish work that was not tied to the organisational paradigm led to some valuable critically oriented scholarship being scattered across other journals, includ-ing the *Australian Journal of Communication* (particularly the 1997 special issue "Public Relations on the Edge", edited by Leitch and Walker, and including a range of contributors from the US, New Zealand and the UK), *Media, Culture and Society* (Davis, 2000; Pieczka, 2002; Tilson, 1993), the *Journal of Business Ethics* (L'Etang, 1992, 1994, 1995), and the *Howard Journal of Communication* (Diggs-Brown & Zaharna, 1995; Kern-Foxworth, 1990). This work probably received more limited exposure among PR scholars as a result. However, it did create the possibility that PR scholarship was seen and read beyond its immediate disciplinary "boundary", potentially helping to improve its status as a more substantial academic discipline.

In the US, liberal analyses of the situation faced by women and ethnic minorities in PR were a minority interest, but even this gentle approach to critique generated conflict between academics and practitioners, making it difficult to develop the topics as a mainstream focus. In fact, the first truly radically critical piece by a US scholar to suggest a transformational approach to PR was Pam Creedon's (1993) powerful article critiquing the 'infrasystem' of patriarchy that dominated systems theory in PR, and advocating radical changes to both practice and scholar-ship. Creedon, however, was a mass communication scholar (see, e.g., Creedon, 1989; Creedon & Cramer, 2007; Rush, Oukrop & Creedon, 2004) and few of her subsequent publications appeared in PR outlets. Hon (1995) published an important article setting out how a feminist theory of PR might look, and arguing for change at individual, organisational and societal level, but as a general rule radical feminist critique remained largely absent from the field. W. Timothy Coombs also published an important critique of the pluralist assumptions underpinning both the systems and the rhetorical approaches to PR, arguing for power issues to be taken more ser-iously by the field (1993). Since this early intervention, and alongside more functional work on crisis management models, he and co-author Sherry Holladay have maintained their calls for a more substantive engagement with the power that PR exerts in society (see, e.g., Coombs, & Holladay, 2007).

Opening up PR: the new century

The first decade of the new century was a time of both building and consolidation for critical thinking. On the basis of the personal connections made during the 1990s, edited books and collaborative work began to appear, while individual scholars also began to find spaces to publish their interpretation of the PR landscape. Publication of critical work accelerated rapidly during the second half of the decade, with a flurry of books and journal articles appearing as critical thinking across the field reached a critical mass. Alternative perspectives of PR became more common, and the horizon for PR research expanded as new publications urged better integra-tion of PR scholarship with other established fields (e.g., political economy, sociology). Personal relationships were also strengthened by collaborative work between the US academy and else-where, and new connections were forged between Scandinavian and UK scholars: an exchange agreement between Stirling and Oslo Universities funded regular exchange visits of academic staff between the two institutions, while Piezcka and L'Etang (then still based at Stirling) devel-oped additional research connections with Örebro University in Sweden.

During the decade, publication boundaries began to weaken as global and critical scholarship appeared more frequently in the major US-based journals. Two new specialist journals were also set up, both initially based in Australia: the *Asia Pacific Journal of Public Relations* (set up in 1999 with support from Deakin University), and the online journal *PRism* (set up 2003 with support from Bond University, and continuing with the support of Massey University). Both provided a space for alternative voices and critical thinking about PR, and *PRism* in particular has become a respected outlet for imaginative scholarship. Its tradition of holding an annual competition for a guest editorship has attracted a range of critical topics, including power in public relations (2012), global public relations (2009) and gender and public relations (2010).

Books and edited collections about PR that incorporated a critical perspective were also published in greater numbers during this period. In the UK, the decade opened with the publication of Kevin Moloney's (2000) *Rethinking Public Relations: The Spin and the Substance.* A political economic analysis, it engaged with the power of PR in broader society and particularly its effects on media, the public sphere, corporate power and democracy. The second edition of the book, *Rethinking Public Relations: PR, Propaganda and Democracy* (2006), and a number of Moloney's journal publications in PR and marketing journals, continued the analysis, with the result that power was placed squarely on the map (for UK scholars in particular) by the middle of the decade. Other political economic analyses of PR appearing at this time included Aeron Davis' *Public Relations Democracy* (2002), an analysis of the ways in which PR was implicated in media, corporate and governmental power networks to the detriment of democracy. Later in the decade, media sociologists David Miller and William Dinan published two highly critical monographs (Dinan & Miller, 2007; Miller & Dinan, 2008) focused on the links between PR and corporate power. Their argument was based on the results of publicly funded research into the use of corporate public relations in UK and multinational companies (Miller, 2005). Finally, Thomas Mickey's *Deconstructing Public Relations* (Mickey, 2002) was an important volume that critiqued PR from a cultural studies perspective, although its uptake was relatively limited among critical scholars, at least initially.

In the US, the first major book publication of this period to extend the audience for critical scholarship was the *Handbook of Public Relations* (Heath, 2001). An extensive volume covering both critical and functional perspectives, the *Handbook* included new approaches to PR alongside normative scholarship and in the process, deliberately positioned critical thinking as a central, rather than marginal interest in the field. The chapters in the opening section included work by McKie, Leitch and Neilson, and Cheney and Christensen, all of which became widely cited for their challenges to normative theory. The *Handbook* also included a critique of PR professionalism by Pieczka and L'Etang, as well as a chapter specifically focused on New Zealand perspectives of PR – perhaps the first that made the case for understanding both practice and scholarship from New Zealand as unique. While these critical chapters only comprised a small portion of the larger book, their presence in such a mainstream, US-published volume confirmed their value to PR scholarship. Five years later, L'Etang and Pieczka (2006) edited a volume explicitly focused on critical debates in the field and including reworked chapters from their original 1996 monograph, for what became a much wider audience. Chapters focused on propaganda, activism, power, discourse, truth, democracy and professionalism, and also included analyses of specialist areas of PR work, including sport, science and religion. As well as making visible the breadth that critical scholarship could encompass, the book, like the *Handbook* before it, brought together voices from different parts of the world and made more visible the community of scholars who had turned away from the Excellence model and were applying a variety of perspectives to PR.

Courtesy of US scholars, postmodernism also made its formal debut into PR theorising during this decade, with articles by Derina Holtzhausen (2000, 2002) – both published in the *Journal of Public Relations Research.* While not consistently critical, her work did outline the ways in which postmodernism could provide a critical perspective that promised to overturn the modernist foundations of the organisational paradigm. Aldoory's (2005) article in the *Journal of Communication* 'reconceived' a feminist paradigm for PR research and set out a new and more critical agenda, encompassing race and class as well as gender. Feminist work in the field also continued with the publication of *Women in Public Relations* (L. Grunig, Toth, & Hon, 2008) which brought together a range of writing – some liberal, some more radical – that continued to push for a feminist agenda in PR. Critical race theory also made its first appearance in PR scholarship at this time, with Pompper (2005) publishing a call for race and class to be addressed more explicitly and critically in the field.

A number of books and articles published between 2005 and 2008 continued the theme of calling for PR scholars to reflect on the gaps in current scholarship. Heath's "Onward into More Fog" (2006) and Karla Gowers' (2006) "Public Relations Research at the Crossroads" – both of which appeared in the *Journal of Public Relations Research* – encouraged scholars to think beyond Excellence and had an important effect on US scholarship. In 2005, McKie and Debashish Munshi guest-edited a special issue of *Public Relations Review* focused on the different perspectives of public relations that were emerging in locations outside the US. The 18 articles included in the special issue drew on scholarship from Iraq to Israel, Norway to New Zealand, and illustrated how a wide range of theories could contribute to a much richer picture of PR that was well equipped to address issues of power and society. McKie and Munshi's (2007) subsequent book, *Reconfiguring Public Relations* drew together some of their previous publications to deliver a manifesto for change in the field, opening up scholarship to ideas such as chaos, complexity and post-colonial theory to deliver new ways of thinking about PR that were concerned more with social, rather than corporate, outcomes.

An important intervention in the same year was the publication of Curtin and Gaither's cultural-economic model of PR (2005, 2007), which represented a clear separation from Excellence theory towards a cultural studies perspective of PR, engaging more explicitly with power and meaning. While using the model need not necessarily lead to critical work, it does require scholars to ask questions about power and how it circulates, courtesy of PR practice. Also in 2007, European and Scandinavian PR scholars made their influence felt perhaps for the first time, with a special issue of *Public Relations Review* focused on social theory and public relations. Edited by Øyvind Ihlen and Betteke van Ruler, the issue – and the subsequent edited book (Ihlen, van Ruler, & Fredriksson, 2009) – also opened up possibilities in the field for pursuing critical sociological analyses of PR by introducing Luhmann, Beck, Habermas, Smith, Weber, Bourdieu and many others. The second edition of *Rhetorical and Critical Approaches to Public Relations* (Heath, Toth, & Waymer, 2009) continued the pattern of using edited books to extend thinking in new and productive ways.

By the end of the decade, critical scholarship was well established. While it still did not receive the same level of attention as normative research, it was a recognisable body of work which was gathering momentum as the field continued to expand. As in the 1990s, new critically oriented scholars had graduated with doctorates to join the field, providing new energy and impetus in the process. They included Natalie Tindall, Jennifer Vardeman-Winter, Damion Waymer and Katie Place in the US; Lee Edwards, Caroline Hodges and Clea Bourne in the UK; Magnus Fredriksson, Josef Pallas and Øyvind Ihlen in Scandinavia; Debashish Munshi and Alison Henderson in New Zealand; and Kristin Demetrious in Australia. New research themes have emerged as a result, including the ways in which race, class and intersectionality affect PR practice, regional and global patterns of hegemony perpetuated by PR, and critical discourse as central to understanding PR.

However, despite this progress, problems remained. Many critical scholars still did not feel there was enough visibility for their work, while journals and reviewers remained wary and sometimes outright unwelcoming of new ideas. Moreover, while edited collections are important as a means of opening up a field, space constraints do not allow contributors to theorise in any depth and so the scope of engagement with new ideas was necessarily limited. Monographs were still in short supply. Finally, connections between US scholars and the rest of the world remained relatively scarce, creating a somewhat lopsided structure to critical scholarship.[2]

Where are we now?

Over the last five years, critical scholarship has arguably come into its own. The volume of critical work being published continues to grow and scholars are taking PR in new directions. While still not straightforward, it is easier to publish critical work within the field, and more is appearing in the mainstream PR journals as well as outside them. Journal special issues on critical topics have appeared, including on "'Race' in/and Public Relations" (Munshi & Edwards, 2011); "Public Relations and Democracy" (Taylor, 2013); "Ethnographic Approaches to PR Research" (L'Etang, Hodges, & Piezcka, 2012) and gender in PR (Daymon & Demetrious, 2010).

Edited collections continue to provide important additions to the range of critical work. Edwards and Hodges (2011) edited *Public Relations, Society and Culture*, a collection specifically focused on developing the "socio-cultural turn" in PR scholarship. Published in the same year, the edited book *Public Relations in Global Cultural Contexts* (Bardhan & Weaver, 2011) included important articles from a range of scholars working in organisational communication, health communication and PR. In 2012, Waymer's edited collection on class, race and culture in PR made its appearance (Waymer, 2012), while in 2013 *Coming out of the Closet* (Tindall & Waters, 2013) introduced a long-overdue exploration of LGBT and queer theory in strategic communication. All these editors – and their contributors – have published journal articles along the way that have expanded critical thinking in the field.

A crucial development since 2012 has been the introduction of a new book series by Routledge, entitled *New Directions in Public Relations Research*. Edited by Kevin Moloney, the series fosters new thinking and has already provided an outlet for monographs that might otherwise be difficult to publish. Publications so far include an edited collection on gender (Daymon & Demetrious, 2013), *Public Relations and the History of Ideas* (Moore, 2014), *Public Relations and Nation Building* (Toledano & McKie, 2013), PR and ethics (Fawkes, 2014), PR, power and diversity (Edwards, 2014) and social media (Motion, Heath, & Leitch, 2015). Routledge has also welcomed stand-alone monographs, publishing *Public Relations, Activism and Social Change* (Demetrious, 2013) as well as a volume on postmodern approaches to PR as activism (Holtzhausen, 2012). With the advent of these longer, more comprehensively theorised works, there is a realistic prospect of greater depth in critical thinking across different areas of PR scholarship. Similarly important has been the advent in 2012 of the new Sage journal *PR Inquiry*. Co-edited by L'Etang, Xifra and Coombs, it has provided a space explicitly dedicated to scholarship that demonstrates more substantial critical engagement with PR than is the case elsewhere.

There is still room for improvement. The US-based PR publications remain dominated by quantitative work and qualitative work tends to be more critically reviewed, making it harder to publish because the benchmark standard seems to be set higher. In *Public Relations Review*, article lengths have become shorter, which limits the degree to which authors can theorise new perspectives effectively, or present qualitative research meaningfully. Across the board, teaching PR is still tightly connected to practice through placements, guest lectures and vocational content, which means new ideas and research are more difficult to pass on to the next generation. However, new programmes are emerging – primarily at taught postgraduate level – that take as their starting point the social, cultural and political effects of PR work, rather than having the organisation at the centre of their curriculum. Scholars still operate in silos; in particular, there are not enough connections between the US and elsewhere, despite the growing strength of critical thinking in North America. Finally, there are still too few doctoral candidates pursuing critical research in PR (indeed, too few doctoral candidates overall); without new faces to drive thinking forward there is a danger that the current wave of creativity will become stale.

Conclusion

History shows that, for critical work to continue to thrive in this rapidly evolving field, certain circumstances need to prevail. Gatekeepers (journal editors, book editors, publishing houses and conference programmers) must continue to invite and allow people to publish differently about PR. Our institutional environment has to be flexible enough to allow us to be adventurous without sacrificing our careers and offer both undergraduate and postgraduate students a broader set of lenses through which they might examine PR (and, I would argue, this will strengthen, not weaken, their skills as practitioners). We must foster intellectually creative thinking among our students and encourage those with the potential and desire to consider pursuing a doctorate in PR.

Of course, we must continue to publish within PR, as well as in journals from fields outside PR (e.g., political communication, queer studies, media studies, ethnic and racial studies, sociology, organisational communication, cultural studies, gender studies), so that the quality of our engagement with other bodies of theory improves and the reputation of PR as a serious academic discipline grows. We must be mobile, fostering relationships across institutions and geographies in order to break down silos, and between us and other fields, to expand our thinking even further.

Most of all, we must retain our desire to change the way the world is. The critical scholars I spoke to before writing this chapter were driven by dissatisfaction with the norm, not only in the PR academy but in the way PR is too often accepted unquestioningly as a matter of course in the increasingly promotional cultures that characterise modern society (Davis, 2013). It is part of our everyday lives, but its influence is multifaceted, not always only good or bad, and mostly somewhere in-between. When academic life is too focused on ticking boxes and meeting targets, critical thinking can be smothered because the personal must necessarily become less political. But if we manage to keep in our sights the right to be angry, to seek and create change, then critical scholarship in PR has a bright future.

Notes

1 Some research on various forms of public relations did appear in other journals (third sector PR, political campaigning, PR as a media source), such as the *Journal of Communication*, the *Journal of Business Ethics*, *Mass Media Ethics* and *Media, Culture and Society*. Some of this work was critical but the majority was also functional, echoing the emphasis on practice that characterised the main body of PR scholarship itself.
2 It is important to note that scholars at the University of Waikato developed strong relationships with organisational communication scholars in the US at an early stage, including George Cheney, Cynthia and Michael Stohl and Linda Putnam. These connections have played an important role in extending the impact of scholarship emerging from the Waikato Management School since the 1990s.

References

Aldoory, L. (2005). A (re)conceived feminist paradigm for public relations: A case for substantial improvement. *Journal of Communication*, 55(4), pp. 668–84.

Bardhan, N., & Weaver, C. K. (Eds). (2011). *Public relations in global cultural contexts: Multi-paradigmatic perspectives*. New York, NY: Routledge.

Botan, C. H., & Hazelton, V. (Eds). (1989). *Public relations theory*. Hillsdale, NJ: Lawrence Erlbaum Associates.

Bournemouth University. (2013). *The archive of the Public Relations Educators' Forum (1994–1999)*. Bournemouth: Bournemouth University. Available at: https://microsites.bournemouth.ac.uk/history-ofpr/files/2010/03/PREF-Archive-1994-1999.pdf

Cline, C., Toth, E., Turk, J., Walters, L., Johnson, N., & Smith, H. (1986). *The velvet ghetto: The impact of the increasing percentage of women in public relations and business communication*. San Francisco, CA: IABC Foundation.

Coombs, T., & Holladay, S. (2007). *It's not just PR: Public relations in society*. Malden MA: Blackwell.

Coombs, W. T. (1993). Philosophical underpinnings: Ramifications of a pluralist paradigm. *Public Relations Review*, 19(2), pp. 111–19.

Creedon, P. (1989). *Women in mass communication: Challenging gender values*. Thousand Oaks, CA: Sage.

Creedon, P. (1993). Acknowledging the infrasystem: A critical feminist analysis of systems theory. *Public Relations Review*, 19(2), pp. 157–66.

Creedon, P., & Cramer, J. (eds) (2007). *Women in mass communication*. 3rd edition. Thousand Oaks, CA: Sage.

Curtin, P. A., & Gaither, T. K. (2005). Privileging identity, difference and power: The circuit of culture as a basis for public relations theory. *Journal of Public Relations Research*, 17(2), pp. 91–115.

Curtin, P. A., & Gaither, T. K. (2007). *International public relations: Negotiating culture, identity and power*. Thousand Oaks, CA: Sage.

Davis, A. (2000). Public relations, news production and changing patterns of source access in the British national media. *Media, Culture and Society*, 22(1), pp. 39–59.

Davis, A. (2002). *Public relations democracy: Public relations, politics and the mass media in Britain*. Manchester, UK: Manchester University Press.

Davis, A. (2013). *Promotional cultures: The rise and spread of advertising, public relations, marketing and branding*. Cambridge, UK: Polity Press.

Daymon, C., & Demetrious, K. (2010). Public relations and gender. *PRism*, 7(4).

Daymon, C., & Demetrious, K. (Eds). (2013). *Gender and public relations: Critical perspectives on voice, image, and identity*. London, UK: Routledge.

Demetrious, K. (2013). *Public relations, activism and social change: Speaking up*. New York, NY: Routledge.

Diggs-Brown, B., & Zaharna, R. (1995). Ethnic diversity in the public relations industry. *Howard Journal of Communications*, 6(1–2), pp. 114–23.

Dinan, W., & Miller, D. (2007). *Thinker, faker, spinner, spy: Corporate PR and the assault on democracy*. London, UK: Pluto Press.

Edwards, L. (2014). *Power, diversity and public relations*. London, UK: Routledge.

Edwards, L., & Hodges, C. E. M. (Eds). (2011). *Public relations, society and culture: Theoretical and empirical explorations*. London, UK: Routledge.

Fawkes, J. (2014). *Public relations ethics and professionalism: The shadow of excellence*. London, UK: Routledge.

Fitch, K. (2014). Professionalisation and public relations education: Industry accreditation of Australian university courses in the early 1990s. *Public Relations Review*, 40(4), pp. 623–31.

Gowers, K. (2006). Public relations research at the crossroads. *Journal of Public Relations Research*, 18(2), pp. 177–90.

Grunig, J. E. (Ed.). (1992). *Excellence in public relations and communication management*. Hillsdale, NJ: Lawrence Erlbaum.

Grunig, J., & Grunig, L. (2002). Implications of the IABC excellence study for PR education. *Journal of Communication Management*, 7(1), pp. 34–42.

Grunig, L., Toth, E., & Hon, L. C. (Eds). (2008). *Women in public relations: How gender influences practice*. New York, NY: Routledge.

Heath, R. (2001). *Handbook of public relations*. Thousand Oaks, CA: Sage.

Heath, R. (2006). Onward into more fog: Thoughts on public relations' research directions. *Journal of Public Relations Research*, 18(2), pp. 93–114.

Heath, R., Toth, E., & Waymer, D. (Eds). (2009). *Rhetorical and critical approaches to public relations II*. New York, NY: Routledge.

Holtzhausen, D. R. (2000). Postmodern values in public relations. *Journal of Public Relations Research*, 12(1), pp. 93–114.

Holtzhausen, D. R. (2002). Towards a postmodern research agenda for public relations. *Public Relations Review*, 28, pp. 251–264.

Holtzhausen, D. (2012). *Public relations as activism: Postmodern approaches to theory and practice*. New York, NY: Routledge.

Hon, L. C. (1995). Toward a feminist theory of public relations. *Journal of Public Relations Research*, 7(1), pp. 27–88.

Ihlen, O., van Ruler, B., & Fredriksson, M. (Eds). (2009). *Public relations and social theory: Key figures and concepts*. New York, NY: Routledge.

Kern-Foxworth, M. (1989). Status and roles of minority PR practitioners. *Public Relations Review*, 15(3), pp. 39–47.

Kern-Foxworth, M. (1990). Ethnic inclusiveness in public relations textbooks and reference books. *Howard Journal of Communications*, 2(2), pp. 226–37.

Kern-Foxworth, M., Gandy, O., Hines, B., & Miller, D. (1994). Assessing the managerial roles of black female public relations practitioners using individual and organizational discriminants. *Journal of Black Studies*, 24(4), pp. 416–34.

Kruckeberg, D. (1998). The future of PR education: Some recommendations. *Public Relations Review*, 24(2), pp. 235–48.

L'Etang, J. (1992). A Kantian approach to codes of ethics. *Journal of Business Ethics*, 11(10), pp. 737–44.

L'Etang, J. (1994). Public relations and corporate social responsibility: Some issues arising. *Journal of Business Ethics*, 13(2), pp. 111–23.

L'Etang, J. (1995). Ethical corporate social responsibility: A framework for managers. *Journal of Business Ethics*, 14(2), pp. 125–32.

L'Etang, J., & Piezcka, M. (1996). Public relations education. In J. L'Etang & M. Pieczka (Eds), *Critical perspectives in public relations*, pp. xxx. London, UK: International Thomson Business Press.

L'Etang, J., & Piezcka, M. (eds). (1996). *Critical perspectives in public relations*. London, UK: International Thomson Business Press.

L'Etang, J., & Piezcka, M. (Eds). (2006). *Public relations: Critical debates and contemporary practice*. Mahwah, NJ: Lawrence Erlbaum Associates.

L'Etang, J., Hodges, C. E. M., & Piezcka, M. (2012). Ethnographic approaches to public relations research [Special Section]. *Public Relations Review*, 38(4).

Leitch, S., & Roper, J. (1998). Genre colonization as a strategy: A framework for research and practice. *Public Relations Review*, 24(2), pp. 203–18.

Len-Rios, M. (1998). Minority public relations practitioner perceptions. *Public Relations Review*, 24(4), pp. 535–55.

McKie, D., & Munshi, D. (2007). *Reconfiguring public relations: Ecology, equity and enterprise*. Abingdon, UK: Routledge.

Mickey, T. J. (1997). A postmodern view of public relations: Sign and reality. *Public Relations Review*, 23, pp. 271–85.

Mickey, T. J. (2002). *Deconstructing public relations: Public relations criticism*. Mahwah, NJ: Lawrence Erlbaum Associates.

Miller, D. (2005). *Corporate public relations in British and multinational corporations*. Swindon, UK: ESRC.

Miller, D., & Dinan, W. (2008). *A century of spin: How public relations became the cutting edge of corporate power*. London, UK: Pluto Press.

Moloney, K. (2000). *Rethinking public relations: The spin and the substance*. London, UK: Routledge.

Moloney, K. (2006). *Rethinking public relations: PR propaganda and democracy* (2nd ed.). Abington, UK: Routledge.

Moore, S. (2014). *Public relations and the history of ideas*. London, UK: Routledge.

Motion, J., & Leitch, S. (1996). A discursive perspective from New Zealand: Another world view. *Public Relations Review*, 22(3), pp. 297–310.

Motion, J., Heath, R., & Leitch, S. (2015). *Social media and public relations: Fake friends and powerful publics*. London, UK: Routledge.

Munshi, D., & Edwards, L. (2011). "Race" in/and Public Relations [Special Issue]. *Journal of Public Relations Research*, 23(4).

Pieczka, M. (1996). Paradigms, systems theory and public relations. In J. L'Etang & M. Pieczka (Eds), *Critical Perspectives in Public Relations*, pp. 124–56. London, UK: International Thomson Business Press.

Pieczka, M. (2002). Public relations expertise deconstructed. *Media, Culture and Society*, 24, pp. 301–23.

Pompper, D. (2005). "Difference" in public relations research: A case for introducing Critical Race Theory. *Journal of Public Relations Research*, 17(2), pp. 139–69.

Rush, R., Oukrop, C., & Creedon, P. (eds). 2004. *Seeking Equity for Women in Journalism and Mass Communication: A 30-Year Update*. New York: Routledge.

Sallot, L. M., Lyon, L. J., Acosta-Alzuru, C., & Jones, K. O. (2003). From aardvark to zebra: A new millennium analysis of theory development in public relations academic journals. *Journal of Public Relations Research*, 15(1), pp. 27–90.

Taylor, M. (2013). Public relations and democracy [Special Issue]. *Public Relations Review*, 39(4).

Tilson, D. (1993). The shaping of "eco-nuclear" publicity: The use of visitors' centres in public relations. *Media, Culture & Society*, 15(3), pp. 419–35.

Tindall, N., & Waters, R. (2013). *Coming out of the closet: Exploring LGBT issues in strategic communication with theory and research*. New York, NY: Peter Lang.

Toledano, M., & McKie, D. (2013). *Public relations and nation building: Influencing Israel*. London, UK: Routledge.

Toth, E., & Cline, C. (Eds). (1989). *Beyond the velvet ghetto*. San Francisco, CA: International Association of Business Communicators.

Toth, E., & Heath, R. (Eds). (1992). *Rhetorical and critical approaches to public relations*. Hillsdale, NJ: Lawrence Erlbaum Associates.

Watson, B., & Riffe, D. (2014). Who submits work to JMCQ and why? A demographic profile and belief summary. *Journalism and Mass Communications Quarterly*, 9(1), pp. 5–16.

Waymer, D. (Ed.). (2012). *Culture, social class and race in public relations: Perspectives and applications*. Plymouth, UK: Lexington Books.

Weaver, C. K. (2014). A history of public relations scholarship in Aotearoa New Zealand: From working on the margins to setting disciplinary agendas. *PRism*, 10(1).

Zerbinos, E., & Clanton, G. A. (1993). Minority practitioners: Career influences, job satisfaction, and discrimination. *Public Relations Review*, 19(1), pp. 75–91.

2

History as a source of critique

Historicity and knowledge, societal change, activism and movements

Jacquie L'Etang

Introduction

This chapter foregrounds the ongoing dilemma of the object of public relations research (Edwards, 2012) and of public relations historical research in particular. This public relations problematic affects the ways in which current public relations practitioners and academics understand their respective public relations practices and operating assumptions, and their ability to affect and shape public relations historicity. The starting point for this chapter is that public relations activities have typically emerged at historical points of emerging change, transformation and contestation (L'Etang, 2011, p. 224) and suggests that public relations histories should be repositioned and embedded within histories of broader societal shifts. This historiographically influenced chapter explores the potential contribution of social theory in relation to evolutionary change, public relations processes, and the historical role for public relations work within these in relation to knowledge and information. Insights from social theory are drawn upon to problematise the relationships among and between public relations, societal change and social movements. This chapter offers an interpretation of public relations history and historiography viewed through a focus on activism and social movements, and gives emphasis to the importance of an orientation away from an organisational focus towards positioning public relations as societal change or process (not progress), calling to mind the process sociologist Elias's concept of *flow*, Simmel's *flux*, *vitalism*, *force* and *energy drive*, and Bourdieu's *creative energies* (Lash, 2005; Papilloud & Rol, 2004; van Krieken, 2001). Within the public relations literature, Edwards (2012) drew on Appadurai to describe public relations as *flow*, highlighting the dynamics of communicative circuits in an approach that was distinctively different to the established portrayal of public relations as organizational function and professionalizing occupation. The chapter is an argument about the necessity to broaden the methodological approaches to public relations history, in particular the way in which public relations historical work is framed by historians – for example within varied concepts and intepretations of modernity, postmodernity, the public sphere, political economy, communicative action, governance and the social imaginary. It is argued that the intersections, processes and dynamics among and between societal change, history, historical knowledge and public relations need closer examination to take into consideration varied levels of analysis and theoretical frames that impact relationships between public relations and society, and different perspectives and readings of those relationships. This stance situates public relations history much more clearly within social theory and political science and thus contributes further to the 'socio-cultural turn' identified by Edwards and Hodges (2011) but effectively a 'tipping-point' since a few critical voices had been present, though somewhat muffled, over the previous 20 years. Finally, the chapter argues that by considering history and historical understanding as dynamic and ever-open to new interpretation and meaning, history itself can be a source of ongoing critique.

First, it is necessary to deal with the ontological issues concerning the object of public relations history and the purposes of public relations histories. In other words, what should the history of public relations be, and why? Public relations historiography has identified the distinction between a narrow focus on the named occupation of public relations and the broader approach that encompasses 'Proto-history' of earlier eras (Bentele, 1997, 2010, 2013; L'Etang, 1995, 2004, 2008, 2014, forthcoming; Watson, 2014a, 2014b). 'Proto-history' is presented by Bentele in a structuralist and, to some degree, progressive, fashion and encompasses practices prior to the establishment of a discrete occupation (public relations). This broader conception stretches through human history to include a range of public communication by regal, political and religious leaders employing a variety of techniques. Typical of this approach in historical public relations literature is that of Cutlip (1995), whose book on US public relations history began with the colonial era and noted the extensive promotional efforts in England to attract immigrants and fundraise; and Cutlip, Center and Broom's (1994, p. 89) reference to, 'a farm bulletin in Iraq that told farmers in 1800 BC how to sow their crops, how to irrigate, how to deal with field mice, and how to harvest their crops'.

The inclusive approach to public relations history bears comparison with ideas in the field of rhetorical studies (Lunsford, 2009) which, although it is primarily focused on language within the context of written records and the dissemination of written ideas, also encompasses archaeological inscription (Enos, 2009), the performative (Wilson & Eberly, 2009) and visual rhetorics (including the carnivalesque), an aspect of communication very relevant both to public relations events and to activism. Although public relations literature has engaged with rhetoric in relation to classical critiques of sophistry and the philosophical conceptualizations of discourse and argument (Heath, 1992, 1997, 2001, 2011; Ihlen, 2002, 2009, 2010; L'Etang, 1996, 1997, 2010; Mackey, 2013; Marsh, 2012) it has not given much attention to performative and dramaturgical aspects of monuments and the built environment. Such broader approaches may position public relations history and historiography within histories of public communication.

There are, of course, some interesting questions about why history has become interesting for public relations academics, and the motivations involved. Is it purely about finding out the truth of claims made by many public relations practitioners who, by the nature of their trade, are oh-so-aware of the importance of being 'the first'? Or is it about finding connections, lineage and respectability? Or from an essentialist perspective seeking some universal societal role? Thus, public relations history may be a quest for respectability or legitimation (part of the struggle for professionalism). This leads to wider questions about the positioning and tensions within public relations and between public relations and the wider world in relation to its role in innovation or tradition, conflict or continuity, and large-scale change such as industrialization, urbanization, bureaucratization and globalization. In other words, all public relations histories contribute to different ways of seeing the world as well as specific public relations worlds or spaces.

It is important to combine sociological insights with historical imagination in order to locate public relations in historical action/societal change while taking into account sociological insights. Closer attention to change processes and the spaces in which public relations-type activities occur can lead to (1) closer recovery of public relations antecedents, and (2) public relations histories that go beyond eventism, and (3) contribute to the development of sociological and critical thinking in public relations – albeit that which is tempered by historical understanding and imagination. This chapter draws attention to activism and social movements since they may be regarded as a form of public relations work concerned with advocacy, promotion, events, lobbying and public affairs, communicating with a wide range of publics, and are clearly directed towards change as a form of social action and the realization of idealized goals. In this way public relations may be understood as intervention directed at collective action, concepts developed sociologically by Touraine (Brincker & Gundelach, 2005; Kivisto, 1984).

The blending of history with sociology has its own history and paradigmatic struggles. These are not the focus of this chapter, although they are, or ought to be, important for all public relations academics tackling historical projects as they affect methodological issues, the tensions between micro and macro levels and overall theorization, as well as important wider considerations such as the role of public relations-type activities in grand transitions such as globalization and neo-liberalism. Self-awareness is also necessary to avoid the trap of ahistoricism – which arises from developmental or evolutionary schemes that can be traced back to Comte and critiqued as mechanistic, and treating '[t]he direction of history as pre-determined, fatalistic, independent of human efforts' (Sztompka, 1986, p. 324).

As noted elsewhere (L'Etang 1995, 2004), initial approaches to conceptualizing public relations history were progressive, based on a particular periodization of US history designed to suggest that public relations practice had developed from basic publicity through public information, to an enlightened, morally desirable and conveniently more effective form of public relations characterized as 'two-way symmetrical communication'. Critiques of the Excellence project, within which the concept of symmetry was located, date back to Pieczka (1996) and challenged the prevailing worldview; as did Motion & Leitch's (1996) Foucault-influenced work on discourse. Part of the history of the discipline has been the privileging of US accounts and paradigms – to the extent that these were widely and uncritically promoted and adopted in a range of cultural contexts. Increasingly there has been recognition of this cultural imperialism, which is beginning to be corrected (Bardhan & Weaver, 2011; Maloney, 2006; McKie & Munshi, 2007; Sriramesh & Verčič, 2012) as part of the 'socio-cultural turn' (Edwards & Hodges, 2011) that took nearly two decades to gain purchase.

Cultural background is significant in approaches to history and sociological history, and needs to be taken into account in tackling public relations history. As Sztompka (1986, p. 326) pointed out, American sociology had radically different origins to European sociology, and not only had a shorter history but was dominated by,

> A single socio-economic system of industrial capitalism and thus unaware of the birth pangs of transition from traditional to modern society, but at the same time [was] exceptionally complex in its racial, ethnic and class composition, ridden with multiple cleavages, contradictions and conflicts.

As a consequence of the historical and cultural context from which they sprang, American sociologists evidently focused on strategies to ensure the smooth functioning of society and were strongly influenced by psychology, social behaviourism, symbolic interactionism and exchange theory, and they were fast to adopt structural functionalism (Sztompka, 1986, p. 327). These important currents can be seen to have shaped the school of American public relations and the take-up of melioristic ideas such as communitarianism, social capital and civil society theses. In contrast, European antecedents (such as Marx, Weber, Gramsci and Lukacs) took a more integrated approach. For example, activistic or praxistic readings of Marx (Topolski, 1968; Sztompka,

1979) as a theory of socio-historical praxis focused on how human agents make history that arises from 'Double dialectics: of actions and conditions (structures and situations within which people act) and of actions and knowledge (social consciousness)' (Sztompka, 1986, p. 325).

It is the interplay among and between actors, actions and structures, and the political and symbolic communication and representation of these, that is where public relations-type work is situated. It is present both in the detailed relational dynamics of building support and in the promotional communications on behalf of interest groups, as well as in the symbolic structuring of organization, space and place.

The interrelationships between historical understandings and societal self-understandings, change dynamics and relationships, and ways of interpreting public relations activities and discourse in ongoing contexts, leads us to understand how public relations may be understood as change agent, or as a resistance to change. It may be understood as action and as discourse. Yet generally, as has now been acknowledged, it is explored at organizational rather than at societal levels. A longer lens, and the use of social theory, may offer new ways of understanding public relations in macro-historical processes, so that public relations history is not solely the history of public relations activities (the occupational development), but rather is positioned more fundamentally within social development. Furthermore, this could trigger an important pedagogical shift from microscopic technical 'case studies' that are valued as 'useful', and evidence that public relations education delivers 'transferable skills', to a broader level education focused on societal dynamics and communication interventions. Macro-sociological and macro-historical approaches may help to generate a new range of critical lines of inquiry central to public relations history/historiography and those who write it – in particular in relation to the following aspects:

- public relations as historical action/change and the multiple levels of involvement/intersections of public relations and the ways in which these affect public relations identities, self-understandings (including public relations academics' and public relations practitioners' senses of their own history), historical roles, and history-making activities and productions
- the relationship between agents/actions and structures, social processes and change, and the role of public relations in these dynamic flows, exchanges, accommodations and conflicts
- public relations as the problematic of social change (focus for conflict) – allowing further reflection on the role of public relations in society, social change and societal processes
- an historicist approach to situating public relations activities as part of social change
- the role of public relations in constructing historical understandings
- the role of public relations in societal self-understandings of past and present
- the role of public relations, or public relations activities, in facilitating historicity
- public relations history as social transformation and collective action.

These problematics are important to public relations historians at both phenomenological and historiographical levels because they generate reflexive historical research and thought in the field. It also highlights the necessity for public relations historians to consider their own presuppositions in relation to their historical work, historical theoretical paradigms (e.g. historical structuralism), and the way in which they determine the objects of 'public relations history'. It also raises questions about where public relations history is located: within institutional history, corporate history, political history, social history or economic history?

The stance taken here is from a conflictual, rather than a consensual perspective. Consensuality has influenced public relations academic values and fashions, both research and teaching. The approach taken here follows Touraine in the notion of conflictual actions as a counterpoint to Habermas's focus on consensus-building and integration. Touraine's emphasis on the centrality of conflictual action means that his concept of communication gives more importance to irreducible differences between participants than it does to consensus-building and projects of reconciliation; instead focusing on conflictual action and difference (Tucker, 2005).

Exploring the overlap and relationship between public relations and social movements, while also drawing on insights from social theory, may be a useful step towards locating public relations within multi-discursive contexts and power struggles. The development of a specialized tradition focusing on social movement rhetoric is a significant source for public relations scholars interested in multi-vocal public address, patterns of public discussion, protest and body rhetorics, and counter-publics (Cox & Foust, 2009). Within social movement theory, some basic questions were asked in the 1980s that are equally relevant to public relations analysts, and not only in relation to social movements,

> How should theorists conceive of the relationship between rhetoric and its object – the social movement? Are movements identifiable phenomena whose life and success depend on rhetoric? Should scholarship emphasise theory-building or historical and critical analysis? Should critics conceive of movements as born of, or engaged in, oppositional struggles with rhetorically defined "enemies"?
>
> *(Cox & Foust, 2009, p. 610)*

The fundamental Othering between activism/social movements and public relations has not always been sufficiently well examined in terms of forces for change and resistance within the public relations literature, or in terms of the internal values, politics and histories of the discipline (but see Holtzhausen, 2011; Demetrious, 2013).

Social movements and activism

In terms of basic definitional hierarchical concepts and linkages, it is possible to understand social movements as long-term campaigns; activism as specific historical events and conflicting agents; and public relations as organizational strategic communication. However, these commonsensical distinctions are not clearly bounded and are open to reinterpretation and new meanings. Approaches to understanding social movements and new social movements (NSMs) are diverse – encompassing the empirical (case studies, campaigns), resource mobilization theory, technological determinism, networks/spaces, political mediation and collective actions. However, as Touraine warned:

> If we call any type of collective action a social movement, it is neither necessary nor even possible to theorize it – no more than doctors can theorize spots or fever as a general type of disease, since very different pathologies can generate such symptoms. Those who think they are making an analysis by describing anything that disturbs the social organization as a social movement are saying nothing. The notion of a social movement is useful only if it allows us to demonstrate the existence of a very particular type of social action that allows a social category – and it is always a particular category – to challenge a form of social domination that is at once particular and general. It does so in the name of general values or social orientations which it shares with its adversary, and it does so in an attempt to deny the adversary's legitimacy.
>
> *(Touraine, 2000, p. 90)*

Touraine argued that a social movement was much more than issue activism or political lobbying, but that it challenged more fundamental decisions about resource allocation, and, in order to distinguish this more fundamental type of challenge, he promoted the use of the term 'societal movement' to describe those that 'challenge[d] society's general orientations' (Touraine, 2000, p. 90). This important distinction should be borne in mind while reading the following review of some public relations sources that may have been influenced by more popular definitional categories that blur the important distinctions that Touraine made, and to which I return later in this chapter.

Public relations and social movements/activism share a number of common features – for example, technical practicalities, campaign focus, and shared challenges of evaluation/impacts. For a substantial period in public relations literature, activism was Othered by a largely hostile public relations dominant paradigm that was reflected in some practitioner worlds; for example, Pieczka's ethnographic account reported practitioners' comments that they perceived activists as frightening, disturbing, distorted reflections of themselves (Pieczka, 2006). Holtzhausen (2011) and Demetrious (2013) reversed the dominant trend but literature on activism, both in and out of public relations, is often functional, case-based, trait-based, under-theorized and often not critical (see Amenta, 2014). Earlier sources within public relations include Anderson (1992), Berger (2005), Dozier and Lauzen (2000), Holtzhausen and Voto (2002), Henderson (2005), McCown (2007), Murphree (1991), Stokes and Rubin (2010). Caution should therefore be exercised not to assume that research into activism is necessarily either critical or radical, and to be wary of such paradigmatic claims. Activism may be attractive to those in the critical paradigm, possibly because it is a closer fit with critical scholars' ideological position and values and because activism is necessarily oppositional, but that does not mean that research itself is critically focused. There are challenging questions to be asked of activists, for example, with regard to propaganda and cultism. Framing public relations as an element within social movements not only repositions public relations ideologically but also challenges those within social movements/activism to acknowledge and face critiques of persuasive communication and propaganda. In other words, it may force those from social movement/activist perspectives to see themselves rather differently as part of public relations practices.

The conceptual relationship between public relations and social movements/NSMs has not been widely subjected to close analysis, but as Eder (2003) pointed out, 'Movements…create communicative spaces…[they become] the mass carrier of the public sphere.' Historically, social movements – and particularly new social movements – played their role in a shift in cultural analysis and the cultural turn in historical theory, opening up multiple subaltern perspectives within social history focused on a range of cultural phenomena such as consumption (relevant to both public relations and marketing history) – with much greater focus on meaning (Hall, 2003, pp. 156–7).

According to Cox and Foust (2009) social theorists focused analysis to interpret movements as foci for identity formulation and as a 'politics of recognition' offering an alternative to the rational-actor resource-mobilization proponents (Zald & McCarthy, 1979). A cultural discursive turn saw movements increasingly understood as sites for rhetoric and not as univocal unity. In comparison, public relations scholarship still writes of organizations as a single unit and references to 'society' and 'culture' are also presented as coherent, consensual, functional units rather than sites of dissensus, conflict and dysfunction. Organizational policies and organizational utterances are presented as representative – embodied in the public relations 'spokesperson' – yet in public relations literature the politics of organizations is not generally taken into consideration. In fact, this represents a challenging area for empirical study: it is a minefield for research ethics protocols since organizations exert considerable dominance over employees (notwithstanding claims of 'engagement') and reconstruct their identities, daily realities and psyches. The concept of 'counter-publics' in organizations is limited to 'the' public of trades unions or the 'employees' in international/employee communications (who in practice are often subjected to management propaganda).

According to sociologist Touraine (2000, p. 92), traditional social movements aim '[t]o abolish a relationship of domination, to bring about the triumph of a principle of equality, or to create a new society'. Such movements are concerned with societal change in relation to human social justice – for example, slavery, worker rights, gender equality, race. The concept of NSMs encompasses a very wide range of expanding issues and rights claims – for example, animal welfare/liberation. Collective action has become fragmented – either defending vested interests, resisting change such as globalization, or engaging in rights appeals for minorities (Touraine, 2000, p. 92). A further category is that of New Religious Movements (NRMs), the last of which have raised issues of distorted manipulative communication/propaganda, a subject given much attention by sociologists and psychologists – for example, Eileen Barker's work on the Moonies at the LSE in early 1980s (Barker, 1984). The rise of network society (Castells, 1996) highlighted increased technological resources that facilitate social movements and issue groups, and converged media offers multiple opportunities (de Jong, Shaw and Stammers, 2005; Lievrouw, 2011; Meikle & Young, 2012). NSMs employ creative performative techniques not accounted for within the Habermasian public sphere (Tucker, 2005, pp. 42–60). The role of fantasy, creativity, experimentation, playfulness and the social imaginary are central to social change, according to Castoriadis, who considered history to be

> The emergence of the radically new, constantly supplying novel forms to society which can be taken up in the social field. All societies have different modes of "historicity"; their definitions of history…the imagination finds its possibilities in the social historical world.
>
> *(cited in Tucker, 2005, p. 51)*

The notion of historicity was central to the sociologist Touraine, whose ideas about the potential that social movements and activism possessed to change society, and his thesis of applied sociology, entailed 'sociological interventions' that were designed to promote social transformation rather than social integration. He aimed to

> Construct the theory of new social movements in the conviction that my theoretical work will have the reflex effect of helping these collective actions to take shape, and that these actions will in fact constitute the struggle of class actors for the social management of a field of historicity.
>
> *(Touraine 1981, p. 42)*

Touraine's ideas are of interest because they embrace and promote a conflict perspective with which this chapter aligns. Likewise, historical sociologist Tilly conceived of the claims of publics on elites as 'contenders', subsequently focusing his research on 'contention' and theorizing about 'contentious politics' (Tilly & Wood, 2013, p. ix). Touraine's ideas fed into the conception and development of action research (recently taken up in public relations by Pieczka & Wood, 2013). Not only does his approach offer relevant critique about the purposes of history, it also offers considerable inspiration and an insight into a conflictual approach to public relations that presents an alternative to the heavily promoted values of consensuality, negotiation, symmetry and dialogue. These ideas are now briefly discussed within the limited context of their implications for public relations historians, and their insights into their underlying assumptions and values.

Historicism and historicity

These broader questions are relevant to public relations historians at both phenomenological and historiographical levels in order to generate reflexive historical research and thought in the field.

Historicity may be understood as the ability of society to initiate and shape its own history, and to reflect and act and be informed by history. The concept raises questions about how historical meaning is generated, circulated and revised in ways that makes society possible in the context of a backdrop of continuous change, flux and transformation. The role of communications and communicative agents within this is clearly relevant to an understanding of public relations history and antecedents. Historicity is thus part of inter- and intra-societal dynamics that in itself generates action. It is therefore a creative process arising as 'self-product of society' (Touraine, 1977). Historicity is thus a process. The past is a raw material for constructing social reality within constraints (Sztompka, 1986); or, as Dubos put it: 'The past is not dead history, it is living material out of which man makes himself and builds the future.' Historicity generates knowledges and shapes understandings and flows of current understandings; therefore control of historicity is of importance to any community. For example, it might be argued that journalists and journalism, and media studies academics, have appropriated public relations historicity and in doing so have largely shaped cultural insights and knowledges about it; there continues to be an ongoing struggle between the collective actors in the fields of public relations and journalism.

Historicism resists the objectification and theorization of concepts across time, arguing, for example, that 'class is a relationship, not a thing, defined by men as they live their own history' (Thompson, 1963, pp. 9–11). Such approaches resist any 'supra-historical framework or any theoretical modelling of generic social processes' (Hall, 2003, p. 155).

The notion of creativity provides an alternative conception of the public sphere, as discussed by Castoriadis who highlighted 'the centrality of fantasy and image rather than rationality as a key to understanding individual and social change' (Tucker, 2005, p. 42). For Castoriadis (1987, pp. 264–5) the social imaginary was informed by history as

> The emergence of the radically new, constantly supplying novel forms to society which can be taken up in the social field. All societies have different modes of "historicity", their definitions of their history. But most historians and social scientists adapt a causal social scientific or historiographic model that limits their understanding to the repetition of the same, events tied to one another, inhibiting their understanding of the possibility of new historical configurations.

Public relations historical work is in its early stages and generally descriptive and explanatory, and contextualizing its emergence – but there is potential for more creative and playful explorations that acknowledge the limits of frameworks.

In Touraine's account, communication is seen as focused around '[t]he conflictual appropriation of historicity by collective actors who struggle for control of it' (Arnason, 1986. p. 144). It is this insight that suggests the importance of considering the relationship between public relations and social movements, and the role of public relations in societal conflict or struggle – including discursive struggle. It also raises interesting questions as to the object of public relations research and the politics of the discipline in relation to its scope and focus. Touraine argued that

The study of society should be replaced by the study of social action [and that we should] reorganise our representation of social life around the notions of social movement, structural conflict and cultural stakes [resources and goals] which are valued and desired by two or more opponents, the most important stake being social control of the main cultural patterns…through which our relationships with the environment are normatively organized… [and] the study of strategies, organization and decisions].

(Touraine, 1985, cited in Arnason, 1996, p. 140)

For Touraine there was a privileged relationship between social movements and historicity; he saw social movements (which he later described as societal movements) as a new paradigm of societal change, causing ongoing interactions and confrontations in time and space, all caught up in macro-historical processes beyond their control. According to Touraine:

The historical system of action, the political system and the organizational system are intermediate levels between the analysis of historicity and that of concrete social units delimited in time and space and responding to historical situations … the transformation of historicity into functioning systems and organized collectivities.

(Arnason, 1986, p. 144)

Touraine argued that struggles in post-industrial society were about information in the cultural sphere; and that consequently, social movements and conflicts struggle for control of historicity (Brincker & Gundelach, 2005, p. 366). Directed and intentional communication – public relations – is crucial to these discursive battles. Touraine's analysis highlights multiple entwined dimensions across societal spaces within which exist discursive power struggles for the control of historicity. Thus, public relations history has a place in political science and sociology within the dialectics of action, structure and process. Public relations and public relations history is part of the generation and circulation of meaning about itself and other primary sponsoring agents. Touraine argued that there remains a central conflict in post-industrial technological/information society that profoundly affects the ability of people to live together,

Can we live together, or will we allow ourselves to become trapped in our differences, or to be reduced to the status of passive consumers of a mass culture produced by a globalized economy? ….Will we become Subjects, or will we be torn, as the whole of social life tends to be torn, between the world of instrumentality and the world of identity? The central conflict in our society is being waged…by a Subject struggling against the triumph of the market and technologies, on the one hand, and communitarian authoritarian powers on the other. This cultural conflict seems to me to be as central to our society as economic conflict was to industrial society, and as political conflict was to the first centuries of our modernity.

(Touraine, 2000, p. 89)

The struggle identified by Touraine raises challenges for the social legitimacy of formal organizational public relations, and also raises questions about individual public relations access, literacies and capacities. The challenge for public relations historians and critics is to trace the role of public relations within processes of the webs of institutionalization, production, marketisation and political economy; and to reconsider the implications for understandings of public relations' societal roles.

Conclusions/implications

This chapter has argued that public relations histories are not fixed static entities, but rather fluid interpretations centred on societal flux and transformation, linked to social movements and activism, and embedded in cultural dynamics and a range of public communication. Understanding public relations in history, and public relations' history-making as blending processes of flow, flux and dynamic energies of dominance positions, the public relations historian is a discursive agent creating texts that generate meanings that are open to new interpretations within and without public relations scholarship and public relations practice communities. Histories contribute to individual and group identities over generations (including the identities of public relations practitioners and activists), and are therefore significant considerations for organized communication, and, indeed, may well be at the root of action. The historian thus plays a crucial role in facilitating ongoing debate within public relations scholarship and practice in terms of knowledge exchange that can help practitioners to reflect upon their historical and societal roles and relationships, and to take actions informed by those histories. Public relations histories that take a sociological slant contribute insights into the conflicts that trigger the need for organized communications, and the various change agents that contribute to that debate. Historicity conceptualizes history in society as a site of struggle over social change and cultural patterns (Touraine, 1985 cited in Arnason, 1986: 140) and such struggles entail rhetoric and persuasion.

Historical understandings and reflections of past societal alignments, social movements and activism can inform ongoing and critical interpretations of past and present public relations practices. These practices include activities that may not be described as public relations, sometimes for ideological reasons. Placing public relations on a continuum that links it to propaganda and persuasion, and activism and social movements, positions it as one of a series of linked activities and terms engaged in the rhetorical and political contexts of societal conflict and change. For this reason public relations histories can be usefully considered by a broad range of philosophical, political and social theorists. Public relations historians are central to understanding how historical meanings about public relations are communicated and debated within the context of societal change, both past and present; and how those understandings inform ongoing and future change. The fluid metaphors promoted in this chapter offer an alternative to the archaeological and sedimentary propositions of Bentele (2010) and permit reflexive histories and historicities that facilitate debate and deeper understandings of the social imaginary (Taylor, 2003).

The chapter has also argued for repositioning public relations as part of wider social change and movements, rather than as a discrete story. Understanding public relations in this way interprets its emergence as part of the professionalization of social movements – a phenomenon that has already been critiqued within activism literature because the institutionalization associated with professionalization is already evident through the disproportionate recruitment of middle class activists and the fear of 'social movement bureaucrats, more interested in forwarding their own organizations and careers than in the welfare of their own constituencies' (Tilly & Wood, 2013, p. 157). Such pessimism continues to have purchase in discussions about the role of public relations in society, and in claims that are made about its ethics and contribution to democratic practice. At the same time, it highlights the need for continuing debates about the construction and interpretation of historical texts in relation to ongoing interpretations of what counts as public relations work and spaces. Communications practitioners' engagement with the processes of self-understanding in relation to their historical role in societal change and history's role in society and societal transformation may contribute a less dichotomous understanding of relations between public relations and activism and their societal, as well as organizational locus.

References

Amenta, E. (2014). How to analyse the influence of movements. *Contemporary Sociology: A Journal of Reviews*, 43(1), pp. 16–29.

Anderson, D. (1992). Identifying and responding to activist publics: A case study. *Journal of Public Relations Research*, 4(3), pp. 151–65.

Arnason, J. (1986). Culture, historicity and power: Reflections on some themes in the work of Alain Touraine. *Theory, Culture & Society*, 3(3), pp. 137–52.

Bardhan, N., & Weaver, C. (2011) (Eds) *Public relations in global cultural contexts: Multi-paradigmatic perspectives*. New York, NY: Routledge.

Barker, E. (1984). *The making of a Moonie: brainwashing or choice?* Oxford, UK: Basil Blackwell.

Bentele, G. (1997). PR-historiographie und functional-integrative schtung. Ein neuer Ansatz zur PR-Geschichtsschriebung. In Szyszka, P. (Ed.), *Auf der suche nach einer identitat. PR-Gesschichte als Theriesbaustein* [In search of identity: PR history as a building block for PR theory], pp. 137–69. Berlin, Germany.

Bentele, G. (2010). *PR-historiography: A functional-integrative strata model and periods in German PR history*. Paper presented to International History of Public Relations conference, University of Bournemouth.

Bentele, G. (2013) Public relations historiography: perspectives of a functional-integrative stratification model. In K. Sriramesh, A. Zerfass & J-N Kim (Eds), *Current trends and merging topics in public relations and communications management* (New York: Routledge).

Berger, B. (2005). Power over, power with, and power to relations: Critical reflections on public relations, the dominant coalition and activism. *Journal of Public Relations Research*, 12(1), pp. 3–22.

Brincker, B., & Gundelach, P. (2005). Sociologists in action: a critical exploration of the intervention method. *Acta sociologica*, 48(4), pp. 365–75.

Castells, M. (1996). *The rise of the network society*. Oxford, UK: Blackwell.

Castoriadis, C. (1987). *The imaginary institution of society*, trans. Kathleen Blamey. Cambridge, MA: MIT Press.

Cox, R., & Foust, C. (2009). Social movement rhetoric. In A. Lunsford (Ed.), *The Sage handbook of rhetorical studies*. Thousand Oaks, CA: Sage.

Cutlip, S. M. (1994). *Public relations: The unseen power: a history*. Hillsdale, NJ: Lawrence Erlbaum Associates

Cutlip, S. M. (1995). *Public relations history: From the 17th to the 20th century. The antecedents*. Hillsdale, NJ: Lawrence Erlbaum Associates.

Cutlip, S.M., Center, A., & Broom, G. (Eds) (1994) *Effective public relations*, 7th edition. Englewood Cliffs, NJ: Prentice-Hall.

De Jong, W., Shaw, M., & Stammers, N. (2005). *Global activism, global media*. London, UK: Pluto Press.

Demetrious, K. (2013). *Public relations, activism and social change: Speaking up*. New York, NY: Routledge.

Diani, M. (2000). Simmel to Rokkan and beyond: Towards network theory of (new) social movements. *European Journal of Social Theory*, 3(4), pp. 387–406.

Dozier, D., & Lauzen, M. (2000). Liberating the intellectual domain for the practice: Public relations, activism and the role of the scholar. *Journal of Public Relations Research*, 12(1), pp. 3–22.

Dubos, René (1968). *So human an animal*. New York: Scribner's.

Eder, K. (2003). Social movements and democratization. In G. Delanty, & E. Isin (Eds), *The handbook of historical sociology*, pp. 276–87. Los Angeles, CA: Sage.

Edwards, L. (2012). Defining the "object" of public relations research: A new starting point. *Public Relations Inquiry*, 1(1), pp. 7–30.

Edwards, L., & Hodges, C. (Eds). (2011). *Public relations, culture & society: Theoretical and empirical explorations*. London, UK: Routledge.

Enos, R. (2009). Rhetorical archaeology: Established resources, methodological tools, and basic research methods. In A. Lunsford (Ed.), *The Sage handbook of rhetorical studies*, pp. 35–52. Thousand Oaks, CA: Sage.

Hall, J. (2003). Cultural history is dead (long live the hydra). In G. Delanty, & E. Isin (Eds), *The handbook of historical sociology*, pp. 151-67. London, UK: Sage.

Heath, R. (1992).The wrangle in the marketplace: A rhetorical perspective of public relations. In E. Toth, & R. Heath, R. (Eds) *Rhetorical and critical approaches to public relations*. Hillsdale, NJ; Lawrence Erlbaum Associates.

Heath, R. (1993).Toward a paradigm for the study and practice of public relations: A rhetorical approach to zones of meaning and organizational prerogative. *Public Relations Review*, 19(2), pp. 141–55.

Heath, R. (1997). Legitimate "perspectives" in public relations: A rhetorical solution. *Australian Journal of Communication*, 24(2), pp. 55–63.

Heath, R. (2001).A rhetorical enactment rationale for public relations: The good organization communicating well. In R. Heath (Ed.), *Handbook of public relations*, pp. 31-50.Thousand Oaks, CA: Sage.

Heath, R. L. (2011) External organizational rhetoric: bridging management and socio-political discourse. Management Communication Quarterly 25(3), pp. 415–435.

Henderson, A. (2005).Activism in "Paradise": Identity management in a public relations campaign against genetic engineering. *Journal of Public Relations Research*, 17(2), pp. 117–37.

Holtzhausen, D. (2011) *Public relations as activism: Postmodern approaches to theory and practice*. New York, NY: Routledge.

Holtzhausen, D., & Voto, R. (2002) Resistance from the margins: The postmodern public relations practitioner as organizational activist. *Journal of Public Relations Research*, 14(1), pp. 57–84.

Ihlen, O. (2002). Rhetoric and resources: Notes for a new approach to public relations and issues management, *Journal of Public Affairs*, 2(4), pp. 259–69.

Ihlen, O. (2009). Good environmental citizens? The green rhetoric of corporate social responsibility. In R. Heath, E. Toth, & D. Waymer, D. (Eds), *Rhetorical and critical approaches to public relations II*, pp. 360–74. New York, NY: Routledge.

Ihlen, O. (2010).The cursed sisters: Public relations and rhetoric. In R. Heath (Ed.), *The Sage handbook of public relations*, pp. 59-70.Thousand Oaks, CA, Sage.

Kivisto, P. (1984). Contemporary social movements in advanced industrial societies and sociological intervention: An appraisal of Alain Touraine's pratique. *Acta Sociologica*, 27, pp. 355–66.

Lash, S. (2005). Lebenssoziologie: Georg Simmel in the information age, *Theory, Culture & Society*, 22(3), pp. 1–23.

L'Etang, J. (1995). *Clio among the patriarchs? Historical and social scientific approaches to public relations: A methodological critique*. Paper presented to the International Public Relations Symposium, Lake Bled.

L'Etang, J. (1996). Public relations and rhetoric. In J. L'Etang, & M. Pieczka (Eds), *Critical perspectives in public relations*. London, UK: International Thompson Business Press.

L'Etang, J. (1997). Public relations and the rhetorical dilemma: Legitimate "perspectives", persuasion, or pandering? *Australian Journal of Communication*, 24(2), pp. 33–53.

L'Etang, J. (2004). *Public relations in Britain: A history of professional practice*. Mahwah, NJ: Lawrence Erlbaum Associates.

L'Etang, J. (2008).Writing PR history: Issues, methods and politics. *Journal of Communication Management*, 12(4), pp. 319–35.

L'Etang, J. (2010). "Making it real": anthropological reflections on public relations, diplomacy and rhetoric. In R. Heath (Ed.), *The Sage handbook of public relations*, pp. 145–63.Thousand Oaks, CA: Sage.

L'Etang, J. (2011). Public relations and marketing: Ethical issues and professional practice in society. In G. Cheney, S. May, & D. Munshi (Eds.), *The handbook of communication ethics*, pp. 221–41. New York, NY: Routledge.

L'Etang, J. (2014). Public relations and historical sociology: Historiography as reflexive critique. *Public Relations Review*, 40(4), pp. 654–60.

L'Etang, J. (2015 in press) Where is public relations historiography? Philosophy of history, historiography and public relations. In Watson, T. (Ed.) *Public relations historiography*. Palgrave Macmillan.

L'Etang, J., & Pieczka, M. (Eds). (1996). *Critical perspectives in public relations*. London, UK: International Thompson Business Press.

Lievrouw, L. A. (2011). *Alternative and activist new media*. Cambridge, UK: Polity Press.

Lunsford, A. (Ed.). (2009). *The Sage handbook of rhetorical studies*.Thousand Oaks, CA: Sage.

McAdam, D., McCarthy, J. D., & Zald, M. N. (Eds.). (1996). *Comparative perspectives in social movements: Political opportunities, mobilizing structures and cultural framings*. Cambridge, UK: Cambridge University Press.

McCown, N. (2007).The role of public relations with internal activists. *Journal of Public Relations Research*, 19(1), pp. 47–68.

Mackey, S. (2013). A sophistic, rhetorical approach to public relations, *Prism*, 10(1): pp. 1–14. Retrieved on 23 April 2015 from http://www.prismjournal.org/

Maloney, K. (2006) *Rethinking PR: PR, propaganda and democracy*: London, UK: Routledge.

Marsh, C. (2012). Converging on harmony: Idealism, evolution and the theory of mutual aid. *Public Relations Inquiry*, 1(3), pp. 313–37.

McKie, D., & Munshi, D. (2007) *Reconfiguring public relations: Ecology, equity and enterprise*. New York, NY: Routledge.

Meikle, G., & Young, S. (2012) *Media convergence: Networked digital media in everyday life*. London, UK: Palgrave Macmillan.

Motion, J., & Leitch, S. (1996). A discursive perspective from New Zealand: Another world view. *Public Relations Review*, 22(3), pp. 297–309.

Murphree, V. (1991) Public relations 1900–1950: Tool for profit or social reform? In Sloan, W. M. (Ed.) *Perspectives on mass communication history*. Hillsdale, NJ: Lawrence Erlbaum.

Papilloud, C., & Rol, C. (2004). Compromise, social justice and resistance: An introduction to the political sociology of Georg Simmel. *Social science information*, 43(2), pp. 205–31.

Pieczka, M. (1996). Paradigms, systems theory and public relations. In J. L'Etang, & M. Pieczka (Eds), *Critical perspectives in public relations*, pp. 124–56. London, UK: International Thomson Business Press.

Pieczka, M. (2006). Public relations expertise in practice. In J. L'Etang, & M. Pieczka (Eds), *Public relations: critical debates and contemporary practice*, pp. 279–302. Mahwah, NJ: Lawrence Erlbaum Associates.

Pieczka, M., & Wood, E. (2013). Action research and public relations: Dialogue, peer learning, and the issue of alcohol. *Public Relations Inquiry*, 2(2), pp. 161–83.

Sloan, W. D. (Ed.). (1991). *Perspectives on mass communication history*. Hillsdale, NJ: Lawrence Erlbaum Associates.

Sriramesh, K., & Verčič, D. (Eds). (2012). *Culture and public relations: Links and implications*. New York, NY: Routledge.

Stokes, A. Q., & Rubin, D. (2010). Activism and the limits of symmetry: The public relations battle between Colorado GASP and Philip Morris. *Journal of public relations research*, 22(1), pp. 26–48.

Sztompka, P. (1979). *Sociological dilemmas: toward a dialectic paradigm*. New York, Academic Press.

Sztompka, P. (1986). The renaissance of historical orientation in sociology. *International Sociology*, 1(3), pp. 321–337. doi:10.1177/026858098600100308.

Tarrow, S. (1996). States and opportunities: The political structuring of social movements. In D. McAdam, J. D. McCarthy, & M. N. Zald (Eds), *Comparative perspectives in social movements: Political opportunities, mobilizing structures and cultural framings*. Cambridge, UK: Cambridge University Press.

Taylor, C. (2003). *Modern social imaginaries*. Durham, NC: Duke University Press.

Thompson, E. P. (1963). *The making of the English working class*. New York, NY: Pantheon.

Tilly, C. (2011). Why and how history matters. In R. E. Goodwin (Ed.), *The Oxford Handbook of Political Science*. Oxford, UK: Oxford University Press.

Tilly, C., & Wood, L. (2013). *Social movements 1768–2012*, 3rd edition. Colorado: Paradigm.

Topolski. J. (1968). *Metodologia historii (Methodology of history)*. Warsaw: Polish Scientific Publishers.

Touraine, A. (1977) *The self-production of society*. Chicago: The University of Chicago Press.

Touraine, A. (1981). *The Voice and the eye: An analysis of social movements*. Cambridge: Cambridge University Press.

Touraine, A. (1985). An introduction to the study of social movements. *Social Research*, 52(4), pp. 749–787.

Touraine, A. (2000). *Can we live together? Equality and difference*. Cambridge, UK: Polity Press.

Touraine, A. (2007). Sociology after sociology. *European Journal of Social Theory*, 10(2), pp. 184–93.

Tucker, K. (2005). From the imaginary to subjectivivation: Castoriadis and Touraine on the performative public sphere. *Thesis eleven*, 83, pp. 42–60.

van Krieken, R. (2001). Norbert Elias and process sociology. In G. Ritzer, & B. Smart (Eds), *Handbook of social theory*, pp. 353–66. London, UK: Sage.

Watson, T. (2014a). Preface. Special issue: Public relations history. *Public Relations Review*, 40(4), pp. 621–2.

Watson, T. (2014b). Let's get dangerous – a review of current scholarship in public relations history. *Public Relations Review*, 40(4), pp. 874–7.

Wilson, K., & Eberly, R. (2009). The common goods of public discourse. In A. Lunsford (Ed.), *The Sage handbook of rhetorical studies*, pp. 423–32. Thousand Oaks, CA: Sage.

Zald, M., & McCarthy, J. (1979). *The dynamics of social movements*. Cambridge, MA: Winthrop.

3

Articulating public relations practice and critical/cultural theory through a cultural-economic lens

Patricia A. Curtin, T. Kenn Gaither and Erica Ciszek

Introduction

In 2009, when asked whether public relations was dead, US industry analyst Brian Solis (2009, para. 5) mused that while still among the living, "PR is in a state of paramount crisis....Perhaps up until now, we have been our own worst enemy." In the years since, many global experts have declared public relations "dead as a strategic management function in large organisations and corporations" (Burns, 2013, p. 1). With "the praxis of public relations...in dire straits," the health of public relations theory is under increasing scrutiny (Venter & Louw, 2012, p. 294). Many scholars have developed much work within an empirical-administrative tradition, closely linking practice and theory, often to the latter's detriment. Others have argued that the development of robust theory "requires a conscious uncoupling of the intellectual agenda from the day-to-day thoughts, actions, and pre-occupations of practitioners" (Dozier & Lauzen, 2000, p. 4).

Increasingly, such uncoupling is occurring through the "socio-cultural turn" in public relations scholarship (Edwards & Hodges, 2011), which examines public relations as a cultural phenomenon immersed in social and political contexts (Ihlen & van Ruler, 2009; Ihlen & Verhoeven, 2012; Weaver, 2011). This scholarship embraces human agency (Leitch & Neilson, 2001), positioning culture as central to meaning-making (Bardhan & Weaver, 2011). Whereas organization-centered perspectives have allowed theorists to distance themselves from the role of public relations in society, a critical/cultural perspective foregrounds processes of continuously renegotiating meaning, making it integral to social functioning (Berger, 1999; Leichty & Warner, 2001).

In this chapter we outline one such approach: the cultural-economic model (CEM) of practice (Curtin & Gaither 2005, 2007). Because a model is not theory but its precursor (Bill & Hardgrave, 1973), we build theory on the model's foundation through development of the concepts of *articulation* and *context*. Applying the resulting theoretical insights to the palm oil industry, we demonstrate how the CEM provides heuristic value at micro, meso, and macro levels of analysis (Dozier & Lauzen, 2000) and is inclusive of areas once deemed outside the realm of public relations praxis and theory, such as activism and social justice (Coombs & Holladay, 2012).

The circuit of culture and the cultural-economic model

The cultural-economic model of public relations (CEM) rests on the Open University's circuit of culture (du Gay, Hall, Janes, Mackay, & Negus, 1997; Figure 1). Its roots lie in Marx's circuit of capitalism and Hall's (1980) subsequent encoding-decoding model, drawing on the Frankfurt School's neo-Marxism. In response to Johnson's criticism (1986–87) that these approaches privileged institutions and modes of production over context and lived experience, scholars developed the circuit to retain structural constraints while incorporating more discursive postmodern traditions (Grossberg, 1986a). For example, the model privileges discourse over semiotics and embraces politics and relative power as central concepts (Kramer, 2004).

The model thus encompasses a shift from classical political-economic thought to that of cultural economy. The resulting tension between structure and context is manifest in the model through the way historicity shapes the bounds of the five moments (regulation, representation, production, consumption, identity), but their interplay is the site of continuously (re)negotiated power dynamics (Curtin & Gaither, 2005). *Regulation* comprises formal and informal controls on cultural activity, such as technological infrastructure, educational systems, laws, and cultural norms. It constructs social order, providing the rules by which we operate and the common sense that guides us. It is in the moment of regulation, for example, that what we label "spin" and what we define as "legitimate" public relations becomes codified.

Representations are formed through language: "We give things meaning by how we *represent* them" (Hall, 1997, p. 3). The meanings contained in representations are part of a fluid, shared, contextually bound cultural space. In the CEM, campaign materials embody organizational discourses, reflecting producers' goals and objectives. Gandy's (1982) notion of information subsidies, which media relations specialists use to shape public agendas, and the use of civil disobedience by some activist groups to drive political agendas, are examples of representations.

Production, both material and symbolic, informs the logistical and ideological boundaries of representations. A number of factors shape the moment of production, such as technological and cultural resources, desired results, and the intersectionalities of class, race, and gender, among others. Many US public relations materials, for example, are produced within a well-resourced corporate culture informed, in part, by white, male privilege and neoliberal economic assumptions.

Production provides a series of possibilities, but *consumption* determines which will be realized because meanings reside not in objects themselves but in the relationships those objects create between producers and consumers (Curtin & Gaither, 2005). Production and consumption form a conjoined cycle because consumption is "not the end of a process but the beginning of another, and thus itself a form of production" (Mackay, 1997, p. 7). The meanings that producers imbue campaigns materials with, then, may not be the meanings that consumers intuit, and the relations that producers intend to establish are often not the relations that result. The CEM emphasizes the necessity of environmental monitoring to track shifting meanings.

Identities derive from the discursive interplay of producers and consumers. Because they arise within multiple contexts (e.g., individual, organizational, national), they are often fractured, conflicting, and always in process. Identities are constructed through difference and power (Hall, 1996): "All signifying practices that produce meaning involve relations of power, including the power to define who is included and who is excluded" (Woodward, 1997, p. 15). Identities are fluid and often self-defined, making the delineation of target audiences for a campaign less of an exact science and more of an art of continuously (re)negotiated engagement.

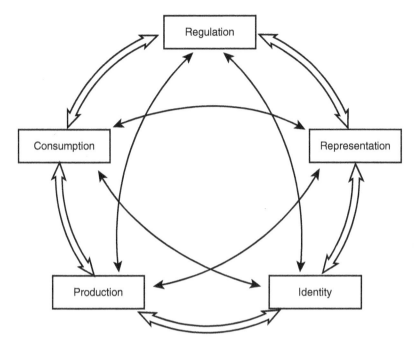

Figure 3.1 The circuit of culture, basis for the cultural-economic model of public relations practice

The five moments conjoin to form "a shared cultural space in which meaning is created, shaped, modified, and recreated" (Curtin & Gaither, 2007, p. 38) in what are termed *articulations*. The term was chosen because of its dual meaning – to express and to join together.

Extending the CEM through articulation theory

The roots of articulation theory lie in Laclau, who rejected the reductionism of classical Marxism in favor of an approach encompassing the struggle to fix meaning and define reality. For Laclau (1977), meaning derives from relationships, or articulations, which are not necessary or given but can be transformed and modified by context, comprising the intertwined and equally important political, economic, and social spheres.

Laclau proposed an extreme degree of relativism, however, that the circuit does not embrace. Within the CEM, articulations are always formed in relation "to material practice and historical conditions" (Grossberg, 1986b, p. 57), although those conditions are not determinative. A constant tension exists between structural constraints and localized agency, making each articulation a "complex set of historical practices by which we struggle to produce identity or structural unity out of, on top of, complexity, differences, contradiction. It signals the absence of guarantees" (Grossberg, 1986a, p. 63). Foucault's (1977) notion of genealogy, which provides an understanding of how relationships arise through contingencies within historical contexts shaped by power (Motion & Leitch, 2009), is similar in approach.

The concept of articulation can provide much insight into public relations theory-building because relationships are forged in and through the articulation process; they are the manifestations of the temporary linkages formed. As such, they are formulated within discourses that enable or write out of consideration a range of possible meanings, actions, and norms. Articulations, then, are the processes of forming relations or alliances to achieve a purpose (Weinstein, n.d.). Relational webs result from the ways in which the CEM's five moments are joined within articulations.

Contrary to relationship management theory, which posits relationships as things that can be measured, articulation theory's emphasis on the process of building relationships highlights human agency, not the relationships themselves. By focusing on process, the CEM examines the strength of the resulting ties, who is included/excluded in the process, what meanings are created (Weinstein, n.d.), and the political and ideological connotations of the resulting webs of relationships (Grossberg, 1986b, p. 55).

At any given historical moment, an articulation is real, but it's not the only reality possible: articulations are "not necessary, determined, absolute and essential for all time. You have to ask, under what circumstances *can* a connection be forged or made?" (Grossberg, 1986b, p. 53; emphasis in original). The articulation process is constrained and can only unify under particular conditions. No one moment guarantees the next, not all articulations are possible, and not all relationships can be created or maintained. Conversely, some relationships will form more readily, appearing "natural."

Although articulations are temporary, contingent junctures and not preordained (du Gay et al., 1997), "some articulations are particularly potent, persistent, and effective" (Slack, 1996, p. 124). When articulations form complex structural webs (i.e., social formations) that persist over time, they are termed *conjunctures* (Grossberg, 2006, 2010). Similar to Foucault's regimes of truth, these webs give the appearance of complete, stable structures and form our common sense knowledge, our reality. As such, they are not easily broken apart (i.e., dearticulated) or reformed into new relational webs (i.e., rearticulated).

Theorizing context

The relative tenacity of articulations is shaped by context: "Different connections will have differing forces in particular contexts…not all connections are equal, or equally important" (Grossberg, 2010, p. 21). Context, however, cannot be considered separate from, or outside of, articulations (Slack, 1996). Contexts are "an active organized and organizing assemblage of relationships…produced even as they 'articulate' the 'facts' or individualities and relations that make them up" (Grossberg, 2010, pp. 30–1). The CEM, therefore, does not propose that relationships are formed within a context of culture, which privileges the anthropological meaning of the term, but instead posits that the process of forming webs of relationships creates meaning, and therefore culture, through discursive practice (Curtin & Gaither, 2005). Culture is not a separate, measurable variable but is integrated into a web of social and material relations (Grossberg, 2006).

As Grossberg (2013) observes, *context* is rarely defined and theorized. Similar to culture, researchers often conceptualize it as a separate, concrete variable rather than as comprising spatial and relational aspects, making it inherently political. Grossberg (2010), building on the work of Deleuze and Guattari, delineates three interrelated aspects of context: *milieu, territory, ontologic*. Although his borrowed terminology is obtuse, his explication is insightful.

Milieus constitute time/space boundaries, or locations. They bridge the discursive and non-discursive realms, the social and the physical, forming the more stable geography of any given articulation. Milieus are the "political, economic, social, and cultural practices" that form the sum of material relations and make certain articulations possible and not others (Grossberg, 2013, p. 37). They are not random but possess a logic that can be examined somewhat independently of their respective territories and ontologies.

Territories constitute the affective realm, our lived reality. They form "a limited space, a dynamic space for carrying out actions" (Grossberg, 2013, p. 36). As such they are always defined in relation to others: a territory "sets up complicated relations between belonging and alienation, identity and identification, subjectivation and subjectification" (Grossberg, 2013, p. 34). Territories are more inherently unstable than are milieus, but they can never be considered separate from them. Instead, milieus and territories connect in contingent and determined ways that are also unpredictable. They don't bound experience; they form the lived topography of experience (Grossberg, 2013).

The *ontologic* encompasses historicity: it is the world we have inherited, but it is not the world as it has to be. It forms, in theoretical terms, the "contingent conditions of possibility of milieus and territories and their relations" (Grossberg, 2010, p. 35). It is our given way of relating to the world, providing us with knowledge of what opportunities exist and where it is possible to go from our current position (Grossberg, 2013). It is the ontologic context that most clearly outlines power flows and demarcates structural factors within the CEM.

The overlapping constructs of context are best viewed not as a "logic of boundaries" but as a "logic of connectivity" (Grossberg, 2010, p. 34) that locates milieus within "webs of relations and practices" (p. 33). Researchers can map this assemblage of relationships among the physical, socially constructed, and historically received realities, although Grossberg (2013, p. 35) cautions that "the best map is not always the articulation of all three together." Such a schematic, however, allows scholars to trace the multiple fracture lines, balancing points, and structural stabilities of the webs of relationships formed through articulations; to trace their underlying logic (Grossberg, 2006); and to examine issues at micro, meso, and macro levels of analysis, while recognizing the connections among them.

Social justice and the context of public relations practice

At the heart of the CEM, shaping the articulation process and resulting relationships, is the Foucauldian notion of power as expressed in relationships, not as an essential property of particular people or things. The CEM provides the contextual framework for power to be enabling and productive because it is key to freedom and agency in every relational web: "If there are relations of power through every social field it is because there is freedom everywhere" (Foucault, 1988, p. 12). Contrary to many critical/cultural approaches that endow structures with power while reducing human agency (Fawkes, 2012), the CEM encompasses human agency and the formation of subjectivities in a fluid form. Through power, subjects construct themselves and consequently systems of inclusion and exclusion (Mumby, 2011).

If public relations practice is conceived as embedded in and formative of cultural, social, and economic discourses in part by how power shapes their contours, then public relations practice cannot be separated from issues of social justice (Curtin & Gaither, 2012). A critical/cultural perspective clearly ties marketplace forces to issues of social justice (Schaefer, Conrad, Cheney, May, & Ganesh, 2011), but the CEM produces social justice possibilities in terms of both/and (rather than either/or) and does not fall prey to the reductionism of false dichotomies (see also Coombe, 2010).

In contrast, some postcolonial theorists have argued that capitalism is inherently unethical, "manipulating the local for the interest of the global" (Dutta, 2011, p. 43). Consequently, practice becomes tarred by the same brush; public relations serves the interests of transnational corporations, maintaining a West-centric hegemony (Dutta & Pal, 2011) and creating an always-silenced "other" (Edwards, 2012). Within this perspective, public relations practice is antithetical to social justice, unless activist public relations that challenge the economic status quo are valorized as the epitome of ethical practice (e.g., McKie & Munshi, 2007).

The CEM instead provides space for competing, multiple discourses and articulations. Transnational corporations, activist groups, INGOs, and others actively engage in creating discourses based on their "vested interests…to shape organizational or public policy" (Roper, 2011, p. 71), and all are consumers of competing discourses. Issues of social justice arise through the relational webs those discourses weave, not through an essentialist moral quality of organizations themselves.

In the following section we use palm oil to illustrate these concepts in practice and demonstrate how the CEM informs public relations theory.

The many articulations of palm oil

The most consumed vegetable oil is beta-carotene rich, trans-fat-free palm oil. Oil palms are native to Africa, but European colonizers spread the trees to tropical countries on other continents, in part because oil palms produce up to two tons of oil for every acre planted – more than any other crop. When synthetic rubber production soared after World War Two, oil palms replaced languishing rubber plantations as the cash crop (Ng & Lim, 2013). In the 1970s, the World Bank and the International Monetary Fund funded oil palm projects in so-called underdeveloped nations (Roberts, 2010) as a "significant source of poverty alleviation" (World Growth, 2011, p. 12). Palm oil, then, is grounded in a milieu of formerly colonized, tropical, resource-rich areas, which drives its articulation with colonialism and the subsequent development of neoliberal economic policies. The legacy of colonization permeates discourse surrounding palm oil in countries that produce it, imbuing messages and actions with specific meanings tied to power imbalances of economics, opportunity, and race/ethnicity, among others.

From 1990 to 2013, global consumption of trans-fat-free palm oil quintupled as manufacturers incorporated palm oil into 50 percent of all processed food after health officials raised concerns about dietary fat (Skinner, 2013). To meet skyrocketing demand, Indonesia and Malaysia, which produce 85 percent of global supply, have cleared large amounts of primary and secondary forestland for new plantations. Consequently, palm oil has become synonymous with deforestation for many stakeholders, sparking boycotts, demonstrations, civil disobedience, and other activist action.

These differing territories, or lived realities, among those who make their living from palm oil and those who potentially consume it have created competing discourses. For the Indonesian and Malaysian governments, palm oil means economic sustainability; it is the "golden egg-laying goose" (Hamid, 2011, para. 6) that helped them survive the Asian fiscal crisis and has contributed to sustained economic growth (Chandran, 2014; CIA World Factbook, 2014a, 2014b). The industry is integral to their poverty eradication programs, providing 4.5 million mainly rural poor workers with access to healthcare and education through corporate philanthropy (World Growth, 2011). For countries such as Indonesia and Malaysia, proposed European environmental labeling standards constitute an affront to national sovereignty, their right to develop, and the assumption of their rightful place in the global economic order (Raghu & Koswanage, 2014). The European Union thus becomes an economic bully working to protect its own soy and sunflower oil producers (Cheng, 2014). This set of articulations conflates neoliberal economic policies with progress, and positions corporations, not governments, as responsible for providing social services, writing out of consideration alternative economic and social policies.

Deforestation provides a competing environmental discourse that has proven particularly potent in the West. Although deforestation has disproportionately contributed to greenhouse gas emissions, severe air and water pollution, and the use of child and slave labor (Skinner, 2013), it is habitat loss that has been the most enduring articulation. Of the many endangered species affected, the orangutan has become the symbol of palm oil devastation, making it a metonym for all of deforestation's ills. Everyone from Greenpeace demonstrators (Curtin & Gaither, 2012), to Girl Scouts (Curtin, 2014), to a punk band in Bali (Smith, 2014) is telling consumers they face a stark choice: palm oil or orangutans. The linkage is so strong that the trade group promoting sustainable palm oil has identified Western zoos as primary opinion leaders for its strategic communication campaign (RSPO, 2013). This articulation creates a simplified, false binary (e.g., palm oil or orangutans, economy or environment), erasing many possibilities and overshadowing others, such as the documented link between palm oil production and human slavery (Skinner, 2013).

Some trade groups are trying to replace environmental discourse with one based in health. The Malaysian Palm Oil Council, for example, uses medical experts to promote palm oil's potential benefits in preventing dementia, heart disease, and cancer (Heisler, n.d.). Such efforts have not been fully successful, however. Although prominent health personalities such as Dr Oz have adopted the health messaging, they also revert to the environmental discourse by noting that any oil consumed should be from a "sustainable" source (Wylde, 2013). The Roundtable on Sustainable Palm Oil (RSPO), comprising corporations, governments and INGOs, was formed in 2004 to establish and enforce sustainability criteria, but the group is frequently seen as inadequate at best, greenwashing at worst (Gies, 2014; Skinner, 2013). Its sustainability discourse is most often called "mere public relations" or "spin" (e.g., C. Wood, 2014), thus dismissing any relationship to meaningful action.

The competing discourses that arise around palm oil highlight the differing identities producers and consumers have imposed upon it, from golden goose, to orangutan killer, to health cure. Each encompasses a web of articulations that has proven relatively potent and persistent in different contexts, and each writes differing possibilities into existence. If palm oil is a golden goose making the lives of 4.5 million citizens better, or a cheap substance that prevents major illnesses, then curtailing production would be ludicrous and oppositional to social justice goals. Conversely, if palm oil is directly responsible for killing an endangered species, then curtailing production may be the only reasonable, and just, action. Organizations use public relations to develop campaigns around each of these identities to create shared meanings with consumers and guide public opinion and policy.

Contributing to the formation of these competing discourses are the conditions of production, such as technology. Activist groups, such as the Bali punk band, are accumulating financial resources through crowdfunding sites such as Kickstarter, to take their message on the road and create a merchandising line (Smith, 2014). Within certain contexts, then, social media have allowed otherwise marginalized groups to accumulate political and economic capital. In turn, these groups can disseminate messages to publics across milieus and socioeconomic strata and help shape discourses that can scorch bottom line businesses and the reputations that public relations ostensibly protects.

Conversely, technologies can constrain production, rather than encourage it. For example, Malaysian oil palm firms, faced with increasing domestic regulations and costs (Ismael, 2012), have been accused of land grabbing in lower-income countries (Hansia, 2014), suggesting the formerly colonized may be the new colonizers. Such actions are coming to light in large part because of new technologies, mainly satellite mapping, which allow governments and INGOs to determine the actual status of remote forestlands (May-Tobin & Goodman, 2014). Satellite imagery has become the panopticon of the palm oil industry, providing continuous surveillance that disciplines behavior (Foucault, 1979). Just the fact of its existence is forcing companies to comply with land use laws and environmental restrictions (Spencer & Chong, 2013).

Technology, then, can be both freeing and constraining. It can help level the playing field or encourage increasing inequality, depending on context.

Distinguishing the CEM from other critical approaches

As the palm oil example demonstrates, the CEM embraces the relative complexity of the interplay of the political, economic, and social spheres. As such, the CEM precludes readily quantifiable approaches at the same time it eschews the reductionism that characterizes many critical approaches. Conversely, the inclusion of historicity avoids the pitfalls of sheer relativism, the hallmark of many more postmodern approaches. What distinguishes the CEM is the continual tension shaped by power flows between structural determinants and situational particulars. This perspective accounts for ontological constraint and focuses scholarly attention on the processes by which public relations practitioners form relationships to serve strategic purposes rather than the relationships themselves. It also allows scholars to extrapolate the intricate topographies of context intersecting at a trio of levels – spatial, lived experience, and structural.

The trade-off is that the CEM provides no set roadmap, easy stock answers, or clear predictive power. It problematizes practice; it doesn't simplify it. What it contributes is heuristic power to previously understudied areas of public relations and a means to recast the discipline and extend theoretical development.

Articulating production and consumption

The CEM, for example, highlights processes, not products, and how constraints and power flows mold those processes. This focus changes the research goal from measurable results or predetermined bottom lines to an exploration of how building relations creates linkages among concepts, their inclusivity (and therefore exclusivity), the shared identities they attempt to create, and their larger sociological, economic, and political implications. One contribution is how multiple producers and consumers participate in shaping competing discourses surrounding an issue. In the case of palm oil, one group's sustainability discourse becomes another's greenwashing discourse; a government's poverty eradication discourse becomes another's environmental degradation discourse.

This discursive dance between producers and consumers stands in stark contrast to traditional public relations theory, which holds that practitioners (producers) create materials (representations), send them to target publics (consumers), and then gather feedback, making resulting theory organization-centric. Conversely, many critical approaches take a Marxist approach, empowering producers and disempowering consumers through the imposition of hegemonic practices, making consumers the passive recipients of corporate messages.

The CEM posits instead that producers write into or out of consideration many facets of an issue, but consumers possess similar power, making the resulting web of relations and consequent meanings a constantly (re)negotiated process. Whereas traditional theory suggests a vertical, linear transmission model between producers and consumers, and critical theory a horizontal top-down model, the relationship between producers and consumers in the CEM is perhaps best conceptualized as a mobius strip. The process of discourse formulation has no clear beginning or end, and producers and consumers are conjoined in an ongoing process, with no bright line of demarcation. The CEM thus erases the sharp distinctions often made, for example, between organizational practitioners and activists, empowered and disempowered, inside and outside. Instead, the CEM "allows us to study public relations…as [an] integral *part of* the larger sociocultural environment, not *apart from* it, providing new conceptual tools to inform public relations scholarship" (Curtin, 2014, p. 24).

Articulation theory provides the CEM the means to unpack how discourses contain and create areas of meaning. It permits scholarly examination of the intersectionalities of discourses by unmasking areas of concern that have been omitted and erased. Stakeholder theory often talks of the need to prioritize stakeholders (Coombs, 1998); articulation theory makes plain the consequences of that action. We can view articulations in some sense as framing an issue – by the very connections made, some issues are no longer included in the picture.

Contextualism: avoiding reductionism and universal truths

Another contribution of the CEM is that context is not simply a physical space that contains events but formative of meanings and how they are used in everyday life. Theorizing context as both spatial and political helps scholars avoid the reductionism of false binaries. One example from current theoretical perspectives is the notion of globalized public relations practice consisting of generic principles combined with localized cultural or contextual variables (e.g., Sriramesh, 2009), which reinforces a global/local dichotomy. In contrast, the CEM embraces a fluid continuum of hybridity, recognizing that the global and local are always blended in ways that reflect the power structures of the ontologic, the lived realities of the territory, and the material processes of the milieu. By parsing context in this way, analysis of global/local flows can take place at micro, meso, and macro levels of analysis, while always being cognizant of the points of contact among them.

The radical contextualism of the model also nullifies the possibility of a universal articulation of justice or ethics, such as the international professional code of ethics espoused by some public relations theorists (Hunt & Tirpok, 1993; Kruckeberg, 1989). To legislate the universal is to negate the agency of the particular and to assume that a dynamic practice can be reduced to a static set of rules that operates independent of power dynamics (Taylor & Hawes, 2011). As in all parts of the model, however, this emphasis on the local is balanced by the ontologic aspect of an articulation's context and the historicity surrounding its formation, which negates radical relativism. Structures play a formative role in allowing opportunities for social justice to emerge – or not. They also are constitutive of how social justice is defined and what it includes and excludes in any given articulation.

Public relations practices, then, may contribute to social justice, although they don't necessarily do so. To paraphrase Grossberg (1986b), who was echoing Hall, a cultural-economic approach to public relations practice comes without guarantees. But unlike many of its critical predecessors, it opens up the possibilities for public relations to contribute to social justice, and it does so in a way that is grounded in praxis and not in normative ideals. Thus the model avoids the general self-interest inherent in public relations ethics in which outcomes are judged in terms of serving client interests (L'Etang, 2011).

Awakening public relations from its coma

The insights of the CEM can be applied to public relations scholarship itself. For example, when attempts are made to dearticulate and rearticulate conjunctions, they become sites of struggle and resistance, evoking crises or "passive revolutions" (Grossberg, 2006, p. 5). Again, similarities to Foucault's thought are evident. Foucault viewed history as a series of disruptions, or epistemic breaks (Mills, 2004). This concept of historicity or disjunctures defies an "evolutionary" perspective of public relations as a discipline (Brown, 2006) and suggests instead that "there is no single, coherent, or unbroken narrative to be told about public relations…despite the typical presentation of itself…in terms of a progressive development" (Cheney & Christensen, 2001, p. 168).

Articulation theory creates space for multiple forms of practice and for the disjunctures of globalized practice, which Appadurai (1996, p. 31) characterized as "a form of negotiation between sites of agency and globally defined fields of possibility." Disjunctures represent the emergence of changing and unexpected relationships, rather than a smooth progression toward a defined goal. Disjunctures shape the possibilities within which "discourse and practice inform each other" (Edwards, 2011, p. 34).

From this perspective, we observe along with Solis (2009) that "PR is broken, but it is far from dead." Or as another industry analyst observed, "*PR is not dead*. It never has been. It's just in a coma" (S. P. Wood, 2014, para. 13). Our extension of the cultural-economic model into fledgling theory presents an inclusionary conceptualization of public relations practice that has demonstrable traction in a hybridized glocal world, awakening the field from its self-induced coma. It avoids easy binaries by examining relationships as dynamic processes among empowered agents, such as positioning producers and consumers as each possessing agency and responsibility and each capable of acting self-reflexively to address the social justice issues raised by global commodities and their conditions of production. As such, the CEM and articulation theory provide the basis for inclusive public relations theory and practice, but without the guarantee of an outcome in any particular instance. But that very absence of guarantees, the tension between the boundaries of the possible and the promise of multiple possibilities, is its strength. The CEM thus fully conceptualizes the place of public relations in the intertwined social, political, and economic formations.

References

Appadurai, A. (1996). *Modernity at large*. Minneapolis, MN: University of Minnesota Press.

Bardhan, N., & C. K. Weaver (2011). Introduction: Public relations in global cultural contexts. In N. Bardhan, & C. K. Weaver (Eds), *Public relations in global cultural contexts: Multiparadigmatic approaches*, pp. 1–28. New York, NY: Routledge.

Berger, B. (1999). The Halcion affair: Public relations and the construction of ideological world view. *Journal of Public Relations Research*, 11(3), pp. 185–203. doi:10.1207/s1532754xjprr1103 _01

Bill, J. A., & Hardgrave, R. L. (1973). *Comparative politics: The quest for theory*. Columbus, OH: Merrill.

Brown, R. E. (2006). Myth of symmetry: Public relations as cultural styles. *Public Relations Review*, 16(3), pp. 206–212.

Burns, W. (2013, July 30). PR is dead. The Centre for Corporate Public Affairs blog. Retrieved on April 11, 2015, from https://accpa.com.au/blog.php?x=50

Chandran, S. (2014, February 15). Eminent palm oil researcher pushing frontiers at 80. *The Star Online*. Retrieved on April 11, 2015, from http://www.thestar.com.my/Lifestyle/People/2014/02/14/Eminent-palm-oil-researcher-pushing-frontiers-at-80/

Cheney, G., & Christensen, L. T. (2001). Public relations as contested terrain: A critical response. In R. L. Heath (Ed.), *Handbook of public relations*, pp. 167–82. Thousand Oaks, CA: Sage.

Cheng, L. (2014, February 15). Standing firm against palm oil boycott threat. *Borneo Post Online*. Retrieved on April 11, 2015, from http://www.theborneopost.com/2014/02/15/standing-firm-against-palm-oil-boycott-threat/

CIA (2014a). Indonesia. *The world factbook*. Retrieved on May 21, 2014, from https://www.cia.gov/library/publications/the-world-factbook/geos/id.html

CIA (2014b). Malaysia. *The world factbook*. Retrieved on May 21, 2014, from https://www.cia.gov/library/publications/the-world-factbook/geos/my.html

Coombe, R. J. (2010). Honing a critical/cultural study of human rights. *Communication and Critical/Cultural Studies*, 7(3), pp. 230–46.

Coombs, T. W. (1998). The internet as potential equalizer: New leverage for confronting social irresponsibility. *Public Relations Review*, 24(3), pp. 289–303. doi:10.1016/S0363-8111(99)80141–6

Coombs, T. W., & Holladay, S. J. (2012). Fringe public relations: How activism moves critical PR toward the mainstream. *Public Relations Review*, 38, pp. 880–887. doi:10.1016/j.pubrev. 2012.02.008

Curtin, P. A. (2014). Renegade Girl Scouts or a merit badge for spin: (Re)articulating activism and public relations through the cultural-economic model. Paper presented to the Association for Education in Journalism and Mass Communication convention, Montreal, Canada.

Curtin, P. A., & Gaither, T. K. (2005). Privileging identity, difference, and power: The circuit of culture as a basis for public relations theory. *Journal of Public Relations Research*, 17(2), pp. 91–116.

Curtin, P. A., & Gaither, T. K. (2007). *International public relations: Negotiating culture, identity and power.* Thousand Oaks, CA: Sage.

Curtin, P. A., & Gaither, T. K. (2012). *Globalization and public relations in postcolonial nations: Challenges and opportunities.* Amherst, NY: Cambria.

Dozier, D. M., & Lauzen, M. M. (2000). Liberating the intellectual domain from the practice: Public relations, activism, and the role of the scholar. *Journal of Public Relations Research*, 12, pp. 3–22. doi:10.1207/S1532754XJPRR1201_2

du Gay, P., Hall, S., Janes, L., Mackay, H., & Negus, K. (1997). *Doing cultural studies: The story of the Sony Walkman.* London, UK: Sage Publications, Inc.

Dutta, M. J. (2011). *Communicating social change: Structure, culture, agency.* New York, NY: Routledge.

Dutta, M. J., & Pal, M. (2011). Public relations and marginalization in a global context: A post-colonial critique. In N. Bardhan, & C. K. Weaver (Eds), *Public relations in global cultural contexts: Multi-paradigmatic perspectives*, pp. 195–225. New York, NY: Routledge.

Edwards, L. (2011). Critical perspectives in global public relations. In N. Bardhan, & C. K. Weaver (Eds), *Public relations in global contexts: Multiparadigmatic approaches*, pp. 29–49. New York, NY: Routledge.

Edwards, L. (2012). Defining the 'object' of public relations research: A new starting point. *Public Relations Inquiry*, 1(1), pp. 7–30.

Edwards, L., & Hodges, C. (2011). Introduction: Implications of a (radical) socio-cultural 'turn' in public relations scholarship. In L. Edwards, & C. Hodges (Eds), *Public relations, society, and culture: Theoretical and empirical explorations*, pp. 1–14. New York, NY: Routledge.

Fawkes, J. (2012). Interpreting ethics: Public relations and strong hermeneutics. *Public Relations Inquiry*, 1(2), pp. 117–40.

Foucault, M. (1977). Nietzsche, geneology, history. In D. F. Bouchard (Ed.), *Language, counter-memory, practice: Selected essays and interviews by Michel Foucault*, pp. 139–64. Ithaca, NY: Cornell University Press.

Foucault, M. (1979). *Discipline and punish: The birth of the prison.* New York, NY: Vintage.

Foucault, M. (1988). The ethic of care for the self as the practice of freedom. In J. Bernauer, & D. Rasmussen (Eds), *The final Foucault*, pp. 1–20. Cambridge, MA: MIT Press.

Gandy, O. (1982). *Beyond agenda setting: Information subsidies and public policy.* Norwood, NJ: Ablex Publishers.

Gies, E. (2014, March 31). Greenpeace report on P&G's palm oil sources could spur industry change. *The Guardian.* Retrieved on April 11, 2015, from http://www.theguardian.com/sustainable-business/greenpeace-procter-gamble-palm-oil-change

Grossberg, L. (1986a). History, politics and postmodernism: Stuart Hall and cultural studies. *Journal of Communication Inquiry*, 10(2), pp. 61–77.

Grossberg, L. (1986b). On postmodernism and articulation: An interview with Stuart Hall. *Journal of Communication Inquiry*, 10(2), pp. 45–60.

Grossberg, L. (2006). Does cultural studies have futures? Should it? (Or what's the matter with New York?) *Cultural Studies*, 20(1), pp. 1–32.

Grossberg, L. (2010). *Cultural studies in the future tense.* Durham, NC: Duke University Press.

Grossberg, L. (2013). Theorising context. In D. Fetherstone, & J. Painter (Eds), *Spatial politics*, pp. 32–43. Chichester, England: Wiley-Blackwell.

Hall, S. (1980). *Encoding/decoding.* In S. Hall, D. Hobson, A. Lowe, & P. Willis (Eds), *Culture, media, language: Working papers in cultural studies 1972–79*, pp. 128–38. London, UK: Unwin.

Hall, S. (1996). Introduction: Who needs 'identity'? In S. Hall, & P. du Gay (Eds), *Questions of cultural identity*, pp. 1–17. Thousand Oaks, CA: Sage.

Hall, S. (1997). The work of representation. In S. Hall (Ed.), *Representation: Cultural representations and signifying practices*, pp. 13–64. Thousand Oaks, CA: Sage.

Hamid, Z. A. (2011, December 22). Making palm oil sustainable. *New Straits Times.* Retrieved on April 11, 2015, from http://www.nst.com.my/opinion/columnist/making-palm-oil-sustainable-1.22693

Hansia, F. (2014, June 16). Papua New Guinea landowners win lands back from Malaysian palm oil plantation. CorpWatch blog. Retrieved on April 11, 2015, from http://www.corpwatch.org/article.php?id=15957

Heisler, T. (n.d.). Nutrition experts renew focus on the health risks of trans fatty acids. News release, Media Relations Inc. Retrieved on April 11, 2015, from http://www.americanpalmoil.com/images/news/Nutrition%20Experts.pdf

Hunt, T., & Tirpok, A. (1993). Universal ethics code: An idea whose time has come. *Public Relations Review*, (19)1, pp. 1–11.

Ihlen, Ø., & van Ruler, B. (2009). Introduction: Applying social theory in public relations. In Ø. Ihlen, B. van Ruler, & M. Fredriksson (Eds), *Public relations and social theory: Key figures and concepts*, pp. 1–20. New York, NY: Routledge.

Ihlen, Ø., & Verhoeven, P. (2012). A public relations identity for the 2010s. *Public Relations Inquiry*, 1(2), pp. 159–76.

Ismail, M. N. (2012, May 10). Oil palm cultivation plan in PNG will benefit KLK. *The Star*. Retrieved on April 11, 2015, from http://palmnews.mpob.gov.my/palmnewsdetails/palmnewsdetail.php?idnews=11705

Johnson, R. (1986–87). What is cultural studies anyway? *Social Text*, 16, pp. 38–80.

Kramer, J. (2004). British studies, cultural studies, British cultural studies? British and cultural studies! Babel: Langages – Imaginaires, *Civilisations*, 9, pp. 45-51.

Kruckeberg, D. (1989). The need for an international code of ethics. *Public Relations Review*, 15(2), pp. 6–18.

Laclau, E. (1977). *Politics and ideology in Marxist theory: Capitalism, fascism, populism*. London, UK: NLB.

Leitch, S., & Neilson, D. (2001). Bringing publics into public relations: New theoretical frameworks for practice. In R. Heath (Ed.), *Handbook of public relations*, pp. 127–38. Thousand Oaks, CA: Sage.

Leichty, G., & Warner, E. (2001). Cultural topoi. In R. Heath (Ed.), *Handbook of public relations*, pp. 61–74. Newbury Park, CA: Sage.

L'Etang, J. (2011). Public relations and marketing: Ethical issues and professional practice in society. In G. Cheney, S. May, & D. Munshi (Eds), *The handbook of communication ethics*, pp. 221–40. New York, NY: Routledge.

Mackay, H. (1997). Introduction. In H. Mackay (Ed.), *Consumption and everyday life*, pp. 1–12. Thousand Oaks, CA: Sage.

May-Tobin, C., & Goodman, L. (2014, March). Donuts, deodorant, deforestation. Union of Concerned Scientists. Retrieved on April 24, 2015, from http://www.ucsusa.org/global_warming/solutions/stop-deforestation/palm-oil-scorecard.html#.VTk9zJMfdpk

McKie, D., & Munshi, D. (2007). *Reconfiguring public relations: Ecology, equity, and enterprise*. New York, NY: Routledge.

Mills, S. (2004). *Discourse: The new critical idiom* (2nd edition). New York, NY: Routledge.

Motion, J., & Leitch, S. (2009). On Foucault: A toolbox for public relations. In Ø. Ihlen, B. van Ruler, & M. Fredriksson (Eds), *Public relations and social theory: Key figures and concepts*, pp. 83–101. New York, NY: Routledge.

Mumby, D. K. (2011). Power and ethics. In G. Cheney, S. May, and D. Munshi (Eds), *The handbook of communication ethics*, pp. 84–98. New York, NY: Routledge.

Ng, A., & Lim, S. S. (2013, November). *The RSPO roulette: How profits win over people and planet*. Penang, Malaysia: Pesticide Action Network Asia and the Pacific.

Raghu, A., & Koswanage, N. (2014, February 20). Palm planters, politicians test Wilmar's new green credentials. Reuters. Retrieved on April 11, 2015, from http://www.reuters.com/article/2014/02/19/environment-palmoil-wilmar-idUSL3N0LC33U20140219

Roberts, J. M. (2010, June 21). World Bank's palm oil development strategy should focus on economic freedom. The Heritage Foundation. Retrieved from http://www.heritage.org/research/ reports/2010/06/world-banks-palm-oil-development-strategy-should-focus-on-economic-freedom

Roper, J. (2011). Environmental risk, sustainability discourses, and public relations. *Public Relations Inquiry*, 1(1), pp. 69–87. doi:10.1177/2046147XII422147

RSPO (2013, July). Request for proposal for communications specialists: Influencers outreach campaign for Europe/US/Australia. Retrieved August 21, 2013, from www.odwyerpr.com/site_images/072513palm-oil.pdf

Schaefer, Z. A., Conrad, C., Cheney, G., May, S., & Ganesh, S. (2011). Economic justice and communication ethics: Considering multiple points of intersection. In G. Cheney, S. May, & D. Munshi (Eds), *The handbook of communication ethics*, pp. 436–56. New York, NY: Routledge.

Skinner, E. B. (2013, July 18). Indonesia's palm oil industry rife with human-rights abuses. *Businessweek*. Retrieved on April 11, 2015, from http://www.businessweek.com/articles/2013-07-18/indonesias-palm-oil-industry-rife-with-human-rights-abuses#p1

Slack, J. D. (1996). The theory and method of articulation in cultural studies. In D. Morley, & K-H Chen (Eds), *Stuart Hall: Critical dialogues in cultural studies*, pp. 112–27. London, UK: Routledge.

Smith, J. (2014, April 25). How Bali punks Navicula took on the palm oil industry. *The Guardian*. Retrieved from http://www.theguardian.com/music/australia-culture-blog/2014/apr/25/how-bali-punks-navicula-took-on-the-palm-oil-industry

Solis, B. (2009, June 8). The state of PR, marketing, and communications: You are the future. Blog post. Retrieved on April 11, 2015, from http://www.briansolis.com/2009/06/state-of-pr-marketing-and/

Spencer, C. C., & Chong, M. P. (2013, July 18). Asia insight: Cost of sustainability; no longer an option. Morgan Stanley Research Asia/Pacific. Retrieved on April 25, 2015, from https://commdev.org/morgan-stanley-asia-insight-cost-sustainability-no-longer-option

Sriramesh, K. (2009). Globalisation and public relations: The past, present, and the future. *Prism*, 6(2). Retrieved on April 25, 2015, from http://www.prismjournal.org/fileadmin/Praxis/Files/globalPR/SRIRAMESH.pdf

Taylor, B. C., & Hawes, L. C. (2011). What are we then? Postmodernism, globalization, and the meta-ethics of contemporary communication. In G. Cheney, S. May, and D. Munshi (Eds), *The handbook of communication ethics*, pp. 99–118. New York, NY: Routledge.

Venter, B-P., & Louw, F. (2012). Is public relations without a future? A South African perspective. *Sociology Mind*, 2(3), pp. 293–301.

Weaver, C. K. (2011). Public relations, globalization, and culture: Framing methodological debates and future directions. In N. Bardhan, & C. K. Weaver (Eds), *Public relations in global cultural contexts: Multi-paradigmatic perspectives*, pp. 250–74. New York, NY: Routledge.

Weinstein, M. (n.d.). Articulation theory for beginners. Retrieved on April 11, 2015, from www.personal.kent. edu/~mweinste/CI67095/Articulation.PDF

Wood, C. (2014, March 24). Perspectives on "sustainable" palm oil: Problematic certification systems and the responsible investor. Portfolio 21. Retrieved on 5 May, 2014, from http://portfolio21.com/blog/new-publication-perspectives-on-sustainable-palm-oil-problematic-certification-systems-and-the-responsible-investor/

Wood, S. P. (2014, March 20). PR is dead! Long live PR! PR Newser. Retrieved on April 11, 2015, from http://www.mediabistro.com/prnewser/pr-is-dead-long-live-pr_b88201

Woodward, K. (1997). Concepts of identity and difference. In K. Woodward (Ed.), *Identity and difference*, pp. 7–50). Thousand Oaks, CA: Sage.

World Growth (2011). The economic benefit of palm oil to Indonesia. World Growth. Retrieved on April 25, 2014, from http://worldgrowth.org/2011/02/the-economic-benefit-of-palm-oil-to-indonesia

Wylde, B. (2013, January 2). Why you should give red palm oil a try. Dr Oz website. Retrieved on April 11, 2015, from www.doctoroz.com/videos/why-you-should-give-red-palm-oil-try

4

Feminism and public relations

Kate Fitch

This chapter explores feminism and public relations. By feminism, I refer to a social movement that seeks to end discrimination on the basis of gender. Like public relations, this movement emerged out of capitalism (Felski, 1989) and modernity (Daymon & Demetrious, 2014; Felski, 1995) and lacks a single and stable definition or meaning. Critical perspectives in feminist public relations scholarship are rare. I therefore explore the relationship between women and public relations in the histories, theories and practices of the field from a critical perspective in order to develop new understandings of the gendering of public relations. I argue feminism remains undertheorised in public relations, despite a body of feminist scholarship stretching back to the 1980s.

This chapter investigates the intersections of public relations and feminism in order to offer an historical and critical overview of feminism in public relations scholarship. First, I consider the feminisation of public relations. Second, I consider how public relations histories have promoted a gendered conceptualisation of the evolutionary development of the field. Then, I consider how concerns about the impact of this feminisation have influenced the construction of a professional identity for public relations. Fourth, I review feminist public relations scholarship to show how it largely adopts liberal and radical feminist perspectives. Finally, I identify gaps in feminist public relations research and call for more critical understandings of public relations in relation to gender and power. Only in this way can the gendered structures underpinning conceptualisations and practices of public relations be revealed and addressed.

Public relations and women

The feminisation of public relations, that is the numerical dominance of women working in public relations that began in the 1980s, is topical in public relations industries in Anglophone countries such as the US, UK and Australia, and in Europe (see, for instance, Fröhlich & Peters (2007) on the industry in Germany; Melgin (2013) in Finland; and Tsetsura (2010) in Russia); and in non-Western countries (see, for instance, Simorangkir (2011) in Indonesia and Al-Jenaibi (2011) in the United Arab Emirates). Concerns are frequently expressed in trade media and even mainstream media about gender pay gaps (Clough, 2014; Yeomans, 2014a), the lack of women in senior public relations roles, the numerical dominance of women (Khazan, 2014), and around its "pink ghetto" and even overtly feminine status (Friedman, 2014; Salzman, 2013; Shepherd, 2012).

Some industry commentators also point to the advantages of being a woman in the public relations industry, and the ways in which women enhance public relations practice (Moore, 2013; Pearce, 2012); the implications are that feminism is redundant. Commentators, for example, question whether there is a systematic discrimination against women in public relations, given that women make up a high percentage of the public relations workforce, pointing to the numerical dominance of women in the public relations industry as an example of how equality has been achieved. One senior Australian practitioner argues that feminisation in the Australian public relations industry was unusual in that "wages and salaries increased, rather than decreased" and "the glass ceiling doesn't seem to exist" (Turnbull, 2012, para. 7; see also Turnbull, 2010, p. 26). However, the limited data available on the Australian industry suggests otherwise. The CEO of Ogilvy PR, one of a number of major female-run agencies in Australia, argues that women are more collaborative than men, and therefore "women of PR … can be a very powerful force in changing the business world to a business world that embraces everyone" (Moore, 2013). Moore suggests that the female dominance in the industry will result in greater equality and increasing the number of women in senior positions is "good business". Similarly, Pearce (2012) argues that "the practice of public relations is an inherently feminine activity" and that therefore "women have a head start". None of these positions are particularly original in that they – possibly unwittingly – articulate particular discourses around women and public relations that do not challenge the status quo and even reinforce gender stereotyping. Suggesting that the glass ceiling does not exist or that feminism is no longer relevant for public relations can be understood as part of a broader societal backlash against feminism. Further, arguing women – as better communicators and more collaborative workers – are beneficial for public relations resorts to essentialist and stereotypical understandings of women.

This feminisation has significant impacts on the public relations industry. In popular culture, female practitioners are frequently and stereotypically associated with trivial work in spheres such as fashion and hospitality rather than corporate or government work (Johnston, 2010; Morris & Goldsworthy, 2008). Industry reports lament the "gender imbalance" and argue that it is "unhealthy" for the communication function (Salt & Schein, 2012). Professional associations document the disparity in seniority and salary along gendered lines; for example, the Public Relations Society of America's (PRSA) Work, Life and Gender survey showed the percentage of women working in public relations was increasing but the gender pay gap was worsening (Sha, 2011). The Chartered Institute of Public Relations (CIPR) (2014) in the UK found that men are twice as likely as women to be directors or partners and that the mean salary for a male public relations practitioner is significantly higher than that for a female practitioner. This phenomenon is by no means unique to public relations and is documented in traditionally female-dominated fields such as teaching (Acker, 1989) and nursing (Rafferty, 1996; Witz, 1992) and in feminising fields such as medicine and accounting (Crompton & Lyonette, 2010).

This gendering of the public relations industry needs to be understood in relation to broader societal structures around women and work (Fitch & Third, 2010, 2014). Although feminisation is not unique to public relations, researching its significance for public relations may offer useful perspectives into both how this gendering occurs and the impact of such gendering. That is, exploring the intersections between feminism (concerned with discrimination against women) and public relations (as an occupational practice that is dominated, at least numerically, by women) may offer significant insights into broader social processes around gender and work. Despite concerns among public relations scholars and overwhelming evidence of gender gaps and the lack of representation of women in senior roles, less attention is paid to understanding why this occurs and the significance for public relations theory and practice.

Gendering of public relations

Historical narratives of public relations establish the field as a history of great white men or "fathers of public relations" (see, for example, Tye (2002), whose book on Edward Bernays is entitled *The Father of Spin*). A recent infographic, "Evolution of the PR Pro", presents images ranging from Julius Caesar to Mark Zuckerberg, which ensures the field's historical narrative is wholly masculine and a steady, linear progression to the modern era (PR Web, 2011). Similarly, official and textbook histories recount the achievements of professional associations and their mostly male members, and demonstrate the field's evolutionary development towards professional standing. The lack of a critical perspective marginalises both the role of women and the technical activity (such as publicity, event management and promotional work) that does not fall into the understanding of public relations as a strategic management profession and primarily a corporate function (thereby excluding other kinds of public relations activity, such as activism and NGO work (McKie & Munshi, 2007)). This stratification of public relations activity occurs along gendered lines.

Only a few scholars have recognised both individual women who have arguably contributed to the historical development of public relations, or more broadly the role of women in the industry. For example, Lamme (2001, 2007) found that although Doris Fleischman was a significant public relations pioneer in the US, she sought less self-promotion than her husband, Edward Bernays. Miller (1997) and Horsley (2009) both lamented the lack of recognition of women's contributions to US public relations history in their respective research into Jane Stewart's work in the 1950s and 1960s and women's leadership contributions between 1940 and 1970. And in her investigation of women's contributions to the development of US public relations, through an analysis of the PRSA's *Public Relations Journal* from 1945–72, Gower (2001) concluded that women initially found it easy to gain employment in public relations, but that institutional barriers to entry increased as the profession matured. I made similar findings in the Australian context, but in relation to a later period; in the 1980s more women, often university graduates, entered public relations and overtook the number of men working in the industry. In 1985 the Public Relations Institute of Australia introduced more rigorous requirements for professional-grade membership (Fitch, 2014; Fitch & Third, 2010, 2014). Women found public relations offered good employment opportunities at entry level and some opportunities for career advancement in particular sectors; however, their employment contributed to a gendered segregation between professional and technical activity that informed conceptualisations of public relations knowledge and expertise.

My historical research into the experiences of women in Australian public relations in the 1980s and 1990s revealed a significant stratification in both the types of public relations work that women performed, and in the public, not-for-profit, and consultancy sectors in which they found it easier to advance into management roles (Fitch & Third, 2014). There is therefore a gendered stratification in public relations work (Fitch & Third, 2010, 2014). These findings are reflected in studies in other countries that found female practitioners in Germany and in the USSR are more likely to work in particular sectors, and that the numerical dominance of women influences and even constrains understandings of public relations as professional work (Fröhlich & Peters, 2007; Tsetsura, 2010). Further, recent research suggests that this gendered stratification continues in contemporary practice in that performing routine social media work, such as maintaining an organisation's Twitter feed, offers less opportunity for those practitioners to build social capital (Bridgen, 2013). I have argued elsewhere that certain types of public relations activity, particularly activity aligned with marketing and promotion or in certain sectors, such as fashion, are marginalised from mainstream understandings of public relations (Cassidy & Fitch, 2013; Fitch & Third, 2010, 2014). In the Australian context, these are precisely the sectors within public relations which traditionally are most feminised, or historically offered pathways for women into public relations work. It is not surprising, then, that such public relations activity is excluded from conceptualisations of public relations as a business management profession that occurs primarily in corporate and government sectors.

Professionalisation and feminisation

Professionalisation marginalises women's work in many industries, and the processes of exclusion and demarcation are not unique to public relations (Davies, 1996; Witz, 1992). These processes include defining and legitimising professional practice, and regulating membership, professional activity and training in order to establish and maintain an elite domain of expertise. According to Edwards (2014), the need to promote a clear occupational identity, in order to justify professional recognition and social legitimacy, results in an exclusionary occupational identity for public relations and contributes to occupational closure. The question of "fit", in terms of social, cultural and even physical capital, points to implicit coding in terms of race, class and gender.

But focusing on the exclusion of women from senior roles within the public relations industry potentially ignores the ways in which women are included. Indeed, the feminisation of public relations provoked anxiety regarding the professional standing of the industry and contributed to the gendered stratification of public relations work; that is, the inclusion of women allows a particular conceptualisation of public relations as professional practice (Davies, 1996). The industry response to its feminisation, at least as I have argued in my historical research into developments in the Australian industry, showed how anxiety about the growing feminisation of the industry contributed to the introduction of new membership structures, greater regulation of the industry, and even helped structure conceptualisations of public relations knowledge and expertise (Fitch, 2014; Fitch & Third, 2010).

Despite the expansion in theoretical perspectives on public relations in the last decade, the dominant paradigm, with its emphasis on functionalist and managerial understandings, still structures much thinking about public relations. It promotes a normative conceptualisation by presenting public relations as an ideal, two-way practice, and ignoring or excluding public relations practices, particularly those aligned with marketing and promotion, or in certain sectors, such as fashion, which do not fit this ideal (Cassidy & Fitch, 2013; Fitch & Third, 2010, 2014; Gordon, 1997). Anxiety about the lack of professional status in public relations contributed to this gendered stratification between different kinds of public relations activity as professional and strategic versus non-professional and technical. The feminisation of public relations, in line with other feminising occupations, therefore contributed to the establishment of these professional structures and to the constitution of public relations knowledge. That is, the introduction of professional structures and the attempts to establish public relations as a profession defined what was, and what was not, public relations activity, and in doing so promoted particular conceptualisations of public relations knowledge, while marginalising others.

This dominant paradigm has contributed to the framing of much feminist research (L'Etang, 2008). Professional associations, and indeed many scholars, seek to establish public relations as a profession (Rakow & Nastasia, 2009). In doing so, the significance of women to public relations is often relegated to the margins of contemporary debates, or explored primarily in terms of their significance for the professional standing of the field. The focus on managerial, organisational and functionalist perspectives in the dominant paradigm inevitably meant that many scholars working within this paradigm fail to consider the broader role of public relations in society (Edwards & Hodges, 2011; Ihlen & Verhoeven, 2009), "to account adequately for the role of power" and to reconceptualise the "limited and somewhat prescriptive research agenda" of much public relations research (L'Etang, 2009, p. 14). Of particular significance to feminist research, the ideology underpinning conceptualisations of public relations as a profession are not contested, even though the very concept of a profession is embedded in masculine concepts (Davies, 1996).

Feminist perspectives on public relations

As I pointed out in the chapter introduction, there is no single or unified feminist movement or theory. In the US, for instance, feminism is predominantly and historically aligned with liberal feminism, emphasising equal rights, and to a lesser extent, radical feminism, campaigning against patriarchy and women's oppression (Mendes, 2011). In contrast, UK feminist movements tended to be more radical and socialist, in that class as well as gender were recognised factors in women's oppression (Mendes, 2011). Despite the diversity in feminist scholarship, feminist public relations scholarship predominantly has been framed within liberal feminism and, to a lesser extent, radical feminism. In this section, I review feminist public relations scholarship to highlight the need for more critical perspectives.

Feminist public relations scholarship exploring the status of women in public relations is longstanding. A landmark US report, *The velvet ghetto: The impact of the increasing percentage of women in public relations and business communication* (Cline, Toth, Turk, Walters, Johnson, & Smith, 1986), commissioned by the International Association of Business Communicators, documented the challenges for female practitioners around lower salary and lesser roles. It identified a number of female attributes – such as lack of ambition – resulting from the socialisation of women that hindered their career advancement in public relations and offered solutions, thereby framing the responsibility for change as that of individual women (Fitch & Third, 2010). Since then, much of the research into feminism and public relations in the 1980s and 1990s, and even into the 2000s, adopts a liberal-feminist approach and focuses on gender inequity in salaries, status and roles (Aldoory, 2003; Fitch & Third, 2010; Rakow & Nastasia, 2009). The liberal feminist focus of much of this research emphasises equality, individualism and the status of women in the industry, with the aim of addressing concerns about the professional development and status of public relations. Roles research, for instance, that focuses on the dichotomy between manager and technician roles in public relations, has spanned several decades, yet, as Wrigley (2010) points out, this focus has limited understandings of alternative perspectives. Liberal feminist public relations scholarship tends to work within the dominant paradigm in that "liberal feminist positions…generally accept the social order as it is, including capitalism, representative democracy, and interest group pluralism but reject sexism within the social order" (Rakow & Nastasia, 2009, p. 272). Liberal feminist scholarship, with its focus on equality, does not challenge the ideological underpinnings of public relations.

It is worth considering postfeminism in the context of public relations. Postfeminist theory has had limited impact on public relations scholarship, but postfeminism, as a backlash against feminism, has its roots in liberal feminism and neoliberalism (Gill, 2007; McRobbie, 2009). It potentially offers critical insights into the ways feminism is simultaneously embraced and rejected in the celebration of personal responsibility and individual choices (Gill, 2007; McRobbie, 2009). Such postfeminist positions – in the sense that public relations no longer requires feminism, as illustrated in the earlier "Public relations and women" section exploring industry commentary – elide the gendered structures underpinning the field even when gender pay gaps and discrimination are acknowledged. That is, the neoliberal market-driven discourse of personal responsibility, individualism and autonomy ignores how gender is manifest in public relations discourse.

Radical feminists sought to change societal structures and overcome patriarchal power relations (Mendes, 2011; Rakow & Nastasia, 2009). Some feminist public relations scholars combined elements of liberal feminism and radical feminism. In "Feminist values in public relations," Grunig, Toth and Hon (2000), for instance, sought to establish public relations' credentials as a profession by linking its ethical practice with traditionally feminine-coded values such as co-operation, respect, caring, intuition and justice. This approach, drawing on essentialist understandings of women, did not contest the dominant paradigm but rather sought to incorporate feminist perspectives within that paradigm. More radical feminist public relations scholars attempted to rearticulate the debate by interrogating the professional structures of public relations, which they considered were underpinned by patriarchy and capitalism (Rakow & Nastasia, 2009). Hon (1995), for instance, recognised public relations was marginalised by its association with women's work, and called for changes at the societal, organisational, industry and individual level. Rakow identified inherent tensions within public relations between "ideologies of individualism and community, of competition and cooperation, or private interest and public good…of masculinity and femininity" and argued that the feminisation of public relations was "nothing less than a gender crisis…fed by a longstanding conflict over these ideologies" (1989, pp. 294, 295).

Much of this feminist public relations scholarship failed to consider the broader social context that produces inequality on the basis of gender. As Pompper points out, "public relations researchers consistently fail to critique vestiges of patriarchy by instead emphasizing that women (somehow) are better communicators anyway" (2014, p. 69). While radical feminist perspectives offer some recognition of the patriarchal and capitalist ideologies underpinning public relations, neither radical nor liberal-feminist scholars are able to move beyond a male-female binary, essentialist understandings of women, or fully challenge the gendered implications of the field's dominant paradigm. Indeed, Aldoory argues that much public relations theory and research "sustain[s] gender stereotypes" and the systematic "devaluation" of women's work (2005b, p. 901). Different research is needed, then, to explore precisely how gender informs conceptualisations of public relations and its role in, and impact upon, society.

Critical feminism and gender

Until recently there has been little critical feminist research in public relations. As the previous sections in this chapter demonstrate, public relations is embedded in certain ideological assumptions such as neoliberalism and heteronormativity that are largely unchallenged (Edwards & L'Etang, 2013). Indeed, various scholars have pointed out feminist public relations scholarship is "narrowly focused" (Aldoory, 2007, p. 339), "underdeveloped" and "uneven" (Rakow & Nastasia, 2009, p. 252). Instead, much feminist public relations research fails to problematise the ways in which women, and indeed public relations, are represented, leading to a focus on the experiences of white, middle-class, heterosexual American women (Aldoory, 2005a) and on gender inequity in salaries, status and roles (Fitch & Third, 2010). There is limited research that adopts a truly critical perspective in terms of challenging the hegemonic assumptions around gender in public relations.

Public relations, however, precisely because of its feminisation, can usefully serve to investigate the constitution, transmission and effects of gender (Fitch & Third, 2010). Gender, drawing on Butler (1999), is understood in terms of a socially constructed identity, allowing the investigation of power and power relations, along with the structural processes that produce gendered discourse. The failure of much feminist public relations scholarship to explore "gender as a social construction guiding public relations practice, or on men as gendered beings that are also affected by the feminization of public relations" (Aldoory, 2007, p. 339) limits research to a focus on women and their role in the professional project.

A critical feminist lens can challenge existing assumptions in public relations, particularly around the professionalising structures that frame understandings of public relations expertise and knowledge. This lens opens up feminist public relations scholarship beyond the dominant paradigm. Recent public relations scholarship has begun to engage with more complex understandings of gender and its intersections with, for instance, race, class and sexuality in the construction of social identities (see, Daymon & Demetrious (2014) and Tindall & Waters (2013)). Drawing on the work of Canadian feminist Dorothy E. Smith, Rakow and Nastasia (2009) identify the need to reframe feminist public relations scholarship by interrogating – rather than working within – the capitalist and patriarchal structures of public relations. Daymon and Demetrious argue that critical feminist theory foregrounds the social impact of "hegemonic assumptions around gender in public relations which continue to be unquestioned and unchallenged" (2014, p. 3).

In this way, more critical feminist research of public relations may be developed. That is, focusing on production of gender in public relations allows scholars to ask different kinds of questions. I offer some examples of new kinds of feminist research which explore the impact of gender on public relations practice and theory. Recent scholarship on LGBT perspectives in public relations illustrates the significance of the dominant heteronormative discourse in public relations research and how gendered binaries shape the research agenda (Edwards & L'Etang, 2013). Vardeman-Winter (2014) employed feminist cultural studies to demonstrate the need for a greater reflexivity towards gender in the development and implementation of health communication campaigns in order to empower publics, and in public relations research. Sison (2014) used postcolonial feminist theory to explore both issues of power and control and how public relations may foster social justice in the social and political context of the Philippines. The lived experiences of women in negotiating professional and personal identities, as another example of critical feminist approaches, reveals new understandings of the impact of gender on public relations. For example, Surma and Daymon (2014) reframe public relations as cultural intermediary work, which can potentially disrupt the neoliberal agenda and draw attention to marginalised others. And Yeomans (2014b) found that the professionalisation of public relations impacts on both male and female practitioners in terms of the ways they negotiate and perform professional, gendered identities. Other scholars use intersectionality as a critical lens to explore the interaction of gender with other social identities (see, for instance, Pompper (2014) on gender, race, and age) and to reconceptualise organisational power in public relations (Vardeman-Winter, Tindall & Jiang, 2013).

Each of these studies reframes feminist public relations scholarship in that they do not focus on the effectiveness of public relations or the representation of women so much as explore the impact of gendered binaries on, and significance for, public relations theory and practice (Edwards & L'Etang, 2013). They also locate public relations within broader societal structures. As Rakow and Nastasia argue,

> a critical feminist public relations theory…would see power not simply nor only in the relations between individual women and men within an organization, but in the structure of society in which powerful institutions produce and enforce meanings about the social order and the place of groups of people within it.
>
> *(Rakow & Nastasia, 2009, p. 272)*

That is, these scholars both problematise the representation of women and men and disrupt the gendered discourses that dominate and inform conceptualisations of public relations.

Conclusions

This chapter investigated feminist public relations scholarship and found that until recently much of this scholarship was dominated by liberal, and to a lesser extent, radical feminism and did not challenge "the hegemonic assumptions in public relations around gender" (Daymon & Demetrious, 2014, p. 3). Instead, much feminist research simply reinforced gender stereotypes by focusing on the significance of women for the field's professional project. Critical feminist scholarship offers new approaches in that it challenges this hegemony. Focusing on gender as a dynamic social construction and its manifestation in the structures and concepts of public relations encourages new understandings of public relations and its role in society. Critical approaches draw attention to the significance of gender for public relations and allow the field to be reconceptualised in terms of gendered power relations by revealing how patriarchal and capitalist ideologies fundamentally inform public relations theory and practice.

References

Acker. S. (1989). *Teachers, gender and career*. London, England: Falmer Press.

Aldoory, L. (2003). The empowerment of feminist scholarship in public relations and the building of a feminist paradigm. *Communication Yearbook*, 27, pp. 221–55.

Aldoory, L. (2005a). A (re)conceived feminist paradigm for public relations: A case for substantial improvement. *Journal of Communication*, 55, pp. 668–84. doi 10.1111/j.1460–2466.2005.tb03016.x

Aldoory, L. (2005b). Women in public relations. In R. L. Heath (Ed), *Encyclopaedia of Public Relations*, vol. 2, pp. 899–902. Thousand Oaks, CA: Sage.

Aldoory, L. (2007). Reconceiving gender for an "excellent" future in public relations. In J. Grunig, L. Grunig, & E. Toth (Eds), *The future of excellence in public relations and communication management: Challenges for the next generation*, pp. 399–411. Mahwah, NJ: Lawrence Erlbaum Assoc.

Al-Jenaibi, B. (2011). Gender issues in the diversity and practice of public relations in the UAE. Case study of PR male managers and female PR practitioners. *International Journal of E-Politics*, 2(3), pp. 35–56. doi 10.4018/jep.2011070104.

Bridgen, L. (2013). The boys are back in town: Rethinking the feminisation of public relations through the prism of social media. *Prism*, 9(1). Retrieved on April 11, 2015, from http://www.prismjournal.org/fileadmin/9_1/Bridgen.pdf

Butler, J. (1999). *Gender trouble: Feminism and the subversion of identity*. New York, NY: Routledge.

Cassidy, L., & Fitch, K. (2013). "Parties, air-kissing and long boozy lunches"? Public relations in the Australian fashion industry. *Prism*, 10(1). Retrieved on April 11, 2015, from http://www.prismjournal.org/fileadmin/10_1/Cassidy_Fitch.pdf

Chartered Institute of Public Relations (CIPR). (2014). *CIPR State of the Profession Survey 2013/14*. Retrieved from http://www.cipr.co.uk/sites/default/files/J9825_CIPR_StateOfTheProfession_2014_V10_AW.pdf

Cline, C. G., Toth, E. L., Turk, J. V., Walters, L. M., Johnson, N., & Smith, H. (1986). *The velvet ghetto: The impact of the increasing percentage of women in public relations and business communication*. San Francisco, CA: IABC Research Foundation.

Clough, E. (2014, July 1). Are women in PR being exploited? *Mumbrella*. Retrieved on April 11, 2015, from http://mumbrella.com.au/men-leading-pr-industry-taking-gender-wage-gap-seriously-235697

Crompton, R., & Lyonette, L. (2010). Women's career success and work-life adaptations in the accountancy and medical professions in Britain. *Gender, Work and Organization*, 18, pp. 231–54. doi:10.1111/j.1468-0432.2009.00511.x

Davies, C. (1996). The sociology of the professions and the profession of gender. *Sociology*, 30, pp. 661–78. doi:10.1177/0038038596030004003

Daymon, C., & Demetrious, K. (Eds). (2014). *Gender and public relations: Critical perspectives on gender, voice and identity*. London, England: Routledge.

Edwards, L. (2014). Discourse, credentialism and occupational closure in the communications industries: The case of public relations in the UK. *European Journal of Communication*, 29, pp. 319–34. doi:10.1177/0267323113519228

Edwards, L., & Hodges, C. (Eds). (2011). *Public relations, society and culture: Theoretical and empirical explorations.* Abingdon, England: Routledge.

Edwards, L., & L'Etang, J. (2013). Invisible and visible identities and sexualities in public relations. In N. Tindall, & R. Waters (Eds), *Coming out of the closet: Exploring LGBT issues in strategic communication with theory and research*, pp. 41–53. New York, NY: Peter Lang.

Felski, R. (1989). *Beyond feminist aesthetics.* London, England: Hutchison Radius.

Felski, R. (1995). *The gender of modernity.* Cambridge, MA: Harvard University Press.

Fitch, K. (2014). Professionalisation and public relations education: Industry accreditation of Australian university courses in the early 1990s. *Public Relations Review.* 40, pp. 623–631. doi:10.1016/j.pubrev.2014.02.015

Fitch, K., & Third, A. (2010). Working girls: Revisiting the gendering of public relations. *Prism*, 7(4). Retrieved on April 11, 2015, from http://www.prismjournal.org/fileadmin/Praxis/Files/Gender/Fitch_Third.pdf

Fitch, K., & Third, A. (2014). Ex-journos and promo girls: Feminization and professionalization in the Australian public relations industry. In C. Daymon, & K. Demetrious (Eds), *Gender and public relations: Critical perspectives on voice, image and identity*, pp. 247–67. Abingdon, England: Routledge.

Friedman, A. (2014, July 18). Why do we treat PR like a pink ghetto? *The Cut.* Retrieved on April 11, 2015, from http://nymag.com/thecut/2014/07/why-do-we-treat-pr-like-a-pink-ghetto.html

Fröhlich, R., & Peters, S. B. (2007). PR bunnies caught in the agency ghetto? Gender stereotypes, organizational factors, and women's careers in PR agencies. *Journal of Public Relations Research*, 19, pp. 229–54. doi:10.1080/10627260701331754

Gill, R. (2007). Postfeminist media culture: Elements of a sensibility. *European Journal of Cultural Studies*, 10, pp. 147–66. doi:10.1177/1367549407075898

Gordon, J. C. (1997). Interpreting definitions of public relations: Self-assessment and a symbolic interactionism-based alternative. *Public Relations Review*, 23, pp. 57–66. doi:10.1016/S0363-8111(97)90006-0

Gower, K. (2001). Rediscovering women in public relations: Women in the *Public Relations Journal*, 1945–1972. *Journalism History*, 27(1), pp. 14–21.

Grunig, L. A., Toth, E. L., & Hon, L. C. (2000). Feminist values in public relations. *Journal of Public Relations Research*, 12, pp. 49–68. doi:10.1207/S1532754XJPRR1201_4

Hon, L. C. (1995). Towards a feminist theory of public relations. *Journal of Public Relations Research*, 7, pp. 27–88. doi:10.1207/s1532754xjprr0701_03

Horsley, J. (2009). Women's contributions to American public relations, 1940–1970. *Journal of Communication Management*, 13, pp. 100–15. doi:10.1108/13632540910951731

Ihlen Ø., & Verhoeven, P. (2009). Conclusions on the domain, context, concepts, issues and empirical avenues of public relations. In Ø. Ihlen, B. van Ruler, & M. Fredriksson (Eds), *Public relations and social theory: Key figures and concepts*, pp. 323–40. New York, NY: Routledge.

Johnston, J. (2010). Girls on screen: How film and television depict women in public relations. *Prism*, 7(4). Retrieved on April 11, 2015, from http://www.prismjournal.org/fileadmin/Praxis/Files/Gender/Johnston.pdf

Khazan, O. (2014, August 8). Why are there so many women in public relations? *The Atlantic.* Retrieved on April 11, from http://www.theatlantic.com/business/archive/2014/08/why-are-there-so-many-women-in-pr/375693/

Lamme, M. O. (2001). Furious desires and victorious careers: Doris E. Fleischman, counsel on public relations and advocate for working women. *American Journalism*, 18(3), pp. 13–33. doi:10.1080/08821127.2001.10739322

Lamme, M. O. (2007) Outside the prickly nest: Revisiting Doris Fleischman. *American Journalism*, 24(3), pp. 85–107. doi:10.1080/08821127.2007.10678080

L'Etang, J. (2008). *Public relations: Concepts, practice and critique.* London, England: Sage.

L'Etang, J. (2009). "Radical PR" – Catalyst for change or an aporia? *Ethical Space: The International Journal of Communication Ethics*, 6(2), pp. 13–18. Retrieved on April 29, 2015, from http://www.communication-ethics.net/journal/v6n2/v6n2_feat1.pdf

McKie, D., & Munshi, D. (2007). *Reconfiguring public relations: Ecology, equity and enterprise.* Abingdon, England: Routledge.

McRobbie, A. (2009). *The aftermath of feminism: Gender, culture and social change*. London, England: Sage.

Melgin, E. (2013). Gender imbalance: Why is the female-dominated PR industry still led by men? Retrieved on April 11, 2015, from International Public Relations Association http://www.ipra.org/itl/10/2013/gender-imbalance-why-is-the-female-dominated-pr-industry-still-led-by-men

Mendes, K. (2011). *Feminism in the news: Representations of the women's movement since the 1960s*. Basingstoke, England: Palgrave Macmillan.

Miller, K. S. (1997). Woman, man, lady, horse: Jane Stewart, public relations executive. *Public Relations Review*, 23, pp. 249–69. doi:10.1016/S0363-8111(97)90035-7

Moore, K. (2013, September 12). PR's lessons in gender equality. *The Australian Financial Review*. Retrieved on April 11, 2015, from http://www.afr.com/p/australia2-0/pr_lessons_in_gender_equality_B8LohZ5cJs2A9VLnETBr7H

Morris, T., & Goldsworthy, S. (2008). *PR – A persuasive industry? Spin, public relations and the shaping of modern media*. Basingstoke, England: Palgrave Macmillan.

Parker, D. (2013, July 18). Is "feminism" a dirty word in PR? *Inside PR*. Retrieved on April 11, 2015, from http://www.prmoment.com/1472/is-feminism-a-dirty-word-in-pr.aspx

Pearce, C. (2012, May 1). Women in PR: Why they win. Retrieved on April 11, 2015, from Public Relations Institute of Australia (PRIA) http://www.pria.com.au/priablog/women-in-pr-why-they-win

Pompper, D. (2014). Interrogating inequalities perpetuated in a feminized field: Using critical race theory and the intersectionality lens to render visible that which should be disaggregated. In C. Daymon, & K. Demetrious (Eds), *Gender and public relations: Critical perspectives on gender, voice and identity*, pp. 67–86). London, England: Routledge.

PR Web. (2011, December). Evolution of the PR pro: A history of public relations progress (Infographic). Retrieved on April 11, 2015, from http://www.bloggingprweb.com/evolution-of-a-pr-pro-infographic

Rafferty, A. (1996). *The politics of nursing knowledge*. London, England: Routledge.

Rakow, L. (1989). From the feminization of public relations to the promise of feminism. In E. Toth, & C. Cline (Eds), *Beyond the velvet ghetto*, pp. 287–98. San Francisco, CA: IABC Foundation.

Rakow, L., & Nastasia, D. I. (2009). On feminist theory of public relations: An example from Dorothy E. Smith. In Ø. Ihlen, B. van Ruler, & M. Fredriksson (Eds), *Public relations and social theory: Key figures and concepts*, pp. 252–77. New York, NY: Routledge.

Salt & Schein. (2012). *2012 Industry snapshot: Our annual quantitative survey of the views of in-house corporate affairs professionals*. Retrieved on April 11, 2015, from Public Relations Institute of Australia (PRIA) http://www.pria.com.au/documents/item/5316

Salzman, M. (2013, June 26). America's PR industry is too feminized and politically correct. *Holmes Report*. Retrieved on April 11, 2015, from http://www.holmesreport.com/opinion-info/13600/Americas-PR-Industry-Is-Too-Feminized-And-Politically-Correct.aspx

Sha, B-L. (2011, March 8). PR women: New data show gender-based salary gap is widening. *Ragan's PR Daily*. Retrieved on April 11, 2015, from http://www.prdaily.com/Main/Articles/PR_women_New_data_show_genderbased_salary_gap_is_w_7468.aspx

Shepherd, T. (2012, March 7). Women create "pink ghettos" in PR and HR sectors. *The Australian*. Retrieved on April 11, 2015, from http://www.news.com.au/business/women-gangs-dominate-business-areas-creating-pink-ghettos/story-e6frfm1i-1226290981814

Simorangkir, D. (2011). The impact of the feminization of the public relations industry in Indonesia on communication practice. *International Journal of Strategic Communication*, 5(1), pp. 26–48. doi:10.1080/1553118X.2011.537602.

Sison, M. (2014). Gender, culture and power: Competing discourses on the Philippine Reproductive Health Bill. In C. Daymon, & K. Demetrious (Eds), *Gender and public relations: Critical perspectives on voice, image and identity*, pp. 177–97. Abingdon, England: Routledge.

Surma, A., & Daymon, C. (2014). Caring about public relations and the gendered cultural intermediary role. In C. Daymon, & K. Demetrious (Eds), *Gender and public relations: Critical perspectives on voice, image and identity*, pp. 46–66. Abingdon, England: Routledge.

Tindall, N., & Waters, R. (Eds). (2013). *Coming out of the closet: Exploring LGBT issues in strategic communication with theory and research*. New York, NY: Peter Lang.

Tsetsura, K. (2010). Is public relations a real job? How female practitioners construct the profession. *Journal of Public Relations Research*, 23, pp. 1–23. doi:10.1080/1062726X.2010.504763

Turnbull, N. (2010). *How PR works – But often doesn't*. Melbourne, Australia: N. S. & J. S. Turnbull. Retrieved on August 30, 2012, from http://noelturnbull.com/wp-content/uploads/2010/06/How-PR-works-but-often-doesnt.pdf

Turnbull, N. (2012, June 5). Come in spinner: PR and the "Samantha Syndrome". *Crikey*. Retrieved on April 29, 2015, from http://www.crikey.com.au/2012/06/05/come-in-spinner-pr-and-the-samantha-syndrome/

Tye, L. (2002). *The father of spin: Edward L. Bernays and the birth of public relations*. New York, NY: Henry Holt.

Vardeman-Winter, J. (2014). Issues of representation, reflexivity, and research-participant relationships: Doing feminist cultural studies to improve health campaigns. *Public Relations Inquiry*, 3, pp. 91–111. doi:10.1177/2046147X13518320

Vardeman-Winter, J., Tindall, N., & Jiang, H. (2013). Intersectionality and publics: How exploring publics' multiple identities questions basic public relations concepts. *Public Relations Inquiry*, 2, pp. 279–304. doi:10.1177/2046147X13491564

Witz, A. (1992). *Professions and patriarchy*. London, England: Routledge.

Wrigley, B. J. (2002). Glass ceiling? What glass ceiling? A qualitative study of how women view the glass ceiling in public relations and communications management. *Journal of Public Relations Research*, 14, pp. 27–55. doi:10.1207/S1532754XJPRR1401_2

Wrigley, B. J. (2010). Feminist scholarship and its contributions to public relations. In R. Heath (Ed), *The Sage Handbook of Public Relations*, pp. 247–60. Thousand Oaks, CA: Sage.

Yeomans, L. (2010). Soft sell? Gendered experience of emotional labour in UK public relations firms. *Prism*, 7(4). Retrieved on April 11, 2015, from http://www.prismjournal.org/fileadmin/Praxis/Files/Gender/Yeomans.pdf

Yeomans, L. (2014a, March 10). The gender gap: What research tells us (blog). *CIPR The Conversation*. Retrieved on April 11, 2015, from http://conversation.cipr.co.uk/2014/03/10/the-gender-gap-in-pr-what-research-tells-us/

Yeomans, L. (2014b). Gendered performance and identity work in PR consulting relationships: A UK perspective. In C. Daymon, & K. Demetrious (Eds), *Gender and public relations: Critical perspectives on voice, image and identity*, pp. 87–107. Abingdon, England: Routledge.

5

The public sphere and PR

Deliberative democracy and agonistic pluralism

Phil Ramsey

It is the contention of this chapter that a critical theory of public relations should involve some reflection on the role that public relations plays within the public sphere. Public relations (PR) has become increasingly influential on activity within the public sphere, and hence in the formation of public opinion. In this chapter we shall seek to introduce the public sphere as a critical category – that is, both sociological and theoretical in its scope – and to understand the role of PR, especially within the domain of news media in North American and European democracies. The chapter will focus on the normative dimension of the account of the public sphere forwarded by the German social theorist Jürgen Habermas, which shapes critical theory understandings of the role of PR in the public sphere. The impact of PR on the public sphere will be discussed through the increased influence of PR in journalism, coming at the expense of original and independent reporting. Further to this, the competing theories of deliberative democracy and agonistic pluralism will be surveyed, and we will see that the basis upon which we think critically about PR greatly differs depending upon which position we take up. Central here is the question of whether or not consensus is possible within the public sphere, or if contestation is rather inevitable.

The theory of the public sphere

The theory of the public sphere is one of the best-known and most frequently adopted theories for understanding contemporary political and social life within critical media and communication studies, and has been influential on critical accounts of PR. Habermas forwarded his early arguments on the subject in *The Structural Transformation of the Public Sphere* (1989) (*STPS*), where he charts the rise of a bourgeois public sphere in eighteenth-century Europe. The central thrust of the Habermasian thesis is that following feudalism as a dominant system, a public sphere emerged as a site of debate and criticism which subjected the state to a new form of scrutiny. By way of defining the public sphere, Habermas's much quoted description provides the most useful introduction: "By 'public sphere' we mean first of all a domain of our social life in which such a thing as public opinion can be formed. Access to the public sphere is open in principle to all citizens" (1997, p. 105). In essence, the (political) public sphere is that "space" in society where citizens discuss a range of political issues, and formulate opinions based on the information that circulates in the public sphere, through rational-critical discussion.

The historical dimension of Habermas's account has long been criticized, particularly on the issue of inclusion, or lack thereof (Curran, 1991, p. 42; Thompson, 1990, p. 112; 1995, p. 73). Perhaps one of the best known critiques comes from Nancy Fraser (1995, p. 289), who argued that the bourgeois public sphere was open only to property-owning, middle-class males, with women historically excluded. It is important to note that writing much later in response to his critics, Habermas (1992, p. 428) accepted failings in his original *STPS* account, arguing, for example, that women were indeed excluded from the bourgeois public sphere. Despite criticisms of Habermas's work, it is striking how the normative dimension of his theory, rather than the sociological and historical basis, has endured for many decades. Garnham (1986, p. 43) argued that the principles contained in the *STPS* public sphere model enable it as "ideal type", and that despite numerous problems these "do not undermine the book's continuing claim to our attention as a fruitful starting point for work on urgent contemporary issues in the study of the mass media and democratic politics" (Garnham, 1992, p. 359).

Applying public sphere theory to public relations

Habermas argues in *STPS* that PR in the West came to "dominate the public sphere" from the 1950s onwards, and that PR techniques "have become a key phenomenon for the diagnosis of" the public sphere (1989, p. 193). Indeed, Graham (2012) has noted that "The very concept of 'public relations' is one that Habermas looks on with suspicion" (p. 34), and it is to this strand of thought that we turn to now. Habermas is suggesting that in our analysis of the public sphere, and the way in which public opinion is generated, the public sphere researcher must turn their attention to PR strategies and practices to further aid their understanding of how public spheres function. Understanding their functioning may encompass reflection on how Habermas "identified public relations as supporting the dominance of elites and reinforcing structural inequalities" (L'Etang, 2009, p. 6). To set the context for understanding why such an analysis of PR is important to Habermas, it is necessary to see how the role of PR can be viewed as part of Habermas's "refeudalization of the public sphere" thesis (in *STPS*). By this, Habermas referred to a return to a type of society that bears more resemblance to the feudal period than it does to the bourgeois public sphere, whereby the public sphere was systematically dismantled due to the greater commercialization of the media, the growing influence of the state and the dissipation of public discourse. If we take each of these three areas, we can expand our critique of PR as viewed through this lens.

First, much PR activity has as its focus the news media, in order to impact the news agenda (Davis, 2007). As we shall see below, changing market conditions in the news media environment have led to a greater reliance on PR materials. Second, state agencies and government departments systematically employ the principles of PR in their political communication (McNair, 2004; Somerville & Ramsey, 2012), and it is thus important to subject this process to assessment. Third, public discourse is undermined by much PR activity which seeks to turn attention to "private" issues (Habermas, 1989), undermining the public interest. In particular, this can be seen in the way Habermas interrogates the role that the state has played in relation to publicity in the refeudalized public sphere, which he argues mirrors the way business operates: "Because private enterprises evoke in their customers the idea that in their consumption decisions they act in their capacity as citizens, the state has to 'address' its citizens like consumers. As a result, public authority too competes for publicity" (Habermas, 1989, p. 195). Here Habermas is arguing that the influence of PR has changed the grounds for communication, because of PR's appeal to the public interest. This argument rests on the distinction that Habermas (1989) makes between PR and advertising, arguing that PR is a technique which makes a claim to political veracity and attempts to manage public opinion among citizens, while advertising is a technique that attempts to influence the public in their role as consumers:

> "Opinion management" is distinguished from advertising by the fact that it expressly lays claim to the public sphere as one that plays a role in the political realm. Private advertisements are always directed to other private people insofar as they are consumers; the addressee of public relations is "public opinion," or the private citizens as the public and not directly as consumers.
>
> *(p. 193)*

While both private sector organizations and governments use PR and advertising today in their communications operations, Habermas is criticizing the manner in which PR purports to be dealing with matters of public importance. However, he argues that the PR practitioner "hides his business intentions in the role of someone interested in public welfare" (Habermas, 1989, p. 193), when it is private gain that is really at stake. With true intentions being hidden, PR works to bestow "on its object the authority of an object of public interest" (Habermas, 1989, p. 194), to give the impression that the public are forming public opinion on the object in the same way as they do for matters of public importance. Given that the public sphere should be the site for the generation of public opinion that follows from rational-critical debate, many techniques practiced as part of PR are therefore necessarily seen by Habermas in critical terms. In this sense, the public sphere has been colonized by private business interests, with PR professionals working on behalf of those who wish to manage public opinion in line with their wider business, economic and strategic interests, so that the subject of their PR becomes something that appears as being in the public, rather than just the private interest. This occurs in a manner that "goes further" than advertising (Boeder, 2005), with the aim of PR being to engender "quasi-political credit, a respect of the kind one displays toward public authority" (Habermas, 1989, p. 194).

In the Habermasian account of the public sphere, debate which is "rational-critical" in its nature is prioritized. Habermas argued that in the historical model of the public sphere, interlocutors would gain prominence of opinion through the strength of their arguments. The public sphere in this sense is the space where opinions may be aired freely, without ridicule or the fear of violence; here rational-critical debate in the public sphere is protected by a "set of basic rights…(freedom of opinion and speech, freedom of press, freedom of assembly and association, etc.) and the political function of private people in this public sphere (right of petition, equality of vote, etc.)" (Habermas, 1989, p. 83). In this conceptualization public opinion is borne out of deliberation – on public matters – and is contingent on freely available information on the affairs of state and of civil society.

Linking Habermas's understanding of rational-critical debate directly to PR, Miller and Dinan (2009) suggest "There is no place in this idealised model for strategic communication and the presentation of private interests as generalizable public interests. Therefore, much of the practice of PR has no place in a rational, deliberative democracy" (p. 254). In this regard, scholars have attempted to build on the work of Habermas in relation to a critical theory of PR. Among them, McNair (2004) notes that in the UK there is a "critical orthodoxy [that] dominates discussion of political public relations" (p. 325), influenced by "Marxian and normative liberal theory", where Habermasian public sphere theory is especially influential. In this tradition, "The manufactured messages of the public relations…professional are seen to subvert the free flow of information in the public sphere, thwarting the citizen's exercise of rational choice" (McNair, 2004, p. 325).

For example, such a view can be seen in the view of Moloney, Jackson and McQueen (2013), who note critically that "PR always has consequences for democracy because it is a powerful set of persuasive techniques available to all interests in the political economy and civil society" (pp. 262–3). However, critical scholarship is divergent on the issue. For example, the media sociologist Davis (2002) eschews the public sphere approach to studying PR for reasons that include his understanding that "While news sources and PR practitioners may act with rational goals, public relations battles, and the public discourses that result, are far from rational" (p. 14).

Taking a rather different approach to what McNair (2004) calls the "critical orthodoxy" (p. 235) of many scholars discussed above, some instead have sought to draw on Habermasian theory in support of PR practice. This position is criticized by Miller and Dinan (2009), who in particular focus on those scholars who have attempted to use Habermasian public sphere theory as a way of "perversely [producing] a normative justification for the increasing use of PR in public communication" (p. 257). Miller and Dinan (2009) focus on the work of James Grunig (and his colleague Todd Hunt), who advanced the "excellence in PR" model, based on the "symmetrical communication model" (see Grunig and Hunt, 1984, p. 22). Here it was suggested "that public relations should be guided by values of equality, reciprocity, and the civic ethos" (Pieczka, 2009, p. 2). For Miller and Dinan (p. 2009), this approach is highly problematic, undermining and misusing Habermasian theory for a very different end:

> this theory is in effect an ideal type that has been used as an apologia or legitimation for the (mal)practice of public relations. It conspicuously avoids questions of strategy and interests in the political communication process, beyond the vacuous assertions that communication in itself is a positive virtue and that liberal democracy is based on the right to communicate, petition and make representations to governance actors.
>
> *(p. 258)*

The impact of public relations on journalism

The extent to which PR has become increasingly influential on the shaping of news and the practice of journalism is an area that has been addressed from the discipline of journalism studies, in particular in relation to the changing political-economic conditions in journalism in North America and Europe. This issue is inexorably tied to the study of the public sphere, as greater influence of PR on journalism would invariably bring a change in the conditions of the public sphere since the information that interlocutors have available to them from the press and news organizations shapes how public opinion is formed (McNair, 2009, p. 238). L'Etang (2009, p. 124) discusses how since the 1950s in the UK, under post-World War Two conditions, journalists who were under greater pressure to fill more space in their newspapers and to deal with their higher production costs saw the use of PR materials as a way of accommodating these conditions: "Economic changes forced increasing dependence on public relations, which challenged the journalists' role and set in motion a seemingly perpetual tension between the two occupations" (L'Etang, 2009, pp. 124–5). Focusing on recent developments in this area in the UK, Lewis, Williams and Franklin (2008a) address "four rumours" that have marked the issue. First, that PR professionals and news agencies have gained a greater role "in shaping and informing the news content of national and local news media", resulting in the notion that "journalists have allegedly become *processors* rather than *generators* of news" (Lewis, Williams & Franklin, 2008a, p. 27). Second, news organizations are expecting more copy from fewer journalists. Third, while journalists increasingly rely on PR materials and agency news copy, a lack of time means that they often cannot check the reliability of those materials, thus giving PR a greater influence.

Given these three, Lewis et al. (2008a) note (fourth) the impression that the press is "less critical" (p. 28), its independence undermined.

Through a series of influential articles (Lewis et al., 2008a, 2008b) and a report (Lewis, Williams, Franklin, Thomas & Mosdell, 2008), this group of scholars has shown that reportage in some of the UK's leading quality newspapers has become widely influenced by PR, often using PR materials (and press agency copy) with little or no adaption. In their empirical study, Lewis et al. (2008a) addressed the content of five UK newspapers, analysing more than 2,000 news stories. They found in their sample "almost a fifth (19 per cent) of stories deriving wholly (10 per cent) or mainly (9 per cent) from PR sources" (Lewis et al., 2008a, p. 30). Given that PR was detected in the sample also in other ways, that left only 46 per cent of stories "containing no evidence of PR sources" (Lewis et al., 2008a, p. 30). Lewis et al. (2008b) also found that while newspapers were, on the whole, attempting to "give the impression" (p. 5) that stories had been written by their own journalists, that "Only 1 per cent of stories were *directly attributed* to Press Association (PA) or other agency services", and that the "data signalled that the *press were far more dependent on copy from these services and other media than conveyed by this initial impression*". Having outlined a critical account of PR from the perspective of public sphere theory, the chapter will proceed to a discussion of two divergent areas that relate to contemporary public sphere theory: that of the theory of deliberative democracy and the critical idea of agonistic pluralism.

Deliberative democracy

The theory of deliberative democracy is one closely aligned to that of the public sphere. Central to the theory, which informs the practice of deliberative democracy, is the notion that the public might be able to debate political issues of central importance, and through deliberation be able to reach reasoned and informed agreement. Talisse (2013) outlines the place of deliberative democracy theory in contemporary political theory, noting, "It is safe to say that deliberative democracy is the prevalent framework for contemporary democratic theory; even views that do not claim to be deliberativist emphasize the importance of public discussion and argument for democracy" (p. 611). Dryzek and Dunleavy (2009) chart this "deliberative turn" (p. 215) to around 1990, though as they note deliberative democracy draws its intellectual roots from theories long preceding that year. The development of a deliberative theory of democracy has been of concern to many leading scholars (Rehg & Bohman, 1996; Bohman, 1996; Cohen, 1997; Benhabib, 1996). Latterly, Fishkin's (1995, 2009) work on deliberative polling (a form of deliberative democracy practice) has been influential in providing empirical evidence for the efficacy of deliberative democracy. Nevertheless, in keeping with much of the rest of the chapter, we turn to the work of Habermas, who has himself drawn on many of these scholars, engaging at turns with their arguments. Dryzek and Dunleavy (2009) note the importance of Habermas's identification with deliberative democracy, along with that by John Rawls, thus cementing the "success of the deliberative turn" (p. 216). From this period on, Habermas framed his relevant work in deliberative terms (1994, 2005), discussing the theory with reference to his contemporary observations on the public sphere (Habermas, 2006).

While the theory of deliberative democracy is not homogeneous, there are a number of principles pointed to by various scholars that mark out the overarching features of the theory. The theory of deliberative democracy suggests that legitimacy may be found in political decisions that have proceeded from specific conditions of deliberation. To this end, like much of Habermasian public sphere theory, his account of deliberative democracy theory is normative in its nature (Rehg & Bohman, 1996, p. 80), important in a tradition of theorists who try to propose and justify the conditions under which they think it is realizable. Thus, for Bohman (1997),

"Deliberation is democratic, to the extent that it is based on a process of reaching reasoned agreement among free and equal citizens" (p. 321). Moreover, in addition to interlocutors being given "equal consideration" (Talisse, 2013, p. 612) to the reasons that they offer in support of their position in a debate, the "process forces citizens to justify their views about the best outcome by appealing to common interests or by arguing in terms of reasons that 'all could accept' in public debate" (Rehg & Bohman, 1996, pp. 80–1). Such a lofty aim means that deliberative democracy has been called "demanding" (Habermas, 2006, p. 413), and one "grounded in an assumption about individuals that stresses their capacity to reflect upon their own preferences, values and judgments in light of their participation in political dialogue with other individuals" (Dryzek & Dunleavy, 2009, p. 216). For Cohen (1997), if deliberative democracy is carried out along the correct lines:

> then democratic politics involves *public deliberation focused on the common good*, requires some form of *manifest quality* among citizens and *shapes the identity and interests* of citizens in ways that contribute to the formation of a public conception of common good.
>
> *(p. 69)*

Habermas's connection to deliberative democracy is one much more developed than his early writings on the public sphere. Rather, Habermasian discourse theory was developed across a number of decades, with Rehg (2013, p. 706) arguing that his "mature position first took shape in the 1970s" and "reached its full expression" in *Between Facts and Norms* (Habermas, 1996). At stake for Habermas is the extent to which political decisions might be said to be legitimate, and in so doing build what Rehg (2013, p.712) calls a normative model based upon the Habermasian "discourse theory of democracy and law". For Habermas, "laws are legitimate insofar as they are enacted according to a procedure whose inclusive and discursive properties warrant the presumption that its outcomes are reasonable for all citizens to accept" (Rehg, 2013, p. 712). Drawing on the work of Rehg and Bohman, Habermas (2006) notes:

> The deliberative paradigm offers as its main empirical point of reference a democratic process, which is supposed to generate legitimacy through a procedure of opinion and will formation that grants (a) publicity and transparency for the deliberative process, (b) inclusion and equal opportunity for participation, and (c) a justified presumption for reasonable outcomes (mainly in view of the impact of arguments on rational changes in preference).
>
> *(p. 413)*

The relevance of a deliberative theory of politics to our study of PR ought to be clear: as citizens deliberate they rely on sources of information to provide backing for their claims, sources of information that can contribute to a deliberative politics that brings about reasonable decisions. While in various versions of deliberative democracy exercises experts are used to provide interlocutors with the information that they require to use in their deliberations (Fishkin, 2009), in contemporary society it is mainly the information circulating in the public sphere – mostly in the media system – that citizens base their deliberations on.

As we have seen above, in democracies like the UK, PR is very influential on the production of news that citizens are consuming. The argument thus follows that the nature of that news and information may have a bearing on the type of deliberation that takes place. Cottle (2003), for example, suggests that through certain "forms of television journalism, 'discursive democracy' can variously come into being and provide resources for wider public deliberation and understanding" (p. 168). If interlocutors are basing their deliberations on news and information that is heavily skewed towards a particular viewpoint, without citizens being aware of the fact, deliberation may be harmed. But what if it is impossible to reach consensus, and to deliberate like rational and reasoned interlocutors, letting the strongest argument win out? Rather than the political sphere being one where consensus need necessarily be reached, what if it is impossible to dispel antagonism between opposing actors? These are the questions at stake for proponents of agonistic pluralism, a competing account of the extent to which consensus through deliberation might be possible, and accordingly relevant for developing a critical theory of PR.

Agonistic pluralism

Crowder (2013) identifies agonistic pluralism as one of the main ways that pluralism in politics is dealt with, of which "The core idea is that human values are irreducibly plural, frequently in conflict, and – crucially – sometimes 'incommensurable' with one another" (p. 353). He notes that the agonistic "school" tends to "interpret incommensurability very strongly to mean that choices among plural values must be non-rational" (Crowder, 2013, p. 353). Moreover, the agonistic approach stands in line with theoretical approaches from scholars who "find that the public sphere model places undue emphasis on consensus as a requirement for a healthy democracy" (Papacharissi, 2010, p. 118). A central proponent of the theory is Chantal Mouffe, who comes in a tradition of postmodern discourse theorists (Rehg, 2013, p. 706). Her account of agonistic pluralism provides a persuasive alternative to deliberative democracy accounts (Mouffe, 1999, 2000, 2005), with her critique of deliberative democracy resting on the basis that the premises that underpin it are wrongly conceived (Mouffe, 1999). Democratic legitimacy cannot come through rationality, since deliberation cannot eliminate antagonism between groups that have competing agendas. On this point, Rehg (2013) notes that Mouffe finds Habermas's "rationalism as profoundly mistaken, based on dangerous illusions about the possibilities of overcoming antagonisms endemic to political life" (p. 715).

The term "agonistic pluralism" is related to "antagonism", but is distinct from it in the view of Mouffe (2000):

> Antagonism is struggle between enemies, while *agonism* is struggle between adversaries. We can therefore reformulate our problem by saying that envisaged from the perspective of 'agonistic pluralism' the aim of democratic politics is to transform *antagonism* into *agonism*.
>
> *(p. 16)*

In direct relation to the alternative to deliberative democracy that she posits, Mouffe (1999) argues:

> Contrary to the model of "deliberative democracy," the model of "agonistic pluralism" that I am advocating asserts that the prime task of democratic politics is not to eliminate passions nor to relegate them to the private sphere in order to render rational consensus possible, but to mobilise those passions towards the promotion of democratic designs.
>
> *(pp. 755–6)*

For proponents of the agonistic approach, the conception of consensus in the deliberative approach is problematic, since "a stabilization of power...always entails some form of exclusion" (Mouffe, 1999, p. 756). Mouffe (1999) does not entirely disallow for the possibility of consensus, suggesting that within a plural democratic system a form of "conflictual consensus" (p. 756) may exist; but for Mouffe consensus without exclusion is not possible. Rather, it is the agonistic account for Mouffe (1999) that is the approach which acknowledges the plural nature of democracy, rather than trying to undermine "democratic contestation": "An 'agonistic' democratic approach acknowledges the real nature of its frontiers and recognizes the forms of exclusion that they embody, instead of trying to disguise them under the veil of rationality or morality" (p. 757).

In direct relation to PR, the deliberative approach and the uncertainty over the extent to which consensus might be found, Motion (2005) attempts to reject "idealized participative processes" (p. 506), being as she is at odds with the Habermasian perspective on deliberative democracy. Instead, participative PR is put forward to "explicitly examine discourse transformation and attempts to involve stakeholders in decision-making processes without necessarily conceding power" (Motion, 2005, p. 506). Taking a Foucauldian perspective, Motion discusses the "Catching the Knowledge Wave" conference held in New Zealand in 2001, an event at which the development of the country's knowledge economy was discussed. She suggests that for PR to be associated with the deliberative approach, to the extent that the deliberative approach involves the "assumption that power relations may be set aside", is "a risky strategy because although it offers a short-term impression of agreement and consensus, in the long-term interests and conflict cannot be suppressed" (Motion, 2005, p. 508). Here she draws on Mouffe's agonistic pluralism perspective, to argue, "The public relations challenge, then, is to bring together multiple conflicting interests, take account of power relations, and achieve a consensus, moral compromise, or resolution" (Motion, 2005, p. 508).

Conclusion

In this chapter we have addressed the public sphere as a normative category, one in which public opinion ought to be formed along rational-critical lines, based on a particular version of deliberation. As we have seen, this theory is further developed by proponents of deliberative democracy, who have suggested how agreement should be formed. In both the deliberative democracy and agonistic pluralism accounts there are implications for the development of a critical theory of PR. The theory of agonistic pluralism provides an increasingly influential critique of deliberative democracy, and a persuasive account regarding the plausibility of consensus being found among parties with different positions on various subjects. It is not enough to say that PR may be considered less problematic when viewed through the agonistic account simply because it is at odds with the deliberative account that is so closely aligned to the public sphere. However, there are clear differences between the two approaches, with deliberative democracy offering more objections to the use of PR than the theory of agonistic pluralism, with relation to the importance of rational-critical debate within the public sphere and the connection between it and the quality of the information that is informing it.

In the case of deliberative democracy, PR can be seen to be impacting negatively on the deliberative democracy process, obscuring the process by which people come to a rational decision, by presenting as something in the public interest when it is really in the private interest. The theoretical basis that it finds in the public sphere places a burden on rational-critical discussion, the kind of discussion that requires balanced and critical reportage to begin from, rather than the starting point of PR which may be utilized to advance the narrow interests of an individual, business or organization. The work of Lewis et al. (2008a, 2008b) shows that PR materials are being incorporated into news media to such an extent that PR is becoming increasingly influential on the quality of news, negatively impacting on the public sphere. In this regard, the perspective of deliberative democracy provides for us a normative position from which to build capacity in our critical theory of PR, offering a persuasive account of why a healthy media system within a democracy ought to be as free from the influence of

PR as possible. Moreover, it allows the theorist to conceive of forms of media reform, to imagine possibilities to improve the conditions under which a more public, and less commercialized media system may take shape (such as through the protection and extension of publicly funded media).

However, in the case of agonistic pluralism it could be argued that the use of PR by those competing groups in society whose interests and aims are ultimately not reconcilable is more *legitimate*, given that a "fully inclusive rational consensus" (Mouffe, 2000) is ultimately impossible. Based on this, the Habermasian critical reflections on PR discussed above hold less value. When you are no longer striving to achieve such consensus between opposing interlocutors or opposing parties, the burden that is placed on communication in the public interest, rather than in the private interest – so important to the former account – is somehow lessened. The argument proceeds that when the possibility of deliberative democracy is given up on, as "demanding" (Habermas, 2006, p. 413) as it might be, that the starting point for a critical theory of PR is somewhat lost.

It could be argued that the agonistic approach allows us to conceive of ways in which PR might be harnessed to further the ends of the agonistic approach, rather than being seen as something intrinsically inimical to the establishment of a critical theory. For example, to return to Mouffe (1999), we saw that she argued "the prime task of democratic politics is not to eliminate passions nor to relegate them to the private sphere in order to render rational consensus possible, but to mobilise those passions towards the promotion of democratic designs" (pp. 755–6). Might PR be utilized for more progressive means, in bringing about such democratic designs, rather than being viewed almost wholly in negative terms by the public sphere and deliberative democracy approaches? In considering this question, many other questions are raised, and a fuller theory of agonistic pluralism in relation to PR would need to be established in order to work through the implications of this. Such a critical theory could fairly point to the ways in which news and journalism have been impacted by PR and the failure of North American and European societies to sustain the forms of media that the correct functioning of a deliberative public sphere relies so heavily upon. Rather than trying to conceive of a better system, it could be argued that effective use of PR is a pragmatic accommodation (maybe even a necessity?) to the actually-existing conditions of society. Proponents of the deliberative democracy and Habermasian public sphere approach might respond by arguing that it is only through sustaining the notion of deliberative politics that we can maintain a normative critique of PR, and instead conceive of a more democratic media system.

References

Benhabib, S. (1996). Toward a deliberative model of democratic legitimacy. In S. Benhabib (Ed.), *Democracy and difference: Contesting the boundaries of the political*, pp. 67–94. Princeton, NJ: Princeton University Press.
Boeder, P. (2005). Habermas' heritage: The future of the public sphere in the network society. *First Monday*, 10. Retrieved on April 12, 2015, from http://firstmonday.org/ojs/index.php/fm/article/view/1280/1200
Bohman, J. (1996). *Public deliberation*. Cambridge, MA: MIT Press.
Bohman, J. (1997). Deliberative democracy and effective social freedom: Capabilities, resources and opportunities. In J. Bohman, & W. Rehg (Eds), *Deliberative democracy: Essays on reason and politics*, pp. 321–48. Cambridge, MA: MIT Press.
Cohen, J. (1997). *Deliberation and democratic legitimacy*. In J. Bohman, & W. Rehg (Eds), *Deliberative democracy: Essays on reason and politics*, pp. 67–92. Cambridge, MA: MIT Press.
Cottle, S. (2003). TV Journalism and deliberative democracy: Mediating communicative action. In S. Cottle (Ed.), *News, public relations and power*, pp.153–70. London, UK: Sage.
Crowder, G. (2013). Pluralism. In G. Gaus, & F. D'Agostino (Eds), *The Routledge companion to social and political philosophy*, pp. 353–63. New York, NY: Routledge.

Curran, J. (1991). Rethinking the media as a public sphere. In P. Dahlgren, & C. Sparks (Eds), *Communication and citizenship: Journalism and the public sphere in the new media age*, pp.27–57. London, UK: Routledge.

Davis, A. (2002). *Public relations democracy: Public relations, politics and the mass media in Britain*. Manchester, UK: Manchester University Press.

Davis, A. (2007). *The mediation of power: A critical introduction*. Abingdon, UK: Routledge.

Dryzek, J. S., & Dunleavy, P. (2009). *Theories of the democratic state*. Basingstoke, UK: Palgrave Macmillan.

Fishkin, J. (1995). *The voice of the people*. New Haven, CT: Yale University Press.

Fishkin, J. (2009). *When the people speak: Deliberative democracy & public consultation*. Oxford, UK: Oxford University Press.

Fraser, N. (1995). Politics, culture and the public sphere: Toward a postmodern conception. In L. Nicholson, & S. Seidman (Eds), *Social postmodernism: Beyond identity politics*, pp. 287–314. Cambridge, UK: Cambridge University Press.

Garnham, N. (1986). Media and the public sphere. In P. Golding, G. Murdock, & P. Schlesinger (Eds), *Communicating Politics*, pp. 37–53. Leicester, UK: Leicester University Press.

Garnham, N. (1992). The media and the public sphere. In C. Calhoun (Ed.), *Habermas and the public sphere*, pp. 359–76. Cambridge, MA: MIT Press.

Graham, G. (2012). Public opinion and public sphere. In C. Emden, & D. Midgley (Eds), *Beyond Habermas: Democracy, knowledge, and the public sphere*, pp. 29–41. Oxford, UK: Berghahn Books.

Grunig, J., & Hunt, T. (1984). *Managing public relations*. New York, NY: Holt, Rinehart & Winston.

Habermas, J. (1989). *The structural transformation of the public sphere: An inquiry into a category of bourgeois society*. Cambridge, UK: Polity.

Habermas, J. (1992). Further reflections on the public sphere. In C. Calhoun (Ed.), *Habermas and the public sphere*, pp. 421–64. Cambridge, MA: MIT Press.

Habermas, J. (1994). Three normative models of democracy. *Constellations*, 1, pp. 1–10.

Habermas, J. (1996). *Between facts and norms: Contributions to a discourse theory of law and democracy*. Cambridge, MA: MIT Press.

Habermas, J. (1997). The public sphere. In R. Goodin, & P. Pettit (Eds), *Contemporary political philosophy*, pp. 105–8. Oxford, UK: Blackwell.

Habermas, J. (2005). Concluding comments on empirical approaches to deliberative politics. *Acta Politica*, 40, pp. 384–92.

Habermas, J. (2006). Political communication in media society: Does democracy still enjoy an epistemic dimension? The impact of normative theory on empirical research. *Communication Theory*, 16, pp. 411–26.

L'Etang, J. (2009). *Public relations in Britain: A history of professional practice in the twentieth century*. Abingdon, UK: Routledge.

Lewis, J., Williams, A., & Franklin, R. (2008a). Four rumours and an explanation: A political economic account of journalists' changing newsgathering and reporting practices. *Journalism Practice*, 2, pp. 27–45.

Lewis, J., Williams, A., & Franklin, R. (2008b). A compromised Fourth Estate? UK news journalism, public relations and news sources. *Journalism Studies*, 9, pp. 1–20.

Lewis, J., Williams, A., Franklin, B., Thomas, J., & Mosdell, N. (2008). *The quality and independence of British journalism: Tracking the changes over 20 years*. Media Wise/Cardiff University. Retrieved on April 12, 2015, from http://www.mediawise.org.uk/wp-content/uploads/2011/03/Quality-Independence-of-British-Journalism.pdf

McNair, B. (2004). PR must die: Spin, anti-spin and political public relations in the UK, 1997–2004. *Journalism Studies*, 5, pp. 325–38.

McNair, B. (2009). Journalism and democracy. In K. Wahl-Jorgensen, & T. Hanitzsch (Eds), *Handbook of Journalism Studies*, pp. 237–49. New York, NY: Routledge.

Miller, D., & Dinan, W. (2009). Journalism, public relations and spin. In K. Wahl-Jorgensen, & T. Hanitzsch (Eds), *Handbook of Journalism Studies*, pp. 250–64. New York, NY: Routledge.

Moloney, K., Jackson, D., & McQueen, D. (2013). News journalism and public relations: A dangerous relationship. In K. Fowler-Watt, & S. Allan (Eds), *Journalism: New challenges*, pp. 259–81. Bournemouth, UK: Centre for Journalism & Communication Research, Bournemouth University.

Motion, J. (2005). Participative public relations: Power to the people or legitimacy for government discourse? *Public Relations Review*, 31, pp. 505–12.

Mouffe, C. (1999). Deliberative democracy or antagonistic pluralism? *Social Research*, 66, pp. 745–58.

Mouffe, C. (2000). Deliberative democracy or agonistic pluralism. *Reihe Politikwissenschaft, Political Science Series*, 72. Vienna, Austria: Institute for Advanced Studies.

Mouffe, C. (2005). *On the political*. Abingdon, UK: Routledge.

Papacharissi, Z. (2010). *A private sphere*. Cambridge, UK: Polity.

Pieczka, M. (2009, September). Public relations as dialogic expertise? Paper presented at Stirling 21 CIPR Academic Conference.

Rehg, W. (2013). Discourse theory. In G. Gaus, & F. D'Agostino (Eds), *The Routledge companion to social and political philosophy*, pp.706–17. New York, NY: Routledge.

Rehg, W., & Bohman, J. (1996). Discourse and democracy: The formal and informal bases of legitimacy in Habermas' *Faktiziät und Geltung*. *The Journal of Political Philosophy*, 4, pp. 79–99.

Somerville, I., & Ramsey, P. (2012). Public relations and politics. In A. Theaker (Ed.), *The public relations handbook*, 4th edition, pp. 38–59. Abingdon, UK: Routledge.

Talisse, R. B. (2013). Democracy. In G. Gaus, & F. D'Agostino (Eds), *The Routledge companion to social and political philosophy*, pp. 608–17. New York, NY: Routledge.

Thompson, J. (1990). *Ideology and modern culture: Critical social theory in the era of mass communication*. Cambridge, UK: Polity.

Thompson, J. (1995). *The Media and modernity: A social theory of the media*. Cambridge, UK: Polity.

6

Dialogue and critical public relations

Magda Pieczka

This chapter aims to answer the question of how dialogue can offer a critical approach to public relations. To do so, it is necessary to reflect on how dialogue has been understood and used in public relations scholarship as well as the ways in which public relations as a field has sought to articulate a critical stance. This discussion starts with a brief definition of critical theory and a sketch of its applications to the field of public relations in order to explore *dialogue* as, on the one hand, the object of critique, and on the other as a method of critique.

Critical theory and public relations

In its most fundamental meaning, the aim of critical theory, and consequently the purpose of a critical stance, is the emancipation of human beings so they can become 'producers of their social life in its totality' (Horkheimer, 1982, p. 244). As a philosophical project, Critical Theory, understood as the work of the Frankfurt School, postulated that theory must be descriptive, practical and normative (Horkheimer, 1972), all at the same time. Its purpose is to reveal the workings of knowledge that structures the social world and human life as well as to articulate how these can be changed so that individuals can regain more freedom and take control over the production of their own shared 'form of life' (Horkheimer, 1993, p. 21). The Enlightenment ideas and their consequences were the original objects of this critique (Habermas, 1984–87; Horkheimer & Adorno, 1972). Subsequently, other critical theories have emerged, such as feminism, or post-colonialism. A critical theory thus identifies and explains the problem, i.e. its specific view of the way in which human freedom is constrained through a particular formation of knowledge: it articulates how action can be taken to change this state of affairs; and it offers a moral argument for such action.

In public relations a critical stance was articulated initially largely from a rhetorical perspective (see Edwards 2012; Heath, Toth & Waymer, 2009; Ihlen, 2010; Marsh, 2003; Toth, 2000; Toth & Heath, 1992); that is, rhetorical study as it was extended and reshaped by 'Marxism, continental philosophy (particularly 'poststructuralism'), and the full development of Burkean (sociologically inclined) criticism' (Cheney, 1992, p. 168). This was followed swiftly by critical approaches to public relations offered from, to mention perhaps the most obvious candidates, the perspectives of: feminist theory (Aldoory, 2009; Demetrious & Daymon, 2014; Grunig, Hon & Toth 2001), postmodern theory (Holtzahausen, 2012); cultural studies (Curtin & Gaither, 2007; Edwards & Hodges, 2011), subaltern studies (Dutta, 2009; Dutta-Bergman, 2005), globalization (Bardhan & Weaver, 2011), or diversity (Edwards 2014). Thus critiques, from their specific theoretical perspectives, have worked to identify various forms of inequality as well as ways in which organizational discourses and persuasive communication exercise power in order to reflect on their consequences for individuals, organizations and society at large.

For the purposes of the present discussion, it is helpful to identify Excellence Theory (Grunig, 1992; Grunig, et al., 2006; Toth 2007) as the object of critique for much of the work that does not neatly fit into more specifically focused theoretical categorizations of critical approaches. Indeed, the main thrust of critical work in public relations has come from what could be seen as an immanent critique of the dominant paradigm (Bardhan & Weaver, 2011; Demetrious, 2013; Dozier & Lauzen, 2000; Fawkes, 2014; Leitch & Motion, 2010; McKie & Munshi, 2007; Moloney, 2006; Pieczka & L'Etang, 1996; Roper, 2005) that is work that probes internal contradictions, deconstructs the ideological edifice, and looks for blind spots of the Excellence Theory. The main lines of this critique could be seen as directed at: the normalization of the liberal-pluralist regime of thought with its lack of attention to ideological and hegemonic processes (Bardhan & Weaver, 2011; Holtzhausen, 2000; McKie & Munshi 2007); the functionalist, and by extension, positivistic approach to knowledge (McKie & Munshi, 2007; Pearson, 1989b; Pieczka & L'Etang, 1996); the teleology of the open systems theory, which underpins the strategic imperative of the Excellence approach, and its moral consequences (Brown, 2006; Edwards, 2012; Heath 2008; Pieczka 1996); a universalist predilection in offering the Excellence Theory as a 'global concept' (Holtzhausen, Petersen & Tindall, 2003; Sriramesh & Verčič, 2012; Verčič & Gruning 2000, cited in McKie & Munshi, 2007, p. 43); and, a tendency to fetishize symmetry, or, to be precise, symmetrical communication (Brown, 2010; Porter, 2010; Stoker & Tusinki, 2006). Each of these, in turn, has led to more detailed and wide-ranging arguments, revealing dialectical tensions in the theory, and reflecting on their practical and theoretical consequences. The purpose of this chapter, however, is to investigate how dialogue can play a part in the critical project in public relations fashioned against this backdrop.

The discussion begins by identifying four, often overlapping strands of dialogue present in public relations scholarship: dialogue as symmetrical communication; rhetorical dialogue; procedural or Habermasian approach to dialogue; and dialogic theory of public relations and its online application.

Dialogue in public relations scholarship

The position of *dialogue* in public relations theory is, as I have argued elsewhere, paradoxical. On the one hand, the term itself and the values and preoccupations it represents, such as trust, openness, or involvement, have been at the heart of public relations for some 30 years; on the other hand, in comparison to other fields of theory and practice, such as deliberative democracy, community development and science communication, dialogue remains rather opaque as an expert practice (Pieczka, 2011). The first critical task is, therefore, to explain how the field of public relations so far has understood and engaged with the concept of dialogue in order to place its current application to public relations in a broader perspective and thus reflect critically on its function.

Dialogue as symmetry

Although *dialogue* was present in the development of the ideas leading to, as well as in the articulation of, the Excellence Theory (Grunig, 1992; Grunig & Hunt, 1984), it appeared largely as self-evident – an apparently unproblematic term and practice used to define symmetrical communication:

> The two-way symmetrical model...consists more of a dialogue than a monologue. If persuasion occurs, the public should be just as likely to persuade the organisation's management to change attitudes or behavior as the organization is likely to change the public's attitudes and behavior.
>
> *(Grunig & Hunt, 1984, p. 23)*

> Symmetrical communication takes place through dialogue, negotiation, listening, and conflict management rather than through persuasion, manipulation, and the giving of orders.
>
> *(Grunig, 1992, p. 231)*

> With the two-way symmetrical model, practitioners use research and dialogue to bring about symbiotic changes in the ideas, attitudes and behaviours of both their organizations and publics.
>
> *(Grunig, 2001, p. 12).*

Thus, while crucial, dialogue also remained unexplored as the debate focused on *symmetry*, understood as the opposite of self-interested persuasion; and on the role of persuasion in public relations more generally (Brown, 2006, 2010; Grunig, 2001; Pfau & Wan, 2006; Porter 2010). This interest was related directly to the public relations professional project and driven by the occupation's need to rethink the basis for its legitimacy away from Lippmann's and Bernays' technocratic view of the role of public opinion management in modern democratic societies.

There is no easy way to disentangle dialogue from symmetry (Kent & Taylor, 2002, p. 23; Theunissen & Wan Noordin, 2012). Grunig, in his own attempt to disambiguate *symmetry*, was tempted to abandon the term altogether in preference to *dialogue* and offered a new explanation of what the term stood for:

> The basic idea was that public relations should go beyond the advocacy of self-interest...to a balance between self-interest and concern for the interests of others....Symmetry might not have been the best choice of a name for the model of public relations I had in mind... mixed motives, collaborative advocacy, and cooperative antagonism all have the same meaning as does symmetry....Simultaneous fusion with the Other while retaining the uniqueness of one's own self-interest seems to describe well the challenge of symmetrical public relations – or perhaps we should begin to say, dialogical public relation.
>
> *(2001, p. 28)*

Dialogue thus emerges here as a process of cooperation premised on a level of recognition that one's actions have to be mindful of the interests of others. It requires a simultaneous orientation to the same object – this is perhaps what in the New Model of Symmetry as Two-Way Practice is represented as the symbiotic changes and the win-win zone (Grunig, 2001, p. 26). This definition, however, also stresses the tension inherent in dialogue's effort to retain the distinctiveness of the different positions. Finally, dialogue is deemed to have happened if the parties have cooperated, irrespective of the outcomes. As far as the manner of this cooperation goes, both persuasion and its opposite, whatever form this non-persuasion might take, are acceptable. Such a definition covers a lot of ground, and while it might work well to articulate an orientation to professional communication work (Hodges & McGrath, 2011; Kent & Taylor, 2002), it does not work well in distinguishing *dialogue* from other forms of communication

Over the years, thus, the meaning of dialogue as symmetrical communication has fluctuated somewhat, but its core is best captured as 'consensus' (Theunissen & Wan Noordin, 2012, p. 7). These two scholars argue that dialogue in this conception is dominated by the 'cybernetic view of public relations', and reduced to managing the organization's (system's) adaptive function. Grunig's own use of a game theory term to describe this process as creating a 'win-win zone', quoted earlier, makes it clear that dialogue here is synonymous with bargaining, or its less combative version – negotiation – a process in which a zone of shared interests or understandings is created while the substantive differences can be bracketed out of the conversation without the need to re-examine them in the light of the encounter. The dynamic of such encounters is that of a trade, and, as Susskind warns, even in its 'mutual gains' approach it 'should not be, as it often is, called a "win-win" approach to negotiation. There is no way for both sides to get everything they want in a negotiation' (Susskind, 2006, p. 282).

Rhetorical dialogue

A different way of working with the concept of dialogue is identified first and foremost with Robert Heath's contributions over the years (1992, 1993, 2000, 2001, 2006, 2008, 2009). Heath draws both on the classical tradition of rhetoric and the New Rhetoric of Kenneth Burke, whose influence he acknowledged in the title of two of his publications (1992, 2009): the wrangle in the marketplace (see also, Heath 2000). To the classical tradition, Heath owes his view of the importance of public persuasion and deliberation for a democratic society. Rhetoric is not seen as shameful sophistry, advocacy for sale, but rather a skill to be put to use responsibly to construct and publicly test arguments that can show the way to the best possible course of action to be taken in matters of public importance (see discussion of Isocrates in Marsh, 2003, 2008). To Burke, Heath owes his marketplace metaphor for a pluralistic political system that values diversity of ideas as the starting point for sound decision-making as well as the rough and tumble of the public, and, therefore, transparent contest of ideas. He sees rhetoric as 'dialogue of opinions, counter opinions, meanings, and counter meanings – the process by which interests are asserted, negotiated, and constrained' (Heath 1993, p. 143).

A number of relevant critical points can be offered here. First, scholars have grappled with the consequences of eliding persuasion/rhetoric with dialogue. Porter (2010, p. 130; see also Brown, 2010) is sceptical of the attempt to 'reconcile persuasion with the symmetrical model' which Heath formulated with the recourse to the term *dialogue* as follows: 'the sort of advocacy that would be comfortable with symmetry.... This paradigm assumes that ideas grow in quality through dialogue as a win-win outcome. As such, advocacy is a virtuous management and communication strategy and philosophy' (Heath 1993, p. 43). Holtzausen (2012) is suspicious of the marketplace metaphor because it 'treats theory building as a form of capitalism, an ideological position' (Fawkes, 2014, p. 19). To this, one could also add the criticism often levelled against pluralist theory more generally for its blindness to power, whether exercised through discourse or other forms of exclusion (Edwards, 2014); Schattschneider, 1960; Weaver, Motion & Roper, 2006). My own objection is to the use of the term *dialogue* in a somewhat indiscriminate way, referring to negotiation, bargaining, and in particular to a practice understood by political and communication scholars as *deliberation* (Dryzek & Hendriks, 2012; Gastil, 2008; Pieczka, 2011).

Despite these criticisms, Fawkes's characterization of the rhetorical approach, as such, is useful to illustrate the meaning of Heath's idea of the rhetorical dialogue (Heath, 2000, p. 71): 'persuasion is seen as central...and the exchange of ideas in the public arena as an essential element in the democratic discourse' (Fawkes, 2014, p. 19). Rhetorical dialogue thus is the Burkean idea of the multiplicity of voices (Burke, 1951, p. 203), each speaking up to express his or her interest and point of view, but operating together in an area delineated by the argument being pursued through such an exchange. However, while the ideas might be refined and sifted in this process, its nature remains opaque: it is not clear whether the improvement in the quality of the ideas is to be judged by the prominent place they come to occupy in the marketplace, and, if so, whether this could be due to the refinement of persuasive appeals associated with them, or whether it must be justified by the shared public examination of the bases of their validity.

Procedural (Habermasian) approach to dialogue

Approaching dialogue as a process rather than its outcomes – a procedural approach – was a feature of Ron Pearson's work on dialogue in the 1980s, the period between the two landmark publications in the development of the Excellence approach (Grunig & Hunt 1984; Grunig, 1992). 'Pearson's work on dialogue as a practical public relations strategy is the earliest substantive treatment of the concept,' write Kent and Taylor (2002, p. 21) in their own influential intervention published a decade after the original Excellence study. Pearson offered an outline of a procedural ethical theory for public relations, but, what is equally important, is that he explicitly employed Habermas's ideas, particularly the ideal speech situation (Habermas, 1970) and communicative action (Habermas, 1984–87) in relation to the emergent notion of symmetry in public relations:

> Habermas' distinction between monological and dialogical rationality nicely articulates the tensions between two approaches to public relations theory – the tensions between asymmetric and symmetric approaches (Grunig 1987). Emphasis on social scientific methodologies and management by objectives techniques suggests an instrumental rationality. Emphasis on symmetry, dialogue, conversation and mutual understanding implies a communicative rationality.
>
> *(Pearson, 1989a, p. 74)*

Habermas's ideas were thus put into circulation in the public relations field, giving the concept of dialogue a philosophical framing in addition to that borrowed from social psychology and the theory of co-orientation.

Pearson (1989b) tackled the question of how dialogue between an organization and people outside it – organization-public dialogue – can be facilitated by borrowing from Habermas's ideal speech situation and adding rules specific to the nature of the communication exchanges that happen between organizations – as anonymous or collective speakers (Cheney, 1992, p. 166) – and individuals. Communication in such situations is often conducted at a physical distance and is mediated through writing and the use of organizational channels of communication. For Pearson, thus, while dialogical rules include the speaker's ability to introduce topics into the conversation freely (one of the ideal speech conditions), overall they are more focused on the criteria for reaching agreement on what actually constitutes dialogue in this context; for example: how much time can separate the dialogic exchanges, or what counts as a response; or how utilization of different channels is to be governed in the constitution of organization-public dialogue (Kent & Taylor, 2002, p. 33; Pearson, 1989b).

While the link between symmetry and dialogue continued to be worked heavily, a more detailed and direct application of Habermas's theory of communicative action also began to emerge from the late 1990s onwards (Burkart 2004, 2009; Leeper 1996; Meisenbach 2006;

Meisenbach & Feldner, 2009). These scholars share the preoccupation with the procedural qualities of communication as well as with the communicators' readiness for challenge of validity claims made on the grounds of truth, truthfulness and legitimacy (Burkart, 2009) or truth, rightness, and sincerity (Meisenbach & Feldner, 2009, p. 256). Dialogue thus comes to be viewed as a structured process by which consensus is built and is offered as a way of both handling and of critiquing public relations as organizational communication. Here consensus is not the give-and-take, win-or-lose dynamic of a negotiation, but rather an agreement reached on explicit criteria of validity which demand interlocutors' alignment in relation to their understanding of the objective world, their respective normative stance, and the authenticity of the positions taken in terms of subjective worlds of experience. Habermas (1984–87) designates these three types of validity as truth, rightness or appropriateness, and sincerity. A challenge can be raised at any of these levels and a transparent process of working through the challenge is required if an agreement is to be reached. Consensus is not an outcome of strategic trading of values, interests and needs, parcelled up and assessed for their bargaining value (see Susskind, 2006), but a comprehensive agreement reached at objective, intersubjective and subjective levels where the three types of validity operate.

Despite its extensive conceptual development and strength, however, this version of dialogue seems less visible in its application to public relations than other versions, including the most recent one referred to as the dialogic theory of public relations discussed in the following section.

Dialogic theory (and its online application)

Dialogue began to be considered more fully as a concept and practice in its own right, rather than an adjunct to symmetry, following Kent and Taylor's (2002) contribution, particularly the publication of 'Toward a dialogic theory of public relations'. The article reinvigorated the interest in, and helped to shift the understanding of, dialogue by offering an introduction to the concept as it had been constituted by the work of a number of philosophers, psychologists, sociologists and communication scholars since around the 1950s. Thus, while Habermas draws on classical sociology (Weber), philosophy (Wittgenstein) and linguistics (Austin, Searle) – primarily to offer a conception of the intersubjective rationality – dialogic theory offered by Kent and Taylor takes the path charted in communication theory by ideas best illustrated by the collection of essays in *Dialogue: Theorizing Difference in Communication Studies* (Anderson, Baxter & Cissna, 2004). In identifying five principles of dialogue – mutuality, propinquity, empathy, risk and commitment – Kent and Taylor take their inspiration from the dialogic legacy of Buber, Bakhtin, Levinas, Gadamer and Bohm. The emphasis in this approach falls less on reason and rationality and more on the phenomenological inspiration, inherent tensions, and a certain element of mystery as fundamental to dialogue. The nature of the intellectual and disciplinary contributions that have been fused into dialogue in its contemporary form as a communication concept are responsible both for its richness but also for its elusiveness (Stewart, Zedicker & Black, 2004). Thus Buber and Levinas are concerned with the individual's experience of the Other, with transcendence and the relational basis of human existence, knowledge and ethics; Bakhtin and Gadamer work on language, communication and culture – dialogue here refers primarily to the presence of other voices and cultural formations retained in language and the resulting openness of meaning; and finally, Bohm's concern is primarily with society, with the 'tacit ground' that holds it together – he sees collaborative, group dialogue as a method of reaching beyond what can be talked about to that foundational, tacit ground that is 'unspoken…[and] cannot be described' (Bohm, 2004, p. 16).

The way in which the dialogic theory of public relations has been used, however, has focused on digitally mediated communication platforms (websites) where dialogue is defined through an earlier scheme (Kent & Taylor, 1998; Madichie & Hinson, 2014) and is understood as a set of characteristics that facilitate particular forms of engagement: Dialogic Feedback Loops, Useful Information, Return Visits, Ease of Interface, and Conservation of Visit time. In this approach 'dialogue is not a process or a series of steps. Rather, it is a product of on going communication and relationships' (Kent & Taylor 2002, p. 24), the application of these ideas to digital communication deals with the set-up for dialogue, which is analysed along the functional dimensions offered by the technology. Subsequently, extrapolations are made about the readiness for dialogue, rather than dialogue itself (Madichie & Hinson, 2014; McAllister, 2012; McAllister-Spooner, 2008, 2009; Uzunoğlu & Kip, 2014). The paucity of dialogue suggested by this research on online communication, and specifically on websites, was offered by McAllister-Spooner (2009) and Hether (2014) as a striking and disappointing finding: 'the dialogic promise of the Web has not yet been realized' (McAllister-Spooner, 2009, p. 321). A broadly similar critique was articulated by Meisenbach and Feldner: 'while public relations scholars recognize the need for a dialogic perspective…most research in the area has failed to examine what this dialogue might look like in practice' (2009, p. 255). In the absence of a systematically advanced explanation for this state of affairs, it is reasonable to ask whether the lack of dialogic public relations practice online is symptomatic of public relations practice in general. This takes us back to the fundamental question of the role of dialogue in the conceptualization of public relations practice raised around the concept of symmetrical public relations.

As the discussion so far shows, dialogue in public relations reflects, if not very directly and extensively, some of the key concerns and contributions to the current understandings of this concept and its philosophical underpinnings: its public significance for social governance, its role as a normative standard of cooperation and consensus building, and its attention to the technique. However, the extent of the field's recognition of dialogue's preoccupation with the world of human experience – with authenticity, the turning to the Other (Buber, 1947/1993, p.35), with the openness and the surprise of dialogue – is particularly limited (Kent & Taylor, 2002; Pieczka & Wood, 2013). Thus, the field draws on the debates about rhetoric and its role in deliberation; it also draws on the principles of communicative action to push back against the world of strategic action of the undeclared self-interest and manipulation it requires. The question at this point becomes what kind of critical re-formation in the field of public relations can be created by *dialogue*.

Critical potential of dialogue

Dialogue resists unequivocal definitions because there are different routes by which it can be reached theoretically. I have sketched one way of thinking about this complexity; Deetz and Simpson (2004) offer another. They explain dialogue through three approaches to meaning production: liberal humanist, critical hermeneutic and postmodern. The first, associated with the work of Maslow, Rogers, Senge and Bohm, is 'rooted in notions of internally located meaning … developed as a normative interaction ideal founded on principles of understanding, empathy and active listening' (Deetz and Simpson, 2004, p. 141). The second, associated with Gadamer and Habermas, 'posits interaction rather than psychological individuals as the locus of meaning production' (p. 142). The third one, inspired by Bakhtin, Foucault, Derrida and Levinas, 'emphasizes, the role of indeterminacy and "otherness" in reclaiming conflicts, resisting closure and opening opportunities for people to be mutually involved in shaping new understandings of the world in which they live and work' (p. 142)

Looking at public relations, we could say that the notion of dialogue as symmetrical communication represents the first, 'native' conception of dialogue (Deetz & Simpson, 2004, p. 142).

This, as we have seen, is constructed from the individualist treatment of dialogue as the creation of negotiated common ground, and while it highlights the importance of humanistic orientation and the relevant dialogic communication skills, it also privileges achievement of consensus over grappling with the issues that defy it. It is, thus, a practically useful way of dialoguing which allows for a degree of agreement to be achieved, albeit at the price of placing fundamental differences outside dialogue and therefore outside the possibility of public intervention or the possibility of transformation. The second, interactional approach, as explicated in particular by Habermas, is represented by the work that draws explicitly on his ideas to guide the development of applied theory in public relations. This includes the work referred to earlier as the procedural approaches to dialogue, but also the work based on a particular instrumentation of the dialogic theory of public relations and its application to online communication platforms. Although at a theoretical level we find examples of confident engagement with these ideas, the indications are that the reach of this conception of dialogue is limited: it serves as a critique rather than applied theory.

Deetz and Simpson's scheme is further helpful in highlighting the problematic nature of the idea of rhetorical dialogue. If rhetoric is understood as a means of persuasion of individuals, as in effect much as Aristotle's technical approach in *Rhetoric* suggests, then there may not be much room for dialogue left because part of the technique is to close opportunities for challenge. If, however, we understand rhetoric in the way proposed by Heath – as used 'to form, assert, and dispute ideas in public' (2000, p. 73) – then we are dealing with the process of public search for good reasons, following Toulmin's (2003) ideas on argumentation and ethics. The preoccupation here is with the acceptability of propositions, and, therefore, in broad terms it is comparable to the aim of Habermas's communicative action. Consequently, we could argue that rhetorical dialogue is, in fact, primarily concerned with argument. The term highlights its traditional roots in rhetoric, but it may be more helpful to think about this practice as *deliberation*, both to clarify its nature but also to connect it more directly with the rich theoretical and empirical work around the idea of deliberative democracy (Elster, 1998; Gutmann & Thompson, 2004; Steiner, 2012).

The discussion so far has demonstrated that the ideas and practices of dialogue in the field of public relations have been mediated primarily through discussion about symmetrical communication and rhetoric – essentially then a discussion about the ethics and legitimacy of public relations itself. These preoccupations have served as critiques and returned the questions of power and reason into the frame of discussion; raised the problem of emasculation of critique through a particular notion of consensus; and inspired a search for practical ways in which these issues might be tackled differently in public relations theory and practice. What has been less explored so far is, for want of a better term, the 'postmodern' approach to dialogue.

Public relations operates in a fiercely modern landscape of organizations driven by strategies, goal-directedness, effectiveness and consistency, i.e. the search for a stable, unitary identity of an organization. In this context, it is particularly important to return to the phenomenological core of dialogue in order to problematize these instrumentally successful ideas. At the core of dialogue lies the intersubjective self, the act of transcending of an individualistic sense of being, as well as an individualistic sense of identity by the empathetic acknowledgement of the reaching out to the Other. Buber talks about it as the I-Thou relationship (1958/2000). In his reading of Buber and Levinas, Arnett (2004, p. 80) argues that 'phenomenologically, the Other makes an "I" possible. Ethics as responsibility for the Other is an act that makes possible human life – without the "Other" there is no "I"'.

This stance is the basis out of which the social world of relationships that empower rather then imprison can arise, of community rather then collectivity, to use Buber's terms:

> [c]ommunity…is the being no longer side by side but *with* one another.…Collectivity is based on an organized atrophy of personal existence, community on its increase, confirmation in life lived with the other. The modern zeal for collectivity is…a flight from the vital dialogic, demanding the shaking of the self, which is at the heart of the world.
>
> *(Buber, 1947/1993, p. 37)*

Dialogic engagement with the world crosses, thus, from the sphere of the individual experience and knowledge to that of social relations.

In this context, it is fruitful to turn to the concept of knowledge as the mediating mechanism that connects experience to action, the individual to the community, and that, in the professional context, creates the basis for expert intervention (Abbott, 1988; Pieczka & L'Etang, 2006). The questions that arise here are about the kind of knowledge that is used in public relations, and about how it is connected to action; or, to put it differently, what is produced by this knowledge. The development of public relations knowledge in recent decades has been driven by the institutional demands of the academia and the profession. This has implications for the way in which knowledge is produced, its form and relationship to action, or the world of practice. The traditional model of scientific knowledge driven by logical-empiricist epistemology has been reshaped by sociological understandings of the importance of institutional influences as well as the messiness of science (for example, Foucault, 1970/2002; Latour & Woolgar, 1979; Lynch & Bogen, 1997; Lyotard, 1984). In this context, we can point to an assumption of a particular division of labour as well as a linear model of knowledge production that moves 'knowledge' from theoretical/empirical work done by scientists to its 'impact', orchestrated by knowledge producers and 'defined as an effect on, change or benefit to the economy, society, culture, public policy or services, health, the environment or quality of life, beyond academia' (REF 2011, para. 140). While the concept of knowledge has been problematized in the sociology of the professions by the recognition of the utility of professional knowledge as a competitive mechanism for creating professional jurisdictions, as well as by the recognition of different forms of professional knowledge (abstract, textbook vs. embodied, tacit knowledge), it could be argued that the profession like science has privileged a linear, hierarchical understanding of knowledge: it is controlled and wielded by the professional who applies it to others and thus ultimately changes lives and institutions in ways that serves the profession's interests, as much as or perhaps more than those it is supposed to serve (Pieczka & L'Etang, 2006).

A very different stance on knowledge has been proposed by action research, an approach that starts with the primacy of practical engagement in the world and the disruption of the division of labour in knowledge production (Reason & Bradbury, 2006a). Action research is a collaborative process of producing 'practical knowledge that is useful to people in the conduct of their everyday lives' (Reason & Bradbury, 2006b, p. 2; see also Park, 2006, p. 83). Dialogic principles, as discussed earlier in relation to Buber, Levinas and Bohm, could be seen as the grounding for the whole range of action research practices (Park, 2006, p. 84). In the context of public relations, Pieczka and Wood's (2013) action research study applied the concept of radical epistemology – a view of knowledge that integrates

> experiential knowing through meeting and encounter, presentational knowing through the use of aesthetic, expressive forms, propositional knowing through the use of words and concepts, and practical knowing-how in the exercise of diverse skills – intrapsychic, interpersonal, political, transpersonal.
>
> *(Heron & Reason, 2006, p. 145)*

This kind of knowledge is produced in direct relation to practical action; it aims at transformation rather than description of the world; and it is enmeshed in the social relations among the people who both produce and use it. In this way knowledge is stripped of its objectifying and also its ideological and hegemonic character. Such an approach to knowledge and action has the potential to respond to Horkheimer's call to return the power to shape the social world to its inhabitants.

Conclusions

A number of conclusions emerge from this discussion of dialogue in public relations scholarship. First of all, I argue that there are four ways in which dialogue has been understood, but we could say now that irrespective of the differences, the presence of dialogue is associated with the normative function of knowledge and scholarship: it takes a position on what should be, on what is 'right'. Second, Deetz and Simpson's (2004) ideas have opened a way to reflect on the critical potential of the various forms of dialogue identified in this discussion, showing that it is unevenly distributed: the native and rhetorical forms of dialogue are perhaps more circumscribed in this respect, while the Habermasian and dialogic approaches, through their roots in extensive theoretical and critical frameworks, offer a clearer argument built around the concepts of communication, reason and knowledge, and the primacy of the lifeworld. Finally, in following the relatively underexplored version of dialogue, this discussion has taken a particular path – from dialogue to knowledge – in order to reflect on the critical contribution that can still be made to both public relations scholarship and practice.

References

Abbott, A. (1988). *The system of professions: An essay on the division of expert labour*. Chicago, IL: University of Chicago Press.

Aldoory, L. (2009). Feminist criticism in public relations. In R. Heath, E. Toth, & D. Waymer (Eds), *Rhetorical and critical approaches of public relations II*, pp. 111–28. New York, NY: Routledge.

Anderson, R., Baxter, L. & Cissna, K. (Eds). (2004). *Dialogue: Theorizing difference in communication studies*. Thousand Oaks, CA: Sage.

Arnett, R. (2004). A dialogic ethic 'between' Buber and Levinas: a responsive ethical 'I'. In I. R. Anderson, L. Baxter, & K. Cissna (Eds), *Dialogue: theorizing difference in communication studies*, pp. 75–90. Thousand Oaks, CA: Sage.

Bardhan, N., & Weaver, C. (Eds). (2011). *Public relations in global cultural contexts: Multiparadigmatic perspectives*. New York, NY: Routledge.

Bernays, E. (1928/1955). *Propaganda*. New York, NY: IG Publishing.

Bohm, D. (2004). *On dialogue*. London, UK: Routledge.

Brown, R. (2006). Myth of symmetry: Public relations as cultural styles. *Public Relations Review*, 32, pp. 206–12.

Brown, R. (2010). Symmetry and its critics: Antecedents, prospects and implications for symmetry in a postsymmetry era. In R. Heath (Ed.), *The SAGE handbook of public relations*, pp. 277–92. Thousand Oaks, CA: Sage.

Buber, M. (1947/1993). Dialogue (R. Gregor Smith, trans.). In *Between man and man*, pp. 1–45. London, UK: Routledge.

Buber, M. (1958/2000). *I and thou* (R. Gregor Smith, trans.). New York, NY: Scribner.

Burkart, R. (2004). Consensus-oriented public relations (COPR): A conception for planning and evaluation of public relations. In B. van Ruler, & D. Verčič (Eds), *Public relations and communication management*, pp. 446–525). Berlin, Germany: Mouton de Gruyter.

Burkart, R. (2009). On Habermas: Understanding and public relations. In O. Ihlen, B. Van Ruler, & M. Fredriksson (Eds), *Public relations and social theory*, pp. 141–64. London, UK: Routledge.

Burke, K. (1951). Rhetoric – old and new. *Journal of General Education*, 5(3), pp. 202–9.

Cheney, G. (1992). The corporate person (re)presents itself. In E. Toth, & R. Heath (Eds), *Rhetorical and critical approaches to public relations*, pp. 165–86. Hillsdale, NJ: Lawrence Erlbaum Associates.

Curtin, P., & Gaither, K. (2007). *International public relations: Negotiating culture, identity and power*. Thousand Oaks, CA: Sage.

Deetz, S., & Simpson, J. (2004). Critical organizational dialogue. In R. Anderson, L. Baxter, & K. Cissna (Eds), *Dialogue: Theorizing difference in communication studies*, pp. 141–58. Thousand Oaks, CA: Sage.

Demetrious, K. (2013). *Public relations, activism and social change: Speaking up*. London, UK: Routledge.

Demetrious, K., & Daymon, C. (Eds). (2014). *Gender and public relations: Critical perspectives on voice, image and identity*. London, UK: Routledge.

Dozier, D., & Lauzen, M. (2000). Liberating the intellectual domain from the practice: public relations, activism and the role of the scholar. *Journal of Public Relations Research*, 3, pp. 3–22.

Dryzek, J., & Hendriks, C. (2012). Fostering deliberation in the forum and beyond. In F. Fischer, & H. Gottweis (Eds), *The argumentative turn revisited: Public policy as communicative practice*, pp. 31–57. Durham, NC: Duke University Press.

Dutta, M. (2009). On Spivak: theorizing resistance – applying Gayatri Chakravorty Spivak in public relations. In O. Ihlen, B. van Ruler, & M. Fredriksson (Eds), *Public relations and social theory*, pp. 278–300. London, UK: Routledge.

Dutta-Bergman, M. (2005). Civil society and public relations: Not so civil after all. *Journal of Public Relations Research*, 17, pp. 267–89.

Edwards, L. (2011). Critical perspectives in global public relations. In N. Bardhan, & C. Weaver (Eds), *Public relations in global cultural contexts: Multiparadigmatic perspective*, pp. 29–49. New York, NY: Routledge.

Edwards, L. (2012). Defining the 'object' of public relations research: The new starting point. *Public Relations Inquiry*, 1, pp. 7–30.

Edwards, L. (2014). *Power, diversity and public relations*. London, UK: Routledge.

Edwards, L., & Hodges, C. (Eds). (2011). *Public relations, society and culture: Theoretical and empirical explanations*. London, UK: Routledge.

Elster, J. (Ed.). (1998). *Deliberative democracy*. Cambridge, UK: Cambridge University Press.

Fawkes, J. (2014). *Public relations ethics and professionalism: The shadow of excellence*. London, UK: Routledge.

Foucault, M. (1970/2002). *The order of things: an archeology of human sciences*. London: Routledge.

Gastil, J. (2008). *Political communication and deliberation*. Los Angeles, CA; Sage.

Gastil, J., & Levine, P. (Eds). (2005). *The deliberative democracy handbook: Strategies for effective civic engagement in the 21st century*. San Francisco, CA: Jossey-Bass.

Gordon, C. (Ed.). (1980). *Power/Knowledge: Selected interviews and other writings 1972–1977 by Michel Foucault*. New York, NY: Pantheon Books.

Grunig, J. (1987). *Symmetrical presuppositions as a framework for public relations theory*. Paper presented to the Conference on the Applications of Communication Theory, Normal, IL.

Grunig, J. (1992). What is excellence in management. In J. Grunig (Ed.) *Excellence in public relations and communication management*, pp. 219–50. Hillsdale, NJ: Lawrence Erlbaum Associates.

Grunig, J. (2001). Two-way symmetrical public relations. In R. Heath (Ed.), *Handbook of public relations*, pp. 11–30. Thousand Oaks, CA: Sage.

Grunig, J. (Ed.) (1992). *Excellence in public relations and communication management*. Hillsdale, NJ: Lawrence Erlbaum Associates.

Grunig, J., & Hunt, T. (1984). *Managing public relations*. New York: Holt, Rinehart & Winston.

Grunig, L., Hon, L., & Toth, E. (2001). *Women in public relations: How gender influences practice*. New York, NY: Guildford Press.

Grunig, J., Grunig, L. & Dozier, D. (2006). The excellence theory. In C. Botan & V. Hazleton (Eds), *Public relations theory II*, pp. 21–62. Mahaw, NJ: Lawrence Erlbaum Associates.

Gutmann, A., & Thompson, D. (2004). *Why deliberative democracy?* Princeton, NJ: Princeton University Press.

Habermas, J. (1970). Towards a theory of communication competence. *Inquiry*, 13, pp. 360–75.

Habermas, J. (1984–87). *The theory of communicative action*, vols 1–2. Boston, MA: Beacon Press.

Heath, R. (1992). The wrangle in the marketplace: A rhetorical perspective of public relations. In E. Toth, & R. Heath (Eds), *Rhetorical and critical approaches to public relations*, pp. 17–36. Hillsdale, NJ: Lawrence Erlbaum Associates.

Heath, R. (1993). A rhetorical approach to zones of meaning and organizational prerogatives. *Public Relations Review*, 19, pp. 141–55.

Heath, R. (2000). A rhetorical perspective on the values of public relations: Crossroads and pathways toward concurrence. *Journal of Public Relations Research*, 12, pp. 69–91.

Heath, R. (2001). A rhetorical enactment rationale for public relations. In R. Heath (Ed.), *Handbook of public relations*, pp. 31–50. Thousand Oaks, CA: Sage.

Heath, R. (2006). A rhetorical theory approach to issues management. In C. Botan, & V. Hazelton (Eds), *Public relations theory II*, pp. 63–100. New York, NY: Routledge.

Heath, R. (2007). Management through advocacy: Reflection rather than domination. In J. Grunig, L. Grunig, & E. Toth (Eds), *The future of excellence in public relations and communication management*. New York, NY: Routledge.

Heath, R. (2008). Rhetorical theory, public relations and meaning. In T. Hansen Horn, & B. Neff (Eds), *Public relations: From theory to practice*. Boston, MA: Pearson Education.

Heath, R. (2009). The rhetorical tradition: Wrangle in the marketplace. In R. Heath, E. Toth, & D. Waymer (Eds), *Rhetorical and critical approaches to public relations II*, pp.17–46. New York, NY: Routledge.

Heath, R., Toth, E., & Waymer, D. (Eds). (2009). *Rhetorical and critical approaches to public relations II*. New York, NY: Routledge.

Heron, J., & Reason, P. (2006). The practice of co-operative inquiry: Research 'with' rather than 'on' people. In P. Reason, & H. Bradbury (Eds), *Handbook of action research*, pp. 144–54. Los Angeles, CA: Sage.

Hether, H. (2014). Dialogic communication in the health care context: A case study of Kaiser Permanente's social media practices. *Public Relations Review*, 40, pp. 856–8.

Hodges, C., & McGrath, N. (2011). Communication for social transformation. In L. Edwards, & C. Hodges (Eds), *Public relations, society and culture: Theoretical and empirical explanations*, pp. 90–104. London, UK: Routledge.

Holtzhausen, D. (2000). Postmodern values in public relations. *Journal of Public Relations Research*, 12, pp. 93–114.

Holtzhausen, D. (2012). *Public relations as activism: Postmodern approaches to theory and practice*. London, UK: Routledge.

Holtzhausen, D., Petersen, B., & Tindall, N. (2003). Exploring the myth of the symmetrical/asymmetrical dichotomy in public relations models in the new South Africa. *Journal of Public Relations Research*, 15, pp. 305–431.

Horkheimer, M. (1972). Traditional and critical theory. In M. Horkheimer (Ed.), *Critical theory: Selected essays*. Toronto, Canada: Herder and Herder.

Horkheimer, M. (1982). *Critical theory*. New York, NY: Seabury Press.

Horkheimer, M. (1993). *Between philosophy and social science*. Cambridge, MA: MIT Press.

Horkheimer, M., & Adorno, T. (1972). *Dialectic of enlightenment*. New York, NY: Seabury.

Ihlen, O. (2010). The cursed sisters: public relations and rhetoric. In R. Heath (Ed.), *The SAGE handbook of public relations*, pp. 59–70. Thousand Oaks, CA: Sage.

Kent, M., & Taylor, M. (1998). Building dialogic relationships through the World Wide Web. *Public Relations Review*, 24, pp. 321–34.

Kent, M., & Taylor, M. (2002). Toward a dialogic theory of public relations. *Public Relations Review*, 28, pp. 21–37.

Latour, B., & Woolgar, S. (1979). *Laboratory life: The social construction of scientific facts*. Beverly Hills, CA: Sage.

Leeper, R. (1996). Moral objectivity: Jurgen Habermas's discourse ethics, and public relations. *Public Relations Review*, 22, pp. 133–50.

Leitch, S., & Motion, J. (2010). Publics and public relations: effecting change. In R. Heath (Ed.), *The SAGEe handbook of public relations*, pp. 99–110. Thousand Oaks, CA: Sage.

L'Etang, J., & Pieczka, M. (Eds) (1996). Critical perspectives in public relations London: International Thomson Business Press.

Lynch, M., & Bogen, D. (1997). Sociology's asociological 'core': An examination of textbook sociology in the light of the Sociology of Scientific Knowledge. *American Sociological Review*, 62, pp. 481–93.

Lyotard, J.-F. (1984). *The postmodern condition: A report on knowledge*. Manchester, UK: Manchester University Press.

McAllister, S. (2012). How the world's top universities provide dialogic forums for marginalized voices. *Public Relations Review*, 38, pp. 319–27.

McAllister-Spooner, S. (2008). User perceptions of dialogic public relations tactics via the Internet. *Public Relations Journal*, 2(1).

McAllister-Spooner, S. (2009). Fulfilling the dialogic promise: A ten-year reflective survey on dialogic internet principles, *Public Relations Review*, 35, pp. 320–2.

McKie, D., & Munshi, D. (2007). *Reconfiguring public relations: Ecology, equity, and enterprise*. London, UK: Routledge.

Madichie, N., & Hinson, R. (2014). A critical analysis of the 'dialogic communications' potential of sub-Saharan African Police Service websites. *Public Relations Review*, 40, pp. 338–50.

Marsh, C. (2003). Antecedents of two-way symmetry in classical Greek rhetoric: The rhetoric of Isocrates. *Public Relations Review*, 29, pp. 351–67.

Marsh, C. (2008). Postmodernism, symmetry and cash values: An Isocratean model for practitioners, *Public Relations Review*, 34, pp. 237–343.

Meisenbach, R. (2006). Habermas's discourse ethics and principle of universalization as a moral framework for organizational communication. *Management Communication Quarterly*, 20, pp. 39–62.

Meisenbach R., & Feldner, S. (2009). Dialogue, discourse, ethics and Disney. In R. Heath, E. Toth, & D. Waymer (Eds), *Rhetorical and critical approaches to public relations II*, pp. 253–71. New York, NY: Routledge.

Moloney, K. (2006). *Rethinking public relations: PR, propaganda and democracy*. London, UK: Routledge.

Munshi, D., & Kurian, P. (2007). The case of subaltern public: Postcolonial investigation of corporate social responsibility (o)missions. In S. May, G. Cheney, & J. Roper (Eds), *The debate over Corporate Social Responsibility*, pp. 438–47. Oxford, UK: Oxford University Press.

Park, P. (2006). Knowledge and participatory research. In P. Reason, & H. Bradbury (Eds), *Handbook of action research*, pp. 83–93. Los Angeles. CA: Sage.

Pearson R. (1989a). Beyond ethical relativism in public relations: Coorientation, rules and the idea of communication symmetry. *Public Relations Research Annual*, vol. 1, pp. 67–86.

Pearson, R. (1989b). Business ethics as communication ethics: Public relations practice and the idea of dialogue. In C. Botan, & V. Hazleton (Eds), *Public relations theory*, pp. 111–31. Hillsdale, NJ: Lawrence Erlbaum Associates.

Pfau, M., & Wan, H. (2006). Persuasions: An intrinsic function of public relations. In C. Botan, & V. Hazleton (Eds), *Public relations theory II*, pp. 101–36. Mahwah, NJ: Lawrence Erlbaum Associates.

Philips, L. (2011). *The promise of dialogue: The dialogic turn in the production and communication of knowledge*. Amsterdam, Holland: John Benjamins.

Pieczka, M. (1996). Paradigms, systems theory and public relations. In J. L'Etang, & M. Pieczka (Eds), *Critical perspectives in public relations*, pp. 124–56. London: International Thomson Business Press.

Pieczka, M. (2011). Public relations as dialogic expertise? *Journal of Communication Management*, 15, pp. 108–24.

Pieczka, M., & L'Etang, J. (2006). Public relations and the questions of professionalism. In J. L'Etang, & M. Pieczka (Eds), *Public relations: Critical debates and contemporary practice*, pp. 265–78. Mahwah, NJ: Lawrence Erlbaum Associates.

Pieczka, M., & Wood, E. (2013). Action research and public relations: Dialogue, peer learning, and the issue of alcohol. *Public Relations Inquiry*, 2, pp. 161–81.

Porter, L. (2010). Communicating for the good of the state: A post-symmetrical polemic on persuasion in ethical public relations. *Public Relations Review*, 36, pp. 127–33.

Reason, P., & Bradbury, H. (Eds). (2006a). *Handbook of action research*. Los Angeles. CA: Sage.

Reason, P., & Bradbury, H. (2006b). Introduction: Inquiry and participation in search of a world worthy of human aspiration. In P. Reason, & H. Bradbury (Eds), *Handbook of action research*, pp.1–14. Los Angeles, CA: Sage.

Research Excellence Framework (REF) (July 2011). *Assessment framework and guidance on submissions*. Retrieved on April 12, 2015, from http://www.ref.ac.uk/media/ref/content/pub/assessmentframeworkandguidanceonsubmissions/GOS%20including%20addendum.pdf

Roper, J. (2005). Symmetrical communication: Excellent public relations or a strategy for hegemony. *Journal of Public Relations Research*, 17, pp. 69–86.

Schattschneider, E. (1960). *The semisovereign people: A realist's view of democracy in America*. New York, NY: Holt, Rinehart and Winston.

Sriramesh, K., & Verčič, D. (Eds). (2012). *Culture and public relations: Links and implication*. New York, NY: Routledge.

Steiner, J. (2012). *The foundations of deliberative democracy*. Cambridge, UK: Cambridge University Press.

Stewart, J., Zediker, K., & Black, L. (2004). Relationships among philosophies of dialogue. In R. Anderson, L. Baxter, & K. Cissna (Eds), *Dialogue: Theorizing difference in communication studies*, pp. 21–38. Thousand Oaks, CA: Sage.

Stoker, K., & Tusinski, K. (2006). Reconsidering public relations' infatuation with dialogue: Why engagement and reconciliation can be more ethical than symmetry and reciprocity. *Journal of Mass Media Ethics*, 21, pp. 156–76.

Susskind, L. (2006). Arguing, bargaining, and getting agreement. In M. Moran, M. Rein, & R. Goodin (Eds), *The Oxford handbook of public policy*, pp. 269–95. Oxford, UK: Oxford University Press.

Theunissen, P., & Wan Noordin, W.N. (2012). Revisiting the concept of dialogue in public relations. *Public Relations Review*, 38, pp. 5–13.

Toth, E. (2000). Public relations and rhetoric: History, concepts, future. In D. Moss, D. Verčič, & G. Warnaby (Eds), *Perspectives on public relations research*, pp. 121–44. London, UK: Routledge.

Toth, E. (Ed.). (2007). *The future of excellence in public relations and communication management: Challenges for the next generation*. Mahwah, NJ: Lawrence Erlbaum Associates.

Toth, E., & Heath, R. (Eds). (1992). *Rhetorical and critical approaches to public relations*. Hillsdale, NJ: Lawrence Erlbaum Associates.

Toulmin, S. (2003). *The uses of argument* (revised edition) Cambridge, UK: Cambridge University Press.

Uzunoğlu, E. & Kip, S. (2014). Building relationships through websites: A content analysis of Turkish environmental non-profit organizations' (NPO) websites. *Public Relations Review*, 40, pp. 113–15.

Verčič, D. and Grunig, J. (2000). The origins of public relations theory in economics and strategic management. In D. Moss, D. Vercic, & G. Warnaby (Eds), *Perspectives on public relations research*, pp. 9–58. London: Routledge.

Weaver, C., Motion, J., & Roper, J. (2006). From propaganda to discourse (and back again): Truth, power, the public interest and public relations. In J. L'Etang, & M. Pieczka (Eds), *Public relations: Critical debates and contemporary practice*, pp. 7–22. Mahwah, NJ: Lawrence Erlbaum Associates.

Westoby, P., & Dowling, G. (2013). *Theory and practice of dialogical community development*. London, UK: Routledge.

7

Critical rhetoric and public relations

Øyvind Ihlen

Pro-choice versus pro-life; terrorist versus freedom fighter; tax burden versus contribution to our community. The list goes on and goes to show that words matter. Each of the mentioned terms invites a certain reading of the issue at hand, as well as its roots and remedies. In short, the terms sell a certain worldview. Public relations practitioners are in the business of coming up with such words and presenting such worldviews on behalf of their organizations. In addition, practitioners are expected to help out with more elaborate strategies, painting organizations green, shielding them from blame in crisis situations, or legitimizing the very existence of their organization through the forging of "win–win situations" with organizational stakeholders or society at large. Think corporate social responsibility. In other words, public relations is in the business of helping organizations position themselves in the societal order. Organizations seek to defend their interests and have issues discussed, defined, and settled with the help of public relations. In this endeavor, language is used to structure social understandings, and it is also the medium that communicates such understandings and perspectives. Organizations in general attempt to achieve specific goals, either political and/ or economic ones, with the help of communication. Hence, researching organizations' communication becomes a crucial academic task so that we can understand social power relations. Or, to quote the blurb on the back of Charles Conrad's book (2011), "Why do governments spend trillions to aid corporations in spite of intense opposition by the vast majority of their citizens?" At least some kind of rhetoric accompanies decisions like this so they can come across as being just and advantageous.

Heath (1992) has postulated that rhetoric is the essence of an organization's relationship to its environment. In other words, one way of studying the communication described above is to adopt a rhetorical perspective and apply rhetorical theory to gain an understanding of how public relations works. Rhetoric here is broadly defined as strategic communication; that is, symbol use that is intended to serve a certain goal. This can be both on the technical, linguistic level as well as that of the societal level. Here it is primarily the latter that will be discussed. While the field of rhetoric initially was oriented toward the study of single speakers, present rhetorical theory also takes into consideration social and structural conditions that have importance for the rhetoric, and vice versa (see, e.g., Lucaites, Condit & Caudill, 1999). Furthermore, scholarly debates have drawn attention to the importance rhetoric has for creating knowledge (Scott,

1967), and for its ability to have a so-called constitutive effect by, for instance, *creating* an audience, not merely addressing an audience that already exists (Charland, 1987). Broadly speaking, rhetoric creates and is created by society.

This chapter discusses the possibilities that a rhetorical perspective offers for critical analysis of public relations. In particular it focuses on the critical rhetoric project (i.e., McKerrow, 1989) and what implications such a perspective has for analysis of public relations rhetoric. Critical rhetoric sees discourse as a site of power struggles and suggests some particular orientations for the critic of these struggles. It is, for instance, argued that domination and freedom are the most important topics for analysis. The critic should expose domination to help create "freedom from," but also help create a reflexivity that enhances "freedom to" (McKerrow, 2001, p. 619). This way, rhetorical analysis not only helps us to grasp how meaning is constructed through communication, but also improves our understanding of the relationship between power and discourse. While neo-Aristotelian rhetorical criticism would ask "did the rhetoric in question fulfil its function," the critical rhetoric project would instead ask "whose interests did the rhetoric serve with what rhetorical means?"

The chapter is structured the following way: first, a short overview of the rhetorical perspectives on public relations is given. Then follows a presentation of the critical rhetoric project, while the third main part of the essay discusses the implications for critique of public relations. The essay is rounded off with a conclusion, arguing that while the critical rhetoric project is useful, we also need other critical perspectives on public relations rhetoric.

Rhetoric and public relations

The link between rhetoric and public relations has been explored by various scholars, most notably Robert L. Heath (1980, 1992, 2001). Later, others have followed suit with broad discussions of the same topic (e.g., Ihlen, 2010; L'Etang, 1996; Marsh, 2012; Toth, 1999). A host of studies have also focused on particular rhetorical concepts: for instance, ethos (Bostdorff, 1992) and paradoxes (Heath & Waymer, 2009).[1]

It is, nonetheless, typically the work of Heath that is addressed when scholars talk about public relations and the rhetorical approach in singular form. Heath sees rhetoric as the essence of an organization's relationship with its environment. Rhetoric provides public relations with both an ethical and a pragmatic program; more specifically, rhetoric can help organizations become "the good organization communicating well" (Heath, 2001, p. 39). Through rhetoric, organizations and stakeholders are thought to co-define and co-create meaning. Lately, Heath has discussed how rhetoric and public relations can contribute to making society "more fully functioning" (Heath, 2011). Public relations is defined as "the management function that rhetorically adapts organizations to people's interests and people's interests to organizations by co-creating meaning and co-managing cultures to achieve mutually beneficial relationships" (Heath, 2001, p. 36).

Heath's approach has been discussed and duly criticized elsewhere (e.g., Cheney & Christensen, 2001; Ihlen, 2010; L'Etang, 1997, 2006). Amid critical arguments about ethics and epistemology, it is particularly the ontological criticism that stands out, at least as it relates to his older writings regarding the "marketplace of ideas" in which resources do not seem to play a role. Heath argues that it is not possible to manipulate others in the long run, and that organizations have to take into account the needs, concerns, and points of view of the public, not only of the organization (Heath, 1993). The question remains, however, whether such a well-functioning marketplace exists (Cheney & Christensen, 2001). It has been claimed that rhetoric still "is a strategy of the powerful, a form of control" (Hartelius & Browning, 2008, p. 33). Heath's position seems to be that public relations can be both things; that is, public relations can play both a constructive and a destructive role in society (Heath, 2011).

Whereas some scholars (i.e., Toth, 1999) have argued that rhetorical scholars have been "too" critical of the practice to enjoy widespread support in the field of public relations scholarship, others have maintained that the critical potential has not really been met. The argument goes that the rhetorical approach has not truly represented an alternative paradigm (L'Etang, 1997). The accusation is that it is the *functional*, rather than the *critical* approaches to rhetoric that has dominated the field. Scholars have largely sought to help organizations reach their goals through, for instance, crisis or issues management rhetoric. Exceptions to this do exist (e.g., Boyd & Waymer, 2011; Coombs & Holladay, 2011). Studies have, for instance, illustrated how public relations rhetoric works to promote particular ideologies (e.g., Crable & Vibbert, 1995; Holloway, 1995). As an example: Cheney, Christensen, Conrad, and Lair (2004) showed how the tobacco industry opposed tax on tobacco and framed the debate as concerning government interference in the free market rather than health issues. Conrad (2011), in a book-length study, has argued that organizational rhetoric has perpetuated an organizational imperative (all good things come from formal organizations), free market fundamentalism, and the myth of leadership in US society.

Still, such studies are so far and few between that there are good reasons to elaborate on a critical rhetorical approach to public relations.

Critical rhetoric

Critical thinking in general involves identifying premises and presumptions and acknowledging the importance of context. It encourages exploration of alternatives and posing questions (see e.g., Browne & Keeley, 2011). Rhetoric is perfectly suited for this task by its very focus on the way that arguments are structured and adapted to particular audiences. Rhetoric helps one to understand what premises are used and/or suppressed in particular communication situations. In short, the rhetorical tradition offers a way to analyze and understand language, its function, and importance. Rhetorical criticism in general seeks to enhance understanding of a rhetorical act (see e.g., Kuypers, 2009b). Thus, rhetorical criticism could be geared towards providing an appreciation of aesthetics, as well as making political evaluation. In going down the latter route, the analyst could choose to apply critical theory in one sense or the other. Of the many approaches found under this umbrella, what seems to be common is an interest in exploring alternative communication practices and helping strengthen democracy in the workplace and elsewhere (see e.g., Deetz, 2005).

As a proper name, critical theory is tied to Frankfurter School critics with resistance and criticism of oppressive ideology as core activities, and emancipation as the main goal (see elsewhere in this volume for a description that is not as crude). Also in the field of rhetoric itself, interest has been expressed concerning the challenges of public deliberation in a Habermasian tradition (e.g., Hauser & Hegbloom, 2009), as well as rhetoric and power (e.g., McGee, 1980, 1999). Much attention has also been paid to the work of Raymie E. McKerrow (1989, 1991, 1999, 2001; 2009 (with St. John)) and what he has called "critical rhetoric."

In the theoretical essay, "Critical rhetoric: Theory and praxis" (1989),[2] McKerrow married rhetoric to critical theory by urging a focus on both domination and freedom. According to McKerrow there are basically two forms of critical analysis: the first one is a critique of domination which has an emancipatory purpose; the second is a critique of freedom, which is a form of self-reflective critique opening up the possibility that social change can be invited and not only inhibited by discourse and power. There is a duality at play here, as power is seen as something that can have a repressive role, establishing or perpetuating certain views or certain interests. At the same time, it can also have a productive role. As a project, critical rhetoric should "serve to identify the possibilities of future action" (McKerrow, 1989, p. 92). Indeed, critical rhetoric serves as "an intellectual backdrop to the critical act" (McKerrow & St. John, 2009, p. 333). Thus, social change is the ultimate goal brought about by the study of how power, consciousness, and resistance are crafted and articulated in and by rhetoric. Critical rhetoric is "not detached or impersonal; it has as its object something which it is 'against'" (McKerrow, 1989, p. 92).

After presenting this theoretical platform, McKerrow (1989) goes on to introduce eight orienting principles for critical practice.

(1) Critique is first and foremost a transformative practice, not a method. Again, the chief aim is to focus on domination and freedom. To this end, no methodological approach should be given privilege over others. Instead, the critic should pursue a type of inquiry that is suitable for the context or situation.

(2) Rhetoric is potentially material, in the sense that it can make a difference in social relations. Ideologies are constituted in and through language, and participants in the social world have the capacity to interact and also modify the discourse. Importantly, critical rhetoric rejects the distinction between discursive and non-discursive practices.

(3) Rhetoric focuses on opinions (doxa), rather than on knowledge (episteme). It is doxastic, not epistemic. While Plato held doxa in disregard as "mere opinion," Aristotle recognized its usefulness building on the contrast between what is certain and what is probable (Herrick, 2001). Since we cannot have certain knowledge, rhetoric deals with the contingent, the probable, or in other words, doxa. In essence, the knowledge of today might look different tomorrow. Following this position means that rhetoric does not focus on what is true or false, but instead examines the forms of power that are embraced in discourse when particular visions are constructed and others are left out.[3]

(4) "*Naming* is the central symbolic act of a *nominalist* rhetoric" (McKerrow, 1989, p. 105). The argument that also follows from the above is that rhetoric is nominalistic rather than universalistic. Meaning does not exist outside particular historical contexts or rhetorical practices. When the name changes, the power relations inherent in the name also change. Thus, looking at the reasons for the emergence of terms, one cannot put one's trust in "fixed, determinative models of inquiry" (McKerrow, 1989, p. 106).

(5) Rhetoric is influential, rather than casual. Rhetoric has the potential for impact, but contradictory impulses and arguments can also be presented.

(6) What is present in discourse is obviously important for meaning formation, but absence can be equally as important to understand and evaluate symbolic action. The critic also has to focus on what is not present in the discourse.

(7) Since different views exist concerning most, if not all, matters, polysemic interpretation is always a potential. Participants are not passive, and critics have to defend their readings by using arguments just like all others.

(8) Rhetorical analysis is an activity that is *preformed* as the critic has to be an inventor who pulls together scraps of discourse across a range of different media types constructed by a range of different actors. This can be seen as a reflection of the fluid and fragmented state of society, and hence also of rhetoric.

If the eight principles above are taken together, they might, according to McKerrow (2001), function as a heuristic for those wishing to craft a rhetorical strategy, as well as for the audience or critic who evaluates or responds to the same rhetoric. Next, I discuss in more detail what service this could do to studies of public relations rhetoric.

Implications for critique of public relations rhetoric

The critical rhetoric project can be aligned with the argument that studies of public relations should not only focus on organizational effectiveness, but also study the consequences that public relations has for society (e.g., Ihlen & Verhoeven, 2012; L'Etang & Pieczka, 1996; Rakow & Nastasia, 2009). Critical rhetoric can help us to understand the role discourse plays in interest struggles and point out how certain interests are presented in "forceful and compelling manners" (McKerrow, 1989, p. 93). Still, the project as outlined by McKerrow seems to have both strengths and weaknesses that I will now proceed to discuss.

At one level, the orientation principles suggested by McKerrow sit comfortably within a wider humanistic non-structuralist tradition. It is urged that critical rhetoric should not be constrained by "the systematicity of method" (p. 102) (Principle #1), as understanding and evaluation are seen as one. Unless the rhetorician is a dogmatist, he will experience struggle in his or her attempts to understand a particular rhetoric, and it is this struggle that ultimately produces new insight. Thus, the argument goes, the critical theorist should operate with certain principles, rather than rely on narrow prescriptive approaches. The aim is to let creativity have its course. Similar ideas have been aired elsewhere and have been the subject of much discussion both outside and within rhetoric (see e.g., Black, 1965/1978; Jasinski, 2001). As formulated by Marie Hochmuth Nichols: beyond "the area of the formula lies an area where understanding, imagination, knowledge of alternatives, and sense of purpose operate....It is reason and judgment, not a [computer], that makes a man [sic!] a critic" (Nichols, as cited in, Kuypers, 2009a, pp. 14–15). Slavishly following a model is to be avoided. This obviously goes for public relations analysis, too. The problem at hand, the context or the situation, should guide the approach of the critic.

The idea that rhetoric is material (Principle #2) sees the distinction between discursive and non-discursive practices being rejected. All practices take "place in terms of discursive practices" (McKerrow, 1989, p. 103). You cannot really escape rhetoric. This discussion is mirrored in the debate concerning the so-called communication constituting organizations (CCO)-perspective (e.g., Putnam & Nicotera, 2008). Talk is really action, as pointed out by Austin (1975). Regarding communication of corporate social responsibility (CSR), for instance, scholars have argued that such communication can create a "creeping" commitment that propels the corporation in such a direction (Christensen, Morsing & Thyssen, 2011). Thus, ambitious CSR communication should not always be held to task for failing to deliver on its promises, but instead be given some leeway since this is what is necessary to create innovation and social change. By presenting ambitious CSR rhetoric *publically*, the corporations create such impetuses.

Since the days of the Sophists, rhetoricians have been taking a stab at the separation between reality and rhetoric, between talk and action. This is also a perspective found in much postmodern theory to the extent that certain strands of the latter discard reality. Here, however, McKerrow has also met resistance from those arguing that he places himself in the relativist camp. This is also due to his claim that rhetoric is doxastic rather than epistemic (Principle #3). McKerrow wants to move beyond a Platonic, neo-Kantian perspective on what constitutes knowledge and what the true role of rhetoric is. Instead, he argues, critical rhetoric invites a focus on "how symbols come to possess power – what they 'do' in society as contrasted to what they 'are'" (p. 104). Hence critical rhetoric is going "one louder" to inform the textual analysis.

Critics, however, lament the sharp disjunctions and dissociations favored by McKerrow as he "dispenses with epistemology" (Murphy, 1995, p. 4). They also see a problematic relativist stance at work, not at least when it is linked with the notion that rhetoric is nominalistic rather than universialistic (Principle #4). The relativist stance would lead to a scrapping of Habermasian discourse ethics (Habermas, 1991) and hence also much of the research that has been undertaken within organization studies (Deetz, 2005). But this also puts the project at odds with itself. What is the status of McKerrow's principles? How can the critics' readings be privileged over others (Cloud, 1994)? Why is it that it is the critics who can reveal the "dense web" of doxa and its oppressive effects? Epistemology should have its place in rhetoric "if only as interlocutor for doxastic reason" (Murphy, 1995, p. 4). Critical rhetoric is thus accused of having a modernist style and purpose, and not recognizing that the new is dependent on the old (Murphy, 1995). Scholars seeking to understand public relations do not need to repeat this mistake.

Importantly too, discourse is not all that matters: "We ought not sacrifice the notions of practical truth, bodily reality, and material oppression to the tendency to render all of experience discursive, as if no one went hungry or died in war" (Cloud, 1994, p. 159). This is a crucial reminder to all scholars that one should not lose sight of the fact that although a bomb was dropped on the Gaza strip, it was dropped even though that critic was not there to witness it (Cloud, 1994). Similarly, while airlines refer to airplane crashes as "involuntarily conversions" (the insurance payout is a one-time gain), real lives are still lost (Greenberg, 2014, p. 9).

On the other hand, it is easy to concur with the non-determinist notion that rhetoric deals in influence and holds a potential for influence (Principle #5). It does not *necessarily* lead to a particular outcome, as other arguments can be presented and override the initial argument. Furthermore, the critic would be hard pressed to be able to point to "concrete evidence" that communication has caused or hindered change. Attempts to pinpoint the influence of public relations rhetoric in political processes and conflicts quickly has to be supplemented by perspectives that also discuss other types of resources. The symbolic should not be treated as a separate domain, and both material and ideal interests should be included in analytical endeavors. Elsewhere (Ihlen, 2002, 2004, 2009), I have argued that in order to grasp complex political processes and the influence of public relations, scholars should research the ethical, emotional, and logical appeals, the topics that are being drawn on, the identification strategies that are being used, the premises the rhetor is attempting to create, and the association and dissociation techniques that are being used. In addition, however, the resources or the context of the rhetorical activities has to be considered. This involves looking at the degree of institutionalization of the organization and its economic, cultural, symbolic, and social capital. Such an integrated approach helps move beyond the common sense insights that resources are valuable and help influence outcomes, and that rhetoric is a powerful persuasive tool. While recognizing that the method of rhetorical criticism should not be limited to a particular approach (confer Principle #1, discussed above), there is still need to recommend some tools that might come in handy for the critic. Here, the critical rhetoric project is silent, but there is a plethora of books that can assist (e.g., Foss, 2008; Kuypers, 2009b), although few are devoted to public relations or organizational rhetoric as such (for an exception, see Hoffman & Ford, 2010).

Returning to other of the principles of McKerrow's program: the argument that absence is important (Principle #6) is recognized from debates with quantitative-oriented scholars who fail to acknowledge that coding schemes for content analysis might miss crucial points. A qualitative scholar would agree that *not* bringing up a particular aspect could be just as important as highlighting others. When an oil company wants to discuss sustainability as a *local* phenomenon – specifically, cleaning up after a well is shut down – the absence of the global perspective and the issue of climate change becomes glaring. A rhetorical analysis would thus invite a critical practice addressing what is not present in the discourse as well. While a coding scheme might be constructed noting some missing aspects, this would have to be preceded by an inductive phase that would at least invite a qualitative analysis of the issue at hand to identify missing elements.

The qualitative-oriented scholar is also likely to agree that texts or rhetorical acts can be read in myriad ways (Principle #7).[4] Furthermore, in a qualitative approach the researcher himelf or herself is the prime research instrument. An important test comes when the constructed narrative of the researcher meets the critical audience. Do the arguments put forward in the scholarly text seem reasonable and convincing? Since I, as a researcher, engage in a rhetorical practice, issues of how, why, who, and power and truth, become central (Kvale, 1996). In the words of McKerrow, then, criticism is a performance (Principle #8) or "a rhetor advocating a critique as a sensible reading of the discourse of power" (McKerrow, 1989, p. 108). The same applies for critics of public relations rhetoric. Conducting and preforming criticism of this kind can obviously also meet resistance. For instance, I have had a reviewer arguing that normative claims must be theoretically accounted for in order to be academically valid. Following this logic, it is does not suffice to, for instance, criticize the current corporate take on sustainability for being an act of strategic redefining of the original ecological concept to stall radical change (e.g., Ihlen & Roper, 2014). In other words, to extend on the logic, the critic should theoretically explain why lying is wrong. While views like this might be unfamiliar to the critical-qualitative tradition and its view of validity and what constitutes criticism, they certainly challenge the critic to go an extra round when presenting an analysis. It also points to the challenge arising when presenting claims outside humanistic academic circles.

McKerrow explicitly points out that his list of principles is not exhaustive. Indeed, in his seminal article there is a range of other implicit principles that could be highlighted, too. McKerrow calls for attention towards the "symbols that address publics" rather on the rhetor disparate pieces of discourse. The critic should be an inventor, collecting fragments not only consisting of great speeches but also focusing on symbols "in all their manifest forms" (McKerrow, 1989, p. 101) across a range of media. In other words, the agent is decentered and the phenomenon under study should be privileged. Indeed, it is argued that "an agent's agency can be understood as an effect" (McKerrow & St. John, 2009, p. 325). Others, however, have taken issue with the absence of a strategic actor, while suggesting other directions for a critical rhetoric (e.g., Kuypers, 1996; Murphy, 1995). It is, for instance, argued that the critical rhetoric described above de-emphasizes the ethical dimension of action and that a prudent critique would reintroduce ethical considerations within a critical rhetoric.

While certainly acknowledging that structure and context matter, researching the strategic intent of the actor is arguably a crucial part of what public relations scholarship is about. Power is not "an impersonal and anonymous force which is exercised apart from the actions and intentions of human subjects" (Best & Kellner, 1991, p. 70). Hence, there needs to be a focus on individual agents. This is, however, not the same as to argue that the focus needs to be nearsightedly concentrated on simple speaker–audience interaction. The rhetoric of single actors can still be analyzed against the backdrop of its cultural, historical, and political setting, and by looking at how the rhetoric is forming and is formed by this setting. There are economic and political interests that seek to structure, frame, and set limits for rhetorical action (Cloud, 1994). The mentioned analysis provided by Conrad (2011) is a good example, as it focuses on social control through the creation of certain societal myths and the corporate colonization of the lifeworld.

Conclusions

All in all, the program of critical rhetoric suggests some principles that are useful for those wanting to understand the role of rhetoric in the context of public relations. McKerrow (2001) is explicitly reluctant to prescribe exemplars or models for fear of "identifying the methods as the only useful one" (p. 620). Instead, readers are challenged to "*consider placing [themselves] inside an orientation that asks questions about the nature of language as it reveals particular formations between and among people, and the productive capabilities of power in enhancing social action*" (McKerrow & St. John, 2009, p. 333, italics in original). As pointed out above, however, there are some very practical challenges that arise from this position, since the potential critic has to start somewhere. Additionally, as argued, in the context of public relations the project of critical rhetoric should also bring back the agent and make use of "old school" rhetorical analysis as devised in some of the referenced books. This, of course, is not the same as to fall back on formula criticism, but something that addresses a practical need.

Of course it can be argued that the particular rhetorical action of a corporation is but one piece in a larger picture. Still, the argument that will be forwarded here is that we need a rhetoric for specific situations and a rhetoric that captures doxa (the former relies on the latter). We need concrete rhetorical analysis and critiques of, for instance, the green rhetoric of corporations. At the same time we can be aware that society's understandings of what sustainability is, is not defined by singular rhetorical acts. What we also need, however, is a critical rhetoric that not only focuses on the macro themes of domination and freedom (although in the end most, if not all, themes can be linked back to these topics). Rhetorical theory offers a plethora of analytical and explanatory tools for social critique in this respect; for instance, regarding the dominance of technical rationality and creation of consent (e.g., Conrad, 2011). But rhetoric also has tools that are helpful to understand other more micro-oriented power configurations; for instance, why certain public relations strategies have paid off in specific conflicts. For instance, the successful rhetoric of immigration activists might be analyzed looking at the use of identification strategies and pathos appeals, pitted against the immigration authorities that are constrained by a bureaucratic ethos (Ihlen & Thorbjørnsrud, 2014). Analyzing such conflicts with the notion of the rhetorical situation (Bitzer, 1968) can help us understand how and why a particular rhetorical strategy was crafted in a certain way. Coupled with a close analysis of media coverage and political decisions, it can provide an understanding of the outcome of the particular immigration cases. This in turn can be discussed in light of a perspective on power and interests.

Linking such analyses back to the macro level of ideology criticism is obviously possible. Still, a perspective building on critical rhetoric should really also be able to focus on the simple question of whose interest is now served without necessarily delving into the language of domination, oppression, and ideology. Such analysis can also be linked to a discussion of ethics and also help theory-building that not only seeks to confirm what we already know. Or, to quote McKerrow: "Assuming the position of a critical [rhetor] is to place critical action within the context of a contingently derived future that is itself open to alteration in an unspecified manner" (McKerrow, 2001, p. 620). In other words, we all need rhetoric, and, what's more, there is hope. Especially, I would like to add, if all eggs are not put in the one proverbial basket.

Notes

1   For an overview of rhetorical research on organizational discourse in general, see Cheney, Christensen, Conrad, and Lair (2004), as well as Hoffman and Ford (2010).
2   The status of the work is singled out by how the essay has been reprinted in the landmark volume *Contemporary Rhetorical Theory: A Reader* (McKerrow, 1999), as well as how critical rhetoric has been made into an entry in the *Encyclopedia of Rhetoric* (McKerrow, 2001); as well as being singled out as a key perspective in *Rhetorical Criticism: Perspectives in Action* (McKerrow & St. John, 2009).
3   Bourdieu presents yet another conception of doxa as that which is taken for granted and unquestioned in a society (Bourdieu, 1977).
4   In the 1989 essay, McKerrow makes an excuse for even mentioning this point, but feels justified to do so given the position of much modernist, ideological criticism.

References

Austin, J. L. (1975). *How to do things with words: The William James lectures delivered at Harvard University in 1955*, 2nd edition. Oxford: Clarendon Press.

Best, S., & Kellner, D. (1991). *Postmodern theory: Critical interrogations*. New York: Guilford Press.

Bitzer, L. F. (1968). The rhetorical situation. *Philosophy and Rhetoric*, 1(1), pp. 1–14.

Black, E. (1965/1978). *Rhetorical criticism: A study in method*. Madison, WI: University of Wisconsin Press.

Bostdorff, D. M. (1992). "The decision is yours" campaign: Planned Parenthood's characteristic argument of moral virtue. In E. L. Toth, & R. L. Heath (Eds), *Rhetorical and critical approaches to public relations*, pp. 301–14. Hillsdale, NJ: Lawrence Erlbaum.

Bourdieu, P. (1977). *Outline of a theory of practice* (R. Nice, trans.). Cambridge, UK: Cambridge University Press.

Boyd, J., & Waymer, D. (2011). Organizational Rhetoric: A Subject of Interest(s). *Management Communication Quarterly*. doi: 10.1177/0893318911409865

Browne, M. N., & Keeley, S. M. (2011). *Asking the right questions: A guide to critical thinking*, 10th edition. Upper Saddle River, NJ: Pearson Prentice Hall.

Charland, M. (1987). Constitutive rhetoric: The case of the Peuple Quebecois. *Quarterly Journal of Speech*, 73(2), pp. 133–50.

Cheney, G., & Christensen, L. T. (2001). Public relations as contested terrain: A critical response. In R. L. Heath (Ed.), *Handbook of public relations*, pp. 167–82. Thousand Oaks, CA: Sage.

Cheney, G., Christensen, L. T., Conrad, C., & Lair, D. J. (2004). Corporate rhetoric as organizational discourse. In D. Grant, C. Hardy, C. Oswick, & L. L. Putnam (Eds), *The SAGE handbook of organizational discourse*, pp. 79–103. London: Sage.

Christensen, L. T., Morsing, M., & Thyssen, O. (2011). The polyphony of corporate social responsibility: Deconstructing accountability and transparency in the context of identity and hypocrisy. In G. Cheney, S. May, & D. Munshi (Eds), *The handbook of communication ethics*, pp. 457–74. New York: Routledge.

Cloud, D. L. (1994). The materiality of discourse as oxymoron: A challenge to critical rhetoric. *Western Journal of Communication (includes Communication Reports)*, 58(3), pp. 141–63.

Conrad, C. (2011). *Organizational rhetoric: Strategies of resistance and domination*. Cambridge, UK: Polity.

Coombs, W. T., & Holladay, S. J. (2011). Self-Regulatory Discourse: Corrective or Quiescent? *Management Communication Quarterly*. doi: 10.1177/0893318911409662

Crable, R. E., & Vibbert, S. L. (1995). Mobil's epideictic advocacy: "Observations" of Prometheus bound. In W. N. Elwood (Ed.), *Public relations inquiry as rhetorical criticism: Case studies of corporate discourse and social influence*, pp. 27–46. Westport, CT: Praeger.

Deetz, S. A. (2005). Critical theory. In S. May, & D. K. Mumby (Eds), *Engaging organizational communication theory & research: Multiple perspectives*, pp. 85–111. London: Sage.

Foss, S. K. (2008). *Rhetorical criticism: Exploration & practice*, 4th edition. Prospect Heights, IL.: Waveland Press.

Greenberg, P. (2014, May 19). The big money surprise about MH370. *Fortune*, pp. 6–10.

Habermas, J. (1991). *Moral consciousness and communicative action* (C. Lenhardt, & S. W. Nicholsen, trans.). Cambridge, MA: MIT Press.

Hartelius, E. J., & Browning, L. D. (2008). The application of rhetorical theory in managerial research: A literature review. *Management Communication Quarterly*, 22(1), pp. 13–39. doi: 10.1177/0893318908318513

Hauser, G. A., & Hegbloom, M. T. (2009). Rhetoric and critical theory: Possibilities for rapprochement in public deliberation. In A. A. Lunsford, K. H. Wilson, & R. A. Eberly (Eds), *The SAGE handbook of rhetorical studies*, pp. 477–96. London: Sage.

Heath, R. L. (1980). Corporate advocacy: An application of speech communication perspectives and skills – and more. *Communication Education*, 29, pp. 370–77.

Heath, R. L. (1992). The wrangle in the marketplace: A rhetorical perspective of public relations. In E. L. Toth, & R. L. Heath (Eds), *Rhetorical and critical approaches to public relations*, pp. 17–36. Hillsdale, NJ: Lawrence Erlbaum.

Heath, R. L. (1993). Toward a paradigm for the study and practice of public relations: A rhetorical approach to zones of meaning and organizational prerogative. *Public Relations Review*, 19(2), pp. 141–55.

Heath, R. L. (2001). A rhetorical enactment rationale for public relations: The good organization communicating well. In R. L. Heath (Ed.), *Handbook of public relations*, pp. 31–50. Thousand Oaks, CA: Sage.

Heath, R. L. (2011). External organizational rhetoric: Bridging management and sociopolitical discourse. *Management Communication Quarterly*, 25(3), pp. 415–35. doi: 10.1177/0893318911409532

Heath, R. L., & Waymer, D. (2009). Activist public relations and the paradox of the positive. In R. L. Heath, E. L. Toth, & D. Waymer (Eds), *Rhetorical and critical approaches to public relations II*, pp. 195–215. New York: Routledge.

Herrick, J. A. (2001). *The history and theory of rhetoric: An introduction*, 2nd edition. London: Allyn and Bacon.

Hoffman, M. F., & Ford, D. J. (2010). *Organizational rhetoric: Situations and strategies*. Thousand Oaks, CA: Sage.

Holloway, R. L. (1995). Philip Morris Magazine: An innovation in grass roots issue management. In W. N. Elwood (Ed.), *Public relations inquiry as rhetorical criticism: Case studies of corporate discourse and social influence*, pp. 135–56. Westport, CT: Praeger.

Ihlen, Ø. (2002). Rhetoric and resources: Notes for a new approach to public relations and issues management. *Journal of Public Affairs*, 2(4), pp. 259–69.

Ihlen, Ø. (2004). Norwegian hydroelectric power: Testing a heuristic for analyzing symbolic strategies and resources. *Public Relations Review*, 30(2), pp. 217–23.

Ihlen, Ø. (2009). On Pierre Bourdieu: Public relations in field struggles. In Ø. Ihlen, B. van Ruler, & M. Fredriksson (Eds), *Public relations and social theory: Key figures and concepts*, pp. 71–91. New York: Routledge.

Ihlen, Ø. (2010). The cursed sisters: Public relations and rhetoric. In R. L. Heath (Ed.), *The SAGE handbook of public relations*, 2nd edition, pp. 59–70. Thousands Oaks, CA: Sage.

Ihlen, Ø., & Roper, J. (2014). Corporate reports on sustainability and sustainable development: 'We have arrived'. *Sustainable Development*, 22, pp. 42–51. doi: 10.1002/sd.524

Ihlen, Ø., & Thorbjørnsrud, K. (2014). Tears and framing contests: Public organizations countering critical and emotional stories. *International Journal of Strategic Communication*, 8(1), pp. 45–60. doi: 10.1080/1553118x.2013.850695

Ihlen, Ø., & Verhoeven, P. (2012). A public relations identity for the 2010s. *Public Relations Inquiry*, 1(2), pp. 159–76.

Jasinski, J. (2001). The status of theory and method in rhetorical criticism. *Western Journal of Communication*, 65(3), pp. 249–270. doi: 10.1080/10570310109374705

Kuypers, J. A. (1996). Doxa and a critical rhetoric: Accounting for the rhetorical agent through prudence. *Communication Quarterly*, 44(4), pp. 452–62.

Kuypers, J. A. (2009a). Rhetorical criticism as art. In J. A. Kuypers (Ed.), *Rhetorical criticism: Perspectives in action*, pp. 13–28. Lanham, MD: Lexington.

Kuypers, J. A. (Ed.). (2009b). *Rhetorical criticism: Perspectives in action*. Lanham, MD: Lexington Books.

Kvale, S. (1996). *InterViews: An introduction to qualitative research interviewing*. Thousands Oak, CA: Sage.

L'Etang, J. (1996). Public relations and rhetoric. In J. L'Etang, & M. Pieczka (Eds), *Critical perspectives in public relations*, pp. 106–23. London: International Thomson Business Press.

L'Etang, J. (1997). Public relations and the rhetorical dilemma: Legitimate "perspectives," persuasion, or pandering? *Australian Journal of Communication*, 24(2), pp. 33–53.

L'Etang, J. (2006). Public relations and rhetoric. In J. L'Etang, & M. Pieczka (Eds), *Public relations: Critical debates and contemporary practice*, pp. 359–71. Mahwah, NJ: Lawrence Erlbaum.

L'Etang, J., & Pieczka, M. (Eds). (1996). *Critical perspectives in public relations*. London: International Thomson Business Press.

Lucaites, J. L., Condit, C. M., & Caudill, S. (Eds). (1999). *Contemporary rhetorical theory: A reader*. New York: Guilford Press.

McGee, M. C. (1980). The "ideograph": A link between rhetoric and ideology. *Quarterly Journal of Speech*, 66(1), pp. 1–16.

McGee, M. C. (1999). Text, context, and the fragmentation of contemporary culture. In J. L. Lucaites, C. M. Condit, & S. Caudill (Eds), *Contemporary rhetorical theory: A reader*, pp. 65–78. New York: Guilford Press.

McKerrow, R. E. (1989). Critical rhetoric: Theory and praxis. *Communication Monographs*, 56(2), pp. 91–111. doi: 10.1080/03637758909390253

McKerrow, R. E. (1991). Critical rhetoric in a postmodern world. *Quarterly Journal of Speech*, 77, pp. 75–8.

McKerrow, R. E. (1999). Critical rhetoric: Theory and praxis. In J. L. Lucaites, C. M. Condit, & S. Caudill (Eds), *Contemporary rhetorical theory: A reader*, pp. 441–63. New York: Guilford Press.

McKerrow, R. E. (2001). Critical rhetoric. In T. O. Sloane (Ed.), *Encyclopedia of rhetoric*, pp. 619–22. New York: Oxford University Press.

McKerrow, R. E., & St. John, J. (2009). Critical rhetoric and continual critique. In J. A. Kuypers (Ed.), *Rhetorical criticism: Perspectives in action*, pp. 321–39. Lanham, MD: Lexington.

Marsh, C. (2012). *Classical rhetoric and modern public relations: An Isocratean model*. New York: Routledge.

Murphy, J. M. (1995). Critical rhetoric as political discourse. *Argumentation and Advocacy*, 32(1), pp. 1–15.

Putnam, L., & Nicotera, A. M. (Eds). (2008). *Building theories of organization: The constitutive role of communication*. New York: Routledge.

Rakow, L. F., & Nastasia, D. (2009). On feminist theory of public relations: An example from Dorothy E. Smith. In Ø. Ihlen, B. van Ruler, & M. Fredriksson (Eds), *Public relations and social theory: Key figures and concepts*, pp. 252–77. New York: Routledge.

Scott, R. L. (1967). Rhetoric as epistemic. *Central States Speech Journal*, 18, pp. 9–16.

Toth, E. L. (1999). Public relations and rhetoric: History, concepts, future. In D. Moss, D. Verčič, & G. Warnaby (Eds), *Perspectives on public relations research*, pp. 121–44. London: Routledge.

8

Sanitising or reforming PR?

Exploring "trust" and the emergence of critical public relations

Kristin Demetrious

This chapter takes a socio-cultural lens to investigate critical public relations (CPR) and its potential to create meaningful reform in public relations which has benefits for the overall quality and strength of public discourse. In exploring these lines of research it considers the intrinsic positioning of CPR within the domain of public relations and how this may run the risk of it being used, or being seen to be used, as a vehicle to sanitise the problems and deep contradictions that beset public relations.

Over the course of the mid to late twentieth century, risk-producing[1] corporations invested in "public relations" (PR) personnel not only to handle queries from the press, but also to confront what they saw as increasing challenges to their business success and long-term viability. PR agents also networked with associates from cognate industries to work through the different tiers of government and the media in order to achieve mutual political ends. One PR strategy was to construct discursive meanings in and through contested social, political and commercial sites; for example, by influencing editorials and news coverage generally, which in turn would impact on politicians and their constituencies. Another strategy was to deploy a "global template" of communication tactics in international contexts to suppress or obfuscate the circulation of information or to discredit opposition (Burton 2007, p. viii). Invoking considerable institutional authority and economic power, this activity successfully influenced the trajectory of PR agendas. Issues that could mobilise this response were the perceived erosion of corporate "privileges" – such as taking action to prevent laws that would increase corporate liability – or encroachments on self-regulation. In the main, these activities were subterraneous and unseen by the so called "publics" that PR sought to influence and control.

In the latter stages of the twentieth century when environmental risks were "among the most pervasive, the most serious and the most feared" (Tindale 1998, p. 54), the opacity of this behaviour and exclusivity of the networks formed and conducted under the banner of "PR" attracted harsh criticism for failing to take account of possible ethical and legal breaches and for the overall damaging effects on public discourse needed, for example, to manage and reduce such risks. Textual critiques of PR emerged from the 1980s onwards, contributing to a distinct genre of corporatist reportage focusing on PR. Written by journalists, political activists, freelance writers and academics from a range of disciplines, they combined socio-political analysis with a satiric, sceptical flavour and highlighted the media's growing dependency on the PR industry.

Examples are: Beder 1997, Burton 2007, Conway & Oreskes 2010, Miller & Dinan 2008, Nelson 1989, Rampton & Stauber 2002, Stauber & Rampton 1995. Exposing the mechanics of PR and the pseudo-scientific evidence on which it sometimes relied, these texts reached new audiences while detailing cases of manipulative and combative communication deployed by the industry to attack activists. As such, they were a counter-hegemonic challenge to wholesome and socially beneficial representations of "PR" promoted by professional institutions such as the Public Relations Society of America (PRSA). They are also significant for rebutting the normative PR notion of "publics" as predictable and innately malleable, demonstrating instead their capacity in the public sphere to be politicised, articulate and forceful.

Sociologist Anthony Giddens argues that in modernity trust is "socially created" and intertwined with risk "that collectively affects masses of individuals" such as is the case in ecological disasters (1995, p. 34). Trust is also linked to the strength of "expert systems". He says: "By expert systems I mean systems of technical accomplishment or professional expertise that organise large areas of the material and social environments in which we live today" (p. 27). Moreover, trust, or *loss of trust*, has a symbolic social significance as it relates to a stabilising coherence or "guarantee" spanning time and space (Giddens 1995, p. 28). At the heart of these criticisms of mainstream PR is an erosion of "trust" linked to risk production, knowledge construction and social development (Beck 1992). Therefore these textual critiques from the 1980s onwards are significant, not only for the ethical issues they raise for individual PR practitioners, or for the industry, but for the ways in which the loss of "trust" connects to the wider "expert systems" in society, such as the regulating industry bodies, allied political and legal institutions and academia.

Around the 1990s, an internal critical stance, challenging mainstream PR and seeking to investigate and address its limitations, emerged in some European and Australasian universities specialising in public relations. Until then, the academy had largely adopted the orthodoxy of a means/ends approach which reflected a positivist and functionalist orientation that was preferred by US industries taking up PR graduates. Overall, the dominant influence of American PR stemmed from its "developed institutional base…big numbers of university courses, big numbers of practitioners associated with the PR Society of America (PRSA) and its PR journals" (L'Etang & Pieczka 2006, p. 270). An example of the interrelationship between business, the academy and PR's institutions is James Grunig and Todd Hunt's 1984 theorisation of PR as: publicity, public information, two-way asymmetrical and two-way symmetrical. Also known as the "Grunigian paradigm" this "four-part typology" has been exported globally and is "still the principal basis of the contemporary academic and operational paradigm about PR" (Moloney, 2006, p. 54). Critical public relations (CPR) emerged as a bifurcation in the field that tolerated rather than suppressed conceptions of PR deviating from the mainstream.

Broadly, CPR can be described as a loose unity of alternative viewpoints that seeks an interdisciplinary, holistic understanding of PR and its social impacts. According to Jacquie L'Etang, one such impact is "how PR serves some classes more than others" (2005, p. 523). For Patricia Curtin and Kenn Gaither these investigations need also to embrace identity and difference and this extends to "race, class and gender simultaneously" (2009, p. 109). On another front, CPR scholars have been active in challenging representations of PR by dominant institutions such as the PRSA and interrogating knowledge bases such as the "Grunigian paradigm" (Curtin & Gaither 2005; Davis 2002; Falkheimer 2009; L'Etang & Pieczka 2006; Moloney 2006).

While as a movement CPR claims to contribute to deepening an understanding of PR and its relationship to society, not everyone is convinced. Bill Huey commented that any reform movement in the academy linked to the PR industry is tainted by this association: "Universities are just farm systems" for a PR business model, "and they appear to like it that way, especially in the U.S." (2008). There are parallels between Huey's comments and a criticism of the business reform movement "Corporate Social Responsibly" (CSR), articulated by Evan Jones who said "CSR is an academic growth industry" and "plays to youthful idealism" (2006). Reflecting on the voguishness of CSR he commented:

> It was the same story fifty years ago when the American corporate PR departments and their academic counterparts invented the concept of the 'soulful corporation'. The inter-war antipathy to corporate business in general was successfully headed off at the pass.
>
> *(Jones 2006)*

In investigating the potential of CPR as a credible means of addressing reform in PR, this chapter has three objectives: first to track movements of meaning in PR over the postwar period of the twentieth century; second to examine the major criticisms of PR over this time and how they interrelate with these developments; and last, to explore the capacity of CPR to address the expressed concerns by people outside the domain.

In examining the major criticisms of public relations, I have chosen to look at some of the areas that have attracted the deepest controversy. This includes "PR" associated with high risk-producing industries such as: asbestos, tobacco, chemical, forestry and energy production. Drawing on testimony from civil campaigners – also referred to as activists – key issues will be identified to better understand the products and social relations of public relations. For the same reason, the chapter also draws on original PR documents, such as minutes, campaign plans and reports sourced from this period. It concludes with a discussion of PR's ambiguities and effects, and CPR's potential to influence and enable reform, as well as a set of questions for scholars to reflect on in order to avoid the false consciousness identified by Huey (2008) and Jones (2006).

Much of the literature reviewed in pursuit of these objectives is sourced from the US, despite considerable PR activity in Europe and Australasia. This is because the US has overwhelmingly swayed global conceptions of PR practice, theory and research (Pieczka, 2006, p. 347) and can be compared with other Western settings around this time.

"Do you believe in PR or don't you?" – postwar PR

In the 1960s and 1970s, dynamic social, economic and cultural influences produced a transitioning and complex era of public relations. This context is a key element in understanding the rise of the CPR movement, its hindrances, and its potential to reform the field.

Throughout the 1940s and 1950s PR was established as a relatively uncontroversial business practice during which politically benign and obedient publics were the norm. Operating with assumptions based on Edward Bernays's (2005, p. 73–4) ideas – namely, that the masses were "herds" following leaders who knew better in forming their thinking – PR consultancies such as Hill and Knowlton had a fairly confident view about how individuals and groups would receive and respond to their messages and tactics. The ease with which they conducted PR activities in defending the reputation of the tobacco industry at this time is described by Miller:

> The agency was able to affect media discussion of issues affecting its clients on innumerable occasions, demonstrated most clearly in the case of tobacco. By creating a seemingly independent organization that was actually a PR strategem, H&K took advantage of the conventions of objectivity and balance, arguing that there existed a medical controversy, as opposed to a clear-cut health hazard. The agency even affected the quantity of news by convincing at least some journalists not to pursue the story. It also influenced media discussion

> simply by providing reporters with information such as statistical data or opinions of the
> industries it represented.
>
> *(Miller, 1999, pp. 189–90)*

By the 1960s, however, it was evident that "publics" and their receptivity to PR were changing. In the US there was a growing environmental awareness, much of it triggered by concerns about the production and consumption of hazardous materials. Public concerns spiked, according to Ingram (2008), "after scientists discovered the presence of Stronitum-90 in cows' milk in 1959, [and] anxieties over nuclear war began to focus in particular on the environmental effects of atomic bomb testing" (p. 21).

The changing receptivity of publics to PR is illustrated in a 1961 report produced by the PR Advisory Committee of the Manufacturing Chemists' Association (MCA). It stated that a growing public awareness of environmental issues saw reputable news sources table the agenda in a series of articles. The PR Advisory Committee wrote to their board of directors: "Here are a few of the titles: *Time* magazine, 'Subtle New Pollutants Endanger Health'; *Good Housekeeping*, 'The Danger In Your Water'; *Science Newsletter*, 'Our Polluted Inheritance'. There can be no doubt of the increasing public interest in pollution control" (MCA, 1961, p. 5). The report also cited that "24 bills (were) introduced in state legislatures restricting and controlling the handling and shipment of the products listed" (1961, p. 7). It cautioned that: "the mind of the public is being reached, almost daily, by those who hold views contrary to our own" (1961, p. 18). The report suggested that – as a remedy – women could be groomed "on a systematic and programmed basis" to adopt redundant ideological and domestic values that would serve the chemical industry's interests (1961, p. 28).

In 1962 such remedial measures were complicated when Rachel Carson's influential book *Silent Spring* (1971) was published. Written in an accessible, lucid style, it appealed to new audiences, including women, who were receptive to an informed discussion of hazardous products such as pesticides and their effects on the environment and on health. Stauber and Rampton (1995, p. 124) argue that the manufacturers of agricultural pesticides responded to this "crisis" by appointing E. Bruce Harrison as "manager of environmental information":

> He was assigned to coordinate and conduct the industry attack on the book. In their campaign to discredit Carson, Harrison and his cohorts used "crisis management" including emotional appeals, scientific misinformation, front groups, extensive mailings to the media and opinion leaders, and the recruitment of doctors and scientists as "objective" third party defenders of agrichemicals.
>
> *(p. 124)*

As social and political awakenings throughout the Western world continued to gather momentum, sceptical "publics" became increasingly politicised. Protest fronts represented movements that were anti-war, pro-environment, pro-civil rights and women's and gay liberation – among others. In general, they challenged the idea of a market-based economy, were disparaging of political conservatism and questioned notions of "progress". Banners, stickers and posters communicated alternative ideas through popular culture and encouraged social experimentation. Notable social indicators were Bob Dylan's song *The Times they are A-Changing* (1963) and Pete Seeger's *God Bless the Grass* (1966) which "became the first album in history wholly dedicated to songs about environmental issues" (Ingram, 2008, p. 22).

In 1972 *Limits to Growth* by Donella H. Meadows, Dennis L. Meadows, Jørgen Randers and William W. Behrens III, was published to critical acclaim and presented the wider-reading public with scientific evidence to project social population pressures on planetary sustainability. "The release of the LtG in 1972 had immediate and ongoing impacts. Environmental issues and the sustainability debate were further popularised as millions of copies were sold, and translated into 30 languages" (Turner 2008, p. 1). Similarly, Steward Brand's *Whole Earth Catalogue* magazines from 1968 to 1972 enlivened a critical consumer culture. Binkley wrote: "American consumers of the 1970s are remembered for the heightened levels of price consciousness, scepticism towards traditional advertising messages, their scrutinizing regard for product information and a market ingenuity for saving money and controlling daily budgets" (2003, p. 288). In the civil realm, protests such as street marches, sit-ins and radical environmentalism gained social traction as legitimate forms of political expression. Individuals and civil groups used media and communication reflexively, through graffiti and hijacking advertising in contested public spaces such as advertising billboards. Klein argues that the term "culture jamming" was coined in 1984 to direct "the public viewer to a consideration of the original corporate strategy" (2000, p. 281). At the extreme end of the protest spectrum was eco-sabotage. According to Letcher, "In the USA, this activity is called 'monkey wrenching' after the 1975 novel *The Monkey Wrench Gang* by Edward Abbey" (2010, p. 154). He argues the equivalent practice in the UK is "pixiening", which reflected a more romantic, neo-paganism approach used to make such practices socially acceptable and "incompatible with the state's view that these are acts of vandalism and criminal damage" (2010, p. 154).

Economic conditions were also changing. McGuigan argues that part of this was a decline in previously understood industry models. From the early 1970s

> the Fordist system of mass production and consumption went into sharp decline in the hitherto advanced capitalist world and capital shifted into a more flexible regime of accumulation and produce specialisation. Large-scale factory production switched increasingly from comparatively high-pay countries and cities in the West to cheaper labour markets on the fringes of the first World and into the Japanese-dominated high-tech Pacific Rim.
>
> *(McGuigan, 1996, p. 98)*

This had two effects for PR. First, it allowed corporations to explore communication management and behaviour control in different ways and in different geo-political jurisdictions; and second, it spurred the formation of new global activist networks. Smith and Pangsapa explain:

> The structural changes in the global economy means that nation-states are less capable of regulating the behaviour of corporations and the effects of capital mobility. This means that other ways of influencing the activities of international capital are seen as more effective, hence the rise of NGOs and transnational networks concerned with sweat shops, human rights abuses, labour standards violations and unsustainable environmental impacts
>
> *(2008, p. 89)*

The communicative activity generated by non-governmental organisations (NGOs) meant social and political contexts had changed substantially for corporations using traditional PR. Wolfsfeld writes:

> Until the 1970s there were no anti-nuclear power frames appearing in the American news media, because such frames were so rare within the general society. This helps explain why a serious nuclear accident that occurred in 1966 in the Fermi reactor, 30 miles south of

Detroit, was barely mentioned in the American press. Later, environmental and anti-nuclear movements played an important role in changing the nature of media discourse about this issue by successfully promoting anti-nuclear frames to compete with those being promoted by the authorities. This led to a very different framing by the news media of the subsequent accidents at Three Mile Island and Chernobyl.

(2006, p. 93)

In these conditions new publics pushed back against the PR tactics. As a result, responses from the industry became more retaliatory and extreme. Holcomb contends that in the US:

The pressures from the social movements of the 1960s and 1970s on corporations were more intense and often more aggressive than those of contemporary interest groups, and the responses by companies were often more immediate and launched with more conviction than those of today.

(2005, p. 31)

This intensification of PR is evident in primary documents of the time. In 1969 the Manufacturing Chemists' Association Inc. (MCA) PR Committee "outlined plans for an aggressive PR program that 'puts us on the offensive instead of on the defensive'" (MCA, 1969, p. 9). In 1984 Cerrell Associates produced a PR plan, entitled "Political Difficulties Facing Waste-to-Energy Plant Siting" for the California Waste Management Board. The report stated: "Public opposition to waste disposal facilities is a recent phenomenon. Prior to the rise of the environment movement in the 1970s, waste facilities aroused little public concern, and rarely were facilities closed due to local opposition" (Cerrell Associates Report, 1984, p. 4).

The ramped-up PR "offensive" had particular consequences for the individual, active, civil participants at the time. They encountered legal intimidation, threats, targeted intelligence gathering, covert infiltration of their groups, media manipulation, unethical use of dirt files and dossiers, amongst other methods (Hager and Burton 1999; Shevory 2007). Moreover, new unethical communication strategies began to emerge. Hass and Kleine (2009) argue that E. Bruce Harrison, the PR executive engaged by the National Agricultural Chemical Association to discredit Rachel Carson's intellectual contribution, was responsible for one such practice:

His new strategy, "green-washing," was a form of corporate camouflage, developed fully in his book *Going Green* and based on his claims that the grassroots environmental movement had become a series of large non-profit organizations whose primary mission was to raise funds in order to enable the movement to remain "green." As a strategy, green-washing aimed to establish corporate-environmental partnerships that provided funding for environmental organizations and, in doing so, subdued them. The overall result was a series of deals that helped corporations deploy their power to subvert the environmental movement.

(p. 273)

Highly effective strategems like green-washing were anathema to some. As a corollary "PR" became characterised as immensely powerful but unaccountable (Nelson 1989). These developments, and an upsurge of a more articulate, persistent and environmentally aware public, may explain a sharp backlash against PR from the late 1980s onwards, with calls for its relationship to democracy and the media to be highly scrutinised (Beder, 1997; Conway & Oreskes 2010; Davis 2002; Ewen, 1996; Hager & Burton, 1999; Miller & Dinan 2008; Stauber & Rampton, 1995).

Pro-business, US-oriented functionalist "PR" was being challenged in the public sphere by a variety of commentators as socially divisive and undemocratic. Moreover, dissent was arising internally from within PR's own ranks. Flagging a change in direction within the academy in 1996, Jacquie L'Etang wrote that "Public relations can be seen to be intrinsically linked to power-broking initiatives in society and therefore a profoundly conservative force in society; the popular concept of PR as 'neutral' seems to privilege the existing order over justice" (L'Etang, 1996, p.105). Drawing on representative literature and theoretical perspectives from Australia, New Zealand and Western Europe, the next section outlines key developments in critical scholarship in PR from the 1990s onwards.

The spirit and intent of CPR

Can CPR "socially create" trust lost by mainstream PR and restore credibility to the field (Giddens 1995, p. 34)? A central theme of CPR research is to understand PR and its impacts in their socially contextualised complexity. Part of its remit is to examine the collective impacts on society. As such it is necessary to prise open the lens through which PR has conventionally been viewed, and scrutinise it from a range of interdisciplinary, synchronic and diachronic perspectives. This position implicitly acknowledges that language is socially constructed and as such its representation as "truth" is linked to societal power relations which are subject to distortion and dominance. Therefore, for Judy Motion and C. Kay Weaver (2005, p. 50), "critical discourse analysis provides PR scholars and practitioners with an ability to conceptualize PR within the context of culture as a symbolic system". Similarly, for Patricia Curtin and Kenn Gaither (2005, p. 110) PR is a complex set of signifiers "that produces meaning within a cultural economy, privileging identity, difference and power because of the central role these constructs play in discursive practice". Thus CPR reflects an interpretivist paradigm, which for Patrick Hughes explains "the social world" which "is not just 'out there' waiting to be interpreted, but 'in here' or 'in us' – it *is* our interpretations" (2001, p. 35).

The interpretivist approach aligns with the related epistemologies of hermeneutics: concerned with meaning-making and the interpretation of texts; and phenomenology: concerned with relationships and shared understandings through "the examination of things according to the lived experiences (and consciousness) of individuals" (Daymon & Holloway, 2009, pp. 180–3). This approach taps into a long-standing academic convention. Jacquie L'Etang (2005) explains that

> Methodologically critical work derives in the continental European context from the German tradition of *quellenkritik* – discursive, argumentative, hermeneutic work. Definitions of "critical" work go beyond the common everyday use of the term, which implies negative evaluation as Morrow and Brown (1994) point out, and include:
> - work that challenges current assumptions in the field;
> - work that alters boundaries and produces a "paradigm shift" (Kuhn, 1970);
> - work that critiques policy or practice in the field;
> - work that specifically draws for its inspiration on the intellectual sociological project known as Critical Theory.
>
> *(p. 521)*

This positioning is the antithesis of the functionalism associated with mainstream PR research (Falkheimer, 2009, p. 104). As Ansgar Zerfass argues, a functionalist orientation does not "answer the fundamental question of why communication is necessary at all within a market system which is, in principle, co-ordinated not via language but via price-relations" (2008, p. 66).

Not surprisingly, some CPR scholars have focused on the problems with public relations' over-reliance on functionalism. One example is the notion of the "dominant coalition". Bruce K. Berger (2005) describes its logic as membership of a powerful decision-making group which "advances the profession's status and allows practitioners to help organizations solve problems and become more socially responsible". He explains:

> A key assumption in this perspective is that practitioners will do the "right" thing once inside the dominant coalition – they will or will try to represent the voices and interests of others and to shape an organization's ideology and decisions to benefit the profession, the organization, and greater society.
>
> *(2005, p. 5)*

However, for Berger this notion "glosses [sic] complex power relations and structural practices inside dominant coalitions that render it difficult for practitioners to do the 'right' thing – even if they want to" (2005, p. 6).

"Faith in numbers" and positivism is another area of counterpoint and knowledge reconstruction for CPR scholars. According to Christine Daymon and Immy Holloway (2011), a quantitative research approach, in which positivism is situated, tends toward a narrow and linear understanding of the world and has often worked in tandem with a managerialist functionalist approach. They argue (p. 5) that "[t]o study complexity, power relations and the co-construction of meaning in a holistic or critical sense requires a different, more flexible type of research where the process of discovery is blended with intuition". In exploring the relations of power in public relations, CPR research approaches draw on interdisciplinary social theory. This may explain why for Judy Motion and C. Kay Weaver (2005)

> The task for the critical public relations scholar is to investigate how PR practice uses particular discursive strategies to advance the hegemonic power of particular groups and to examine how these groups attempt to gain public consent to pursue their organizational mission. We also argue that discourses deployed for PR purposes can only be fully understood in relation to the political, economic, and social contexts in which they operate.
>
> *(p. 50)*

These ideas, which challenge the legitimacy and social benefit of public relations, have gained traction within the associated disciplines operating within the academy. In 2005, Jacquie L'Etang wrote:

> Critical work in PR has blossomed in the last decade. It has challenged current assumptions, defined and critiqued a "dominant paradigm" (and thus in the process defined itself and marked new boundaries), applied critical theory (especially those who have been influenced by media sociology) and critiqued policy and practice.
>
> *(p. 522)*

Similarly, Jane Johnston (2013) wrote:

> By the 1990s, Australian, New Zealand and British scholars had become increasingly critical of the dominance of the North American texts which were seen to present limited

paradigms for understanding the industry and contexts which were inconsistent with other cultures or discourses.

(p. 4)

In 2008 a community of scholars came together for a "Radical PR Roundtable" hosted by the University of Stirling which sought to connect PR up with "contemporary debates" and focus on "societal impacts rather than organizational need" (About Radical PR, 2008, pp. 1–3). However, for Bill Huey (2008), the exercise may have merely been tokenism within academe, since he sees that the real power for reform resides in industry practices:

> "Radical PR" may happen someday, but it won't be at a university conference. It will be when PR changes its business model, i.e., hiring a bunch of young ladies to work phones while billing five or six times their hourly cost plus a considerable overhead tax.

CPR scholars may laudably aim for reform, but the social history of PR to date, and entrenched relations of power which underpin its place in society, present challenges which cannot be underestimated. In particular the nexus between the PR practice, the PR industry and academe may be a significant impediment to creating the complex notion of "trust" as discussed by Giddens (1995, p. 34). Therefore, understanding the historical role, contradictions or even the vague ambiguities of PR practice in depth, is fundamental in establishing the capacity of the CPR movement to effectively rebuild knowledge and address reform.

Understanding PR, power, discourse and interpretation

This section reports on experiences of PR practice from the 1970s to the end of the millennium, applying CPR as a heuristic to analyse the emergent themes. I interviewed civil participants or activists who had encountered PR from the 1970s onwards. I adopted a critical-interpretative, qualitative approach to the research and CPR as the lens for analysis. This is a fusion of an interpretative method – which sees an individual's reality both constructed and contextualised by their social world – with a critical method which "takes account of power and inequalities in society" (Daymon and Holloway, 2011, pp. 102–3). This synthesis aims to produce a better understanding of the interactions between activists and PR while directing the research to marginalised areas of the social world that may have been overlooked by mainstream PR. This approach also complements my interest in uncovering new ways of thinking about PR and activism, challenging orthodoxies and contributing to substantive reform (Daymon and Holloway, 2011, p. 5; Demetrious, 2013). I argue that identifying the extent of the problems in PR and analysing these through the lens of CPR is a key step in understanding the extent of its social impacts and finding new ways to address this.

To this end, six informants, who had closely observed and/or participated in activist and community action campaigns in Australia and New Zealand over 1970–2000, were interviewed. The participants were asked to comment on PR campaigns and to describe any aspects that caused them concern. These civil participants had encountered PR associated with the asbestos, tobacco, forestry, fishing, petroleum and chemical industries. Some had multiple participation within NGOs, or in grassroots community action groups, across a number of different industries in different geo-political jurisdictions. They were also asked if any PR actions they witnessed had interfered with the democratic processes of debate or discussion by citizens. Participants were also asked to discuss ways the PR industry could be reformed to reach higher ethical standards. Finally, they were asked to describe their own communicative activities and detail what was done differently. Themes arising from these interviews contributed to an understanding of potential agendas for reform, which are discussed in the conclusion.

Lived experiences of PR: citizenry and social change

Over the last 40 years, mainstream PR has been the target of much criticism from outside the domain, especially in relation to manipulative techniques to attack civil campaigners. To understand this contradiction in its complexity I turned to the lived experience of PR through its interactions with citizens engaged in contentious and contested public debates.

Claims of ethically grey activity as part of a PR offensive were routinely made by the informants. A key issue raised by all but one was the spying, monitoring and infiltration of activist groups by paid PR personnel, to the extent that they were "going through people's rubbish bins" (Matt Ruchel, interview, 6 March 2014). Robert Vojakovic, an asbestos awareness campaigner, believed that industry had paid people to monitor their activities, gather information, and claimed that listening devices had been installed and that "we also had our phones tapped" (Robert Vojakovic, interview, 10 July 2014).

Cath Wallace (interview, 30 January 2014) said she: "first got involved in activism in the late 70s" in a range of environmental conservation campaigns in New Zealand. In discussing the infiltration and surveillance of forest protection and other groups, and anti-activist PR tactics, she said:

> It's particularly deplorable when it's state-owned companies hiring PR companies to spy on groups, infiltrate groups, and undertake other surveillance as happened with both a state-owned forest logging company and a state-owned coal mining company. New Zealand's Ministry of Fisheries also funded private fishing industry PR campaigns. There are really questionable relationships between private interests and the public purse and government's support for PR when it's being done to counter legitimate civil society concerns.
>
> *(Wallace, 2014)*

Nicky Hager (interview, 18 February 2014), who opposed the logging activities of the New Zealand state-owned organisation, Timberlands, experienced similar infiltrations by PR personnel. He said:

> When groups discover they've been infiltrated and they are not sure they can trust the people they work with – which is a very common factor in the political targeting of public interest groups – [then] people just walk away, and they don't do it in a conscious way, they just don't feel comfortable anymore and when a turning point comes in their lives or something happens and they can make a choice of keeping on fighting or doing it, they're just not there anymore. I think that's a very important thing: fragility.
>
> *(Hager, 2014)*

These comments indicate that the covert spying on activist groups by PR personnel has compound, detrimental ramifications beyond the issue at hand for individuals and communities. This sheds light on the entrenched trustworthiness issues at the core of criticisms about PR and the multiplier effect this has for an individual's confidence and participation in the democratic and judicial systems (Giddens, 1995).

Another damaging effect identified was the slurring of activists for their moral stances on civil issues and the deploying of highly resourced media relations that frustrated legitimate debate. In 1978 Bill Musk was part of a group of doctors who formed the Australian Council of Smoking and Health (ACOSH). However, some colleagues framed the activist doctors as "extremists": "Not many doctors smoked, but there were a few that still smoked, and they would sort of say that we were extremists…and they sort of thought that it was not the role of doctors to be involved in these sort of activities (Bill Musk, interview, 11 July 2014). In contrast, careful PR management of individual reputations within corporations was used to buttress industries from public scrutiny and criticism. Robert Vojakovic said that asbestos producer Jim Reid, the executive director of James Hardie, was a "pillar of society" and "untouchable", and that therefore "[h]is influence was far beyond our ability to sort of have any victory, if you like, or any final position from that point of view because those guys were sheltered by state and federal governments" (Vojakovic, 2014). These examples show that the lived effects of "reputation management" by PR is far from simple and needs greater understanding. Often a standard activity for a PR practitioner, it can have complex disempowering effects for individuals and organisations, instilling a belief that it was not in their best interests to "confront" PR problems of an offending company by making a complaint.

Some activists believed that they were victimised and falsely identified as the likely instigators of an industrial accident. Matt Ruchel was a local activist who later worked for Greenpeace as a campaign manager. As a local activist he had concerns about the safety of a volatile chemical storage facility in Melbourne, Australia, called Coode Island. He said:

> There was a bid for Melbourne to get the Olympics…and we made ourselves very unpopular by writing a submission to the Olympic Committee and the Greek Olympic Committee to say why Melbourne was unsafe to host the Olympic Games. That was fairly controversial at the time – but it certainly put the Coode Island issue on the agenda and then it blew up – like a year or so later. In the media's mind we were proved to be right. But a few days after the fires the police held a press conference accusing local activists, saying that fire was likely started by local activists. A protest gone wrong. There was found to be no basis to it but they did the press conference anyway. And it was an unusual media conference in the sense as it was speculation from the police, but it was very well timed. It was later found by coronial inquiry that in the end someone left a cap off a tank and it blew up. That's what caused it. But it was convenient strategy to deflect flack.
>
> *(Ruchel, 2014)*

In the asbestos campaign Robert Vojakovic believed an industry opponent "set up" and falsely accused the activists of extremism: "They delivered a tape recorded message to the *Western Australian* newspaper" which discussed an "organisation, you know, that wants to kill…every minister, and they demanded for every claim several million dollars. They came to our house, with a search warrant…and ransacked our office…they didn't find nothing.…The whole media ridiculed them for that because they knew it was a set-up" (Vojakovic, 2014).

These incidents illustrate the extent to which the interviewees believe that industry, state and media power and interests are entwined and linked to unethical PR practice. It suggests that for CPR to be credible to a wider public it must vigorously confront and tackle these issues, otherwise it may be both ineffective and/or regarded as another form of corporate camouflage, which deepens scepticism.

Over-resourced and protectionist PR campaigns, costing millions of dollars and mounted by risk-producing industries, were derided as self-serving and not in the community interest. Matt Ruchel said that when he worked for Greenpeace International he was aware that Burson-Marstellar "very cynically" developed the "'Responsible Care' code of practice, [which] was rolled out globally by the chemical industry in response largely to Bhopal and a couple of shockers in the US".

Nicky Hager also commented on the resourcing of PR campaigns:

> What happened with Timberland, as happened with these kinds of PR campaigns, is that they didn't just want to have their say – they wanted to win. And this is where it gets tricky…the Timberland tactics fell into two groups. The first one was creating a campaign in favour of logging where there hadn't been one. And you know the tactics:…the funding of expertise over time, the cultivation of journalists who are temperamentally unkind to your story, and the more aggressive the sponsorship (for) all those things that can buy you influence. The reality of PR is the more money, the more you can do.
>
> *(Hager, 2014)*

Ruchel's and Hager's comments suggest that the over-resourcing of PR campaigns provides greater opportunity for legal or ethical misuse. As such, budgeting is another aspect of practice that CPR scholars could analyse from alternative perspectives, especially in risk-producing industries where the potential for immediate harm is greater, or which may be incubating and irreversible over the longer term (Beck 1992).

The participants saw their own communicative activities differently. Rose Marie Vojakovic (interview, 10 July 2014) said that the Asbestos Diseases Society of Australia's public communication activities are underpinned by the values of "truthfulness, yes, [and] sincerity so that we mean what we say and that we carry those promises through". According to Robert Vojakovic, asbestos producer "CSR never had the values. They were happy to have us die like flies you know… James Hardie had the same thing you know…they didn't believe that they could be blamed for anything whatsoever" (Vojakovic, 2014).

Cath Wallace said: "What we do is advocacy and networking and trying to reform." Matt Ruchel explained: "PR companies will say we are lobbyists – we're not lobbyists. We are very constrained by law." In discussing reform for PR, Cath Wallace said: "I don't have a problem with PR firms writing things and publishing them – but I think they need to disclose that that's who they are and that they are 'hired guns' in that respect." She further reported: "I think there have to be some rules around disclosure, rules around not infringing civic rights to engage in protest" (Wallace, 2014).

Similarly, Nicky Hager said that

> [e]thical things PR people can do [is] they can get a more real appreciation of what they're dealing with. That it's not enough to just say we had our say and we had a robust fight about this. That actually people who participate in politics for money who are ethical should be aware that they can tread on and break the other side; that they can actually harm the political system, the political environment that they are working in.
>
> *(Hager, 2014)*

Understanding the value and practice of intellectual rigour was seen as critical by all. Matt Ruchel made that point that "[p]eople need to be trained in checking the evidence. [There is] not a great deal of ecological literacy". Nicky Hager said:

> The broad issue is, I believe, that in a kind of mixed democratic society everyone's got a right to have a say but I don't think everyone is equal. I've never heard a version of democracy which talks about the rights of companies, for example, and much less foreign

companies. My interpretation of democracy is about the citizens of a country but that's a different matter from freedom of speech...you have to allow a logging company or a foreign bank to express their point of view and their version of the facts. That's the kind of society we live in and I like that.

The interviews with civil campaigners interacting with PR in contentious political debates in the latter stages of the twentieth century reveal key areas for attention in CPR research. Significantly, the interviewees made accusations of collusion between the state, industry and the media; false representation; surveillance; covert infiltration of civil groups; and breaches of privacy. They believed some issues they opposed, such as asbestos production, attracted multiple PR responses from a range of self- interest groups such as manufacturers, insurance companies and government. They also revealed that there was a sense of futility in bringing these communication practices to the attention of industry or their professional associations. In part, this was because they believed the offending individuals and industry had disproportionate privileges in society that provided impunity and shielded them from public criticism.

The overarching issue for these civil campaigners is PR's aggressive promotion of "environments of risk" and the erosion of trust in political and other systems (Giddens, 1995, p. 35). Playing into this space is the complex impact of reputational management of individuals and of corporations, the over-resourcing of PR campaigns, the global reach of PR, the replication and impact of ethically dubious campaign tactics, and the lack of transparency and rules around disclosure.

Conclusion: the social cost of doing nothing

CPR is a significant development in PR linked to the increasing politicisation of publics over the latter part of the twentieth century. Without new perspectives from within the PR domain, the problems outlined thus far are likely to continue, albeit in different forms due to globalisation and the rapid techno-economic developments characterising contemporary society. Intrinsically positioned within the field, CPR espouses distinct paradigmatic and epistemological beliefs about knowledge and methodological orientations to mainstream public relations. Yet as Huey (2008) alludes, how this activity translates into the lived experiences of PR practitioners and citizens is yet to be determined.

The empirical evidence of civil campaigners opposing business interests has brought to light the complex interrelationships and entwinement of power relations between industry, government and other bodies with vested interests. In addition, their experiences of multi-fronted communication responses through the instrument of public relations warrants investigation and a reply from CPR scholars. Thus, at this point, CPR can only claim that the capacity of the field to respond to problems has increased.

Credible CPR approaches to research need to acknowledge the ambiguities of PR and seek to understand not just the impacts of individual practitioners or businesses on specific issues, but complex ways in which this activity has collectively impacted on social trust and public discourse for society. To progress the practical application of CPR research, perhaps a starting point may be a reflexive and sceptical stance which considers: what are the intrinsic ambiguities and contradictions within CPR that need to be examined? And to what extent could CPR be "culture bound" by mainstream PR and subject to dominant institutional orientations? Further questions distilled from the research that may deserve attention are: how are the identities of individuals and groups (publics) within political debates being constructed, described and distributed within varied media environments? How can individuals and groups (publics) formally report PR interventions, impacts and effects so that these understandings are circulated to the wider public and effectively reviewed? Moreover, how, and in what ways, do reputational factors both for the corporation and for the individual or group impact on a complaints process?

On another front, the civil participant evidence suggests that some PR activities require particular scrutiny; for example, the high-budget PR used by hazardous and risk-producing industries such as the energy, chemical and forestry industries that impact on the natural environment and human health to a far greater extent than other more benign ones (Beck 1992). According to Giddens "the prime condition of requirements for trust is not lack of power but lack of full information" (1995, p. 33). Thus, disclosure about *failures of practice*, especially within *risk-producing* industries, paradoxically could go some way toward restoring *trustworthiness* in PR and the expert systems that surround it. Trust flowing from this could in turn nourish innovation, invention and enterprise within society.

All civil participants accepted the right of commercial organisations to lobby the state on behalf of their self-interest through the public channels of the communicative process: but with provisions. Key areas identified for organisations and practitioners are: being willing to disclose information relating to involvement; a primary understanding and respect for the political systems in which PR and civil groups interact; and the checking of evidence in view of a deeper understanding of the proliferation of meanings through the tools of their trade. Other themes emerging are consistent with the concerns of CPR in that they centrally position power relations, discourse and interpretation as contested sites. In other words, these views of the civic campaigners and CPR scholars are not widely divergent. Both believe in the democratic mix of voices in political debates and fairness. Both positions see a conceptual weakness in public relations, that, unaddressed, perpetuates bad practice and the erosion of public debate. This suggests that extrinsic and intrinsic critics of PR may share common ground and they could possibly work together to develop practical steps to build coherence and stability in "expert systems" (Giddens 1995, p. 27).

In furthering a CPR reform agenda, this chapter argues there is a need to consider "trust" and the proximity of "expert systems" with vested interests such as industry associations. The idea of PR as represented by the PRSA is "a strategic communication process that builds mutually beneficial relationships between organizations and their publics" (2014). Yet this is demonstrably not true in relation to the PR deployed in support of the tobacco, asbestos and polluting industries which worked, and in some cases continues to work, actively against the common good. If CPR scholars attempting to gain credibility in academe do not interrogate the close proximity of this relationship, then their own legitimacy within this "expert system" (Giddens 1995, p. 27) may be further eroded in ways suggested by Huey (2008) and Jones (2006).

A level of scepticism toward CPR is justified, not least because reform is complex and connected to a chain of social relationships that cut through, and across, time and space. Moreover, there is a risk that CPR may get caught up in a voguish wave of academic opportunism, which, in part, may obscure and complicate the problems in the field further. Nevertheless, opportunity exists for CPR to confront PR with a self-reflexive interrogation of its practices. If the movement does not recoil from the difficult themes noted in this chapter, its intrinsic positioning presents a distinct stance which may well be a potent driver for change and renewal.

Notes

1   Risks such as radioactivity or toxic contamination produced in late modernity "induce systematic and often *irreversible* harm, generally remain *invisible*, are based on *casual interpretations* and thus initially only

exist in terms of the (scientific or anti-scientific) *knowledge* about them" (Beck 1992, pp. 22–3, italics in original).

Reference

Beck, U. (1992). *Risk society: Towards a new modernity*. London: Sage.

Beder, S. (1997). *Global spin: The corporate assault on environmentalism*. Melbourne: Scribe Publications.

Berger, B. K. (2005). Power over, power with, and power to relations: Critical reflections on public relations, the dominant coalition, and activism. *Journal of PR Research*, 17:1, pp. 5–28.

Bernays, E. (2005). *Propaganda*. New York: IG Publishing.

Binkley, S. (2003). The seers of Menlo Park: The discourse of heroic consumption in the "Whole Earth Catalog". *Journal of Consumer Culture*, 3, pp. 283–313.

Burton, B. (2007). *Inside spin, the dark underbelly of the PR industry*. Crows Nest, NSW: Allen and Unwin.

Carson, R. (1971 [1962]). *Silent Spring*. Harmondsworth: Penguin.

Cerrell Associates, Inc. (1984). *Political Difficulties Facing Waste-to-Energy Conversion Plant Siting*, pp. 1–60, California.

Conway, E., and Oreskes, N. (2010). *Merchants of doubt: How a handful of scientists obscured the truth on issues from tobacco smoke to global warming*. New York: Bloomsbury Press.

Curtin, Patricia A. & Gaither, T. Kenn. (2005). Privileging identity, difference, and power: The circuit of culture as a basis for PR theory, *Journal of PR Research*, 17(2), pp. 91–115.

Davis, A. (2002). *PR democracy: Public relations, politics and the mass media in Britain*. Manchester: Manchester University Press.

Daymon, C., & Holloway, I. (2011). *Qualitative research methods in PR and marketing communications*. London and New York: Routledge.

Demetrious, K. (2013). *Public relations, activism and social change: Speaking up*. New York: Routledge.

Ewen, S. (1996). *PR! A Social History of Spin*. New York: Basic Books.

Falkheimer, J. (2009). On Giddens: Interpreting PR through Anthony Giddens's structuration and late modernity theory. In Ihlen, O., Van Ruler, B., & Fredriksson, M. (Eds), *PR and social theory – key figures and concepts*. London: Routledge.

Giddens, A. (1995). *The consequences of modernity*. Cambridge, UK: Polity Press.

Grunig, J., & Hunt, T. (1984). *Managing public relations*. New York: Holt, Rinehart and Winston.

Hager, N., & Burton, B. (1999). *Secrets and lies, the anatomy of an anti-environmental PR campaign*. Munroe, ME: Common Courage Press.

Hass, B., & Kleine, M. (2009). The rhetoric of junk science, *Technical Communication Quarterly*, 12(3), pp. 267–84. doi: 10.1207/s15427625tcq1203_3

Holcomb, J. (2005). Public affairs in North America, US origins and development. In Harris, P., & Fleisher, C. S. (Eds), *The handbook of public affairs*. London: Sage Publications.

Huey, B. (15 September 2008). Reply to radical PR: Alternative visions and future directions. Retrieved on 10 October 2014 from http://radicalpr.wordpress.com/about/

Hughes, P. (2001). Paradigms, methods and knowledge. In MacNaughton, G., Rolfe, S., & Siral-Blatchford, I. *Doing early childhood research: International perspectives on theory and practice*. Sydney: Allen & Unwin.

Ingram, D. (2008). "My Dirty Stream": Pete Seeger, *American Folk Music, and Environmental Protest, Popular Music and Society*, 31(1), pp. 21–36.

Johnston, J. (2013). Breaking from tradition. In Horsley, M.,, & Brien, D. *Textbooks and educational texts in the 21st century: Writing, publishing and reading*, Text Special Issue 23, October 2013.

Jones, E. (20 May 2006). Corporate social non-responsibility in alert and alarmed blogspot. Retrieved on 5 July 2006 (in possession of the author) from http://alertandalaramed.blogspot.com/200 6/05corporate-social-non…

Klein, N. (2000). *No logo, taking aim at the brand bullies*. London: Flamingo.

Kuhn, T. (1970). *The structure of scientific revolutions*. Chicago: University of Chicago Press.

L'Etang, J. (1996). Corporate responsibly and public relations ethics. In L'Etang, J.,, & Pieczka, M. (Eds), *Critical perspectives in public relations*. London: International Thomson Business Press.

L'Etang, J. (2005). Critical public relations: Some reflections, *PR Review*, 31 (4), pp. 521–6.

L'Etang, J., & Pieczka, M. (1996). *Critical perspectives in public relations*. London: International Thomson Business Press.

L'Etang, J., & Pieczka, M. (Eds). (2006). *Public relations, critical perspectives and contemporary practice*. Mahwah, NJ: Lawrence Erlbaum Associates.

Letcher, A. (2010). The souring of the shire: Fairies, trolls and pixies in eco-protest culture, *Folklore*, 112(2), pp. 147–61.

McGuigan, J. (1996). *Culture and the public sphere*. London, New York: Routledge.

Manufacturing Chemists' Association (MCA), Inc. (14 February 1961). *A Report to the Board of Directors by The Public Relations Advisory Committee*, CMA 067883. Retrieved on 16 October 2014 from http://www.chemicalindustryarchives.org/dirtysecrets/pr/pdfs/067883.pdf

Manufacturing Chemists' Association (MCA), Inc. (27 September 1962). Minutes of Meeting, Air Pollution Abatement Committee, CMA 085250, Dearborn, Michigan, Retrieved on 16 October 2014 from http://www.chemicalindustryarchives.org/search/PDFs/cma/19620927_00001640.pdf

Manufacturing Chemists' Association (MCA), Inc. (29 November 1969). Minutes of Meeting, Public Relations Committee, New York City, CMA 134266.

Meadows, D. H., Meadows, D. L., Randers, J., & Behrens, W. (1972). *The limits to growth: A report for the Club of Rome's project on the predicament of mankind*. London: Potomac Associates.

Miller, D., & Dinan, W. (2008). *A century of spin: How PR became the cutting edge of corporate power*. London: Pluto Press.

Miller, K. (1999). *The voice of business: Hill & Knowlton and post war public relations*. Chapel Hill: The University of North Carolina Press.

Moloney, K. (2006) *Rethinking public relations: PR propaganda and democracy*. London: Routledge.

Morrow, R. A., & Brown, D. D. (1994). *Critical theory and methodology*. London, Sage.

Motion, J., & Leitch, S. (1996). A discursive perspective from New Zealand: Another world view'. *PR Review*, 22(3), Autumn, pp. 297–309.

Motion, J., & Weaver, C. (2005). A discourse perspective for CPR research: Life sciences network and the battle for truth, *Journal of PR Research*, 17(1), pp. 49–67.

Nelson, J. (1989). *Power in societies*. Toronto, Ontario: Macmillan.

Pieczka, M. (2006). Paradigms, systems theory and public relations. In L'Etang, J., & Pieczka, M. (Eds), *Public relations critical debates and contemporary practice*. Muhwah. NJ: Lawrence Erlbaum Associates, Inc.

PR Society of America (PRSA) (2014). What is public relations? PRSA's widely accepted definition. Retrieved on 15 October 2014 from http://www.prsa.org/AboutPRSA/PublicRelationsDefined/#.VD32vvmSy5K

Radical PR https://radicalpr.wordpress.com/about/ Accessed 6/7/2015

Rampton, S., & Stauber, J. (2002). *Trust Us, We're Experts!* New York: Penguin Putman.

Shevory, T. (2007). *Toxic burn the grassroots struggle against the WTI incinerator*. University of Minnesota Press, Minneapolis.

Smith, M., & Pangsapa, P. (2008). *Environment and citizenship: Integrating justice, responsibility and civic engagement*. London and New York: Zed Books.

Stauber, J., & Rampton, S. (1995). *Toxic sludge is good for you: Lies, damn lies, and the PR industry*. Monroe, ME: Common Courage Press.

Tindale, S. (1998). Procrastination and the global gamble. In Jane Franklin (Ed.), *The politics of risk society*. Cambridge: Polity Press in association with the Institute for Public Policy Research.

Turner, G. (2008). A comparison of the limits to growth with thirty years of reality. In *Socio-Economics and the Environment in Discussion*, CSIRO Working Paper Series 2008–09, Canberra, Australia.

Weaver, C., Motion, J., & Roper, J. (2006). From propaganda to discourse (and back again): Truth, power, the public interest and PR. In L'Etang, J., & Pieczka, M. (Eds), *PR critical debates and contemporary practice*. Muhwah, NJ: Lawrence Erlbaum Associates.

Wolfsfeld, G. (2006). The Political Contest Model. In Cottle, S. (Ed.), *News, PR and power*. London: Sage Publications.

Zerfass, A. (2008). Corporate communication revisited: Integrating business strategy and strategic communication. In Zerfass, A., Van Ruler, B., & Sriramesh, K. (Eds), *PR research: European and international perspectives and innovations*. Wiesbaden VS: Verlag.

Part II
Orientations and reorientations

9

Extending PR's critical conversations with advertising and marketing

Clea D. Bourne

Advertising, marketing and public relations (PR) have experienced phenomenal occupational growth throughout the past century. In large, mature markets, particularly in Europe and North America, the three fields have emerged as separate specialisms, disciplines and professional projects. From the outside looking in, few might regard advertising, marketing and PR as necessarily *separate*. This is particularly so in small and emerging markets, where practitioners may operate flexibly across PR, advertising and marketing activity. Indeed, in an increasingly globalised and digital world, distinctions between advertising, marketing and PR are often blurred, perceived as part of the same set of advanced techniques in modern commercial culture.

From a critical perspective, advertising, marketing and PR can be seen collectively as a set of practices and discourses which have helped to constitute and shape modern social relations. Yet the evolution of the three fields as *separate* disciplines is an important subject for the critical lens. This is because the emergence of distinctions between the fields is a story of interprofessional tensions, as advertising, marketing and PR struggle for dominance over one another. Practitioners within the respective fields have also struggled to formalise their managerial status and establish themselves as trusted experts to client organisations.

Professional tensions between the fields are also visible in academic discourses, which have played an accompanying role in formalising advertising, marketing and PR techniques. Nearly 40 years ago, well-known marketing theorist, Philip Kotler, writing with Mindak (1978), questioned whether PR and marketing would evolve as "partners or rivals", critiquing a perceived lack of scientific discipline within the public relations field. A decade later, Kotler, together with other US marketing scholars, met their PR counterparts at a colloquium designed to mark out conceptual domains and "operational turf" between the PR and marketing disciplines (Broom, Lauzen & Tucker, 1991). Similarly, influential theorists in Critical Marketing are inclined to regard both advertising and PR as "aspects" or "sub-fields" of a general marketing discourse (Skålén, Fougère & Fellesson, 2008). I have myself encountered on the conference circuit, critical theorists from other fields who dismiss the very notion of "Critical PR"; arguing either that PR is merely part of advertising or marketing, and can only be critiqued as a subset of these activities, or that PR itself is so malodorous that critiquing PR activity would be unproductive, since PR ought not to exist.

My own critical efforts have no such cynical outlook, and are driven instead by a quest for new and more productive understandings of PR practices and techniques. My quest is informed by more than 20 years spent as a practitioner, working variously in advertising, marketing and PR. As an academic, I have also taught in each of the three fields. More recently, as convenor of a new postgraduate programme, I tasked myself with collating critical perspectives from three separate academic fields – Critical Advertising, Critical Marketing and Critical PR. In doing so, I have been struck by how much there is to learn about PR itself by exploring PR's disciplinary struggles with its nearest professional counterparts. If reconfiguring PR means changing its conversations (McKie & Munshi, 2007, p. 2), I believe that PR's conversations can be expanded, quite productively, by throwing open the windows that currently separate the three sets of critical literature. My objective in this chapter is, therefore, to cast advertising, marketing and PR as distinct professional projects, and to move directly to the points of tension and overlap in order to discern deeper understandings about PR itself by exploring the struggles of its closest professional neighbours.

Genesis of critique on advertising and marketing

Whereas Critical PR is only just emerging as an academic field, critical perspectives of advertising and marketing have existed since at least the 1970s. The trajectory of research has also differed; in part because advertising and marketing have often evolved in different university departments; in part, because the scholars who critique advertising and marketing wear their critical hats at different "angles". Scott (2007, p. 4) explains this by pointing to the different ways in which the term "critical" is construed across advertising and marketing literature. For some advertising and marketing scholars, for example, critical means "interpretive" or "qualitative"; while others wear their "Critical" with a capital "C", explicitly meaning "Marxist". Still others adopt a "critical" stance on larger social issues – such as globalisation or environmentalism – using advertising or marketing for socially progressive purposes. Finally, there are "critical" theorists who choose to resist more mainstream approaches to the study of advertising and marketing (Scott, 2007), a pursuit which chimes well with much existing Critical PR scholarship.

Earlier critical advertising and marketing work was dominated by literary critique, using semiotics, rhetoric, poststructuralism and postmodernism to deconstruct the *products* of advertising and marketing as forms of representation (Scott, 2007, p. 5). Some of this work, maintains Scott, has become canonical, including John Berger's (1973) *Ways of Seeing* and Judith Williamson's (1979) *Decoding Advertisements*. Williamson's classic, in particular, posited that consumers could not escape advertising's false meanings; that advertising had "a life of its own", persuading consumers to buy goods against their real class interests (Williamson, 1979, p. 13). These and many other authors offered an analytical gaze on the "pervasiveness of imagery in late twentieth-century culture" (Nava, 1997, p. 47). The combined perspectives resulting from this earlier work gave rise to a new sub-discipline, "cultural studies", typically housed in English departments or communications schools (Scott, 2007).

Cultural Studies explored the "culture industries" and processes of enculturation, taking in all those institutions and industries involved in some way with the production of popular culture (Ellis, Fitchett, Higgins, Jack, Lim, Saren & Tadajewski, 2011, p. 43). Advertising and marketing were positioned as a key site of negotiation between the economic and cultural spheres (Leiss, Klein, Jhally & Botterill, 2005, p. 15), with advertising and marketing practitioners cast as cultural intermediaries educating the masses in the pleasures of consumption (Willmott, 1999, p. 208). Other early critical scholarship adopted postmodernist perspectives, with successive studies focused on themes such as fragmentation of markets into ever-smaller segments, including supposed "one-to-one marketing"; hyperreality – exemplified by the many studies of shopping centres, fantasy worlds of theme parks; the "pretence" of typical service encounters in which customer service representatives deliver rote responses as they follow preordained scripts; and pastiche television commercials and display advertising represented by self-referentiality (Skålén et al., 2008, p. 10).

Some of these critical approaches proved both questionable and problematic. It became increasingly apparent that Cultural Studies was providing a way for many advertising and marketing academics to legitimise their discipline in relation to campus radicalism and the "culture wars" of the 1990s (Arvidsson, 2008). At the same time, some early critical advertising and marketing scholarship promoted Marxist political agendas, thinly disguised as research (Scott, 2007). Moreover, Cultural Studies was so often characterised by a "Critical" perspective that, by the 1990s, the two had become synonymous, and viewed by a new generation of critical theorists as too negative and despairing in tone, too dogmatic and proscriptive in approach (Scott, 2007).

Revisionist scholars (Arvidsson, 2008; Nava, 1997; Scott, 2007) argue that earlier critical work portrayed people primarily as "consumers", thus marginalising other subjectivities such as citizenship. Meanwhile, those same consumers – particularly women – were too often portrayed as weak, malleable and unable to resist so-called neoliberal ideologies imposed by the "marketing-media-branding complex" (Hackley, 2009). Early critical scholarship is also accused of focusing relentlessly on industrial capitalism as the major source of oppression, thus failing to encompass other forms of economic organisation, particularly in more traditional, agrarian societies. One exception to these revisionist critiques, concedes Scott (2007), may be the emancipatory efforts of Cultural Studies regarding cultural representations of women.

Leiss et al. (2005) further contend that earlier debates about advertising and marketing focused too greatly on their role in shaping individual consumer choices. By privileging consumer markets, and the most visible outputs and effects of advertising and marketing – such as display and television advertising – earlier critical work helped to mask a wide range of "hidden" techniques; from sales and marketing "control technologies" which are defined by their very invisibility – such as concealed microphones and cameras, or mystery shoppers – to disciplinary practices such as training, compensating and the setting of sales quotas, practices which are also invisible to the onlooker, thus never framed as forms of power (Skålén et al., 2008). (Similarities can be seen in critiques of PR scholarship, for its failure to delve deeply into hidden activity such as lobbying, focusing on more visible outputs such as media relations and corporate communications.) Likewise, B2B (business-to-business) marketing remained less visible and under-represented in earlier critical scholarship, even though B2B markets are generally larger with B2B, organisations trading more products and services than business-to-consumer (B2C) organisations (Ellis et al., 2011). What also remained hidden in earlier critical work were the everyday activities and techniques employed by advertising and marketing practitioners (Leiss et al., 2005; Lien, 1997), aided by the "invisible" history of these occupations where, in the absence of formal industry-wide training schemes and formalised knowledge, myth and oral history predominate (Lury, 1994).

Advertising, marketing and PR – assuaging producer anxiety

As critical perspectives of advertising and marketing have evolved, authors have increasingly unmasked the activity taking place "behind-the-scenes" of advertising and marketing work. These behind-the-scenes studies include explorations of efforts to professionalise the fields (Chalmers, 2001; Lien, 1997; Willmott, 1999). My objective here is to integrate some of this literature with similar discussions in Critical PR, and with broader sociological perspectives of professionalisation, to yield new understandings of all three fields vis-à-vis one another I begin by positioning advertising, marketing and PR as "entrepreneurial professions" or "expert labour" (Muzio, Ackroyd & Chanlat, 2008, p. 25). Entrepreneurial professions have borrowed several features from traditional professions such as medicine or law, but, as Muzio et al. (2008) point out, this is largely a symbolic exercise. Advertising, marketing and PR have neither the professional credentials nor other independent sources of knowledge, remaining largely open and governed by market mechanisms. Their professional associations are embryonic, with no mandatory membership or official credentials, and minimal special education is required to become a practitioner in any of the three fields (Muzio et al., 2008, p. 4).

As a result, *de facto* control over the advertising, marketing and PR professions is weak – deliberately so, argue Muzio et al. (2008), because entrepreneurial professions are highly responsive to the organisations and cultures they serve. Not only are such professions active in the construction of knowledge through their use of language and relations skills with client organisations, they are also continually developing *new* forms of knowledge together with different methods for its production, organisation and delivery, adopting "radically different strategies and organisational configurations" as needed (Muzio et al., 2008, p. 4). But why would promotional professions deliberately undermine their own professional projects in this way? One answer emerges in scholarship which personifies the corporate body, in order to highlight the anxiety levels which now plague the contemporary client organisation.

Writing about advertising and marketing, Lury and Warde (1997) contend that the constant shifting and changing in these professions has been in response to "producer anxiety or uncertainty" (p. 87). Organisations which seek out advertising and marketing counsel have a perpetual problem – that of finding sufficient consumers for the volume of goods they produce – knowing that they cannot force people to buy their products, services or ideas now or in the future (Lury & Warde, 1997). Any legitimacy possessed by the advertising and marketing professions has therefore evolved through practitioner efforts to assuage producer anxiety by promoting advertising and marketing as the appropriate disciplines for "guiding, controlling, influencing and predicting what consumers will be prepared to buy" (Lury & Warde, 1997, p. 92). Similarly, Marchand (1998) argues that an array of twentieth century PR initiatives was undertaken by client organisations in a quest to create a "corporate soul". Corporates were intent on legitimising newly amassed power, not just to others but to themselves. PR techniques were consequently used to assuage the anxiety of corporations keen to restore their social role in the eyes of the public, and to be accepted members of the larger community, by establishing the "rightness" of their expansion activities (Christensen, Morsing & Cheney, 2008; Marchand, 1998). Boyd (2012) even ascribes middle-class sensibilities and angst to modern corporations as a partial explanation for the growth of CSR activities, which are themselves often driven by PR techniques. Hence advertising, marketing and PR are located as part of a growing number of professions concerned with assuaging the anxiety of decision-makers concerned with "managing uncertainty, calculating probability and minimising risk" (Lury & Warde, 1997, p. 99).

Contemporary client organisations are therefore likely to resist professionalisation strategies (Lury & Warde, 1997) adopted by advertising, marketing and PR, stripping these forms of professional advice of their moral authority and recasting the fields as a technical resource or commodity that is subject to corporate needs (Lury & Warde, 1997; Muzio et al., 2008). Broadly speaking, organisations, regardless of whether they are in the private, public or not-for-profit sectors, are defined by the overarching need to produce reliable, stable alliances with their key stakeholders (Lien, 1997). The implications for advertising, marketing and PR's professional projects are stark. Whereas traditional professions are customarily understood to produce their own ideology, which in turn establishes their professional status and universal validity conferred via expertise (Larson, 2012), the combined critical literatures suggest that it is organisational ideology which has produced advertising, marketing and PR. This represents a "reverse" ordering of professionalisation, in which professional development is shaped not by the professions but by the organisations they serve (Muzio et al., 2008). As a result, advertising, marketing and PR are forced into a never-ending pursuit of legitimation strategies which will help them remain relevant to client organisations. This never-ending pursuit for relevance further defines the interprofessional tensions within and between the three promotional fields.

Advertising, marketing and PR – legitimation strategies

The contemporary anxieties "experienced" by client organisations are defined by a constant series of challenges – from entering new markets to holding on to customers in existing ones; from adopting new technologies and media channels to meeting new regulatory requirements. What then are the legitimation strategies developed by advertising, marketing and PR? And how successful have these strategies been in assuaging organisational anxieties? Across the promotional professions, a significant portion of the expertise is based on social capital, informal knowledge, soft skills and emotional labour, as well as formal, scientific and managerial knowledge more closely associated with professional influence.

The social capital underlying the promotional fields is complex. In Western Europe and North America, for example, the most powerful promotional roles tend to be white, male and middle class (Edwards, 2011; Lury, 1994; Nixon, 2003). Applicants to advertising, marketing and PR are, today, typically university-educated, but the type of degree is less important than the associated peer-group influence, since many promotional practitioners come to rely on their social networks for professional advancement. This is particularly true for consultancy-based practitioners for whom new business contacts are professional "currency". The "white, male, middle-class" profile is not replicated globally, of course, but what remains important is that the promotional professions should replicate, as far as possible, the social capital of their client organisations. For this reason, where diversity may have become an organisational imperative in some fields, for promotional professions, diversity in respect of gender, race or class is "useful" only insofar as it allows client organisations to engage better with external audiences (Edwards, 2011).

Informal knowledge is, of course, hard to pin down, in part because of deliberate efforts to separate personal knowledge from achievement of professional identity (Lien, 1997). Promotional practitioners bring a range of pertinent knowledge gleaned as citizens, consumers and other subjectivities to their daily tasks; yet as Lien (1997) argues, such competence remains largely invisible or unarticulated. Other forms of informal knowledge are elusive, known only to certain professionals. Advertising, for example, has engendered a "cult of creativity" and mythology of artistry-plus-genius – in which creative directors and art directors, typically male, have elite status and wield great influence (McStay, 2010: Nixon, 2003). Client organisations valorise creativity for its "newness", and its ability to break new boundaries and establish new genres (Nixon, 2003). Through creativity, advertising professionals (and to some extent PR and marketing) are able to assuage client anxiety by meeting the demand for ever-more sophisticated campaigns in highly competitive markets (Faulconbridge, Beverstock, Nativel & Taylor, 2011). The UK is just one country that has assigned economic value to creativity in public policy, with advertising a designated industry in the "creative economy", and London a designated centre of "creative excellence" (House of Commons, 2013; Nixon, 2003, p. 6). Yet advertising's supposed dominance over creativity may have infringed on PR territory in some contexts, since London's early emergence as a centre for industrial design in the 1950s was itself associated with the rise of UK public relations in the twentieth century (L'Etang, 2004). Contemporary debates in the PR trade press suggest that, in a battle for market share, global PR firms are recolonising marketing communications by reclaiming "creativity" as a public relations specialism – hiring creative directors and "creative catalysts", and entering creative competitions that were previously the domain of advertising (Rogers, 2014).

All three promotional professions rely heavily on soft skills such as communication. Lien (1997) points out that this is true of marketing, despite the profession's efforts to privilege its "hard" skill sets. For Lien (1997), marketing is communicative on two levels; first, by translating and interpreting consumers' needs and preferences; and second by selecting the characteristics of product (or service), then visualising and textualising these characteristics for target groups. Such soft skills are often part of emotional labour – that is, the management of "feeling" in the workplace (Hochschild, 2012). In PR, for example, Yeoman (2010, p. 6) points to the emotional labour of managing client relationships, earning trust and respect by "making the client happy". Many PR practitioners also cater to journalists as another important stakeholder group, where emotional labour involves "not upsetting or alienating" journalists, earning their trust and respect by not "wasting their time or sending them irrelevant press releases" (Yeoman, 2010, p. 6).

Scientific/managerial discourse

Despite the importance of informal knowledge, advertising, marketing and PR have all come to be dominated by a managerial discourse in which formal knowledge, and particularly scientific knowledge, confers most power (Hackley, 2009, p. 44). Scientific knowledge relies on credibility gained through the use of epistemology, the collation of facts and the application of scientific method (Willmott, 1999). The need to recast promotional work as scientific and managerial has come about, in part, due to a sense of intellectual inferiority experienced by those working within promotional professions (Lury & Warde, 1997), but also the need to vie for credibility against the claims of other, more established management disciplines such as accounting or operations. Promotional professionals therefore engage in a "Darwinian corporate game" (Pitcher, 2002, p. 62) to outdo each other in managerial and technical expertise.

Marketing has been particularly successful in systematising formal, technical knowledge, due perhaps to its "headstart". Marketing as an academic discipline itself evolved as a branch of applied economics concerned with the distribution of goods and buying behaviour (Hackley, 2009). Marketing then replaced the economists' assumption of "perfect information in competitive markets" with theories of advertising persuasion drawing from social psychology and other fields (Hackley, 2009, p. 117); while also adopting approaches from engineering and sales management (Skålén et al., 2008, p. 68). Concepts such as the Unique Selling Proposition, the "4Ps" – Product, Price, Place and Promotion (later extended to "7Ps") – market segmentation and Integrated Marketing Communication (IMC) became widely used terms that can be attributed to the success of marketing's managerial discourse. Such terms appeal to client organisations not just because they provide a well-defined, theorised set of practices but because of their inherent promise of progress and rationality (Christensen et al., 2008). Checklists such as the "4Ps" offer clients a sense of engineering precision from their marketing advisors. Meanwhile, other terms such as B2B, and CRM (Customer Relationship Management) have introduced further specialisation in marketing practice, creating new, distinct sub-fields of expertise. Some of these scientific methods will now be examined in further detail.

Market segmentation and surveillance

Perhaps the most powerful set of legitimation strategies used by promotional professions are those which manipulate stakeholders, producing subjectivities and binding targeted groups more tightly to organisations (Skålén et al., 2008). Segmentation and other forms of market surveillance, for example, employ researchers to produce contextualised knowledge regarding the sorts of products or services an organisation's customers want (Lury & Warde, 1997). By tracking and tracing consumers, market segmentation acts as a "vast panoptic system of observation and social control" (Brownlie, Saren, Wensley & Whittingham, 1999, p. 8). Methods of marketing surveillance have intensified dramatically since the widespread introduction of digital technologies in the promotional fields. Digital advertising is a prime example. Much of it is unbranded, like classified advertising, and based on algorithms which aim to engender relevance to the consumer (McStay, 2010). It is therefore "hidden" from view, unlike the more creative forms of display advertising which featured heavily as exemplars of visual representation in earlier Cultural Studies work. Dataveillance produced through advertising algorithms invoke Foucauldian views of discipline, argues McStay (2010), involving surveillance, individuation and behavioural correction, and creating docile bodies that are more powerful yet easier to direct and subjugate, because they are more calculable, thus "easier to know".

Relationship management paradigm

Also connected with surveillance techniques is relationship management, a parallel paradigm in public relations and marketing. As an orthodoxy, the relationship paradigm has defined the formalisation of the PR and marketing professions, particularly in *mature* markets. There, PR and marketing have been compelled not just to promote products, services, people or ideas to stakeholders as counterparts in an exchange, but to "engage" with stakeholders as long-term partners, even a "spouse" (Skålén et al., 2008 citing Gummeson, 2002); in the hope that resulting long-term relationships will secure profits and recognisable gain. The "relationship management" orthodoxy is further driven by the imperative to create value during the consumption of goods or services. In service-oriented firms, value creation is mutually created with the customer through long-term relationships (Skålén et al., 2008). The customer, or the key stakeholder, becomes the core of the organisation's strategic process. Any occupation which can govern this "ultimate organisational imperative"(Skålén et al., 2008) gains a strategic role within the firm through expertise on key stakeholder relations. For this reason, relationship marketing and relationship management have become important joint sources of power through which PR and marketing simultaneously "legitimise" their managerial expertise (Skålén et al., 2008). The "relationship" paradigm has contributed to ever-more "complex methods of observation" (Foucault, 1989 [1963]), a form of "gaze" over individuals and organisations. In marketing, the relationship paradigm has been coupled with technologies such as Customer Relationship Management systems. Similar forms of "gaze" are apparent in PR practice, where a plethora of indices and surveys are conducted by national and global PR consultancies in an effort to measure trust, goodwill and mutual understanding among key stakeholder groups (Bourne, 2013).

Managerial discourses in advertising, marketing and PR are replete with issues – the promotional fields are accused, for example, of an over-reliance on bad science, exaggerated or "made-up" metrics, and counterproductive scientism (Brownlie et al., 1999; Turow, 2011). Furthermore, managerial discourses are often gendered discourses, reproducing technical expertise as a central defining feature of the senior male professional's role, while relegating more routine tasks and much of the emotional labour to junior, often female, personnel (Chalmers, 2001). Ultimately, while managerial discourses may articulate promotional activity on behalf of large, complex organisations, they do not adequately express the nature of wide-ranging promotional activity undertaken on behalf of small, ephemeral or non-corporate entities such as activist groups or one-man bands (McKie & Munshi, 2007).

Globalising

The final legitimation strategy reviewed here is that of globalising, in which there is an ever-increasing reliance on advertising, marketing and PR to develop, spread and sustain new markets for products and services (Faulconbridge et al., 2011; Sriramesh & Verčič, 2007). The need to globalise markets as a means of assuaging corporate anxiety has changed the shape of the promotional industries. All three have experienced convergence, with an increasing number of national consultancies now acquired by large, global groups with phenomenal reach. Global communication firms have real clout with client organisations because they are in a position to employ *all* of the preceding legitimation strategies, whether formal or informal, on a global dimension, thus achieving efficiencies of scale. Global consultancies can also act quickly, offering campaigns and other services which mimic "just-in-time" manufacturing processes. A new advertising campaign can, for example, be tailored not just to specific reflexive consumers, but also to their "reactions and interpretations of recent global- or country- or region-specific events", with campaigns appearing almost immediately after key political and sporting mega-events, attempting to reflect consumer responses to them (Faulconbridge et al., 2011, p. 13).

Unsurprisingly, the globalising of promotional activity has been heavily criticised by critical scholars across advertising, marketing and PR (Leiss et al., 2005; McKie & Munshi, 2007; Witkowski, 2008), particularly since the promotional fields have provided strategies and tactics for spreading a "dominant world culture" via an "influx of ideas, values, products, and lifestyles from the rich countries", ultimately debasing developing countries' cultures (Witkowski, 2008, p. 220). Meanwhile, the success of global communication firms in exporting the "ideas, images, products, services and brands" of multinational organisations (Ellis et al., 2011, p. 221), only intensifies critiques of global advertising, marketing and PR as forms of cultural imperialism.

Struggles within and between the fields

The struggles within and between advertising, marketing and PR can be further seen within the context of broader professional struggles. Advertising has, for example, found it necessary to converge with or protect itself from specialisms such as media buying, web design and social media campaigning. The past 25 years have seen the rise of media buying agencies, together with an array of satellite companies which feed them technology and data (Turow, 2011). Whereas media buying was once a "backwater" of advertising, its hegemony over digital technologies has now closed this field of knowledge to those in the upper reaches of advertising who lack the technical knowledge or expertise to grasp the nature of this specialism (Turow, 2011). Digital media has also increased blurred lines between advertising and marketing, with websites providing an excellent example of convergence since they act as both web advertising as well as a "virtual shop window" for marketing activity (McStay, 2010, p. 116).

Whereas PR has "divorced" its professional project from that of fields such as journalism or advertising (McKie & Munshi, 2007, citing Toledano, 2005), PR has also struggled with colonisation by the marketing discipline, which increasingly includes activities traditionally ascribed to PR such as fostering and maintaining goodwill among relevant stakeholders (Christensen et al., 2008). Jurisdictional threats to PR also come from human resources, in-house legal counsel, investor relations and risk management professionals, all of whom are concerned with issues management and reputation management. More recently, the PR profession has itself pointed to management consultancy and professional services as the disciplines now in the best position to "eat PR's lunch" (PRCA, 2012). As with advertising's relationship with media buying, PR also struggles to maintain its professional identity against its own "hybrids". Corporate communications has, for example, established itself as a managerial vision that promises to establish and maintain a unified organisational identity by regulating and controlling *all* communicative activity, encapsulating not just PR, but advertising and marketing, as well as HR (Christensen et al., 2008).

Of the three fields, advertising and PR may encounter greater jurisdictional threats, but marketing is by far the greatest aggressor. This is perhaps unsurprising, since marketing discourses frequently explicate marketing as warfare through notions of "competition", "conquest" and the importance of "capturing market share" (Lien, 1997). Marketing's assertive approach has not only achieved greater success in *deepening* the field's expertise through scientific and managerial discourses, marketing has also increased status and influence by *broadening* its relevance and reach (Willmott, 1999). Whereas marketing initially emerged as a professional jurisdiction by "divorcing" itself from sales (Chalmers, 2001; Willmott, 1999), it has since gone on to contest other fields – not just advertising and PR – by reconstructing and stretching established definitions of marketing. The marketing concept has been universalised, extending from consumer markets to wholesale markets, as well as the public and not-for-profit sectors (Hackley, 2009). While within organisations, marketing's "exceptionalism" has thwarted the jurisdictional roles of accountants, engineers, HR managers and project managers (Eriksson, 1999; Willmott, 1999).

Marketing's efforts to "universalise" its expertise has meant that, particularly in service organisations, "everyone is a marketer now", with front-line employees considered part-time marketers, albeit with ill-defined marketing roles (Skålén et al., 2008). On the one hand, the concept of part-time marketer is "ingenious" according to Skålén et al. (2008), who argue that it resolves potential conflict between marketing and operational functions by rearticulating marketing as a "cross-functional dimension" rather than as a threat to, or replacement of, other functions (Skålén et al., 2008, p. 134). By contrast, Brownlie et al. (1999, p. 186) describe this universalising effect of marketing as a "bridge too far". The broader marketing becomes, they argue, the further it thrusts itself into domains "for which it is ill equipped", and the less exclusive is its expertise – a view which sounds a warning for other fields, including public relations.

Conclusion

This chapter has presented a sample of arguments from Critical Advertising and Critical Marketing scholarship, through which Critical PR as a discipline might contextualise its own emerging perspectives. It is useful, for example, to explore PR's professional project, not in isolation, but as part of a wide range of entrepreneurial professional projects constantly struggling to make themselves relevant to decision-makers. This helps to illuminate some of the questions that occupy PR scholars, such as the constantly evolving nature of PR definitions and expertise. An exploration of other bodies of critical literature further suggests that the ebbs and flows which constantly erode and reshape PR's jurisdiction and professional identity are by no means unique to the field.

Exploring the critical perspectives generated in other disciplines is also a reminder that PR scholarship must simultaneously embrace theory, including critical theory, while remaining suspicious of it (Maclaran & Stevens, 2008). Theory can not only broaden the development of Critical PR, it can skew perspectives as well: Critical PR scholars will no doubt want to guard against the sort of insularity which has defined certain areas of normative PR scholarship. Exploring Critical Advertising and Critical Marketing is also a reminder to Critical PR scholars that PR cannot solve *all* the problems that exist in organisations or societies, since contemporary organisations and cultures are diverse and different. Further bodies of critical work also serve as a cue to Critical PR scholars to guard against using their critical perspectives to "suppress, silence and devalue other theoretical voices" (Maclaran & Stevens, 2008, p. 347). The solution proposed by Maclaran and Stevens is one that Critical PR scholars arguably already apply; that is, engaging with and theorising the *human* side of PR, while constantly asking "Who is marginalised in our field?" and "Who does PR dominate or silence?"

References

Arvidsson, A. (2008). The function of cultural studies in marketing. In M. Tadajewski, & D. Brownlie (Eds), *Critical marketing: Issues in contemporary marketing*, pp. 329–44. Chichester, UK: Wiley & Sons.

Berger, J. (1973/2008). *Ways of seeing*. London, UK: Penguin Classics.

Bourne, C. (2013). Reframing trust, power and public relations in financial services. *Public Relations Inquiry*, 2(1), pp. 51–77.

Boyd, J. (2012). The corporation-as-middle-class-person: Corporate social responsibility and class. In D. Waymer (Ed.), *Culture, social class, and race in public relations*, pp. 45–55. Lanham, MD: Lexington Books.

Broom, G. M., Lauzen, M. M., & Tucker, K. (1991). Public relations and marketing: Dividing the conceptual domain and operational turf. *Public Relations Review*, 17(3), pp. 219–25.

Brownlie, D., Saren, M., Wensley, R., & Whittingham, R. (Eds). (1999). *Rethinking marketing: Towards critical marketing accountings*. London, UK: Sage Publications.

Chalmers, L. V. (2001). *Marketing masculinities*. Westport, CT: Greenwood Press.

Christensen, L. T., Morsing, M., & Cheney, G. (2008). *Corporate communications: Convention, complexity and critique*. London, UK: Sage Publications.

Edwards, L. (2011). Diversity in public relations. In L. Edwards, & C. Hodges (Eds), *Public relations, society and culture: Theoretical and empirical explorations*, pp. 75–89. Abingdon, UK: Routledge.

Ellis, N., Fitchett, J., Higgins, M., Jack, G., Lim, M., Saren, M., & Tadajewski, M. (2011). *Marketing: A critical textbook*. London, UK: Sage Publications.

Eriksson, P. (1999). The process of interprofessional competition. In D. Brownlie, M. Saren, R. Wensley, & R. Whittingham (Eds), *Rethinking marketing: Towards critical marketing accountings*, pp. 188–204. London, UK: Sage Publications.

Faulconbridge, J., Beaverstock, J. V., Nativel, C., & Taylor, P. J. (Eds), (2011). *The globalization of advertising*. Abingdon, UK: Routledge.

Foucault, M. (1989 [1963]). *The birth of the clinic*. Abingdon: Routledge Classics.

Gummesson, E. (2002). *Total relationship marketing*, 2nd edition. London: Butterworth-Heinemann.

Hackley, C. (2009). *Marketing: A critical introduction*. London: Sage Publications.

Hochschild, A. (2012). *The managed heart: Commercialization of human feeling*. Berkeley, CA: University of California Press.

House of Commons (2013). *Supporting the creative economy*, HC 674, 26 September, The Stationery Office.

Kotler, P., & Mindak, W. (1978). Marketing and public relations. *Journal of Marketing*, 42(4), pp. 13–20.

Larson, M. S. (2012). *The rise of professionalism: Monopolies of competence and sheltered markets*. Piscataway, NJ: Transaction Publishers.

Leiss, W., Klein, S., Jhally, S., & Botterill, J. (2005). *Social communication in advertising: Consumption in the mediated marketplace*. Abingdon, UK: Routledge.

L'Etang, J. (2004). *Public relations in Britain: A history of professional practice in the twentieth century*. Mahwah, NJ: Lawrence Erlbaum Associates.

Lien, M. E. (1997). *Marketing and modernity: An ethnography of marketing*. New York, NY: Bloomsbury Academic.

Lury, A. (1994). Advertising: Moving beyond the stereotypes. In R. Keat, N. Whitely, & N. Abercrombie (Eds), *The authority of the consumer*, pp. 84–93. London, UK: Routledge.

Lury, C., & Warde, A. (1997). Investments in the imaginary consumer. In M. Nava, A. Blake, I. MacRury, & B. Richards (Eds), *Buy this book: Studies in advertising and consumption*, pp. 87–102. London, UK: Routledge.

McKie, D., & Munshi, D. (2007). *Reconfiguring public relations: Ecology, equity, and enterprise*. Abingdon, UK: Routledge.

Maclaran, P., & Stevens, L. (2008). Thinking through theory. In M. Tadajewski, & D. Brownlie (Eds), *Critical marketing: Issues in contemporary marketing*, pp. 345–61. Chichester, UK: Wiley & Sons.

McStay, A. (2010). *Digital advertising*. London, UK: Palgrave Macmillan.

Marchand, R. (1998). *Creating the corporate soul: The rise of public relations and corporate imagery in American big business*. Berkeley, CA: The University of California Press.

Muzio, D., Ackroyd, S., & Chanlat, J.-F. (Eds). (2008). Introduction: Lawyers, doctors and business consultants. In D. Muzio, S. Ackroyd, & J.-F. Chanlat (Eds), *Redirections in the study of expert labour: Established professions and new expert occupations*, pp. 1–30. Basingstoke, UK: Palgrave Macmillan.

Nava, M. (1997). Framing advertising: Cultural analysis and the incrimination of visual texts. In M. Nava, A. Blake, I. MacRury, & B. Richards (Eds), *Buy this book: Studies in advertising and consumption*, pp. 34–50. London, UK: Routledge.

Nixon, S. (2003). *Advertising cultures*. London, UK: Sage Publications.

Pitcher, G. (2002). *The death of spin*. Chichester, UK: Wiley & Sons.

PRCA. (2012). *The future of the PR industry: Initial report*. London, UK: Public Relations Consultants Association.

Rogers, D. (2014). Cannes' crowning glory, *PR Week*, July–August, pp. 46–8.

Scott, L.M. (2007). Critical research in marketing: An armchair report. In M. Saren, P. Maclaran, C. Goulding, R. Elliott, A. Shankar, & M. Catterall (Eds), *Critical marketing: Defining the field*, pp. 3–17. Burlington, MA: Butterworth-Heinemann.

Skålén, P., Fougère, M., & Fellesson, M. (2008). *Marketing discourse: A critical perspective*. Abingdon, UK: Routledge.

Sriramesh, K., & Verčič, D. (2007). Introduction to this special section: The impact of globalization on public relations. *Public Relations Review*, 33, pp. 355–59.

Toledano, M. (2005). *Public relations in Israel: the evolution of public relations as a profession in Israel's changing political, socio-cultural and economic environment*. Unpublished thesis, University of Paris 8, France.

Turow, J. (2011). *The daily you: How the new advertising industry is defining your identity*. London, UK: Yale University Press.

Williamson, J. (1979). *Decoding advertisements*. London, UK: Marion Boyar.

Willmott, H. (1999). On the idolization of markets and the denigration of marketers. In D. Brownlie, M. Saren, R. Wensley, & R. Whittingham (Eds), *Rethinking marketing*, pp. 205–22. London: Sage Publications.

Witkowski, T. H. (2008). Antiglobal challenges to marketing in developing countries. In M. Tadajewski, & D. Brownlie (Eds), *Critical marketing: Issues in contemporary marketing*, pp. 211–44. Chichester, UK: Wiley & Sons.

Yeomans, L. (2010). Soft sell? Gendered experience of emotional labour in UK public relations firms. *PRism* 7(4), pp. 1–14. Retrieved from http//www.prismjournal.org

10

Public relations, the postcolonial *other* and the issue of asylum seekers

Jane Johnston

It's simple: they're different. Plus,
Illegals, they chose their fates:
There are words for it – human waste.
And the words for us?
> *(Australian poet Judith Rodriguez: 'There are no*
> *words for this', in Scott & Keneally, 2013, p. 205)*

Introduction

This chapter draws on postcolonial theory to examine how public relations is used to frame and perpetuate power imbalances within cultural, social and political settings. It examines how post-colonial concepts are embedded within the public and political discourse on asylum seekers in Australia, analysing the role of public relations in developing policies and practices which rely on deeply ingrained attitudes of nationalism and sovereignty. Drawing on the work of Edward Said, in particular his analysis of the Middle East and the plight of Muslims in the West, it examines the treatment of asylum seekers within a neoliberal context, developing the themes of nationalism, sovereignty and the concept of the *other* to create a deeper understanding of this contemporary issue; and it echoes in the words from Australian poet Judith Rodriquez above. This critical study considers how asylum seekers, as subaltern and marginalised people, are caught within the liminal space between their own countries and the country in which they seek refuge, with little or no opportunity to voice their case for asylum. Dutta (2011, p. 11) suggests how "silence" within the subaltern sectors in neo-liberal policy structures is deeply intertwined with marginalising policies. The "silence" which surrounds asylum seekers, the policies of exclusion and the discursive practices that accompany them, along with sites of local, national and international resistance that have emerged in response, are each examined within this chapter.

Australia's own Human Rights Commission (AHRC) (2013, p. 3) notes that "Australia maintains one of the most restrictive immigration detention systems in the world. It is mandatory, not time limited, and people are not able to challenge the need for their detention in a court of law." Underpinning this policy is the discourse that drives the key messages to the Australian people, described as a "fraught, distorted war of words" (Scott & Keneally, 2013, back cover). Government public relations and communications specialists are among those who have been targeted for purposefully creating a sense of "them and us" through this discourse, positioning asylum seekers as *others*: queue jumpers, terrorists and fraudsters. Two of Australia's most respected contemporary authors, Rosie Scott and Tom Keneally (2013, p. 1) call this a "storm of venom and cliché", arguing:

> The language of this discussion has been debased to such an extent that spin-doctor flacks and people on the extremist fringes of Australian politics are largely responsible for the tone and direction of one of the central moral issues of our time.

As far back as 2002, the United Nations criticised the Australian government for vilifying those seeking asylum, urging improved accuracy and up-to-date information on asylum seekers "based on facts rather than negative stereotyping" (UN, 2002). More than a decade later the United Nations High Commissioner for Refugees (UNHCR) again reaffirmed this call (UNHCR, 2014). The UN is joined by Amnesty International, Human Rights Watch and no less than 200 Australian non-government and community groups (Refugee Council of Australia, 2014), plus thousands of individuals like Scott and Keneally to condemn the exclusionary and restrictive nature of these migration practices and the discursive practices that surround them.

Not since Australia's "White Australia Policy" during the early part of the twentieth century has the Australian government shown such resistance to entry from non-Anglo nations. According to the AHRC, the top five countries whose nationals sought asylum in Australia in 2012 (arriving by boat without a valid visa) were Afghanistan, Pakistan, Iran, Iraq and Sri Lanka (AHRC 2013); their dominant religion, Islam. Briskman (2011) points out that almost half of the world's 16 million refugees come from Muslim countries. Cultural disquiet about this religion and related migration policies have been likened to Australia's fear of Jews in the 1940s. As one of Australia's foremost political commentators notes: "Jews then. Muslims today. We should learn from this moment in our history: not to exploit fear of refugees; not to toss decency overboard into the cesspit of racism" (Adams, 2009, p. 6). One British study describes this as "Islamophobia" (Runnymede Trust, 1997, p. 4): an unfounded hostility toward Islam, and the discrimination and exclusion that results from it. It is therefore highly appropriate that Said's work should be used as a framework for this chapter's critique, given that much of his writing incorporated a focus on challenges for Muslims in Western society.

Postcoloniality, public relations and the *other*

This chapter draws together three problematised fields, notably postcolonialism, public relations and asylum seekers. Each is complex in its own right and, collectively, they provide many varied and interweaving strands of thought. The common link to them all is the concept of the *other* which, as we will see, describes those who do not fit with a particular worldview. Following McKie and Munshi (2007) and Curtin and Gaither (2012) the chapter covers a range of interconnected themes incorporating subaltern culture, cosmopolitanism, sovereignty and nationalism. These all strike at the centre of the Australian asylum seeker policy – "Operation Sovereign Borders" – which will be examined in the second part of the chapter.

While postcolonialism is variously defined, Amoko (2006) outlines it as the study of "the history and legacy of colonialism from the disciplinary perspectives of literature and culture" (p. 133). Postcolonial theory is commonly associated with Edward Said, initially his work *Orientalism* (1978), written as a critique of the discursive production of the Orient in Western scholarship. His work later expanded the critique of culture, imperialism and nationalism to the Palestinian struggle and Islam more broadly within the global context (see, for example, 1981, 1993, 1994, 2000). Kennedy (2013) explains that this latter portion of Said's critique looks squarely at the "Arabo-Islamic world and its relationship with and representation by the west" (p. 1); it is this perspective that is particularly useful for analysing the phenomenon of modern day asylum seekers. The concept of the *other* has been used to analyse issues of social and cultural exclusion on both a global level and within national or continental borders. Said (1978) called it "the act of emphasizing the perceived weaknesses of marginalized groups as a way of stressing the alleged strength of those in positions of power" (p. 5). For Said (1981), these people are scapegoats "for everything we do not happen to like in the world's new social, political and economic patterns" (p. xv). Other scholars have considered this issue in Canada (Moss, 2003) Britain (Weedon, 2004) and New Zealand (Drichel, 2007) in research which has examined how subaltern or marginalised groups who constitute the *other* are represented pejoratively within national narratives, often in order to enhance border security and keep boundaries safe; or within borders, as people who are excluded from the mainstream.

Huggan (1997) notes that the prefix "post" should not imply that the colonial era is over. Moreover, postcolonialism has arisen "*to account* for neo-colonialism, for continuing modes of imperialist thought and action across much of the contemporary world" (p. 22, his emphasis). Similarly Dutta (2011) couples colonialism and neocolonialism under postcolonial theory in exploring the intersections of discursive representation, economic interests and forms of control. This clarification is important for this chapter, which includes colonialism and neocolonialism within its understanding of postcolonialism and the examination of a contemporary global issue.

In seeking paradigms and parameters for reading global culture (Amoko 2006) a postcolonial approach sits comfortably within critical public relations scholarship, which has for some time demanded greater attention to non-Western approaches and insights, as well as deeper critiques of public relations power roles (L'Etang & Pieczka 1996, 2006; McKie & Munshi 2007; Sriramesh 2002;,Sriramesh & Verčič, 2009; Weaver, Motion & Roper 2006). As McKie and Munshi (2007) observe: "Understanding the link between old colonist agendas and the modern-day neo-colonist strategies is central to the process of decolonising PR" (p. 62). Though postcolonial theory gained prominence in the 1970s, it was not until the mid-2000s that it came to the attention of public relations scholars as a means of critical reflection on the role of cultural communication, interpretation and information management by dominant hegemonies within the global environment (Curtin & Gaither, 2012); Dutta & Pal, 2011; McKie & Munshi, 2007). The relatively late engagement with this theory is somewhat surprising given its axiomatic fit and neat application to public relations' intersections with cultural and political knowledge and practice. In their recent treatise on the links between the two, Curtin and Gaither (2012) identify public relations as "a powerful hegemonic tool to secure [governments'] legitimacy and set the global agenda" (p. 318). As this chapter will show, public relations' role in establishing the asylum seeker discourse aptly illustrates Curtin and Gaither's position.

Nationalism, cosmopolitanism and sovereignty

It is important at this juncture to consider two competing but fundamental elements of postcolonial thinking that provide a foundation for better understanding the asylum seeker issue: nationalism and cosmopolitanism. Nationalism has been called "the strongest and most emotional of the world's ideologies" (Roskin & Berry, 2007, p. 118). While there are many definitions for it, this chapter finds a useful one as: "a people's sense of identity and unity, often exaggerated and focussed on foreigners" (Roskin & Berry, 2007, p. 118). Dutta (2011) argues that the nation state is "the vital entry point for the enactment of hegemonic discourses" (p. 6) in postcolonial thinking. And others confirm that nationalistic discourses relegate falsehood and inferiority to outsiders, using language of national pride, collective sentiments and group passions to exacerbate difference (Rao, 2010). These essentialist approaches to nationalism, forged through cultural stereotyping, myth-making, nation-building and branding, reinforce the "them" and "us" approach that enables the *other* to exist. They represent what Curtin and Gaither (2007) call "binary oppositions of identity" (p. 175), a concept that is epitomised in Said's division between the Middle East and the West.

But Said's approach to the Middle East also presents what Rao (2010) calls a "Saidian paradox" (p. 128) because of a tension which exists between the equally important, but often conflicting positions of nationalism and cosmopolitanism. In contrast to nationalism, cosmopolitanism considers individuals as the ultimate unit of moral and political concern, with individuals all of equal importance, irrespective of their nationality. This approach suggests that boundaries are not significant in themselves, but become so if they are of significance to individuals. Cosmopolitanism also suggests that government policies should weigh up the position of *all* individuals who might be affected, even those beyond a nation's borders (Rao, 2010, p. 5). Nationalism thus sits in tension with cosmopolitanism, as nationalism's legitimacy is based on "the sovereignty of a cultural or historically distinctive people in a polity that expresses and protects those distinctive characteristics" (Snyder, 2012, p. 146). Briskman (2011) notes how in Australia, throughout the history of white settlement, and now relating to asylum seekers, a nationalistic approach has been focused on enforcing sameness, repressing diversity and diminishing the rights of those seen as outsiders.

The concept of sovereignty, the cornerstone of the "Operation Sovereign Borders" policy, is a political manifestation of nationalism. Sovereignty is defined as "the right of individual states to determine for themselves the policies they will follow" (Shimko, 2013, p. 6). Thomas Hobbes, in his seventeenth century work *Leviathan*, argued that under a strong central government citizens have a "social contract", surrendering individual rights for other benefits including protection from the state (Tétreault & Lipschutz, 2005, p. 2). This idea is fundamental to the concept of "positive sovereignty", which is seen as a state's capacity to enforce its authority throughout its territory (p. 85). Devadas and Prentice (2007) suggest that in the contemporary global environment "a new form of sovereignty is manifesting itself". They cite the "violence of the Australian and American nation-state against asylum-seekers, refugees, migrants (legal and illegal); the building of fences along the United States border with Mexico; [and] the killing of Muslims and Hindus in the Indian subcontinent in the name of the nation" as examples.

Such approaches to sovereignty and border protection leave some people more likely to be excluded than others. Skilled workers and those with money are usually welcome across international borders – not so the poor, unskilled, or those from subaltern groups. Curtin and Gaither (2012) point out that people from low income postcolonial nations are more likely to face immigration restrictions when trying to migrate to richer countries. They are also more likely to be subject to search or arrest. "The wealthy have no problems crossing borders: they and their money are welcome everywhere" (Tétreault & Lipschutz, 2005, p. 98). However, lack of wealth is not the sole obstacle to border access; as the asylum seeker analysis illustrates, patterns of ethnic and religious exclusion are also apparent.

Charlesworth (1999) suggests that Australian sovereignty needs to have a clearer understanding of its place in the world and a greater focus on human rights. She argues that national laws which celebrate sovereignty, particularity, self-sufficiency and isolation must, in the twenty-first century, be considered alongside international laws which look beyond the individual polity. In arguing for an "enhanced citizen sovereignty", Charlesworth (1999) calls on Australia to develop a more contemporary approach to sovereignty, one which takes greater account of its place in the international environment and is less inward-looking. This legal argument finds common ground with the cultural understanding expressed in the Saidian paradox – one which accepts a duality of cosmopolitanism and nationalism.

Asylum seekers as *others*

There are two key elements of the current Australian asylum seeker policy that deserve close attention as they relate to public relations, communication practice and information management. The first is the development of the specific discourse, including the rhetorical devices and narrative construction that position asylum seekers as *other*. Such political discourse establishes certain "truths" about asylum seekers in the minds of the citizenry, in a process that perpetuates power imbalances and reduces the legitimacy of individuals and groups in society, thus positioning them as *other*. Michel Foucault (1984) argues that the role of discourse can be both strategic and controlling: "It is in discourse that power and knowledge are joined together" (p. 100). Importantly, while discourse regimes not only govern what is said, they can also exclude or prohibit certain language, controlling "what can be known" (Malpas & Wake, 2006, p. 175). The second part of the policy that demands consideration is the lack of information made available to the media and the wider community, controlled and managed via media briefing sessions and restrictions placed on media access to asylum seekers living on temporary protection visas and within detention centres.

The first element, the development of the government asylum seeker discourse, was to reach a crescendo in mid-2013 when Australia's conservative party, the Liberal-National coalition (then in opposition, now in government) launched its "Operation Sovereign Borders" (OSB) policy. The policy (Liberal-National Coalition, 2013) argued: "border protection crisis [is] a national emergency", and highlighted this in a campaign which centred around key messages of "stop the boats", "combat people smuggling", "protect our borders", "military-led response", "queue-jumpers" and other emotionally charged language. Ultimately, the government argued that its election win in September 2013 included a mandate to "stop the boats", but as one commentator noted, policies by both major parties – the Liberal-National coalition and the Labour Party – were equally as unpalatable: "So at last we are being offered a real choice on asylum seekers by the two major parties: dumb and dumber" (Manderson, 2013). Human Rights Watch (2013) affirmed the bilateral government position by noting how successive governments engaged in scare-mongering politics at the expense of the rights of asylum seekers and refugees (p. 292).

"Operation Sovereign Borders" followed more than a decade of fear-inducing language about asylum seekers. In 1999, then immigration minister Phillip Ruddock, with the previous conservative government, captured news headlines by saying that Australia faced a national emergency because whole villages were packing up in the Middle East to flood into Australia (Briskman, 2011). Two years later the government found itself at the centre of a major international controversy relating to claims that a boatload of asylum seekers en route to Australia threw their children overboard. Ruddock announced that "a number of children had been thrown overboard" from a vessel suspected of being an "illegal entry vessel" (Cook, 2002, p. xxi). What was to become known as the "Children Overboard" scandal saw a subsequent government inquiry finding the claims to be false. The report summed up the capacity for a government to incite fear and condemnation of asylum seekers and how this was tied to notions of sovereignty and nationalism:

The peculiar sensitivity associated with the claim that children had been thrown overboard was that it was made at the beginning of, and sustained throughout, a Federal election campaign, during which "border protection" and national security were key issues. That asylum seekers trying to enter Australia by boat were the kinds of people who would throw their children overboard was used by the Government to demonise them as part of the argument for the need for a "tough" stand against external threats and in favour of "putting Australia's interests first."

(Cook, 2002, p. xxi)

The events of 11 September 2001 in the US followed soon after, and with them came heightened claims of threats to national safety and security and the opportunity for the government to further exploit the international hysteria of the time. As Briskman (2011) points out, once political fear is established, governments can manipulate that response to achieve political aims. "They will often use propaganda and the media to communicate risk to their populations in order to gain public support for policies by appealing to public fears" (p. 3). Weedon (2004) argues that the post 9/11 "Islamophobia" which gained momentum at the same time as Muslim fundamentalism, compounded the *othering* of Islam by the West creating "monolithic images" (p. 141) and ideas of an oppressive religion. The information about asylum seekers from the government and the media, in turn, assumes an aura of authenticity, resulting in groups being defined on the basis of these attributes, thus rationalising and normalising their discriminatory treatment (Briskman, 2011). Indeed, the development of this calculated discourse was to see quite specific positioning of those seeking asylum. In October 2013, shortly after the new government came to office, the Australian media reported that the new immigration minister, Scott Morrison, had instructed his department and detention centre staff to change their terminology from the previous government's description of "irregular maritime arrivals" to "illegal maritime arrivals"; and from "clients" to "detainees". Another popular part of the rhetoric was the adoption of the word "transferees", used to describe people en route to offshore detention centres. Such words dehumanise asylum seekers, described by one critic as "language-by-manipulation" (Hardaker, 2013). Award-winning journalist, linguist and Middle East expert David Hardaker (2013) has been highly critical of the government's choice of words: "It all starts, of course, with the objectification of a population. The technique of turning people into objects is propaganda 101 [basic propaganda]. If we don't think we are dealing with people then horrible actions become that much easier to commit."

The government, however, was to remain unrepentant in its use of such language. Morrison (2013) responded to criticisms by noting "our language calls it as we see it. We are not going to soften our language to condone illegal entry to Australia by boat".

The second element of the current asylum seeker policy which deserves scrutiny is the change in the way the government released information. Once in power, the new government ceased delivering ad hoc press conferences and notifications relating to boat arrivals and other asylum seeker news, scheduling instead once-weekly press conferences – effectively introducing a very strategic and curtailed line of information to the media. Not surprisingly, this was widely criticised as propagandist, with one political cartoon illustrating three placards: "Stop the boats", "Stop the people Smugglers", "Stop the Truth" (Moir, cited in Haigh, 2013). Former diplomat-turned-media-commentator Bruce Haigh (2013) noted: "State-imposed secrecy, with respect to managing minorities, dissidents or groups judged to be antithetical to the interests of the ruling elite, leads to oppression through lack of accountability."

Again, the government defended its position, this time focusing on its information black-outs and media restrictions, but also identifying its position in keeping asylum seekers uninformed.

We are not going to reveal the posture of our border protection assets at sea, by revealing the time, place and intercepting vessel as the previous government did....Nor are we going to provide open access to centres for media as not only does this raise false hopes among detainees who believe media coverage of their plight will change the outcome of their case, but also can encourage non-compliant behaviour [by asylum seekers].

(Morrison, 2013)

Public relations' complicity

While public relations and communication departments are clearly not singularly responsible for either the marginalisation of these people or the public access restrictions, connections between the developed discourse and information management are all too obvious. Public relations' capacity for developing and communicating a certain position within popular narratives has been key to the development of a now widely accepted discourse across Australia, and across political parties. Dutta and Pal (2011) call these "public relations practices that manufacture, reproduce, and circulate symbolic representations and interpretive frames that carry out...agendas" (p. 195).

In a scathing critique of the way the Australian government has handled the communication about asylum seekers, Hardaker (2013) is highly critical of government public relations, arguing that the profession is pandering to "suspicion and bigotry which is being manipulated and forged into hatred by wordsmiths on the government payroll". He further claims: "It's a practice of the black art of propaganda which is despicable and verges on evil. It comes from those clever enough to know the power of language to manipulate and immoral enough to care little of the consequences". Hardaker (2013) raises issues of nationalism, sovereignty and neocolonialism, castigating those who have created and perpetuated this version of the truth beyond the sympathies of the Australian public:

The authors of the phrasing will no doubt have a hundred ways to justify it. "Protecting Australia" will be among them. But those who play with words for a living know the dark side of their patriotic message....The masterstroke is to now erase the idea of "asylum seekers" altogether.

A counter-narrative

Dutta (2011, p. 19) notes that social change can occur at the local level while simultaneously having an effect on the national and global political environment. Such a response has been described in critical scholarship as "the informally mobilized body of non-government discursive opinion, that can serve as a counterweight to the state" (Outhwaite, 1994, p. 483). Indeed, as indicated earlier, a groundswell of public opinion has emerged in resistance to the discursive practices of the government. Accordingly, as the government has escalated its position on asylum seekers, so too has the counter-narrative, illustrating the power of the collective response. Hardaker (2013), cited above, is joined by a raft of other media commentators, journalists, academics, authors, and church, community and activist groups (e.g., Haigh, 2013; Mogelson, 2013; Scott & Keneally, 2013; Tsiolkas, 2013) who have not only loudly and openly expressed condemnation for the asylum seeker policies and the discursive practices associated with them, but have provided compelling alternative counter-points. Award-winning author Christos Tsiolkas (2013), for example, drew on cosmopolitanism and nationalism: "The reality is that there isn't 'one nation' that makes up Australia, only competing notions of 'nationhood'....Asylum seeker rights are easily understood and supported by cosmopolitan Australians." Tsiolkas thus also supports the concept of the "Saidian paradox", the idea of nationhood or nationalism co-existing with cosmopolitanism, arguing that the Australian citizenry is capable of this.

Likewise, the national broadcaster, the Australian Broadcasting Corporation (ABC) has challenged the government's position on this asylum seeker issue which has, in turn, brought charges that the broadcaster is unpatriotic. Former head of the ABC, David Hill, was quick to defend its independence: "The inference to be drawn from this is that patriotism should now become part of the ABC editorial responsibility and the ABC should deny the public access to news and information" (Hill, 2014).

This counter-narrative which sits in opposition to the government has provided a potent voice for the asylum seeker *other* both through institutional voices such as churches and the United Nations, as well as activists, public interest groups and concerned individuals. At the same time as the Australian government was rolling out "Operation Sovereign Borders" in 2013, an eight-metre-tall banner was erected in one of the country's largest cities, calling on Australians to "fully welcome refugees". The banner, hung outside St Paul's Cathedral in Melbourne's CBD, was in stark contrast to the official government "Stop the boats" mantra. In imploring the country to embrace asylum seekers, the Dean of Melbourne, Rev. Andreas Loewe (2013) explained how Australia was alone among the signatory nations to the United Nations Convention on Refugees in denying people asylum based on their mode of arrival.

Meanwhile, one of the most damning critiques of the OSB policy was expressed in the 2014 report from the international NGO, Human Rights Watch, which was highly critical of the politicising and scare-mongering of the asylum seeker issue "at the expense of the rights of asylum seekers and refugees" (Human Rights Watch, 2013, p. 292). Likewise, the Australian Human Rights Commission (AHRC) expressed major concerns about Australia's treatment of asylum seekers, noting that "The United Nations Human Rights Committee has repeatedly found Australia to be in breach of its international obligations" (AHRC, 2012).

Neocolonialism in the Pacific

A fundamental pillar of the Australian government's position on asylum seekers lies in its offshore detention and relocation programme. While it is unequivocal in its policy of no-settlement on its *own* shores – with its Customs and Border Protection website reading: NO WAY YOU WILL NOT MAKE AUSTRALIA HOME – it has negotiated with two poor Pacific neighbouring islands, Nauru and Manus Island (in Papua New Guinea) to house its offshore detention centres and relocation sites. At the very least, this presents issues relating to the unequal power balance between these islands and Australia.

The two islands have much in common: Nauru has a population of just 9,000 people, Manus Island 10,000; both house detention centres with capacities of around 1,500 people; and, importantly, both are heavily dependent on Australia for international aid. The management of these centres is outsourced to multinational companies, in a process described as "vulture capitalism at its worst" (Loewenstein, 2013). To date both islands' detention centres have been mired by riots, claims of human rights abuses and instances of self-harm, reports of rape and attempted suicides, and severe restrictions on media access and claims of censorship (AHRC, 2013; Duncan, 2013; Loewenstein, 2013). In March 2014 one man was killed and 70 were injured on Manus Island following a riot. The incident followed months of commentary about the potential for disaster and tragedy, with one commentator noting six months before the riot: "[I]t is hard to see the Nauru and Manus Island ventures becoming anything but a complete debacle" (Duncan, 2013, p. 3).

The Australian government's most recent "solution", has been to move the asylum seekers housed in these Pacific Islands further afield: this time to the south-east Asian country of

Cambodia. Amid further claims of secrecy, the deal with Cambodia was described as "shameful and illegal" by that country's Centre for Human Rights (Ou, in ABC 2014). Critics argue that Cambodia is not equipped with the infrastructure to resettle refugees, nor does it possess health and education services to assist them. As Duncan (2013) notes:

> Under the Refugee Convention, Australia is not required to settle all refugees in our own country, but ensure that if refugees go to a third country they are treated well, with reasonable security and support. If all nations simply pushed asylum seekers and refugees out to other countries, particularly very poor ones, the whole Refugee Convention would collapse.
>
> *(p. 3)*

Stringer (2007) describes neocolonialism as "a moment in which the objectives, relations and effects of the colonial syndrome do not merely reverberate but resurge" (para. 7). Such a reverberation and resurgence is manifest in these detention and relocation programmes, described as "solutions". The Australian government's increasing use of these countries to process and manage its part in this international crisis, and the discourse and information management that has accompanied it, has simply compounded the hegemonic, postcolonial position by shifting the problem offshore.

Conclusion

Said argued for criticism and a critical consciousness that should take account of "the realities of power and authority as well as those of resistance" (Kennedy, 2013, p. 10). In the case of asylum seekers in Australia, the voices of the powerful have been dominant and strategic, while potent voices of resistance have taken up the plight of the *other*. Kennedy (2013) points out that Said's theory of postcolonialism was premised on enabling such criticism, thereby creating awareness within society: "For him, it is one of the functions of the intellectual in the wider world to work toward this change in reality and awareness" (p. 11). It seems fitting, therefore, that Said's critical position and explanations of the *other* should provide a foundation for the examination of such an important international issue. In doing so, this chapter provides a prism for illuminating the power relationships between the hegemony and the marginalised asylum seekers, together with the strategic discourses of nationalism and sovereignty, and the counter-narratives that have emerged.

Scholars in public relations are increasingly calling for alternative (Demetrious, 2013; McKie & Munshi, 2007) and negotiated (Curtin & Gaither, 2012) positions, which break free from the dominance of strategic discursive practices of powerful organisations and governments. Said's approach to critical scholarship affirms this need: "[T]he intellectual should not be seduced by power or official approval, but should remain unco-opted if not uncommitted, ready to challenge" (Kennedy, 2013, p. 3). Such an approach is consistent with Charlesworth's (1999) and Tsiolkas's (2013) call for an "enhanced citizen sovereignty" which enables the voices of weaker players in the world system and encompasses a more cosmopolitan understanding of *others* in a national context. As the chapter has shown, alternative responses have emerged from many sectors. Rev. Loewe says St Paul's Cathedral will continue to fly its eight metre banner until Australia changes its asylum seeker policies (Loewe, 2014): "I am convinced that future generations of Australians will judge this policy for what it is: inhumane to those seeking our protection, and demeaning to Australia as a nation." Words and actions such as this, enabled by both public relations practitioners and other outspoken individuals which challenge the prevailing discourse, illustrate Dutta's (2011) notion that tensions between government power bases and the resistance that seeks to transform structures of injustice and inequality are inevitable. Public relations, therefore, has a role within both sides of this complex international issue: through the government discourses that serve certain ends, and by the rhizomic community responses that emerge as the counter-narrative. Whether resistance, and these voices of protest, will continue to gain traction, and whether this will provide sufficient impetus for social and political change, remains to be seen.

References

Adams, P. (2009, 14–15 November). Don't forget the war, *Weekend Australian Magazine*, p. 6.

AHRC (Australian Human Rights Commission). (2012). Asylum seekers, refugees and human rights - Snapshot Report. Retrieved from https://www.humanrights.gov.au/publications/asylum-seekers-refugees-and-human-rights-snapshot-report

Amoko, A. (2006). Race and postcoloniality. In S. Malpas, & P. Wake (Eds), *Routledge companion to critical theory*. London, UK: Routledge.

Australian Broadcasting Corporation (2014, September 26) Human rights groups describe Cambodia deal as shameful. Retrieved on 13 April 2015 from http://www.abc.net.au/news/2014-09-25/cambodia-asylum-seeker-deal-shameful-human-rights-group/5767810

Australian Human Rights Commission (2013). Asylum seekers, refugees and human rights – snapshot report. Retrieved on 13 April 2015 from https://www.humanrights.gov.au/publications/asylum-seekers-refugees-and-human-rights-snapshot-report

Briskman, L. (2011, April). Fear of the other: asylum seekers, religion and culture. Multi-Faith Centre, Griffith University Multifaith Centre. Retrieved on 13 April 2015 from http://blogs.curtin.edu.au/human-rights-education/wp-content/uploads/sites/15/2011/05/Multifaith-Centre-Briskman-2011.pdf

Cook, P. (2002). *A select committee on a certain maritime incident* (Children Overboard Report), Commonwealth of Australia. Retrieved on 13 April 2015 from http://www.aph.gov.au/binaries/senate/committee/maritime_incident_ctte/report/report.pdf

Charlesworth, H. (1999). *Globalisation, the law and Australian sovereignty: Dangerous liaisons* (Papers in Parliament, No. 33). Retrieved on 13 April 2015 from http://www.aph.gov.au/About_Parliament/Senate/Research_and_Education/pops/pop33/charlesworth

Curtin, P. A., & Gaither, T. K. (2007). *International public relations: Negotiating culture, identity, and power.* Thousand Oaks, CA: Sage Publications.

Curtin, P., & Gaither, K. (2012). *Globalization and public relations in postcolonial nations: Challenges and opportunities.* Amherst, NY: Cambria Press.

Demetrious, K. (2013). *Public relations, activism, and social change: Speaking up.* London, UK: Routledge.

Devadas, V., & Prentice C. (2007). Editorial: Postcolonial politics, *Borderlands e-journal*, 6(2). Retrieved on 13 April 2015 from http://www.borderlands.net.au/vol6no2_2007/device_editorial.htm

Drichel, S. (2007). Of political bottom lines and last ethical frontiers: The politics and ethics of "the Other", *Borderlands e-journal*, 6(2). Retrieved on 13 April 2015 from http://www.borderlands.net.au/vol6no2_2007/drichel_other.htm

Duncan, B. (2013). Asylum seekers: breakthrough or debacle? *Social Policy Connections.* Retrieved 13 April 2015 from http://gallery.mailchimp.com/8125f451e8c2734b5c5d00eb3/files/bduncan_asylum_seekers_aug13.2.pdf?ct=t(SPC_New

Dutta, M. (2011). *Communicating social change: Structure, culture and agency.* New York, NY: Routledge.

Dutta, M., & Pal, M. (2011). Public relations and marginalisation in a global context: A postcolonial critique. In N. Bardham, & K. Weaver (Eds), *Public relations in a global cultural context: Multi-paradigmatic perspectives*, pp. 195–226. New York, NY: Routledge.

Foucault, M. (1984). *The history of sexuality, vol 1: An introduction* (R. Hurley, Trans.). Harmondsworth, UK: Penguin.

Haigh, B. (2013, 15 November). Scott Morrison's no-show-and-tell on asylum seekers is already starting to unravel. *Canberra Times*. Retrieved on 13 April 2015 from http://www.canberratimes.com.au/comment/scott-morrisons-noshowandtell-on-asylum-seekers-is-already-starting-to-unravel-20131114-2xjkx.html#ixzz2vF2v0APi

J. Johnston

Hardaker, D. (2013, 22 July). Stop the boats? Stop the propaganda, *The Drum*, ABC. Retrieved from http://www.abc.net.au/news/2013-07-22/hardaker-stop-the-propaganda/4835328

Hill, D. (2014, 31 January). Patriotism lies in unbiased journalism not in censorship, Mr Abbott. Comment, *Sydney Morning Herald*. Retrieved on 13 April 2015 from http://www.smh.com.au/comment/patriotism-lies-in-unbiased-journalism-not-in-censorship-mr-abbott-20140130-31p9t.html#ixzz2vcp75JHD

Hobbes, T. (1651). *Leviathon*. London, UK: Penguin.

Huggan, G. (1997). The neo-colonialism of postcolonialism: A cautionary note. *Links and letters*, 4, pp: 19–24.

Human Rights Watch. (2013). World report: Events of 2012. Retrieved on 20 April 2015 from https://www.hrw.org/sites/default/files/wr2013_web.pdf

Kennedy, V. (2013). *Edward Said: A critical Introduction*. Hoboken, NJ: Wiley.

L'Etang, J & Pieczka, M. (1996). *Critical perspectives in public relations*. London: International Thomson Business Press.

L'Etang, J., & Pieczka M. (Eds). (2006). *Public relations: Critical debates and contemporary practice*. Mahwah, NJ: Lawrence Erlbaum.

Liberal-National Coalition (2013). *The Coalition's Operation Sovereign Borders Policy*, pp. 1–20, Retrieved on 13 April 2015 from http://www.nationals.org.au/Portals/0/2013/policy/The%20Coalition%E2%80%99s%20Operation%20Sovereign%20Borders%20Policy.pdf

Loewe, A. (2013). Australian Cathedrals say: "Let's fully welcome refugees". *News at St Paul's Cathedral*. Retrieved on 13 April 2015 from http://www.stpaulscathedral.org.au/news/article/australian_cathedrals_say_lets_fully_welcome_refugees

Loewe, A. (2014). Banner to stay until asylum policies change. *News at St Paul's Cathedral*. Retrieved on 13 April 2015 from http://www.stpaulscathedral.org.au/news/article/banner_stays_put_till_policies_change

Loewenstein, A. (2013, 22 July). Australia's deal with Papua New Guinea is vulture capitalism at its worst. *The Guardian*. Retrieved on 13 April 2015 from http://www.theguardian.com/commentisfree/2013/jul/22/vulture-capitalism-papua-new-guinea-australia

Malpas, S., & Wake P. (Eds). (2006). Names and terms. In S Malpas, & P. Wake (Eds), *The Routledge companion to critical theory*, pp. 141–269. London, UK: Routledge.

Manderson, D. (2013, 27 August) Stop the boats? Change tack. *Sydney Morning Herald*. Retrieved on 13 April 2015 from http://www.smh.com.au/comment/stop-the-boats-change-tack-20130826-2sm3f.html#ixzz2vEvJTRM2

McKie, D., & Munshi D. (2007). *Reconfiguring public relations: Ecology, equity and enterprise*. New York, NY: Routledge.

Mogelson, L. (2013, 15 November). The dream boat. *New York Times Magazine*. Retrieved on 13 April 2015 from http://www.nytimes.com/2013/11/17/magazine/the-impossible-refugee-boat-lift-to-christmas-island.html?hpw&rref=magazine&_r=1&

Morrison, S. (2013, 29 October). We stop the circus to stop the boats – Op-ed. *Daily Telegraph*. Retrieved on 20 April 2015 from http://www.dailytelegraph.com.au/news/opinion/we-stop-the-circus-to-stop-the-boats/story-fni0cwl5-1226748465033

Moss, L. (2003). *Is Canada postcolonial?* Waterloo, Canada: Wilfred Laurier University Press.

Outhwaite, W. (1994) *Habermas: A critical introduction*, Cambridge, UK: Polity Press.

Rao, R. (2010). *Third World protest: Between home and the world*. Oxford, UK: Oxford University Press.

Refugee Council of Australia (2014) Members. Retrieved on 13 April 2015 from http://www.refugee-council.org.au/about-us-2/members/

Rodriguez, J. (2013). Five Poems. In R. Scott, & T. Keneally (Eds), *A country too far*. Melbourne, Australia: Penguin.

Roskin, M. G., & Berry, N.O. (2007). *IR: The new world of international relations*. Upper Saddle River, NJ: Prentice Hall.

Runnymede Trust. (1997). *Islamophobia: A challenge for all of us*. London: Runnymede Trust.

Said, E. (1978). *Orientalism*. New York, NY: Pantheon.

Said, E. (1981). *Covering Islam: How the media and the experts determine how we see the rest of the world*. New York: Pantheon.

Said, E. (1993). *Culture and imperialism*. New York, NY: Knopf/Random House.

Said, E. (1994). *The politics of dispossession: The struggle for Palestinian self-determination, 1969–1994*. New York, NY: Pantheon Books.

Said, E. (2000). *The end of the peace process: Oslo and after*. New York, NY: Pantheon.

Scott, R., & Keneally, T. (2013). *A country too far*. Melbourne, Australia: Penguin.

Shimko, K. (2013). *International relations: Perspectives, controversies & readings*. Boston, MA: Wadsworth.

Snyder, J. (2012). *Power and progress: International politics in transition*, London, UK: Routledge.

Sriramesh, K. (2002). The dire need for multiculturalism in public relations education: An Asian perspective. *Journal of Communication Management*, 7(1), pp. 54–77.

Sriramesh, K., & Verčič, D. (Eds) (2009). *The global public relations handbook: Theory, research, and practice*, 2nd edition. New York: Routledge.

Stringer, R. (2007). A nightmare of the neocolonial kind: Politics of suffering in Howard's Northern Territory intervention, *Borderlands ejournal*, 6(2). Retrieved on 13 April 2015 from http://www.borderlands.net.au/vol6no2_2007/stringer_intervention.htm

Tétreault, M. A., & Lipschutz, R. D. (2005). *Global politics as if people mattered*. Lanham, MD: Rowman & Littlefield.

Tsiolkas, C. (2013, September). Why Australia hates asylum seekers *The Monthly*. Retrieved on 13 April 2015 from http://www.themonthly.com.au/issue/2013/september/1377957600/christos-tsiolkas/why-australia-hates-asylum-seekers

United Nations (UN) (2002). UNHCR urges Australia to review policy of detaining asylum seekers. Media Release. Retrieved on 13 April 2015 from http://www.un.org/apps/news/story.asp?NewsID=2785&Cr=australia&Cr1=asylum

United Nations High Commissioner for Refugees (UNHCR) (2014). 2014 UNHCR regional operations profile – East Asia and the Pacific. Retrieved from http://www.unhcr.org/cgi-bin/texis/vtx/page?page=49e487af6

United Nations High Commissioner for Refugees (UNHCR) (2015) 2015 UNHCR regional operations profile – East Asia and the Pacific. Retrieved on 13 April 2015 from http://www.unhcr.org/cgi-bin/texis/vtx/page?page=49e487af6

Weaver, C. K., Motion, J., & Roper, J. (2006). From propaganda to discourse (and back again): Truth, power, the public interest, and public relations. In J. L'Etang, & M. Pieczka (Eds), *Public relations: Critical debates and contemporary practice*, pp. 7–23. Mahwah, NJ: Lawrence Erlbaum.

Weedon, C. (2004). *Identity and culture: Narratives of difference and belonging*. New York, NY: McGraw Hill.

11

Critical discourse analysis

A search for meaning and power

Judy Motion and Shirley Leitch

A critique is not a matter of saying that things are not right as they are. It is a matter of pointing out on what kinds of assumptions, what kinds of familiar, unchallenged, unconsidered modes of thought the practices that we accept rest.

(Foucault, 1988, p. 154)

To be perfectly candid, our early scholarship was driven by a desire to criticize, as well as critique, public relations. With backgrounds in government and environmental activism, we shared political experiences that placed notions of power and resistance at the centre of our understanding of public relations. Yet, as we explored North American public relations scholarship, it became clear that the field lacked theories and methods for analysing power relations. There really was no choice – from the outset of our academic careers we had to seek out alternative explanatory concepts and research methods to theorize public relations. From our political perspectives, a very different approach was called for that would open up the field of public relations scholarship and practice for critique. Although the Excellence project offered an idealized view of public relations and normative insights for best practice, it did not resonate with the more complicated, pluralistic practices that we had observed and engaged in. Why, we wondered, were discussions of politics and activism seemingly absent from public relations scholarship? Where were the interrogations of power and resistance that underpinned our own experiences of public relations? Further, we wanted to theorize public relations as a system of meaning production that reinforced or intersected with power relations. For this challenge, the rhetorical scholarship of Toth and Heath (1992) provided frameworks for exploring meaning-oriented perspectives and established conceptual starting points. The key task, then, was to determine how to introduce notions of politics, power and resistance into public relations scholarship that would intersect with the extant rhetorical work on meaning production and sense-making.

Our first scholarly ventures in public relations were explicitly political. Shirley had attended a conference in Australia and after the conference she was led outside and asked if she would take a box of archived evidence that documented a campaign to "bust" or undermine union power in Western Australia. Simultaneously, Judy was researching media representations of women politicians and the modes of public relations that were deployed to create particular gendered public personas. An immediate challenge we faced was to identify theories that would resonate with the datasets we were analysing – in these particular instances our critiques were explicitly driven by empirical approaches. Examination of post-structuralist theory led us to the work of Michel Foucault and then Norman Fairclough, which seemed to offer possible ways of thinking about public relations that informed the analysis of our data and linked to our interests in power, culture and language. The work of Foucault offered insights for problematizing the social construction of discursive regimes, interrogating the relationships between power and knowledge, and analysing technologies of governmentality, agency and the self. Scholarship emerging from critical linguistics, in particular the work of Norman Fairclough offered a critical approach to the study of social change, discourse and language. At the same time that we were exploring these approaches in the early 1990s, other groups of scholars were also trying to open up possibilities for rethinking public relations – Robert Heath in North America became an invaluable mentor and in Scotland Jacquie L'Etang and Madga Pieczka were important allies in this task, along with many of our colleagues in the fields of organizational studies and communication. As more colleagues joined our research team in New Zealand, we became confident that we had the momentum to offer a diverse range of critical analyses of public relations. We very deliberately interrogated the role of public relations in establishing and sustaining particular regimes of power and discursively shaping socio-cultural practices. In the following sections we outline the critical agenda that underpinned our research, explain how the work of Michel Foucault and Norman Fairclough is both salient and vital for critical scholarship, and offer insights into how their work opens up possibilities for re-imagining public relations.

A critical agenda

As idealistic, relatively young scholars, we wanted to not only move beyond organizational modes of conceptualizing public relations – we also wanted to open up the discipline for critique and consider how it may be reconfigured and transformed by social and democratic agendas. Normative conceptualizations of public relations, such as the Excellence project, were also concerned with how public relations should function within society, but it seemed that the emphasis on organizational imperatives meant that interrogations of the political and socio-cultural impacts of public relations were not part of that agenda. So, within our initial research agenda, we sought to offer a critique and criticism of the role of public relations in society and to develop frameworks for analysing how public relations actually functioned within society.

Although the early work by Trujillo and Toth (1987) had classified public relations paradigms according to the goals or intentions of an organization, it also provided ways of talking about the agenda of our scholarship. In the Trujillo and Toth (1987) framework, public relations scholarship was classified into three broad categories: functional, interpretive and critical paradigms. Functional approaches that were concerned with the effectiveness and efficiency of organizations most definitely did not correlate to our approach. Interpretive approaches that were concerned with symbolic meaning seemed salient. However, the description of the third paradigm, *critical public relations*, as an approach that "treats organizations as ideological and material arenas for power, influence and control" (p. 216) seemed the most appropriate characterization of our work. Within the critical paradigm, Trujillo and Toth (1987) suggested that scholars may research issues relating to inequitable power relations, opaque or dishonest communicative efforts, and manipulative public relations practices – and argue for radical social change. Positioning our agenda within a critical paradigm provided us with a space for experimenting with and making sense of public relations ideas and practices.

Michel Foucault, critique and problematization

Although we have discussed the value of Foucault's work for public relations scholarship in previous publications (Motion & Leitch, 2007; Motion & Leitch, 2009), in this chapter the discussion focuses specifically on how his work opens up possibilities for critical public relations scholarship. Critique was central to Foucault's work and he offered a number of insights into its practice. The quotation at the beginning of the chapter points to how Foucault conceived critical practice – the task of a critical scholar is to question the structures and frameworks that underpin discourses, knowledge/power relations, and practices of the self, rather than to simply judge them. For Foucault, the problem with judgement was that it established a polemic based upon a form of legitimacy that an adversary was denied. Thus, possibilities for deliberation and discussion were closed down. Clearly, at times our early work strayed from a Foucauldian understanding of the practice of critique – yet by criticizing public relations we were opening it up for appraisal and attempting to create a new agenda for public relations scholarship.

Within his own work, Foucault was concerned with the critical history of thought. He explained, "It seems to me that there was one element that was capable of describing the history of thought: this was what one would call the element of problems, or more precisely, problematizations" (Foucault, 1996, p. 420). Arguably, for those who wish to take up a critical endeavour in public relations, the most important contribution that may be derived from Foucault's work is techniques for the analysis of problematization. Foucault (1997a, p. 118) explained quite simply that problematization should be understood "not [as] an arrangement of representations but as a work of thought". Within his work, Foucault attempted to analyse how conditions such as madness were problematized in particular ways and how certain solutions became normalized. For critical projects, this approach offers insights into "how the different solutions to a problem have been constructed; but also how these solutions result from a specific form of problematization" (Foucault, 1996, p. 422). In other words, the task was to understand how certain solutions have been made possible by the ways in which specific conditions are framed as problems. It is, however, important to note that problematization may also act as a method of inquiry, interrogation and interpretation. As critical scholars we may draw upon problematization as a research technique for analysing the machinations of public relations that influence how certain systems of thought and practices come to be conceived in a particular way, to highlight paradoxes, difficulties, and "the conditions in which human beings 'problematize' what they are, what they do, and the world in which they live" (Foucault, 1984, p. 10). Questions about how particular meanings and practices have come to dominate have the potential to open up public relations problematization strategies to examination and critique. Within our own work we sought to understand and problematize public relations practices that were designed to normalize discourse transformations and create legitimacy for privileged power regimes or instances of power relations. In line with Foucault's interest in transgression and the possibilities for resistance, our work sought to interpret public relations as *a set of practices* that may be deployed across multiple domains by multiple participants.

A starting point for utilizing problematization as a research technique is to analyse the problem context, to investigate the historical, socio-cultural, economic or political conditions that influence how public relations may be practiced. A series of questions may then be posed that seek to explore "how and to what extent it might be possible to think differently, instead of legitimating what is already known" (Foucault, 1984, p. 9). At a more general level, the following questions that Foucault posed relating to strategy, relations and power effects may establish directions for critical endeavours: "What took place here?" "Can one speak of interests here?" (Foucault, 1980, p. 204). "What does struggle mean here?" (Foucault, 1980, p. 209). To this set of questions we would suggest that it is important to consider "why does this matter?" and "what is at stake here?" At this more specific level, a repertoire of problematizations may be developed that examine how ideas are "put into discourse" (Foucault, 1978, p. 11), by identifying "instances of discursive production," "the production of power" and "the propagation of knowledge" (Foucault, 1984, p.12). In Chapter 1 of the first volume of the *History of Sexuality* (1978), Foucault explored what he termed a series of "doubts" and outlined a number of questions that formed the foundation of his problematization of the repressive hypothesis. The questions were designed to provide an account of "a transformation into discourse, a technology of power, and a will to knowledge" (Foucault, 1978, p. 12). The repertoire of questions may provide a resource for developing a set of problematizations that interrogate the role of public relations in social transformation. These general and more specific problematizations may form the foundation for critiques of the role of public relations in establishing, contesting, normalizing and legitimating particular meanings, power relations, truth and knowledge.

Norman Fairclough and critical discourse analysis (CDA)

The work of Norman Fairclough has made important contributions to the theoretical debates underpinning the development of public relations research over the past two decades (Leitch & Motion, 2010; Motion & Leitch, 1996, 2007, 2009). Fairclough's (1992, 1995) early works were groundbreaking in their combination of linguistics and critical social theory. This work may be seen as part of the broader movement within the social sciences, which is known as the "turn to language". In combining the insights of critical theory and linguistic methodology, Fairclough has been a central figure in the development of CDA, which is now well-established as a methodological approach within many disciplines, including education (Rogers, 2011), organization studies (Grant, Hardy & Putnam, 2011) and human resources management (Ainsworth & Hardy, 2004).

CDA is a subset of discourse analysis, which is a broad and overlapping field of study (Alvesson & Karreman, 2000; Clegg, Courpasson & Phillips, 2006; Meyer, 2001; Mumby, 2004; van Dijk, 1993; Wodak & Meyer, 2001). There are, however, a number of features that distinguish CDA from other forms of discourse analysis (Leitch & Palmer, 2010). As an offshoot of critical theory, perhaps the most pronounced of these features is the clear focus on major social issues and the power relations that are produced, reproduced, or challenged by these issues. In this respect, the work of Foucault (1972, 1979) has been influential on the development of CDA and is heavily referenced within the work of Fairclough (1992, 1995, 2003). In relation to Foucault, Fairclough (1992) is, however, careful to point out the clear distinction between his approach (which he refers to as "textually oriented discourse analysis") and Foucault's more abstract, historical analysis. It is Fairclough's focus on everyday texts that has made his work so relevant for public relations practice, which itself is heavily focused on the production of texts.

Undertaking a Faircloughian CDA of a public relations problem means adopting a three-dimensional approach to research. These three dimensions comprise: the text; the discourse practices associated with the production, distribution and interpretation of texts; and the broader social practices within which these discourse practices are embedded. Discourse practices and social practices combine to provide the micro-, meso- and macro-level contexts for our analysis. Fairclough emphasizes that while all three dimensions should be considered within CDA, the degree to which each dimension is considered is dependent upon the nature of the research problem and the corpus of data that is accessible by the researcher. For example, Leitch and Davenport's (2007) study analysed the way in which the keyword "sustainability" had been negotiated and deployed by a variety of competing discourse actors or stakeholders, with the goal of dominating public policy debates in relation to biotechnology. This study's detailed textual analysis was situated within the broader societal context of the controversy over the introduction of genetically modified organisms. The study also included an intertextual analysis to demonstrate the relationship between the key texts and highlight the discourse practices associated with these texts.

The textual dimension of CDA typically focuses on written language, including transcripts of spoken language. However other elements of text, such as static and video images, objects, spaces, music and sounds, may also be included. While the primary focus remains upon language, these additional elements are now routinely included in the analysis of texts. Given the centrality of digital communication to public relations, this multi-modal focus which takes CDA beyond the written word, makes it particularly well-suited for public relations research. A CDA project might, for example, include texts as varied as a Twitter hashtag, a Facebook page, a public relations strategy document, a series of video media releases, or the proceedings of a public meeting, among its targets for data collection.

Public relations is very much an applied field of endeavour. For this reason, the second dimension of Faircloughian CDA – discourse practices – provides a very fruitful ground for public relations research. Research projects that take discourse practices as the starting point of analysis, might, for example, examine the social media communication strategies associated with a crisis or issue. The organization of work within a public relations practice, the processes of client relationship management, or the collaboration between multiple agencies on a campaign, would all constitute good datasets or research sites for a CDA project that began at the discourse practice level of analysis.

All public relations work is undertaken within broader organizational, social, economic and political contexts. These contexts are infused with systems of thought, which are termed "ideologies." Fairclough (1992, p. 88) argues that ideology is both a property of institutional structures and a property of events. From a structural perspective, ideology appears to reinforce existing power relations between people and institutions. From an events perspective, ideologies appear open to challenge by the actions of individuals or organizations which seek to change existing power relations. A purely structural view of ideology would tend to overemphasize the stability of existing institutional arrangements, while a purely events-based view would tend to overemphasize moments at which change in these arrangements has occurred. Public relations work has been used to serve the structural interests of existing institutions that actively strive to preserve the status quo. Public relations has also been used to progress change agendas. In either case, research projects focused on either institutional stability or change could usefully deploy a CDA for which social practices are the starting point of analysis.

The three-dimensional character of Faircloughian CDA requires the linking of texts to contexts. Linking the macro-level of social practices, with the meso-level of discourse practices and the micro-level of texts, can be a difficult exercise (Leitch & Palmer, 2010). Fairclough (2005) emphasizes that these multi-levelled linkages must be demonstrated empirically through the analysis of data rather than simply asserted. When undertaking a CDA project, researchers must always be self-reflexive in determining "what can be said" based on the corpus of available data (Leitch & Palmer, 2010). One common pitfall is to assume that the intentions of those who create texts translates in any straightforward manner into the interpretations of texts by those who experience them. Research that equates click-throughs, retweets or page views with public relations campaign success falls into this trap.

It is also important to note that undertaking three-dimensional research does not necessarily mean undertaking a CDA. Throughout his work, Fairclough (1992, 1995, 2003) emphasizes that a CDA research project starts with a social problem or issue. CDA research is therefore characterized by explicit explanations of data choices that are framed in terms of how these choices will advance our understanding of the nominated social problem. Leitch and Palmer (2010) found that some research claiming an affiliation with CDA focused on a group of texts or an organization, but did not explain why the texts or organization came to be the focus of study. The researcher's motivations and decision-making process for choosing data or research sites are thus obscured. CDA research requires that such motivations and processes are both explicit and explicitly linked to a broader social problem or issue.

A critical public relations manifesto

Fundamentally, the work of Foucault and Fairclough draws attention to the ways that social problems and change are entangled with power relations. At the heart of those power relations are organizational public relations efforts that seek to protect or damage identities and reputations, convey or deny legitimacy, and normalize or contest the status quo. Understanding public relations as a set of practices shifts our attention to the purpose and outcomes of public relations. Public relations that is conducted by or for organizations is part of a broader structure that shapes society. Within the sections above we discuss how our work has theorized public relations as a discourse technology (see also, Edwards, 2011). Our critique in this section focuses upon public relations as a professional organizational practice with a wide range of communication practices designed to influence societal power relations and decision-making processes. In particular, our critique is driven by problematization of the purposes and outcomes of those practices and aims to open up discussion and development of a critical manifesto. Questions about how organizational public relations contributes to society and the world we live in are the defining feature of a critical gaze and endeavours. Studies of humanitarian, environmental and democratic projects, and what we may learn from the public relations efforts that support such projects, underpin a critical manifesto. Critical scholars need, of course, to continue to identify transgressions or fractures in societal fault lines in terms of how professional public relations complies with societal expectations and norms, but the aim of these critiques must be to reassert humanitarian, environmental and democratic principles within our critiques. In this respect we echo the call from McKie and Munshi (2007) to "develop the field away from insularity and in the direction of environmental improvement, inclusive egalitarianism and sustainable enterprise" (p. 145). This call for action is explicitly political.

Action begins with collaboration. As critical scholars we need to abandon our own particular preoccupations in favour of expanding the boundaries that delimit how we engage with the field of professional public relations. The challenge is to establish critical agendas that problematize the relationships and intersections between political, socio-cultural and environmental concerns, rather than deal with each of these concerns separately. Collaboration also means that we need to be fully engaged with the practice of public relations – a defining feature of critical public relations could be a shift from external critique to collaboration within the field. Alternatively, we could join forces with those who critique the field of organizational public relations by joining activist groups.

Governance of professional public relations, we suggest, is a significant target for problematization and a potentially useful starting point for critical scholarship and research activism. A key activist strategy would be to challenge and politicize the self-regulation of the industry and the process by which organizational public relations intervenes in democratic decision-making processes. Normalization of self-regulation has meant that organizational public relations can be conducted in the shadows and with impunity. It is crucial that self-regulation is questioned again and again – why should organizational public relations have the right to self-regulate? Voicing concerns about the role of organizational public relations and publicly calling into question the governance of public relations is a significant reminder that society has the power to legitimate or delegitimate particular sectors. Ultimately, from this perspective, the role of a critical public relations manifesto is to focus on reclaiming participative democracy – we need to challenge organizational public relations and those professional sense-making practices that seek to influence political processes and contribute to the redistribution of power relations in such a way that civil society voices may be heard and taken into account. Holtzhausen's (2014) view of public relations as activism is an important insight for these efforts – our project must be safeguarding "a radical democracy that ensures equality for all, respects cultural plurality and requires a confrontational intolerance of injustice" (p. 239). Safeguarding a form of democracy that privileges civil society, rather than corporations, and does not grant institutions the same rights as human beings, may be achieved by mobilizing public opinion as a legitimating or delegitimating voice for a wider set of socio-cultural, technical and political factors in governance processes (Macnaghten, Kearnes & Wynne, 2005). If government is failing in its duty to regulate professional public relations, then critical public relations has to assume a governance role. The task cannot simply be talking to each other – we now have to step outside the academy and take a stand. Independent regulatory bodies may need to be called for and established. Drawing upon the work of Stirling (2008), we suggest that our critical public relations efforts may be evaluated according to whether they succeed in opening up or closing down the democratic, deliberative and decision-making roles of civil society.

A critical public relations manifesto may usefully draw upon recent studies of activism. Ganesh and Zoller (2012) advise that activist politics "should not privilege consensual dialogue as the best form of social change" (p. 84). Social justice, they suggest, must be central to activist politics. Holtzhausen (2014) poses a series of understandings about the relationship between the postmodern condition and public relations that serve as a foundation and justification for public relations activism. She reminds us that public relations is complicated, pluralistic and political, but, more importantly, she reasserts the need for responsible, moral postmodern public relations that strives for participative democracy. The recent work of Demetrious (2013), exploring public relations, activism and social change, suggests a set of guidelines for sustainable communication that includes the following considerations:

> [O]penness to ideas; a commitment to truthfulness; the development of depth of discussion in public debate; the tendency to explain choices facing the public, rather than engage in persuasion or derision; the encouragement of a broad culture of participation; a long-term commitment to the group's objectives and the ability to main a critical distance from their subjectivities.
>
> *(pp. 136–7)*

These principles may be usefully explored as a starting point for external or independent regulation and review of professional or organizational public relations. Our own work with Kay Weaver on activism suggests that a potential pathway towards a manifesto for change includes the tasks of asserting a stake in the issue, establishing societal priorities, establishing a general agenda for change, articulating a governance plan, challenging and inserting social concerns into public relations, and potentially manufacturing or mobilizing dissent (Motion, Leitch & Weaver, forthcoming).

As a corollary to this focus it is essential that we also develop an agenda for critical public relations education because that is where we may have the greatest impact and possibly affect change within the practice of public relations. Public relations practices that succeed in opening up issues in ways that enable publics to define problems and consent to or dissent from proposed societal changes must form the core of what we teach so that our graduates can negotiate boundaries between commercial, socio-cultural and political imperatives. It is not just that we must become activists – so must our students. That is, of course, easier to achieve when we teach outside public relations in disciplines that are linked to politics, law, social and environmental justice.

Within our education efforts we also need to collaboratively explore possibilities for new ways of thinking about public relations – what Foucault (1997b, p. 232) refers to as "scintillating leaps of the imagination". Within these imaginative moments the critical endeavour may transform from criticism into curiosity – curiosity about how public relations practices may enhance the human condition. Perhaps more playful critiques could open up the transformational potential of critical public relations education and suggest new avenues for a more positive, creative engagement with public relations practice. In this way our work may prove even more successful at questioning, subverting, transgressing and ultimately transforming the less acceptable, less equitable aspects of public relations.

References

Ainsworth, S.A., & Hardy, C. (2004). Critical discourse analysis and identity: Why bother? *Critical Discourse Studies*, 1(2), pp. 225–9.

Alvesson, M., & Kärreman, D. (2000). Varieties of discourse: On the study of organizations through discourse analysis. *Human Relations*, 53(9), pp. 1125–49.

Clegg, C., Courpasson, D., & Phillips, N. (2006). *Power and organizations*. London, UK: Sage.

Demetrious, K. (2013). *Public relations, activism, and social change: Speaking up*. New York, NY: Routledge.

Edwards. L. (2011). Critical perspectives in global public relations: Theorizing power. In N. Bardham, & C. K. Weaver (Eds), *Public relations in global contexts: Multi-paradigmatic perspectives*, pp. 29–49. New York, NY: Routledge.

Fairclough, N. (1992). *Discourse and social change*. Cambridge, UK: Polity.

Fairclough, N. (1995). *Critical discourse analysis*. New York, NY: Longman.

Fairclough, N. (2003). *Analysing discourse: Textual analysis for social research*. London, UK: Routledge.

Fairclough, N. (2005). Peripheral vision: Discourse analysis in Organization Studies: The case for critical realism. *Organization Studies*, 26(6), pp. 915–39.

Foucault, M. (1972). *The archaeology of knowledge*. London, UK: Tavistock.

Foucault, M. (1978). *The history of sexuality: An introduction* (R. Hurley, Trans.). London, UK: Penguin.

Foucault, M. (1979). *Discipline and punish: The birth of the prison*. Harmondsworth, UK: Penguin.

Foucault, M. (1980). *Power/knowledge: Selected interviews and other writings 1972–1977*. New York, NY: Pantheon.

Foucault, M (1984). *The use of pleasure: The history of sexuality*, vol. 2 (R. Hurley, Trans.). London, UK: Penguin.

Foucault, M. (1988). Technologies of the self. In L. Martin, H. Gutman, & P. Hutton (Eds), *Technologies of the self: A seminar with Michel Foucault*, pp. 16–48. Amherst, MA: University of Massachusetts.

Foucault, M. (1996). Problematics. In S. Lotringer (Ed.), *Foucault live: Collected interviews, 1961–1984*, pp. 416–22. New York, NY: Semiotexte.

Foucault, M. (1997a). Polemics, politics and problematizations. In P. Rabinow (Ed.), *Michel Foucault: Ethics: subjectivity and truth. The essential works of Foucault 1954–1984*, vol. 1 (R. Hurley, Trans.), pp. 111–19). New York, NY: The New Press.

Foucault, M. (1997b). The masked philosopher. In P. Rabinow (Ed.), *Michel Foucault: Ethics: subjectivity and truth. The essential works of Foucault 1954–1984*, vol. 1 (R. Hurley et al., Trans.), pp. 321–8). New York, NY: The New Press.

Ganesh, S., & Zoller, H. M. (2012). Dialogue, activism and democratic social change. *Communication Theory*, 22(1), pp. 66–91.

Grant, D., Hardy, C., & Putnam, L. (Eds). (2011). *Organizational discourse studies*. Thousand Oaks, CA: Sage.

Holtzhausen, D. R. (2014). *Public relations as activism: Postmodern approaches to theory and practice*. New York, NY: Routledge.

Leitch, S., & Davenport, S. (2007). Strategic ambiguity as a discourse practice: The role of keywords in the discourse on sustainable biotechnology. *Discourse Studies*, 9(1), pp. 43–61.

Leitch, S., & Motion, J. (2010). Publics and public relations: Effecting change. In R. Heath (Ed.), *The SAGE handbook of public relations*. Thousand Oaks, CA: Sage.

Leitch, S., & Palmer, I. (2010). Analyzing texts in context: Current practices and new protocols for critical discourse analysis in Organization Studies. *Journal of Management Studies*, 47(6), pp. 1194–212.

Macnaghten, P., Kearnes, M. B., & Wynne, B. (2005). Nanotechnology, governance and public deliberation: What role for social sciences? *Science Communication*, 27(2), pp. 268–91.

McKie, D., & Munshi, D. (2007). *Reconfiguring public relations: Ecology, equity and enterprise*. London, UK: Routledge.

Meyer, M. (2001). Between theory, method and politics: Positioning of the approaches to CDA. In R. Wodak, & M Meyer (Eds), *Methods of critical discourse analysis*. London, UK: Sage.

Motion, J., & Leitch, S. (1996). A discursive perspective from New Zealand: Another world view. *Public Relations Review*, 22(3), pp. 297–309.

Motion, J., & Leitch, S. (2007). A toolbox for public relations: The oeuvre of Michel Foucault. *Public Relations Review*, 33(3), pp. 263–8.

Motion, J., & Leitch, S. (2009). On Foucault: A toolbox for public relations. In O. Ihlen, B. van Ruler, & M. Frederiksson (Ed.), *Public relations and social theory: Key figures and concepts*. New York, NY: Routledge.

Motion, J., Leitch, S., & Weaver, C. K. (forthcoming). Popularizing dissent: A civil society perspective. *Public Understanding of Science*.

Mumby, D. (2004). Discourse, power and ideology: Unpacking the critical approach. In D. Grant, C. Hardy, C. Oswick, & L. Putnam (Eds), *The SAGE handbook of organizational discourse*, pp. 237–58. London, UK: Sage.

Rogers, R. (2011). *Critical discourse analysis in education*, 2nd edition. New York, NY: Routledge.

Stirling, A. (2008). "Opening up" and "closing down": Power, participation and pluralism in the social appraisal of technology. *Science, Technology and Human Values*, 33(2), pp. 262–94.

Toth, E. L., & Heath, R. L. (Eds). (1992). *Rhetorical and critical approaches to public relations*. Hillsdale, NJ: Lawrence Erlbaum.

Trujillo, N., & Toth, E. L. (1987). Organizational perspectives for public relations research and practice. *Management Communication Quarterly*, 1(2), pp. 199–281.

van Dijk, T. A. (1993). Principles of critical discourse analysis. *Discourse and Society*, 49(2), pp. 249–83.

Wodak R., & Meyer, M. (Eds). (2001). *Methods of critical discourse analysis*. London, UK: Sage.

12

Changes to be encouraged

Radical turns in PR theorisation and small-step evolutions in PR practice

Kevin Moloney and David McKie

In this chapter we take critical theory as a conceptual canopy covering an array of diverse but interlinked perspectives. Under that canopy our focus rests on three key features: scepticism about the legitimacy of existing knowledge configurations and methods; an interdisciplinary and political approach; and a justice agenda with a commitment to human emancipation. We highlight the term "turn" as a marker of significant, or potentially significant, changes favouring progress in or with critical PR. In addition, to give credit where it is due, we identify initiators and major players in such "turns" by naming them as "turners" – with apologies to the many important "turners" omitted for lack of knowledge or lack of space. We look back to Saul Alinsky's work to give context to current considerations of activism and the activist "turn".

From the outset we acknowledge that this is a subjectively influenced, and unquestionably "interested", interpretation. Rather than a more complete academic survey – although these have their place (see Edwards, this volume) – we aim to stimulate discussions about how critical PR (CPR) can better contribute to equality and justice. In the process, we position PR as ideologically neutral technique by noting how techniques cross over from activist PR to mainstream business PR. We then argue that the professional consequences of crossover justify an equality of esteem for those working in both areas of practice. We also hope stimulation also comes from developing two new descriptors of activist PR. We finish with a short retrospective on the work of the American radical community organiser Paul Alinsky and ask what relevance he may have to modern PR.

"Turns" and significant shifts

The deployment of "turn" as a marker signalling a potentially significant shift can be seen in the so-called "linguistic turn" that gained a larger circulation and become part of mainstream discourse across many disciplines. Although associated with many different intellectual currents from the Vienna Circle to Cambridge-based philosophers Bernard Russell and Ludwig Wittgenstein, the linguistic turn has gained wider traction over time. It helps express at a meta-level how scholars, especially in philosophy and the humanities, had reoriented their studies to focus on the relationship between language and the discursive nature of "reality". The linguistic turn has also expanded to encompass challenges to the assumed neutrality of language in economics and the sciences. In the more updated and politicised form of a discursive turn, it arrived relatively late into the PR field (Motion & Leitch, 1996) but still feeds into PR today informed by the work of Michel Foucault and heavily informed by Fairclough's (2013) critical discourse analysis (CDA).

Keeping those backgrounds in mind, this chapter connects various "turns" in scholarly writing in PR and in earlier influencers of both critical theory and critical practice. We argue that, in pluralist liberal democracies with big businesses, open markets and active civil societies, it has been decades since public relations was an exclusive tool for, nearly exclusively, the rich and powerful. We argue, however, that we PR academics have been slow in absorbing shifts away from the few-but-very-powerful to the many-but-less-powerful.

But catch-ups are now visible in a number of attempts to create a turn in the discipline. We identify, albeit with overlaps, the following range of potential contenders: (1) the postmodern turn; (2) the turn to power and the associated revision of activism both of which also link with the sociological and the socio-cultural turn; (3) the postcolonial turn, which we'll also broaden to include issues of race. All of these might be seen, more controversially, as part of the critical turn itself, which is partly marked by the publication of this first handbook of critical PR.

The first of these possible turning points in PR was the postmodern. It emerged outside of the field as a periodisation called postmodernism or postmodernity, which claimed to go beyond the modern or modernity, with a new set of values and tools that would redress the deficiencies of the modern period. In PR, that turn is mainly associated with the work of Holtzhausen (2000, 2002, 2012). In terms of critical theory, the titles of Holtzhausen and her collaborators clearly side with the less powerful against the powerful. That partisan position is explicit in their article and book titles such as "Resistance from the Margins: The Postmodern Public Relations Practitioner as Organizational Activist" (Holtzhausen & Voto, 2002), and *Public Relations as Activism: Postmodern Approaches to Theory and Practice* (Holtzhausen, 2012).

Although she is the most prominent PR postmodernist, Holtzhausen was neither the first nor the last to suggest a postmodern turn. Mickey (1997) was a notable predecessor and both have since been followed by Radford (2012) and Tyler (2005), who explicitly reframed crisis from "a postmodernist perspective" to see it "as a disruption in the dominant narrative that members of an organization's power elite wish to perpetuate" (p. 566). In line with Holtzhausen's (2000) contention that "the postmodern public relations practitioner wants to set the disorder of discourse free from the tight web of constraints that inhibits it" (p. 105), Tyler's (2005) language choice and attitude are typically postmodern, and fit with critical theory egalitarianism in how they welcome "disruption" of "the dominant narrative" of the "power elite" (p. 566).

Revisiting and resisting the postmodern turn

Yet almost all postmodern PR sits in relative isolation from major critical issues on postmodernism outside the field. In Cultural Studies, a decade before the end of the twentieth century, Frow (1991) was posing the question "What Was Post-Modernism?" and within six years Eagleton (1996), in Literary Studies, published the dismissive *The Illusions of Postmodernism*. Other critical scholars in other fields made equally unflattering assessments by contesting the idea of postmodernity as any kind of critical intervention because of its social conformity with market forces. From Cultural Geography, David Harvey (1989) argued convincingly that postmodernism undermined its potential for social liberation because it was also the cultural manifestation of late capitalism and, in that role, was comfortably complicit with the continuing economic and social exploitation of that period.

Other critical theorists sided more with Harvey and challenged the accuracy of calling the period "postmodern". Leading sociological challengers to the postmodernists featured Beck's (1992) *Risk Society*, Bauman's (2000) *Liquid Modernity*, and Beck, Giddens and Lash's (1994) *Reflexive Modernization*. Their alternative periodisations arose because of their dissatisfaction with the minimal social critique and emancipatory potential in postmodernism. These authors converged in positioning the postmodern as embedded in, and comfortably complicit with, neo-liberalism and neo-capitalism (Derrida & Malabou, 2004), and their existing elites.

Over a decade on, Holtzhausen (2011) still argues "The Need for a Postmodern Turn in Global Public Relations" (p. 161). Although few in the PR academy have publicly enrolled to make it a lasting turn within the field, PR postmodernists have assisted in making PR more critical. They have exhibited a determination to understand how societies really work and a sceptical attitude to the legitimacy of existing knowledge configurations. They have adopted an interdisciplinary and politically oriented approach to whatever subject they consider, whether it be crisis or history. Their language and approaches combine to illustrate a commitment to human freedom and social justice. Their output remains less experimental, formally, than Grisoni and Kirk's (2006) "Verse, Voice and Va Va Voom!: Illuminating Management Processes through Poetry", or Stephen Brown's (2006) *The Marketing Code*, a creative copy of Dan Brown's *The Da Vinci Code*, and a thriller revealing "the secrets of 21st century marketing" (e.g., "sometimes you have to make a kill to make a killing") (http://www.amazon.co.uk/The-Marketing-Code-Stephen-Brown/dp/1904879888).

Nevertheless, the only formal experiment in critical PR writing is McKie and Munshi's (2009) structuring of a chapter – "Theoretical Black Holes: A Partial A to Z of Missing Critical Thought in Public Relations" – in the postmodern form of an alphabet. That chapter offers a stylistic experiment rare in PR in opening up ways of representing reality, but it is even rarer in designing the form to introduce critical theorists (e.g., Arjun Appadurai, Pablo Neruda, Amartya Sen, Slavoj Zizek) concerned with social justice.

All of this has been made possible by adapting ideas from disciplines and critical scholars outside PR, as in Holtzhausen's (2012) view "that there needs to be some criteria on which a life of activism can be built, even if those criteria are always contested and might change from situation to situation" (p. 3). Ironically, for a movement named after a period in time, that very provisionality acts as a reminder that critical theory has also to adapt to changing environments.

The turn to power and the socio-cultural "turn"

In the turn to power in the contemporary world, PR has also had to engage with global dimensions, with the associated cultural differences. Bardhan and Weaver (2011b) record how the "last two decades have radically changed the way people, organizations, and systems communicate and operate across national and cultural borders" (p. 1) and co-edit a collection on *Public Relations in Global Cultural Contexts* (Bardhan & Weaver, 2011a) to address it. Similarly, in theorising power, Lee Edwards (2011) engages explicitly with PR "situated in a global environment" (p. 29).

In both collections, this turn, despite the enlarged spatiality, continues to be characterised by a focus on the less powerful than the powerful, and the use of interpretive, non-quantitative methodologies to explore these matters. Another prominent example of addressing power directly includes the Edwards and Hodges (2011a) collection, whose opening chapter claims a different turn that they term "a (Radical) Socio-Cultural 'Turn' in Public Relations Scholarship" (Edwards & Hodges, 2011b, p. 1).

Similar turners, such as Ihlen, van Ruler and Fredriksson (2009), delved back into the classic social theorists – many of whom used critical theory – to bring a broader social breadth to contemorary PR. Many pre-turners, especially in calling into question the Grunigian symmetry paradigm, addressed issues of power (e.g., L'Etang & Pieczka, 1996), activism (e.g., Moloney, 2000; 2006), culture and race (e.g., Munshi & Edwards, 2011), methods (McKie, 1997) and history (e.g., L'Etang, 2004; Pearson 1992).

This more critical movement has been accompanied by fresh theorisations in relation to activism that might almost earn the title of an "activist turn" in its own right for it places activists at the core of public relations. Coombs and Holladay (2011, 2012), Demetrious (2013), and McKie and Munshi (2007) all feature in this movement. They follow a few early and often forgotten voices – Alinsky (1971), Carey (1995), and Ewen (1996) – who are seen as outsiders, or as marginal, to the PR academy and so under-recognised for their contributions to CPR.

Society before PR industry

A revealing feature of the work of the authors of the turn is their placement of societal interests above PR industry interests. They argue for PR to be researched, taught and done as a persuasive tool for strengthening a pluralist democracy, and for making elected governments and free markets more responsive. Examples include challenging inequalities on the grounds of race, gender and sexual orientation; questioning hierarchies – especially gender hierarchies – in organisations; interrogating the ethics and politics of capitalist investment; attacking multinational corporations for tax evasion, and markets for their lack of transparency and sustainability.

To liberal and left of centre academics, the list above is a hymn sheet to societal virtue and could merit the title "progressive PR". We personally welcome that trend but would be disappointed if the academy's future output is *only* liberal and left-leaning. If that happens, it will be in one respect, at least, a regrettable "return" to a feature of the intellectual mood status quo *ante bellum* when the dominance of the Grunigian paradigm limited the academy's thinking by concentration on organisation-centric operational symmetry. This would be an unintended consequence that we contend should be avoided. If "symmetry" once dominated our thinking, no single, guiding idea should replace it. For example, we do not say that contemporary, post-turn activist PR is a specific tool for achieving the *d*-word "democracy" (Holtzhausen 2012, p. 157). Admirable and rare as activist PR employees are in wanting organisational equity, they remain subject to contract law and to a dominant business culture of management's "right to manage". Also in public affairs, the rich and powerful are still frequent, committed, skilled and *active* users of PR who invariably fight against strong regulation by democratically elected governments (*Guardian*, 2008; Bureau of Investigative Journalism, 2012.)

We hope that the un-rich and un-powerful catch up these powerful players in efficiency and effectiveness, but we do not believe that PR per se is, or will be, the decisive change agent. We say this to remind ourselves that being PR scholars can lead to the distortions of the single perspective; to the emphasis associated with devotion to single-subject study, and to the solipsistic belief that the matter one studies is *the* universal prime mover. Also, we can be a closed group, too disconnected from PR practice and from the forces that call it up to serve them. To date, for us, the turn is mainly a domestic matter for the PR academy and its fuller title is "'turn' in PR thinking" and its most distinguishing feature is the role of power in the creation and delivery of PR messaging. But that power is not inherent in PR messages: it lies instead in the political, economic and social forces which call up PR to serve their own ends. What empowers PR is not the quality of its messaging but the power quotients of those who put it into action.

For us, therefore, the turn demonstrates that PR remains what it has always, but not apparently, been – a neutral set of communicative tools. These were available to its founding generation of users amongst the powerful, but *only recently* available to PR activists on the left, centre and right in the last 20 to 30 years. PR is used by partisans of all stripes. It is not technically partisan, although the switch from big media to social media ensures greater access for the production and distribution of persuasion. It is thus now immeasurably more difficult for PR to be captured by elites. It has become the communication of choice by society-wide forces and it is these that shape the contents of its messaging and stimulate and refine its techniques. The "signified" can bring the "signifier" into existence like never before. This universalism can put all of our turns into their broadened social, cultural and political significance.

Let's not be too serious

Another feature of the turn, for us, is that replacing symmetry with power has shaken us up, made us more questioning of other features of the PR phenomenon. For example, PR's own identity, as a practice and an academic field, could move away from its usual po-faced, over-seriousness about its own importance. A cheering, cheeky and very small sign of this was a conference at London College of Communications (10 July 2013) in the vibrant working-class London inner suburb of Elephant and Castle – with the title "PR and Disruption: Embracing and Surviving Change". In some emails, "Disruption" had a K in its spelling, and outside the building banners welcomed people to the "London College of Exhibitionists". Lecture titles included "PR and Disruptive Society", "PR and Disruptive Media" and "PR and Disruptive Skills". We note that these papers were given by the social media head of an international supermarket chain and by mainstream academics. Perhaps the conference's enthusiasm for its subject was ahead of its ability to find speakers in the "disruptive" tradition?

The conference, however, spurs us on to explore "PR and disruptive skills" as a skills crossover from activist PR into business. A current example is the insertion of flash mobbing into market promotion. The *Wall Street Journal* (2013) described the trend with the headline "Spontaneity for Hire: Flash Mobs Go Corporate: Companies Hire Dancers to Break Out in Public; Shimmying for Shoes, Chicken". The article signalled crossover from the first reported street flash mob in 2003 to the corporate event ten years later with "one difference: this mob was paid for".

Technique transfer to business

Another, more established example of crossover from outsider to insider practice is the "front" interest group, apparently speaking for the declared, named interest but funded by a hidden or rarely mentioned source. Sourcewatch (2013), part of the American-based Center for Media and Democracy and one of the most established and persistent critics of PR, lists partial, substantial or full examples in the US, Canada, Australia, Europe and the UK. The crossover of these "fronts" is to mimic groups of, say, environmentalists, consumer advocates, healthcare reformers, educationalists, springing up from "grassroots" individuals and having a local, regional or national presence. An example of "front" crossover is in the pro-smoking movement in the UK where the *Guardian* (2012) reported two groups (Forest and Freedom2choose)[1] campaigning against the public places smoking ban. Whether or not there is funding by the tobacco industry, there is a co-incidence of interest between these groups and the industry.

Mention "grassroots" and we can see why "fronts" are also known as "astroturf" organisations (Lubbers, 2002, p. 64). What corporate bodies want from crossover is a share of the public voice and support, and lobbying influence that groups like Friends of the Earth, Greenpeace, CND and Amnesty International have accumulated over time. Front groups are the compliment of technical imitation paid to such radical PR activists by big business. This sincerest form of flattery suggests a closer look at contemporary PR professionalism. If PR technique is not partisan, then framing any debate about the state of relationships between PR professionals in business, and in active advocacy bodies as a "disruption", is more a promotional trope than a forensic act. Besides the needs of conference organisers to attract an audience, what we have, more substantially, in the crossover phenomenon, is the knowledge transfer and skills exchange of a *common set of good communication practices*. Modern PR is becoming, we argue, a unified set of skills across all its users. This connects with our view that PR now must not be framed as a pro-capitalist or pro-activist exclusive skill set. We seek equality of esteem between PR practitioners whether they work for capitalist, non-capitalist or anti-capitalist interests. However, there is one necessary condition before that award of equal esteem is made, and the "astroturf" word shows it: PR practice should not attract esteem if deceit is used.

Refining our terms

Our argument of equal standing for corporate and activist PR lets us argue for another addition to the definition of the "turn". In the spirit of small-step evolution, this paper pushes the turn a little further by suggesting that two new terms, "dissent PR" and "protest PR", can better describe the wider field of activist PR. Our Google searching did not reveal these terms, nor does the literature show them to be extant, except that "dissent PR" has another small-step evolution in a sense different to the one developed here. An example is Reber and Berger (2006), who further develop PR role theory and professional ethics to include "dissent PR" not as an analytical category but as a professional practice (i.e., when practitioners in organisations argue against what they judge to be bad senior management decisions). Holtzhausen (2012) is the most forceful proponent of this reformation of PR away from organisational modernist thinking, which she sees as bounded by unchallenged assumptions and includes people in a hierarchical order who rarely (if ever) dissent from their seniors. She wants professionals to be evangelical PR protestants who dissent inside their employing organisation because her postmodern PR "is egalitarian, democratic and participative, not representative. Activist practice invited everyone to the discussion table and does not privilege management's views over those of stakeholders" (p. 238).

Our experience of corporate PR suggests that this small-step evolution will not thrive in our lifetimes. It is the practice of very brave and very rare corporate PR whistle blowers. But core features of Holtzhausen's postmodern PR are alive and well in many national and international cause and pressure groups such as Occupy, trade unions (the Living Wage campaign in the UK), and in their grass roots. See also protest and dissent PR described in the account of a PETA anti-fishing and anti-dairy campaign (Brummette, Zoch & Miller, 2013). They are also described as a collective experience inside the territory of protest camps (Feigenbaum, Frenzel & McCurdy, 2013) where activists develop "dynamic media ecologies;…innovative media strategies, experiment with new technologies, create independent media, crowdsource data and proactively debate issues of representation and media management" (p. 112). In our reading of Holtzhausen (2012), she fails to recognise the egalitarian, democratic and participative features of postmodern PR in the practice of these external, non-corporate dissenters. This omission neglects vital evidence of her desired reformation in what we consider to be another, more promising, setting.

There are at least three other interesting features to this activist "turn". The first is the near-automatic association of "dissent" with left wing causes. We would argue that this is academic "group thinking" that needs to be challenged. We remember a conference of the heartland institution of British capitalism (the Confederation of British Industry) in the 1970s, when a suggestion to start privatising nationalised industries was met with incredulity. Look what happened within a decade! A major cause of this earthquake of opinion was the dissenting PR from the British right wing thinktanks: The Adam Smith Institute and The Institute of Economic Affairs. Their thinking, amplified by effective PR through the national media, changed the policy agenda in the UK. So we have to let the rich and powerful back into our examination of modern "turned" PR, and note that when British (and other) bankers lobbied against reforms to their operations after the 2008 global financial crash, they are doing "dissent PR", if not its "protest" follow-up.

The second feature is definitions. If any of us has something new and differentiating to say, we need matching concepts to utter it. If we drill into the established but under-differentiated descriptor "activist", we find the distinction between two new concepts: "dissent PR" and "protest PR". The first is the dissemination of ideas, commentaries and policies through PR techniques in order to change current, dominant thinking and behaviour in private and public life (think of campaigns for gay marriage). The second term, "protest PR", follows on and it uses not ideas but techniques such as marches, rallies, stunts, strikes, boycotts and lawsuits to create influence on policy-makers (think black anger over police violence in the US). Note the August 2013 article in the right wing British *Express* group of newspapers welcoming opposition to fracking in the Conservative heartland county of Sussex. This intrusion of oil exploration into the southern English Home Counties comes after some two years of scientific and media debate about its pros and cons as a solution to cutting the UK's strategic dependency on foreign-sourced oil. (See the 2013 July report by the American Center for Science and Democracy for the case for and against this energy source.) Such reports are the raw material for dissent PR messaging by interested businesses. Listen also for new vocabulary from the protesters: to "controversalise" the fracking issue is one of their aims.[2]

Protest and dissent by the *Rules*

The third interesting feature of the academic turn away from near-exclusive use by the rich and powerful is exploring possible early influences on it. One candidate is Saul Alinsky's work on community organising in the American 1960s. Olson, Viola and Fromm-Reed (2011) have taken a psychologistic approach to analysing his 1971 *Rules for Radicals* rulebook. They note that social psychologists look at the informational influences and normative influences on campaigning. The first are concerned with truth statements and the latter focus on power relations. The informational influences bring out "the best and fullest pool of arguments, emphasizing intellect and research to raise the consciousness of everyone involved" (p. 52). On the other hand, the normative influences produce membership, intensity of beliefs, demonstrations, marches and protests (p. 52). These two influences are revealing descriptors, taken from another discipline (social psychology), and throw an independent light on our terms in that dissent PR aligns with informational influence and protest PR aligns with normative influence.

On the non-partisan quality of PR techniques, Namit (1983) noticed that establishment bodies also learned the *Rules* and knew how to neutralise them. He called, for example, on Californian school managers, when facing a possible teachers' strike, to prepare "a defense which consists of using the 'offense' by having a good public relations program to present their position" (abstract).

We also note that Alinsky himself pitches these informational influences highly in his "rulebook": *Rules for Radicals*. He thus assigns communications skill to be a very high level factor in creating pressure against powerful opponents: "One can lack any of the qualities of an organiser – with one exception – and still be effective and successful. The exception is the art of communications" (p. 81). Coombs and Holladay (2007) have come close to claiming Alinsky for PR.

They say that he developed a social activism in which they identify what today's practitioners call "issues management" and "research-based communications", and in so doing "he articulated a vision of activists that correlates with public relations more strongly" (pp. 68–70).

We do not, however, see Alinsky's (1971) *Rules* as a read-across to PR as strongly as Coombs and Holladay. First, community organising is a skill set much more overtly political. Community organising explicitly wants government or corporate policy change. It is not a politically or corporately neutral activity like PR. Community organising is a cause: PR is a communicative style. Change-seekers do community organising: conservatives and left radicals do PR. There is some read-across, however. We can imagine six of his rules underpinning PR techniques of messaging via words, visuals and events. These are signalled with square brackets below:

Thirteen rules of community organising, by Saul Alinsky (1971)

(1) "Power is not only what you have, but what the enemy thinks you have."
(2) "Never go outside the expertise of your people." [PR transferable]
(3) "Whenever possible, go outside the expertise of the enemy." [PR transferable]
(4) "Make the enemy live up to its own book of rules." [PR tranferable]
(5) "Ridicule is man's most potent weapon." [PR transferable]
(6) "A good tactic is one your people enjoy."
(7) "A tactic that drags on too long becomes a drag."
(8) "Keep the pressure on. Never let up."
(9) "The threat is usually more terrifying than the thing itself." (PR transferable)
(10) "The major premise for tactics is the development of operations that will maintain a constant pressure upon the opposition."
(11) "If you push a negative hard enough, it will push through and become a positive." [PR transferable]
(12) "The price of a successful attack is a constructive alternative."
(13) "Pick the target, freeze it, personalize it, and polarize it."

(From: http://en.wikipedia.org/wiki/Rules_for_Radicals)

Perhaps, readers, you can see more transfers?

There is another reason for our seeing only weak links with Alinsky's *Rules*, and for not claiming him for PR. We don't believe that PR is part of every public communicative act and we are therefore not inclined to see it everywhere. PR is not part of every communicative act but communication is part of every PR act. PR is not ubiquitous, and sometimes we suspect that as career academics in PR studies we are imperialist, wanting to see our object of study in action everywhere.

We claimed that PR today has escaped monopoly use by the rich and powerful while noting that the rich and powerful are also dissenters and protesters when their interests are threatened. An example is businesses registering headquarters in low tax countries. We welcome this catholic use of PR by the universe of interest, pressure, and cause groups in our pluralist, liberal, capitalist and market-orientated democracies. In doing so, we know that PR can have great persuasive effect, but we also know that it is too specific and too limited in its methods to be always the key persuasive factor in all circumstances of dissent and protest. We also know that there is a repertoire of persuasive activity (advertising; brand marketing; satire; street and building art; music, song and humour) that can be mixed to produce more effective campaigns than pure PR ones alone. But all campaigns in a democracy are still up against two factors that are hard to manipulate, however fully funded and multi-sourced. These are the balance of public opinion for and against them, and the balance government chooses between votes cast and sectional pressure applied.

Conclusion

Under the broad canopy of critical theory's key features we explored more deeply the possibilities for critical PR. We identify a central consequence of this postmodern turn in academic thinking as the replacement of symmetry by power. We note the retheorisation of activism as another consequence. We also identify some small-step evolutions in our discipline. First, activist PR analysis is refined by sub-sets of dissent and protest. Second, activist PR is now done by capitalist and anti-capitalist interests and occupies a significant acreage of liberal and pluralist political economies and civil societies. It has claimed centre stage. Third, activist PR can henceforth claim parity of esteem with business PR. Fourth, a reminder that PR as technique is neutral; and it is message content that is biased. Finally, we looked back on the work of the radical American community organiser Saul Alinsky, especially his rules of organisation, to continue debates about activist PR and explore how it can become more effective.

Notes

1   Forest is funded by the UK tobacco industry as well as individuals. See http://www.forestonline.org /about/faq/ (accessed 11 September 2013). It is part of the wider libertarian movement. See http://www. forestonline.org/about/message-from-our-director/ (accessed 11 September 2013). Freedom2choose state that they have no funding from industry and are supported by individual donations.
2   First heard by Kevin Moloney on the *Today* news programme, British BBC Radio 4, 7.55am, 20 August 2013.

References

Alinsky, S. (1971). *Rules for radicals: A pragmatic primer for realistic radicals*. New York, NY: Random House.
Bardhan, N., & Weaver, C. K. (Eds). (2011a). *Public relations in global contexts: Multi-paradigmatic* perspectives, pp. 140–66. New York & London: Routledge.
Bardhan, N., & Weaver, C. K. (2011b). Public relations in global cultural contexts. In N. Bardhan, & C. K. Weaver (Eds), *Public relations in global contexts: Multi-paradigmatic* perspectives, pp. 1–28. New York & London: Routledge.
Bauman, Z. (2000). *Liquid modernity*. Cambridge, UK: Polity Press.
Beck, U. (1992). *Risk society: Towards a new modernity*. London, UK: Sage.
Beck, U., Giddens, A., & Lash, S. (1994). *Reflexive modernization: Politics, tradition, and aesthetics in the modern social order*. Stanford, CA: Stanford University Press.
Brown, S. (2006). *The marketing code*. London, UK: Cyan Communications.
Brummette, J., Zoch, L. M., & Miller, L. (2013). *PETA: Media reputation and press agentry in the context of animal rights activism*. Paper presented at the International Public Relations Conference, Miami, March 2013.
Bureau of Investigative Journalism. (2012). Revealed: The £93m city lobby machine. Retrieved on 19 September 2013 from http://www.thebureauinvestigates.com/2012/07/09/revealed-the-93m-city -lobby-machine/
Carey, A. (1995). Taking the risk out of democracy: Propaganda versus freedom and liberty. In A. Lohrey (Ed.), *Taking the risk out of democracy: Propaganda in the US and Australia*. Sydney, Australia: University of New South Wales Press.
Center for Science and Democracy. (2013). Science, democracy, and community decisions on fracking. Retrieved 5 August 2013 from http://www.ucsusa.org/center-for-science-and-democracy/events/ community-decisions-on-fracking.html
Coombs, W. T., & Holladay, S. J. (2007). *It's not just PR: Public relations in society*, Oxford, UK: Blackwell Publishing.

Coombs. W. T., & Holladay, S. J. (2011). Privileging an activist vs. a corporate view of public relations history in the U.S. *Public Relations Review*. doi: 10.1016/j.pubrev.2011.11.010

Coombs. W. T., & Holladay, S. J. (2012). Fringe public relations: How activism moves critical PR toward the mainstream. *Public Relations Review*, 38(5), pp. 880–7.

Demetrious, K. (2013). *Public relations, activism, and social change: Speaking up.* Abingdon, UK: Routledge.

Derrida, J., & Malabou, C. (2004). *Counterpath: Travelling with Jacques Derrida* (D. Wills, Trans.). Stanford, CA: Stanford University Press.

Eagleton, T. (1996). *The illusions of postmodernism*. Oxford, UK: Blackwell.

Edwards, L. (2011). Critical perspectives in global public relations: Theorizing power. In N. Bardhan, & K. Weaver (Eds), *Public relations in global cultural contexts: Multi-paradigmatic perspectives*, pp. 20–49. New York, NY: Routledge.

Edwards, L., & Hodges, C. (Eds). (2011a). *Public relations, society, and culture: Theoretical and empirical explanations.* Abingdon, UK: Routledge.

Edwards, L., & Hodges, C. (Eds.). (2011b). Introduction: Implications of a (radical) socio-cultural "turn" in public relations scholarship. In L. Edwards, & C. Hodges (Eds), *Public relations, society, and culture: Theoretical and empirical explanations*, pp. 1–14. Abingdon, UK: Routledge.

Ewen, S. (1996). *PR! A social history of spin*. New York, NY: Basic Books.

Express (2013). Balcombe backs anti-fracking protest. Retrieved on 4 August 2013 from http://www.express.co.uk/news/uk/419532/Balcombe-backs-anti-fracking-protest

Fairclough, N. (2013). *Critical discourse analysis: The critical study of language*. New York, NY: Routledge.

Feigenbaum, A., Frenzel, F., & McCurdy, P. (2013). *Protest camps*. London, UK: Zed Books.

Freeland, C. (2012). *Plutocrats: The rise of the new global super-rich and the fall of everyone else*. New York, NY: Penguin.

Frow, J. (1991). *What Was Postmodernism?* Sydney, Australia: Local Consumption Publications.

Grisoni, L., & Kirk, P. (2006). Verse, voice and va va voom!: Illuminating management processes through poetry. *Management Decision*, 44(4), pp. 512–25.

Harvey, D. (1989). *The condition of postmodernity*. Oxford, UK: Blackwell.

Holtzhausen, D. (2000). Postmodern values in public relations. *Journal of Public Relations Research*, 12, pp. 93–114.

Holtzhausen, D. (2002). Towards a postmodern research agenda for public relations. *Public Relations Review*, 28, pp. 251–64.

Holtzhausen, D. (2011). The need for a postmodern turn. In N. Bardhan, & C. K. Weaver (Eds), *Public relations in global contexts: Multi-paradigmatic* perspectives, pp. 140–66. New York & London: Routledge.

Holtzhausen, D. (2012). *Public relations as activism: Postmodern approaches to theory and practice*. New York, NY: Routledge.

Holtzhausen, D., & Voto, R. (2002). Resistance from the margins: The postmodern public relations practitioner as organizational activist. *Journal of Public Relations Research*, 14, pp. 57–84.

Ihlen, O., van Ruler, B., & Fredriksson, M. (Eds). (2009). *Public relations and social theory: Key figures and concepts*. New York, NY: Routledge.

L'Etang, J. (2004). *Public relations in Britain: A history of professional practice in the 20th century*. Mahwah, NJ: Lawrence Erlbaum Associates.

L'Etang, J. (2008). *Public relations: Concepts, practice and critique*. London, UK: Sage.

L'Etang, J., & Pieczka, M. (Eds). (1996). *Critical perspectives in public relations*. London, UK: International Thomson Business Press.

Lubbers, E. (Ed.). (2002). *Battling big business: Countering greenwash, infiltration and other forms of corporate bullying*. Monroe, ME: Common Courage Press.

McKie, D. (1997). Shifting paradigms: Public relations beyond rats, stats and 1950s science. *Australian Journal of Communication*, 24(2), pp. 81–96.

McKie, D., & Munshi, D. (2007). *Reconfiguring public relations: Ecology, equity, and enterprise*. London, UK: Routledge.

McKie, D., & Munshi, D. (2009). Theoretical black holes: A partial A to Z of missing critical thought in public relations. In E. L. Toth, R. L. Heath, & D. Waymer (Eds), *Rhetorical and critical studies in public relations*, 2nd edition, pp. 61–75. Mahwah, NJ: Lawrence Erlbaum Associates.

Mickey, T. (1997). A postmodern view of public relations: Sign and reality. *Public Relations Review*, 23(3), pp. 271–85.

Moloney, K. (2000). *Rethinking public relations: The spin and the substance*. Abingdon, UK: Routledge.

Moloney, K. (2006). *Rethinking public relations: PR propaganda and democracy*. London, UK: Routledge.

Motion, J., & Leitch, S. (1996). A discursive perspective from New Zealand: Another world view. *Public Relations Review*, 22(3), pp. 297–309.

Munshi, D., & Edwards, L. (2011). "Race" in/and Public Relations [Special issue]. *Journal of Public Relations Research*, 23(4).

Namit, C. (1983). Advocacy communications: A game plan to win public support at National School Board's Association Convention. San Francisco, June. Retrieved on 18 July 2013 from http://ehis.ebscohost .com/eds/results?sid=558f1a0b-1a07-46af-b021eeb9f961216e%40sessionmgr15&vid=14&hid= 4&bquery=Namit,+Charles,+J.&bdata=JnR5cGU9MCZzaXRlPWVkcy1saXZlJnNjb3 BlPXNpdGU=

Olson, B., Viola, J., & Fromm-Reed, S. (2011). A temporal model of community organising and direct action. *Journal of Social Justice*, 23, pp. 52–60.

Pearson, R. (1992). Perspectives on public relations history. In R. Heath, & E. Toth (Eds), *Rhetorical and critical approaches to public relations*, pp. 111–30. Hillsdale, NJ: Lawrence Erlbaum Associates.

Radford, G. (2012). Public relations in a postmodern world. *Public Relations Inquiry*, 1(1), pp. 49–67. doi: 10.1177/2046147X11422143

Reber, B., & Berger, B. (2006). Advocate, exit, or something else? Doing the "right thing" in PR when organisations misstep. Paper presented at the International Communications Association Conference (PR Division), Dresden, Germany.

Sourcewatch. (2013). Front groups. Retrieved 30 August 2013 from http://www.sourcewatch.org/index. php/Front_groups

The *Guardian*. (2008). Financial regulations: Banks fight new rules to prevent repeat of Rock run. Retrieved on 19 September 2013 from http://www.theguardian.com/business/2008/sep/15/northernrock. banking

The *Guardian*. (2012). Pro-smoking activists threaten and harass health campaigners. Retrieved on 11 September 2013 from http://www.theguardian.com/society/2012/jun/01/pro-smoking-activists-health-campaigners

Tyler, L. (2005). Towards a postmodern understanding of crisis communication. *Public Relations Review*, 31(4), pp. 566–71.

Wall Street Journal. (2013, 8 May) Spontaneity for hire: Flash mobs go corporate. Retrieved 28 August 2013 from http://online.wsj.com/article/SB10001424127887323798104578453172650031706.html

13

A reflexive perspective on public relations

On leaving traditional thinking and uncovering the taken-for-granted

Jesper Falkheimer and Mats Heide

A decade ago we published a book in Swedish entitled *Reflexiv kommunikation: Nya tankar för strategiska kommunikatörer* [Reflexive communication: New thoughts for strategic communication professionals] (Falkheimer & Heide, 2003) in which we introduced the concept of reflexive communication. The book aimed to turn established ideas upside-down and to contribute to a reflexive turn of public relations by integrating social and organizational theories. In the book we questioned several communication myths. We did not explain myths as being equal to lies, but rather as being equal to stories, discourses or taken-for-granted ideas. We challenged the idea that information was the same thing as knowledge (and the strong belief in new information systems and media technologies), the concept of target group (since we found this to be based in a transmission view on communication), the myth that publicity effects may be statistically generalized based on counting exposure (as a simplification of interpretative processes), the boundary between external and internal communications (since this was and is in flux), the idea that a monolithic organizational identity is possible and preferable (leading to simplistic and dangerous management), and the myth that theory and practice may be totally separated. Several of our questionings may not be regarded as totally new or radical; still, several practitioners showed interest in the approach. But this approach was harder to find when consulting the literature on public relations, and it still is.

We have been struck by the fact that the rational, modernistic paradigm and representationalism, which builds on a being-realism ontology (see Chia, 1996), still predominates mainstream public relations literature. We are, obviously, provocative and over-exaggerate to a certain point, but the tendency is salient. We are astonished that there are so few alternative and critical perspectives available to the dominating perspective, although there are exceptions such as Gilpin and Murphy (2008), Holtzhausen (2012), and Ihlen and Verhoeven (2012). Our concern is, however, not new. Already in the first *Handbook of public relations* McKie (2001) concludes that "public relations theory cannot stick with the traditional 'value-free and neutral scientific observations'…of old research paradigms" (p. 91). McKie believes that the field is too insular. Gower (2006) states, in the same vein, that "we need to bring into our literature new theories from other disciplines to enhance our conceptual understanding of the field and explore more fully the implications of postmodern theories for the practice of public relations" (p. 177). Botan and Hazleton (2006) withhold that the Excellence theory is excellent, but urge that the next stage of development of the field would be a struggle of paradigms. European PR scholars had already started this struggle at the beginning of the 1990s, but there is a heavy US bias in public relations research and such research has mainly had a functionalistic approach (L'Etang, 2005, 2008). They mention co-creation as an important new, and possibly paradigmatic, trend. A special issue of *Public Relations Review* aims to widen the theoretical framework of public relations through the use of prominent social theorists (Ihlen & van Ruler, 2007). Elizabeth Toth (2010) argues in the newest *Handbook of Public Relations* that there exist at least six alternative paradigms to the dominant one.

However, we do not agree with Toth since these six "paradigms" are not at an equal level. Some of those that Toth mentions, such as the crisis communication and tactical paradigm, are research interests; while others are merely perspectives – such as the feminist and the rhetorical "paradigm". The only one of the six that we believe could be counted as an authentic paradigm is the critical theory paradigm; it has a different ontological and epistemological approach compared to the dominant, functionalistic paradigm. While the critical theory paradigm, with its foundation in neo-Marxism, exclusively analyses public relations from a power perspective, a reflexive perspective is broader and includes other aspects from different "turns" within organization theory, such as the cultural, practice and paradox turn, as well as late modern social theory.

Hence, this chapter proposes a *reflexive perspective* on public relations research and practice. The "reflexive turn" within academic theorizing is a result of an increasing interest among scholars to be aware of, and discuss, the active role they have in constructing the reality that is to be researched. This turn stands in contrast to the still-dominating belief that researchers have an objectivist status. The aim of this conceptual and meta-theoretical chapter is to challenge and question public relations theory and present an alternative, reflexive and holistic perspective that connects theory and practice in a new way.

This chapter starts with a somewhat personal reflection on the research in public relations that we have experienced during our careers as scholars. We then present and discuss the dominating, functionalistic and managerial approach within public relations research. The third section focuses on the concept of reflexivity and its bearing on public relations, and ends with a discussion about the relationship between theory and practice.

Experiences and reflections on public relations research

We have read dozens of textbooks and chapters in anthologies as well as hundreds of research articles that have a functionalistic approach based in a positivistic paradigm. We have reviewed a lot of manuscripts that clearly could be placed within the functionalistic approach. Further, we have attended numerous research conferences listening to presentation after presentation with a functionalistic approach. An archetypal conference presentation contains a hypothesis, empirical research questions, graphs, pie charts and various statistical measures that are delivered in an elegant, but often speedy fashion. The presenters are often proud of the somewhat limited results that they have found, but never reflect or discuss the quality of the research or philosophy of science aspects. From a reflexive perspective these studies may be criticized from an epistemological and ontological approach but also from a *why* perspective. Why is it interesting to conduct a survey into this? What gains are made from the results?

Another problem is that practitioners often find that the elegant, but often too abstract, statistic correlations and measurements are distant from their everyday work, and it is, consequently, hard for them to adopt and use the results (see Alvesson, 1996b). Even if we were proponents of the positivistic paradigm we could challenge and reflect upon several of the studies from a methodological perspective. These conference presenters always tend to claim that the response rate of the investigation is good or acceptable, although it is usually somewhere between 40 per cent down to the extreme of as little as 6 per cent. At the same time methodology literature and courses teach students that an acceptable response rate is at least 60 per cent. A consequence of a low response rate is that the sample becomes so small that it is not possible to make any advanced statistical analysis. We have witness presentations where N = 10 and the scholar presented statistical measures and drew several general conclusions. But how can we accept research that is based on such a low response rate and N number, when it is impossible to run any statistical tests? Another pattern that we find in many studies within public relations is the tendency to use student sampling in experiments or surveys. But how is it possible to draw general conclusions from a student group? Students belong to an exclusive group with certain and unique prerequisites. Further, students tend to be rather homogenous (Peterson, 2011). Sears's (1986, p. 515) widely cited article proposes several problems with student sampling: "[C]ompared with older adults, college students are likely to have less-crystallized attitudes, less-formulated senses of self, stronger cognitive skills, stronger tendencies to comply with authority, and more unstable peer group relationships." Accordingly, it is very problematic to use student sampling, with low external validity, for drawing any generalizable conclusions.

Thus, one might wonder how it is feasible that this kind of research is accepted for publication in well-established journals? One possible explanation is that there is a large demand on modern scholars to publish articles to make academic careers. Another answer is that many scholars at the same time have limited financial resources, which makes it convenient to use convenience samples of students. Students are also used because it is hard to "draw nonstudents to the lab" (Kam, Wilking & Zechmeister, 2007, p. 416). Henry (2008) has identified the same tendency in psychology research, and he requests that scholars be more aware of the problems and limitations of student sampling and that they become more self-reflective. We all sit in the same boat, so to speak, and there is a large pressure to be productive and get articles published (see Alvesson & Sandberg, 2014).

Depicting the dominant research approach

One can easily identify a main approach within public relations research – the functionalistic applied approach. There is no doubt that this approach has dominated and still dominates the field of public relations (Holtzhausen, 2002, 2012; Ihlen & Verhoeven, 2012; Toth, 2002; Wehmeier & Winkler, 2013). One reason may be that public relations research has emanated from practitioners' need of simple and standardized models. Another reason is that the ideal of positivism and what is widely taken-for-granted as real "scientific research" has dictated for a long time. This ideal has also been reproduced since many scientific journals primarily welcome positivistic research. One explanation why the functionalistic research, which is based in a positivistic epistemology, dominates, is that many scientific journals within the area of public relations have a certain publication formula that produces and reproduces tacit blueprints (see Fairhurst, 2014). The publication formula is taken-for-granted as something natural that is both rational and good. There are many academic and methodological expectations of rationality and clarity that are rather easy to fulfil with a study that follows a positivist tradition (and vocabulary), but it is more of a challenge for alternative, reflexive or social constructionist research.

In positivistic social science research scholars understand the world as constituted of discrete and identifiable material and social entities, and there is a fairly large risk that they develop an intellectual understanding that Whitehead (1925/1985) calls "the fallacy of misplaced concreteness". In the lion's share of textbooks, articles, and, not least, consultancy books (i.e., pop-management or "airport-management-books") concerning public relations, we can identify a strong belief in rational choice theory, with the American economist Gary Becker (see, e.g., Becker & Murphy, 1988) being one dominant proponent. Different to research in closely related fields such as organizational communication, public relations is still bound to a predominating static understanding of concepts such as "organization", "strategy", "communication" and "environment", whose ontological status is not problematized at all. Thus, there is strong agreement that information is equal to "data", which we may collect using scientific and standardized methods, helping us to uncover and understand the real truth that is "out there".

The functionalistic approach is characterized by an over-confidence in information per se (Christensen & Cornelissen, 2011). It is believed that organizations are a stable phenomenon in an objective world, and the research is mainly focused on producing normative, applied knowledge (often in the form of models or tools) that can help managers to make organizations and their communication strategies even more efficient and effective. The social reality is believed to exist "out there", external to individuals and produced before human activity (Putnam, 1983). Hence, functionalism is based in realist epistemology, and natural science is the ideal role model. It is often assumed that an objective and value-free social science is possible (Burrell & Morgan, 1979; Morgan, 1980).

There is also a strong element of *managerialism* (Alvesson & Sveningsson, 2011) in the public relations literature. Managerialism is an ideology based on the notion that managers of various kinds are rational actors, and essential for running effective organizations. Consequently, it is taken-for-granted that organizations, to a greater extent, can control and manage internal and external development and various publics and opinions. This traditional understanding and thinking produces "rational" theories and models that are rhetorically convincing and rather seductive; they explain the complex reality in a linear and straightforward fashion.

Effects of boxed-in research in public relations

A great problem with one dominating approach within public relations research is that the rather tight frames and particular mindset tends to produce fragmented knowledge and uncreative thinking, which Alvesson and Sandberg (2014) call *boxed-in research*. This kind of research often is rather uncreative and uninteresting and only tries to bridge a small knowledge gap that has been identified, leading to results with little relevance for either scholars or practitioners. Alvesson and Sandberg (2014) distinguish between different types of research boxes that scholars tend to stay inside, leading to non-innovative and predictable research – these may indeed gain individual researchers meaningful careers and serve to fulfil institutional demands for a high publication rate, but they do not advance research or societal development. First there is the perspective box, which means that the scholar always uses the same theoretical framework: e.g., image repair theory or agenda-setting theory. Second there is a domain box, meaning that a scholar specializes in one small field, e.g. national branding or social media use, and mainly replicates earlier studies. Third, there is a methodology box, where the scholar consistently applies the same method approach and technique in empirical research.

Alvesson and Sandberg conclude that boxed-in research is very problematic: "We regard the following disadvantages as particularly problematic for valuable knowledge production: over-specialization, silo mentality, fragmentation, box identity, suspiciousness, intra-box communication, polarization and unquestioning attitudes" (p. 8). The critique mentioned mainly concerns management and organizational research, but we – sadly enough – think that it is even more applicable to public relations research. We would also like to add a fourth box that is valid for public relations – the practitioner-expectation box. A common pattern at some public relations conferences is for some attending practitioners to claim that scholars are not willing enough to develop "useful", applied theories that can help organizations to become even more efficient and excellent in their public relations.

And we also often meet the same expectation in our contacts with practitioners; they request theories that can help them to show the "real value" of public relations, mainly for the CEO and the corporate executive board; and they would like to know how different practical problems can best can be solved. Many PR scholars also experience this practitioner expectation from national public relations associations. There is, consequently, a large pressure on PR scholars to develop "useful" theories. However, we question this expectation, not least since the field of public relations is biased by a functionalistic approach. We do not believe that "more of the same" will develop the field. On the contrary, there is a larger need for more critical and reflexive research on public relations, and we are certain that such research will advance the discipline. It is also important to raise the question "do we have something interesting to say", something that gives new, astounding or alternative insights into the phenomena under study (Alvesson, 2013).

Reflexivity

There have been several calls to develop the field: "public relations ought to become even more intellectually expansive, more critically reflective, and more cognizant of the diverse forms of organizational activity in today's world" (Cheney & Christensen, 2001, p. 179). One way to reach this is to apply a reflexivity approach to public relations research. The concept of reflexivity has been used in several ways and we could have spent the whole chapter reflecting on it. Social theorists (e.g., Beck, Giddens & Lash, 1994) have, in different ways, described late modern society as increasingly reflexive, creating notions of uncertainty, ambiguity and risk for societies, organizations and individuals. While social theorists often discuss reflexivity at a societal level, other scholars have focused more on the relationship between the nature of knowledge and how we can produce knowledge about the complex reality.

The communication scholar Frederick Steier (1991) is interested in this relationship and how reflexivity affects social constructionist research. Steier discerns two forms of reflexivity – first-order and second-order. In the first-order reflexivity scholars pay attention to organizational accounts and how they form the reality of organizational members; and in the second-order reflexivity, or what often is labelled meta-reflexive theorizing, scholars reflect on their own notions and claims. In this chapter we mainly focus on second-order reflexivity and discuss public relations research, but we also discuss public relations practice in organizations and society from a reflexive approach.

Many social and organizational theorists have used reflexivity as a concept in several academic fields, and in different ways. Reflexivity as a generic scientific concept, used in mathematics as well as the social sciences, interprets relationships as bidirectional and challenges unidirectional dichotomies between structure and agency or cause and effect. A reflexive approach would mean that both strictly functionalistic-instrumental and neo-Marxist-critical theories are viewed as being deterministic and non-reflexive. Holtzhausen (2002, p. 256) states that "[r]eflexivity is a postmodern process whereby scholars critique their own theories". The social theorist Giddens is one of the main proponents of a reflexive approach in the social sciences, analysing the bidirectional relationships between structure and agency as well as between macro and micro levels of societal and human life. Giddens (1984, 1990) interprets contemporary society as a radicalized and reflexive modernity where individualism, detraditionalization, uncertainty and increased information flow are challenging old relationships between structure and agency.

Reflexive society may be interpreted as a crucial premise for the evolvement and expansion of public relations as a late modern expert system that handles reflexivity processes between organizations and society. Following this thinking, public relations may be viewed as a reflexive organizational process or system aiming to create, defend or increase legitimacy in reflexive modernity processes inside organizations and between organizations and society. The evolvement of social media and new media, and their behaviours, is making reflexivity processes even more relevant from an analysis point of view, since they transgress borders between the private and the public and what we used to term "senders" and "receivers". Organizational members and publics are reflexive agents in a bidirectional relationship with organizations and social entities.

According to Verčič, van Ruler, Bütschi and Flodin (2001), European communication professionals ideally are "reflexive". They use the concept "reflexive" in relation to business intelligence and adaptation to current societal values, meaning that practitioners "analyze changing standards and values in society and discuss these with the members of the organization, in order to adjust the standards and values of the organization regarding social responsibility and legitimacy" (Verčič, et al., 2001, p. 380). Using reflexivity in this sense is possible, but is not very new in public relations. The practice of one of the so-called fathers of public relations, Ivy Lee, may be debated, but he did in fact explain his public relations ideal in a similar way: "[N]o company can succeed permanently which does not deserve and receive the confidence of both its own employees and the public" (Lee, quoted from a bulletin after the Colorado coal strike 1913–14, cited in Hallahan, 2002, p. 299).

We, on the other hand, use "reflexive" as an ontological and epistemological concept, similar (to some extent) to Holmström (2010), who, based in the social systems theory of Luhmann, proposes reflectivity as a central concept describing the ability to question the taken-for-granted one "truth" or understanding of reality. Holmström (2005, p. 499) writes about the evolution of public relations and its relation to social processes, and about how the field is now entering a reflective paradigm: "As opposed to reflexivity, reflection means that a social system is able to relate to itself and its perspective or worldview." This interpretation is certainly correct using Luhmann's definition, but we do not use his theory here and we do not really see any clash between reflexivity and reflectivity. Hence, we understand reflexivity as a meta-theory that can be used to gain new insights and knowledge on public relations as a social or organizational phenomenon. We acknowledge that there are ideological aspects behind every theory, model and research. And with the reflexivity approach we should challenge different dominating perspectives and welcome alternatives (see. Alvesson & Kärreman, 2013). In the majority of public relations books and articles there is a concealed managerial and rationalistic perspective that colours our understanding and knowledge of public relations. The research in public relations is socially legitimized by society, and the hegemony of certain kinds of public relations research has profound effects on individuals, organizations and society.

Apart from the dominating positivistic approach within public relations, the reflexivity approach focuses on how we understand the reality (ontology) and how we can produce new knowledge on this reality (epistemology). In the traditional (neo-)positivistic approach, reality is believed to be objective and external, and accordingly it is possible for it to be discovered and described by scholars using scientific methods (for "scientific methods" read "questionnaires"). Communication is then regarded as a simple tool to describe the already-fixed reality (i.e., a transmission view of communication), that then can be used to develop models or theories that describe and prescribe how the reality functions. However, it is important here to underline that there are also many scholars who use qualitative methods using the same ideals that rule positivistic research – such as hypothesis testing, objectivity and inter-rater reliability (see Alvesson, 1996b).

One such example is Glaser and Strauss's (1967) grounded theory. Following the reflexivity approach means that scholars are hesitant to see communication only as a simple vehicle to describe the reality "out there"; rather communication is understood as a means to produce and reproduce a social reality (see Mickey, 1997). Being reflexive embraces the notion that scholars understand that they also are part of the social reality themselves, and that they contribute to the production of this reality. This means that scholars must consider how they and their own interests, backgrounds, and so forth, influence the results that are produced. Empirical "data" are never stable, mirroring an objective reality; but rather constructions produced by the scholar and in some degree in interaction with the persons that are part of the study (Alvesson & Sköldberg, 2009). By interpreting the empirical material through the lens of different theories, the scholar can produce one of many conceivable interpretations and results.

Accordingly, there are always alternative explanations and interpretations, and it is ideal for the reflexivity approach for one to never take things for granted and to continually search for alternative understandings. One effective way to attain this ideal is to use several different philosophical traditions and theories concerning any given empirical material. A very elegant example of this procedure is performed by Alvesson (1996a), who analyses a business meeting at an industrial company. Alvesson interpreted the empirical material, in the form of observations, with the help of culture theory, Foucault's theory of power *and* Habermass' theory of communicative action. These different theories and traditions put different aspects of the socially constructed reality into the limelight, and proposed different understandings. The use of different theories makes us open to alternative understandings of an all-too-often taken-for-granted reality, and to be stuck in the first descriptive first-order interpretation.

Another part of being methodologically reflexive is to consider how the scholar's background, values, ideas, interests and so forth influence the result, and to consider how these aspects both open and close different interpretive possibilities (Alvesson, 1996b). However, Gilmore and Kenny (2015) maintain that self-reflexivity in published qualitative studies often is treated "somewhat mechanistically within the methods section" (p. 20). Their recipe for reaching meaningful conclusions in organization studies is to conduct reflexive pair interviewing, whereby two or more scholars work together within the same research study. This technique helps to reach a deeper reflection on both the research process per se, and to the "self-as-researcher", both of which are more difficult to attain by an individual scholar acting alone. In the same vein, there is the idea of presenting interim interpretations to participants of the study in order to receive new and different perspectives upon the interpretations. These perspectives and ideas are often very rewarding, and can help the scholar to see alternative solutions and understandings. However, we do not believe in the idea of respondent validation that is proposed by Lincoln and Guba (1985) (among others), as a way to increase the validity of a study. Respondent validation is grounded in a realist understanding under which it is assumed that there is an objective and "correct" reality out there, and one that scholars can reach with the help of their respondents (Silverman, 2013).

Hibbert, Sillince, Diefenbach and Cunliffe (2014) have developed the relationally reflexive approach, which they believe offers a better prerequisite for more generative theorizing, encompasses new ideas, assists in the development of scholars and their practices and relationships, and provides thought-action repertoires for practitioners. Many other reflexive comprehensive scholars, including Alvesson and Sandberg (2013), also conclude that there is far too little innovative and high-impact research within organization studies. PR is similarly guilty, as we pointed out in the earlier discussion of boxed-in research. A practice of relationally reflexive research practice entails three stages: (1) pre-research, (2) the research process, and (3) refining theories in context. In the first stage the scholar should try to go beyond preferred theories, and thereby challenge the taken-for-granted worldview. One way to achieve this is to develop long-term relationships with scholars from different fields and with different interests and backgrounds.

An advantage of engaging in multidisciplinary conversations is that one's assumptions become more visible (Hibbert et al., 2014). During the research process scholars can discuss the emergent theorizing with different actors (e.g., other scholars and practitioners) so that traditional or expected theoretical conclusions are drawn. We have noticed that critical scholars within the fields of public relations and organization studies too often deliver expected conclusions; i.e., that different power dimensions affect the persons under study. The last stage is refining theories in context, and Hibbert et al. claim that such a procedure can expand the richness of the conclusions. Our experience is that conversations with the subjects of study contribute greatly to the results and give inspiration for new lines of thought and alternative interpretations. Hibbert et al. note that such conversations and interactions make practitioners part of the theory construction process. These conversations are thus valuable occasions for scholars to undertake several kinds of reflection.

We had an analogous idea for a Swedish anthology (Falkheimer & Heide, 2011). The aim of the anthology was to review and present some of the research in strategic communication that Swedish scholars have studied. Each chapter would contain one, longer, section, in which a scholar would present on an issue (e.g. lobbying, institutionalism, political strategic communication); a closing section in which a.practioner would respond to the previous text would then follow. This way of working seemed very promising and also contributed to a wider group of readers than usually is the case for research anthologies. Traditionally, practitioners are experts on practice and scholars analyse texts, acts, data and so forth. By collaborating with practitioners, or (as in the case of the anthology mentioned above), opening up the literature for practitioner comments, the process becomes bidirectional. One possible implication is that research might effect a larger impact upon practice; conversely, another implication is that practice would have a larger impact upon research.

Finally: the relationship between theory and practice

In comparison to critical theory that mainly focuses on challenging the source and legitimacy of dominating ideas from a power and structural perspective (L'Etang, 2005), we do not view public relations from a deterministic perspective. We believe – based on long experience and collaboration with communication practitioners – that public relations practice is a double-edged sword. Public relations may be used as an instrument for domination or manipulation, but it may also be used also as a tool for increasing organizational and societal transparency, participation and motivation. There has, over the last decade or so, been a slight increase in critical public relations research. This is beneficial for the development of the discipline, but sometimes we think that critical research takes an elitist position, watching practice from an ivory tower with a poor connection to what is going on in the diverse practice. An example of this is when media scholars do research about "spin" or "news management" based on the assumption that publicity is all that public relations is, and that all practitioners are basically propagandists. We know that public relations is a diverse field of practice and that there are examples of manipulation as well as work that actually may have positive organizational or societal impact, and we welcome more public relations research from a practice perspective and also research projects in collaboration with practitioners. Hence, we believe in an ideal where critical and reflexive research can be combined with a constructive practitioner-oriented approach and result in a new, interesting and productive knowledge of public relations.

The relationship between theory and practice is crucial in public relations. It is a fact that public relations research is and has a strong relationship to practice. A semantic network analysis of keywords in the titles of articles published in *Public Relations Review* and the *Journal of*

Public Relations Research between 1975–2011 show that "communication", "PR", "public" and" practitioner" were the most prominent keywords: "The most salient association was 'PR' and 'practitioners' across time periods. This suggests that PR scholars have persistently tried to link scholarship and practice" (Kim, Choi, Reber & Kim, 2014, p. 118). Many scholars – including ourselves – have a background in practice and work with consultancy.

From a critical perspective one may question the strong bond between practitioners and researchers, especially since mainstream research also has a managerial approach and tries to answer research questions formulated in practice. We do not think that a total separation between research and practice is possible, or indeed preferable, but we do think that the relationship between researchers and practitioners should be viewed differently than it usually is. From a traditional perspective researchers are supposed to be experts, and practitioners laymen. From a reflexive perspective the relationship is bidirectional, not unidirectional. This means that new knowledge is developed as part of a process whereby researchers problematize, question and con-textualize, while practitioners supply experiences and concrete knowledge.

There is an increasing demand on public relations practice to demonstrate outcomes. This is not new but the demands are becoming stronger in parallel to the increase in public relations practice globally and the expectations that follow this. Practitioners ask for methods and tools that can show their organizations that their practice leads to measurable effects and offer a return on investment (e.g., considering public opinion, behavioural change, image perception, trust or co-worker identity). One may question if this is what public relations research is for, but the demand for effects research is understandable. We do not think that the solution is that research-ers prioritize to solve organizations' communication problems since practitioners do this a lot better by themselves. But what we may do is to carry out research work in the actual field of practice – from a reflexive and, of course, an ethical perspective.

References

Alvesson, M. (1996a). *Communication, power and organization*. Berlin: Gruyter.

Alvesson, M. (1996b). Leadership studies: From procedure and abstraction to reflexivity and situation. *Leadership Quarterly*, 7(4), pp. 455–85.

Alvesson, M. (2013). Do we have something to say? From re-search to roi-search and back again. *Organization*, 20(1), pp. 79–90.

Alvesson, M., & Kärreman, D. (2013). The closing of critique, pluralism and reflexivity: A response to Hardy and Grant and some wider reflections. *Human Relations*, 66(10), pp. 1353–71.

Alvesson, M., & Sandberg, J. (2013). *Constructing research questions. Doing interesting research*. London: Sage.

Alvesson, M., & Sandberg, J. (2014). Habitat and habitus: Boxed-in versus box-breaking research. *Organization Studies*, 35(7), pp. 967–87.

Alvesson, M., & Sköldberg, K. (2009). *Reflexive methodology: New vistas for qualitative research*, 2nd edition. London: Sage.

Alvesson, M., & Sveningsson, S. (2011). Management is the solution: Now what was the problem? On the fragile basis for managerialism. *Scandinavian Journal of Management*, 27(4), pp. 349–61.

Beck, U., Giddens, A., & Lash, S. (1994). *Reflexive modernization: Politics, tradition, and aesthetics in the modern social order*. Stanford, CA: Stanford University Press.

Becker, G. S., & Murphy, K. M. (1988). A theory of rational addiction. *The Journal of Political Economy*, (4), pp. 675–700.

Botan, C. H., & Hazleton, V. (2006). Public relations in a new age. In C. H. Botan, & V. Hazleton (Eds), *Public relations theory II*, pp. 1–18. Mahwah, New Jersey: Lawrence Erlbaum.

Burrell, G., & Morgan, G. (1979). *Sociological paradigms and organizational analysis*. Aldershot: Gower.

Cheney, G., & Christensen, L. T. (2001). Public relations as contested terrain: A critical response. In R. L. Heath (Ed.), *Handbook of public relations*, pp. 167–82. Thousand Oaks, CA: Sage.

Chia, R. (1996). The problem of reflexitivity in organizational research: Towards a postmodern science of organization. *Organization*, 3(1), pp. 31–59.

Christensen, L. T., & Cornelissen, J. (2011). Bridging corporate and organizational communication: Review, development and a look to the future. *Management Communication Quarterly*, 25(3), pp. 383–414.

Fairhurst, G. T. (2014). Exploring the back alleys of publishing qualitative organizational communication research. *Management Communication Quarterly*, 28(3), pp. 432–39.

Falkheimer, J., & Heide, M. (2003). *Reflexiv kommunikation: Nya tankar för strategiska kommunikatörer* [Reflexive communication: New thoughts for strategic communicators]. Malmö, Sweden: Liber.

Falkheimer, J., & Heide, M. (Eds). (2011). *Strategisk kommunikation: Forskning och praktik.* [Strategic communication: Research and practice]. Lund, Sweden: Studentlitteratur.

Giddens, A. (1984). *The constitution of society: Outline of the theory of structuration.* Cambridge, England: Polity Press.

Giddens, A. (1990). *The consequences of modernity.* Cambridge, England: Polity.

Gilmore, S., & Kenny, K. (2015). Work-worlds colliding: Self-reflexivity, power and emotion in organizational ethnography. *Human Relations*, 28(1), pp. 55–78

Gilpin, D. R., & Murphy, P. J. (2008). *Crisis communication in a complex world.* Oxford: Oxford University Press.

Glaser, B. G., & Strauss, A. L. (1967). *The discovery of grounded theory: Strategies for qualitative research.* Chicago, IL: Aldine Publishing.

Gower, K. K. (2006). Public relations research at the crossroads. *Journal of Public Relations Research*, 18(2), pp. 177–90.

Hallahan, K. (2002). Ivy Lee and the Rockefellers' response to the 1913–1914 Colorado coal strike. *Journal of Public Relations Research*, 14(4), pp. 265–315.

Henry, P. J. (2008). Student sampling as a theoretical problem. *Psychological Inquiry*, 19(2), pp. 114–26.

Hibbert, P., Sillince, J., Diefenbach, T., & Cunliffe, A. L. (2014). Relationally reflexive practice: A generative approach to theory development in qualitative research. *Organizational Research Methods*, 17(3), pp. 278–98.

Holmström, S. (2005). Reframing public relations: The evolution of a reflective paradigm for organizational legitimization. *Public Relations Review*, 31, pp. 497–504.

Holmström, S. (2010). Reflective management: Seeing the organization as if from outside. In R. L. Heath (Ed.), *The SAGE handbook of public relations*, pp. 261–76. Thousand Oaks, CA: Sage.

Holtzhausen, D. R. (2002). Towards a postmodern research agenda for public relations. *Public Relations Review*, 28(3), pp. 251–64.

Holtzhausen, D. R. (2012). *Public relations as activism: Postmodern approaches to theory and practice.* New York, NY: Routledge.

Ihlen, O., & Verhoeven, P. (2012). A public relations identity for the 2010s. *Public Relations Inquiry*, 1(2), pp. 159–76.

Ihlen, Ø., & van Ruler, B. (2007). How public relations works: Theoretical roots and public relations perspectives. *Public Relations Review*, 33(3), pp. 243–8.

Kam, C. D., Wilking, J. R., & Zechmeister, E. J. (2007). Beyond the "narrow data base": Another convenience sample for experimental research. *Political Behavior*, 29(4), pp. 415–40.

Kim, S. Y., Choi, M. I., Reber, B. H., & Kim, D. (2014). Tracking public relations scholarship trends: Using semantic network analysis on PR journals from 1975 to 2011. *Public Relations Review*, 40(1), pp. 116–18.

L'Etang, J. (2005). Critical public relations: Some reflections. *Public Relations Review*, 31, pp. 521–6.

L'Etang, J. (2008). *Public relations: Concepts, practice and critique.* London: Sage.

Lincoln, Y. S., & Guba, E. G. (1985). *Naturalistic inquiry.* Beverly Hills, CA: Sage.

McKie, D. (2001). Updating public relations: "New science", research paradigms, and uneven developments. In R. L. Heath (Ed.), *Handbook of public relations*, pp. 75–91. Thousand Oaks, CA: Sage.

Mickey, T. J. (1997). A postmodern view of public relations: Sign and reality. *Public Relations Review*, 23(3), pp. 271–84.

Morgan, G. (1980). Paradigms, metaphors and puzzle solving in organizational theory. *Administrative Science Quarterly*, 25, pp. 605–22.

Peterson, R. A. (2011). On the use of college students in social science research: Insights from a second order meta-analysis. *Journal of Consumer Research*, 28(3), pp. 450–61.

Putnam, L. L. (1983). The interpretive perspective: An alternative to functionalism. In L. L. Putnam, & M. E. Pacanowsky (Eds), *Communication and organization: An interpretive approach*, pp. 31–54. Beverly Hills, CA: Sage.

Sears, D. O. (1986). College sophomores in the laboratory: Influences of a narrow data base on social psychology's view of human nature. *Journal of Personality and Social Psychology*, 51(3), pp. 515–30.

Silverman, D. (2013). *Doing qualitative research: A practical handbook.* London: Sage.

Steier, F. (Ed.). (1991). *Research and reflexivity*. London: Sage.

Toth, E. L. (2002). Postmodernism for modernist public relations: The cash value and application of critical research in public relations. *Public Relations Review*, 28(3), pp. 243–50.

Toth, E. L. (2010). Reflections on the field. In R. L. Heath (Ed.), *The SAGE handbook of public relations*, pp. 711–22. Thousand Oaks, CA: Sage.

Verčič, D., van Ruler, B., Bütschi, G., & Flodin, B. (2001). On the definition of public relations: A European view. *Public Relations Review*, 27(4), pp. 373–87.

Wehmeier, S., & Winkler, P. (2013). Expanding the bridge, minimizing the gaps: Public relations, organizational communication, and the idea that communication constitutes organization. *Management Communication Quarterly*, 27(2), pp. 280–90.

Whitehead, A. N. (1925/1985). *Science and the modern world*. London: Free Association Books.

14

Double deconstruction

Transparency, dialogue and social media from a critical post-structuralist perspective

Oliver Raaz and Stefan Wehmeier

Jacques Derrida (1976) taught us to look twice at texts and concepts: a first reading reveals and reconstructs the "dominant" perspective of the author(s) and a second reading (re-)interprets the dominant perspective, fills it with different meaning, reveals blind spots and by this transforms the dominant perspective into a series of undecidable meanings (deconstructive double reading – see Kakoliris, 2004). In public relations theory and practice, we can find a dominant mindset arguing from an identity-centred view on society that public relations is a means to establish an integrated and well-functioning social sphere. Therefore, public relations is associated with high-value words like "transparency" and "dialogue" that indicate the possible realization of such a "fully functioning society" (Heath, 2006).

In this chapter we want to deconstruct this myth by addressing two common and intertwined assumptions: first, the assumption of social media fostering transparency and, second, the assumption that online public relations foster dialogue between corporations and stakeholders. In doing so, we basically refer to critical post-structuralist social theory – especially the discourse theory inaugurated by Ernesto Laclau and Chantal Mouffe (Laclau & Mouffe, 1985). Being deeply influenced by the work of the French philosopher Jacques Derrida, Laclau and Mouffe promote a difference-oriented view on society that sharply contrasts with the prevalent paradigm of public relations research.

Translating the distinction between a dominant perspective and its reinterpretation into Heinz von Foerster's (1981) more usable vocabulary, we distinguish between a first and a second order perspective of observation. We demonstrate that social media hopes of transparency and dialogue fail in both perspectives. First, by referring to second order perspective, we show that transparency and dialogue do not meet advanced communication-theoretical and epistemological findings – which means that communication scholars should not adopt them unawares – rather, they rest on an identity-centred view on society and may only serve as part of indispensable aims for a first order perspective of observation. Second, in a further step, we introduce the Habermasian idea of the ideal speech situation as an adequate representation of this first order perspective. Taking a closer look at the existing corpus of empirical research on online PR dialogue capacity that has been conducted for the last one-and-a-half decades, we demonstrate that this framework may serve as a theoretical basis for the dominantly applied categories. Third, as the results of this research indicate, prerequisites for transparency and dialogue have not even been accomplished on the first order level.

In effect, our contribution to a critical "boundary breaking" (L'Etang, Xifra & Coombs, 2012) of the dominant public relations perspective is specific and twofold: on the one hand we coincide with one *leitmotif* of critical interventions (see L' Etang, 2005) and offer a difference-oriented rejection of basic categories of the functionalist public relations discourse; yet being obliged to a constructive notion of critique, on the other hand we show that this criticism of their academic application does not lead to a rejection of these categories in general. They remain necessary parts of public relations (social media) practice. Along with proposals for future research we will discuss the implications of this move for critical research, as well as for reflective practice, in our conclusion.

Introduction

Whenever new media enter the field of social communication, this process usually is accompanied by a wide range of discourses that emphasize the democratic potential of such media. Schmidt and Zurstiege (2000) grasp this fact as one of the constants of media evolution. From this emphatic point of view, media innovations help audiences to gain insight into previously arcane social spheres. We call this the (alleged) "transparency function". Along this line of argumentation for the majority of people, TV and the internet are the only means to indirectly gather experiences from different social spheres such as distant social groups, (supra-)national political procedures, or juridical routines. In line with this argumentation, new media often are said to overcome traditional borders between heterogeneous social units. Thus they contribute to human understanding and social integration. On the other hand, however, mainstream discourse on new media highlights their ability to facilitate access to public discourse by minimizing the costs, requisite technical equipment, and expert knowledge of content production and dissemination. We call this the (alleged) "participation function". Historically, even the radio (during its period of consolidation) was conceived as an outstanding instrument, capable of repairing fragmented and power-biased public discourses. Prominent intellectuals like the German playwright Bertolt Brecht proposed that it could transform mass media communication from pure distribution into reciprocal communication (Silberman, 2000).

The same kind of arguments can be traced back by observing the introduction of social media into the organizational communication area. According to the mainstream academic literature, online public relations fosters interactivity, transparency and dialogue between organizations and stakeholders of all kind (Ingenhoff & Koelling, 2009; Kent, Taylor & White, 2003; Naudé, Froneman & Atwood, 2004). Within this literature the internet is perceived as one of the most powerful communication channels, enabling symmetric communication between organizations and publics. Following this mindset, social media do not only allow organizations to portray themselves in an unfiltered and truthful way (transparency function), but also by means of instant feedback mechanisms (as in forums or blogs) they contribute to vibrant dialogic communication. In this line of argument, blog communication, for example, is described as highly interactive, transparent, authentic, dialogic and, therefore, very credible (Pleil, 2007; Seltzer & Mitrook, 2007; Zerfass & Boelter, 2005). A recent analysis of academic articles about social media and public relations reveals that social media in particular are currently seen as the silver bullet for building symmetric, transparent and dialogic relations with publics (Schultz & Wehmeier, 2011).

Transparency and dialogue: first and second order observations

Second order cybernetics teaches us to distinguish between a first (corresponds with Derrida's dominant perspective) and a second (corresponds with Derrida's reinterpretation) order perspective of observation (von Foerster, 1981). In first order perspective, an agent takes his social and material day-to-day experiences for granted. For example, a public relations counsellor in routine situations will neither doubt the reality of the newspaper in his hands nor the correctness of the moral standards he is socialized with. This idea is reflected in Alfred Schütz's social-phenomenological remarks on the natural attitude in the mundane life-world. Expressed very briefly, they state that within this attitude everyone knows that his or her social and natural, respectively, material environment can be perceived in the same way by everyone else, and shares the same meaning for everyone else (Schütz, 1967).

In contrast, second order perspective takes a closer look at the attitudes of the first order perspective-holders themselves and thus uncovers their irreducible contingency. Historical and intercultural comparisons show that there can or could be found totally different types of intellectual understanding of the world and its elements, as well as forms of social coexistence. As a prominent expression of second order observation, Thomas S. Kuhn's (1962) historical analyses of science depict how now-negated world elements like "ether" were once grasped as an accepted part of scientifically ennobled theory. Not only historical and intercultural investigations, but also our own experiences in a highly differentiated society can confront us with the multiplicity of different moral standards and polarized lifestyles. Insights from second order observation may serve as a means to be aware of the contingency of social processes and to avoid treating knowledge and moral standards as absolutes (Rorty, 1979).

To sum up, first order observation imparts the impression of a well-structured, morally integrated world, and thus promotes the notion of an identity-centred account of society. Second order observation, meanwhile, focuses on the ruptures and fragmentations within social sense structure and strictly emphasizes that every observation – moral ideals and judgements included – depends on the "uncloseable" (cognitive and social) context of the observer.

In pushing this distinction forward, emphatic notions of transparency and dialogue can be conceived as illustrations of a first order observation. They, at least implicitly, converge in a specific, identity-centred account of social communication. In the following, we will provide a short sketch of this concept. Although such a portrayal is unavoidably simplified and generalized, we think it catches the core structure of the idealistic account in favour of a systematic approach. This will help to accomplish a comparison to the difference-centred account that we promote. We will organize our sketch along the three elements of communication, "information", "utterance" and "understanding" (Luhmann, 1995, p. 141), which in varying forms are part of the most widespread communication theories (see Krallmann & Ziemann, 2001).

Conventional theory comprehends communication as a mode of social interaction which enables different human beings to exchange (utterance) their thoughts, views and impressions (information), principally in order to coordinate their prospective actions in a reciprocally satisfying way (understanding). While many communication scholars who promote the normative ideas of dialogue and transparency admit the absence of a total congruence between the interpretations of different communicators, usually they assert an approximate convergence between the respective sets of symbols as well as their deployments. This convergence – in their eyes – permits us to understand other communication participants in a more or less objective way.

As a consequence, dialogue and transparency appear as two deeply connected, intertwined normative concepts. Presuming this concept of communication to be true, dialogue can then be conceived as an ongoing communication process between social agents (encompassing each communication element mentioned above), in which they mutually adapt their views and intentions, and find a consensus-based coordination for their future actions. Further on within this framework, transparency may then be understood as the corresponding term for the quality and completeness of the (truthful) pieces of self-information an agent receives from his counterpart during the dialogue process. Therefore, it serves as a requisite condition for the consensus-building process of successful dialogue happening at all. Considering communication as the essential element of social processes, and turning our attention to society as a whole – according to the identity-centred view – transparency and dialogue preserve the opportunity for consensus on the macro level. In other words, they represent themselves as constitutive mechanisms of social integration.

Turning the perspective to the second order view, this understanding of transparency and dialogue cannot stand scrutiny. Sociologist Niklas Luhmann (1995) teaches us that all three components of the communication process have to be understood as contingent selections within a complex world. Due to this complexity, there is no neutral access to (social) reality; rather, reality as a singular term, de facto, comes out as realities (plural): there exist just as many realities as social and cognitive systems (see Luhmann, 2000). When deployed to our topic of social media, transparency and dialogue, this has the following meaning: whenever a corporation provides new self-regarding content on a social media platform (such as a video or a podcast), this content is highly selective. While the corporation cannot itself comprehend all the complex processes taking place within its boundaries, it has to make a choice according to specific relevance systems and standards (which are also the result of selection processes). Thus, it is not ironic to draw attention to the fact that requests "for transparency…are rarely directed toward issues like the color of the canteen furniture or the number of daily telephone calls" (Christensen, Morsing & Thyssen, 2011, pp. 464–5). The same applies for the selection of the mode of utterance. Here, too, the corporation has the opportunity to choose between different (social media) channels as well as between different pre-existing modes of communication, like a report, a plea, news forms, etc.

Finally, understanding also turns out to be a selective process. On the one hand, the recipient – due again to reasons of complexity – cannot oversee all features of the communication offer (he may, for example, disregard an intentionally placed logo). More important, by distinguishing between information and utterance, he makes his own decision (but this is not to be understood as intentionality!), regardless of whether he interprets the company's activities as communication efforts or merely as ever-passing social events rather than directed action. Consequently, he may interpret corporate social media efforts as genuine dialogue-oriented communication offers, or purely as the epiphenomena of routine strategic behaviour. His insinuation will influence the progress of communication, which, in the end, has to be modelled as an ongoing process solely based on insinuations.

Given these insights, communication loses its capacity to preserve the potential of social integration by means of transparency and dialogue. On the one hand, transparency cannot attach to its identity-centred meaning, insofar as the handling of symbols and information is not stabilized by a neutral access to reality but is instead at the mercy of a heterogeneity of possible interpretations – none of which can claim a superior status. On the other hand, dialogue forfeits its emphatic connotation, insofar as it is nothing more than an insinuation of (at least) one party that may err. And even if both parties should insinuate a dialogue, with the transparency function already deconstructed, it is impossible for them to draw on a common basis of knowledge. Moreover, even if both parties should assume a consensus, this consensus might collapse just a moment later as a result of a different interpretation. Eventually, the assumption that transparency and dialogue are part of an identity-centred communication process has to be substituted by understanding them as pure insinuations. They are part of a communication process that is based on different worldviews which cannot be reduced to one another and thus compel a difference-oriented conception of society.

Yet the effect of second order insights should not be to denounce social media practice that is based on first order observation, but rather we should respect it as a form of practice of its own right. While first order observation was said to neglect the structural conditions of observation and thereby essentialize its observations, in some way this holds true for second order observation as well (Luhmann, 1994). It is capable of visualizing the latent structures of other (first order) observers, but, in parallel, cannot reflect its own latent structures. From this point of view, every second order observation at the same time displays a first order observation. Hence, in the words of Hofstadter's (1979) analysis of circular systems, the relation between first and second order of observation can be referred to as a "tangled hierarchy" (p. 690).

Transparency and dialogue as part of normative discourse requisites

In this section we want to demonstrate how normative concepts like transparency and dialogue maintain their importance for first order practice, even though they are deconstructed by second order observation. Helpfully, the concept of "tangled hierarchies" already points into a direction that is most elaborately formulated within the post-structuralist account of Laclau and Mouffe (1985). Devoting their work to the development of hegemonic processes, academics in this tradition engage themselves in the analysis of diffuse normative concepts like freedom or social market economy. As the label "post-structuralism" already suggests, their work thereby appears as a (typical second order perspective) endeavour to overcome classical structuralist, homeostatic conceptions of society that correspond with the first order perspective. Structuralists like the linguist Ferdinand de Saussure (1977) think of systems as closed sets of elements, whose meaning derives from their connection to other elements in the system. Although meaning depends on the difference between the elements, the system, as a closed entity, still guarantees the meaning as fixed and stable. That is why this way of conceptualizing reality still has to be labelled as identity-oriented.

In contrast, post-structuralists – in accordance with the Luhmannian communication model expressed above – emphasize the primacy of differences (Marchart, 2007). First of all, they indicate that it is impossible to signify a single element, or a totality like a system, without marking a difference to other entities. Taken seriously, this idea finds it is impossible to resort to specific signs and symbols with a fixed position that could guarantee transparency and dialogue. Consequently, one cannot think of a higher unity or a closed system like a harmonically integrated society that could evade the fundamental play of differences (Derrida, 1978). Furthermore, the remarkable role of temporality and action lead to permanent shifts in the network of differences and subvert ever-stable meaning. Again, we have to accept difference as the basic category of scientific analysis.

Nevertheless, even though elements can only exist in the fluidity of multiple differences, the same is true the other way round. As at the later Heidegger (1967) teaches us, differences can only be experienced through the different elements and identities they constitute. Therefore, despite of the primacy of differences, social processes rely heavily on the construction of identities. While only the primacy of differences allows meaning to evolve and change, pure differences without identities – regardless of whether they are only partial and temporary in character – would make any meaning impossible because social processes could not inform themselves any more. Instead of "organized complexity" (Weaver, 1948, p. 536), indistinguishable chaos would prevail and undermine any chance of structured social evolution. That is why it is not surprising when

Laclau and Mouffe notice that society consists of permanent attempts to resist the fundamental play of differences. Social agents always try to establish stable meaning and a fixed social order. These attempts range from the assumption of shared social meaning to the implementation of detailed political conceptions. Nevertheless, though these attempts inevitably fail, they epitomize the process of generating temporary identities, which is indispensable for social evolution. As part of these identity-oriented attempts, specific concepts arise which dominate the discourse for a period. These concepts serve as points of orientation and thus fulfil the function of the necessary identities. In respect of the fundamental play of differences, these concepts – even more than any other word or concept – have to be polyvalent and flexible in meaning. Otherwise, they could not fit with the heterogeneous differences in discourse and provide a temporary anchor in the fluidity of social processes. Accordingly, Laclau (1996) calls such concepts "empty signifiers" (pp. 36–46).

Transferred to the analysis of dialogue and transparency, both emphatic concepts can be comprehended as representations of empty signifiers. Like other empty signifiers, such as socialism or the social market economy, they convey the picture of a society that is possibly smooth and integrated. Likewise, their emptiness is visible: they appeal to a range of different, even contradicting discourses. Apparently, the pursuit of transparency and dialogue by means of social media suits either a business or a moral case, if one just mentions the most prominent "rival doctrines" (Hood, 2006, p. 20). Providing points of orientation that enable social evolution at all, like empty signifiers in general, they are typically accompanied by moral postulates. Organizations that do not follow the rule of transparency and dialogue are subject to public moral denunciation. These postulates are designed to protect their self-asserted state as self-evident landmarks of discourse, and to make their contingent meaning invisible (see for the analogous case of CSR: Schultz, 2011, pp. 55–71). In this, they neglect the latent possibility of deviating from incommensurable interpretations and communications. Yet these neglects contradict the "true nature" of social processes and communication described above. Because of this, transparency and dialogue are necessary, but necessarily failing attempts of the institutionalization of society.

Empirical investigations I: a Habermasian framework

As our theoretical argument has shown, transparency and dialogue cannot hold within a second order observation perspective. Yet first order practice fundamentally depends on the circulation of those empty signifiers and is not able to dismiss them. The second part of our argument is that in spite of the necessity of concepts such as transparency and dialogue, the first order practice of organizations has not succeeded in at least preparing the prerequisites of their use in social media behaviour. For this purpose we rely on the existing corpus of recently conducted research. A huge part of this research refers to the five principles of dialogue that were proposed by Kent and Taylor (1998). From our point of view these five principles lack a clear theoretical structure. For that reason we start by deriving them from the classical Habermasian idea of the "ideal speech situation" (Habermas, 1992, pp. 86ff.). To avoid misunderstandings: we do not think that Habermas's theory complies with the results of second order observation. Instead, we opt for it because we regard it as the account which best mirrors current first order practice intuitions concerning communication and dialogue. In the same vein Rorty (2006), in his popular conception of a "liberal ironist", even grasps Habermas as a favourable complementary account to Derrida's post-structuralism. Furthermore, it stands out for its highly systematic profile.

Habermas's (1984, 1987) paramount theoretical concerns lie with the problem of preserving the concept of rationality. Emphasizing the value and existence of rationality he (at least implicitly) promotes the ideal of an identity-centred society and thus has to be categorized as doing first order observing. In a shift away from subject philosophy to an intersubjective account he does not situate rationality within the cognition of individual subjects, but rather locates it in the procedural structure of human communication and language. In its pure form, rationality is represented in the mode of communicative action, with its inherent aim of understanding and consensus (for the impact on public relations theory see Wehmeier, 2013). Habermas acknowledges that empirically one also finds other forms of egocentric, instrumental-oriented actions – and fuses them into the term "strategic action" (Habermas, 1984, p. 333). Very prominently, Habermas has pointed to the problematic displacement of communicative action by strategic interests within the public sphere, referred to as "structural transformation of the public sphere" (1989).

However, for him these strategic forms are somehow discernible as corruptions or parasites of emancipative communicative action, which remain the elementary form of communication. Therefore, his main argument is that even strategic communication, like a lie, has to presume and simulate communicative action, because otherwise it would not work. From his point of view, people who reject the idea of rationality inherent in communication commit a "performative contradiction" (Habermas, 1992, p. 80), because their speech is already grounded on its rational qualities. Otherwise, it would not make sense to make any objection at all. The idea of performative contradiction also serves him as a methodological means to reconstruct all the rational elements of discourse that cannot be suspended. If the principles of communicative action are followed appropriately, concrete-empirical communication approximates the ideal speech situation. Although this situation can never be reached totally, it serves as a normative measure for real communication sequences. Habermas (1992) retrieves four types of "validity claims" (pp. 58ff.) inherent in the ideal speech situation that are of special importance for our purpose. In order to prepare a rational consensus and coordinative action, each participant in communicative action has to make validity claims in terms of:

(1) (theoretical) truth (concerning the objective world)
(2) subjective truthfulness (concerning one's subjective thoughts and intentions)
(3) normative rightfulness (concerning the accepted moral standards of a social entity)
(4) intelligibility as basic claim that underlies the three other forms (concerns the (grammatically) correct use of language and meaning).

Whenever one of those complementary claims is challenged, communication should be able, or at least should be able to try, to restore it by means of sound arguments, and should thus come to an intersubjectively accepted consent as a basis for further (communicative) action. These four validity claims cannot only be understood as prerequisites for (1) functioning dialogue and communicative action, but they do also include (2) transparency as reflected in the second claim. Thus, they perfectly harmonize with our research focus and can shed light on the up-to-this-date used empirical criteria.

Until now, Kent and Taylor's (1998) five principles of dialogue prevail in the (content) analysis of the dialogue capacity of the internet. In a later publication, together with White, the authors categorize these principles with the help of a technical design and a genuine dialogic cluster (Taylor, Kent & White, 2001, pp. 277–8). The five principles are: (1) ease of interface (2) usefulness of information and (3) conservation of visitors belonging to the technical and design category; whereas the (4) generation of return visits and the (5) dialogic loop itself, manifest the genuine dialogic cluster. Each of these principles is defined by a list of features whose appearance is counted by means of content analysis and then summed up as a value for each principle. Thus, the realization of the dialogic potential can be measured and compared for each principle. In a next step, the values of the single principles can be summed up themselves with a general value of the dialogue capacity of any specific internet application. Eventually, and again in a comparative

Table 14.1 Dialogic principles as expressions of validity claims

Dialogic principle	Validity claim
(1) Ease of interface	Intelligibility
(2) Conservation of visitors	Intelligibility
(3) Usefulness of information	(Theoretical) truth – (subjective) truthfulness
(4) Generation of return visits	Normative rightfulness
(5) Dialogic loop	Normative rightfulness

approach, different applications can be compared for their general dialogue capacity as well as with respect to certain principles. As we see below, this happened in various instances and cases.

Every principle can easily be read as an expression of one of the Habermasian validity claims (see Table 14.1). The "Ease of interface" is a structural condition for any communication at all, and thus corresponds with the overall claim of intelligibility. The same counts for the "Conservation of Visitors", which encompasses "Important info available on 1st page", "Short loading time (less than 4 seconds)", and "Posting of last updated time and date" (Taylor et al., 2001, p. 273) and hence also refers to structural conditions. In contrast, the last element of the technical and design cluster, the "Usefulness of information", inherently refers to the claim of truthfulness as another term for transparency.

Here, completely relevant information about the organization or person in question is requested in order to make it possible to expect his or her further actions and to evaluate them according to the self-set standards. Because claims about the objective world here are made as well, it is also connected with the dimension of (theoretical) truth. As the categorization of Kent et al. (2003) already suggests, "Dialogic loop" and "Generation of return of visits" relate to the claim of normative rightfulness. On the one hand, "Generation of return visits", characterized by items like "explicit statement invites user to return" or "calendar of events", is responsible for enabling further dialogue and keeping such dialogue attractive. On the other hand, "Dialogic loop", by providing the "opportunity for user-response" or the "opportunity to vote on issues", establishes the mechanisms for feedback by recipients. Together, both categories measure the conditions for dialogic communication actually taking place according to accepted normative standards. That is why, in respect of dialogue capacity, these principles may legitimately demand the highest status among the five principles.

Empirical investigations II: results of research

The mainstream corpus of empirical research on online dialogue capacity relies on the framework of Kent and Taylor, which we could substantiate by coupling it with the Habermasian idea of the ideal speech situation. During the last one-and-a-half decades, this framework has been applied to a multitude of different social areas and industry sectors. Referring to this corpus of work, we aim, as a last step, to show that even in first order practice, transparency and dialogue have not yet lived up to their promise. We consciously concentrate on the genuine dialogic cluster (claim of normative rightfulness) and also take it as an indicator for transparency. This is because, in order to understand transparency properly, it cannot be measured by previously published information as in the mere technical items of "Usefulness of information". In contrast, it rather represents the quality of open and respondent communication behaviour in dialogue processes and thus is represented adequately in the dialogic cluster.

Our point of departure is McAllister-Spooner's (2009) literature review. There, she evaluates the research tradition inaugurated by Kent and Taylor (1998). Providing an overview of the results of this research tradition, McAllister-Spooner (2009) concludes that dialogic tools are "very poorly used" (p. 321). By taking a closer look at the body of empirical research in this area, this judgement can be expanded upon. Typically, the "Generation of return visits" and "Dialogic loop" achieve the lowest scores in the content analyses. This is problematic, since they correspond with the claims of normative rightfulness and thus represent the core component of dialogic preconditions. This diagnosis empirically holds true for different organizational types such as environmental watchdogs and activist organizations (Sommerfeldt, Kent & Taylor, 2012; Taylor et al. 2001), Fortune Global 500 companies (Kim, Nam & Kang, 2010), colleges (Gordon & Berhow, 2009), or Spanish museums (Capriotti & Pardo Kuklinski, 2012). Deviations can hardly be called real exceptions. For example, in McAllister and Taylor's (2007) article on US colleges, "Dialogic loop" ranges on the last, but "Generation of visitors" "only" the third last place. Yet here "dialogic feedback loop features scored very low" (McAllister & Taylor, 2007, p. 231). While mobile-ready Fortune Global 500 websites at least achieve better results in respect of the "Dialogic loop", they also fail in "Return visit engagement" (McCorkindale & Morgoch, 2013).

As further investigations suggest, these general observations on the internet dialogue capacity, which mainly focus on websites, can also claim validity for the social media sphere. Interestingly, some organizations, like Swiss charitable non-profit organizations (Ingenhoff & Koelling, 2009, pp. 68–9) and Latin American governments (Searson & Johnson, 2010, p. 124) hardly make use of social media tools. Seltzer and Mitrook have conducted a direct comparison between the blogs and traditional websites of environmental activist groups. Their results show that while blogs succeed in terms of "Ease of interface" and "Conservation of visitors", while falling short in terms of "Usefulness [of information] to volunteers", there "were no significant differences in terms of usefulness to media, generation of return visits, and dialogic loop" (Seltzer & Mitrook, 2007, p. 228). McAllister's (2012) study on the new media usage of the world's top 100 universities confirms the insufficient occurrence of dialogic features within social media employment. Universities increasingly involve new media like Facebook, Youtube, blogs, iTunes, Flickr, FriendFeed, etc. Yet as McAllister (2012) states, "organizations are not adequately utilizing new media tools to generate dialogic communication" (p. 326). Concentrating her interest on Facebook she shows that although half of the analysed Facebook sites dispose of message boards (49 per cent) and active walls (54 per cent), only 16 per cent integrate links to addresses for commentaries, and only 15 per cent enable their users to post and respond. Hence, "85% of the universities [are] utilizing their Facebook pages for one-way communication messages" (McAllister, 2012, p. 326). Again, "Dialogic loop" and "Generation of return visits" rank low, though undercut by "Usefulness of information" – which is explainable by the fact that universities do not design these pages to become information platforms.

The low implementation of the core dialogic traits that represent the claim of normative rightfulness verified by content analysis is also reinforced by interviews with practitioners (though they naturally do not use the five principles framework). Metropolitan PR practitioners "are slower to integrate more technologically complicated tools that cater to a niche audience" (Eyrich, Padman & Sweetser, 2008, p. 414). Moreover, interviews with PR practitioners from 75 transnational NGOs indicate that they do not focus on two-way communication and prefer not to use social media tools at all (Seo, Kim & Yang, 2009, p. 124).

Concluding remarks

Being devoted to critical post-structuralist thought, the main purpose of this article was to perform a double deconstruction by challenging the assumption that social media foster the emergence of dialogue and transparency. Converting deconstructive double reading into Heinz von Foerster's distinction between (1) first, and (2) second order observation, we incrementally demonstrated that transparency and dialogue fail on both levels. On the one hand we show that both transparency and dialogue correspond with identity-centred conceptions of society (see Kent, 2013) that do not comply with modern communication and social theory, emphasizing the role of difference in social evolution. On the other hand, this theoretical deconstruction does not lead to a total rejection of both concepts. In contrast, post-structuralist inspired analysis shows them to be indispensable normative orientation points of first order practice that can be labelled as "empty signifiers". They are necessary, but necessarily failing attempts of the institutionalization of society.

Nevertheless, their deconstruction should remind scholars to be cautious in their deployment. They should not identify with their normative implications unreflectively. For example, a critical and distanced analysis shows that the pursuit of transparency may also lead to uniformity and superficial "pornographic" communication (Han, 2012). In order to determine the empirical status of the usage of transparency and dialogue with respect to social media in first order practice we examined the corpus of existing empirical investigations. For the benefit of theoretical closure we connected the criteria of this research with the Habermasian notion of the ideal speech situation, which may count as the most plausible expression of first order practice intuitions. The results of our literature review suggest that prerequisites for transparent and dialogue-oriented communication have not yet been implemented. The categories "Generation of return visits" and "Dialogic loop" as expressions of dialogic and transparency-related efforts consistently rank low.

Thus, our critical approach has particular implications for public relations research and practice: first of all, the deconstruction of practical high value words like "transparency" and "dialogue" should remind scholars to be cautious about deploying them. On the one hand, they have to be aware of the theoretical inadequacy of transparency and dialogue: these concepts claim to harmonize society, while de facto they are elements of (potentially) contradicting discourses seeking social hegemony in an always rhizomatic and ruptured social world. Yet since transparency and dialogue represent indispensable components of first order practice, critical research should show understanding for their deployment in the practical sphere and should not develop any academic arrogance towards practitioners. Here, the same tolerance and understanding requested for other paradigms (Edwards, 2012) has also to be given to other working cultures.

Of course, interpreting transparency and dialogue as indispensable parts of first order practice, and the claimed respect for this (public relations) practice, in no way means that every practical deployment of these concepts is unproblematic and valuable. In contrast, here we find another main task of future critical public relations research: to find suitable practical solutions and measurements in order to bridge the gap between second order insights and first order practices – which is part of the broader agenda of reconciling difference-oriented epistemology with genuine normative thought (Raaz, 2014). Therefore, scholars (ideally working together with practitioners) have to shape the normative idea and the practical use of transparency and dialogue within social media contexts in a way that reflects the irreducible heterogeneity of social processes. While our discussion, for different reasons (see above), focused on a Habermasian framework, it is also possible to refer to genuine post-structuralist concepts like Mouffe's "agonistic pluralism" (Mouffe, 2005). This may lead to a polyphonic instead of a univocal policy of transparency (Christensen & Langer, 2009). Another task of critical public relations, then, will be to compare these theoretically informed standards to an actual dealing with dialogue and transparency and thus induce efforts for improved practical solutions (first order) on the one hand, and theoretical solutions (second order) on the other. Following this programme of critical public relations, the idea of criticism will embrace both of its classical dimensions, identifying social injustice as well as challenging theoretical and practical ideas and concepts (L'Etang, 2008).

Future critical research should expand the post-structuralist theoretical basis and combine it with modern organizational theory. Adapting to the Luhmann-inspired version of the CCO perspective (Schoeneborn, 2011), for instance, it would be possible to analyse how empty signifiers like dialogue and transparency are incorporated into the network of different demands and decisions that an organization is confronted with. In addition, a theoretical framework of this kind could serve as a basis for future empirical research. That research should not become bogged down in content analyses of mere technical standards, but rather it should observe (for example by means of participant observation or non-standardized interviews) the whole (communication) process of how and why transparency-related and dialogic values are (or are not – perhaps due to the prevalence of other communication channels) implemented (for instructive insights see von Groddeck, 2011) in the use and creation of corporate social media. Yet, irrespective of the specific theoretical and methodical design, following the post-structuralist mindset one insight unquestioningly remains: that transparency and dialogue in and outside social media communication will never be fully achievable – paraphrasing Derrida, they maintain a transparency and dialogue "to come" (Derrida, 1994).

References

Capriotti, P., &, Pardo Kuklinski, H. (2012). Assessing dialogic communication through the Internet in Spanish museums, *Public Relations Review*, 38(4), pp. 619–26.

Christensen, L. T., & Langer, R. (2009). Public relations and the strategic use of transparency: Consistency, hypocrisy and corporate change. In R. L. Heath, E. L. Toth, & D. Waymer (Eds), *Rhetorical and critical approaches to public relations*, 2nd edition, pp. 129–53. New York: Routledge.

Christensen, L. T., Morsing, M., & Thyssen, O. (2011). The polyphony of corporate social responsibility: Deconstructing accountability and transparency in the context of identity and hypocrisy. In G. Cheney, S. May, & D. Munshi (Eds), *Handbook of communication ethics*, pp. 457–74. New York, NY: Routledge.

Derrida, J. (1976). *Of grammatology*. Baltimore, MD: John Hopkins University Press.

Derrida, J. (1978). *Writing and difference*. Chicago, IL: Chicago University Press.

Derrida, J. (1994). *Specters of Marx: The state of the debt, the work of mourning, and the new international*. New York, NY: Routledge.

Edwards, L. (2012). Defining the "object" of public relations research: A new starting point. *Public Relations Inquiry*, 1(1), pp. 7–30.

Eyrich, N., Padman, M. L., &, Sweetser, K. D. (2008). PR practitioners' use of social media tools and communication technology. *Public Relations Review*, 34(4), pp. 412–14.

Gordon, J., & Berhow, S. (2009), University websites and dialogic features for building relationships with potential students. *Public Relations Review*, 35(1), pp. 150–15.

Habermas, J. (1984). *The theory of communicative action. Volume 1. Reason and the rationalization of society*. Boston, MA: Beacon Press.

Habermas, J. (1987). *The theory of communicative action. Volume 2. Lifeworld and system: A critique of functionalist reason*. Boston, MA: Beacon Press.

Habermas, J. (1989). *The transformation of the public sphere*. Cambridge, UK: Polity.

Habermas, J. (1992). *Moral consciousness and communicative action*. Cambridge, MA: MIT.

Han, B.-C. (2012). *Transparenzgesellschaft*. Berlin, Germany: Matthes & Seitz.

Heath, R. L. (2006). Onward into more fog: Thoughts on public relations' research directions. *Journal of Public Relations Research*, 18(2), pp. 93–114.

Heidegger, M. (1967 [1927]). *Being and time*. London, UK: SCM Press.

Hofstadter, D. (1979). *Gödel, Escher, Bach: An eternal golden braid*. New York, NY: Basic Books.

Hood, C. (2006). Transparency in historical perspective. In C. Hood &, D. Heald (Eds), *Transparency: The key to better governance?*, pp. 3–23. Oxford, UK: Oxford University Press.

Ingenhoff, D., & Koelling, A. M. (2009). The potential of web sites as a relationship building tool for charitable fundraising NPOs. *Public Relations Review*, 35(1), pp. 66–73.

Kakoliris, G. (2004). Jacques Derrida's double deconstructive reading: A contradiction in terms? *Journal of the British Society of Phenomenology*, 35(3), pp. 283–92.

Kent, M. L. (2013). Using social media dialogically: Public relations role in reviving democracy. *Public Relations Review*, 39(4), pp. 337–45.

Kent, M. L., & Taylor, M. (1998). Building dialogic relationships through the World Wide Web. *Public Relations Review*, 24(3), pp. 321–34.

Kent, M. L., Taylor, M., & White, W. J. (2003). The relationship between website design and organizational responsiveness to stakeholders, *Public Relations Review*, 29(1), pp. 63–77.

Kim, D., Nam, Y., & Kang, S. (2010). An analysis of corporate environmental responsibility on the global corporate web sites and their dialogic principles. *Public Relations Review*, 36(3), pp. 285–288.

Krallmann, D., & Ziemann, A. (2001), *Grundkurs kommunikationswissenschaft*. München, Germany: Fink.

Kuhn, T. S. (1962). *The structure of scientific revolutions*. Chicago, IL: University of Chicago Press.

Laclau, E. (1996). *Emancipation(s)*. London, UK: Verso.

Laclau, E., & Mouffe, C. (1985). *Hegemony & socialist strategy: Towards a radical democratic politics*. London, UK: Verso.

L'Etang, J. (2005). Critical public relations: Some reflections. *Public Relations Review*, 31(4), pp. 521–6.

L'Etang, J. (2008). *Public Relations: Concepts, practice and critique*. London, UK: Sage.

L'Etang, J., Xifra, J., & Coombs, T. (2012). Breaking boundaries. *Public Relations Inquiry*, 1(1), pp. 3–6.

Luhmann, N. (1994). The modernity of science. *New German Critique*, 61(1), pp. 9–23.

Luhmann, N. (1995). *Social systems*. Stanford, CA: Stanford University Press.

Luhmann, N. (2000). *The reality of the mass media*. Stanford, CA: Stanford University Press.

McAllister, S. M. (2012). How the world's top universities provide dialogic forums for marginalized voices. *Public Relations Review*, 38(2), pp. 319–27.

McAllister, S. M., & Taylor, M. (2007). Community college web sites as tools for fostering dialogue. *Public Relations Review*, 33(2), pp. 230–2.

McAllister-Spooner, S. M. (2009). Fulfilling the dialogic promise: A ten-year reflective survey on dialogic internet principles. *Public Relations Review*, 35(3), pp. 320–2.

McCorkindale, T., & Morgoch, M. (2013). An analysis of the mobile readiness and dialogic principles on Fortune 500 mobile websites. *Public Relations Review*, 39(3), pp. 193–7.

Marchart, O. (2007). *Post-foundational political thought: Political difference in Nancy, Lefort, Badiou and Laclau*. Edinburgh, UK: Edinburgh University Press.

Mouffe, C. (2005). *On the political*. London, UK: Routledge.

Naudé, A. M. E., Froneman, J. D., & Atwood, R. A. (2004). The use of the internet by ten South African non-governmental organizations – a public relations perspective. *Public Relations Review*, 30(1), pp. 87–94.

Pleil, T. (2007). Online-PR zwischen digitalem Monolog und vernetzter Kommunikation. In T. Pleil (Ed.), *Online-PR im Web 2.0. Fallbeispiele aus Wirtschaft und Politik*, pp. 10–31. Konstanz: UVK.

Raaz, O. (2014). La normativité et la transparence: Une combinaison problématique dans le processus scientifique. In A. Catellani, C. Hambursin, & T. Libaert (Eds), *La communication transparente. Communication, organisations et transparence*. Louvain-la-Neuve, France: Presses Universitaires de Louvain.

Rorty, R. (1979). *Philosophy and the mirror of nature*. Princeton, NJ: Princeton University Press.

Rorty, R. (2006). Habermas, Derrida and the functions of philosophy. In L. Thomassen (Ed.), *The Derrida-Habermas reader*, pp. 46–65. Chicago, IL: University of Chicago Press.

Saussure, F. de (1977 [1916]). *Course in general linguistics*. Glasgow, UK: Fontana/Collins.

Schmidt, S. J., & Zurstiege, G. (2000). *Orientierung Kommunikationswissenschaft. Was Sie kann, was Sie will*. Reinbek bei Hamburg: Rowohlt.

Schoeneborn, D. (2011). Organization as communication: A Luhmannian perspective. *Management Communication Quarterly*, 25(4), pp. 663–89.

Schultz, F. (2011). *Moral – organisation – kommunikation: Funktionen und implikationen normativer konzepte und theorien des 20. und 21. Jahrhunderts*. Wiesbaden, Germany: VS Verlag für Sozialwissenschaften.

Schultz, F., & Wehmeier, S. (2011). Medieninnovationskommunikationen in Wissenschaft und Kommunikationsberatung: Zur Konstruktion und Bedeutung von Online Relations. In: J. Wolling, A. Will, & C. Schumann (Eds), *Medieninnovationen. Wie Medienentwicklungen die Kommunikation in der Gesellschaft verändern*, pp. 391–408). Konstanz: UVK.

Schütz, A. (1967). *The phenomenology of the social world*. New York: Northwestern University Press.

Searson, E. M., &, Johnson, M. A. (2010). Transparency laws and interactive public relations: An analysis of Latin American government web sites. *Public Relations Review*, 36(2), pp. 120–6.

Seltzer, T., & Mitrook, M. A. (2007). The dialogic potential of weblogs in relationship building. *Public Relations Review*, 33(2), pp. 227–9.

Seo, H., Kim, J. Y., & Yang, S-U. (2009). Global activism and new media: A study of transnational NGOs' online public relations. *Public Relations Review*, 35(2), pp. 123–6.

Silberman, M. (2000). *Brecht on film and radio: A critical edition*. London, UK: Methuen.

Sommerfeldt, E. J., Kent, M. L., & Taylor, M. (2012). Activist practitioner perspectives of website public relations: Why aren't activist websites fulfilling the dialogic promise? *Public Relations Review*, 38(2), 303–312.

Taylor, M., Kent, M. L., & White, W. J. (2001). How activist organizations are using the internet to build relationships. *Public Relations Review*, 27(3), pp. 263–84.

von Foerster, H. (1981). *Observing systems*. Seaside, CA: Intersystems.

von Groddeck, V. (2011). Rethinking the role of value communication in business corporations from a sociological perspective: Why organizations need value based semantics to cope with societal and organizational fuzziness. *Journal of Business Ethics*, 100(1), pp. 69–84.

Weaver, W. (1948). Science and complexity. *American Scientist*, 36, pp. 536–44.

Wehmeier, S. (2013). Habermas, Jürgen, on public relations. In R. Heath (Ed.), *Encyclopedia of public relations*. Thousand Oaks, CA: Sage Publications.

Zerfass, A., & Boelter, D. (2005). *Die neuen Meinungsmacher. Weblogs als Herausforderung für Kampagnen, Marketing, PR und Medien*. Graz: Naunser & Naunser.

15

"Critical public relations is so critical!"

Objections, counter-objections, and practical applications to critical-cultural public relations work

Jennifer Vardeman-Winter

Public relations' critical-cultural connection

Critical inquiry of public relations questions assumptions about practice, practitioners themselves, and the environmental contexts in which practice exists. Cultural inquiry of public relations requires reflection and introspection of how our ontology and epistemology contributes to practice, and where and how differences across cultures within a public relations relationship affect society. The two forms of inquiry are inextricably linked because to question history is an act requiring the consideration of cultural norms and traditions; conversely, to examine differences among cultures inevitably stumbles upon the recognition of power differences across cultural groups and the subsequent questioning of how these differentials occurred, persist, and can change from the status quo (Edwards, 2011). Thus, it is nearly impossible to distinguish one form of inquiry without addressing the other.

Furthermore, public relations is an increasingly important site of critical-cultural interrogation. Organization-public communication enables the exponential connections of technology, interdisciplinary management, global business, activism, travel, and participation in all levels of governance. Public relations lies at the heart of how these movements come together and affect one another (Sriramesh, 2010). Thus, we see critical-cultural work burgeoning in public relations as it becomes a global and cross-cultural intellectual discipline (Toth, 2009).

However, critical-cultural work struggles for acceptance and implementation in academe and in practice as "fringe public relations" (Coombs & Holladay, 2012, p. 880). Some dissent is explicit, while most is implicit; some is intentional as well as unrealized. Furthermore, much opposition is due to theoretical and methodological loyalties (Gregory, 2012), whereas some remains ingrained in the "normal" processes of scholarship and practice ingrained in an "'empirical-administrative' tradition" (Curtin & Gaither, 2005, p. 92, citing Dozier & Lauzen, 2000, p. 8). Evidence of this dissention manifests as: the dearth of critical-cultural work (Coombs & Holladay, 2012), particularly since "the social scientific (modernist) systems functionalist approach still dominates the field" (Bardhan & Weaver, 2011b, p. 2); the chronic privileging of quantitative methods over qualitative methods (Gregory, 2012); and the historical and current positioning of Western public relations as the norm, despite a growing need for global and inter-cultural paradigms – among other reasons. Unfortunately, critical work is less easily measured and oftentimes not even reported.

Why argue for critical work in a critical public relations handbook?

To these points, I found in an experience teaching a "Critical and Cultural Public Relations" course in 2011 that I designed for graduate students, the difficulty is not in engaging them in these debates but in convincing them that these critical discourses are indeed valuable to have and continue to have. In fact, the quote in the title of this essay comes from a graduate student in this course, in a moment of frustration for her to see the purpose and tangible outcomes of critical work. I've reflected on her comment and students' struggles and discomfort with committing to critical and cultural work many times during and since teaching this course. In a city that thrives off some ardently mainstream and traditional industries like energy/oil/gas, healthcare and manufacturing, I have gathered that graduate students are hesitant to wander far from the corporate-based philosophies and practices of public relations for fear of not getting a job. In fact, another graduate student emailed me after her graduation, asking me if she was "selling out" because she was interested in applying for a public relations job at a global oil and gas company.

Interactions with students such as these led me to develop a final project option for students to create a training programme for organizational executives, teaching them the reasons for adopting a critical-cultural perspective in public relations (discussed later in this essay). The assignment also included a section on predicting objections from training students and counter-arguments to use in response. I developed that part of the assignment, and this essay, using the point-counterpoint model[1] as a way to build a philosophy behind a perspective toward critical work, to anticipate objections to the tenets of the philosophy, and to develop counter-arguments to the objections. This makes for a more cogent foundation for critical work.

For this chapter, I first provide a brief conceptualization of critical public relations and cultural public relations, as well as an analysis of how they are related. Then I provide seven major objections that scholars have had toward critical work in the field. After each objection, I provide counter-objections to the objections as ways to rethink the contributions of critical-cultural work to the field. Finally, I end the chapter by looking at innovative ways by which we can bring these theoretical discourses about critical work into the applications of practice and pedagogy.

Critical public relations

Critical scholarship questions our assumptions about the factors, roles, processes and consequences of public relations in publics' lives, organizational settings and social systems, including policy (Motion & Weaver, 2005). As critical work is "concerned with issues of power" (Gower, 2006, p. 179), this form of inquiry is "interested in exposing how public relations may support and contribute to systems of oppression, and, additionally how its role in such oppression can be obscured by normative theories of practice" (Bardhan & Weaver, 2011b, p. 15). Taken extremely broadly, critical public relations can arguably include theories of feminism, postmodernism, poststructuralism, postcolonialism, critical race, queer studies and cultural studies, and this essay adopts the broad categorization of critical theory due to my admitted bifurcation of inquiry of public relations between modernist/positivist theory-building and postmodern/

critical/interpretivist theory-building[2] for the purposes of establishing a platform for which to present objections and counter-objections to critical work.

Cultural public relations

As a separate but related body of public relations scholarship, cultural public relations has developed into two fairly distinct forms of inquiry. The first research agenda regards the application of seemingly generic principles of effective public relations on non-US national practices of public relations to describe and evaluate the likeness of principles internationally, and, as such, interculturally (Wakefield, 2011). The second research agenda – which is given attention in this essay – refers to the broad trend toward multiculturalism from a critical orientation focusing on how power, identity and economy affect the factors and efforts of public relations. As multiculturalism is a "blind spot" in public relations (Macnamara, 2004), it is relevant in this text to understand why and how culture is perpetually neglected in public relations, using critical inquiry.

To this point, I argue that critical and cultural works in public relations are systemically linked and simultaneously grow from one another because of the essence of identity in both forms of inquiry. Individual, public, organizational and social identities are only known when they are compared to those with different identities; furthermore, based on scarcity of organizational and social resources, identities are cognitively and physically linked with different types and quantities of power. Therefore, identity and culture are political constructions. Furthermore, public relations helps stabilize power differentials in cultures (Holtzhausen, 2011). Politics of identity are laid bare in global and international work because practitioners are forced to consider "whether their identity is uniquely cultural or rather ethnic chauvinism…whether it is global or international practice, practitioners will come in contact with local social and cultural practices that will affect their practice" (Holtzhausen, 2011, p. 152). Since critical work questions taken-for-granted assumptions about authoritative figures (in this context, I refer to public relations practitioners and organizations), then "the context of globalization for public relations work refocuses the lens of critical analysis onto the complexity of power in an overwhelmingly connected environment" (Edwards, 2011, p. 43).

Responding to objections of critical-cultural work

We should reflect on the merits of the objections, for "it is through our own arguments and counter-arguments that our theories achieve the criteria of explanatory power and organizing of knowledge for increased understanding of the field" (Toth, 2009, p. 58). This chapter attempts to identify and address common and potential arguments that suggest critical-cultural public relations research, philosophy, and practice are unproductive, through seven major objections: the navel-gazing objection, the overly abstract objection, the unrealistic application objection, the confusing pedagogy objection, the stigmatization objection, the contrarian objection, and the corporate privilege objection. Each objection is responded to with counter-objections that I hope will strengthen our discourse around critical work, particularly for objectors.

1. The navel-gazing objection: critical-cultural work involves too much self-analysis, identity politics and "navel-gazing"

L'Etang (2008) wrote that "there is a danger that public relations academics and students can be too introspective or 'navel-gazing', working convergently within rigid railway grooves rather

than wandering freely and creatively in search of useful insights" (p. 7). The self-reflection practice inherent in critical theories like cultural studies, feminism and postcolonialism exacerbates
this critique, leading some authors to lay bare their identities, assumptions and epistemologies in
every piece of writing. Weaver (2011) critiqued systems theory's effects on public relations' definitions and noted that, "just as systems Excellence theorists have their own paradigmatic cultural
biases, so do critical theorists" (p. 259).

Counter-objection: reflecting upon our backgrounds and our situated positions helps us know why we make the decisions we do

If we don't do critical work, we continue to know only one frame of our affect on the world.
By examining our history, we contextualize the professionalism process – including the study
of habitus – that sets us differently from other discursive structures (e.g., marketing) in the
globalization of public relations. Without examinations of the "structured structures" of public
relations, we miss examinations of those in/out of power, particularly in ever-increasing glo-
bal/international contexts (see Edwards, 2011, p. 36; McKie & Munshi, 2007). Finally, critical
work illuminates micro-politics between our publics and us, in the hope of reducing those gaps
(Pompper, 2010).

Alternatively, if we do *not* conduct critical and postmodern reflection of our practices,
then "local public relations practices can be discriminatory and naïve, particularly when
practitioners are not educated in the practice" (Holtzhausen, 2011, p. 154). Without critical
work we cannot develop activist models, practitioners and pedagogy (Holtzhausen & Voto,
2002) that advocate for resistance strategies via dissensus, decentralized decision-making,
the privileging of marginalized stakeholder voices, "living consciously in daily mic,roprac-
tice", and the "enabling of social action" (Holtzhausen, 2011, pp. 156–7). Critical work is
not only necessary, it requires the conscious effort of delving into the theoretical body of
public relations: "It is important that academics in social scientific fields *consciously* nourish
paradigmatic variety rather than suppress it, promote equitably shared academic space, and
encourage interaction between paradigms, rather than separation" (Edwards, 2012, p. 10, italics in original).

2. The overly abstract objection: critical-cultural work is overly abstract and does not apply or test theory rigorously

Power – individual, political and societal – is difficult to conceptualize and operationalize;
therefore, inquiring into the composition and the effects of power does not conform as
easily to the traditional social scientific method of data collection and analysis. Specifically,
critical-cultural work is largely based in qualitative and ethnographic methodology and does
not easily translate to quantitative inquiry. For public relations, in particular, as we talk about
relationships across different social groups (i.e., publics and organizations and societies),
Weaver (2011) acknowledged, "for positivists and post-positivists, the intentionally subjective
and activist agenda of critical theory can be both perplexing and nonsensical" (p. 259). She
also noted that "much of this postcolonial work is conducted at a purely theoretical level, as
indeed is a significant amount of critical writing in public relations" (Weaver, 2011, p. 261).
Finally, critical work tends to focus on one context (e.g., campaigns, organizational structure),
or one organization, rather than theorizing across "cultural flows" (Appadurai, 1996, cited in
Edwards, 2011).

Counter-objection: critical scholarship actually encompasses a variety of theoretical and methodological approaches

To Botan and Hazelton's (2006) argument that public relations theory is not developed enough, critical theory provides fertility to the body of scholarship by interrogating our ideas to find how interdisciplinary ideas can fill holes as well as blossom into new areas of research. (For a review of various critical research projects, see Bardhan & Weaver, 2011a). Indeed, without essays and studies like Holtzhausen's (2011), and her agenda of documenting postmodern practices in public relations, our field might not have thought distinctly about the differences between critical theory, postmodern theory and social theory; and, this being the case, foci on discourse, story-telling and activism – particularly from global perspectives – would be flatter, less nuanced and without theoretical discernments from sociological theorists like Lyotard and Foucault. Holtzhausen's analysis of a "metanarrative of progress" is one such application, perpetuated by global public relations practitioners and which can have unintended positive consequences on a society but which requires from practitioners awareness, reflection and rejection of predetermined assumptions (Holtzhausen, 2011). Furthermore, in the nuanced analyses brought forth by postmodernism's commitment to deconstructing "normal" discourses and actively seeking out dissenting messages or resistance strategies, Holtzhausen illuminated a dangerous consequence in intercultural public relations that "critiquing culture has become one of the communication taboos" (p. 162), advocating instead that "while postmodernism argues for respect of difference, it is important to understand and acknowledge when cultural practices are repressive" (p. 162).

Counter-objection: increasingly, critical-cultural work is operationalizing macro-, meso- and micro-processes and contexts in order to link them to public relations factors and outcomes

Critical-cultural work has been applied quantitatively (e.g., O'Neil, 2003), and, therefore, tested rigorously according to traditional positivist protocols. Furthermore, qualitative research consists of a different set of rigorous methodological standards based on achieving validity via techniques like methodological triangulation, member checks, reflexivity and "strong objectivity". These methods enhance transparency, consistency, comparability and other characteristics that enable theory-building. (See Curtin & Gaither, 2005; Edwards, 2011; Sriramesh, 2010; Vardeman-Winter, Jiang & Tindall, 2013.)

In conjunction with the *overly abstract objection*, Gregory (2012) warned against these micro-analyses of theory in her suggestion that scholarship tests too much theory, and in ways that perhaps practitioners may not need. This problem arises from a perception that since our research is conducted by a group of "non-practicing academics, we are not solving the problems of practitioners anymore" (p. 3). This culminates in ongoing "obsessions" in scholarship, which

> include role research, evaluation, "new" media, ethics and, increasingly definitions and the naming of the field....Our obsessions seem small compared to the challenges facing practitioners who are called upon to counsel their organisations and governments as they try to engage with these critical and complex issues.
>
> *(Gregory, 2012, p. 3).*

In response to Gregory's warning, I defer to Mumby's (1997) advocacy of critical interrogation of existing communication theories. He argued that we identify weaknesses in more productive ways than simply scrapping old theories to make way for the production of new ones:

> Instead of seeing the Enlightenment as the gradual and ineluctable progression toward freedom and responsibility, critical modernists recognize the complex relations among communication, power, and identity as mediating this progress. Freedom is not won by the creation of new scientific techniques but rather by careful examination of the socially constructed character of the systems of oppression that limit humans' ability to critically reflect on their conditions of existence.
>
> *(Mumby, 1997, p. 13)*

3. The unrealistic application objection: *critical-cultural work is too difficult to enact in real business situations, and it does not result in practical solutions*

Critical-cultural research continues to receive dissent from "advocates of the functionalist systems Excellence theory...that critical theory fails to make a contribution to public relations practice" (Bardhan & Weaver, 2011b p. 17) because the research is "not necessarily instructive with respect to actual practice" (Gower, 2006, p. 180, citing Curtin & Gaither, 2005). Furthermore, critical work is driven by questioning; therefore, some scholars believe critical-cultural work creates more problems and does not replace current theories/models with either solutions or new frameworks (Tyma, 2008). Moreover, Gregory (2012) explored this critique through an elucidation of the practitioner-academic divide:

> Why [does] the academy appear increasingly irrelevant to the practice from which it was born[?] I would argue that just as public relations practice has a primary duty to serve the public interest, academics too have a wider responsibility to serve the whole of the field: the academy and the practice.
>
> *(p. 3)*

Without honoring this responsibility, she argued, we are not solving the problems of practice anymore.

Counter-objection: *critical-cultural scholarship can exist in theory and in practice untethered from functionalist public relations scholarship*

Because of essential differences in epistemology, critical-cultural scholars may not need to adapt to mainstream critiques, since "criticisms...are, however, symptomatic of functional academics' paradigmatic mindset that scholarship, research, and theory should necessarily serve the interests of professional practice" (Bardhan & Weaver, 2011b, p. 17). Furthermore, there seems to be some unspoken but unwarranted obligation that critical scholars must answer to functionalist scholars (L'Etang, 2005, cited in Bardhan & Weaver, 2011). In reality, scholars are increasingly introducing innovative theories, methods and practices based on reflection and micro-political social action in attempts to resolve gaps left by traditional models. For example, theories like critical race (Pompper, 2005), feminism (Hon, 1995), intersectionality (Vardeman-Winter et al., 2013) and queer theory, are non-communication theories that scholars have applied to public relations contexts to resolve problems that we experience with power differentials based on identity. All of the above have expanded theory within the necessary mainstream framework of public relations theories, and suggested actionable strategies for improving conditions for both practitioners and publics.

Similarly, critical-cultural scholars have provided concrete methods for asking traditional questions while considering our privileged standpoints and assumptions. For example, Mumby (1997) explicated four "postmodern communication conditions" – communication is (im)possible, is political, is for self-de(con)struction, and is subjectless (pp. 16–22) – as a response to a reviewer's question: "What 'cash value' does postmodernism have for communication?" Similarly, in proposing ways that practitioners and educators can address interracial and inter-class gaps, Vardeman-Winter (2011a) suggested "microrevolutionary research" acts like dialogue circles and coalition-building.

4. The confusing pedagogy objection: we are trying to teach students to learn the basics of public relations so let's not cloud their understanding with critiques of the practice

Many public relations programmes are patterned curricula that build on previous classes, require significant time to include all lessons about general and specific public relations strategies, and increasingly demand significant hands-on internship experience to prepare students for post-graduation jobs. Many educators find that while it is important to teach theory to students, it is also difficult to teach in an applied discipline like public relations. To these points, Gregory (2012) argued that critical scholarship does not respect traditional theory and the history of public relations as it should:

> Many papers I receive not only challenge, but also disparage alternative insights, particularly of the founding scholars. This is not right: all deserve respect for the contributions they have made. At some stage no doubt there will be some "settling" in the field where some of "the old" will be regarded as having great worth while new and powerful insights take root and rightfully gain acceptance as the field matures, but hopefully never stultifies.

(Gregory, 2012, p. 3)

Counter-objection: arming students with objections and counter-objections empowers them to defend their practice better against outside critics

Applying the above will enable students to understand public relations more cogently and they will have stronger convictions about why their practice can be ethical, thoughtful, strategic and meaningful. Furthermore, critical work respects the foundations that traditional theory lays, and works to improve it. To this point, deconstructions of traditional educational texts actually "broaden[s] our discussion of public relations, and open[s] our scholarship and teaching to new possibilities" (Duffy, 2000, p. 297) rather than limiting students to a few metanarratives based on propaganda.

For example, Courtright, Wolfe and Baldwin (2011) explain the myriad contributions made by scholars applying Hofstede's (1984) cultural dimensions theory; meanwhile, Courtright et al. (2011) highlighted critiques of the homogeneity circumscribed in intercultural communication research through the continued use of Hofstede's dimensions, and applied the theory to a global campaign (i.e., Dove's "Campaign for Real Beauty") to evince the main critiques that the theoretical dimensions are neither exhaustive nor are they necessarily congruent with "national cultures" rather than individual behaviours. Their findings suggested that according to Hofstede's dimensions, the Dove campaign could be considered multicultural; however, Courtright et al.'s analysis suggested that there were shortcomings in applying the theory because of continued ethnocentric messaging about the primacy of Western notions of beauty that were evident in the campaign.

In fact, Worley (2000) contextualized critical scholarship within the responsibilities of educators and scholars in order to best prepare students for the dynamic business environments that await them after graduation: "The next generation of practitioners will inherit a world of complexity, contradiction, and discontinuous change. They need to be prepared for the requirements of this world – both as citizens and as professionals" (p. 377).

5. The stigmatization objection: we shouldn't be disagreeing with one another – critical public relations work makes us look bad, and we already fight enough stigma as an industry

Again, Gregory (2012) pointed out that we are already a challenged field that experiences a "constant battle for us to increase the status of our own academic journals" (p. 4). For example, Holtzhausen (2011) argued that the term "culture" has been used as a decoy, or a salve, to reject claims of inequity; further, a danger exists when

> assuming all practice is culture, [which] leads to public relations being used to build relationships with local power holders who do not necessarily pursue or support principles of equality and democracy or look out for the interests of subaltern groups.
>
> *(p. 153)*

As such, public relations helps stabilize power differentials in cultures for the benefit of elites as a result of practices like the personal influence model. Furthermore, asserting the socially moral nature of public relations is certainly conflicting – at best – to critics of public relations: "Seeing public relations as a critical and emancipatory set of practices and theories, rather than public relations looking for more persuasive, economic, and efficient ways to complete goals for the dominant coalition, may seem paradoxical" (Tyma, 2008, p. 195).

Counter-objection: we destigmatize the field by critically examining cultural practices within the field

Critiquing our work is aligned with evaluating our work and actually adds credibility to our field (Curtin & Gaither, 2005). Reflective work actually allows outsiders to see that we are thoughtful about our processes and claims, as an industry. For example, through resistance strategies and acts of dissensus (Holtzhausen & Voto, 2002), "postmodernism offers opportunities for dialectical interventions that could enable public relations practitioners working in international or global contexts to navigate and preserve the inherent complicity in the global environment while resisting discriminatory and anti-democratic practices" (p. 155). It is through all this critical work – like Edwards's work on habitus (2009), understanding the power within the practice – and the *constructive* reflection involved, that we attempt to destigmatize public relations as a haphazard, unethical, callous, manipulative discipline. As it is the "logical and ethical responsibility" of researchers to question the basic knowledge of the field, then "critical theory becomes a logical methodology for such work" (Tyma, 2008, p. 196).

6. The contrarian objection: *critical work is contrary to a basic purpose of public relations by asking too many questions and not providing enough solutions*

The basic purpose of public relations is to help organizations promote the bottom line via business continuity and maximization of profit (Duffy, 2000, citing Wolff, 1992). But critical scholarship all too often illuminates problems and does not provide solutions (Gregory, 2012; Grunig, 2001; Tyma, 2008): "Toth (2002) and J. E. Grunig (2001) challenged the critics of the modern, functional approach to come up with their own theories to replace two-way symmetrical, arguing that, in a practical field such as public relations, scholars have a responsibility to develop research that assists practitioners" (Gower, 2006, p. 180). In providing solutions to problems, new forms of practice and applicable research frameworks will emerge, but only if solutions are provided:

> Many papers deconstruct and criticise the work of others in skilful and insightful ways, but this is not enough. It is the responsibility of scholars to advance knowledge, not just by pointing out flaws in the arguments and scholarship of others, but by offering something that is potentially better and which in turn is open to criticism and debate. From that healthy clash there might be a basis on which to move the field forward…it is not good enough to stand on the sidelines and criticise, you have to come up with a viable alternative.
>
> *(Gregory, 2012, p. 2)*

The effect of a stale contrarian stance against functional theories can "lead to an overwhelming determinism that paralyzes actual practice" (Curtin & Gaither, 2005, p. 95) under the constant "discourse of suspicion" (Mumby, 1997, p. 9).

Counter-objection: *critical work forces us out of our stale theories and complacent practices*

Theories are never strengthened until outliers to the average outcomes are identified and explored (Edwards, 2012). The same goes for practice: critical work encourages practitioners to adopt a mindset of: have our normal processes been working for us? For example, in the special issue of *Journal of Public Relations Research* in an article entitled "Identity, Difference, and Power", alterative models of public relations addressed concerns that "functional models of practice do not capture the dynamic characteristics of relationships and discursive nature of meaning, which form the core of public relations practice" (Curtin & Gaither, 2005, p. 91). If this is the case, what can we do differently? Although some critical work requires resources to implement new ideas, new ideas can save organizations money in the long run.

Counter-objection: *entire organizational cultures have been built around questioning the norm rather than settling for the status quo*

By adopting a critical-practical mantra (Woodward, 2003), each critical-cultural project should explore how to enact solutions. For example, critical scholars suggest that the bottom line may not necessarily always be the end-goal of public relations processes; rather, an important public relations goal is to create a better environment for employees and other important publics. Addressing this point, Holtzhausen and Voto (2002) asserted that within examinations into the diverse philosophies and strategies that practitioners desire and embody – a postmodern attempt to diversify our field's understandings of the composition of the workforce – "this lack of insight would limit [practitioners'] ability to bring about organizational change" (p. 79).

To this point, actionable alternatives to the norm abound, particularly in recent texts like: *Public Relations in Global Cultural Contexts* (Bardhan & Weaver, 2011a); *Rhetorical and Critical Approaches to Public Relations II* (Heath, Toth & Waymer, 2009, although first published in 1992, and edited by Toth and Heath); *Gender and Public Relations: Critical Perspectives on Voice, Image and Identity* (Daymon & Demetrious, 2014); and in a new peer-reviewed journal, *Public Relations Inquiry (PRI)* (not to mention this current handbook of critical perspectives). One recent article appearing in *PRI* conducts critical analysis of traditional notions of engagement in public relations, and, in turn, offers useable insight from the *kaupapa* Maori principles in New Zealand. The *kaupapa* Maori values propose that power to create knowledge is concentrated among participants rather than researchers (Weaver, 2011). Specifically, public relations refers to engagement based in power-sharing among sovereign, reciprocating, negotiating bodies that participate in "practical turn-taking and spatial mechanisms [that] ensure equal share of voice and freedom of expression" (Love & Tilley, 2014, p. 37). This alternative framework for engagement is one of many solutions provided to the public relations community that also is committed to the basic goals of public relations of relationship-building and cultural empowerment.

7. The corporate privilege objection: *because critical work is based on illuminating power problems in traditional theories and practice, corporate-based theories and practices remain dominant*

"Critical work continues to privilege the voices of dominant groups as it challenges them" (Edwards, 2011, p. 30) in critiques of corporate and governmental authorities, leading to a lack of privileging of *othered* voices like activist and community groups (Dutta & Pal, 2011). Furthermore, while critical-cultural work privileges marginalized groups, some critics suggest critical work does not actually empower or alleviate conditions for *others* (Weaver, 2011).

Counter-objection: *the corporate-critical dominance tautology is why global public relations and globalization theory are so important to study because they identify the distribution of power across global and local entities*

Since "global public relations work is produced locally, disseminated nationally and globally, and deconstructed locally again, often far removed from its origins" (Edwards, 2011, p. 30), continued interrogations at the power structures between dominant and marginalized groups in global relationships helps deconstruct harmful assumptions. Moreover, deconstruction is not only focused on which voices are/are not empowered in messages; rather, deconstruction is also largely concerned with how public relations structures organizations, how it distributes economic resources, and in what ways it values human participation (Edwards, 2011, p. 43). In short, in conducting postcolonial examinations of knowledge production in public relations, the "deconstructive move uncovers the taken-for-granted assumptions in mainstream approaches" (Dutta & Pal, 2011, p. 217), which is especially helpful in theorizing about public relations because

> it explores the ways in which: (a) public relations practices serve the interests of [transnational corporations] and the free market logic that upholds their dominance; (b) public relations theories maintain the hegemony of West-centric articulations of modernity and development… and (c) resistive politics among the subaltern sectors seek to transform the global inequities in knowledge production, participation in, and resource distribution. (Dutta & Pal, 2011, p. 196)

Implications for researchers

The *overly abstract, stigmatization, contrarian* and *corporate privileging* objections address researchers, and I would suggest that critical scholars make some specific affirmations. First, to realize that likely, most public relations scholars understand and support the need for competing paradigms and theories (Edwards, 2012), with a view to seeing relationships between multiple paradigms as well as the contradictions inherent in them. Improving our "intellectual flexibility is a skill that is not simply advisable but necessary...in global cultural contexts" (Bardhan & Weaver, 2011b, p. 15). Second, although it is recognized that "historically many research outlets had been 'unkind' to critical public relations research" (Coombs & Holladay, 2012, p. 886), critical scholars should "maintain their pressure by continuing to produce, to present and to publish quality research" in efforts to "move critical public relations from the fringe to the center of public relations orthodoxy" (p. 886).

Implications for educators/students

The *navel-gazing, unrealistic applications* and *confusing pedagogy* objections address concerns we have as educators. I suggest that it is not only important to include critical scholarship in public relations theory and management curricula (where critical theories are typically listed in the latter halves of syllabi), but also to include it as a discussion in *each session* of a course. One important reason for ingraining critical thought in each discussion is that without critical-cultural work, some students will simply abandon our programmes because they may feel they do not have a "place" in public relations since they don't conform with traditional notions of communication.

To address the applications for teaching/learning critical thought, Duffy (2000) proposed a postmodern pedagogy for public relations that would:

> present public relations history as a series of stories told from different perspectives of public relations workers...perhaps it would pair a story of public relations success in influencing legislation favorable to the corporation with the [sic] a story of the impact of that legislation on individuals or other organizations. Most importantly is [sic] would encourage students to become skeptical rather that [sic] credulous readers and become aware that organizational activities are not neutral and that there is not only one objective reality that can be known.
>
> *(Duffy, 2000, p. 313)*

In my own critical-cultural public relations course, I gave graduate students the option to conduct one of the following for their final project: produce a graduate-level syllabus around a critical or cultural theory, including reflective writing about the readings assigned each week; develop a practical model for campaign development based on a critical-cultural theory, or; prepare an executive/communicator training programme. These projects addressed the significant challenge in critical-cultural public relations of convincing those around us (e.g., dominant coalition, other communicators, partners, publics) of the need for recognizing the diverse interests/preferences of our publics (and transforming our organization to fit those needs better). The projects suggested above required students to develop executive-level arguments as to why such work was needed, while at the same time teaching the fundamentals of doing critical work (Vardeman-Winter, 2011b).

Conclusion

Therein lies the importance of reflecting on critical work and projecting a defence of it: without organization of our critical arguments, we may lose the opportunity to gain credibility among our peers, our supervisors, those who report to us, our partners and our publics. In traditional research a scientist bolsters credibility through a set of validation techniques; but although critical and cultural scholars do not necessarily align with the methodological practices of traditional research, organization around an argument, and engaging in an intellectual debate about the merits of each perspective, is based in the classic rhetorical tradition. This tradition is a mainstay of persuasion and basic communication theory. So, if we propose that students, scholars, researchers and practitioners organize their philosophies about their work, imagine how this work can be made even better through the utilization of critical-cultural thought. Furthermore, being able to defend our position can only serve to strengthen the practice as a whole. This is an important exercise for a field that continues to carry a stigma about its credibility and value.

Notes

1   I adopted the framework for this essay from an assignment given to a graduate seminar, "Ethics and Philosophy in Public Relations," taught by Professor Larissa Grunig at the University of Maryland.
2   Several authors have explicated the differences between various interpretivist theories and methodologies in relation to communication and public relations. See Gower, 2006; Holtzhausen and Voto, 2002; and Mumby, 1997, for some distinctions.

References

Bardhan, N., & Weaver, C.K. (Eds) (2011a). *Public relations in global cultural contexts: Multi-paradigmatic perspectives*. New York: Routledge.
Bardhan, N., & Weaver, C. K. (2011b). Introduction: Public relations in global cultural contexts. In N. Bardhan, & C. K. Weaver (Eds), *Public relations in global cultural contexts: Multi-paradigmatic perspectives*, pp. 1–28. New York: Routledge.
Botan, C. H., & Hazelton, V. (2006). Public relations in a new age. In C. H. Botan, & V. Hazelton (Eds) *Public relations theory II*, pp. 1–17. Mahwah, NJ: Lawrence Erlbaum Associates.
Coombs, W. T., & Holladay, S. J. (2012). Fringe public relations: How activism moves critical PR toward the mainstream. *Public Relations Review*, 38, pp. 880–7.
Courtright, J., Wolfe, R., & Baldwin, J. (2011). Intercultural typologies and public relations research: A critique of Hofstede's dimensions. In N. Bardhan, & C. K. Weaver (Eds), *Public relations in global cultural contexts: Multi-paradigmatic perspectives*, pp. 108–39). New York: Routledge.
Curtin, P. A., & Gaither, T. K. (2005). Priviling identity, difference, and power: The circuit of culture as a basis for public relations theory. *Journal of Public Relations Research*, 17, pp. 91–115.
Daymon, C., & Demetrious, K. (Eds). (2014). *Gender and public relations: critical perspectives on voice, image and identity*. London: Routledge.
Dozier, D., & Lauzen, M. (2000). Liberating the intellectual domain from the practice: Public relations, activism, and the role of the scholar. *Journal of Public Relations Research*, 12(1), pp. 3–22.
Duffy, M. E. (2000). There's no two-way symmetric about it: A postmodern examination of public relations textbooks. *Critical Studies in Media Communication*, 17, pp. 294–315.
Dutta, M. J., & Pal, M. (2011). Public relations and marginalization in a global context: A postcolonial critique. In N. Bardhan, & C. K. Weaver (Eds), *Public relations in global cultural contexts: Multi-paradigmatic perspective*, pp. 195–225. New York: Routledge.
Edwards, L. (2009). Symbolic power and public relations practice: Locating individual practitioners in their social context. *Journal of Public Relations Research*, 21, pp. 251–72.

Edwards, L. (2011). Critical perspectives in global public relations: Theorizing power. In N. Bardhan, & C.K. Weaver (Eds), *Public relations in global cultural contexts: Multi-paradigmatic perspectives*, pp. 29–49. New York: Routledge.

Edwards, L. (2012). Defining the "object" of public relations research: A new starting point. *Public Relations Inquiry*, 1, pp. 7–30.

Gower, K. (2006). Public relations research at the crossroads. *Journal of Public Relations Research*, 18, pp. 177–90.

Gregory, A. (2012). Reviewing public relations research and scholarship in the 21st century. *Public Relations Review*, 38, pp. 1–4.

Grunig, J. E. (2001). Two-way symmetrical public relations: Past, present, and future. In R.L. Heath (Ed.), *Handbook of public relations*, pp. 11–30. Thousand Oaks, CA: Sage.

Heath, R. L., Toth, E. L., & Waymer, D. (Eds). (2009). *Rhetorical and critical approaches to public relations II*. New York: Routledge.

Hofstede, G. H. (1984). *Culture's consequences: International differences in work-related values*, abridged edition. Beverly Hills, CA: Sage.

Holtzhausen, D. (2011). The need for a postmodern turn in global public relations. In N. Bardhan, & C. K. Weaver (Eds), *Public relations in global cultural contexts: Multi-paradigmatic perspectives*, pp. 140–66. New York: Routledge.

Holtzhausen, D., & Voto, R. (2002). Resistance from the margins: The postmodern public relations practitioner as organizational activist. *Journal of Public Relations Research*, 14, pp. 57–84.

Hon, L. C. (1995). Toward a feminist theory of public relations. *Journal of Public Relations Research*, 7, pp. 27–88.

L'Etang, J. (2005). Critical public relations: Some reflections. *Public Relations Review*, 31(4), pp. 521–26.

L'Etang, J. (2008). *Public Relations: Concepts, Practice and Critique*. Thousand Oaks, CA: Sage.

Love, T., & Tilley, E. (2014). Acknowledging power: The application of kaupapa Maori principles and processes to developing a new approach to organization-public engagement. *Public Relations Inquiry*, 3, pp. 31–49.

Macnamara, J. (2004). The crucial role of research in multicultural and cross-cultural communication. *Journal of Communication Management*, 8, pp. 322–34.

McKie, D., & Munshi, D. (2007). *Reconfiguring public relations: Ecology, equity and enterprise*. Abingdon, UK: Routledge.

Motion, J., & Weaver, C. K. (2005). A discourse model for critical public relations research: The Life Sciences Network and the battle for truth. *Journal of Public Relations Research*, 17, pp. 49–67.

Mumby, D. K., (1997). Modernism, postmodernism, and communication studies: A rereading of an on-going debate. *Communication Theory*, 7(1), pp. 1–27.

O'Neil, J. (2003). An analysis of the relationships among structure, influence, and gender: Helping to build a feminist theory of public relations. *Journal of Public Relations Research*, 15(2), pp. 151–79.

Pompper, D. (2005). "Difference" in public relations research: A case for introducing critical race theory. *Journal of Public Relations Research*, 17(2), pp. 139–69.

Pompper, D. (2010). Researcher-researched difference: Adapting an autoethnographic approach for addressing the racial matching issue. *Journal of Research Practice*, 6(1). Retrieved on 28 January 2011, from http://jrp.icaap.org/index.php/jrp/article/view/187

Sriramesh, K. (2010). Globalization and public relations: Opportunities for growth and reformulation. In R.L. Heath (Ed.), *The SAGE handbook of public relations*, 2nd edition, pp. 691–707. Thousand Oaks, CA: Sage Publications, Inc.

Toth, E. L. (2002). Postmodernism for modernist public relations: The cash value and application of critical research in public relations. *Public Relations Review*, 28, pp. 243–50.

Toth, E.L. (2009). The case for pluralistic studies of public relations. In R.L. Heath, E.L. Toth, & D. Waymer (Eds), *Rhetorical and critical approaches to public relations II*, pp. 48–60. New York: Routledge.

Toth, E.L., & Heath, R.L. (1992). *Rhetorical and Critical Approaches to Public Relations*. Mahwah, NJ: Lawrence Erlbaum Associates.

Tyma, A. (2008). Public relations through a new lens: Critical praxis via the "Excellence Theory". *International Journal of Communication*, 2, pp. 193–205.

Vardeman-Winter, J. (2011a). Confronting Whiteness in public relations campaigns and research with women. *Journal of Public Relations Research*, 5(4), 412–41.

Vardeman-Winter, J. (2011b). *Critical and cultural public relations: Final project assignment*. COMM 7397. Unpublished manuscript. University of Houston.

Vardeman-Winter, J., Jiang, H., & Tindall, N. T. J. (2013). Information-seeking outcomes of representational, structural, and political intersectionality among health media consumers. *Journal of Applied Communication Research*, 41(4), pp. 389–411.

Wakefield, R. (2011). Critiquing the generic/specific public relations theory: The need to close the transnational knowledge gap. In N. Bardhan, & C. K. Weaver (Eds), *Public relations in global cultural contexts: Multi-paradigmatic perspectives*, pp. 167–94. New York: Routledge.

Weaver, C. K. (2011). Public relations, globalization, and culture: Framing methodological debates and future directions. In N. Bardhan, & C. K. Weaver (Eds), *Public relations in global cultural contexts: Multi-paradigmatic perspectives*, pp. 250–74. New York: Routledge.

Woodward, W.D. (2003). Public relations planning and action as "practical-critical" communication. *Communication Theory*, 13, pp. 411–31.

Worley, D. A. (2000). Public relations as postmodern: Reply to Margaret E. Duffy. *Critical Studies in Media Communication*, 17, pp. 374–77.

16

What is critical about critical public relations theory?

Robert L. Heath and Jordi Xifra

The title "What is Critical about Critical Public Relations Theory" is designed to not only answer that question but also to spark discussions about that question. This *Handbook* challenges authors to make the case that critical theory can do more than criticize public relations to bring it back from the brink of malfeasance. As inspiration and guidance, critical theory of public relations aspires for a social critique that leads to human and social emancipation.

The incentive to change aspires to improve the conceptualization of public relations and ultimately to create a discipline, in study and practice, that produces an ever more constructive approach to critical public relations. That approach should not only make the practice better, and more moral, but also guide it to add value where public relations must serve more than corporate and other elite interests. Such aspiration begins by acknowledging society as a collision of interests (the logics of mind, self, and society); as George Herbert Mead (1934) reasoned: "the difficulty is to make ourselves recognize the other and wider interests, and then to bring them into some sort of rational relationship with the more immediate ones" (p. 389).

With the publication of this *Handbook*, probes made now can become more seriously developed themes and theoretical perspectives for later critical work. To that end, one prompting probe is the emancipating theme that is often at the center of public relations. Traditional public relations has presumed that people want, need, and yearn for direction from some elite, whether corporate or state. Are people, individually or more collectively, capable of self-determination and self-reliance? Do they expect some elite to render assistance to solve their problems, and if so, how? Does the incentive to create agentic social coordination move upward and outward, or is it only functional if it comes from some dominant coalition? Such judgments may be the critical turning points on which a critical theory of public relations rests.

We start by investigating the meaning of the term "critical" as an important adjective used by various disciplines and in different contexts. Many common-use definitions of the term "critical" can be found, for example, in *Webster's New Twentieth Century Dictionary* (1983). Woven together, the definitions found there shed light on how and why "critical" means a *vital turning point(s)* and implies *vital evaluations, standards and interpretations* regarding some matter. As such, the term suggests that judgments of specific kinds are vital at the important turning points in both the routine and vital matters of the human condition.

Critical methodology and evaluative standards: One definition of "critical" emphasizes the standards that are used by those who engage in criticism in areas such as art, film, or literature. Critical judgement presumes that explicit standards can be developed and used to judge the relative quality and moral value of a specific work, body, or genre of work. Generations of critics craft standards to make their judgments insightful and valued, not only for consumers of art but also for those who create it. Why does one painting deserve more acclaim and appreciation than another? Is one critical system better than others? Are standards of aesthetics static or ever-changing? Innovations in visual art, by that line of reasoning, occur when paradigms shift, but critics are right to ask whether the shifts, or turning points, add to the technical quality, aesthetic impact, and moral value of the art. For instance, the shift from realism to impressionism and post-impressionism was debated as a loss of commitment to realistic detail, and a substitution of "daubing" for painting. Can emotion, social concern, moral judgment, and aesthetic expression truly shape the critical ability of the individual viewer who studies a painting of dancers or families on outings?

Some critical methodologies and evaluations are quite pragmatic. A definition of scientific variables presumes that critical measures guide sound judgment and action such as those needed to launch and guide astronauts to and from the moon. Similarly, in metallurgy, standards are carefully developed to analyze compositions that affect the strength of steel. Although few drivers appreciate the critical science of an arc, the science of turning radius guides how a driver negotiates a turn and how automobile steering mechanisms are engineered. There is a critical point in the arc of a turn when the steering wheel cannot be safely turned if the vehicle is to maueuver safely at various speeds.

Similarly, in the judgment of organizational structures and functions, it is reasonable to ask if some decisions actually open an organization up to more criticism. Or, conversely, whether the organization strategically adds to the uncertainty involved in making an enlightened choice by flooding the societal cognitive space with so much information that critical judgment is difficult or impossible. Championing transparency is not in and of itself a sufficiently critical judgment.

Critical moment: Timing, sometimes, is critical. A critical moment can refer to cell division in biology, or in mathematics the statistical moment of a trend shift at a specified degree of probability that predicts one candidate's likelihood of victory or defeat. One can imagine a critical point when the temperature of a sick child results in brain damage or death. In landing a plane, what is the critical moment; when is lift no longer appropriate; and at what speed does it come into play to keep a plane in the air?

In public relations, a critical moment might be when a response or other statement is expected for the appropriate discussion of some matter, and its eventual resolution. Traditionally, "no comment," meant just the opposite: an unwillingness or an inability to comment. In the recent case of the Ebola scare, when is a message too early or late for the turns societies need to make to provide humane care and security for key populations?

Critical criticism: Literary criticism may not predict the market success or failure of a work. Nor does critical judgment emphasize finding fault, carping, and even denigrating. This definition might include mere expressions of taste, bias, or whim; it suggests that "carping," for instance, might be unwisely opinionated and not well guided by standards of judgment that are applied by critics whose opinions are most worthy of consideration. This definition assumes both standards of judgment and turning points where some matter progresses from being "right" to "wrong," "correct to incorrect," "proper to improper," "moral to immoral" or "legitimate" to "illegitimate." Critical criticism is at its best when it corrects and inspires in the same way that a teaching surgeon improves a student's skill with a scalpel.

In public relations, carping can be a rhetorical stance taken by activists (critical moment) who believe that an organization is not meeting the best standards of environmental responsibility. Public relations can give a critical voice to those who can make a critical difference. Consider biologist Rachel Carson, who noted a decline in the sounds of birds that typically welcomed spring. Spring was becoming silent because chemicals in the environment were reducing the bird population. Did public relations publicize her findings to arouse a sleeping population, or serve as a corporate tool in opposition?

The organic quality of critical theory presupposes standards that are developed and refined, but which change rather than serve as static universal guidelines. Sometimes the choice in the practice of public relations is that of one word rather than another. What verbs and modifiers best serve various interests and empower various voices? If "global warming" is threatening, does the substitution of "climate change" make such matters easier to discuss?

Critical agency: Agency refers to the ability of an individual, organization, or society to establish itself as efficacious. Failure to achieve the critical level of agency needed to prevent or respond to the manifestation of a risk produces crisis. Is there a turning point between crisis and "not" crisis, or "not" crisis and crisis? Is there a critical turning point where reputation has been harmed, where the organization is no longer deemed legitimate?

As a medical turning point, crisis might occur if a person's blood sugar level is critically high or low. In public relations, it might mean a point at which an issue position is no longer tenable. What critical standard affirms the height of a retaining wall designed to protect a nuclear generating facility from a sea surge caused by a tsunami? All systems of a rocket must operate synchronously at the same instant, or in sequence, for propulsion to occur. As such, this definition, as do others, implies that critical decisions can prevent a turning point, or must respond strategically and morally to a turning point.

Critical agency implies standards of personnel, skills, position, timing, and tools (material or equipment). It presumes the ability to foresee, as well as the willingness and ability to plan for and respond to changing critical conditions. It presumes a kind of legitimacy challenge where the voice of an organization is no longer deemed as of sole value among a community of voices.

Critical narratives, ideas, and interpretative frames: Humans live by narratives, co-create ideas to guide their actions, and develop interpretative frames with which to make critical judgments. "Critical" implies some condition, context, or action that is dangerous, risky, or perilous. Thus, individuals, organizations, and societies need a critical understanding of the conditions of risk to avoid the point at which humans, other animals, and living things are harmed, say, by exposure to some chemical. Critical judgment presumes that at some moment measures must be taken to protect a population.

As a preventative, critical means essential – as in the case of critical care or critical defense. It can refer to the amount of nutrition or water a person or group needs. What is the critical moment when the body is so dehydrated that it can no longer function? How is sustainability to be achieved, and what role does critical public relations theory play? Can contemporary critical public relations exclude the environment?

Thus, societies (through complex dialogues among individuals and on behalf of organizations) craft narratives, formulate ideas (critical ideology), and develop interpretative frames that increase the critical agency of individuals, organizations, and communities.

As an adjective, the dictionary points to the following examples: critical angle (at what point will a leaning tower topple?), critical constant (freezing point), critical philosophy (where, for instance, morality becomes immorality), critical point, critical pressure, critical state, and critical temperature. From this list, it is reasonable to conclude that "critical" means known, socially constructed standards by which some turning point must be identified and preventative or corrective responses undertaken. A critical point is not only a call for engagement, it is also knowing how and when to shift positions and strategies to help move engagement toward critical resolution, rather than some confounded trajectory on the matter.

Reflecting on these generic definitions, insights can be formed to develop a critical theory of public relations. This is needed to answer the questions of what does "critical" mean with regard to the role of public relations in society, in the viability and success of an organization as it makes critical managerial decisions, of the quality of life of some populations, or of the understanding and agreement various groups and organizations have on some matter. Pondering such matters can help an academic discipline and professional practice develop analytical standards by which turning point events can be identified so that appropriate corrections can be made.

Communication for centuries has been empowered by the rationale of turning points. Aristotle's theory of rhetoric (as the foundation for the Western heritage of rhetoric) was based on the prevailing belief that human society must deliberate in ways that lead to enlightened choices and judgments, as turning points between guilt and innocence, expedience or inexpedience, or praise or blame – for instance. Rhetorical theory presumes, said Isocrates (and Aristotle and others), turning points in the history of an idea or issue that are vital to an individual, organization, or society. It presumes the citizenship's responsibility to engage, or remain silent.

At what point, and by what criteria, then, is an organization's reputation such that it deserves the right to reward and the right to operate – or not? Is the company known for producing (un)safe products and (un)justified profits, or as exerting (in)appropriate amounts of power and control over employees, consumers, or communities where it operates? Can it control the institutions, including scientific decision-making, by which it is allowed to manufacture and sell pharmaceuticals that are (un)safe and (in)efficacious? In that sense, does the organization or industry (or government) develop and apply knowledge that tautologically justifies its existence and operations? Do organizations organize to communicate or communicate to organize?

What critical points are used to determine when or why an organization is tolerated or sanctioned? Is there a critical evaluation by which the legitimacy of an organization can be determined? Is it critically sufficient to assume that an organization is legitimate because it continues to operate? Does an organization increase its legitimacy by being tolerant of conflicting opinions? What is the critical judgment of a "quality relationship" by which an organization is a legitimate participant in society so that it deserves reward and the right to operate? Does it create risk, abate risk, shift risk, or put some populations unfairly at risk? Are there critical requirements to judge when an organization bends society to its own interests, or a society's ability to bend the organization to its interests? Does public relations help organizations to be tolerated?

In sum, *critical as a concept* refers to vital turning points as moments, evaluations/judgments, measures, training, cognitive and professional skills, and intervals (between good and bad, stop and go, positive and negative, for instance). These points are not absolutes as societal judgments. They are not the sole purview of some entity called the "dominant coalition." They are subject to the discourses of each community.

A critical moment is one where judgments and actions can make a vital difference. Is the ultimate influence of critical public relations theory the knowing of critical moments, the empowering of ideologies and narratives, and the strategic changes in management decision-making and operations. By that logic, what critical turning point judgments and actions differentiate more rather than less fully functioning judgments critical to human affairs? Is critical public relations' role in society interdependent with such critical judgments?

Critical concepts for critical theory

Critical theory needs to meet the challenge of determining what concepts are critical to critical public relations. Does an organization empower or disempower other entities in a community? Is empowerment rewardable or merely a matter of morality? Do certain actions and narratives actually empower others, or only seemingly do so? Discussions of power as a resource, narrative, and ideology give vitality to public relations theory and focus attention on the factors of critical judgment. As Edwards (2013) observed, "Those who enjoy symbolic power tend to be positioned at the top of the social hierarchy, enjoying a status underpinned by attributions of symbolic value that give them the power to construct a version of reality that others are unlikely to contest" (p. 673).

McKie's (2013) discussion of "Critical Theory" offers a staking point for the trajectory of critical public relations. In that entry, he featured "traditions of thought," "a set of methods that vary over time but consistently draw from different disciplines to examine root assumptions about knowledge," and "involves critical views of social power arrangements in society" (p. 229). What are those root assumptions? How and why do they vary? What are the outcomes of changes in social power arrangements? Are these universal principles or recurring social constructions? Are some words critical to the quality and full functioning of society and therefore to the challenge of critical public relations?

To answer such questions, it can be proposed that language is an instrument by which societies, through individual communicativeness, socially construct themselves, and co-construct their views of reality and of the relationships between individuals as well as with organizations. Kenneth Burke, American philosopher of language and society, reasoned that the essential nature of humans is their symbolicity, their symbolic action. They are by nature able to create and use language to become part of the world, but also to separate themselves from reality and divide themselves from one another. They are by nature ethical animals who socially construct the moral judgments in which they swaddle and justify themselves. They are variously supportive of – and at war over – the power arrangements of society. At one extreme, words are objective definitions of some matter. At the other extreme they are social constructions of some matter and can be lived as though they are that matter. They move from being descriptions to prescriptions, and even evaluations.

Public relations academics and practitioners are wise to consider Burke's argument that if language allows the management of cooperation and communion, it is also the source of the dysfunctions in such aspects of the human condition. Critical judgment wisely embraces Burke's (1934) warning: "If language is the fundamental instrument of human cooperation, and if there is an 'organic flaw' in the nature of language, we may well expect to find this organic flaw revealing itself through the texture of society" (p. 330).

Terms are orderings. They are the foundations of narratives; key terms can be descriptive and prescriptive narratives. Consider terms such as race, gender, profession(al), value, age, capital, functional, privilege, loyalty, identity, opposition, dialogue, banker, lawyer, physician, laborer, sanitation worker, energy producer, job creator, terrorist, and relationship (which itself is the tip of a lexicon). Ponder the narrative power of these words: deliberative democracy, collaboration, empowerment, we/they, and "others." Words' meanings come into being through enactments that are critical rationale for, and challenges to, public relations as an academic discipline and professional practice.

Humans enact themselves through language (Burke, 1966, 1969). Such enactment is as flawed as the language that rationalizes the enactment. Since public relations is essentially a profession of wordsmiths, then words craft ideology and communities and serve as critical moments in the analysis of how fully functioning a society is.

Another concept, and one entangled with the first two, points to the rationale for organizations, language, and society as legitimacy. Assessment of legitimacy is inherently critical in all of the ways mentioned above. When and why does a gap in legitimacy develop or become identified between what an organization does and how (un)favorably it is judged against the legitimacy expectations used by complexes of stakeholders to determine when and why they will grant or hold their resources? Assuming that gaps always and necessarily exist, when does any gap with any set of stakeholders constitute a critical turning point? As in the case of a driver negotiating a turn, when is the start of the legitimacy strain and after which moment is recovery not possible?

Such discussions of legitimacy imply the critical concept of social capital, the benefits/costs and quality of collective trust distributed within a community and between the entities that create it and those who need it and reward it. The social capital of trust results from and supplies the foundation for the balance of preferential treatments and enacted cooperation (empowerment and marginalization) among the members of a society.

Legitimacy is fundamentally the right to operate and the right to reward. It is both the limits on entitlement and the moral rationale for empowered agency. It presumes that organizations are challenged to represent themselves and construct relationships that meet the standards of societal legitimacy. That challenge presumes that organizations contribute at least as much moral and financial/pragmatic capital to communities, in balance for what they take as a resource granting their operations and roles in that society. Such assessments need a socially constructed critical rationale that justifies the legitimacy of organizations but that also offers the critical rationale for the individuals and organizations to challenge such organizations.

Along with legitimacy, the concept of hegemony is connected with the roots of critical theory in the social sciences, Marxism is in all views on political economy, and the pursuit of morality as the rationale of enlightened choice and a community's social capital. Such challenges have found voice in the well-known formulation of one of the first Marxist thinkers who was critical of Marx's ideology: Antonio Gramsci.

Karlsson (2013) captured how the writings of Gramsci (1971) have been particularly influential in the humanities and social sciences:

> Gramsci uses key concepts such as hegemony, culture, and common sense in order to argue that ideology and culture are crucial in the ambition of achieving hegemony and establishing what common sense is in a given society. State ideology and propaganda are thus important tools for (re)producing asymmetric relations of power.
>
> *(p. 25)*

Another important influence that draws on such thinking can be found in the writings of Michel Foucault (1980), who sought to undermine and enrich concepts such as truth and knowledge by linking them to power, authority, and the marginalization of the abnormal. As Siddall (2013) noted, "the parameters of these influences have led to highly political and cynical assessments of ideology and propaganda" (p. 135).

These concepts are essential to the field of public relations, and fundamental to a theory of critical public relations. Indeed, as Heath (2008) stated, "power and control are two of the molar concepts in the theory, research, and best practice of public relations" (p. 2). Acknowledging the tensions between power and control, Heath (2008) argued that power and control are related to legitimacy, in that legitimacy "gives an organization (or individual with a public image) the public right to make arguments relevant to its position, even if that is against current public opinion" (as summarized in Hansen-Horn, 2013, p. 675).

Other scholars have shown how public relations practitioners use communication to create power – and power to create communicativeness: "Practitioners create discourses that present and justify their view of the world. When publics accept the practitioner's view of the world, hegemony is created and publics cede power to the organizations" (Coombs & Holladay, 2012, p. 881). Agreement and accepting perspectives embedded in discourse do not inherently shift power resources, but if they should, or do, then public relations' judgments become essential to either affirming this or for putting matters right.

Already, some critical public relations writing links power to Gramsci's (1971) concept of hegemony (Coombs & Holladay, 2012), or to "domination without physical coercion through the widespread acceptance of particular ideologies and consent to the practices associated with those ideologies" (Roper, 2005, p. 70). Gramsci (1971), as Gregory and Halff (2013) pointed out, claimed that dominant classes exercise power in different spheres, including the economic, political, and cultural; but they also, and crucially, extend it "to the state and civil society. It was in these spheres that hegemony was created and maintained" (p. 418). In such judgments, it is imperative to realize that "dominant classes" are not something predetermined in the human condition, but the result of the development of hegemony that reflexively justifies the empowerment of the voices that dominate discourse. Thus, critical public relations openly identifies battlegrounds where power elites, dominant coalitions, and all other configurations compete. Each seeks to presume the rights and powers of various organizations and individuals to shape society in their image – as the justification of their reputation and foundation for their legitimacy, and as the means for their need to offer their preferred solutions to problems relevant to satisfying their resource dependency.

No wonder, then, that the Gramscian concept of hegemony has formed part of the research agenda of critical public relations scholars since it "operates…through a power of attraction exerted by the social group onto one or more groups" (Hoare & Sperber, 2013, p. 95). From this standpoint, Nye's (2002, 2004) concept of soft power – which "can be studied as the ontological power of public relations practice" (Xifra & McKie, 2012, p. 822) – is also an updated version of Gramsci's notion of hegemony. Soft power is the iron hand in the velvet glove, the elite with a smile.

Hegemony helps analyze how power is exercised, and the role communication plays during different historical periods. This claim justifies a contestation over the antecedents of modern public relations as residing in the distant and veiled past, and thus cut off from relevance to contemporary corporate public relations as its "real start" in the early twentieth century (Lamme & Russell, 2010).

Moreover, as Macciocchi (1974) indicated, Gramsci's hegemony cannot be understood without another of his key concepts – namely the historical bloc. Hegemony unites civil and political society in the same historical bloc, with intellectuals having the role of contributing via ideological diffusion. The complex framework by means of which the ruling classes hold power over the people is via the intermediation of intellectuals and via social communication processes (Hoare & Sperber, 2013). The dissemination of, and access to, these messages in these communications constitute the functional and structural elements of these processes. Thus, the concept of historical bloc offers an additional key for unlocking a critical approach to the history and historiography of public relations.

Marx and Engels (1848) proposed that the economic recessions and practical contradictions of a capitalist economy would provoke the working class to proletarian revolution, depose capitalism, restructure societal institutions (economic, political, and social) for the rational models of socialism, and thus begin the transition to a communist society. Therefore, dialectical changes in how the economy functions in a society determine its social superstructures (culture and politics), and the composition of its economic and social classes. To this end, Gramsci (1971) proposed a strategic distinction between a war of position and a war of *maneuver*. The war of position is an intellectual and cultural struggle wherein the anti-capitalist revolutionary creates a proletarian culture whose native value system counters the cultural hegemony of the bourgeoisie. As further rationale for change management, the dialectic predicts an unending journey as long as tensions reveal new challenges and ideological options and oppositions as corporativism and statism often use public relations to turn the interests of people against themselves and to the advantage of power elites.

To achieve a balance, i.e. a fully functioning society, the voices of the disadvantaged and marginalized need to reach the media, mass organizations, and educational institutions to guide and manage more egalitarian change. To Gramsci (1971), any class that wants to take political power must overcome its simple economic interests, exercise moral and intellectual leadership, and build partnerships and commitments with a range of social forces (Portelli, 1972). Gramsci (1971) called this union of social forces the historical bloc (success in this war of position would allow the communists to start the war of *maneuver*, or the insurrection against capitalism, with the support of the masses). Such hegemony, which is variable in time and space, is indissoluble from the historical bloc; that is, an overall historical situation where we distinguish between, on the one hand, a social structure – the classes – which is directly dependent on the productive forces and, on the other, an ideological and political superstructure. Structure and superstructure are united through the actions of intellectuals.

Within each bloc, action by intellectuals – in communication in general and in persuasion in particular – stands out (Hoare & Sperber, 2013): the "new intellectual [is a]…'permanent persuader' and not just a simple orator" (Gramsci, 1971, p. 10), and persuasion plays an integral role in the hegemonic process (Coombs & Holladay, 2012). At the heart of the historical bloc, the intellectuals of the historically ruling class exercise their power of attraction – their soft power – on intellectuals of other social groups, and eventually unite them with the ruling class.

This role of intellectuals in the process of ideologically developing both the superstructure (civil society and political society) – and structure (economic relations with regard to production and exchange) (Gramsci, 1971) – is the same as that developed by different agents and elites along the histories (hegemonies of history) of humankind. From this standpoint, the critical study of the role of public relations practitioners can be approached from the perspective of Gramsci's intellectual, and, furthermore, can be examined through the critical analysis of cultural and political hegemony in different periods of history.

Given that Gramsci's concept of hegemony is built on the idea of intellectual persuasion and negotiation (Hoare & Sperber, 2013), these forces recur throughout history. Accordingly, approaching them from the perspective of public relations may offer a new opportunity to overcome organization-centric public relations promoted by corporate spokespersons and the four dimensions model of their theoretical apologists (see Grunig & Hunt, 1984), and offer a critical view of public relations historiography. This critical standpoint should be used to investigate the processes of hegemony and/or domination, as well as existing forms of activism, in every age. The analyses should seek to determine the role of communication, information, persuasion, and moral evaluation, and to understand to what extent they were comparable processes to those used today by corporations, nation states, and other organizational forms to impose their ideological hegemony over their environment.

Central to such discussion of critical public relations theory is the inherent need to examine public relations practice in light of political economy. McKie and Munshi (2009, p.81) claimed the following:

> No discipline is an island. Public relations education cannot be independent of, or be indifferent toward, the society in which it operates. Without a sense of different ways that society might be theorized, public relations students and practitioners are limited in their participation in broader dialogues about how public relations contributes to public communication.

Laying down that gauntlet is similar to what Pearson (1990) did when he noted how views of political economy shaped competing views of the roles and social capital of public relations. Reflecting on the challenges posed by Pearson, McKie and Munshi, we question if political economies shape public relations, or does public relations similarly shape political economies?

Analyses that view public relations less as an organizational function and more as a flow in the tides and turbulence of conflict and cooperation already exist (Edwards, 2011). Such analyses ask whether humans can live without organizations, as well as live well with them? As such, public relations is organizational, sociological, cultural, and meaning-centered insofar as relationships are complex, discursively shaped, and a matter of co-created meaning. As a result, no matter how valuable or influential structural and functional processes are to public relations, critical public relations is fundamentally the challenge of the means by which humans co-construct the ideas of social arrangement. Meaning matters and, therefore, so do those forces that shape the meanings that bend society.

Conclusion: towards a critical definition of public relations

This chapter suggests motives to move toward a critical review of public relations and thereby to create a critical theory of public relations. Such a challenge does not deny influence or mute interests. It champions interest as the fundamental aspect of the human condition and serves as the rationale for communication to overcome the prevailing condition of uncertainty. In that way, public relations is a discipline connected in nature and purpose with the condition of continual change management in communities that are multi-dimensional, multi-layered, and multi-textual.

General systems theory, which variously informs different theories of public relations, reasons that uncertainty and entropy are fundamental conditions of reality and choice – human choice. If entropy, then what is the trajectory toward disorder? Can public relations as an academic discipline, moral condition, and cognitive challenge, presume to prevent entropy, and serve all of the interests that are affected by that trajectory into the future. Such a future, and the human approach to it, is shaped by the uniquely human condition of language, and the morality of choices that are as small as individual acts of kindness and as daunting as a political economy in which rewards are amalgamated and used selfishly, or as the enactment and empowerment of shared interests.

One theme of public relations presumes an organizational-centric approach to such challenges. The human condition presumes organization. But the human condition also presumes the virtue of organizations serving to build community resources of social and symbolic capital rather than instrumentalizing publics to distribute resources to the benefit of some for no other rationale than the dictates of power and hegemony. Who does public relations empower? Does it create and apply infrastructures of decision-making to serve the community? How does it reconcile the tensions between power and knowledge? Does it provide a social critique that leads to human and social emancipation?

In these ways, that which is critical seems so because it is sensitive to the demands and logics of turning points. Critical public relations theory has a commitment to learning what critical turns allow for moral change management to free humanity. Such theory should not be templated, and perhaps can never be, but should rather be a dynamic process of explorations, challenges, false starts, and successful landings. It should challenge academics and professionals to be thoughtfully ethical and more egalitarian in choices of strategy, purpose, and practice.

The critical theory of public relations does not presume to have final answers to these and other challenges. Nevertheless, it should commit itself to a journey that presumes as the ultimate, fundamental, choice that organizations are as obligated to bend themselves to community interests as they are to bend those interests and resources to the benefit of their organization.

References

Burke, K. (1934, May 2). The meaning of C. K. Ogden. *New Republic*, 78, pp. 328–31.
Burke, K. (1966). *Language as symbolic action*. Berkeley, CA: University of California Press.
Burke, K. (1969). *A grammar of motives*. Berkeley, CA: University of California Press.
Châtelet, F., & Pisier-Kouchner, E. (1981). *Les conceptions politiques du XXᵉ siècle*. Paris, France: Presses Universitaires de France.
Coombs, W. T., & Holladay, S. J. (2012). Fringe public relations: How activism moves critical PR toward the mainstream. *Public Relations Review*, 38(5), pp. 880–7.
Edwards, L. (2011). Defining the "object" of public relations research: A new starting point. *Public Relations Inquiry*, 1, pp. 7–30.
Edwards, L. (2013). Power, symbolic. In R. L. Heath (Ed.), *Encyclopedia of public relations*, 2nd edition, pp. 673–74. Thousand Oaks, CA: Sage.
Foucault, M. (1980). *Power/knowledge: Selected interviews and other writings 1972–1977*. New York: Pantheon.
Gramsci, A. (1971). *Selections from the prison notebooks*. New York, NY: International Publishers.
Gregory, A., & Halff, G. (2013). Divided we stand: Defying hegemony in global public relations theory and practice? *Public Relations Review*, 39(5), pp. 417–25.
Grunig, J., & Hunt, T. (1984). *Managing Public Relations*. New York: Holt, Rinehart and Winston.
Hansen-Horn, T.L. (2013). Power resource management theory. In R. L. Heath (Ed.), *Encyclopedia of public relations*, 2nd edition, pp. 674–6. Thousand Oaks, CA: Sage.
Heath, R. L. (2008). Power resource management: Pushing buttons and building cases. In T. L. Hansen-Horn, & B. D. Neff (Eds), *Public relations: From theory to practice*, pp. 2–19. Boston. MA: Pearson.
Hoare, G., & Sperber, N. (2013). *Introduction à Antonio Gramsci*. Paris, France: La Découverte.
Karlsson, M. (2013). *Early neo-Assyrian state ideology: Relations of power in the inscriptions and iconography of Ashurnasirpal II (883–859) and Shalmaneser III (858–824)*. Uppsala, Sweden: Institutionen för lingvistik och filologi.
Lamme, M. O., & Russell, K. M. (2010). Removing the spin: Toward a new theory of public relations history. *Journalism & Communication Monographs*, 11(4), pp. 281–362.
Macciocchi, M. A. (1974). *Pour Gramsci*. Paris, France: Seuil.
McKie, D. (2013). Critical theory. In R. L. Heath (Ed.), *Encyclopedia of public relations*, 2nd edition, pp. 229–32. Thousand Oaks, CA: Sage.
McKie, D., & Munshi, D. (2009). Theoretical black holes: A partial A to Z of missing critical thought in public relations. In R. L. Heath, E. L. Toth, & D. Waymer (Eds), *Rhetorical and critical approaches to public relations*, pp. 61–75. New York, NY: Routledge.
Marx, K., & Engels, F. (1848). *Manifest der Kommunistischen Partei*. London, UK: Druck von R. Hirschfeld, English & Foreign Printer.
Mead, G. H (1934). *Mind, self and society*. Chicago, IL: University of Chicago Press.
Nye, J. S., Jr. (2002). *The paradox of American power. Why the world's only superpower can't go it alone*. New York, NY: Oxford University Press.
Nye, J. S., Jr. (2004). *Soft power. The means to success in world politics*. New York, NY: Public Affairs Press.
Pearson, R. (1990). Perspectives on public relations history. *Public Relations Review*, 16(3), pp. 27–38.

Portelli, H. (1972). *Gramsci et le bloc historique*. Paris, France: Presses Universitaires de France.
Roper, J. (2005). Symmetrical communication: Excellent public relations or a strategy for *hegemony*? *Journal of Public Relations Research*, 17(1), pp. 69–86.
Siddall, L. R. (2013). *The reign of Adad-nīrāñ III*. Leiden, Holland: Brill.
Webster's New Twentieth Century Dictionary (1983). New York, NY: Simon & Schuster.
Xifra, J., & McKie, D. (2012) From realpolitik to noopolitik: The public relations of (stateless) nations in an information age. *Public Relations Review*, 38(5), pp. 819–24.

Part III

Perspectives from different locations

17

A post-socialist/communist perspective

From foreign-imposed to home-grown transitional public relations

Ryszard Ławniczak

This chapter suggests how recent developments in international public relations research extend critical theory on post-socialist/communist countries. It also aims to fill a gap in the critical public relations body of scholarship in relation to the specificity of the political and socio-economic environment of post-socialist/communist nations. It also adds to the literature on econo-centric public relations in arguing that public relations strategies and instruments were and are used to promote, and, sometimes, to impose, political and socio-economic models of the market economy with the help of foreign-imposed public relations. As a result, in the first years of transition, most of the European transition countries and Russia adopted a kind of Anglo-Saxon model based on prescriptions of the Washington Consensus. On the other hand, it considers how Viktor Orbán, the prime minister of Hungary, is trying to change this model of development with what this chapter calls home-grown transitional public relations.

Most public relations theory and analysis – critical and mainstream alike – continue to focus primarily on the United States and some Western European countries. Along with the resulting "scarcity of empirical evidence about public relations practices from other regions of the world" (Sriramesh, 2014, p. 1), the highly developed population of over 1.7 billion people, which consists of the countries of Central and Eastern Europe (CEE), the former Soviet Union, China, North Korea, and Cuba are also neglected. Since the early 1990s those populations have experienced a unique historical process as a group of former "socialist," centrally planned economies (or communist countries and societies) are undergoing a process of transition from planned to market economies, from party dictatorship to democracy, and from socialism to capitalism. There have been no precedents in the last two centuries of such a comprehensive transition from one political and economic system to another.

A key factor – in making this change successfully – will be the degree to which social awareness can be changed. This would include the immediate elimination of negative habits related to "socialist" thinking and attitudes towards work, along with the removal of fears and prejudices towards capitalism. This chapter argues that a specific kind of international public relations strategy and instruments – *transitional public relations* (TPR) – have proved to be a useful tool in helping to achieve such transformations in social consciousness in a short timeframe and with a relatively smooth transition from one political and socio-economic system to another.

The concept of *transition* as applied to post-socialist/communist countries entails two aspects:

- the political one (Sussman, 2006), defined as a transition from a single-partisan authoritarian political system to a democratic and pluralistic civil society, and
- the economic one (Wedel, 2000, 2001), seen as the transition from a centrally planned economy, based on state ownership of means of production, to a market economy relying on private ownership and property rights.

The chapter is limited to a discussion of economic transition, and specifically addresses such issues as the socio-economic model of development to be adopted, and how to achieve that adoption. Such an *econo-centric approach* is based on the assumption that using the contribution of analysts of comparative economic systems enables greater consideration of differences between economic systems defined as sets of "mechanisms and institutions for decision-making and the implementation of decisions concerning production, income, and consumption within a given geographic area" (Gregory & Stuart, 1989, p. 5). Differences between those elements in market economy countries and transition economies have a strong effect on public relations strategies and practices in all countries in transition.

In the first years of transition in the early 1990s, one of the most important questions posed was: which variant/model of capitalism would be most suitable for a given country and society in a specified geographic location, time and original environment? The question was neither academic nor new. For years, leading world powers (e.g., United States, Germany, Great Britain, France, Japan) have been continuously using their "soft power" – culture, investment, foreign aid – to "win the battle of hearts and minds." The aim was to promote their own political and socio-economic model of market economy/capitalism, mainly in their own interests. This type of outside assistance, as part of the so-called public diplomacy, has been provided more or less discreetly by international public relations activities (Hiebert, 1992, 1994; Sussman, 2006; Wedel, 1998a, 2001; Ławniczak, 2001, 2003).

In the early years, most of the European transition countries and Russia adopted a kind of Anglo-Saxon model of economic development based on prescriptions of the Washington Consensus and neoliberal ideology. This chapter argues that such development was to a great extent the result of *foreign imposed transitional public relations*. However, this model seems to win only temporary acceptance by the publics in some of the transition economies (e.g., Poland and Hungary). After an early period of expectations, the growing disappointment led to radical and nationalist parties winning elections. These parties were trying to change their economic policy in the direction of a model of capitalism with a human face, similar to a European-style social market economy. For such a successful U-turn in political and socio-economic development, the evolution of communication policy – from *foreign-imposed* to *home-grown transitional public relations* – is crucial.

This chapter, based on case studies of Poland and Hungary, has two main aims. The first is to analyze the role of international public relations and the competition between Western developed countries striving to impose the model most suitable for their political and socio-economic development interests. The second aim is to present the arguments for the more home-grown radical and unorthodox reforms of the Victor Orbán government in Hungary. This approach should be also considered as filling a gap in the critical public relations body of scholarship because it has failed to take into consideration the specificity of the political and socio-economic environment of post-socialist/communist countries.

From admiration to criticism: stages of attitude change toward mainstream US scholarship

There are two basic, but competing, approaches in the public relations theory: the first approach assumes that "public relations have flourished as management practice because practitioners have persuaded organizations to act in society's interest" (Culbertson, Jeffers, Sone & Terrell, 1993, p. 112); and the second, which says that "business and industry have used techniques of the field to promote their own self-interest at the expense of society" (p. 112).

It took almost 20 years for scholars from the post-socialist/communist countries to dare to raise doubts about the universality of the first approach and make their first criticisms of mainstream US PR theory (Ławniczak, 2008, 2011). Even in 2005, when two special issues of the field's leading journals – *Public Relations Review* and *The Journal of Public Relations Research* – demonstrated substantial opposition not only to the US but also generally to the Anglophone dominance in public relations research, the critical research perspective from countries of post-socialist/communist "margin" was still absent. At this point in time, this chapter distinguishes the following three stages of the attitude of transition countries' scholarships towards mainstream theory: stage one of admiration and multiplication, stage two of slowly growing skepticism and the first original concepts, and stage three of critical research (Ławniczak, 2011).

It is, however, necessary to underline that different countries are at different phases of their transitions towards market economy and pluralistic democratic political systems (see, e.g., Chen, 2008; Gruban, Verčič & Zavrl, 1994; Gruban, 1995; Krylov 2003; Lawniczak, 2001, 2003, 2007; Tampere, 2003; Tsetsura, 2004). However, even today in most of the post-socialist/communist countries, the admiration and multiplication stage is still in progress. The scholars are further on in digesting Western theories and multiplying their main concepts in textbooks written by locals. It will take some time before more critical research develops.

Transitional public relations (TPR): the new phase in the development of international public relations

Alongside the historically unprecedented experience of transition, the new phase in the development of international public relations also began (Tampere, 2003). For the first time in the history of public relations, its strategies, policies, and instruments could be applied to assist in the peaceful transition from one political and socio-economic system to the other. This happened not only in one country and society, but also in a group of countries with the common heritage of a socialist command economy.

This "transitional" role/function of international public relations may be defined as helping to introduce and adopt the mechanisms and institutions of the market economy and democracy in former command economies. It is enacted by practitioners, with different intensity in different countries of transition. They apply public relations in the following areas: state-run enterprises, privately owned businesses, government institutions, "new" market economy institutions (e.g., stock exchanges), and city, region, and nation promotions (Ławniczak, 2001). Ławniczak (2001) has also postulated that public relations strategies and instruments have proved useful in helping initially, in the pre-transitional period, to abolish the "old" socialist (communist) system (Hiebert, 1992) and subsequently: to achieve a desirable transformation of public awareness by reversing, or at least mitigating, the fears and prejudices toward "ruthless capitalism" instilled during the "old socialist era"; to adopt the mechanisms and institutions of market economy and democracy, in effect to facilitate an effectively functioning market economy (Holmström, 2003; Ławniczak,

2001, 2003; Tampere, 2003), and to promote alternative market economy models and pluralistic political systems.

Public relations' role in shaping an optimal development model

Previously, centrally planned economies had to decide which model of the market economy to implement. The existing economic literature (Albert, 1992; Coates, 2000; Hall & Soskice, 2001; Szomburg, 1993) distinguishes the following four basic models of market economy capitalism: (1) the Anglo-Saxon (American); (2) the European, social market economy; (3) the Asian, which is either communitarian Japanese-style capitalism, or the authoritarian market economy of the so-called "New Japans": Korea, Taiwan, Hong Kong, and Singapore, who have refined the adopted Japanese model; and (4) the Latin American, dependent market economy.

Theoretical explanation of the problem of choice of the most appropriate model of development for the post-socialist/communist countries was provided by the former president of the National Bank of Hungary, Peter A. Bod (1992). He formulated a thesis on a triangle of rules and conditions – all of which must be harmonized – for any country undergoing an economic and political transition. The three elements of the triangle are swift change, peaceful change, and self-reliance. The problem is that these three goals conflict with one another. If the transition is swift – akin to Klein (2007, pp.180–1) shock therapy – and is to take place in a democratic framework, then it must be financed externally (as in the former GDR and Poland). If there is no external financing and the nation has to rely on its own resources, the transition can be swift but it will need strong authoritarian government (as in the Orbán-governed Hungary since 2010); and if the transition is to be peaceful and self-financing, it takes time (a gradual approach is needed). According to Bod no nation can escape this triangle. Poland as well as Hungary may provide a good verification of Bod's observation (Fleck & Lawniczak, 1993; Kowalik, 2009; Kołodko, 2008; Szomburg, 1993; Szondi, 2014).

Foreign-imposed transitional public relations: the case of Poland

The societies of transition countries have been exposed to public relations strategies and tools aiming to shape their specific model of market economy. The process has involved not only both a country's governmental and private institutions, but also primarily – and more or less openly – institutions from abroad.

Internal versus external sources of change of the socio-economic model (the case of Poland)

Undoubtedly, *internal factors* played a decisive role when a given country faced more or less profound changes of the political system, government, or the political, social, and economic model within a political system. This type of change results from growing dissatisfaction, and social unrest, all of which, in Poland, culminated in the establishment of the "Solidarity" trade union movement. After a series of strikes and a period of martial law, the government agreed to round-table talks with "Solidarity" representatives. The result was the parliamentary election of June 1989, and by the fall, the first non-communist government in postwar history was established.

The shape of any particular social and economic model is affected also by *external factors*. As Freitag (2004) notes, the adoption of a particular social and economic model in a given country, or group of countries, is of significance to other nations. Following a sense of a mission to propagate their own and, in their opinion, the best model of democracy or market economy, these nations often strive to – more or less openly – affect the design of a social, economic, and political model in other countries (Wedel, 1998b, 2001; Sussman, 2006).

Since the end of World War Two the US, and its successive administrations, have been particularly active in promoting the American model of democracy and market economy. In the late 1970s the US – inspired by the German "model of democracy assistance" – developed its own "public and private mechanism" of financing their support for "the battle of ideas" and "progress in the realm of implementing human rights" (www.ned.org). The model was based upon the concept of affecting other countries by means of certain types of non-governmental organizations, the so-called QUANGO's (quasi autonomous – or seemingly autonomous – non-governmental organizations). In fact, it was financed by the government and non-governmental organizations. This method of affecting other countries' societies by means of so-called "non-state actors" is one of several forms of public diplomacy and interpreted as "direct government" (Malone, 1988).

Methods of influencing the direction of transition

To impose a certain model of socio-economic development, Malone (1988) suggests, the initiators should apply information, education, and culture to influence the citizens of a foreign country in order to affect their governments. Such activities include scholarships for representatives of a given country's political and intellectual elites. Another form is the exchange of artists, sports people, local government activists, etc. Lately, material and financial support for various types of non-governmental organizations abroad has become very popular. Current public diplomacy tools include all types of information channels like TV and radio programs, websites, social media, and supplies of equipment such as copiers, fax machines, computers, and devices usually intended for the opposition abroad.

Public relations activities promoting the neoliberal economic system have been also regularly implemented primarily by the "aid-funded private organizations" (Wedel, 1998a). These included Polish think tanks such as the Centre for Social and Economic Research (CASE), the Adam Smith Centre, and the Gdansk Institute for Market Economics, and, in the past few years, the National Bank of Poland. These institutions have organized a series of scientific conferences, the outcomes of which were delivered to media in the form of press releases (Ławniczak, 2007).

The most important slogan of the PR campaign to promote the neoliberal model was TINA (There Is No Alternative) pushing the idea that there was no alternative to such a mode of growth: "Polish media, just like in several other developed countries, have been monopolized by TINA.... Where there is no alternative, there is nothing left to discuss" (Zakowski, 2005, p. 9). As a result of such campaigns, the promotion of other models (e.g., the Scandinavian one), has failed.

The first years of market reforms and transformation of the political and socio-economic system in Poland seem to resemble the German model of "social market economy." Article 20 of the new Constitution of April 2, 1997 says the "social market economy, based upon economic freedom, solidarity, dialogue and cooperation between social partners constitutes the basis for the economic system of the Republic of Poland." In reality, however, the model implemented in Poland until the present can be defined as a neoliberal model of the so-called "shock therapy" and Washington Consensus, applied by the majority of the successive governments over the 25-year transition.

The victory of the neoliberal concept, at that first stage of the Polish transition (with the short break after the 2006 elections), can be attributed to the following factors:

• privatisation of the media and the taking control of them by Western capital, which in such a manner was able to effectively shape public opinion, (Andrzejewski, 2009; Roth, 2014)

- "by the receptiveness of the Poles to liberal economics, which is evidently not the case in the other parts of the regions" (Kiss, 1993, p. 5)
- strong pro-American feelings, and
- successful, financed and outside-managed public relations activities, promoting neoliberal concepts (Kołodko, 2008; Ławniczak, 2007; Pomykało, 2014).

That's why the variety of public relations applied to transform the political and socio-economic system in Poland is labelled *foreign-imposed transitional public relations*.

The aims of *foreign imposed transitional public relations* may be summarized as follows:

- inwards – to impose, in the interest of the rich/developed countries (their governments and corporate groups) their own value systems, political and economic theories, development models, institutions (like pension funds), or NGOs as models of civil society groups (in reality quangos and gongos).
- outwards – to sell such development model as a success, to encourage further countries in transition to apply it (Ukraine, Belarus, North Korea, Cuba, China).

Growing demand for a new model of capitalism after more than 20 years of transition

The results of the Polish parliamentary elections' of the fall of 2006, as well as the elections to the European Parliament of 2014, encourage a hypothesis that – just as in Peru (Freitag, 2004) campaigns promoting the neoliberal model were in fact fruitful only for some time: "Such global electioneering on behalf of neoliberal capitalism is likely to lead to resistance in targeted countries as they become wiser to these means of political manipulation, particularly by outside forces" (Sussman, 2006, p. 14).

In Poland it took about 15 years before such serious resistance emerged. In 2005 three parties: PiS (Law and Justice), SAMOOBRONA (Self-defense) and Liga Polskich Rodzin (League of Polish Families) came into power through criticism of this model. Their election campaigns juxtaposed a "liberal Poland" versus a "Poland showing solidarity," thereby undermining the TINA ideology (Zakowski, 2005). The leader of the PiS Party – Jaroslow Kaczynski – challenged the neoliberal model, claiming that: "we oppose a certain way of thinking...too much of the state, too little of the market, too high taxes, too high labour costs*" (Puls Biznesu*, September 2, 2005).

That might be interpreted as an indication of Polish society approving the market economy, but not its extremely neoliberal version. However, in 2006 this coalition had not succeeded in introducing its anti-liberal, alternative model of capitalism, because they lost the next 2007 elections. In spite of that, Kaczynski and his party, PIS, with the lasting popular support of about 35 per cent of the population, have a good chance of winning the elections in 2015. It means that the "Bavarian," or rather today, the "Hungarian model" of Viktor Orbán, may have a chance of being promoted to a much broader extent.

The transition path of reforms based on Polish experience may be illustrated by Figure 17.1 below.

After the global crisis of 2008–09, one could observe the disappointment and growing criticism of the neoliberal globalization era. It came to the point that the participants of London Rothschild's "Inclusive Capitalism" conference of the world's richest people (May 27, 2014), insisted on the need for a thorough repair of capitalism, referring to the social-democratic order dominating in the European postwar period (*Gazeta Wyborcza*, 31 May–1 June, 2014). Paradoxically, a few years earlier, it was Viktor Orbán in Hungary who made a bold attempt

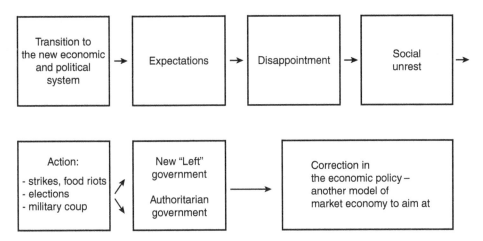

Figure 17.1 The transition path of post-socialist/communist reforms

to move away from the neoliberal market economy model. Orbán's radical reforms infringed the interests of powerful financial groups and many governments. Accordingly, for the effective implementation and defense of his reform, his government needed to use a new variety of transitional public relations – the *home-grown transitional public relations.*

Orbán's home-grown transitional public relations

In deciding which model of market economy to adopt, Hungary followed almost the same path as Poland from the Antall government's (1990–93) attempt to build a "social market economy," through a stage of development based on the "Washington Consensus," to the crisis of 2008–09 (Szondi, 2014), and back to the call for a "new social contract." This was announced by Orbán in his speech to the Hungarian Parliament in June 2010. In reality, it meant a U-turn back to the "social market economy" concept. In the opinion of Hungarian expert Hieronymi (2013): "The choice from the start by the Antall Government of the 'social market economy' as a model for the transformation and reconstruction of the Hungarian economy…at the time of the early 1990s…has been derided as old-fashioned" (p. 9).

From the perspective of this chapter, however, it was derided with the "help" of the *foreign-imposed transitional public relations*, which was also applied in Hungary in the first years of transition (Hiebert, 1992, 1994; Szondi, 2014), to promote the "model of ultra-liberalism and institutional and financial neo-orthodoxy" exercised in practice until 2010.

Political and economic environments of the FIDESZ electoral victory in April 2010

One reason for the electoral victory of Viktor Orbán's party, FIDESZ, in April 2010 was the major riots of 2006. Another reason was a leaked admission by the prime minister, Ference Gyurcsany, that his government had been lying to the people about the country's economic performance and about many other issues. What further enabled Orbán's electoral victory of 2010 was the legacy of the socialist-liberal governments.

As a result, in the opinion of one Hungarian expert

By 2010, a large majority of Hungarians had reached the conclusion that the liberal consensus which had provided the foundation for politics of all colors after 1989 was not much more than a thinly veiled attempt by the national elite to legitimize the exploitation of Hungary's labor and assets by "foreign powers" – transnational capital ("big business") and the international organizations acting in the interests thereof ("big brother").

(Szombati, 2014, p. 1)

Radical reforms of Orbán's FIDESZ government

With a two-thirds majority in Parliament, the Orbán government had a mandate to change laws, including the Constitution. He has used this power to consolidate his grip on key institutions and promised a new era of patriotic government, economic security, and social justice. Since taking power the FIDESZ government has put high importance on undertaking measures that aimed "to find the form of community organization, the new Hungarian state, which is capable of making our community competitive in the great global race for decades to come." This is because

the most popular topic in thinking today is trying to understand how systems that are not Western, not liberal, not liberal democracies and perhaps not even democracies, can nevertheless make their nations successful…in this sense the new state that we are constructing in Hungary is an illiberal state, a non-liberal state. It does not reject the fundamental principles of liberalism such as freedom…the central element of state organization, but instead includes a different, special, national approach.

Orbán formulated these ideas in his already most famous speech at Tusnadfurdo (Baile Tusnad) on July 26, 2014 (see www.kormany.hu/en, the website of the Hungarian government, July 30, 2014).

In seeking to achieve such a model of development, Orbán shocked the international financial markets and unnerved investors, as well as European and international institutions, with the following radical steps:

- In the political sphere:
  - changing the Constitution, and
  - regaining control over the media through media reforms
- In the economic sphere introducing:
  - controversial pension changes allowing the state to effectively seize up to $14 billion in private pension assets to reduce the budget gap
  - new taxes on banks and mostly foreign-owned businesses that helped to avoid implementing new austerity measures
  - renationalization (or de-privatization) of several companies
  - punitive corporate taxes on foreign multinationals
  - an unorthodox, high-risk fiscal recovery strategy designed to force the International Monetary Fund out of Hungary's affairs
  - the possibility to repay mortgages in foreign currencies at a below-market level exchange rate; and
  - a declaration that he will not extend a 20 billion euro loan deal with the European Union and the International Monetary Fund, and will no longer submit Hungary's policies to oversight by any other body other than the EU.

Obviously, most of the costs of such policies had to be borne by international corporate players such as the foreign banks, retailers, and utility companies. This was because, in FIDESZ's view, such companies had benefited too much at the expense of Hungarian citizens. After the

April 2014 elections FIDESZ still gained a two-thirds majority, and no serious change could be observed in these radical governmental policies.

The global campaign of discrediting the Orbán reforms

Orbán had no doubt that the international financial circles and international organizations that he had offended with his radical economic policies would take revenge on both his country and on him personally. In fact, it didn't take much time for the global campaign of discrediting Orbán's reforms to start (Sadecki, 2014). The reasons seem obvious and may be summarized as follows: (1) the infringement of the interests of the Western capital, and (2) the fear that, if such reforms succeed (as in the case of Malaysia), this "plague" could also extend to other transition countries. According to Sounders (2011) and Schoepflin (2014), "the international media have run a quite unbelievably vicious campaign against Hungary, plausibly backed by a sophisticated public relations operation" (p. 2).

The importance of a new type of communication policy to the success of the radical reforms

These radical reforms – both political and economic – challenge the dominating prescriptions recommended for, or forced onto, transition countries by the IMF. So far only two countries in the world have dared to challenge such IMF advice: Malaysia and Venezuela. In the event that the radical reforms introduced by Victor Orbán's government succeeded, they would encourage other countries to follow suit. That could threaten the interests of Western governments and powerful corporations. Hence, for the reforms to succeed, the change of the model of communication policy was also absolutely essential. The new model sought liberation from *foreign-imposed transitional public relations* and the application of a new variety – *home-grown transitional public relations*.

The Orbán government recognized that sound communication inwards and outwards would be key to the success of its radical and unorthodox reforms (Kaiser, 2010). The former involved explaining the basic concept, purpose, and benefits flowing from them, in order to gain public support for its implementation and to win the elections. For the latter, outwards, it meant strengthening the international communication in defense of Hungary's image; and to promote the reasons, concepts, and rationality for the change, to encourage both foreign investors as well as expand international cooperation.

Orbán's government communication strategy since the 2010 election victory

The communication strategy was based on the following guidelines:

- inwards, constantly reminding voters that:
  - "this government is 'different' and functions 'differently' to the previous government" (Kaiser, 2010, p. 120)
  - Hungary is now presented with a major opportunity, which its voters have opened up with their choice for change
  - the FIDESZ government is "the only bulwark against the evils lurking around the corner: the IMF, transnational capital, the Socialist 'kleptocracy' and most recently, 'Jobbik'" (Szombati, 2014, p. 3)
  - the fundamentals of the Hungarian economy remain sound

– the Hungarian government will wage war against the enemies of the country; and
– Orbán himself is the defender of popular interests.
- Outwards, the Hungarian government is trying to lead a two-pronged strategy of communication. On the one hand, it stresses that in Hungary there is nothing terrible happening, with no totalitarianism or the compromising of people's rights. On the other hand, the government emphasizes its strong social mandate and its political independence from other states. The message is clear: nobody is in a position to criticize the Hungarian government, which has a clear mandate given to it by the voters. People have granted consent to reforms that were openly declared, and the government is going to stand by its electoral promises.

The unorthodox methods, tools and measures applied

For inward communication the Inter Media Group (IMG) and the company Young & Partners were chosen as the government's two biggest communication partners. Additionally, the PM's Office contracted Medúza Event and Waldorf Catering to organize protocol events, hired Mega Film Publishing House to manage PM Viktor Orbán's presence on social media sites, and Vármegye Publishing House to run the premier's website at www.orbanviktor.hu (Balla, 2012).

In his inward communication, according to Balla (2012), the second Orbán government frequently used such tools as:

- spectacular billboards and full-page newspaper ads
- BTL communication tools "to discuss important matters with the citizens"
- so-called "consultations," usually consisting of mass mailshots sent out with or without forms and envelopes to answer certain questions, or to write down one's view on the matters under discussion (e.g. the "Economic Consultation" of May 2012, the "Social Consultation" of July the same year, consultations with pensioners relating to private pension funds, and another consultation on the rewritten Constitution)
- using two-word or three-word slogans to appeal to those voters who barely read newspapers and are all but uninformed about the world (Szily, 2013).
- finally, Orbán himself, as an excellent communicator, appeared often amongst "the people," frequently using folk expressions and proverbs, showing himself as a football fan and a politician committed to protecting Hungarians' right to brew brandy at home.

In the most controversial internal communication campaigns:

- posters and billboards were used showing former socialist prime ministers Gordon Bajnai and Ferenc Gyurcsány with the slogan: "They destroyed the country together"
- various media outlets were deployed in the anti-IMF campaign of October and November 2012. According to a government document, the campaign was run "in order to inform the people of Hungary, due to an unforeseen reason, and with extreme urgency" (Balla, 2012).

To communicate outwards, the following controversial (Szily, 2013, p.4) foreign communications tools were applied:

- Hungarian ambassadors were encouraged "to pen militant letters to the editor right away, should they read articles critical of Hungary"
- the "movement for the intellectual defense of the homeland," aimed at reacting to any form of criticism of Hungary

- "the ban imposed on the directors of Hungarian cultural institutes abroad on commenting publicly without prior consultation with head office in Budapest"
- "the blog of the state secretary in charge of embarrassment, Ferenc Kumin...an effort to defend the government's measures"
- "the website 444.hu...that praised Fidesz Fundamental Law"
- Orbán himself as a charismatic leader and excellent communicator, who after assuming the rotating presidency of the European Union on January 1, 2011, "shocked Europe with his outspoken defense of rigid policies" (Sounders, 2011, p. 2); and
- engaging the government's communication minister, Zoltan Kovacs, who was very active and efficient in defending his government's reforms, including writing open letters to the editors of the *Financial Times*, the *Washington Post*, and other influential newspapers.

To help to restore its public image abroad, as well as persuade foreign investors not to withdraw from Hungary, the government appointed two London PR and lobbying firms: Financial Dynamics – to handle financial communications; and Project Associates – to carry out PR on political issues (Bryant, 2011).

Conclusions

Today, after 25 years of transition, there are now two distinct types of *transitional public relations* (TPR):

- foreign-imposed TPR – primarily in the interest of developed market economies, and
- home-grown TPR, aiming to correct the development path/model to suit the interest of the local population ahead of foreign interests.

The Orbán government adopted the home-grown TPR variant in defense of his radical political and economic reforms.

This chapter concludes that, so far, Orbán's reforms and their associated and innovative communication policies are having positive effects. This argument is supported by one Hungarian expert's view that "the communication strategy pursued by the Fidesz government will be taught as a textbook example of successful political communication in university departments across Europe" (Szombati, 2014, p. 2). What this chapter has labeled the *"home-grown variety of TPR"* is deeply embedded in the recent communication histories of the post-socialist/communist countries and should be of interest to critical public relations.

References

Albert, M. (1992). *Capitalisme contra capitalisme*. Paris, France: Edition du Seuil.

Andrzejewski, P. (2009) *Własność mediów a public relations na rynku prasowym* [Media ownership and public relations on the media market]. Poznań, Poland: Wydawnictwo Uniwersytetu Ekonomicznego.

Balla, B. (2012) Message with a price tag, *The Budapest Business Journal*. Retrieved from bbj.hu_files, December 10.

Bod, P. A. (2011). The unloved Hungarian capitalism. *Hungarian Review*, V(4), July 25.

Bryant, Ch. (2011). Hungary wants a face lift. *Financial Times*, March 4. Retrieved on April 23, 2015, from http://blogs.ft.com/beyond-brics/author/chris-bryant/

Chen, N. (2008) Evolutionary public relations in China, Japan, and South Korea: A comparative analysis. In A. R. Freitag, & A. Q. Stokes (Eds), *Spanning borders, spanning cultures: Public relations in a global setting*, pp.137–62. New York, NY: Rutgers.

Coates D. (2000). *Models of capitalism: Growth and stagnation in the modern era*. Cambridge, UK: Cambridge University Press.

Culbertson, H., Jeffers, D., Stone, D., & Terrell, M. (1993). *Social, political, and economic contexts in public relations: Theory and cases*. Hillsdale, NJ: Lawrence Erlbaum Associates.

Fleck, H.-G, & Lawniczak, R. (Eds). (1993). *Alternative models of market economy for economic transition economies*. Poznan, Poland: Printer.

Freitag, A. (2004). Peru's Fujimori: The campaign to sell the administration's neoliberal policies. In D. Tilson, & E. C. Alozie (Eds), *Toward common good: Perspectives in international public relations*, pp.83–102. Boston, MA: Pearson.

Gregory, P. R., & Stuart, R. C. (1989). *Comparative economic systems*. Boston, MA: Houghton Mifflin.

Gruban, B., Verčič, D., & Zavrl, F. (1994). *Odnosi z javnostmi v Sloveniji:raziskovalno porocilo 1994* [Public Relations in Slovenia: Research Report 1994]. Ljubljana, Slovenia: Pristop.

Gruban, B. (1995). Performing public relations in Central and Eastern Europe. *Public Relations Quarterly*, 40, pp. 20–4.

Grunig, J. E., & Grunig, L. (2005). The role of public relations in transitional societies. In R. Ławniczak (Ed.), *Introducing market economy institutions and instruments: The role of public relations in transition economies*, pp. 3–26. Poznan, Poland: Piar.pl.

Hall, P., & Soskice D. (Eds). (2001). *Varieties of capitalism: The institutional foundations of comparative advantage*. Oxford, UK: Oxford University Press.

Hiebert, R. E. (1992). Global public relations in a post-communist world: A new model. *Public Relations Review*, 18(2), pp. 117–26.

Hiebert, R. E. (1994) Advertising and public relations in transition from communism: The case of Hungary, 1989–1994. *Public Relations Review*, 20(4), pp. 357–72.

Hieronymi, O. (2013). The economic and social policies of the Orbán government: A view from outside. *Hungarian Review*, II(4), retrieved on May 29, 2014, from http://www.hungarianreview.com

Holmström, S. (2003). *Between independence and interdependence*. Paper presented at an International EUPRERA Conference in Tallinn, Estonia. September.

Horcher, F. (2014). *Conservative or revolutionary? Three aspects of the second Orbán government (2010–2014)*. Budapest, Hungary: Danube Institute.

Hungarian Spectrum (2011). Viktor Orbán's vision of the international financial world. November 30.

Kaiser, H. (2010). Upheaval in Hungary, *KAS International Reports*, 7, pp. 110–20.

Kiss, K. (1993). Western prescriptions for Eastern transition. In H.-G. Fleck, & R. Ławniczak (Eds), *Alternative models of market economy for economic transition economies*, pp. 29–53. Poznan, Poland: Printer.

Klein, N. (2007). *The shock doctrine: The rise of disaster capitalism*. London, UK: Penguin Books.

Kołodko, G. (2008). *Wędrujący świat* [Walking world]. Warszawa, Poland: Prószynski i S-ka.

Kowalik, T. (2009). *Polska transformacja*. [Polish transition]. Warszawa, Poland: MUZA SA.

Krylov, A. (Ed.). (2003). *Public relations im osteuropaischen Raum*. Frankfurt am Main, Germany: Peter Lang.

Ławniczak, R. (Ed.). (2001). *Public relations contribution to transition in central and eastern Europe: Research and practice*. Poznan, Poland: Printer.

Ławniczak, R. (2003). Intermezzo: The transitional approach to public relations. In B. van Ruler, & D. Verčič (Eds), *Public relations and communication management in Europe*, pp.217–27. Berlin, Germany: Mouton de Gruyter.

Ławniczak, R. (Ed.). (2005). *Introducing market economy institutions and instruments: The role of public relations in transition economies*. Poznan, Poland: Piar.pl

Ławniczak, R. (2007). Public relations role in a global competition "to sell" alternative political and socio-economic models of market economy. *Public Relations Review*, 33(4), pp. 377–87.

Ławniczak, R. (2008). *Mainstream commandments versus transition realities: The roots of the transitional public relations approach*. Paper presented at the Stirling Conference on Radical PR, June 22.

Ławniczak, R. (2011). *From admiration to critical approach: The historical evolution of post-socialist/communist PR scholarship*. Paper presented at International History of Public Relations Conference, Bournemouth University, July 6–7.

Ławniczak, R, Rydzak, W., & Trebecki, J. (2003). Public relations in an economy and society in transition: The case of Poland. In K. Sriramesh, & D. Verčič (Eds), *The handbook of global public relations*, pp. 257–80. Mahwah, NJ: Lawrence Erlbaum Associates.

Malone, G. (1988). *Political advocacy and cultural communication: Organizing the nation's public diplomacy*. Lanham, MD: University Press of America.

Markowski, K. (2002). Ekonomicznie poprawni [Economically correct]. *Trybuna*, May 31.

Prime Minister Viktor Orbán's Speech at the 25th Balvanyos Summer Free University and Student Camp. (2014, July 26). (Retrieved from the website of the Hungarian government on August 27, 2014).

Pomykało, W. (2014). Mało znane oblicze przewrotu ustrojowego dokonanego w Polsce w 1989 i jego skutki [A little-known face of political coup in Poland in 1989 and its effects]. Author's blog. Tuesday, July 22.

Roth, J. (2014). An interview for a Polish weekly, *WPROST.* Published on June 1.

Sadecki, A. (2014). *Państwo stanu wyższej konieczności. Jak Orbán zmienił Węgry* [The state of necessity. How Viktor Orbán has changed Hungary], p. 41, April. Warszawa, Poland: Centre for Eastern Studies.

Schoepflin, G. (2014). Hungarian elections and after. *Hungarian Review,* V(4), July 6. Retrieved on July 28, 2014, from www.hungarianreview.com

Sounders, D. (2011). Hungary's Victor Orbán and the ascent of Europe's democratic authoritarians. Retrieved from http://dogsounders.net/2011/01/hungary-orban-fides/

Sriramesh, K. (2014). Spreading the word. *Communication Director, 2.*

Stasiński, M. (2014). Szefowa MFW straszyła miliarderów Karolem Marksem [The chief of the IMF has threatened the billionaires with Karol Marks]. *Gazeta Wyborcza,* May 31–June 1.

Sussman, G. (2006). The myths of "Democracy Assistance": U.S. political intervention in post-Soviet Eastern Europe. *Monthly Review,* 58(2). Retrieved on May 3, 2013, from http://monthlyreview.org/2006/12/01/the-myths-of-democracy-assistance-u-s-political-intervention-in-post-soviet-eastern-europe/

Szily, L. (2013). Getting the wrong message across. *The Budapest Times,* 11(35), August 30–September 5.

Szomburg, J. (1993). Jaki kapitalizm? [What capitalism?]. *Przegląd Polityczny.* (Wydanie specjalne).

Szombati, K. (2014). Hungary: What can we expect from the next Orbán government? Budapest, Hungary: Heinrich Boell Foundation. April 21. Retrieved from http://www.boell.de/en/2014/04/23/

Szondi, G. (2004). Hungary. In B. van Ruler, & D. Verčič (Eds), *Public relations and communication management in Europe,* pp. 185–221. Berlin, Germany: Mouton De Gruyter.

Szondi, G. (2006). International context of public relations. In R. Tench, & L. Yeomans (Eds), *Exploring public relations,* pp. 112–41. London, UK: FT/Prentice Hall.

Szondi, G. (2014). Hungary. In T. Watson (Ed.), *Eastern European perspectives on the development of public relations: Other voices,* pp. 41–54. London, UK: Routledge.

Tampere, K. (2003). *Public relations in a transitional society, 1989–2002.* Jyväskylä, Estonia: Jyväskylä Studies in Humanities, p. 8.

Tsetsura, K. (2004). Russia. In B. van Ruler, & D. Verčič (Eds), *Public relations and communication management in Europe,* pp. 331–47. Berlin, Germany: Mouton de Gruyter.

Van Ruler, B. (2000). Future research and practice of public relations: A European approach. In D. Verčič, J. White, & D. Moss (Eds), *Public relations, public affairs and corporate communications in the millenium: The future.* Ljubljana, Slovenia: Pristop Communications.

Watson, T. (Ed.). (2014). *Eastern European perspectives on the development of public relations: Other voices.* New York, NY: Routledge.

Wedel, J. R. (1998a). *Collision and collusion: The strange case of Western aid to Eastern Europe, 1989–1998.* New York, NY: St. Martin's Press.

Wedel, J. E. (1998b). The Harvard boys do Russia. *The Nation.* May 14

Wedel, J. E. (2000). U.S. assistance for market reforms: Foreign aid failures in Russia and the former Soviet bloc. *The Independent Review,* IV(3), pp. 395–418.

Wedel, J. R. (2001). *Collision and collusion: The strange case of Western aid to Eastern Europe, 1989–1998.* New York, NY: St Martin's Press.

Wedel, J. R. (2007). *Prywatna Polska* [The Private Poland]. Warszawa, Poland: Wydawnictwo Trio.

Żakowski, J. (2005). *antyTINA.* Warszawa, Poland: Wydawnictwo Sic.

18

Public relations and humanitarian communication

From persuasion to the creation of a community of equals

Jairo Lugo-Ocando and Manuel Hernández-Toro

Introduction

Public relations has broadly sought to empower organisational actors (Holtzhausen, 2000; Holtzhausen & Voto, 2002; Ihlen, 2005; Radford, 2012) and its practice tends to be underpinned by functionalist/positivist approaches (Barquero Cabrero & Castillo Esparcia, 2011; Trujillo & Toth, 1987), particularly in the Anglophone context (L'Etang, 2004, p. 18). This prevalent paradigm sees professional communication in non-profit organisations dealing with humanitarian causes as focusing on the interactions among the different stakeholders such as the media, donors and recipients (Beaudoin, 2004; Naude, Froneman & Atwood, 2004).

In this context, public relations is mainly understood as a set of actions that can help increase the legitimacy of organisational and institutional actors while, at the same time, promoting their efforts to build and manage multiple relationships with stakeholders (Burchell & Cook, 2008; Roper, 2005). This is an effort that ultimately seeks to support the channelling of resources and the acquisition of power and influence as to mitigate suffering. This last has been, generally speaking, the predominant approach for many practitioners in the humanitarian sector (Deegan, 2001; Wiggill, 2014a).

It is one that calls for public relations to support the aims of the organisation in the context of humanitarian communication (Holtzhausen, 2014; Wiggill, 2014b). Because of this approach, practitioners have focused their efforts in convincing people to donate to and support their organisations in their quest to deliver humanitarian aid. This is by means of mobilising the media and public opinion so as to influence governments, corporations and individuals (Seo, Kim, & Yang, 2009, p. 123), while legitimising such calls for power and resources using the discourse of civil society (Dutta-Bergman, 2005, p. 267).

It is not, of course, all about cynicism. We do recognise that public relations does play a pivotal role in modern humanitarian communication, as some scholars have suggested (Kang, & Norton, 2004; Taylor, 2000). This function is now even more important as over the past few years the public in the West, as a whole, has become increasingly reluctant to engage with humanitarian efforts (Barton, 2010; Young-Powell, 2012); suffering from what some scholars have called "compassion fatigue" (Höijer, 2004; Kinnick, Krugman & Cameron, 1996; Tester, 2001). The question then arises among many public relations practitioners as to what to do in order to restore their ability to mobilise the public in the wider context of humanitarian politics.

However, as we will argue in this chapter, this is the wrong question to ask as it only reinforces the power relations that led to the exhaustion of the traditional model of public relations practice dealing with humanitarianism – one which tends to be characterised by a utilitarian ethics (Bivins, 1987, p. 196; Bowen, 2005, p. 191) as it was historically developed in a commercial and profit-driven environment (Miller and Dinan, 2007) that seems at times incompatible with the objectives and aims of non-profit organisations.

Furthermore, by reproducing these practices in which the prevalent action is to foster a feeling of "pity for those suffering" – often packaged as solidarity – public relations has contributed to the "othering" of those who suffer. To us this is problematic as these "regimes of pity" (Boltanski, 1999; Chouliaraki, 2006, 2013) end up allocating more power to the observer while hindering the possibility of audiences and sufferers seeing each other as a community of "equals". In light of this, we question if this is in fact the role that professional communication ought to have in the context of these non-profit organisations.

Instead, we suggest that it is by means of creating spaces of dialogue that public relations can ultimately foster this "society of equals" (Rosanvallon, 2012) in which individuals can share perceptions of risks and vulnerability.

Indeed, "risk" is listed as one of the principles of dialogue in public relations (Pieczka, 2011; Theunissen & Wan Noordin, 2012); the others being mutuality, propinquity, empathy and commitment (Kent & Taylor, 2002, p. 25). In so doing, we suggest, public relations can have a role in promoting more structural solutions to the challenges we face and finally leave behind, once and for all, the diminishing role of simply providing the rhetoric to justify temporary palliative actions.

Scholars have already pointed out that humanitarian communication needs to reinvent itself so it stops being just about promoting "our" common humanity in the West and about highlighting "our" feelings for distant others (Chouliaraki, 2010, 2013) in order to achieve organisational goals such as donations and political influence. Indeed, one of the key paradoxes of humanitarian communication is that while it claims to speak the language of common humanity, nevertheless the spectacle of vulnerability that it puts forward by means of professional communication evokes the language of power; ultimately reinforcing the existing global divides (Chouliaraki, 2013, p. 29).

Likewise, Luc Boltanski (1999) has argued that the legitimacy of current humanitarian communication is not simply a problem of appeal but also a problem in the very relationship between humanitarianism and politics. Consequently, to explore this argument, one would need to examine not only the current role but also the potential of public relations to generate the emotional/rational frameworks of understandings that are required. Thus, there is a need to discuss the actions, discourses and narratives that could allow the audiences to relate to the suffering and their tragedies in a different way and therefore confer to public relations an alternative role in the evolving framework of international humanitarian communication.

Discourses of humanitarianism

Overall, one of professional communicators' main aims, in the context of neoliberal discourses and humanitarianism, has been to foster regimes of pity as frameworks of understanding (Kamat, 2004, p. 155), while focusing on deploying campaigns to attract resources (Seo et al., 2009, p. 123) that can help to sustain the bureaucracies and activities of the NGOs that make use of public relations (Polman, 2010, p. 162). These regimes have been traditionally achieved by media and relational campaigns that put forward specific representations to allow spectators to link on an emotional level with those who suffer.

However, the current communication of solidarity in the West faces a turning point in which the separation between the public logic of economic utilitarianism and the private logic of sentimental obligation towards vulnerable, others, is becoming blurred. For Lilie Chouliaraki, this transformation in the aesthetics and ethics of solidarity reflects a wider mutation in the communicative structure of humanitarianism. It is a turning point leading to what she calls post-humanitarianism (Chouliaraki, 2013, p. 12). By this she refers to how humanitarian communication has moved from emotion-oriented to post-emotional styles of appealing and how it now tends to engage with practices of playful consumerism (Chouliaraki, 2010, p. 107).

In the post-humanitarian scenario, as she explains, there is no longer the theatrical element in which the encounter between the spectator and the vulnerable, other, meet as an ethical and political event. Instead, she continues, the spectators and the victims of tragedy and suffering meet in a mirror structure where this encounter is reduced to an often narcissistic self-reflection that involves people like "us" feeling good about mediated performances of compassion. The end result is the marketisation and corporatisation of public messages coming from international non-profit organisations (NPOs and NGOs) and other actors campaigning on behalf of those who suffer (Dogra, 2012, p. 140). Any radical alternative to this dominant utilitarian ethics of solidarity, Chouliaraki (2013) argues, needs to start by reclaiming the "theatricality" (p. 171) in the public realm.

However, we ought to remember that this "theatricality", which is often so present in humanitarian and development public relations and marketing communication practices, is nevertheless articulated from a position of power. That means that those living in the nations and working for the corporations that created this suffering in the first place (Churchill, 2003, p. 14) are mostly in control of the resources and heavily influential in dictating the agenda of the organisations crafting the policies and palliatives that aim at addressing these humanitarian crises.

David Spurr (1993) typified these as the "incoherencies" created by the legacy of colonial humanitarianism. This is because they keep conferring power to those with the resources to stage media events and campaigns. Those event and campaign managers then highlight the suffering of others and therefore mobilise the media and their publics around the agenda of the centres of power. As a result, public relations campaigns mainly address the consequences but not the causes of suffering and exclusion, that is inequality in the distribution and access to wealth (Dorling, 2011; Lansley, 2012; Piketty, 2013; Wilkinson & Pickett, 2010). For example, for all Bono's campaigns for alleviating poverty, he has equally shown to be equally committed to tax havens that favour the rich (Neate, 2014).

It is in this context that we can argue that public relations dealing with humanitarian communication needs to reinvent itself if it is "to overcome the narcissist and increasingly corporate discourses of solidarity" (Chouliaraki, 2013). Therefore, for those working for NPOs, multilateral organisations or foreign governments, the main challenge is to re-think practice. So far this practice has been restricted to making sure that communication efforts focus on appeals to bring about quantifiable outcomes; donations, cause-related marketing (CRM), political leverage, an acceptable measure of policy change and overall a certain type of public engagement; by which we mean public participation at the different levels of decision-making and decision-taking (Rowe & Frewer, 2005, p. 251). Consequently, humanitarian organisations are making use of professional communication to turn the suffering of others into a spectacle/commodity to be exchanged for donations, support and political leverage. This is, in our view, both ethically wrong and operationally counterproductive in the long run.

Little support for change

One of the key problems that public relations practice faces in addressing these issues is that NPOs cannot be easily placed in any ideological or institutional camp (Lewis & Kanji, 2009, p. 51) and public relations scholars have been at pains trying to figure out how to approach NPOs. At times they are predominately conceptualised as activist, and therefore seen as belonging to a more complex network or social movement (Kang & Norton, 2004; Rondinelli & London, 2003). In these cases, public relations faces the challenge of reconciling donors who provide the financial support with the flammable rhetoric of the NPOs and the social movements in which they are inscribed (Den Hond & De Bakker, 2007, p. 901). Hence, public relations practice in the context of these organisations cannot be considered just as conduits of rhetorical efforts aiming at gathering resources, since, in the end, NPOs are not commercial or corporative activities.

Despite this, most research on NPOs and professional communication has concentrated on assessing how well the functionalist postulates, approaches and frameworks translate to the circumstances surrounding these organisations. This is noticeable, for instance, in Holtzhausen's (2014) study of South African NPOs where relational and corporate identity management theories are examined. It is also present in Wiggill (2014a, 2014b), who analyses the applicability of two-way symmetrical communication and relational theory to NPOs, also operating in South Africa. Crisis and issues management approaches are also tested and subsequently prescribed to those NPOs facing reputational problems in other scholarly work (Sisco, Collins & Zoch, 2010).

Despite the fact that many public relations scholars and practitioners remain of the view that NPOs are not that different from for-profit organisations in relation to their professional communications needs, there are, nevertheless, some distinctive approaches. Indeed, Hume and Leonard (2014) suggest, contrary to more traditional voices, that there is a link between NPOs' distinctive nature and more "specific management needs". For them, it is problematic to prescribe to NPOs functionalist approaches or basic principles of "traditional strategic management" (Hume & Leonard, 2014, p. 2). This is an area that calls for further research.

What is more, the changing environment, characterised by geo-political multi-polarity, digitalisation and fragmentation of audiences, is remodelling the way NPOs interact with the external world. Society in general is interlinking in different ways and that is challenging public relations practice within organisations and corporations in relation to the need to change the current social paradigm (Dinamarca, 2011, p. 79). Jeremy Rifkin (2009) refers to the emergence of an "empathetic civilisation" in order to highlight how the world is becoming more emotionally and rationally interconnected. In this context, some public relations scholars allude to the challenging times and climate to highlight the forces driving the reconfiguration of NPOs into sustainable organisations (Holtzhausen, 2014, p. 286). Other scholars refer to these "social enterprises" (SEs) as "creating a new milieu of initiatives, which necessitates more study and different approaches" (Pang, Mak & Lee, 2011, p. 295).

However, the key problem remains: the fact that the "professionalisation" of NPOs ultimately weakens their transformative potential as it "bureaucratises" them as a whole (Corwall, 2007, p. 476) and, that professional communication has contributed overall with this process of bureaucratisation. They do so by aiding the domestication of NPOs to be compliant with the prerogative of the neoliberal status, hence making these organisations part of the flourishing outsourcing industry in the area of humanitarian aid. This is despite the fact that they were originally conceived as promoters of social change (Lewis & Kanji, 2009, p. 13).

Within public relations, these utilitarian views remain prevalent. This continues despite a vast historical critique recorded against functionalist approaches (Cheney & Christensen, 2001;

L'Etang & Pieczka, 1996; Pieczka, 1996) and historical revisions of the role that public relations has played in reinforcing power structures (Burt, 2012; Dinan & Miller, 2013; Miller & Dinan, 2007). This functionalist perspective remains embedded to the organisational domain as the essential focus of this scholarship (Edwards, 2012, p. 13).

The obsession with the organisational domain is partially rooted in concerns about the financial sustainability of NPOs (Wiggill, 2014a, p. 278) – for example, in terms of 'who will pay the bills?' Not surprisingly, a great deal of attention from scholars and practitioners is put upon those stakeholders "who matter financially" (the donors) and upon designing more efficient fundraising campaigns (Ingenhoff & Koelling, 2009; Kang & Norton, 2004; Swanger & Rodger, 2013).

Certainly, while public relations scholarship on NPOs focuses on analysing in detail the causal links of survival/sustainability relationships and survival/sustainability communication, the study of other NPO stakeholders has received little attention. For instance, the recipients of help as a category has been overlooked by research in this area (Lugo-Ocando, Kent & Narváez, 2013, p. 286). Consequently, many scholars looking at NPOs' professional communication tend to underplay the essential role that other stakeholders, such as communities and individual sufferers, can have in shaping policy and action. Indeed, under the current media arrangements – reinforced by public relations practice – those who suffer are not seen as equals (Lugo-Ocando, 2014, p. 125). Instead, the prevalent assumption is that of accessing resources that can then trickle down from wealthy donors to the hands of the NPOs who manage them according to their own worldviews. These donations are then presented as a charitable gift and not as a gesture of reciprocal responsibility of the donors towards those who are suffering.

At this point is worth making reference to Marcel Mauss' anthropological notion of *potlatch*; a gift-giving feast practised by the indigenous peoples of the Pacific North-west Coast of Canada and the United States (1954). For these communities, the gifts must be reciprocated, for, if they are not, the recipients lose face. Moreover, an unreciprocated gift makes inferior the person who has accepted it. In the context of foreign aid, this translates that those in receipt are given no possibility or opportunity for reciprocity, "in a sense they have received a gift for which they are unable to reciprocate: they are then *potlatched*" (Pawlett, 2013, p. 60), and hence they have become inferior.

This matters, both in ethical terms and in professional communication practice within NPOs. Indeed, over the years, practitioners have had to deal increasingly more with an "ironic spectator" (Chouliaraki, 2013) who is reluctant to participate in this type of engagement. These spectators are either sceptical or suffer from "compassion fatigue" (Moeller, 1999) and thus refuse to engage with issues that, to them, perhaps seem too recurrent, too detached, or both. Under these circumstances, traditional communicative action, in the form of propaganda, is no longer a valid way to engage with these matters as it reinforces the notions of superior/inferior.

Many professional communication practitioners working in NGOs have known and experienced this for some time (Kurzyp, 2013; Pohl, 2014; Seu, Orgad & Flanagan, 2012). However, organisational cultures and day-to-day pressures mean that many professionals keep approaching the problem in functionalist terms. That is to say they think about strategies to re-engage with the public in the same utilitarian ethical terms. It is true that some of these approaches have been successful and have given some new impetus to humanitarian causes, such as the "Make Poverty History" campaign (Oxfam, 2005). However, these experiences are nowadays a rarity with a temporary effect that ultimately only delays scepticism and compassion fatigue. Overall, the public's engagement with the suffering of others has declined together with the ability to mobilise private support to their causes, at least in terms of accessing funding (Stoddard, 2009). In view of this scenario, traditional public relations' functionalistic approaches and practices have become increasingly "inadequate".

Overcoming paradigms

Overall, public relations needs to rethink the nature and purpose of what it does in the context of humanitarian communication. In so doing, it requires to rethink the objective of public engagement, refocusing instead on developing a community of equals. By this, we are referring to the fact that these professionals can no longer deliver the attention of the audiences following traditional approaches in an age of multiplying media, political disillusionment and time-scarcity. This is no longer plausible. Instead, as some authors have pointed out, there is a need to develop what they call "public connections" (Couldry, Livingstone & Markham, 2007, p. 5). These connections – or forms of engagement – will require, however, a level playing field that allows some equality in the communication by means of assuring transparency and accountability between the organisation and the stakeholders.

This means going beyond the narrow organisational objectives of mobilisation and resources allocation – as important as they may seem at that moment – so as to be able to foster a relationship space in which spectators and sufferers do not see each other as distant parties but as equals in terms of citizenship and humanity. This space should be understood as a different type of regime of empathy defined not only by emotionality but also, and above all, by rationality. Something that we believe can not only help turn around the declining trend in public engagement with these causes but also create new forms of commitments in terms of public participation and resource allocation.

This rationality has precedent in our times and derives from the notion of risk that led in the twentieth century to the creation of the welfare state. This was well summarised by John Rawls (1971) in his classic *A Theory of Justice*, in which he suggested that when individuals assume the possibility of risk destitution and suffering as their own, then they are more willing to accept a collective action and responsibility. This rationale can use the notion of shared risk to negotiate with publics, resolve conflict and promote mutual understanding and respect among the different stakeholders. Consequently, this understanding of "risk" needs to be able to accommodate a "plurality of distinctions" (Luhmann, 1993, p. 16).

Therefore, professional communication in relation to humanitarianism needs to be able to communicate risk effectively in a way that allows donors and recipients of aid to appreciate the situations as a challenge for both parts. This is not by assuming "risk" in terms of fear – as used by governments and corporations to advance particular agendas (Klein, 2007) – but as a rational and paused understanding that the individuals on the other side of the screens are equals, and that therefore we could all be exposed to similar tragedies. This notion of risk is still, to a certain point, utilitarian as it aims at reducing potential pain. Nevertheless, it does convey an important amount of empathy that allows those suffering to "de-potlatch" and those in the West to feel a shared sense of responsibility.

In this context, the appeal for donations would not be done in terms of a "gift" derived from pity coming from the powerful, but instead would have to be articulated as a moral "retribution" for the suffering and pain that our own Western society has caused in the first place by means of its own consumerist patterns and historical structures of colonial power. Indeed, let us not forget that in modern times the social production of wealth is followed by the social production of risk in the way the former is distributed (Beck, 1998, p. 29); consequently the function of humanitarian communication should address the issues of distribution and wealth from a rhetorical and dialogical perspective.

This, of course, goes against the utilitarian notion of public relations practised in corporation and commercial environments, which tends to be obsessed with "organisations" and "systems"; that sees the public solely as potential commodities for which relationships and communications are a means of achieving specific outcomes. More importantly, it will need to be a new rationale that recognises that NPOs are not commercial entities but social agents for change. Therefore, those working in them are required to embrace the implementation of regimes of empathy by means of collaborative agreements. These agreements need to allow a dialogue that can help to deliver distinctive frameworks of rational and emotional understanding for civic engagement and political action. In so doing, professional communication can help to create a space in which all parts see each other as equals and engage in a negotiated construction of reality. This in turn can support the establishment of a more permanent relationship between the spectators and those who suffer by transforming both into stakeholders in equal terms and with equal rights. Doing so will provide, we believe, a different type of legitimacy to the role that public relations plays in the context of humanitarian communication.

References

Althusser, L. (1971). *Ideology and ideological state apparatuses (Notes towards an investigation): Lenin and philosophy and other essays.* Brooklyn, NY: Verso.

Barquero Cabrero, J. D., & Castillo Esparcia, A. (2011). *Marco teórico y práctico de las relaciones públicas.* Barcelona, Spain: McGraw Hill/ESERP.

Barton, N. (2010). Donations Dropped 11% at Nation's Biggest Charities Last Year. Retrieved on 11 October 2014 from http://philanthropy.com/article/A-Sharp-Donation-Drop-at-Big/125004/

Beaudoin, J. P. (2004). Non-governmental organisations, ethics and corporate public relations. *Journal of Communication Management,* 8(4), pp. 366–71.

Beck, U. (1998). *La sociedad del riesgo: Hacia una nueva modernidad.* Barcelona, Spain: Paidos.

Bivins, T. H. (1987). Applying ethical theory to public relations. *Journal of Business Ethics,* 6(3), pp. 195–200.

Boltanski, L. (1999). *Distant suffering: Morality, media and politics.* Cambridge, UK: Cambridge University Press.

Bowen, S. A. (2005). A practical model for ethical decision making in issues management and public relations. *Journal of Public Relations Research,* 17(3), pp. 191–216.

Burchell, J., & Cook, J. (2008). Stakeholder dialogue and organisational learning: Changing relationships between companies and NGOs. *Business Ethics: A European Review,* 17(1), pp. 35–46.

Burt, T. (2012). *The dark art: The changing face of public relations.* London, UK: Elliott & Thompson.

Cheney, G., & Christensen, L. T. (2001). Public relations as contested terrain: A critical response. In R. Heath (ed.), *Handbook of Public Relations.* Thousand Oaks, CA: Sage.

Chouliaraki, L. (2006). *The spectatorship of suffering.* London, UK: Sage.

Chouliaraki, L. (2010). Post-humanitarianism: Humanitarian communication beyond a politics of pity. *International Journal of Cultural Studies,* 13(2), pp. 107–26.

Chouliaraki, L. (2013). *The ironic spectator: Solidarity in the age of post-humanitarianism.* Cambridge, UK: Polity.

Churchill, W. (2003). *On the justice of roosting chickens: Reflections on the consequences of US imperial arrogance and criminality.* Oakland, CA: AK Press.

Corwall, A. (2007). Buzzwords and fuzzwords: Deconstructing development discourse. *Development in Practice,* 17(4–5), pp. 471–84.

Couldry, N., Livingstone, S. M., & Markham, T. (2007). *Media consumption and public engagement: Beyond the presumption of attention.* Basingstoke, UK: Palgrave Macmillan.

Deegan, D. (2001). *Managing activism.* London, UK: Kogan Page.

Den Hond, F., & De Bakker, F. (2007). Ideologically motivated activism: How activist groups influence corporate social change activities. *Academy of Management Review,* 32(3), pp. 901–24.

Dinamarca, H. (2011). Challenge for public relations management: A comprehensive. *Revista Internacional de Relaciones Publicas,* 1(2), pp. 79–106.

Dinan, W., & Miller, D. (2013). *Thinker, faker, spinner, spy: Corporate PR and the assault on democracy.* London, UK: Pluto Press.

Dogra, N. (2012). *Representations of global poverty: Aid, development and international NGOs.* London, UK: I.B. Tauris.

Dorling, D. (2011). *Injustice: Why social inequality persists.* Bristol, UK: Policy Press.

Dutta-Bergman, M. J. (2005). Civil society and public relations: Not so civil after all. *Journal of Public Relations Research,* 17(3), pp. 267–89.

Edwards, L. (2012). Defining the "object" of public relations research: A new starting point. *Public Relations Inquiry*, 1(1), pp. 7–30.

Grunig, J. E. (Ed.). (1992). *Excellence in public relations and communication management*. Hillsdale, NJ: Lawrence Erlbaum.

Hall, S. (2011). The march of the neoliberals. The *Guardian* Retrieved on 1 May 2014 from http://www.theguardian.com/politics/2011/sep/12/march-of-the-neoliberals

Höijer, B. (2004). The discourse of global compassion: The audience and media reporting of human suffering. *Media, Culture & Society*, 26(4), pp. 513–31.

Holtzhausen, D. R. (2000). Postmodern values in public relations. *Journal of Public Relations Research*, 12(1), pp. 93–114.

Holtzhausen, L. (2014). Non-profit organisations bridging the communication divide in a complex South Africa. *Public Relations Review*, 40, pp. 286–93.

Holtzhausen, D. R., & Voto, R. (2002). Resistance from the margins: The postmodern public relations practitioner as organizational activist. *Journal of Public Relations Research*, 14(1), pp. 57–84.

Hume, J., & Leonard, A. (2014). Exploring the strategic potential of internal communication in international non-governmental organisations. *Public Relations Review*, 40, pp. 294–304.

Ihlen, Ø. (2005). The power of social capital: Adapting Bourdieu to the study of public relations. *Public Relations Review*, 31(4), pp. 492–6.

Ingenhoff, D., & Koelling, A. M. (2009). The potential of web sites as a relationship building tool for charitable fundraising NPOs. *Public Relations Review*, 35(1), pp. 66–73.

Kamat, S. (2004). The privatization of public interest: Theorizing NGO discourse in a neoliberal era. *Review of International Political Economy*, 11(1), pp. 155–76.

Kang, S., & Norton, H. E. (2004). Nonprofit organizations' use of the World Wide Web: Are they sufficiently fulfilling organizational goals? *Public Relations Review*, 30(3), pp. 279–84.

Kent, M., & Taylor, M. (2002). Toward a dialogic theory of public relations. *Public Relations Review*, 28(1), pp. pp. 21–37.

Kinnick, K. N., Krugman, D. M., & Cameron, G. T. (1996). Compassion fatigue: Communication and burnout toward social problems. *Journalism & Mass Communication Quarterly*, 73(3), pp. 687–707.

Klein, N. (2007). *The shock doctrine: The rise of disaster capitalism*. New York, NY: Macmillan.

Kurzyp, R., 2013. NGOs need to tell better stories. Retrieved on 19 October 2014 from http://www.whydev.org/ngos-need-to-tell-better-stories/

Lansley, S. (2012). *The cost of inequality*. London, UK: Gibson Square Books.

Ledingham, J. A., & Bruning, S. D. (2000). *Public relations as relationship management: A relational approach to the study and practice of public relations*. London, UK: Routledge.

L'Etang, J. (2004). *Public relations in Britain: A history of professional practice in the twentieth century*. Mahwah, NJ: Lawrence Erlbaum Associates.

L'Etang, J., & Pieczka, M. (Eds). (1996). *Critical perspectives in public relations*. London, UK: International Thomson Business Press.

L'Etang, J., & Pieczka, M. (Eds). (2006). *Public relations: Critical debates and contemporary practice*. Mahwah, NJ: Lawrence Erlbaum.

Lewis, D., & Kanji, N. (2009). *Non-governmental organizations and development*. London, UK: Routledge.

Lugo-Ocando, J., Kent, G., & Narváez, A. (2013). Need a hand? No thanks! Media representations and peace building indicators: The case of UK foreign aid programs in Colombia. *Journal of Intervention and Statebuilding*, 6(1), pp. 285–312.

Lugo-Ocando, J. (2014). *Blaming the victim: How global journalism fails those in poverty*. London, UK: Pluto.

Luhmann, N. (1993). *Risk: A sociological theory*. New Brunswick, NJ: AldineTransaction.

Mauss, M. (1954). *The gift: The form and reason for exchange in archaic societies*. New York, NY: Norton.

Miller, D., & Dinan, W. (2007). *A century of spin: How public relations became the cutting edge of corporate power*. London, UK: Pluto Press.

Moeller, C. (1999). *Compassion fatigue. How the media sells disease, famine, war and death*. New York, NY: Routledge.

Naude, A. M., Froneman, J. D., & Atwood, R. A. (2004). The use of the internet by ten South African non-governmental organizations – a public relations perspective. *Public Relations Review*, 30(1), pp. 87–94.

Neate, R. (2014). Bono: Controversial tax laws have brought Ireland the only prosperity it's ever known, The *Guardian*. Retrieved on 12 October 2014 from http://www.theguardian.com/world/2014/oct/12/bono-tax-laws-bring-ireland-prosperity-apple-google-u2

Oxfam, 2005. Make Poverty History. Retrieved on 1 October 2014 from http://www.makepovertyhistory. org/takeaction/

Pang, A., Mak, A. & Lee, J. (2011). Significance of sector-specific corporate social responsibility initiatives, status and role in different sectors. In O. Ihlen, J. Bartlett, & S. May (Eds), *The handbook of communication and corporate social responsibility*, pp. 295–315. Chichester, UK: Wiley-Blackwell.

Pawlett, W. (2013). *Violence, society and radical theory: Bataille, Baudrillard and contemporary society*. Farnham, UK: Ashgate.

Pieczka, M. (1996). Paradigms, systems theory and public relations. In J. L'Etang, & M. Pieczka (Eds), *Critical perspectives in public relations*. London, UK: International Thomson Business Press.

Pieczka, M. (2011). Public relations as dialogic expertise? *Journal of Communication Management*, 15(2), pp. 108–24.

Piketty, T. (2013). *Capital in the twenty-first century*. Cambridge, MA: Harvard University Press.

Pohl, L. E. (2014). Collecting stories with program vs. communications staff. Retrieved on 21 October 2014 from http://www.ngostorytelling.com/2014/04/23/collecting-stories-with-program-vs-communications-staff/

Polman, L. (2010). *War games: The story of aid and war in modern times*. London, UK: Viking.

Radford, G. P. (2012). Public relations in a postmodern world. *Public Relations Inquiry*, 1(1), pp. 49-67.

Rawls, J. (1971). *A theory of justice*. Cambridge, MA: Belknap Press.

Rifkin, J. (2009). *The empathetic civilization*. New York, NY: Penguin.

Rondinelli, D. A., & London, T. (2003). How corporations and environmental groups cooperate: Assessing cross-sector alliances and collaborations. *The Academy of Management Executive*, 17(1), pp. 61–76.

Roper, J. (2005). Symmetrical communication: Excellent public relations or a strategy for hegemony? *Journal of Public Relations Research*, 17(1), pp. 69–86.

Rosanvallon, P. (2012). *La Sociedad de los Iguales*. Barcelona, Spain: RBA Libros.

Rowe, G., & Frewer, L. J. (2005). A typology of public engagement mechanisms. *Science, Technology & Human Values*, 30(2), pp. 251–90.

Seo, H., Kim, J. Y., & Yang, S. U. (2009). Global activism and new media: A study of transnational NGOs' online public relations. *Public Relations Review*, 35(2), pp. 123–6.

Seu, B., Orgad, S., & Flanagan, F. (2012). Knowing about and acting in relation to distant suffering: Mind the gap! Retrieved on 21 October 2014 from http://www.lse.ac.uk/media@lse/Polis/documents/Who-Cares.pdf

Sisco, H., Collins, E., & Zoch, L. (2010). Through the looking glass: A decade of Red Cross crisis response and situational crisis communication theory. *Public Relations Review*, 36, pp. 21–7.

Spurr, D. (1993). *The rhetoric of empire: Colonial discourse in journalism, travel writing, and imperial administration*. Durham, NC: Duke University Press.

Stoddard, A. (2009). *Humanitarian NGOs: Challenges and trends*. HPG Report. Retrieved on 26 April 2015 from http://mercury.ethz.ch/serviceengine/Files/ISN/38273/ichaptersection_singledocument/32e99f4d-0bd8-4d25-b26a-eb87b140316d/en/Chap3.pdf

Swanger, W., & Rodger, S. (2013). Revisiting fundraising encroachment of public relations in light of the theory of donors relations. *Public Relations Review*, 39, pp. 566–8.

Taylor, M. (2000). Media relations in Bosnia: A role for public relations in building civil society. *Public Relations Review*, 26(1), pp. 1–14.

Tester, K. (2001). *Compassion, morality, and the media*. Buckingham, UK: Open University Press.

Theunissen, P., & Wan Noordin, W. N. (2012). Revisiting the concept "dialogue" in public relations. *Public Relations Review*, 38(1), pp. 5–13.

Trapp, L. (2012). Corporation as climate ambassador: Transcending business sector boundaries in a Swedish CSR campaign. *Public Relations Review*, 38, pp. 458–65.

Trapp, L. (2014). *Stakeholder involvement in CSR strategy-making? Clues from sixteen Danish companies*. *Public Relations Review*, 40, pp. 42–9.

Trujillo, N., & Toth, E. L. (1987). Organizational perspectives for public relations research and practice. *Management Communication Quarterly*, 1(2), pp. 199–231.

Wiggill, M. N. (2014a). Donor relationship management practices in the South African non-profit sector. *Public Relations Review*, 40, pp. 278–85.

Wiggill, M. N. (2014b). Communicating for organisational legitimacy: The case of the Potchefstroom Fire Protection Association. *Public Relations Review*, 40, pp. 315–27.

Wilkinson, R., & Pickett, K. (2010). *The spirit level: Why equality is better for everyone*. London, UK: Penguin.

Young-Powell, A. (2012). Charity donations and donors decrease, says survey. The *Guardian*. Retrieved on 10 October 2014 from http://www.theguardian.com/voluntary-sector-network/2012/nov/13/charity-donations-donors-decrease-survey

19

Science, medicine, and the body
How public relations blurs lines across individual and public health

Katie R. Place and Jennifer Vardeman-Winter

Communication campaigns for public health are often based on empirical and social scientific research that produce findings about health problems that need to be remedied, and often a remedy includes educating a population about a problem to which they may be at risk. To this point, public relations in the public health and health technology sector is growing rapidly due to the increasing acknowledgment by governmental, non-governmental, and for-profit organizations that communication is necessary in helping consumers become healthier. Given the complexity of the digital environment, evolving policies, and changing demographics and sociographics of publics, communicators are using technologies and techniques in new ways that blur lines between traditional and progressive communication values.

The discipline of science and technology studies (STS) – also called social studies of science (SSS) – examines the ways in which scientific knowledge is produced. STS scholars argue that socially and scientifically accepted knowledge that is produced by scientific findings and technological advancements is subjectively researched, generated, and communicated. To understand the dynamics and dimensions of knowledge production is to investigate "the stakes, alliances, and action of a much-enhanced array of constituents and producers of what may count as fact" (Haraway, 1997, p. 270). As a boundary object between science, culture, and technology and nature (Mamo & Fishman, 2001), STS and SSS scholars argue that the human body is a site where knowledge is produced differentially across types of bodies. Thus, the knowledge produced about bodies creates further complicated power relations for the way society treats different bodies (Hess, 1997). For example, scientific discourse has operationalized and simplified the complexities of the human body by creating divisions that construct the natural world and social world, the body and the mind, and "male" and "female" as polar opposites. These divisions have created boundaries and "dualisms" (Fausto-Sterling, 2000; Haraway, 1991, 1997; Harding, 1991; Naples, 2003) that falsely homogenize publics.

Critical public health research and public relations

Public relations is the foundation upon which commodification and biomedicalization of bodies – and subsequently communities – occur. For instance, advocacy organizations use academic research they have funded, and therefore, commodified, in order to validate arguments to the media:

> Commodities are seen as commensurable with each other through the medium of money. When academic research becomes a commodity, it loses any explicit association with either particular scientific communities or society as a whole, and it becomes reduced to a possession of individual agents that can be exchanged on the market.
>
> *(Brown, 2010, p. 259)*

Organizations commodify isolated information about bodies in states of distorted health to attract attention toward an organization for the purposes of achieving its mission.

The communication campaign, thus, is the primary packaging material and delivery vehicle through which publics learn about themselves as defined by organizations. Social scientists and communications do not appropriately identify with the cultural assumptions they inject into their research and campaigns; thus, campaigns for public consumption tend to be based on knowledge as understood and produced *by* the institution *for* the ultimately exclusive benefit of the organization sponsoring the research and campaign. Specifically, as "information campaigns arise out of a particular configuration of social relations in this country which gives institutional power over individuals" (Rakow, 1989, p. 164), institutions will segment publics and produce campaigns in order to sell their commodity to the publics. Individuals, therefore, become recipients of calculated discursive strategies intended to advance an organization's mission or political ideology, solidify hegemonic power over particular publics, and generate public consent (Motion & Weaver, 2005, p. 50).

Despite the important relationships between STS/SSS and public relations scholarship, the public relations field lacks theoretical development of its effect on the body as a specific site for technoscientific development. STS/SSS scholars indict marketing, advertising, and public relations techniques as culpable in their critiques of communication campaigns and messaging by pharmaceutical and biomedical technology manufacturers (e.g., Fishman, 2004; Haraway, 1997; Mamo & Fishman, 2001; Shim, 2005). However, public relations scholars have not explored the extent to which public relations enables manufacturers, advocacy groups, and governmental bodies to utilize the body for monetary and political profit. This chapter attempts to instigate such a research agenda within the public relations body of knowledge.

Purpose and implications of this chapter

The purpose of this chapter is to introduce public relations scholarship to recent work in the STS/SSS fields (see roadmap below). We predict we will find few empirical studies utilizing such theories in health contexts. We propose that public relations scholars can look at the variety of SSS/STS theories in the following public relations frame:

- theories of biopolitics, biopower, and biological citizenship combined as the underlying context – or paradigm – by which public relations comes to appropriate meaning of health and medicine to publics
- assumptions that preclude communication work, particularly in how we know public relations as a practice and body of practitioners; these assumptions emerge from producer-consumer culture gaps, actor-network and practice theories, and assumptions of ignorant lay publics
- the public relations processes of research, partnerships, and commoditizing identities in images, which contribute to the ongoing "administration of life," and
- consequences of commoditizing, the making of persons, biomedicalization, and the technoscientific cyborg.

Thus, we will broaden the review to include studies that interrogate the knowledge production of science, medicine, and the body using public relations strategies and techniques (e.g., Vitellone, 2001; Vardeman-Winter, 2012). The chapter offers a roadmap for future research agendas for social studies of health public relations.

Biopolitics: a critical context for public relations and health

Biopolitics, biopower and biological citizenship

The concepts of biopolitics, biopower, and biological citizenship form an underlying context – or paradigm – by which public relations comes to appropriate meanings of health and medicine to publics. First, biopolitics represents the regulatory control and supervision of the human body (Foucault, 1978) by myriad "techniques, technologies, experts and apparatuses for the care and administration of life" (Rose, 2001, p. 1). Scientific and medical advancements, in particular, have created and legitimized new forms of knowledge, authority, and practice (Rabinow & Rose, 2006, p. 197) that have influenced notions of human worth and capacity, contributing to the discrimination of, constraint, or exclusion of individuals deemed "biologically abnormal" (Rose, 2001, p. 2).

Public relations, advertising, and marketing have played significant roles in the biopolitical "will to health" (Rose, 2001, p. 17) through the development of consumer health markets and the promotion of health discourse in the media. More powerful, however, is the way in which strategic communication creates new vocabularies, altering knowledge and experience to align with evolving values systems, practices, and desires (Rose, 2001, p. 18). Individuals thus become active participants, subjects, and consumers in a complex biopolitical structure (Rose, 2001, p. 20).

Thus, an "era of biopower" has emerged in the wake of techniques that seek to take control of life and discipline the body (Foucault, 1978, p. 140). Biopower refers to the mix of state-run and institutional strategies to compose and manage a population, "made possible by forms of specialized knowledge and self-governing participants" (Raman & Tutton, 2010, p. 715). Likewise, it is intrinsically tied to capitalism and economic growth, involving the control and use of the human body for means of production (Foucault, 1978, pp. 141–3).

Applied to health contexts, biopower is evident in the categorization and production of genetic knowledge by science and health professionals and researchers in complex structures and political dynamics. This knowledge often takes the form of social statistics, public health, infection controls, or policy interventions (Ramon & Tutton, 2010, pp. 715–27). Rose (2001) explains that this power to create scientific knowledge is both "pastoral" and "relational" (p. 9). "Pastoral" denotes the oversight of health knowledge by health professionals, researchers, associations, and companies; whereas "relational" denotes how publics' access to health knowledge often depends on the guidance and interpretation of that knowledge by science or medical personnel (p. 9).

Described variously as "cultural intermediaries" (Bourdieu, 1984; Curtin & Gaither, 2005, 2007; L'Etang, 2012), workers of capitalistic control and consent (Kellner, 1992), and "tools" to promote political or economic agendas (Motion & Weaver, 2005), public relations professionals play central roles in the production and dissemination of health communication, scientific knowledge, and biopower. Raman and Tutton (2010) urge for STS and like-minded scholars to analyze these structures of control at various levels and to examine the systems of relations that constitute scientific knowledge. Scholars, therefore, must examine how health public relations research, audience segmentation, strategy, and tactics contribute to systems of pastoral and relational (Rose, 2001) biopolitical power, scientific knowledge dissemination, population management, and economic growth. How does public relations contribute to health disparities or new trends and tactics of health communication? Moreover, public relations scholars must explore biopower in public relations not only as a means of disciplining public relations professionals themselves, but in how public relations functions within a larger societal system to discipline publics and communicate a corporate body politic. Ultimately, acknowledging biopower may at least foster more reflexivity into our theorizing of power, health communications (Kasabov, 2004, p. 8), and citizenship.

In an era of biopolitics and biopower, critical scholarship must explore public relations' role in fostering notions of biological citizenship. The term 'biological citizenship' encompasses programs, politics, and ethics (Petryna, 2004; Rose, 2001, p. 36) that relate the concept of citizen to concepts of human biological existence (Rose & Novas, 2005, p. 2). Therefore, as individuals become a resource for the generation of intellectual property or biotechnological innovation, they generate biovalue (Waldby, 2000, as cited in Rose & Novas, 2005, p. 3). At the same time, however, individuals have come to acquire and expect protection over their dignity, their bodies, and their biological existence (Petryna, 2004; Rose, 2001), offering them access to resources or protection from invasive policies or procedures (Rose & Novas, 2005, p. 4). Controversies surrounding biological citizenship, however, rest on how scientific knowledge is unnaturally collapsed to form new categories of citizenship and entitlement, questioning who receives the "right" to citizenship (or access to medical, political, economic attention) and who does not (Petryna, 2004, p. 251).

The notion of biological citizenship offers rich directions for critical exploration into the ties between public relations and scientific knowledge transfer, healthcare market creation, and relationship-building among strategic publics. Knowledge of how social norms and scientific knowledge is produced through political and economic institutions (i.e., Petryna, 2004) is critical for practitioners' ability to communicate ethically with respect for the diversity and plurality of strategic publics. How does public relations serve as the communicative link between medical, political, and economic entities and the (dis)empowerment of publics seeking political and *biological* recognition (Petryna, 2004)? How can public relations professionals play an activist role (Holtzhausen & Voto, 2002) in critiquing market practices which communicate to and about publics in an essentializing manner?

Assumptions: producer-consumer culture gaps, knowledge of lay publics, and actor-network and practice theories

Below, we explore assumptions that preclude communication work, particularly in how public relations is critically explored as a practice and a collective of practitioners. Producer–consumer cultural gaps have been explored in public relations as contextual factors that influence whether communication messages resonate with publics. The inherent gap between producers and consumers results in producers oftentimes assuming certain limits on lay publics' knowledge about science, medicine, and technology. To interrogate how these assumptions are ingrained in the everyday routines and behaviors of producers, we suggest that actor-network theory and practice theory can be useful to public relations scholarship.

Producer-consumer cultural gaps

Certain sociocultural factors enable public relations to provide the communication vehicles that deliver messages about self-surveillance to public health publics. First, there is growing interest among public relations scholars for interrogating the differences between the culture of public relations producers and the cultures of public relations publics (e.g., Aldoory, 2009; Curtin & Gaither, 2007; Motion & Weaver, 2005; Place & Vardeman-Winter, 2013). For example, public relations often maintains the perspectives of powerful groups over those who have fewer opportunities, skills, and resources (Curtin & Gaither, 2007). Some multinational corporations have a gross domestic product (GDP) larger than that of several developing nations. This economic advantage, in turn, often affords these organizations greater media access and discursive power over their publics and competitors, while contributing to assumptions of "developed world moral superiority" (Curtin & Gaither, 2007, pp. 241–3).

The effect of this phenomenon is reflected in the public relations assumption that publics rarely have power of choice or preference over which discourses they receive (Motion & Weaver, 2005, p. 63). For example, Motion and Weaver (2005), in their critical discourse analysis of the Life Sciences Network in New Zealand found that campaigns offer *select* discourses framed as "truth" intended to gain and shape public consent over an issue. More recently, Place and Vardeman-Winter (2013) found that public relations professionals perceive themselves as "brokers of information" that produce and regulate discourses between organizations and publics. Despite the prominence, and gravity that technological developments have brought to publics' ability to advance issues in a public arena – seen in phenomena like citizen journalism and expert blogging – corporations and organizations still have more media, political, and economic access to message-framing. From the sociocultural perspective, class, educational attainment, and race are often distinct from publics, intricately linked, influential of the organizational messages created in campaigns, and accepted and made popular by mass culture (Curtin & Gaither, 2007; Vardeman-Winter, Jiang, & Tindall 2013).

Similarly, SSS/STS scholars emphasize the body as a site for cultural clashes because of sociocultural differences between medical authorities and lay publics. Science, medicine, and politics have used the body as a site of research, culture, and exclusion, working to universalize, operationalize, and simplify concepts regarding the body through boundaries, "border wars" (Haraway, 1991), and "dualisms" (Fausto-Sterling, 2000; Haraway, 1991, 1997; Harding, 1991; Naples, 2003). In particular, boundaries were constructed to divide male from female and nature from culture (Haraway, 1997; Hess, 1997). The scientific revolution in sixteenth-century Europe, for example, defined the white male as the "qualified" scientist in a private lab setting regulated by the Church (which served as the key governmental and scientific force of a community), while enforcing a values system that excluded women, non-independent men, or non-heterosexual men from the study of science and medicine (Haraway, 1997; Hess, 1997). Thus, scientific and medical knowledge from the perspective of women and certain classes of men were systematically ignored and classified as non-science.

Assumptions of ignorant lay publics

Second, some scholars argue that producers assume lay publics to be inherently illiterate about health, medicine, technology, and media about health (Lupton, 1994). It is critical for public relations professionals to openly address their assumptions and how "campaign messages reflect a social formation" (Moffitt, 2011, p. 30). Practitioners must increasingly privilege audience viewpoints by organizing communications with respect for publics' diverse traits, cultural backgrounds, and life experiences (pp. 29–30). The assumption of lay ignorance inevitably harkens back to cultural practices of medical professionals (and, through association, communicators), particularly in the "closed-loop" of ideas that circulate among them. In his call for research investigating the "ontology of relationality" – a critique of the cultural practice of medical professionals' networking – Law (2004) reiterated that "the public interprets science, it does not misunderstand it" (p. 2).

Actor-network and practice theories

Actor-network theory (ANT), attributed to French scholars Bruno Latour and Michel Callon, offers new avenues for critical health public relations scholarship by examining how scientific practices foster understanding and connection between people and things, as "science in the making" (Thompson, 2005, p. 46). Through this theoretical lens, scientific knowledge and technology is viewed as a "product" of the ongoing processes that stabilize or take for granted scientific "truths" – in a process called "black boxing" (Thompson, 2005, p. 47). ANT cautions that scientific truth is always affected by human interaction, instrumentation, testing, observation, and analysis of an object or phenomenon (p. 47). Thus, ANT questions the centrality and subjectivity of humans and human knowledge to networks, exploring the inherent connectedness among all things (Somerville, 1999, p. 9).

Similar to ANT, practice theories encompass the interest in the everyday life and life world, as well as the language acts and performances of routine and identity characteristics of a group. Reckwitz (2002) situated the study of praxis into knowledge production studies in her argument that practice theory naturally "explains action by having recourse to individual purposes, intentions and interests; social order is then a production of the combination of single interests… explains action by pointing to collective norms and values, i.e., to rules which express a social 'ought'" (p. 248). Reckwitz reasoned that the traditional forms of practice theory contain a "blind spot" in which practice theory neglects tacit knowledge, particularly those knowledges that "lay down which desires are regarded as desirable and which norms are considered to be legitimate" (p. 248).

Public relations theory has traditionally prioritized the human subject while marginalizing the non-human and non-social (Somerville, 1999, p. 11). The application of ANT and practice theory to public relations contexts can help scholars to examine particular hierarchies of knowledge, complicate our understanding of networks, examine the semiotics and cognitive-symbolic structures of practice as in campaign texts, and question the "taken for granted" and "modern" assumptions regarding public relations practice (p. 11). Human subjects are simply one element of a larger complex of networks encompassing humans, objects, and technologies as "micro-actors," and institutions and governmental agencies as "macro-actors" (Somerville, 1999, p. 10). Critical health scholars, therefore, may want to explore the vast micro and macro networks of actors, technologies, and "truths" that comprise current institutionalized health public relations practices. Such an approach would be especially fruitful for detailing how communication and public relations professionals build networks among humans and non-humans, communicate about the role of public relations, and forge new relationships in an ever-evolving society of science and technology (Verhoeven, 2008, p. 133).

Processes: public relations as apparatus for "administration of life"

Drawing upon the aforementioned assumptions of publics and culture, public relations is integral to the systemization of scientific knowledge in public relations. More specifically, through public relations' campaign strategies and tactics, and the microprocesses of campaign work, public relations serves as an essential apparatus for the "administration of life" upon which our macro-societal systems function in the public health industry. Consequences of the "administration of life" are evidenced through practices such as the standardization of identities, public surveillance, and medicalization of bodies. Here, we offer a foundation for detailing public relations as apparatus for "administration of life."

Campaigns consist of strategies and tactics – or microprocesses of surveillance work – that contribute to the administration of life of health publics, such as the use of scientific research; the publicity of partnerships, and, specifically, the fetishization of celebrities, authorities, and disease survivors/victims; and the commoditization of identities in images.

Research as a microprocess

First, the *use of scientific research* in public health campaigns encourages publics to employ "technologies of the self" (Foucault, 1977; 1978). For instance, in order to validate arguments to the media, public health advocacy organizations will often use supportive statistics from studies they have funded:

> Although the organization is funded directly by the [construction] industry, which clearly has a vested interest, it is very successful in having its numbers accepted by the media and legislators because the latter groups don't possess the resources to derive their own statistics.
> *(Salmon, 1990, p. 33)*

As discussed previously, STS examines the ways in which scientific research is used to validate organizational interests and support public health claims (Clarke, Mamo, Fishman, Shim & Fosket, 2003; Rose & Novas, 2005). STS scholars are also concerned with the perceived relationship among the selling, sponsoring, marketing/promoting, and tailoring of research to specific interests' needs across the sponsor, producer, and users of the research (Mamo & Fishman, 2001). For example, an excavation of the relationships between pharmaceutical companies, government regulation agencies, and academic researchers found that "researchers thus contribute to the commodification of new drugs and diseases, while promoting and marketing their own medical expertise and legitimacy" (Fishman, 2004, p. 188).

Partnerships as a microprocess

Second, campaigns also seek partnerships with well-known advocacy, governmental, and corporate entities to add credibility and to leverage complementary resources to aid the campaign's success. Communicators also commit significant resources to *publicizing the partnerships* in order to brand the campaign and to suggest credibility of the effort to publics. In the past decade, partnerships have surged into media salience, as they have become the commodities by which organizations sell the mission of their campaigns. Campaigns also fetishize the voices and portrayals of celebrity, authorities, and disease survivors/victims – the "faces" or "value" of disease prevention. Thus, a network of commercial, health industry, not-for-profit, media, and academic actors produce small and large campaigns.

The explicit consequences of these relationships are represented by the wealth of messages and activities available for consumption, as well as the disease-specific products that may emerge among affected (and sometimes, unaffected) populations as a result of communication efforts. However, implicit consequences exist as well, such as the blurring of disciplinary, operational, and potentially ethical lines between governance, education, and commerce (Fishman, 2004, p. 207).

This point can be further examined by following Fishman's (2004) instigation of examining the tangents between education and marketing within the context of this entity that proficiently and proudly employs marketing: the US governmental health agencies (e.g., Health and Human Services, National Institutes of Health, Food & Drug Administration, etc.). Taken directly from the basic elements of marketing theory – which are product, placement, promotion, and price – social marketing has emerged as a respected model (among government communication personnel and their marketing and communications contractors) used for "the planning and implementation of programs designed to bring about social change using concepts from commercial marketing" (Social Marketing Institute, n.d.). According to this theory, social marketing action is "undertaken whenever target audiences believe that the benefits [of the physical or intellectual innovation] they receive will be greater than the costs they incur," and messages should be differentiated among audiences because, "target audiences are seldom uniform in their perceptions and/or likely responses to marketing efforts and so should be partitioned into segments." Thus, the relationships between education and commerce within the context of a governmental marketing operation for women's health elaborate the combined theories of commodity fetishism and commodification of bodies and knowledge. Knowledge and experiencing fear about health is sold and fetishized to consumers, and the driver behind this effort is the government, supported financially, intellectually, and proximately by corporate and non-governmental groups that may or may not otherwise have specific vested interests in the health of certain US populations.

Commoditizing identity as a microprocess

Without necessarily intending to do so, campaigns standardize identities of publics through the images, branding, and messages of the campaign. They do this through the commodification of bodily health. There are explicit commodification practices adopted among the multidirectional, multi-sited technologies produced and promoted, which include the "infomercial as education" model that Fishman (2004) claimed blurs the lines of education and commerce (p. 200); the use of Bob Dole as the celebrity spokesperson of Viagra to highlight traditional masculine sexual values and identity (Mamo & Fishman, 2001); and marketing racial difference (Mamo & Fishman, 2001; Shim, 2005) in racializing the Viagra user via perfunctorily incorporating diversity by portraying same-race couples, but excluding mixed-race couples (Mamo & Fishman, 2001). The commodification of these new relationships between potential consumers, for-profit biomedical companies, biomedical researchers, and media technologies further sullies who gets to claim knowledge as veritable – although these relationships are "built on an assumed need for patients to become knowledgeable consumers in the marketplace" (Fishman, 2004, p. 208).

Consequences: commoditizing identity and the making of persons

The marketing of biomedical relationships also holds implicit, socially consequential effects. By normalizing the union of technology with the natural body, and selling the vehicle by which to achieve this union, scientific information becomes fetishized, and the scientific claims may be given more credence to impact social and cultural norms than may be possible (Fishman, 2004; Whitehead, 1929). Furthermore, in the union of technology with the body, identities are inevitably altered, as Mamo and Fishman (2001) found: not only did the advertising and scientific promotion behind Viagra differentiate between acceptable and deviant sexual orientations, sexual abilities, genders, ages, and races, these distinctions further reified hegemonic beliefs about proper uses for technology by certain bodies. In this co-productive process of hegemonic identity and technoscientific adoption, "bodies are changed by and also change technological innovations, representations and medical practices" (Mamo & Fishman, 2001, p. 30). Within the contexts of production and consumption, and biomedical knowledge, the fetishization of commodified bodies and knowledge can easily lead to blurred distinctions between education and commerce (Fishman, 2004; Haraway, 1997).

Furthermore, to Mamo and Fishman's (2001) point, race as a particular social construction of identity is commodified in biomedical industries (Haraway, 1997; Shim, 2005). In the making and marketing of race, details of how race functions in the public discourse and across multiple communications reveal disconnects in perception, reception, and application. Problems such as stereotyping, profiling, other-ascribing instead of self-avowal, and systematic marginalization perpetuate the "errors" (Whitehead, 1929) of assuming social and cultural purity across genetics and biology. To this point, Haraway (1997) hinted that "in these zones, uninvited associations and dissociations are sure to undo one's sense of the self same, which is always neatly prelabeled to forestall moral, epistemological, and political scrutiny" (p. 215). Because of these crossed disassociations of identity, ways of knowing are further racialized and thus privileged or marginalized among scientific and untrained understanding alike.

Consequences on gender and sexuality

Critical science and health scholars argue that scientific knowledge has artificially categorized notions of sexuality and gender as binaries, ignoring "shades of difference" (Butler, 1990; Fausto-Sterling, 2000, pp. 3–5). These "dualisms" are often constructed via naming and defining of phenomena, standardized scientific practices, and utilization of the "instrument" as an objective means of discovery. Likewise, socially constructed beliefs regarding sexuality and gender affect the scientific production of knowledge about the human body. Over time, certain "truths" about sexuality and gender have become institutionalized and internalized (Fausto-Sterling, 2000, pp. 3–5).

Because public relations is central to the production, distribution, and consumption of scientific and medical discourse, it plays a role in the shaping of norms regarding sexuality and gender. In particular, public relations has been found to perpetuate values systems and hegemonic discourses that equate heterosexuality as the norm (Edwards & L'Etang, 2013; Tindall & Waters, 2013). Under this "heterosexual matrix" (Butler, 1990, as cited by Edwards & L'Etang, 2013) public relations research has rarely critiqued its heteronormative values or lack of attention to sexuality (p. 50). Queer theory – which attempts to understand the evolution of sexual and gender categories, and "debunk" them (Jagose, 1996, pp. 2–3) – offers one such means of critique. Deconstructing and debunking essentializing norms may assist public relations professionals to avoid communicating about gender and sexuality in a highly managed way that conceives of some publics as "dominant" and the rest as "other" (Munshi, 2005, p. 47, as cited in McKie & Munshi, 2009, p. 69).

Making and marketing of race

Race is a synthetic category through which biomedicine identifies organizations' needs to establish boundaries of purity and difference for the social institutions of politics, economics, and culture. The US, for example, is culturally and politically preoccupied with choreographing the borders and relationships among "pure breeds of Americans" and "mixed breeds of Americans" with foreigners, which results in racial and sexual violence upon the psyche of individuals, and works deep into cultural and scientific institutions (Haraway, 1997). In the capitalist tradition of stretching the possibilities of profit into biomedicalized commodification, marketing strategies position race as not only the motive for obtaining new technology but also as the reason that health disparities affect particular populations. Specifically, commercial interests have crafted clinical trial data to promote race-specific pharmaceuticals. These so-called remedies for so-called health disparities help medical practitioners, policy-makers, and marketers rationalize the race segmentation of disciplines like health promotion, physical-patient communication, and drug regulation (Kahn, 2004). For example, the relatively recent approval of BiDil – indicated specifically to treat high blood pressure in African Americans – sparked debate about assumptions of an interaction between the phenotype of skin color and drug efficacy. Assuming race to be commonly differentiating across biological and genetic expressions threatens committing the "fallacy of reification" (Duster, 2005, p. 1050), a type of "misplaced concreteness" that Whitehead (1929) warns of to avoid widely assuming racial categories as absolute.

In the making and marketing of race, details of how race functions in the public discourse and across multiple communication venues reveals disconnects in consumer perception, reception, and application. Problems such as stereotyping, profiling, committing microaggressions, and systemic marginalization perpetuate the "errors" (Whitehead, 1929) of assuming social and cultural purity across genetics and biology. Differences in meaning-making about race becomes problematic when one knowledge is valued over another, and the product of that knowledge (e.g., epidemiological studies which drive communication campaigns) retains predictive and explanatory power about the connection between identity and disease (Shim, 2005).

Consequences: biomedicalization and the technoscientific cyborg

Biomedicalization

Biomedicalization is the larger consequence of the standardization of identities, combined with the making of scientific facts. Biomedicalization is credited with widening the concept of health to not only include the absence of illness/sickness but to encompass sociocultural meanings about normalcy (Clarke et al., 2003). However, as a product of technoscientific discovery, biomedicalization privileges some actors with information, access, and resources about ideals of health, whereas others are marginalized, and their knowledge is withheld in the production and dissemination of technology (Haraway, 1997). For example, Kaufman, Shim and Russ (2006) argued that the favoring of certain actors' knowledge and interests can be seen in the aging process: it is increasingly framed as a pathology and an awkward condition in life that must be fixed, such that to dissent from remedying the aging "disease" is to deny the patient, the patient's network of loved ones, the patient's healthcare providers, and the sociocultural value of maximizing life.

Researchers have mapped the sources of biomedicalization to such practices as epidemiological culture's process of segmenting populations according to varying risk levels (Clarke et al., 2003), which critics argue increases the commodification of health, and thus, difference. This process seems to serve as a systematic "othering" of groups that does not represent normative embodiment of health, particularly through supposed low self-surveillance. This framing of the increasing emergence of customized, specific health administration contests the seemingly well-intentioned intellectual and practical recommendation of culturally competent/sensitive messaging within health education and communication. The acts of segmentation of populations, scientific facts, and communication messaging echoes Foucault's (1977; 1978) depiction of the asymmetrical interests of a governing power enacting discipline via standards, surveillance, and control over population members to achieve socioeconomic benefits for government. Thus, it is important to ask to what extent are such "intellectual technologies" like segmentation equally beneficial across populations?

Technoscientific cyborg

Haraway (1991, 1997) proposed that humans are increasingly machinated, computerized, and made technical through science, medicine, and technology. She offered up the metaphor of the "cyborg" and later "witness-as-muted surfer" to critique false dichotomies of male/female, science/ nature, and human/machine depicted by science and medicine. A cyborg, Haraway explained, is a human-machine who finds pleasure in the blurring of scientific binaries and boundaries. This metaphor contradicts any notion of unity among individuals, instead advocating for the pluralistic "speaking in tongues." Referencing the Internet and technology, Haraway (1997) has also invoked a "witness-as-muted-surfer" metaphor to illustrate a more pluralistic, co-created way in which to envision and destabilize science. Unlike a "modest witness" – who operates in a laboratory culture free of racial, gendered, or socio-economic identities – a witness-as-muted-surfer explores and validates multiple co-created identities and subjugated knowledges. Rather than completely deconstructing the work of modern science, Haraway's cyborg and surfer metaphors advocate for responsibility for the consequences involved in building scientific thought.

To this point, SSS/STS scholars question how medical technologies create meaning for humans about humans' bodies; specifically, studies of science behooves readers to consider the ontological and epistemological consequences of not knowing how information about our bodies and life processes have been selected and communicated to us. Extending to public relations applications, scholars pursuing SSS questions have asked, how are representations of our bodies used and repackaged to us? (Tindall & Vardeman-Winter, 2011); and, what information is left out of the conversation about what technologies tell us? (Vardeman-Winter, 2012). Furthermore, communication framing research should examine to what extent a technology dictates our personhood to us; and how does the technology know a body, and, ultimately, a human being? In fact, SSS/STS scholars have implied an extension of STS work into the communication discipline by revealing the need for members of a culture to engage in reflexivity about the articulation between social meaning and biomedical meaning (i.e., the discrepancy between the ascribed meaning of physiological phenomemon, and personal, self-produced value of one's body) (Dumit, 2004; Joyce, 2005).

Conclusion

From this chapter, a critical roadmap for the further exploration of public relations in health and scientific contexts emerges. While this sampling is neither exhaustive nor fully representative of the vast spectrum of theoretical approaches to science, medicine, and technology, it provides a preliminary menu of topics relevant to the development of a critical health public relations paradigm. Deconstructing health public relations from the lenses of biopolitics and biopower, drawing upon Science and Technology (STS) and Social Studies of Science (SSS) literature situates public relations culture, practitioners, and communication tactics within a complex system of political and economic power. Critical-cultural approaches to public relations, actor-network theory, and practice theory offer three methods of addressing the multiple assumptions of lay public knowledge and practitioner-public relationships that public relations practice may perpetuate. Finally, contemplating health public relations as a function and consequence of biomedicalization, but conceiving of individuals as capable of multiple, flexible, "cyborg" (Haraway, 1991, 1997) identities, offers a richer and more complex theorizing of public relations in health contexts. Scholars must remain critically aware that practitioners are active players in a powerful culture of knowledge production and distribution, whereas publics are increasingly active producers of knowledge, defining for themselves how they will experience science, technology, medicine, and their bodies.

References

Aldoory, L. (2009). Feminist criticism in public relations: How gender can impact public relations texts and contexts. In R. L. Heath, E. L. Toth, & D. Waymer (Eds), *Rhetorical and critical approaches to public relations II*, pp. 110–24. New York, NY: Routledge.

Bourdieu, P. (1984 [1979]). *Distinction: A social critique of the judgement of taste*. Boston, MA: Harvard University Press.

Brown, M. B. (2010). Coercion, corruption, and politics in the commodification of academic science. In H. Radder (Ed.), The commodification of academic research: Science and the modern university, pp. 259–76. Pittsburgh, PA: University of Pittsburgh Press.

Butler, J. (1990). *Gender trouble and the subversion of identity*. New York, NY: Routledge.

Clarke, A. E., Mamo, L., Fishman, J. R., Shim, J. K., & Fosket, J. R. (2003). Biomedicalization: Technoscientific transformations of health, illness, and U.S. biomedicine. *American Sociological Review*, 68, 161–194.

Curtin, P. A., & Gaither, T. K. (2005). Privileging identity, difference, and power: The circuit of culture as a basis for public relations theory. *Journal of Public Relations Research*, 17(2), pp. 91–115.

Curtin, P. A., & Gaither, T. K. (2007). *International public relations: Negotiating culture, identity, and power*. Thousand Oaks, CA: Sage Publications.

Dumit, J. (2004). *Picturing personhood: Brain scans and biomedical identity*. Princeton, NJ: Princeton University Press.

Duster, T. (2005). Race and reification in science. *Science*, 307(5712), pp. 1050–1.

Edwards, L., & L'Etang, J. (2013) Invisible and visible identities and sexualities in public relations. In N. T. J. Tindall, & R. D. Waters (Eds), *Coming out of the closet: Exploring LGBT issues in strategic communication with theory and research*, pp. 41–56. New York, NY: Peter Lang.

Fausto-Sterling, A. (2000). *Sexing the body: Gender politics and the construction of sexuality*. New York, NY: Basic Books.

Foucault, M. (1977). *Discipline & punish: The birth of the prison*. New York: Random House, Inc.

Foucault, M. (1978). *The history of sexuality: Vol. 1, An introduction*. New York: Vintage Books.

Fishman, J. R. (2004). Manufacturing desire: The commodification of female sexual dysfunction. *Social Studies of Science*, 34, pp. 187–218.

Haraway, D. (1991). *Simians, cyborgs, and women: The reinvention of nature*. New York, NY: Routledge.

Haraway, D. (1997). *Modest_Witness@Second_Millennium.Female_Man_Meets_OncoMouse*. New York, NY: Routledge.

Harding, S. G. (1991). *Whose science? Whose knowledge? Thinking from women's lives*. New York, NY: Cornell University Press.

Hess, D. J. (1997). *Science studies: An advanced introduction*. New York, NY: New York University Press.

Holtzhausen, D. R., & Voto, R. (2002). Resistance from the margins: The postmodern public relations practitioner as organizational activist. *Journal of Public Relations Research*, 14(1), pp. 57–84.

Jagose, A. (1996). *Queer theory: An introduction*. New York, NY: New York University Press.

Joyce, K. (2005). Appealing images: Magnetic resonance imaging and the construction of authoritative knowledge. *Social Studies of Science*, 35(3), pp. 437–62.

Kahn, J. (2004). How a drug becomes "ethnic": Law, commerce, and the production of racial categories in medicine. *Yale Journal of Health Policy, Law, and Ethics*, 4(1). Retrieved on April 14, 2014, from http://digitalcommons.law.yale.edu/yjhple/vol4/iss1/1

Kasabov, E. (2004). Power and disciplining: Bringing Foucault to marketing. *Irish Marketing Review*, 17.

Kaufman, S. R., Shim, J. K., & Russ, A. J. (2006). Old age, life extension, and the character of medical choice. *Journals of Gerontology Series B: Psychological Sciences and Social Sciences*, 61(4), S175–S184.

Kellner, D. (1992). *Critical theory, Marxism and modernity*. Baltimore, MD: The Johns Hopkins University Press.

Law, J. (2004). Enacting naturecultures: A view from STS. Retrieved on April 15, 2014, from http://www.heterogeneities.net/publications/Law2004EnactingNaturecultures.pdf

L'Etang, J. (2012). Public relations, culture and anthropology: Towards an ethnographic research agenda. *Journal of Public Relations Research*, 24(2), pp. 165–83.

Lupton, D. (1994). Toward the development of critical health communication praxis. *Health Communication*, 6(1), pp. 55–67.

McKie, D., & Munshi, D. (2009). Theoretical black holes: A partial A to Z of missing critical thought in public relations. In R. L. Heath, E. L. Toth, & D. Waymer (Eds), *Rhetorical and critical approaches to public relations II*, pp. 61–75. New York, NY: Routledge.

Mamo, L., & Fishman, J. R. (2001). Potency in all the right places: Viagra as a technology of the gendered body. *Body & Society*, 7(4), pp. 13–35.

Moffitt, M.A. (2011). Critical theoretical considerations of public relations messaging around the globe: Tools for creating and evaluating campaign messages. *Journal of Promotion Management*, 17, pp. 21–41.

Motion, J., & Weaver, C. K. (2005). A discourse perspective for critical public relations research: Life sciences network and the battle for truth. *Journal of Public Relations Research*, 17(1), pp. 49–67.

Munshi, D. (2005). Through the subject's eye: Situating the other in discourses of diversity. In G. Cheney, & G. Barnett (Eds), *International and multicultural organizational communication*, pp. 45–70. Cresskill, NJ: Hampton Press.

Naples, N. A. (2003). *Feminism and method: Ethnography, discourse analysis, and activist research*. New York, NY: Routledge.

Petryna, A. (2004). Biological citizenship: The science and politics of Chernobyl-exposed populations. *Osiris*, 19, pp. 250–65.

Place, K. R., & Vardeman-Winter, J. (2013). Hegemonic discourse and self-discipline: Exploring Foucault's concept of bio-power among public relations professionals. *Public Relations Inquiry*, 2(3), pp. 305–25.

Rabinow, P., & Rose, N. (2006). Biopower today. *BioSocieties*, 1(2), pp. 195.

Rakow, L. F. (1989). Information and power: Toward a critical theory of information campaigns. In C. T. Salmon (Ed.), *Information campaigns: Balancing social values and social change*, pp. 164–84. Newbury Park, CA: Sage Publications.

Raman, S., & Tutton, R. (2010). Life, science, and biopower. *Science, Technology & Human Values*, 35(5), pp. 711–34.

Reckwitz, A. (2002). Toward a theory of social practices: A development in culturalist theorizing. *European Journal of Social Theory*, 5(2), pp. 243–63.

Rose, N. (2001). The politics of life itself. *Theory, culture & society*, 18(6), pp. 1–30.

Rose, N., & Novas, C. (2005). *Biological citizenship*. In A. Ong, & S. Collier (Eds), *Blackwell companion to global anthropology*, pp. 439–63. Oxford, UK: Blackwell Publishing.

Salmon, C. T. (1990). God understands when the cause is noble. *Gannett Center Journal*, 4(2), pp. 23–34.

Shim, J. K. (2005). Constructing "race" across the science-lay divide: Racial formation in the epidemiology and experience of cardiovascular disease. *Social Studies of Science*, 35, pp. 405–36.

Social Marketing Institute. (n.d.). Social Marketing. Retrieved on April 10, 2006, from http://www.social-marketing.org/sm.html

Somerville, I. (1999). Agency versus identity: Actor-network theory meets public relations. *Corporate Communications: An International Journal*, 4(1), pp. 6–13.

Thompson, C. (2005). *Making parents: The ontological choreography of reproductive technologies*. Cambridge, MA: MIT Press.

Tindall, N. T. J., & Vardeman-Winter, J. (2011). Complications in segmenting campaign publics: Women of color explain their problems, involvement, and constraints in reading heart disease communication. *Howard Journal of Communication*, 22, pp. 280–301. Retrieved on April 24, 2015, from http://dx.doi.org/10.1080/10646175.2011.590407

Tindall, N. T. J., & Waters, R. D. (Eds) (2013). *Coming out of the closet: Exploring LGBT issues in strategic communication with theory and research*. New York: Peter Lang.

Vardeman-Winter, J. E. (2012). Medicalization and teen girls' bodies in the Gardasil cervical cancer vaccine campaign. *Feminist Media Studies*, 12(2), pp. 281–304. doi: 10.1080/14680777.2011.597106

Vardeman-Winter, J., Jiang, H., & Tindall, N. T. J. (2013). Information-seeking outcomes of representational, structural, and political intersectionality among health media consumers. *Journal of Applied Communication Research*, 41(4), pp. 389–411.

Verhoeven, P. (2008). Who's in and who's out? Studying the effects of communication management on social cohesion. *Journal of Communication Management*, 12(2), pp. 124–35.

Vitellone, N. (2001). Watching AIDS, condoms and serial killers in the Australian "Grim Reaper" TV campaign. *Continuum: Journal of Media & Cultural Studies*, 15(1), pp. 33–48.

Waldby, C. (2002). Stem cells, tissue cultures and the production of biovalue. *Health*, 6(3), pp. 305–23.

Whitehead, A. N. (1929). *The function of reason*. Princeton, NJ: Princeton University Press.

20

A postcolonial critique of public relations

Mohan J. Dutta

Postcolonial theory examines closely the processes and artifacts that produce colonialism, the problematics and contexts of colonialism, and the processes of transformation in the decolonizing project (Shome & Hegde, 2002). In opening up a conversation between postcolonial theory and communication studies, Shome and Hegde (2002) offered that the "politics of postcoloniality is centrally imbricated with the politics of communication" (p. 249). Situating interpretation and meaning as constitutive of the global processes of erasure integral to unequal imperial formations attends to the politics of knowledge production amid global histories, geographies, and colonial modernities (Chakrabarty, 2009; Shome & Hegde, 2002). Public relations, broadly understood as the strategic deployment of meanings to shape public opinion and public relationships through persuasion, circulates these knowledge claims as universal values that work toward maintaining the global inequalities along the lines of race, nation, gender, and imperialism (McKie & Munshi, 2007; Munshi, 1999). A postcolonial critique of public relations attends to the interplays of culture and power in processes of communication within the realm of geopolitics, unequal power relationships, and colonial relationships of exploitation and oppression.

In this chapter, I will argue that the post in postcolonial needs to be engaged in a theoretical framework that draws upon concepts of colonialism and material inequalities in global flows of power to understand contemporary global relationships, terrains of power, and international division of labor. The current shifts in global terrains of power continue to maintain a US-led core tied to US economic, geostrategic, and military interests in an imperial frame, connecting this core with multiple nodes of power that are dispersed across the globe as sites of colonial modernities (Dutta, 2011). Colonialism thus is structured into new relationships of material flow that simultaneously reproduce the structures of US imperialism, reconfigured under the logic of neoliberal governance that privileges the ideology of the free market as the overarching organizing framework for political, social, and economic relationships. International financial institutions (IFIs) such as the World Bank (WB), International Monetary Fund (IMF), and World Trade Organization (WTO) work in collusion with powerful nation states in the Global North to exert pressure on economies in the Global South to open up, and simultaneously enable new forms of flow that create new market opportunities for emerging economies such as China and India (Harvey, 2005).

Thus, a new form of colonialism emerges on the global map that reifies imperialism – maintaining US hegemony – aligning with newly emerging forms of hegemony such as the Chinese and Indian hegemonies, and working within transnational networks of collaboration that bring these hegemonic actors together in mutually beneficial relationships in the global arena. As transnational corporations (TNCs) operating across global boundaries depict the shifts in the nodes of power into the hands of the owners of private capital, these shifts are enabled by powerful nation states engaged in the active promotion of the free market, situated within global cartographies of power and working through the powerful role of civil society as instruments of imperialism (Dutta, 2005a, 2005b). The civil society sector, as an elite network of control operating across local-national-global spaces, usurps the language of communities, participation, and bottom-up development to carry out the agendas of transnational capital. This consolidation of power in the hands of the global elite corresponds with the increasing inequalities witnessed across the globe, the dramatic decline in employment opportunities across the globe, the weakening of the organizing capacity of the working classes, and the increasing incorporation of the subaltern sectors across the globe into global chains of profiteering and exploitation (Dutta, 2011; Harvey, 2005).

Public relations, as the communication function that generates knowledge and disseminates it, lies at the heart of this neocolonial project, materializing new colonial relationships through the images and narratives that are circulated in knowledge claims, press releases, and media representations (Munshi & Kurian, 2005). Public relations tools, as instruments in the hands of transnational corporations, circulate dominant frameworks of meanings and interpretations that consolidate power in the hands of the global elite, working hand-in-hand with universities, think tanks, non-governmental organizations, and the mainstream media to erase particular forms of knowledge and simultaneously produce other forms of culturally sensitive, multicultural, and inclusive knowledge that constitute the new colonial modernities (Dutta, 2009). Public policies, programs, and practices are constituted amid corporate-driven public relations functions of meaning production that are actively at work in promoting specific configurations of global policies that reinforce the power of transnational hegemony and generate newer avenues of profiteering, continuing to reproduce imperial structures rearticulated in the language of culture (Dutta, 2009, 2011; McKie & Munshi, 2007; Munshi, 1999; Munshi & Kurian, 2005). Tools of public relations such as "corporate social responsibility" and "sustainable development" are put in place to co-opt subaltern communities and to thwart opportunities for resistance driven by grassroots democratic participation (Dutta, 2009, 2011; Dutta & Pal, 2011; Munshi & Kurian, 2005). New forms of colonialism thus embody the geographic inequities between the North and the South/the West and the East in distributions of power, and simultaneously create new zones of imperial domination through global collaborations of elites in networks of power such as in the examples of the emerging global dominance of China and India, working through language to shape interpretive frames that normalize these forms of domination, (re)producing knowledge claims in global networks of elites, managers, NGO workers, academics, bureaucrats, and experts. As in the examples of the US, China, and India, the state is reconfigured into the structures of transnational profiteering, with large sums of investment into electoral processes – as in the examples of recent elections in India and the US – and with strong interpenetrating ties between the state and owners of capital, as in the examples of China, India, and the US. Moreover, new forms of imperialism – such as the Chinese imperial controls being asserted over Africa in relationships of investment in extractive projects and accompanying projects of development masqueraded as improving the well-being of local communities; and the leasing out of Indian mineral resources by the state to powerful transnational corporations once again in the name of development. These are just some examples of the integral role of public relations practices in the establishment of resource exploitation and domination as normative to economic growth.

The postcolonial cartographies in current global spaces witness the emergence of new power formations – such as the global emergence of China, India, and Brazil – even as these new formations reify the Eurocentric values of individualism, free market capitalism, and economic fundamentalism underlying the neoliberal project grounded in fundamentally Western articulations of atomized individualism as solutions to human problems (Dutta, 2011; Dutta & Pal, 2011; Pal & Dutta, 2008a, 2008b). For instance, the emergence of China in the global context reproduces neoliberal hegemony by incorporating underpaid and exploited Chinese labor into global circuits of production, and at the same time creates new forms of colonialism in the Global South in the form of Chinese extractive industries distributed across spaces in the Global South. Chinese mining corporations operating across sites in Africa carry out their public relations functions through community building and infrastructure development efforts, framing extraction as sustainable development and leveraging public relations tools of community and media relations to narrate a story of development that justifies the large-scale expropriation of mineral resources from these African countries. Africa thus configures in the global narrative of power flows as a site to be exploited not only by TNCs located in the familiar sites of colonialism in the US, but also in new relationships of exploitation with emerging hegemonic powers such as China and India, all carried out through public relations functions of framing such resource extraction as promoting development and economic growth. Moreover, the local elites at these sites of exploitation in the Global South collaborate with the interests of transnational capital, enabling multiple globally dispersed layers of profiteering through resource extraction.

The subaltern communities living in these spaces of exploitation in the Global South, as well as in the South within the North, remain erased from sites of discourse and discursive articulation (Dutta, 2009, 2011). Displaced subaltern communities, uprooted from their spaces of livelihood by top-down structural adjustment programs carried out in the language of participatory development and grassroots-driven empowerment, are dislocated as disposable and exploited bodies of subaltern migrant labor at the cosmopolitan centers of neoliberal capitalism (Dutta, 2011). The body of the subaltern and her/his resources of everyday living, erased from discursive spaces, emerge as sites of profiteering, co-opted into narratives of culture and development, and connected with global networks of biocapitalism that are framed as forms of development interventions through the commoditization of life resources. Biocapitalism, the new phase of capitalism linking life forms to information capitalism, finds new spaces of wealth extraction through the piracy of subaltern knowledge, through the patenting of life as private commodity, and through the large-scale global marketing of such knowledge as scientific-technical solutions of development and well-being. Subaltern knowledge formations, incorporated into ethno-botany investigations and culturally situated explorations of natural resources, generate knowledge claims that are privatized and patented by TNCs, removed from the very subaltern communities that hold ownership to these forms of knowledge (Dutta, 2011).

The ongoing conversation between the postcolonial studies and public relations literature offers a valuable framework for interrogating the role of communication in global structures of power, especially within the context of material and communicative inequalities that enable resource extraction in these new colonialisms (Dutta, 2009; McKie & Munshi, 2007; Munshi, 1999; Munshi & Kurian, 2005). In this essay I will engage in dialog with this emerging body of theorizing and research in public relations to suggest some tentative entry points for conversations regarding the flows of power, colonialism, and communication within global structures of neoliberal hegemony and the material relationships of inequality reflecting and reproducing these structures. I will specifically attend to the communicative inequalities in access to spaces for articulation and dialog, suggesting that communicative inequalities are built into neocolonial modes of neoliberal governance, and that public relations is an integral tool in the circulation of these inequalities. The erasure of subaltern communities lies at the heart of public relations processes that reify and reproduce the image of a global order propped up on the narrative of development and progress through individualization and participation in the free market, albeit rearticulated in a variety of multicultural and culturally localized messaging strategies that foreground diversity incorporated into neoliberal knowledge management functions.

Public relations, communicative inversions and communicative erasures

Communicative inversions refer to the uses of communication to shift symbolic representations to signify the opposite of the material formations that communication seeks to represent (Dutta, 2011). Inversions thus are communicative turns that shift material representations, dislocating them from their underlying structural configurations and material bases. Historically, public relations as a practice of communication connected to processes of image-making and propaganda played a key role in achieving these communicative inversions during World War Two, achieving consensus and orchestrating public opinion (L'Etang, 2006a, 2006b). The Office of War Communications, as one of the earliest exemplars of public relations, was rooted in the notion of communicative inversions, and formed the basis of funding the persuasion strategies that constituted the disciplinary bulwark of communication studies. Noting the opinion formation role of public relations in serving the interests of power structures, L'Etang (2006b, p. 9) suggests "the real value of propaganda lies not in its dissemination and promotion of *ideas*, but in its ability to orchestrate public opinion and social action that supported the ruling elite."

In the post-World War Two Cold War climate, the public relations function of communicative inversion was taken up by state-funded development agencies such as the United States Agency for International Development (USAID) that deployed development communication programs as instruments for creating economic opportunities for US-based corporations and for serving US geostrategic interests abroad. The narrative of development serve as a public relations device to serve US economic, military, and geostrategic goals across the globe. As depicted in the examples of Chile, Nicaragua, and the Philippines, development assistance, often channeled through elite power networks, worked to open up economies for US-based corporations (Dutta & Pal, 2011). The emergence of neoliberalism on the global arena was brought about through networks of power strategically deploying public relations through linkages with elite civil society groups, often carried out within the ambits of development – with many of the democracy promotion initiatives being funded by USAID (Robinson, 1996).

Communicative inversions are marked by discrepancies between the symbolic representations and the material manifestations. These discrepancies become apparent in the realm of development communication campaigns when the material markers of outcomes in targeted communities are compared with the rhetoric of development. Development knowledge, plotted in a linear narrative of movement from the state of underdevelopment to the state of development, is projected as the solution to problems of poverty, lack of access, and poor health. The material markers of development, in the form of access to economic opportunities among the poor, access to food, access to employment, etc., remain hidden from discursive sites of articulation. Contemporary neoliberal forms of global control, captured in the notion of the free market, are replete with such communicative inversions achieved through cycles of public relations as spin, reformulated under the seemingly neutral and universal labels of civil society, social capital, participation, and democracy.

Communities, engagement, and power

The community is framed in the public relations literature as a site of organizing relationships between the corporation and its publics (Kruckeberg & Starck, 1988). Community relations activities connect communities to organizations through a variety of relationship-building activities. Spivak (2000), in her essay entitled "*The new subaltern: A silent interview*," refers to the new subaltern as a contemporary form of subalternity under neoliberal restructuring, where the subaltern is connected to global sites of power as a resource for exploitation in global capitalist networks. Community relations activities, carried out in the form of building schools, hospitals, roads, etc., and framed as bringing development into the community, have emerged as the new faces of transnational capitalism in subaltern communities. The new subaltern is marked by her incorporation into these global circuits of capital as a site of, and resource for, profiteering. Her body, knowledge, and everyday culture are scripted into transnational capitalist structures as exploitable resources. Spivak (1999) notes:

> Today the "subaltern" must be rethought. S/he is no longer cut off from lines of access to the centre. The centre, as represented by the Bretton Woods agencies and the World Trade Organization, is altogether interested in the rural and indigenous subaltern as source of trade-related intellectual property or TRIPs.
>
> *(p. 326)*

Agriculture, for instance, is being reorganized as transnational corporate agriculture predicated on the privatization of the seed as a profitable resource, removed from community knowledge and community ownership of seeds, accomplished through the accelerated introduction of bio-technology as a global panacea, funded by major foundations and governments in the Global North and in collaboration with NGOs, academics, the private sector, and government bureaucrats in the Global South. Biotechnology, as the new imperialism, reproduces the colonial patterns of value extraction, extracting local knowledge, rendering it valueless, and introducing newly engineered products at higher prices (Shiva, 2002).

Subaltern communities across the global margins residing in resource-rich mineral zones are the subjects of directed public relations strategies through a variety of community relations activities framed in the narrative of development. Mining companies seeking to extract resources from spaces that have been inhabited by subaltern communities use narratives of development and growth to displace subaltern communities from their spaces of livelihood, often with the deployment of altruistic community relations activities under the aegis of corporate social responsibility (CSR); and at other times through the use of force (Padel & Das, 2010; Dutta, 2011). The goals of community engagement are thus often tied to the instrumentalist logics of transnational capitalism, deploying the interpretive frame of development to secure community "buy-in" for mining operations. The role of communication in its relationship to community in such instances lies in minimizing resistance to the processes of exploitation through resource extraction, performing the façade of sustainability, listening, dialog, and participation to co-opt the voices of community members.

Knowledge production, democracy and civility

The circulation and reproduction of knowledge are powerful instruments of neoliberal hegemony, working within spaces of global inequalities to further reify such inequalities (McKie &

Munshi, 2007). The articulation of knowledge as a symbolic resource attached to power maintains the inequities in global distributions of power, with knowledge itself serving a public relations function, circulating specific images and claims that reify global hegemony and simultaneously erase alternative claims that threaten these hegemonic structures. The emergence of the expert, managerial, and professional classes in contemporary global configurations is tied to knowledge claims that mark the other as the site and subject of the intervention, while at the same time maintaining the networks of power in global flows of capital and labor. For instance, the language of empowerment is often deployed in public relations campaigns seeking to intervene in communities at the margins, reifying implicit differentials in power and targeting communities with knowledge claims that are directed at "giving power." Intrinsic to such logics of empowerment are material differentials in the flow of power, accompanied by implicit assumptions about the knowledge deficits in communities that are the targets of intervention. The margins are marked as the "other," devoid of knowledge and agency to determine their own courses of actions, offering the justification for colonial interventions that are carried out in the form of public relations functions. Moreover, as a public relations tool, the narrative of empowerment works toward serving specific neoliberal goals of privatizing public resources, foregrounding entrepreneurship as a mechanism for weakening state support systems, and fostering open spaces for private investments.

Academic knowledge structures operate within these colonial terrains of power, making pronouncements rooted in specific values tied to their US and Eurocentric roots, and simultaneously treating these values as universals. For instance, the articulations of democracy within knowledge networks of US imperial power serve as the basis for US democracy promotion efforts, at the same time obfuscating the colonial logics of power and control that are often built into these democracy promotion efforts (Robinson, 1996). The goals of the US to pry open markets for transnational corporations rooted in the US, and to serve US geostrategic interests through the agenda of democracy promotion, remain erased in academic discourses of democracy promotion. As countries get conceptualized and mapped into the hegemonic articulations of democracy, racist depictions of the "other" as primitive, tribal, and incapable of democracy are formulated into these structures of knowledge claims as normative states of "otherness." Within the realm of the US imperial invasion of Iraq, academics employed to conduct the "Iraqi tribal studies" are guided by the objectives of mapping out Iraqi culture through military-sponsored human terrain research, ethnographic research, and multicultural analyses, parsing out the key themes and characteristics of the culture, and suggesting strategies for intervention, military management, and control through such efforts of mapping out the geographic terrain, social structure, and culture of Iraq (Eisenstadt, 2007).

The differential access to sites of power and the spatial rootedness of the new colonialism is evident in the construction of disciplines, disciplinary expectations, and normative ideals. Broadly, in the discipline of communication, and more specifically within the public relations literature, the normative ideals that are circulated embody the values of US hegemonic structures, tied to notions of democracy embedded within capitalist power structures. Culture emerges within this dominant framework of public relations as a tool for guiding culturally sensitive campaigns for expanding the power and control of transnational capital (see Curtin & Gaither, 2005). The language of cultural studies, folded into the structures of culturally sensitive public relations, is deployed to further reify the hegemony of a monolithic neocolonial structure of neoliberal capitalism. The very critique of US-Eurocentric theorizing of public relations practice is deployed to refashion a culturally packaged public relations structure of neoliberal governance that takes culture into account in developing even more powerful and effective global public relations campaigns, further consolidating the power of transnational capitalism. Ironically, the language of openness, invitation, and multiculturalism works as a form of communicative inversion, foreclosing debate even as it calls for openness. As a result, postcolonial interrogations of the dominant value structures are often dismissed, co-opting postcolonial arguments into the folds of the White mainstream, foreclosing these arguments by suggesting that similar arguments have already been made by White scholars or that these arguments have nothing new to offer or reducing postcolonial critiques as fashionable tools for effective multicultural public relations campaigns. (On this, see the critical piece by Broadfoot and Munshi, 2007, and the response by Mumby and Stohl, 2007 defending the White mainstream knowledge production processes in the language of openness and multiculturalism; see also the absence of serious postcolonial theorizing in Curtin and Gaither's (2005) treatment of postcolonialism as a tool for international public relations.) The language of multiculturalism, diversity, and openness is played out precisely to silence those voices from the Global South that disrupt the very assumptions of multiculturalism and diversity. Decolonizing thought that seeks to interrogate the workings of power is dismissed as non-empirical, out of touch, uncivil, or radical. As a result, academic structures in the mainstream continue to perpetuate US-based value frames positioned as universal values of progress and development, incorporating culture into the folds of multicultural structures. In doing so, academic knowledge production becomes an exercise that itself serves a public relations function for exerting and reproducing US global hegemony, framing concepts of civility, civil society, and the free market as the universal markers of progress and simultaneously obfuscating articulations of knowledge that invite alternative possibilities that challenge transnational hegemony. Organizational structures of knowledge production co-opt the language of culture and difference within the ambits of diversity to perpetuate the agendas of silencing.

As exemplars of communicative inversion, normative ideas of civil society foreclose opportunities for dialog and conversation by constraining the realms of acceptability of communication (see my earlier criticism of civil society efforts in Dutta, 2005a, 2005b). The notion of civility as intrinsic to a functioning civil society gets intertwined with dominant configurations of the realms of acceptable speech and communication. Communication that is transformative and threatens the existing configurations of the status quo is labeled as uncivil, and, therefore, beyond the realm of participation. Participation, democracy, and collaboration work within the realms of acceptability as defined by the dominant structure, with the codes of participation and normative ideas of communication having been preconfigured by the dominant actors. Struggles for decolonization thus are often labeled as emotional, violent, and angry, and hence beyond the realms of acceptable speech within the dominant colonial structures of civil society.

Civil society, as a space for elite participation, works closely with the market and the state as a site of elite control and elite consolidation of power (Petras, 1997). Participation in civil society is predicated on fulfilling the requirement of literacy. Thus, the realm of participation as articulated in dominant configurations of civil society is limited to the elite and bourgeoisie classes that have access to resources in order to participate along the guidelines that are dictated by the dominant structures. In contemporary processes of globalization, civil society – as a marker of participation – services market forces by creating opportunities, as well as by greenwashing the images of transnational corporations. Large non-governmental organizations (NGOs), driven by large managerial structures and organizational processes, are tied to corporate funders and foundations for resources, thus achieving particular outcomes to serve the interests of the funders. Although the language of participation takes center-stage in much NGO talk, the opportunities for participation are constituted within the goals, objectives, and agendas of dominant social actors. Even as communities enact their agency in participating in struggles of resistance that challenge the material inequalities of neoliberal globalization, these communities become the subjects of exploitation and co-optation by networks of NGOs and academics performing solidarity with community voices. Academic representations of subaltern struggles within dominant knowledge structures reproduce the hierarchies of knowledge production refashioned in the language of participation and community, co-opting subaltern voices and subaltern scripts into academic products that are far removed from the politics and embodied risks of everyday struggles.

Public relations, public diplomacy and power circuits

The public relations function in public diplomacy renders visible the powerful role of knowledge in serving the agendas of dominant global actors, circulating specific knowledge claims as the bases for shaping beliefs, attitudes, and behaviors of elite and general populations in target countries (L'Etang, 2006a, 2006b). L'Etang suggests that the functions of public relations and public diplomacy fall along a spectrum, and differentiates between public diplomacy efforts targeted at elite publics and cultural diplomacy efforts targeted at the wider population of target countries. Large public relations budgets are dedicated to top-down communication driven by the underlying logic of persuasion and public opinion formation of elites and general populations in target countries, tied to various forms of public diplomacy. The targeting of beliefs and attitudes in recipient countries becomes particularly critical within the realm of imperial invasions, depicting the imperial support function of communication as a one-way flow carried out under the flag of the nation state and married to the agendas of TNCs in extracting profits from global spaces by opening up markets through the powerful communication instruments deployed by the sender nation state. For instance, many private strategic communication firms and private media organizations handled the US public diplomacy portfolio in Iraq, complemented by specific public relations functions carried out by transnational corporations with economic interests in Iraq. Moreover, the funding for the development of the media infrastructure in Iraq from USAID was driven by the objective of promoting a neoliberal agenda in Iraq – creating, controlling, and manipulating the media system there to support pro-market agendas and to shape the outcome of elections that would be favorable to the establishment of a pro-market government (Barker, 2008).

US public diplomacy efforts in the Middle East have been configured against the backdrop of US invasions of Iraq and Afghanistan, situating the work of public diplomacy as a tool for generating support among a population that has been invaded; and subsequently establishing a neoliberal structure of governance (Dutta, 2005b, 2006, 2011; Harvey, 2005). The persuasive function of public relations in shaping public opinion is driven by an underlying framework of communication that treats communication as an instrument for circulating images, understanding communication as vital to shaping beliefs, interpretations, and values. For instance, the language of listening played out in US public diplomacy efforts in Iraq against the backdrop of "Operation Iraqi Freedom" co-opts the framework of listening to serve the imperial agendas of the US (Dutta, 2005b). These communicative inversions, which invert the representation of material realities away from their material bases, therefore work to perpetuate the interests of transnational actors at sites of global power, and play an instrumental role within neoliberal configurations to utilize the language of two-way communication even as the very formation of the communicative process is one-way and constituted within the hidden agendas of power structures that invest resources into the public relations efforts to serve their objectives. In the midst of the US invasions of Iraq and Afghanistan, US public diplomacy efforts were reframed as transformational diplomacy (Dutta, 2005b; Dutta & Pal, 2011). The language of transformational diplomacy highlighted participation, listening, and community collaboration – even as the US was deploying material force to invade these spaces; and even as it was investing development and reconstruction funds to shape Iraq and Afghanistan into the pro-market image of the invader, thus creating new markets for US TNCs.

Imaginations and new cartographies: a decolonizing agenda

In the framework of the CCA, participation and reflexivity offer entry points for disrupting neoliberal globalization.

Participation as transformative

Challenging the dominant ideas of participatory communication that circulate in the mainstream, participatory forms of communication emerging from subaltern communities at the margins depict their collective agency and offer alternative discourses that seek to transform the structures constituted by neoliberalism (Boal, 1985, 1998; Dutta, 2011). For instance, the struggles of the Dongria Kondh in the Niyamgiri Hills of Odisha, India, threatened with displacement by a mining operation operated by the UK-based mining company TNC Vedanta, depicts the power of participation in challenging the dominant narrative of development written into neoliberalism (Padel & Das, 2010). The story of development circulated by think tanks, NGOs, media, and academics, many of whom have been paid by Vedanta to produce particular forms of knowledge claims, is disrupted by stories of the subaltern communities of the Dongria Kondh – who voice their collective ownership of the mountains, the sacredness of Niyamraja (the divine presence that rules over the mountains), and the health threats they face from the mining operation. Participation as the performance of everyday politics fosters transformative spaces that challenge the communicative inversions of neoliberal public relations.

Voicing a relationship rooted in the collective and in the broader ecological framework of the sacredness of nature, the Dongria Kondh resist the mining operation and simultaneously offer a value system that makes impure the assumptions that are taken for granted in the narrative of neoliberal development. The promises of growth and employment are resisted by narratives of indigenous rights, sacredness of land, ecology, and well-being. Subaltern participation in processes of change offers a framework for transforming the structures of neoliberal development by reframing the narrative of development, and by interrupting the very assumptions underlying neoliberal interventions. Similarly, the participation of the Ogoni in Nigeria against the colonial extraction of local resources by Shell, and the participation of the nation state in legitimating and enabling this extraction, becomes an entry point for an anticolonial struggle against neoliberal imperialism, directly opposing the co-optive politics of public relations deployed by Shell (Munshi & Kurian, 2005).

Reflexivity as theoretical invitation

As a theoretical invitation, reflexivity fosters openings for interrogations of the very sites of privilege within which knowledge is produced, turning the lens on the communicative processes of knowledge production and the communicative processes that position knowledge within public relations plans (Dutta & Pal, 2011). A culturally centered approach to public relations suggests the need to continually dislocate the very bases that serve as the foundations of knowledge claims, interrogating the articulations of diversity and multiculturalism in postcolonial instruments of transnational capitalism, simultaneously placing these knowledge claims in conversations with the material structures they seek to represent. Postcolonial interventions are also material – mapping the symbolic circulations of knowledge within trajectories of power, disrupting through continuous movements between the outside and the inside in communicative practices of structural transformation.

Reflexivity thus suggests the turning of the lens inward as an activist intervention that dislocates the objective value-free invisible position of the scholar, instead questioning the very hierarchies that are produced by knowledge formations. By acknowledging the participation and role of the academic within the discursive space, the notion of reflexivity fosters openings for dialog that place within the discursive realm one's own value positions and register of articulation. Reflexivity, moreover, interrogates the embodied possibilities of solidarity amid bourgeoisie desires that direct the scholar away from subaltern communities and into networks of other academics who find these subaltern spaces as convenient resources to be exploited for furthering academic careers in elite structures of neoliberal decision-making. Notions such as informed consent, community participation, benefits to the community, and translation of knowledge as community resources are reinterpreted in a language that is meaningful to the lived experiences of subaltern communities and to the relationships that scholars hold with communities articulated in transformative imaginations. The realms of accountability are shifted into the conversations with subaltern communities rather than in the structures of academic elite knowledge production.

Intervening in knowledge structures

Noting that the production of knowledge lies at the heart of the claims that are made and offered as justifications for neoliberal transformations, decolonizing processes need to engage with the possibilities of intervening in the very knowledge structures where articulations are generated and recycled, acknowledging the co-optive politics emboldened in stances of listening to subaltern voices, and working through this acknowledgment to imagine a politics of social change in partnership with subaltern communities (Spivak, 1990a, 1990b, 1996, 1999). Examining the taken-for-granted assumptions in communicative frameworks offers opportunities for situating these frameworks against the backdrop of neoliberal flows of power. For instance, examining the nature of participation in campaigns that claim to be participatory disrupts the co-optation of participation as an instrument of one-way communication. Critically interrogating claims to dialog by situating these claims amid material flows interrupts the hegemonic narratives that circulate within knowledge structures. Critically interrogating democracy and civil society intervenes in the imperial space that renders these terms as neutral, distanced from the politics of ontologies (Chakrabarty, 2009). Working toward fostering invitational opportunities for subaltern communities to participate as co-creators in discursive spaces of knowledge production fosters new openings for knowledge claims, working hand-in-hand with everyday subaltern politics.

The claims of development and economic growth that are often pushed as monolithic narratives justifying the privatization of resources and the hegemony of the free market are disrupted in subaltern articulations of collective ownership, cooperative participation, and the harmonious relationship with nature. For instance, the participation of women farmers from grassroots communities in South India disrupts the monolithic narrative of *bacillus thuringiensis* (Bt.) cotton and cash crop-based agriculture as solutions for development – instead offering alternative frameworks of seed sovereignty, seed rights, and women's ownership of collective agricultural processes (Thaker & Dutta, 2014). Activist-academic collaborations foster openings for disrupting the very structures of knowledge production where claims are made. In doing so, the dominant function of public relations as an instrument for perpetuating dominant knowledge claims that serve the status quo is inverted, and replaced by an activist framework of public relations that is rooted in listening to the voices of subaltern communities.

Intervening in dominant structures of knowledge production calls for continual theoretical engagement with the erasures that are tied to our own participation as academics within these knowledge structures. Reflexivity, as an overarching commitment in the theoretical and methodological framework of the CCA, calls for continual movements across spaces – which opens up possibilities for disruption. The intervention, as opposed to being targeted at an audience in a subaltern context, is reformulated as a disruption of the mainstream processes of knowledge production – targeting policy-makers, elites, and powerful state, market, and civil society actors that actively perpetuate the disenfranchisement of subaltern communities. Thus, the CCA works toward learning the language of public relations as an inverted strategy for resisting the co-optation of subaltern cultures, and formulating creative strategies from the grassroots to disrupt the structures of the state, market, and civil society, while simultaneously putting forth alternative rationalities of cultural, social, political, and economic organizing.

Conclusion

In this chapter I offered some tentative areas of consideration for the theorizing of postcolonial communication processes within the realm of public relations theorizing, research, and practice. Theorizing the role of public relations in dominant structures of knowledge production draws attention to the interpenetrating relationship between neocolonialism and neoliberalism, depicting the ways in which the enterprise of knowledge production is in itself a public relations activity. Further, the chapter aims to create a dialogic space with the culture-centered approach of CCA, seeking to explore spaces for listening to subaltern voices in resistance to the hegemonic processes of manipulation and cultural co-optation. The voices of subaltern communities in conversations with the researcher-activist continually work toward imagining alternative possibilities of local-national-global political-economic organizing.

References

Barker, M. J. (2008). Democracy or polyarchy? US-funded media developments in Afghanistan and Iraq post 9/11. *Media, culture, and society*, 30(1), p. 109.

Berger, B. K. (2005). Power over, power with, and power to relations: Critical reflections of public relations, the dominant coalition, and activism. *Journal of Public Relations Research*, 17, pp. 5–28.

Boal, A. (1985). *Theater of the oppressed*, trans. C. A., & M. L. McBride. New York, NY: Theater Communications Group.

Boal, A. (1998). *Legislative Theatre*, trans. A. Jackson. New York, NY: Routledge.

Broadfoot, K. J., & Munshi, D. (2007). Diverse voices and alternative rationalities imagining forms of postcolonial organizational communication. *Management Communication Quarterly*, 21(2), pp. 249–67.

Chakrabarty, D. (2009). *Provincializing Europe: Postcolonial thought and historical difference*. Princeton, NJ: Princeton University Press.

Curtin, P. A., & Gaither, T. K. (2005). Privileging identity, difference, and power: The circuit of culture as a basis for public relations theory. *Journal of Public Relations Research*, 17(2), pp. 91–115.

Dutta, M. (2005a). Civil society and public relations: Not so civil after all. *Journal of Public Relations Research*, 17, pp. 267–89.

Dutta, M. (2005b). Operation Iraqi Freedom: Mediated public sphere as a public relations tool. *Atlantic Journal of Communication*, 13, pp. 220–41.

Dutta, M. (2006). US public diplomacy in the Middle East. *Journal of Communication Inquiry*, 30, pp. 102–24.

Dutta, M. J. (2009). On Spivak: Theorizing resistance – applying Gayatri Chakravorty Spivak in public relations. In O. Ihlen, B. van Ruler, & M. Fredriksson (Eds), *Public relations and social theory: Key figures and concepts*, pp. 278–300. New York, NY: Routledge.

Dutta, M. (2011). *Communicating social change: Structure, culture, agency*. New York, NY: Routledge.

Dutta, M. J., & Pal, M. (2011). Public relations and marginalization in a global context: A postcolonial critique. In N. Bardhan, & C. K. Weaver (Eds), *Public relations in global cultural contexts*, pp. 195–225. New York, NY: Routledge.

Eisenstadt, M. (2007). Iraq: Tribal engagement lessons learned. *Military Review*, 87(5), p. 16.

Harvey, D. (2005). *A brief history of neoliberalism*. Oxford, UK: Oxford University Press.

Kent, M. L., & Taylor, M. (2002). Toward a dialogic theory of public relations. *Public Relations Review*, 28, pp. 21–37.

Kim, I. (2007). A subaltern studies approach to crisis communication. Paper presented at the Annual Meeting of the Public Relations Division of the National Communication Association. Chicago, IL.

Kruckeberg, D., & Starck, K. (1988). *Public relations and community: A reconstructed story*. New York, NY: Praeger.

Landry, D., & MacLean, G. (1996). *The Spivak reader: Selected works of Gayatri Chakravorty Spivak*. New York, NY: Routledge.

L'Etang, J. (2006a). Public relations and propaganda: Conceptual issues, methodological problems, and public relations discourse. In J. L'Etang, & M. Pieczka (Eds), *Public relations: Critical debates and contemporary practice*, pp. 23–40. Mahwah, NJ: Lawrence Erlbaum Associates.

L'Etang, J. (2006b). Public relations as diplomacy. In J. L'Etang, & M. Pleczka (Eds), *Public relations: Critical debates and contemporary practice*, pp. 373–88). Mahwah, NJ: Lawrence Erlbaum Associates.

McKie, D., & Munshi, D. (2007). *Reconfiguring public relations: Ecology, equity, and enterprise*. London, UK: Routledge.

Mumby, D. K., & Stohl, C. (2007). (Re)disciplining Organizational Communication Studies: A response to Broadfoot and Munshi. *Management Communication Quarterly*, 21(2), pp. 268–80.

Munshi, D. (1999). Requisitioning variety: Photographic metaphors, ethnocentric lenses, and the divided colours of public relations. *Asia Pacific Public Relations Journal*, 1, pp. 39–51.

Munshi, D., & Kurian, P. (2005). Imperializing spin cycles: A postcolonial look at public relations, greenwashing and the separation of publics. *Public Relations Review*, 31, pp. 513–20.

Padel, F., & Das, S. (2010). *Out of this earth: East India adivasis and the aluminium cartel*. Hyderabad, India: Orient Blackswan.

Pal, M., & Dutta, M. J. (2008a). Public relations in a global context: The relevance of critical modernism as a theoretical lens. *Journal of Public Relations Research*, 20, pp. 159–79. Retrieved from http://dx.doi.org. libproxy1.nus.edu.sg/10.1080/10627260801894280

Pal, M., & Dutta, M. J. (2008b). Theorizing resistance in a global context. In C. S. Beck (Ed.), *Communication yearbook 32*, pp. 41–87. New York, NY: Routledge.

Petras, J. (1997). Imperialism and NGOs in Latin America. *Monthly Review*, 49. Retrieved on October 31, 2013, from http://monthlyreview.org/1997/12/01/imperialism-and-ngos-in-latin-america

Pratt, C. (2006). Reformulating the emerging theory of corporate social responsibility as good governance. In C. Botan, & V. Hazleton (Eds), *Public Relations Theory*, pp. 249–77. Mahwah, NJ: Lawrence Erlbaum Associates.

Robinson, W. (1996). *Promoting polyarchy: Globalization, US intervention, and hegemony*. Cambridge, UK: Cambridge University Press.

Said, E. W. (1978). *Orientalism*. Harmondsworth, UK: Penguin.

Said, E. (1988). Foreword. In R. Guha, & G. C. Spivak (Eds), *Selected Subaltern Studies*, pp. v–xii. New York, NY: Oxford University Press.

Shiva, V. (2002). Seeds of suicide: The ecological and human cost of globalization of agriculture. In V. Shiva, & G. Bedi (Eds), *Sustainable agriculture and food security: The impact of globalization*, pp. 169–83. New Delhi: Sage.

Shome, R., & Hegde, S. R. (2002). Postcolonial approaches to communication: Charting the terrain, engaging the intersections. *Communication Theory*, 12, pp. 249–70.

Smith, J., Pagnucco, R., & Chatfield, C. (1997). Social movements and world politics. In J. Smith, C. Chatfield, & R. Pagnucco (Eds), *Transnational social movements and global politics*, pp. 59–77. Syracuse, NY: Syracuse University Press.

Spivak, G. C. (1990a). The post-colonial critic. In S. Harasym (Ed.), *The postcolonial critic: Interviews, strategies, dialogues*, pp. 67–74. NY: Routledge.

Spivak, G. C. (1990b). Questions of multi-culturalism. In S. Harasym (Ed.), *The postcolonial critic: Interviews, strategies, dialogues*, pp. 59–66. NY: Routledge.

Spivak, G. C. (1996). Bonding in difference: Interview with Alfred Arteaga. In D. Landry, & G. MacLean (Eds), *The Spivak reader: Selected works of Gayatri Chakravorty Spivak*, pp. 15–28. NY: Routledge.

Spivak, G. C. (1999). *A critique of postcolonial reason: Toward a history of the vanishing present*. Cambridge, MA: Harvard University Press.

Spivak, G. C. (2000). The new subaltern: a silent interview. In Vinayak Chaturvedi (Ed.), *Mapping subaltern studies and the* postcolonial, pp. 324–40. London: Verso.

Sriramesh, K., & Verčič, D. (2003). A theoretical framework for global public relations research and practice. In K. Sriramesh, & D. Verčič (Eds), *The global public relations handbook*.

Taylor, M., Kent, M. L., & White, W. J. (2001). How activist organizations are using the Internet to build relationships. *Public Relations Review*, 27, pp. 263–84.

Thaker, J., & Dutta, M. (2014). *Bt Cotton, scientific studies, and power circuits: Culturally-centering science*. Singapore: Center for Culture-Centered Approach to Research and Evaluation White Paper Series.

21

Who's afraid of the big bad wolf?

Critical Public Relations as a cure for Media Studies' fear of the dark

C. Kay Weaver

It is commonly said that the relationship between public relations and the media is an uneasy one (DeLorme & Fedler, 2003; Macnamara, 2014; Moloney, Jackson & McQueen, 2013; White & Hobsbawn, 2007) – one of mutual dependency and loathing, with the loathing residing more with media professionals than with public relations practitioners. These tensions play out not only in the media and communication industries, but are also evident in academia, where public relations is often dismissed as the ventriloquist of dark self-interested undemocratic agendas by scholars in what could be regarded as closely associated disciplines of Media and Communication Studies (e.g., Davies, 2009; Herman & Chomsky, 2008; Miller & Dinan, 2008a; Rushkoff, 1998; Sussman, 2011). Any public relations academic who has conversed with Media Studies colleagues about public relations will recognise the suspicion and even disdain with which our subject is sometimes perceived. Even those of us who have traversed both camps, and perhaps especially those of us who have relocated from Media Studies to Public Relations departments, will be familiar with the assertions that we have "sold-out", are turncoats, or traitors. While such jibes may be made in the best of collegial humour, the pejorative views of public relations educators and public relations practice that underpin them are largely based on suppositions that teaching and researching public relations must involve working with, and advocating for, the public relations industry and anti-democratic government and/or corporate interests.

Given that normative functional public relations scholarship and its widespread espousal in the tertiary education classroom does support Western neoliberal capitalist business agendas (McKie & Munshi, 2007, 2009; Weaver, 2011), and that the history of the public relations industry is intimately connected to the history of capitalism and neoliberalism (Demetrious, 2006; Miller & Dinan 2000), there are grounds for these fears. Yet what do these concerns about public relations and public relations education say about Media Studies, how it understands and engages with public relations, and how it engages with and contributes to critical public relations scholarship? And why, when public relations "occupies a central position in today's wider promotional culture" (Cottle, 2003, p. 3), does Media Studies itself not place "the public relations question" at its very heart?

In this chapter I explore why a gulf exists between the academic fields of Public Relations and Media Studies, and why this continues despite the ever-growing presence and influence of public relations in culture and media output, and the rise of the self-defined area of Critical

Public Relations scholarship. In outlining the often-tense relationships between public relations and Media Studies, I argue that there are important opportunities for collaboration and dialogue between Critical Public Relations and Media Studies, especially in the context of the digitisation of global information flows.

Common disciplinary birthings

Public Relations and Media Studies are both relatively young fields of academic education and inquiry, though both share a common – albeit troubled – parentage in communication research. Walter Lippmann, Robert Parks, John Dewey and Harold Lasswell pioneered communication research in the 1920s in the US through their various foci on issues of public opinion formation and the role played by the mass media in urbanisation and democratic participation. However, while these authors are frequently cited as providing the foundational building blocks for Communication and Media Studies (Buxton, 2008; Morrison, 1998), the term "communication" was rarely used until the 1950s (Sproule, 2008). Similarly, while James Carey (1989, p. 75) credits Walter Lippman's (1922) *Public Opinion* as the founding book in American Media Studies, Media Studies would only begin to emerge as an academic discipline in the 1960s. Nevertheless, the 1920s was an important period in terms of the emergent (tense) relationship between Media Studies and public relations.

During this time Lippman raised important questions about the potential for representative democracy and the role the media play in shaping public opinion. While Lippman's project was concerned with public knowledge and the achievement of (albeit technocratic) democratic ideals, it also raised concerns about the possibilities of engineering public consent (Duff, 2013; Jansen, 2008, 2013; Weaver, Motion & Roper, 2006). Meanwhile Harold Laswell, commonly regarded as one of the founding "media effects theorists" (Lubken, 2008), was working at "understanding and discerning patterns in the propaganda process [that] would reveal its strategies and ultimate effectiveness" (Jowett & O'Donnell, 2006, p. 102). Coming from a quite different and Machiavellian political agenda, Edward Bernays drew on many of the theoretical and philosophical ideas developed by his contemporaries – especially Lippman's – in making the case for the purposive engineering of public opinion to advantage business and government. Bernay's *Crystalizing Public Opinion* (1923) and *Propaganda* (1928) remain seminal texts in introducing techniques of propaganda, public opinion management, and public relations, and he is commonly described as the "father of public relations" (Ewen, 1996; Jansen, 2008; Tye, 1998).

There is little question that the early years of communication and media research were intricately bound up with questions about the role, strategies and practices of propaganda, and what Bernays termed, "public relations counsel" in public opinion management, social consensus formation and mass communication. Pioneering researchers of this period adopted a range of positions in relation to these matters (Buxton, 2008), and the extent to which some advocated for the social engineering of public opinion remains highly contested (see Barsamian & Chomsky, 2001; Jansen, 2008). What is clear, however, is the genuine importance placed on inquiring into the role that public relations and propaganda – as well as the strategies and techniques available to those seeking to manipulate and influence public thinking – played in social culture and its management.

It is generally agreed that there is a direct relationship between Bernays' espousal of propaganda techniques in *Crystalizing Public Opinion* (1923) and *Propaganda* (1928) and the rise of German fascism, the Third Reich, and support for the holocaust engineered by Hitler and his minister of propaganda, Joseph Goebbels. Goebbels is said to have owned a copy of *Crystalizing Public Opinion* (Barsamian & Chomsky, 2001; Jansen, 2008; Tye, 1998). The Nazi Party's horrifically successful use of propaganda and "public relations" techniques contributed to cementing such forms of communication being overwhelmingly associated with unethical communication – the strategic manipulation of audiences through mass media, and the corruption of democracy by (especially) governments and corporations. Consequently, where Media Studies has engaged with public relations, as I discuss in the next section, it is mostly in terms of its pejorative positioning as propaganda. This has worked to constrain the development of a holistic critical inquiry into, and intelligent debate about, the role of public relations in society.

The Media Studies disciplinary project

It is notoriously difficult to describe exactly what Media Studies is. Media scholar William Merrin (2012, p. 40) explains that:

> Our introductory media modules and textbooks explain what media studies argues, but not what it is. They offer little information about its origins and history, its development, its relationship to other disciplines and its strengths and limitations. They don't reveal its lacunae, its failings, its logic, its historical complicity with government and the industries it studies, its biases, its misrepresentation of media, its hostility to certain positions or authors, or the underlying philosophical assumptions that frame its approaches and claims.

It is, indeed, perilous to attempt a definition of Media Studies, especially for the purposes of assessing its relationship to public relations, and where its failings and blindness might be in that relationship. It is also necessary to appreciate that while Media Studies has become a well-established discipline in the UK and Australasia, in the US the nomenclature is often different – with Mass Communication, Communication Studies or Communications being commonly used to describe the field entitled Media Studies elsewhere. A further complication is that linked to Media Studies are an ever-evolving range of medium-specific disciplines such as Film Studies, Television Studies, Radio Studies, Journalism Studies, Screen Studies and, more recently, Internet Studies. To complicate matters further, there is Cultural Studies. All of these disciplines share significant similarities as well as differences, and have some common as well as specific "founding" theorists, concepts, key terms and trajectories. All have also produced at least some historical analyses of how they have been touched by and/or implicated with the public relations and propaganda industries (e.g., Combs & Combs, 1994; Horten, 2002; Jowett & O'Donnell, 2006; Kilborn, 2006; Reeves, 1999; Strinati, 2000; Taylor, 1999). Difficult as it may be, though, and with apologies to disciplinary purists, I do want to at least attempt to outline where Media Studies positions itself in relation to public relations and critical public relations scholarship.

In the UK, Media Studies programmes were being established in polytechnics and universities from the 1960s onwards, with many of the pioneering departments having grown out of English and literary criticism. In the UK and in Australasia, the development of Media Studies was significantly influenced by the cultural theorists Raymond Williams, Richard Hoggart, E. P. Thompson and Stuart Hall (Davis, 2007; Worrall Redal, 2008). Other key influencers were theorists associated with the "Frankfurt School" established in 1923 in Germany's University of Frankfurt – Herbert Marcuse, Max Horkheimer, Theodore Adorno and Jürgan Habermas (Berry, 2012). Their collective work played a key role in shaping the critical direction of the disciplinary project. Consequently, even in its beginnings, Media Studies was focused on identifying and theorising how the "mass media, controlled by advertising and commercial imperatives, serve the needs of dominant corporate interests and play a major role in ideological reproduction in creating subservience to the system of consumer capitalism" (Burkart, 2009, p. 141). This was scholarship with a moral agenda which also asked "how can the role of culture be understood in the quest for a better world? How can it be influenced in the service of such a goal? How can intellectual practice, at its heart, also be political practice?" (Worrall Redal, 2008, p. 271). Underlying this work was a critical belief that the media has considerable responsibilities in and to society, and to supporting democratic ideals. Over 50 years later media scholars are still motivated by such principles. For example, Nick Couldry (2012), one of the most influential and respected and of twenty-first century Media Studies theorists, has stated that: "The point, for me, of 'media studies' is to study how media contribute to conditions of knowledge and agency in the world, and so to our possibilities of living well together."

Media Studies and the question of consent

When Media Studies programmes were being established, the same type of issues that early twentieth-century public opinion theorists were asking continued to provide a focus for research agendas, but now through a broader range of media content. As Aeron Davis (2007, p. 75) explains: "'The consent question' – how the majority consented to and/or resisted the inequalities imposed by the dominant class – was to be a key object of enquiry." The impact of the media on cultural life and relationships between groups, communities, institutions, media and popular culture was central to this research, through the study of, for examples, the press, current affairs and entertainment television, pop music, Western movies, crime fiction and advertising. During this period of the 1970s, Media Studies also began to draw on a range of European post-structuralist critical, social and cultural thinkers – Antonio Gramsci, Roland Barthes, Pierre Bourdieu, Jürgen Habermas and Michael Foucault – whose perspectives injected more complex ways of theorising the role of media and culture in social life. This vastly complicated the question of whether people consented to power and what they had to gain in so doing. Media and cultural researchers concluded that "Culture is itself far from being a simple tool of repression or resistance. It is also autonomous, pleasurable, polysemic and productive" (Davis, 2007, p. 76). Led especially by John Fiske (1987, 1989), including work by, among others, Ien Ang (1985), Kim Christian Schrøder (1989) and Dorothy Hobson (1982), and drawing on theories of pleasure developed by Foucault (1980, 1990), together with Baudrillard (1985) and Lyotard's (1984) notions of postmodern individualism, this "revisionist" (Curran, 1990) argument placed the power of social and cultural meaning-making in the hands of autonomous media audiences/users.

Arguing that public opinion can be engineered and manufactured became much more difficult when pluralists asserted that audiences are "capable of manipulating the media in an infinite variety of ways according to their prior needs and dispositions" (Curran & Gurevitch, 1977, pp. 4–5). From this point, media were theorised by many Media and Cultural Studies scholars as having very limited effects, and audiences as active and, in a form of "semiotic democracy" (Curran, 1990), having agency to resist and negotiate message content. Indeed, audiences were argued to have such agency as to be able to subvert and create their own sub-cultural meanings out of media content. Consequently, arguments that public relations and propaganda are capable of manipulating and influencing public opinion and culture became less than fashionable.

With pluralists abandoning notions of media power and its elite control, it has been those with a particular interest in the social and political construction of knowledge, and primarily those involved in journalism research, who have continued to touch on matters related to the question of public relations. They have done this in the context of studies of news production and research into how news sources and information subsidies impact on what information is made available to civil society via the news media (e.g., Davis, 2000; Lewis, Williams & Franklin, 2008; Miller, 2004; Schlesinger, 1989).

Media Studies' perspectives on public relations

The notion of the public sphere and concerns about how public relations professionals and the organisations they represent attempt to strategically manage access to information in that sphere has provided an important underpinning for discussions about the role of public relations in news management and the dissemination of information in society (Roper, 2005; Weaver et al., 2006). The concept of the public sphere is a much-debated one, and anyone who appropriates the term also has to negotiate the many criticisms levelled at it (Lunt & Livingstone, 2013). It is a concept that Habermas revised following disparagement of his idealisation of a public space where communicative action and deliberation occurs, his acknowledgement of the complexities of modern democracies, and the roles that institutions – including media institutions – play in civil society. While the concept continues to be debated, less debated among many media scholars is that in relation to the public sphere, public relations is a highly problematic and undemocratic strategic communication practice (Herman & McChesney, 1997; Miller & Dinan, 2008b).

Habermas was highly critical of public relations regarding it – along with marketing and advertising – as contributing to the erosion of the public sphere through its "strategic attempt to control the agenda of public discussion and the terms in which that discussion takes place" (Weaver et al., 2006, p. 17). Consequently media academics make statements such as that made by Dinan and Miller (2007): "the PR industry is antidemocratic in intent and effect" (p. 3). Public relations is not, then, regarded by the critical and radical Media Studies project as a communicative practice that enhances the possibilities of "living well together" (Couldry, 2012). On the contrary, as Brian McNair states (2006, p. 46),

> public relations and its linked professions came to be viewed within critical media sociology as an industry of dishonest persuasion, an infrastructure of propaganda…public relations is perceived to have usurped the free flow of information between politician and citizen, and to have distorted reality itself in favour of private interests, which have used it as a means of translating their economic dominance into intellectual, ideological and cultural dominance.

McNair's analysis of how public relations has been analysed and theorised by media sociologists is particularly useful in understanding the different lenses applied to it.

McNair separates Media Studies approaches to public relations into two perspectives: the control paradigm and the chaos paradigm. Scholars aligned to the control paradigm are most likely to address public relations under the pejorative term "propaganda", and position it as supporting neoliberalism's globalising colonial forces. For example, Gerald Sussman (2011, p. 5) states:

> we link the growth of propaganda and promotion to the neoliberal regime of capitalist accumulation, characterised by the almost unfettered expansion of transnational corporate trade and investment, corporate mega mergers (with millions of jobs lost) convergent technologies (functionally and through ownerships), massive cuts in social spending, government deregulation, tax "reform" for the rich, militarism, escalated assaults on labour organizations, the privatization and outsourcing of public institutions and services and increasing moral deregulations.

From this perspective public relations is associated with a vast range of social ills and injustices and fails to make any positive contribution to the betterment of society. It is this overly simplified view of public relations which influences media scholars' judgements and dismissal of those who work within public relations departments in tertiary institutions. Within this paradigm, "the controlling power of public relations has been seen to reside in the ability of its practitioners to cover up, manufacture or 'spin' information in various ways, thus deceiving populations without their being aware of that deceit" (McNair, 2006, p. 47).

Herman and Chomsky's (2008) *Manufacturing Consent*, first published in 1988, provided the war cry for many media sociologists to align with the control paradigm's political economy model of public relations. From this perspective, the public sphere has been "re-feudalised", and news production "subjected entirely to the interests of economically and politically motivated groups" (Palmer, 2000, p. 157). The greater the amount of resources a group, government or organisation has in the form of social, political and/or financial power, the greater its ability will be to determine news agendas and effectively marginalise dissenting voices. Conversely, the less resourced an organisation, government or group is, the less ability it will have to influence news agendas through public relations activities and information management.

The massive downsizing of print media in the last decade, the move to online journalism, and cost-cutting that has been forced on media organisations which struggle to identify business models in the digital context, has added grist to the control paradigm's view that public relations is contaminating the potential for a healthy public sphere. In this context, journalists, working to 24/7 deadlines, who have higher workloads than their predecessors and who are required to produce more "copy" with fewer resources, have been identified as increasingly reliant on information provided through public relations sources to produce "news" (e.g., Boyd-Barrett, 2010; Forde & Johnston, 2013).

Many media researchers continue to espouse the political economy control paradigm of public relations – recently caricatured as arguing "capitalism is bad, propaganda is generally bad, and the two working together are eroding our political and social systems" (Heydon, 2013). Yet in the context of digital environments, a pluralist perspective on public relations has found some traction in Media Studies scholarship. McNair (2006) terms this the "chaos paradigm", while Cottle (2003) defines it in terms of "communicative action" or a "communicative frame". Here, financially and/or politically dominant groups are not theorised as having power through the use of public relations to "manufacture" or construct news and determine how issues are framed by the media Rather, news "*emerges* from the interacting elements of the communication environment which prevails in a given media space. These spaces contain many social actors striving to manufacture and shape the news, but none has any guarantee of success" (McNair, 2006, p. 49, italics in original).

The evolution of digital technologies has certainly added to the plurality of media that information audiences are able to access. Within Western contexts, the internet is now a primary route through which information is disseminated. Large proportions of internet users seek that information from social networking sites, and increasingly audiences are engaging with news online (Schrøder & Larsen, 2010). Thus, audiences – once dependent on others to define and communicate the "news of the day" – can now actively identify their own news from a vast range of information sources, and share that news among their networks. This creates a whole new context for Media Studies researchers to examine and reflect on the role of public relations in social culture. However, it is one they would be better equipped to address if they were more open to a wider range of perspectives on public relations, and engaged with that trail already blazed – and which is discussed further below – by Critical Public Relations scholars. To date, there has been barely any acknowledgment of this group and its contribution to researching and theorising public relations within Media Studies.

The Public Relations disciplinary project

The establishment of Public Relations as a discipline in the academy was driven by very different agendas than the critical ones which underpinned the evolution of Media Studies. The development of public relations education, which began as early as the late 1940s in the USA and Canada, and the 1950s in the UK, has been widely driven by professional bodies seeking to enhance and legitimise the professionalisation of the field (L'Etang & Pieczka, 2006; Weaver, 2013; Wright, 2011). L'Etang and Pieczka (2006, p. 435) also outline how one of the themes in the development of public relations education has been the desire to establish and maintain public relations as a subject area independent from other disciplines. Consequently, public relations education has overwhelmingly emphasised practical vocational training over and above theory development, and academics who have dominated the discipline have shunned the introduction of critical perspectives in teaching and research (Grunig, 2001). Furthermore, in the US, public relations is often taught within journalism schools (Wright, 2011) which deliver a vocational training, publicity, and media relations-based curriculum, rather than a philosophical and theoretically driven one.

In the public relations discipline, Grunig and Hunt's (1984) influential Excellence "theory", and the four models of public relations which it propounded, sought to provide public relations with a conceptual distance from propaganda and advance it as an ethical form of communication. Within these models, propaganda is equated with unethical practices of publicity and press agentry. Positioning ethical public relations as dialogic, and contributing to public debate in the laissez-faire marketplace of ideas, the Excellence project – despite its managerialist and scientific orientations (McKie, 1997; Weaver, 2011) – sits in a fascinating alignment with the celebration of "active audiences" and "sovereign consumer pluralism" (Curran, 1990, p. 140) which predominated in Media Studies in the late 1980s and early 1990s. Just like the liberal pluralist position in Media Studies, the dialogic model of public relations places considerable power in the hands of publics to actively participate in dialogue and negotiate with organisations about goals and policies (Weaver et al., 2006). Ultimately, in the dialogic model, the needs and interests of the public play a determining role in organisational decision-making and policy formation.

Both public relations Excellence theory, and liberal pluralism in Media Studies have been heavily critiqued for considering their object of study in isolation from relations of power, or for situating that object of study within a model of society in which power is widely diffused (Dutta & Pal, 2011; Edwards, 2014). It was those informed by, and working from, critical perspectives who drove the turn to address questions of how public relations is implicated in social-cultural power structures, but who also, unlike Media Studies researchers, were prepared to consider how public relations might be used to challenge dominant power structures.

The Critical Public Relations project and the socio-cultural turn

Critical Public Relations scholars have consistently drawn attention to the lack of consideration of social relations of power in functionalist public relations theory and, in these terms, they do share a social justice agenda with critical Media Studies. Indeed, where Nick Couldry (2012) positions Media Studies as concerned with examining the "conditions of knowledge and agency in the world, and so to our possibilities of living well together", Critical Public Relations pioneer, Jacquie L'Etang (2005, pp. 521–2) explains that the critical approach in her field aims to:

transform those social, political and economic structures which limit human potential. It seeks to identify, challenge, and debate the strategies of domination that are implicit in such structures. Such investigation and debate have the potential to raise awareness and act as a catalyst for change.

There are an increasing number of public relations theorists who work to bring some of the theoretical frameworks and theorists found in Media Studies to bear on the theorising of public relations (see, for example, many of the chapters in L'Etang & Pieczka, 2006b). Meanwhile, Media Studies itself, and those who are researching and writing about public relations within that disciplinary context, appear largely unaware of this Critical Public Relations project – certainly they do not make reference to it in their own work on public relations or propaganda.

Unlike radical and critical Media Studies scholars, Critical Public Relations theorists are far less likely to position public relations as propaganda and dismiss it as the villainous tool of neoliberalism. Some Critical Public Relations scholars such as Kevin Moloney (2006) – who works at Bournemouth University (one of the few tertiary institutions to include public relations teaching and research within a Media School) – have explored the relationship between public relations and propaganda, and asked whether these are different forms of communication practice (see also Weaver et al., 2006). Quite rightly it is concluded that public relations and propaganda are inseparable, but that does not mean these "communicative modes" of practice (Moloney, 2006, p. 176) are inherently unethical. As Critical Public Relations researchers have argued, if public relations is theorised as a form of discursive practice, its ethics can only be judged in relation to the context in which it is applied. In these terms, sweeping and dismissive generalisations about the unethical nature of public relations and propaganda – such as those made by Media Studies scholars (e.g., Sussman, 2011) – simply lack credibility.

Critical Public Relations researchers have also introduced a sophisticated range of theoretical perspectives to public relations research and analysis which have added much-needed depth to the understanding of its role in culture. Dutta and Pal, (2011), McKie and Munshi (2007), Munshi (1999) and Munshi and Kurian (2005), for example, have applied postcolonial lenses in theorising how public relations supports nation-building, colonisation and globalisation processes. Coombs and Holladay (2012), Demetrious (2006, 2008, 2013), Heath and Waymer (2008), Henderson (2005) and Weaver (2010, 2014) have theorised the use of public relations strategies and tactics by activist groups, and how such groups have challenged dominant interpretations of social issues. Others (e.g., Ihlen, Bartlett & May, 2011); L'Etang, 1994, 1995, 1996; Roper, 2004, 2012) have examined public relations' contribution to corporate social responsibility (CSR) and sustainability discourses, identifying how these are used to legitimise organisations and also how organisations have responded to public pressure to change CSR practices. Critical researchers have also explored the many and varied relationships between gender and public relations (see chapters in Daymon & Demetrious, 2014), race and public relations (see chapters in Logan, 2011; Munshi & Edwards, 2011; Pompper, 2005; Waymer, 2012), ethics and public relations writing (Surma, 2013), and even terrorism and public relations (Baines & O'Shaughnessy, 2014; Heath & Waymer, 2014a, 2014b; Holbrook, 2014; Somerville & Kirby, 2012). These few examples illustrate the breadth of concerns that Critical Public Relations scholars are bringing to their field. Neither restricted by a need to examine public relations' connections with, and use of, mass media to spread its message, nor constrained by a limitation of paradigmatic disciplinary perspectives and prejudices, Critical Public Relations researchers are examining the very broad range of ways that public relations is used to shape social culture, public opinion, political processes and globalisation.

Certainly it is only in very recent years that critical public relations has reached a critical mass to such a point where there are now clear avenues for the submission and dissemination of its research and theorising. The publishing of the *Public Relations Inquiry* journal since 2012 is providing a significant new route through which Critical Public Relations work can be more fairly reviewed, published and critiqued. However, there remains more to be achieved and it is crucial that we do not become an enclave of scholars speaking only among ourselves. As Holladay and Coombs (2013) have argued, it is also important that we use our Critical Public Relations agendas to develop public relations literacy among citizens.

Future directions – collaborative Critical Public Relations and Media Studies agendas

It is vital that we continue to examine the significance of public relations within and to the media in digital environments. The media has undergone massive and rapid change in the last decade, research into which Critical Public Relations and Media Studies scholars are well equipped to collaborate on researching and educating students about. Widely described as "in crisis" (Franklin, 2010, Levy & Nielsen, 2010; Mancini, 2013) because of its loss of cultural authority to determine what news is, mainstream journalism has innovated with interactive web and social media platforms in efforts to re-engage audiences (Lewis, 2012; Schlesinger & Doyle, 2014). So too, however, have commercial and non-profit organisations (Agarwai, Mondal & Nath, 2011), politicians, bloggers and civil society groups (Bennett & Segerberg, 2012), who now communicate their "news" directly to their publics. In the context of this radical global upheaval of information dissemination, the rise of alternative news makers and news distribution networks, media researchers are just beginning to ask fundamental questions about the contemporary communicative relationship of news: Who produces news for whom, and how is the value of news judged in terms of shared public endeavours? This shift away from controlled and mass mediated contexts poses a significant challenge to Media Studies research to make sense of the changes in news production and dissemination that has occurred, with power moving away from journalists to public relations workers (Davies, 2009). Studies show that most news is now initiated by former journalists working in the wider professional communication sector (Lewis et al., 2008), reaching audiences either through public relations press releases that are reproduced in "old" news media (Sissons, 2012), or through new digital communication channels. How Media Studies will theorise the major disjuncture between traditional journalistic methods of newsgathering and analysis, dependent on standardised news sources and experts, and an emergent cultural milieu of information sharing, connection, and an openness to diverse voices and perspectives (Spyridou, Matsiola, Veglis, Kalliris & Charalambos, 2013) remains to be seen. As is evident, in the context of assessing the relationship between media and public relations, the centrality of the media has shifted, and where public relations is present in social culture becomes harder to assess and yet vitally important to track. Conducting research into the cultural meaning and consequences of this is a vast and challenging undertaking. The challenge is for Media Studies and Critical Public Relations scholars to come together and share the load in this endeavour, putting prejudices about each other aside for the greater good of continuing to investigate how public relations contributes to shaping social culture in the twenty-first century.

References

Agarwai, S., Mondal, A. & Nath, A. (2011). Social media – the new corporate playground. *International Journal of Research and Reviews in Computer Science*, 2(3), pp. 696–700.

Ang, I. (1985). *Watching Dallas*. London, UK: Methuen.

Baines, P. R., & O'Shaughnessy, N. J. (2014). Al-Qaeda messaging evolution and positioning, 1998–2008: Propaganda analysis revisited. *Public Relations Inquiry*, 3(2), pp. 163–91.

Barsamian, D., & Chomsky, N. (2001). *Propaganda and the public mind*. London, UK: Pluto Press.

Baudrillard, J. (1985). The ecstasy of communication. In H. Foster (Ed.), *Postmodern culture*, pp. 126–34. London, UK: Pluto Press.

Bennett, W. L., & Segerberg, A. (2012). The logic of connective action. *Information, Communication & Society*, 15(5), pp. 739–68.

Bernays, E. L. (1923). *Crystalizing public opinion*. New York, NY: Boni & Liveright.

Bernays, E. L. (1928). *Propaganda*. New York, NY: Horace Liveright.

Berry, D. (Ed.). (2012). *Revisiting the Frankfurt School: Essays on culture, media and theory*. Farnham & Burlington, UK: Ashgate.

Boyd-Barrett, O. (2010). National news agencies in the turbulent era of the internet. In O. Boyd-Barrett (Ed.), *News agencies in the turbulent era of the internet*, pp. 5–21. Barcelona: Generalitat de Catalunya/ Col-leccio Lexikon.

Burkart, R. (2009). On Habermas: Understanding public relations. In O. Ihlen, B. Van Ruler, & M. Fredriksson (Eds), *Public relations and social theory*, pp. 141–63. New York, NY: Routledge.

Buxton, W. J. (2008). From Park to Cressey: Chicago sociology's engagement with media and mass culture. In D. W. Park, & J. Pooley (Eds), *The history of media and communication research: Contested histories*, pp. 345–62. New York, NY: Peter Lang.

Carey, J. (1989). *Communication as culture: Essays on media and society*. Boston, MA: Unwin Hyman.

Combs, J. E., & Combs, S. T. (1994). *Film propaganda and American politics: An analysis and filmography*. New York, NY: Routledge.

Coombs, T. W., & Holladay, S. J. (2012). Fringe public relations: How activism moves critical PR towards the mainstream. *Public Relations Review*, 38(5), pp. 880–7.

Cottle, S. (2003). News, public relations and power: Mapping the field. In S. Cottle (Ed.), *News, public relations and power*, pp. 3–24. Thousand Oaks, CA: Sage.

Couldry, N. (2012). Relegitimation crisis: Beyond the dull compulsion of media-saturated life. *Divinatio*, 35, pp. 81–92.

Curran, J. (1990). New revisionism in mass communication research: A reappraisal. *European Journal of Communication*, 5(2), pp. 135–64.

Curran, J., & Gurevitch, M. (1977). *The audience, mass communication and society; Block 3*. Milton Keynes, UK: Open University Press.

Davies, N. (2009). *Flat earth news: An award-winning reporter exposes falsehood, distortion and propaganda in the global media*. London, UK: Vintage Books.

Davis, A. (2000). Public relations, news production and changing patterns of source access in the British national media. *Media Culture and Society*, 22(1), pp. 39–59.

Davis, A. (2007). *The mediation of power: A critical introduction*. New York, NY: Routledge.

Daymon, C., & Demetrious, K. (Eds). (2014). *Gender and public relations: Critical perspectives on voice, image and identity*. New York, NY: Routledge.

DeLorme, D. E., & Fedler, F. (2003). Journalists' hostility toward public relations: An historical analysis. *Public Relations Review*, 29(2), pp. 99–124.

Demetrious, K. (2006). Active voices. In J. L'Etang, & M. Pieczka (Eds), *Public relations: Critical debates and contemporary practice*, pp. 93–107. Mahwah, NJ: Lawrence Erlbaum Associates.

Demetrious, K. (2008). New activism and communication in Australian risk society: A case study of the Otway Ranges Environmental Network. *Third Sector Review*, 14(2), pp. 113–26.

Demetrious, K. (2013). *Public relations, activism, and social change: Speaking up*. Abingdon & Oxon: Routledge.

Dinan, W., & Miller, D. (2007). *Thinker, faker, spinner, spy: Corporate PR and the assault on democracy*. London, UK: Pluto Press.

Duff, A. (2013). Pundit for post-industrial times? Walter Lippmann as an information society theorist. *Information, Communication and Society*, 16(6), pp. 967–88.

Dutta, M. J., & Pal, M. (2011). Public relations and marginalization in a global context: A postcolonial critique. In N. Bardhan, & C. K. Weaver (Eds), *Public relations in global contexts: Multi-paradigmatic perspectives*, pp. 195–225. London, UK: Routledge.

Edwards, L. (2014) *Power, diversity and public relations*. London, UK: Routledge.

Ewen, S. (1996). *PR: A social history of spin*. New York, NY: Basic Books.

Fiske, J. (1987). *Television culture*. London, UK: Methuen.

Fiske, J. (1989). *Understanding popular culture*. Boston: Unwin Hyman.

Forde, S., & Johnston, J. (2103). The news triumvirate. *Journalism Studies*, 14(1), pp. 113–29.

Foucault, M. (1980). *Power/knowledge: Selected interviews and other writings 1972–1977*. New York, NY: Pantheon.

Foucault, M. (1990). *The history of sexuality*. London, UK: Penguin.

Franklin, B. (2010). Introduction. *Journalism Practice*, 4(3), pp. 246–67.

Grunig, J. (2001). Two-way symmetrical public relations: Past, present and future. In R. L. Heath (Ed.), *Handbook of public relations*, pp. 11–30. London, UK: Sage.

Grunig, J. E., & Hunt, T. (1984). *Managing public relations*. New York, NY: Holt, Rinehart & Winston.

Heath, R. L., & Waymer, D. (2008). A case study of Frederick Douglass' "Fourth of July Address". In R. L. Heath, E. L. Toth, & D. Waymer (Eds), *Rhetorical and critical approaches to public relations II*, pp. 195–215. New York, NY: Routledge.

Heath, R. L., & Waymer, D. (2014a). John Brown, public relations, terrorism, and social capital: "His Truth Goes Marching On." *Public Relations Inquiry*, 3(2), pp. 209–26.

Heath, R. L., & Waymer, D. (2014b). Terrorism: Social capital, social construction, and constructive society? *Public Relations Inquiry*, 3(2), pp. 227–44.

Henderson, A. (2005). Activism in "paradise": Identity management in a public relations campaign against genetic engineering. *Journal of Public Relations Research*, 17(2), pp. 117–37.

Herman, E. S., & Chomsky, N. (2008) *Manufacturing consent: The political economy of the mass media*. London, UK: Bodley Head.

Herman, E. S., & McChesney, R. W. (1997). *The global media: The new missionaries of global capitalism*. London, UK: Cassell.

Heydon, J. (2013). Review: The propaganda society: Promotional culture and politics in global context. *Canadian Journal of Communication, North America*, 38(3). Retrieved on 20 April 2015 from: http://www.cjc-online.ca/index.php/journal/article/view/2755/2401

Hobson, D. (1982). *Crossroads*. London, UK: Methuen.

Holbrook, D. (2014). Approaching terrorist public relations initiatives. *Public Relations Inquiry*, 3(2), pp. 141–61.

Holladay, S. J., & Coombs, T. W. (2013). Public relations literacy: Developing critical consumers of public relations. *Public Relations Inquiry*, 2(2), pp. 125–46.

Horten, G. (2002). *Radio goes to war: The cultural politics of propaganda during World War II*. Berkeley, CA: University of California Press.

Ihlen, O., Bartlett, J. L., & May, S. (Eds). (2011). *The handbook of communication and corporate social responsibility*. Chichester, UK: John Wiley.

Jansen, S. C. (2008). Walter Lippmann, straw man of communication history. In D. W. Park, & J. Pooley (Eds), *The history of media and communication research: Contested histories*, pp. 71–112. New York, NY: Peter Lang.

Jansen, S. C. (2013). Semantic tyranny: How Edward L. Bernays stole Walter Lippmann's mojo and got away with it and why it still matters. *International Journal of Communication*, 7, pp. 1094–111.

Jowett, G. S., & O'Donnell, V. (2006). *Propaganda and persuasion*, 4th edition. Thousand Oaks, CA: Sage.

Kilborn, R. (2006). A marriage made in heaven or in hell? Relations between documentary film makers and PR practioners. In J. L'Etang, & M. Pieczka (Eds), *Public relations: Critical debates and contemporary practice*, pp.187–204. Mahwah, NJ: Lawrence Erlbaum Associates.

L'Etang, J. (1994). Public relations and corporate social responsibility: Some issues arising. *Journal of Business Ethics*, 13(2), pp. 111–23.

L'Etang, J. (1995). Ethical corporate social responsibility: A framework for managers. *Journal of Business Ethics*, 14(2), pp. 125–32.

L'Etang, J. (1996). Corporate responsibility and public relations ethics. In J. L'Etang, & M. Pieczka (Eds), *Critical perspectives in public relations*, pp. 82–105. London, UK: International Thomson Business Press.

L'Etang, J. (2005). Critical public relations: Some reflections. *Public Relations Review*, 31(4), 521–526.

L'Etang, J., & Pieczka, M. (2006). Public relations education. In J. L'Etang, & M. Pieczka (Eds), *Public relations: Critical debates and contemporary practice*, pp. 433–42. Mahwah, NJ: Lawrence Erlbaum Associates.

Levy, D., & Nielsen, R. (Eds.). (2010). *The changing business of journalism and its implications for democracy*. Oxford, UK: The Reuters Institute for the Study of Journalism.

Lewis, J., Williams, A., & Franklin, B. (2008). A compromised fourth estate? *Journalism Studies*, 9(1), pp. 1–20.

Lewis, S. C. (2012). The tension between professional control and open participation: Journalism and its boundaries. *Information, Communication & Society*, 15(6), pp. 836–66.

Lippmann, W. (1922). *Public opinion*. New York, NY: Macmillan.

Logan, N. (2011). The white leader prototype: A critical analysis of race in public relations. *Journal of Public Relations Research*, 23(4), pp. 442–57.

Lubken, D. (2008) Remembering the straw man: The travels and adventures of hypodermic. In D. W. Park, & J. Pooley (Eds), *The history of media and communication research: Contested histories*, pp. 19–42. New York, NY: Peter Lang.

Lunt, P., & Livingstone, S. (2013). Media studies' fascination with the concept of the public sphere: Critical reflections and emerging debates. *Media, Culture & Society*, 35(1), pp. 87–96.

Lyotard, J-F. (1984). *The postmodern condition*. Manchester, UK: Manchester University Press.

Macnamara, J. (2014). *Journalism and PR: Unpacking "spin", stereotypes, and media myths*. New York, NY: Peter Lang.

McKie, D. (1997). Shifting paradigms: Public relations beyond rats, stats, and 1950s science. *Australian Journal of Communication*, 24(2), pp. 81–96.

McKie, D., & Munshi, D. (2007). *Reconfiguring public relations: Ecology, equity and enterprise*. London, UK: Routledge.

McKie, D., & Munshi, D. (2009). Theoretical holes: A partial A to Z of missing critical thought in public relations. In R. L. Heath, E. L. Toth, & D. Waymer (Eds), *Rhetorical and critical approaches to public relations II*, pp. 61–75. New York, NY: Routledge.

McNair, B. (2006). *Cultural chaos: Journalism, news and power in a globalised world*. New York, NY: Routledge.

Mancini, P. (2013). Media fragmentation, party system, and democracy. *The International Journal of Press/Politics*, 18(1), pp. 43–60.

Matthews, J., & Cottle, S. (2012) Television news ecology in the United Kingdom: A study of communicative architecture, its production and meanings. *Television and New Media*, 13(2), pp. 103–23.

Merrin, W. (2012) *Media Studies 2.0*. New York, NY: Routledge.

Miller, D. (2004). Information dominance: The philosophy of total propaganda control. In Y. Kamalipour, & N. Snow (Eds), *War, media and propaganda: A global perspective*, pp. 7–16. Lanham, MD: Rowman & Littlefield.

Miller, D., & Dinan, W. (2000). The rise of the PR industry in Britain, 1979-98. *European Journal of Communication*, 15(1), pp. 5–35.

Miller, D., & Dinan, W. (2008a). Introduction. In D. Miller, & W. Dinan (Eds), *A century of spin: How public relations became the cutting edge of corporate power*, pp. 1–7. London, UK: Pluto.

Miller, D., & Dinan, W. (Eds). (2008b). *A century of spin: How public relations became the cutting edge of corporate power*. London, UK: Pluto.

Moloney, K. (2006). *Rethinking public relations: PR, propaganda and democracy*. Oxford, UK: Routledge.

Moloney, K., Jackson, D., & McQueen, D. (2013). News journalism and public relations: A dangerous relationship. In S. Allan, & K. Fowler-Watt (Eds), *Journalism: New challenges*, pp. 259–81. Poole, UK: Centre for Journalism & Communication Research, Bournemouth University.

Morrison, D. E. (1998). *The search for a method: Focus groups and the development of mass communication research*. Luton, UK: University of Luton Press.

Munshi, D. (1999). Requisitioning variety: Photographic metaphors, ethnocentric lenses, and the divided colours of public relations. *Asia Pacific Public Relations Journal*, 1(1), pp. 39–51.

Munshi, D., & Edwards, L. (2011). Understanding "race" in/and public relations: Where do we start and where should we go? *Journal of Public Relations Research*, 23(4), pp. 349–67.

Munshi, D., & Kurian, P. (2005). Imperializing spin cycles: A postcolonial look at public relations, greenwashing, and the separation of publics. *Public Relations Review*, 31(4), pp. 513–20.

Palmer, J. (2000). *Spinning into control: News values and source strategies*. Leicester, UK: Leicester University Press.

Pompper, D. (2005). "Difference" in public relations research: A case for introducing critical race theory. *Journal of Public Relations Research*, 17(2), pp. 139–69.

Reeves, N. (1999). *Power of film propaganda: Myth or reality?* New York, NY: Continuum.

Roper, J. (2004). Corporate responsibility in New Zealand. *The Journal of Corporate Citizenship*, 14, pp. 22–5.

Roper, J. (2005). Symmetrical communication: Excellent public relations or a strategy for hegemony? *Journal of Public Relations Research*, 17(1), pp. 69–86.

Roper, J. (2012). Environmental risk, sustainability discourses, and public relations. *Public Relation Inquiry*, 1(1), pp. 69–87.

Rushkoff, D. (1998). *Coercion*. New York, NY: Riverhead.

Schlesinger, P. (1989). From production to propaganda. *Media Culture & Society*, 11(3), pp. 283–306.

Schlesinger, P., & Doyle, G. (2014). From organizational crisis to multi-platform salvation? Creative destruction and the recomposition of news media. *Journalism*, First published 12 May, as doi:10.1177/1464884914530223.

Schrøder, K. C. (1989). The playful audience: The continuity of the popular cultural tradition in America. In M. Skovman (Ed.), *Media fictions*. Åarhus, Denmark: Åarhus University Press.

Schrøder, K. C., & Larsen, B. S. (2010). The shifting cross-media news landscape: Challenges for news producers. *Journalism Studies*, 11(4), pp. 524–34.

Sissons, H. (2012). Journalism and public relations: A tale of two discourses. *Discourse and Communication*, 6(1), pp. 273–94.

Somerville, I., & Kirby, S. (2012) Public relations and the Northern Ireland peace process: Dissemination, reconciliation and the "Good Friday Agreement" referendum campaign. *Public Relations Inquiry*, 1(3), pp. 231–55.

Sproule, M. J. (2008). "Communication" from concept to field to discipline. In D. W. Park, & J. Pooley (Eds), *The history of media and communication research: Contested histories*, pp. 163–78. New York, NY: Peter Lang.

Spyridou, L., Matsiola, M., Veglis, A., Kalliris, G., & Charalambos, D. (2013). Journalism in a state of flux: Journalists as agents of technology innovation and emerging news practices. *International Communication Gazette*, 75(1), pp. 75–76.

Strinati, D (2000). *An introduction to studying popular culture*. New York, NY: Routledge.

Surma, A. (2013). *Imagining the cosmopolitan in public and professional writing*. Basingstoke, UK: Palgrave Macmillan.

Sussman, G. (Ed.). (2011). *The propaganda society: Promotional culture and politics in global context*. New York, NY: Peter Lang.

Taylor, P. M. (1999). *British propaganda in the twentieth century: Selling democracy*. Edinburgh, UK: Edinburgh University Press.

Tye, L. (1998). *The father of spin: Edward L. Bernays and the birth of public relations*. New York, NY: Crown Publishers.

Waymer, D. (Ed.). (2012). *Culture, social class, and race in public relations: Perspectives and applications*. Lanham, MD: Lexington Books.

Weaver, C. K. (2010). Carnivalesque activism as a public relations genre: A case study of the New Zealand group Mothers Against Genetic Engineering. *Public Relations Review*, 36(1), pp. 35–41.

Weaver, C. K. (2011). Public relations, globalization, and culture: Framing methodological debates and future directions. In N. Bardhan, & C. K. Weaver (Eds), *Public relations in global contexts: Multi-paradigmatic perspectives*, pp. 250–74. New York, NY: Routledge.

Weaver, C. K. (2013). A history of public relations scholarship in Aotearoa New Zealand: From working on the margins to setting disciplinary agendas. *Prism*, 10(1). Retrieved on 20 April 2015 from http://www.prismjournal.org/fileadmin/10_1/Weaver.pdf

Weaver, C. K. (2014). Mothers, bodies, and breasts: Organising strategies and tactics in women's activism. In C. Daymon, & K Demetrious (Eds), *Gender and public relations: Critical perspectives on voice, image and identity*, pp.108–31. New York, NY: Routledge.

Weaver, C. K., Motion, J., & Roper, J. (2006). From propaganda to discourse (and back again): Truth, power, the public interest and public relations. In J. L'Etang, & M. Pieczka (Eds), *Public relations: Critical debates and contemporary practice*, pp. 7–22. Mahwah, NJ: Lawrence Erlbaum Associates.

White, J., & Hobsbawn, J. (2007). Public relations and journalism. *Journalism Practice*, 1(2), pp. 283–92.

Worrall Redal, W. (2008). Making sense of social change: Studying media and culture in 1960s Britain. In D. W. Park, & J. Pooley (Eds), *The history of media and communication research: Contested histories*, pp. 270–90. New York, NY: Peter Lang.

Wright, D. K. (2011). History and development of public relations education in North America. *Journal of Communication Management*, 15(3), pp. 236–55.

22

The need for critical thinking in country promotion

Public diplomacy, nation branding, and public relations

Alina Dolea

This chapter discusses how countries promote themselves across borders (a phenomenon generically called "country promotion" in this chapter) and aims (1) to review the evolution in conceptualizing country promotion in the literatures of public diplomacy, nation branding, and public relations, (2) to call for exploring further the emergent critical thinking in these literatures and apply it to the study of country promotion, and (3) to illustrate how a critical, social constructivist paradigm can give voice to previously ignored issues (e.g., power relations, structures, and social inequalities).

The interest of scholars and practitioners from political science and international relations (public diplomacy), economics and marketing (nation branding) and communication science (public relations) for the practice of country promotion, as well as for finding concepts and theories to explain the phenomenon, has been constantly augmenting during the twentieth century under the spread of neoliberalism. It reached a climax in the beginning of the twenty-first century, also due to the accelerated development of information technologies, the Internet and social media, those new "battlefields" for "winning the war on hearts and minds" (Nye, 2008). As a result, a variety of specializations and actors emerge in country promotion, previously considered to be the province of governments. The increasing role of culture leads to the coagulation of a consistent corpus dedicated to cultural diplomacy (Mark, 2009); as new actors come into country promotion, new concepts are being formulated, such as media diplomacy (Gilboa, 1998), non-state actor diplomacy (Langhorne, 2005), corporate diplomacy (Henisz, 2014; Ordeix-Rigo & Duarte, 2009), digital diplomacy and public diplomacy 2.0 (Cull, 2013). Although these concepts are new and subject to debate (see Melissen, 2005), they are an indication of how the practice and interdisciplinary thinking about country promotion has recently evolved, especially during the last decade.

The new media and social media offer these newcomers in international politics new opportunities to gain visibility and to emerge as public actors in an attempt to be recognized by states as dialogue partners. As Snow and Taylor (2009) put it:

> whereas public diplomacy in the 20th century emerged from two world wars and a balance of power Cold War framework between the communist East and capitalist West, the 21st

century trend is a post 9/11 environment dominated by fractal globalization, preemptive military invasion, information and communication technologies that shrink time and distance, and the rise of global non-state actors (terror networks, bloggers) that challenge state-driven policy and discourse on the subject

(p. ix)

In research, there remains a predominance of functionalist approaches and a rather positivist and commercial understanding of country promotion, as actors use public diplomacy, nation branding and public relations for competitive advantage in the global neoliberal market. This dominant instrumental view of country promotion has largely ignored the broader social, political and cultural context, as well as important aspects related to the access to resources, existing inequalities and the issue of power. With the global crisis, critical thinking started to (re)gain momentum and offers fertile ground for further exploring the kinds of issues that have been marginalized thus far. It is time to go beyond the prescription of "how to" promote the country, to address instead the hard "why" questions, thus problematizing and contextualizing the phenomenon, its implications and, above all, its impact at social level.

Consequently, this chapter calls for using the emerging critical thinking, the so-called "socio-critical turn" especially prevalent in public relations (e.g., Edwards, 2011, 2012; Ihlen & van Ruler, 2009; L'Etang, 2005;), but also in nation branding (Aronczyk, 2008; Kaneva, 2011a, 2011b) and public diplomacy (Dutta-Bergman, 2006; Snow, 2009) for analysing country promotion. This makes it possible "to define assumptions which are taken for granted with a view to challenging their source and legitimacy" (L'Etang, 2005, p. 521). The Critical Theory School is an interdisciplinary approach that can be used in order to look at country promotion as a social phenomenon, revealing aspects related to power structures and relations, stratification and inequalities that are characteristic for the contemporary society and that cannot be left aside when analysing the phenomenon of country promotion. Building on the key statements of social constructivism (Berger & Luckmann, 1966), the conceptualization of power and discourse of Foucault (1972) and critical discourse analysis (Fairclough, 2001; Wodak, 2001), country promotion can be seen as the social construction of discourses about the country: both as social process (of socially constructing discourses) and as outcome (the discourses themselves) that are subject to power relations within society. Discourses about the country are constructed and reconstructed in time, through the constant interaction and negotiation between various social actors who try to impose their own definitions and interpretations, certain significations and symbols, and even manipulate meanings in order to temporarily impose frames. Ultimately, this chapter illustrates how a critical social constructivist paradigm invites reflection and challenges the domination of the functionalist paradigms in order to give voice to previously neglected issues in the country promotion literature.

Country promotion: a growing preoccupation under neoliberalism

While the preoccupation of states for promoting their images outside borders can be traced to the early history of humankind (Kunczik, 1997), country promotion has gained momentum during the last decades and with the ascent of neoliberalism. Following a transformational twentieth century, the twenty-first century is characterized by a "complex interdependence" (Keohane & Nye, 1972) that redefines the relationships between a variety of actors who are active and have a say in domestic and foreign affairs issues: governments, corporations, non-governmental organizations, activists and media. This "complex interdependence" also redefines society as a whole, theorized as a "network society" (Castells, 2004, 2008) that follows the information age and emphasizes the need of these actors to network and gain visibility in the global arena.

Neoliberalism, with its view of the world as a global marketplace in which not only corporations, but also governments and NGOs all compete, contributed extensively to the emergence of country promotion on these actors' agenda since it augmented their need to be visible. With "the world (i.e. the international system) understood as a large and complex communication network, in which the mass media cannot be treated in isolation" (Kunczik, 1997, p. 12), the various actors go beyond information to seek a competitive advantage in terms of attention and visibility. Their ultimate goal is to impose themes on the international agenda, since media (including social media) have become "key networks and primary sources of messages and images that reach people's minds" (Castells, 2004, p. 3). In this quest, institutional and state actors have adopted strategies and tactics from the business sector in order to become visible, to gain and to preserve a favourable image. In fact, they are competing for symbolic power, which was conceptualized in 1990 as soft power by Nye (2008) or even postmodern power (van Ham, 2008). These generally refer to the changes in international relations and in the relationships between states since military, economic and political power were losing importance against the growing importance of a "good image". While the initial conceptualization of soft power was within the realm of international relations, it spread quickly and infiltrated other domains. Moreover, scholars (e.g., Gilboa, 2008; van Ham, 2008) have started to consider favourable image and reputation among the sources of power traditionally linked to the size of a territory, its population and its wealth of raw materials – the state itself being conceptualized as a "brand state" (van Ham, 2008), a "postmodern state" or a "competition state" (Cerny, 1997, cited in van Ham, 2008).

In fact, these preoccupations for country promotion have followed a constant process of institutionalization throughout the twentieth century, a process that has brought with it much debate about how to understand, conceptualize and research the phenomenon. In addition, the incorporation of new practices from the business sector (public relations, marketing and branding) consecrated the emergence of new professions in society and, consequently, of consistent lines of research and specific fields of study within traditional disciplines: international relations and public diplomacy within political sciences; marketing and branding within economics; and public relations within the communication sciences. The way states and institutions are equipped for the competition going on in the marketplace, and how they can be promoted (more efficiently), became a constant theme of inquiry for both practitioners and scholars. This led to a significant corpus of literature dominated by functionalist approaches meant to describe ideal models of practising the new professions, prescribing roles for practitioners and setting a normative paradigm of how things should be done, in general, and how countries should be promoted, in particular, in an efficient and effective way. The following section discusses in detail how the thinking about country promotion evolved within the new fields of study of public diplomacy, nation branding, and public relations for nations.

Main conceptualizations of country promotion

In diplomacy, the transformation from the traditional approach characterized by official communication between governments, usually behind closed doors, to a new approach labelled "public diplomacy", is considered to have started in the 1920s (Gregory, 2008). Although the term "public diplomacy" has been in use since 1856 (Cull, 2008), it was only in 1965 that Edmund Gullion defined it as dealing with the influence of public attitudes on the formation and execution of foreign policies. It encompasses dimensions of international relations beyond traditional diplomacy; the cultivation by governments of public opinion in other countries; the interaction of private groups and interests in one country with another; the reporting of foreign affairs and its impact on policy; communication between those whose job is communication, as diplomats and foreign correspondents; and the process of intercultural communications.

(p. 19)

While other scholars have also defined it in their studies (e.g., Malone 1985; Tuch 1990), "public diplomacy" does not have a generally accepted definition. There is rather more interest in establishing the variety of activities encompassed by public diplomacy and the actors involved in it. Melissen (2005) introduced the concept of new public diplomacy, pointing to the shift in the activity itself (that moves from promoting positive aspects of a country to foreign publics towards engaging with foreign audiences), but also in the actors that engage in diplomacy.

Melissen (2005) shows the definitions of diplomacy

have either stressed its main purpose ("the art of resolving international difficulties peacefully"), its principal agents ("the conduct of relations between sovereign states through the medium of accredited representatives") or its chief function ("the management of international relations by negotiation"), [therefore,] in a sense, such definitions do not take into account the transformation of the environment in which diplomacy is at work.

(p. 5)

Besides this, in Melissen's opinion the main problem is that defining diplomacy as "the mechanism of representation, communication and negotiation through which states and other international actors conduct their business still suggests a neat international environment consisting of a range of clearly identifiable players" (p. 5). The major transformation in international relations is that diplomacy cannot be seen in the same traditionalist view as a

game where the roles and responsibilities of actors in international relations are clearly delineated, because this picture no longer resembles the much more fuzzy world of postmodern transnational relations – a world, for that matter, in which most actors are not nearly as much in control as they would like to be.

(p. 5)

While there is agreement among both practitioners and scholars that people and publics have come to play a significant role in public diplomacy, a major debate has been articulated on the exact role of these publics and the extent to which they exert it: for some, the transformation in diplomacy is encompassed in the government-to-people equation which is defined as public diplomacy, since states don't only address their peers, but also the publics of their peers. For others, the very role of the key player (the state) is questioned, as scholars basically argue that a variety of actors now can be involved in public diplomacy and that the state loses its supremacy in diplomacy. The state is no longer the sole actor when it comes to public diplomacy – it is just one of many actors, together with nongovernmental organizations, corporations and activists: "the truth is that foreign publics now matter to practitioners of diplomacy in a way that was unthinkable as little as 25 years ago", observes Melissen (2005) in his Introduction (pp. xix-xx). This people-to-people model would define the new public diplomacy that is emerging. The implications for country promotion when it comes to this later approach is that other actors can develop public diplomacy programmes in pursuit of their own agenda, which can be very different to that of the state.

Compared with public diplomacy, cultural diplomacy as a distinct concept and practice has attracted little scholarly attention until recently. Yet it has a long history of intersection with a range of subjects (e.g., diplomacy, national identity, and the Cold War), and has a substantial investment in it by some practitioners. Mark (2009) emphasizes that

> the discipline of International Relations has almost entirely ignored cultural diplomacy and even studies on diplomacy have paid little attention due to the following facts: politicians and diplomats, have, in the main, regarded cultural diplomacy as a lesser tool of diplomacy which in its turn is regarded by some as a lesser tool of foreign policy, the difficulty in determining cultural diplomacy's long term impact on the behavior of audiences, and the lack of clarity about what precisely the practice entails.
>
> *(pp. 2–4)*

Contemporary scholars look more and more to the potential of cultural diplomacy, documenting the practice of public and cultural diplomacy in a given country (Bustamante & Sweig, 2008 – Cuba and Venezuela; Fitzpatrick, 2010 – USA; Ryniejska-Kiełdanowicz, 2008 – Poland; Wang, 2008 – China); or exploring aspects like exchange programmes (Scott-Smith, 2008; Snow, 2008), or international broadcasting (Price, Haas & Margolin, 2008), with a clear domination of US-centric studies.

Reviewing the literature, Glassgold (2004) identifies four distinct stages in the study of public diplomacy and the main ideas corresponding to each stage. Her study is valuable in reflecting upon the evolutions in public diplomacy – starting with the 1960s when the concept was coined, and continuing up to the present. Glassgold (2004) distinguishes between: (1) the early research period – the 1960s – when "John Lee and Arthur Hoffman recognized the emergence of public diplomacy due to mass communication that makes people-to-people dialogues more important than the communication between governments" (p. 2); (2) the late 1970s to the late 1980s, which comprised studies such as Abshire's (1976) and Adelman's (1981), "focused on US public diplomacy analyzing the management of public diplomacy, its content and direction and its integration within US foreign policy" (Glassgold, 2004, p. 3); (3) the late 1980s to the mid-1990s when scholars and practitioners (e.g. Fisher, 1987; Hansen, 1989; Malone, 1988; Manheim, 1994) "devoted more systematic attention to the relationship between communication and public diplomacy than previously" and "the focus shifted to administration, foreign public opinion, communication technology" (Glassgold, 2004, p. 6); (4) after 9/11, scholars (e.g. Brown, 2002; Campbell & Flournoy, 2001; Hachten & Scotton, 2002; Price, 2002) conducted "studies focused heavily on the role of media, radio and TV networks in public diplomacy and especially on the US public diplomacy" (Glassgold, 2004, p. 21). The changes occurring in public diplomacy are clearly traced in this chronology that shows how the emergence of new actors and the increasing role of media and international broadcasting have shaped the practice: from a government-to-government approach there has been a transition towards a government-to-people and even a people-to-people approach. Most studies reflecting on these evolutions are rather normative, describing how public diplomacy should ideally be, and how practitioners can improve their practice. Therefore, the dominant approach in research falls into a functionalist paradigm since it is meant to identify better instruments for crafting messages and to furnish solutions for improving the practice in general, drawing heavily on the (new) roles of practitioners.

In a similar way, the history of conceptualizing nation branding starts before the coining of the concept itself: the country-of-origin effect was formulated at the beginning of the 1960s from a classical marketing perspective to investigate the relationship between a product and its place of origin. Starting in the second half of the 1960s, the literature on country-of-origin (COO) effect flourished, several studies were published, and the definitions also evolved to include not only products but also services: "the effect that a product or service's origin has on consumer attitudes and behavior towards that product or service" (Dinnie, 2008, 84). The growing interest of researchers in this topic is confirmed by the number of materials published: Zeugner-Roth and Diamantopoulos (2009) quote a review of Usunier (2006) that estimates the number of publications relating to COO at well over 1,000.

During the period of the 1970s to the 1990s, studies focused on country images and consumer buying decisions from a similar marketing perspective. Zeugner-Roth and Diamantopoulos (2009) point out a predominance of cognitive approaches on the image of countries, while the affective component is rather little researched. After 1990, place marketing emerged as a new area of investigation within the field of study of marketing, starting from the idea that "places" can be strategically marketed. The works of Kotler (1993), and Kotler and Gertner (2002), are considered to be the major place marketing texts; they originate from traditional marketing, and include a combination of best practices and theoretical discussion.

Once the term "nation brand" was coined in the 1990s, more studies were dedicated to how nation branding and place branding work, and to furnish solutions for better and more efficient "branding" of places. The focus of academics and practitioners was to clearly distinguish between marketing places and branding places, to explain why there is a need for them, and to describe how they function and what benefits they bring. Olins (1999, 2004, 2005) and Anholt (2002, 2004, 2007, 2010) both noticed the considerable reluctance with which the idea of nation as a brand was first received: putting together the term "nation" that stands for statecraft and is deeply rooted in the traditional discipline of political science, and the term "brand" that emerges from a new and sometimes misunderstood field of study deriving from marketing, was in the 1990s almost inconceivable. This added to the difficulty of conceptualizing nation branding. Moreover, the focus of Anholt and Olins on positioning and legitimizing nation branding as a new area of study led to an emphasis in the literature on description (of the global context, manifestation and practice of nation branding) and efficiency (of branding when applied to nations). Authors underlined more the need for nation branding, rather than defining what, exactly, nation branding is. They based their entire argumentation on the neoliberal assumption that the world has changed and is now a global market in which several actors compete for more than just political power. They conceive this new reality as a datum and therefore follow a rather normative approach. In this context the critics of nation branding appeared, all the more so since nation branding itself had both soft and hard conceptualizations: while some authors consider it an instrument or tool of strategic management, others go much further and assume it to be an art of statecraft. Anholt (2007) recommended replacing the concept of nation branding with the concept of "competitive identity" – because "branding [itself] has a bad brand" (p. 3).

Despite the debates on the theory and practice of nation branding over the last 15 years since it was officially coined, nation branding has followed a quick process of institutionalization. As noted by Kaneva (2011b), Anholt is "the most prolific author on the subject" and one who made "efforts to institutionalize it as an academic field with scientific legitimacy" (p. 117); but Szondi (2010) considers that he abandoned his brainchild before it had the chance to reach maturity.

Tracing the public relations history of investigating the promotion of countries and national images, Grunig (1993) argues that "although concern about the effects and ethics of international public relations activities seems to be recent, public relations firms and counselors have been working for governments and other international organizations at least throughout this century" (p. 149). Some of the authors investigating the use of public relations in country promotion preferred to use the term "international public relations" because of the international dimension of the communication process between countries. Signitzer and Coombs (1992) define international public relations as "the planned and organized effort of a company, institution or government to establish mutually beneficial relations with the publics of other nations" (p. 137). Kunczik (1997) also prefers international public relations and international image cultivation, considering "public relations between nations…is arguably the most difficult of all public relations work" (p. 2).

In contrast to public diplomacy and nation branding, public relations scholars chose to explore the convergence and differences between public relations for nations and public diplomacy (e.g., Fitzpatrick, 2007; Grunig, 1993; L'Etang, 1996, 2009; Signitzer & Coombs, 1992; Signitzer & Wamser, 2006; van Dyke & Verčič, 2009), of public relations for nations and nation branding (Szondi, 2010), and of public diplomacy and nation branding (Szondi, 2008b); or in formulating a theoretical framework that integrates public diplomacy, nation branding, and public relations (Szondi, 2008a; Buhmann & Ingenhoff, 2013). It is within public relations that the interdisciplinary approach to country promotion emerged as a consistent line of research in current literature.

Other categories of studies include: historical accounts of international image cultivation by governments (Kunczik, 1997, 2003a); empirical studies on the use of Grunig's public relations model to public diplomacy, using the technique of interviews (Yun, 2006); empirical studies on the use of public relations and the role of media in promoting certain messages and images about specific countries, with two distinct lines of research: (1) some scholars (Albritton & Manheim, 1985; Kunczik, 2000, 2003b; Lee, 2006, 2007) applied mass media theories such as cultivation, agenda-setting and theories of image management to investigate how certain images of nations are promoted to other audiences and focus, in the case of Kunczik, also on the further effects they have in society. These studies employed mainly quantitative methods, especially content analysis, and focused on the media relations component of public relations; (2) Other scholars (Drumheller & Benoit, 2004; J. Zhang & Benoit, 2004; E. Zhang & Benoit, 2009; Peijuan, Ting & Pang, 2009) conducted studies on international incidents and crises using discourse analysis and building on the theory of image repair discourse. Such studies bring a qualitative approach to analyzing media coverage, conceiving it as discourse – not merely a quantitative result of public relations activity, but also considering various actors and a plurality of voices and not just one single actor. They would also reveal the dynamic of the process of image repairing.

While focusing on the same practices of country promotion, the research in public diplomacy, nation branding, and public relations has developed along parallel lines: it mainly used concepts and theories from their "mother" disciplines, with little in the way of an interdisciplinary approach, which ultimately impacted on methodologies and on imposing a certain limited and determinist way of thinking about country promotion.

A cha(lle)nging context: emergent critical thinking

During the past years there has been a (re)emergence of critical thinking in reaction to the latest social developments and also to the global crisis that spilled beyond economic and political arenas, impacting also the scientific world. As a consequence, there are theories that question the established political and economic models, policies and systems (e.g., Couldry, 2010). It seems as if the economic crisis has led somehow also to a crisis in knowledge and science, since scholars have started to question the existing paradigms and rethink analytical criteria, methodologies and so on.

The auto reflexivity turn within the scientific community impacts also the new fields of study (such as public diplomacy, branding, public relations), with approaches from critical studies and sociology recently starting to coagulate. These approaches critically discuss, among other things, the existence of a "promotional culture" (Wernick, 1991), which includes all the "promotional" practices (e.g., public relations, branding, public diplomacy) that ultimately serve the purposes of those organizations and actors that hold power in society. The focus of scholars embracing such perspectives is more on how these new conceptualizations and practices impact upon society and democracy. The focus on the effects and impact that public relations, branding and public diplomacy have in society has come to complement the functionalist perspectives with their emphasis on instrumentalism and efficiency. Therefore, scholars discuss public space and the public sphere, and not only in relation to the market but also in relation to democracy and social actors.

From describing and prescribing, public relations has moved its focus towards reflexivity and interpretation. The implication of these evolutions for the study of country promotion resides in looking at the phenomenon from a more nuanced perspective that is ultimately reflected in methodologies: "understanding public relations in its societal context entails a focus on such concepts as trust, legitimacy, understanding, and reflection, as well as on issues of power, behavior, and language" (Ihlen & van Ruler, 2009, p. 8). Critical scholarship (e.g., L'Etang, 2005, 2009) brings forward issues of power and can explore how the public relations of a specific country is used as a resource by its government to promote its image, how it is understood and defined by the actors employing it, and what its impact and effects are in that society.

Dutta-Bergman (2006) also formulated a culture-centred approach to public diplomacy as an alternative to the traditional one-way models, while the new emerging approaches from sociology (e.g. Castells, 2008; Yun & Toth, 2009) and media studies (e.g., Entman, 2008) challenge the insularity of the concept. For Castells (2008), a sociological conceptualization of public diplomacy

> contributes to the building of the global public sphere in which diverse voices can be heard in spite of their various origins, distinct values, and often contradictory interests…the goal of public diplomacy, in contrast to government diplomacy, is not to assert power or to negotiate a rearrangement of power relationships…it is to induce a communication space in which a new, common language could emerge as a precondition for diplomacy, so that when the time for diplomacy comes, it reflects not only interests and power making but also meaning and sharing.
>
> (p. 91)

These new arguments open, in fact, a new line of research on public diplomacy since it has become too complex a concept to be reflected upon through the "lens" of a single discipline. New fields of study (e.g., public relations, place branding) have developed various theoretical and methodological approaches. Newer conceptualizations of diplomacy reveal this new trend, as the focus shifts from the functionalist approaches towards a sociological perspective that reflects on the process itself, its dynamics, and the role of public diplomacy in society.

In the nation branding literature, scholars (e.g., Dinnie, 2008) now look at the importance of national identity issues that were previously ignored, and more scholars from other fields (e.g., cultural studies) are questioning the practices of country promotion: "nation branding promotes a particular organization of power, knowledge and exchange in the articulation of collective identity" and "intends to show, [that] culture – as category, discourse, and reproductive practice – continues to matter for the ways in which value, meaning and self-understanding are made" (Aronczyk, 2008, p. 46). In fact, cultural studies open a new line of research (Kaneva 2009, 2011b; Kaneva & Popescu, 2011 Volcic, 2008; Volcic & Andrejevic, 2011) that focuses mainly on formulating a critique to nation branding and its implications for the representation of national identity: "nation branding as a discourse privileges the logic of value exchange, while concealing alternative possibilities for narrating the nation" (Kaneva, 2011a, p. 12). These studies question "the imputed equivalence of global marketization and democratization, by connecting the discourse of nation branding to constructivist ideas of nationhood, and by historicizing the texts and practices of nation branding and exposing their linkage to relations of social power" (Kaneva, 2011b, p. 128).

Conclusion

Current research on country promotion has mainly focused either on conceptual convergences or on answering "how to" questions. Accordingly, critical thinking needs to be explored and further used in country promotion to extend the frames of reference and the ways of reflecting about country promotion: they can bring forward new perspectives and critically discuss "the other side of the coin" in country promotion. Consequently, the very object of research, changes: it is not reduced anymore to the communication products and campaigns, but is extended to include their context, the conditions of their production, the types of discourses they embody, and how these are perceived and debated within society. These open perspectives and levels such as: (1) the relationship between countries in certain political contexts and the "quest" for a good image and to "be seen" as eligible and trustworthy so as to gain important positions within international organizations. This process has ended up generating and/or deepening unequal positions, since it takes the expenditure of consistent levels of resources to keep "performing" in this global competition; (2) the type of discourses and visions about the country that governments have gradually come to assume in order to fulfil certain expectancies and construct an imaginary that correspond to what the global "eyes" want to see. Therefore, governments have come to promote external projections and even stereotyped images that might not be fully covered by the reality existing within the country; (3) the use of government's powerful status in society in order to impose certain discourses about the country has had internal effects that have dominated the public agenda. Thus, other social actors and their alternative discourses about the country have been marginalized, or even excluded, in the government's quest for promoting internationally "competitive" images about the country.

Missing so far from the literature dedicated to country promotion is a critical analysis focusing on the internal debates taking place within the countries about governments' initiatives concerning country promotion. I would argue that a constructivist paradigm would be particularly useful for the study of country promotion at the internal level, as governments become but one of the social actors which contribute to the construction process of country promotion. In addition, constructivism brings forward aspects related to the historicity of a communication process, its dynamics, the interplay and the constant negotiation between a variety of social actors involved in the process; and can thus illustrate how, in particular socio-historical contexts, certain social actors with different power resources and positions interact, construct and reconstruct established significations and practices, and negotiate and manipulate meanings in order to temporarily impose frames. Moreover, a constructivist research paradigm gives researchers in country promotion the liberty to use a wider diversity of complementary methodological instruments ranging from critical discourse analysis, pragmatics and rhetoric studies to content analysis of social documents, interviews or focus groups.

Building on the key statements of constructivism, on Foucault's (1972) idea that "in every society the production of discourse is at once controlled, selected, organized, and redistributed according to a certain number of procedures" (p. 216), and on critical discourse analysis with its focus on the relationships between discouses, power and social structures, country promotion can be ultimately conceptualized as the social construction of discourses about the country. Therefore, country promotion is seen both as social process (of socially constructing discourses) and as outcome (the discourses themselves) that are subject to power relations within society. Within this framework, it is possible to address power relations in country promotion with such questions as: why do countries come to engage in country promotion? Is the theme on the agenda of the state? In this case, how did this theme come to be a priority on the government's agenda? Is it also on the agenda of other social actors in that society? Or is it a public issue that concerns the entire society? Did it lead to the emergence of new institutional structures? Ultimately, are social actors imposing dominant and, even, counter discourses about the country?

In a social constructivist and interdisciplinary approach, country promotion is conceptualized as a dynamic social process with two distinct phases: one internal – within the nation, which was often neglected; one external – communicating and engaging with foreign audiences. In the internal phase, several social actors contribute to the construction of what is representative about their nation and their national identity: they construct their own definitions about the country, try to dislocate existing significations in society and to impose others in constant negotiation and interaction with each other. This leads to a social construction of country promotion, while the typification of practices related to country promotion leads eventually to institutionalization. In the external phase of country promotion, the final products – the campaigns aimed at foreign audiences – are considered to stand for a temporarily imposed definition about the country. However, the external phase does not necessarily follow the internal phase, as in an ideal setting: on the contrary, there are internal debates that emerge within the society after governments have launched campaigns, thus making use of their position to impose a discourse and vision about the country that does not necessarily reflect its national or cultural identity.

A social constructivist and interdisciplinary approach for the study of country promotion continues research initiated by public relations scholars (e.g., Szondi, 2008a, 2008b, 2010; L'Etang, 2009), the constructivist perspectives introduced in both public relations (e.g., Bentele, 2008), and public diplomacy from the perspective of international relations (e.g., van Ham, 2008). Elements of constructivism are also included in the critical approaches to nation branding (e.g., Kaneva & Popescu, 2011), but these scholars focus exclusively on nation branding as ideology and a type of discourse, and not on the entire process of country promotion. Building on all these approaches, a social constructivist and interdisciplinary one not only develops existing research, but also fills a consistent gap in the literature investigating the issue of country promotion: it takes a step forward and bridges the constructivist and the interdisciplinary approaches that allow the analysis of the entire process of country promotion – the internal debate about what is representative for the nation and the external communication campaigns aimed at foreign audiences.

Such an approach can be useful also for carrying out comparative studies, investigating how various countries have come to engage in country promotion and whether there are differences between "consolidated" and "new" democracies. It seems in post-communist countries, the topic of country promotion became a public issue as part of the national identity reconstruction process, while in Western countries this appears to be a theme on the specialized agenda of the experts in communication and branding or on the agenda of the governments. Therefore, the following questions arise: is country promotion a public issue only in post-communist countries due to their transition and redefinition of national identity (dominant questions in the public space – who are we as a nation and what are our values?), while in consolidated democracies there are only "expert" debates between specialists and officials that don't reach the public agenda because the "identity issue" already gained a social consensus?; or is country promotion also a public issue in consolidated democracies, but one which generates other types of discourse?

Moving the focus of analysis from the communication campaigns and the dominant functionalist perspective in current literature to a more profound understanding of country promotion as a social construction and a product of a national society, the constructivist and interdisciplinary approach privileges the multiplicity of voices that can be expressed and the symbolic negotiation of competing definitions placed in the public debate.

This approach opens new paths for thinking and analyzing country promotion beyond specific concepts that have become mere labels and ultimately ended up narrowing the research horizon of scholars. Raising more questions than answers, this approach allows researchers to look at the phenomenon itself and to question it, without the constraints of having to, a priori, integrate their inquiry within a particular literature (be it public relations, public diplomacy, or nation branding). Thus, they can explore new methodologies and concepts beyond the disciplines that have traditionally studied the efforts of countries to promote themselves across borders. Complementary to the predominant positivist, technical and instrumental view of the topic, the constructivist and interdisciplinary approach offers a dynamic, social-centred view of this complex and interdependent process and can, ultimately, advance the study of country promotion.

Acknowledgement

This work was supported by a grant from the Romanian National Authority for Scientific Research, CNCS – UEFISCDI, project number PN-II-ID-PCE-2011-3-0968, *Diaspora in the Romanian Media and Political Sphere: From Event to the Social Construction of Public Issues* (project coordinator: Professor Camelia Beciu).

References:

Abshire, D. M. (1976). *International broadcasting: A new dimension of Western diplomacy*. Beverly Hills, CA: Sage.

Adelman, K. L. (1981). Speaking of America: Public diplomacy in our time. *Foreign Affairs*, 59, pp: 913–36.

Albritton, R. B., & Manheim, J. B. (1985). Public relations efforts for the Third World: Images in the news. *Journal of Communication*, 35, pp. 43–59.

Anholt, S. (2002). Foreword. *Journal of Brand Management*, 9(4–5), pp. 229–39.

Anholt, S. (2004). Nation-brands and the value of provenance. In N. Morgan, A. Pritchard, & R. Pride (Eds), *Destination branding: Creating the unique destination proposition*, 2nd edition, pp. 26–39. Burlington, MA: Elsevier.

Anholt, S. (2006). Editorial. Public diplomacy and place branding: Where's the link? *Place Branding*, 2, pp. 271–5.

Anholt, S. (2007). *Competitive identity: The new brand management for nations, cities and regions*. New York, NY: Palgrave Macmillan.

Anholt, S. (2010). *Places, identity, image and reputation*. New York, NY: Palgrave Macmillan.

Aronczyk, M. (2008). "Living the Brand": Nationality, globality and the identity strategies of nation branding consultants. *International Journal of Communication*, 2, pp. 41–65.

Bentele, G. (2004). New perspectives of public relations in Europe. In B. van Ruler, & D. Verčič (Eds), *Public relations and communication management in Europe*, pp. 485–96. Berlin, Germany: Mouton de Gruyter.

Bentele, G. (2008). Public relations theory: The reconstructive approach. In A. Zerfass, B. van Ruler, & K. Sriramesh (Eds), *Public relations research: European and international perspectives*, pp. 19–31. Wiesbaden, Germany: Springer.

Bentele, G., & Wehmeier, S. (2007). Applying sociology to public relations: A commentary. *Public Relations Review*, 33, pp. 294–300.

Bentele, G., & Wehmeier, S. (2008). Commentary: Linking sociology with public relations. Some critical reflections in reflexive times. In Ø. Ihlen, B. van Ruler, & M. Fredriksson (Eds), *Public relations and social theory*, pp. 341–62. New York, NY: Routledge.

Berger, P., & Luckmann, T. (1966). *The social construction of reality: A treatise in the sociology of knowledge*. Garden City, NY: Doubleday.

Botan, C., & Taylor, M. (2004). Public relations: State of the field. *Journal of Communication*, 54(4), pp. 645–61.

Brown, J. (2002). *The purposes and cross-purposes of American public diplomacy*. Chapel Hill, NC: American Diplomacy Publishers.

Buhmann, A., & Ingenhoff, D. (2013). Advancing the country image construct from a public relations perspective. European Public Relations Education and Research Association Annual Congress (EUPRERA) Annual Conference. Strategic Public Relations. Public Values and Cultural Identity. October 3–5, 2013, Barcelona.

Bustamante, M., & Sweig, J. E. (2008). Buena vista solidarity and the axis of aid: Cuban and Venezuelan public diplomacy. *The Annals of the American Academy of Political and Social Science*, 616(1), pp. 223–56.

Campbell, K. M., & Flournoy, M. A. (2001). *To prevail: An American strategy for the campaign against terrorism*. Washington DC: The CSIS Press.

Castells, M. (2004). Informationalism, networks, and the network society: A theoretical blueprint. In M. Castells (Ed.), *The network society: A cross-cultural perspective*, pp. 3–45. Boston, MA: Edward Elgar.

Castells, M. (2008). The new public sphere: Global civil society, communication networks, and global governance. *The Annals of the American Academy of Political and Social Science*, 616(1), pp. 78–93.

Cerny, P. G. 1997. Paradoxes of the competition state: The dynamics of political globalization. *Government and Opposition* 32(2), pp. 251–74.

Couldry, N. (2010). *Why voice matters: Culture and politics after neoliberalism*. London, UK: Sage Publications.

Cowan, G., & Arsenault, A. (2008). Moving from monologue to dialogue to collaboration: The three layers of public diplomacy. *The Annals of the American Academy of Political and Social Science*, 616(1), pp. 10–30.

Cull, N. J. (2008). "Public diplomacy" before Gullion: The evolution of a phrase. In N. Snow, & P. M. Taylor (Eds), *Routledge handbook of public diplomacy*, pp. 19–23. London, UK: Routledge.

Cull, N. J. (2013). The long road to public diplomacy 2.0: The Internet in U.S. public diplomacy. *International Studies Review*, 15(1), pp. 123–39.

Der Derian, J. (2009). *Critical practices in international theory. Selected essays*. Abingdon, UK: Routledge.

Dinnie, K. (2008). *Nation branding: Concepts, issues, practice*. Oxford, UK: Butterworth Heinemann Dutton.

Drumheller, K., & Benoit W. L. (2004). USS Greeneville collides with Japan's Ehime Maru: Cultural issues in image repair discourse. *Public Relations Review*, 30, pp. 177–85.

Dutta-Bergman, M. (2006). U.S. public diplomacy in the Middle East: A critical cultural approach. *Journal of Communication Inquiry*, 30(2), pp. 102–24.

Edwards, L. (2011). Defining the "object" of public relations research: A new starting point. *Public Relations Inquiry*, 1(1), pp. 7–30.

Edwards, L. (2012). Looking for the needle of public relations in a disciplinary haystack. Unpublished presentation at Barcelona Meeting #2: International Conference on Social E-Xperiences 2012, Barcelona, July 2012.

Entman, R. M. (2008). Theorizing mediated public diplomacy: The U.S. case. *Press/Politics*, 13(2), pp. 87–102.

Fairclough, N. (2001). Critical discourse analysis as a method in social scientific research. In R. Wodak, & M. Meyer (Eds), *Methods of critical discourse analysis*, pp. 121–38. London: Sage Publications.

Fisher, G. (1987). *American communication in a global society*, revised edition. New York: Praeger.

Fitzpatrick, K. (2007). Advancing the new public diplomacy: A public relations perspective. *The Hague Journal of Diplomacy*, 2(3), pp. 187–211.

Fitzpatrick, K. (2010). U.S. Public Diplomacy's Neglected Domestic Mandate. *CPD Perspectives on Public Diplomacy*, Los Angeles: Figueroa Press. Retrieved on 10 January 2013 from http://uscpublicdiplomacy.org/sites/uscpublicdiplomacy.org/files/legacy/publications/perspectives/CPDPerspectivesNeglectedMandate.pdf

Foucault, M. (1972). *The archaeology of knowledge*. London, UK: Routledge.

Gilboa, E. (1998). Media diplomacy: Conceptual divergence and applications. *International Journal of Press/Politics*, 3(3), pp. 56–75.

Gilboa, E. (2008). Searching for a theory of public diplomacy. *The Annals of the American Academy of Political and Social Science*, 616(1), pp. 55–77.

Glassgold, S., M. (2004). *Public diplomacy: The evolution of literature*. Thesis. USC Annenberg School of Communication. Retrieved on 7 October 2009 from http://uscpublicdiplomacy.org/pdfs/Stacy_Literature.pdf

Gregory, B. (2008). Public diplomacy: Sunrise of an academic field. *The Annals of the American Academy of Political and Social Science*, 616(1), pp. 274–90.

Grunig, J. E. (1993). Public relations and international affairs: Effects, ethics and responsibility. *Journal of International Affairs*, 47(1), pp. 137–61.

Hachten, W. & Scotton, J. F. (2002). *The world news prism: Global media in an era of terrorism*. Ames: Iowa State Press.

Hansen, A. C. (1989). *USIA: Public diplomacy in the computer age*. New York: Praeger.

Henisz, W. (2014). *Corporate diplomacy: Building reputations and relationships with external stakeholders*. Sheffield, UK: Greenleaf.

Ihlen, Ø., & van Ruler, B. (2009). Introduction: Applying social theory to public relations. In Ø. Ihlen, B. van Ruler, & M. Fredriksson (Eds) *Public relations and social theory*, pp. 1–20. New York, NY: Routledge.

Kaneva, N. (2009). *Critical reflections on nation branding as discourse and practice*. Paper presented at the International Conference, Images of Nations: Strategic Communication, Soft Power and the Media, Athens, Greece.

Kaneva, N. (2011a). Nation branding in post-communist Europe: Identities, markets, and democracy. In N. Kaneva (Ed.), *Branding post-communist nations. Marketizing national identities in the new Europe*, pp. 3–22. New York, NY: Routledge.

Kaneva, N. (2011b). Nation branding: Toward an agenda for critical research. *International Journal of Communication*, 5, pp. 117–41.

Kaneva, N., & Popescu, D. (2011). National identity lite: Nation branding in post-communist Romania and Bulgaria. *International Journal of Cultural Studies*, 14(2), pp. 191–207.

Keohane, R., & Nye, J. (1972). *Transnational relations and world politics*. Cambridge, MA: Harvard University Press.

Kotler, P. (1993). The major tasks of marketing management. *Marketing Management*, 2(3), pp. 52–6.

Kotler, P., & Gertner, D. (2002). Country as brand, product, and beyond: A place marketing and brand management perspective. *The Journal of Brand Management*, 9(4–5), pp. 249–61.

Kunczik, M. (1997). *Images of nations and international public relations*. Mahwah, NJ: Lawrence Erlbaum.

Kunczik, M. (2000). *Globalization: News media, images of nations and the flow of international capital with special reference to the role of rating agencies*. Paper presented at the IAMCR Conference, Singapore, 17–20 July 2000. Retrieved on 3 January 2013 from http://www.giga-hamburg.de/content/publikationen/archiv/duei_arbeitspapiere/ap_04_0102.pdf

Kunczik, M. (2003a). Transnational public relations by foreign governments. In K. Sriramesh, & D. Verčič (Eds), *The global public relations handbook. Theory, research, and practice*, pp. 399–424. Mahwah, NJ: Lawrence Erlbaum Associates.

Kunczik, M. (2003b). *The image of India in German schoolbooks. An explorative study of textbooks in geography, religion, German lessons and history*. Paper presented at the ICA Conference.

Langhorne, R. (2005). The diplomacy of non-state actors. *Diplomacy and Statecraft*, 16, pp. 331–9.

Lee, S. (2006). An analysis of other countries' international public relations in the U.S. *Public Relations Review*, 32, pp. 97–103.

Lee, S. (2007). International public relations as a predictor of prominence of US news coverage. *Public Relations Review*, 33, pp. 158–65.

Leong, P., & Sriramesh, K. (2006). Romancing Singapore: When yesterday's success becomes today's challenge. *Public Relations Review*, 32, pp. 246–53.

L'Etang, J. (1996). Public relations as diplomacy. In J. L'Etang, & M. Pieczka (Eds), *Critical perspective in public relations*, pp. 14–34. London, UK: International Thomson Business Press.

L'Etang, J. (2005). Critical public relations: Some reflections. *Public Relations Review*, 31, pp. 521–6.

L'Etang, J. (2009). Public relations and diplomacy in a globalized world: An issue of public communication. *American Behavioral Scientist*, 53(4), pp. 607–26.

Malone, G. (1985). Managing public diplomacy. *Washington Quarterly*, 8(3), pp. 199–213.

Malone, G. (1988). Political advocacy and cultural communication: Organizing the nation's public diplomacy. Lanham, MD: University Press of America.

Manheim, J. B. (1994). Strategic public diplomacy and American foreign policy: The evolution of influence. Oxford: Oxford University Press.

Mark, S. (2009). A greater role for cultural diplomacy. Netherlands Institute of International Relations (Clingendael). Discussion Papers in Diplomacy, 114. Retrieved on 23 August 2012 from http://www.clingendael.nl/sites/default/files/20090616_cdsp_discussion_paper_114_mark.pdf

Melissen, J. (2005). The new public diplomacy: Between theory and practice. In J. Melissen (Ed.), *The new public diplomacy: Soft power in international relations*, pp. 3–27. New York, NY: Palgrave Macmillan.

Nye, J. S. Jr. (2008). Public diplomacy and soft power. *The Annals of the American Academy of Political and Social Science*, 616(1), pp. 94–109.

Olins, W. (1999) *Trading identities: Why countries and companies are taking on each others' roles*. London, UK: Foreign Policy Centre.

Olins, W. (2004). Branding the nation: The historical context. In N. Morgan, A. Pritchard, & R. Pride (Eds), *Destination branding: Creating the unique destination proposition*, 2nd edition, pp. 17–25. Oxford, UK: Elsevier.

Olins, W. (2005). Making a national brand. In J. Melissen (Ed.), *The new public diplomacy. Soft power in international relations*, pp: 169–79. New York, NY: Palgrave Macmillan.

Ordeix-Rigo, E., & Duarte, J. (2009). From public diplomacy to corporate diplomacy: Increasing corporation's legitimacy and influence. *American Behavioral Scientist*, 53(4), pp. 549–64.

Peijuan, C., Ting, L. P., & Pang, A. (2009). Managing a nation's image during crisis: A study of the Chinese government's image repair efforts in the "Made in China" controversy. *Public Relations Review*, 35, pp. 213–218.

Price, M.E., Haas, S., & Margolin, D. (2008). New technologies and international broadcasting: Reflections on adaptations and transformations. *The Annals of the American Academy of Political and Social Science*, 616(1), pp. 150–72.

Ryniejska-Kiełdanowicz, M. (2008). *Cultural diplomacy as a form of international communication*. Paper presented at the 16th BledCom International Public Relations Symposium, 3–4 July 2009, Bled, Slovenia. Retrieved 13 June 2012 from http://www.instituteforpr.org/wp-content/uploads/Ryniejska_Kieldanowicz.pd

Scott-Smith, G. (2008). Mapping the undefinable: Some thoughts on the relevance of exchange programs within international relations theory. *The Annals of the American Academy of Political and Social Science*, 616(1), pp. 173–95.

Signitzer, B., & Coombs, T. (1992). Public relations and public diplomacy: Conceptual convergences. *Public Relations Review*, 18(2), pp. 137–48.

Signitzer, B., & Wamser, C. (2006). Public diplomacy: A specific governmental public relations function. In C. Botan, & V. Hazleton (Eds), *Public relations theory II*, pp. 435–64. Mahwah, NJ: Lawrence Erlbaum.

Snow, N. (2008). International exchanges and the U.S. image. *The Annals of the American Academy of Political and Social Science*, 616(1), pp. 198–222.

Snow, N, (2009). Rethinking public diplomacy. In N. Snow, & P. M. Taylor (Eds), *Routledge handbook of public diplomacy*, pp. 3–11. London, UK: Routledge.

Snow, N., & Taylor, P. M. (2009). Preface and introduction. In N. Snow, & P. M. Taylor (Eds), *Routledge handbook of public diplomacy*, pp: ix–xi. London, UK: Routledge.

Szondi, G. (2008a). Central and Eastern European public diplomacy. In N. Snow, & P. M. Taylor (Eds), *Routledge handbook of public diplomacy*, pp. 292–313. London, UK: Routledge.

Szondi, G. (2008b). *Public diplomacy and nation branding: Conceptual similarities and differences*. Netherlands Institute of International Relations (Clingendael). Discussion Papers in Diplomacy, 112.

Szondi, G. (2010). From image management to relationship building: A public relations approach to nation branding. *Place Branding and Public Diplomacy*, 6(4), pp. 333–43.

Taylor, M., & Kent, M. (2006). Public relations theory and practice in nation building. In C. Botan, & V. Hazleton (Eds), *Public relations theory II*, pp. 341–59). Mahwah, NJ: Lawrence Erlbaum.

Toth, E. (2009). The case for pluralistic studies in public relations: Rhetorical, critical, and excellence perspectives. In R. Heath, E. Toth, & D. Waymer (Eds), *Rhetorical and critical approaches to public relations II*, pp. 48–60. New York, NY: Routledge.

Tuch, H. (1990). *Communicating with the world: US public diplomacy overseas*. New York, NY: St. Martin's.

Usunier, J. C. (2006). Relevance in business research: The case of country-of-origin research in marketing. *European Management Review*, 3(2), pp. 60–73.

van Dyke, M. A., & Verčič, D. (2009). Public relations, public diplomacy, and strategic communication: an international model of conceptual convergence. In K. Sriramesh, & D. Verčič (Eds), *The global public relations handbook. Theory, research, and practice*, pp: 822–42. Mahwah, NJ: Lawrence Erlbaum Associates.

van Ham, P. (2008). Place branding: The state of the art. *The Annals of the American Academy of Political and Social Science*, 616(1), pp. 126–49.

Volcic, Z. (2008). Former Yugoslavia on the world wide web. Commercialization and branding of nation-states. *The International Communication Gazette*, 70(5), pp. 395–413.

Volcic, Z., & Andrejevic, M. (2011). Nation branding in the era of commercial nationalism. *International Journal of Communication*, 5(1), pp. 598–618.

Wang, Y. (2008). Public diplomacy and the rise of Chinese soft power. *The Annals of the American Academy of Political and Social Science*, 616(1), pp. 257–73.

Wernick, A. (1991). *Promotional culture: Advertising, ideology, and symbolic expression*. London, UK: Sage.

Wodak, R. (2001). What CDA is about – a summary of its history, important concepts and its developments. In R. Wodak, & M. Meyer (Eds), *Methods of critical discourse analysis*, pp. 1–13. London, UK: Sage Publications.

Yun, S. H. (2006). Toward public relations theory-based study of public diplomacy: Testing the applicability of the excellence study. *Journal of Public Relations Research*, 18(4), pp. 287–312.

Yun, S.-H., & Toth, E. (2009). Future sociological public diplomacy and the role of public relations: Evolution of public diplomacy. *American Behavioral Scientist*, 53(4), pp. 493–503.

Zeugner-Roth, K. P., & Diamantopoulos, A. (2009). Advancing the country image construct. *Journal of Business Research*, 62(7), pp. 726–40.

Zhang, J., & Benoit W. L. (2004). Message strategies of Saudi Arabia's image restoration campaign after 9/11. *Public Relations Review*, 30, pp. 161–7.

Zhang, E., & Benoit, W. L. (2009). Former Minister Zhang's discourse on SARS: Government's image restoration or destruction? *Public Relations Review*, 35, pp. 240–6.

Zhang, J. (2006). Public diplomacy as symbolic interactions: A case study of Asian tsunami relief campaigns. *Public Relations Review*, 32, pp. 26–32.

23

Critical race and public relations

The case of environmental racism and risk bearer agency

Damion Waymer and Robert L. Heath

What would the discipline of public relations look like if "race" was placed at the center of research inquiry, design, and execution? This chapter is our effort to provide a thoughtful, reflective response to this guiding question. In so doing we begin by introducing and defining Critical Race Theory (CRT); next, we briefly highlight some of the critical public relations research that both parallels and sets the stage for a critical discussion of race in public relations; then we situate this discussion of race and/in public relations into broader academic discussions taking place in organizational and management communication to provide initial answers to the opening question. Finally, we introduce and analyze a vignette that pertains to risk equity (environmental racism and risk bearer agency) to more fully address our guiding question.

Critical Race Theory (CRT)

CRT, an academic discipline and social movement initiated by critical legal scholars during the 1980s, applies critical theory to explore and illuminate the intersections of law, power, and race in society (Delgado & Stefancic, 2012). More specifically, CRT is used to examine ways in which the law actually functions to establish, protect, and reproduce White racial power in the United States (Harris, 1993) – even though the law is supposed to be objective and neutral (Delgado & Stefancic, 2012). As Logan (2011) put it in her application of CRT to public relations research:

> CRT scholars understand racism as endemic to American life; are skeptical of dominant legal claims of neutrality, objectivity, colorblindness, and meritocracy; insist on a contextual/historical analysis of contemporary conditions; presume that racism contributes to all contemporary manifestations of group advantage and disadvantage; argue that the experiential knowledge of people of color is significant in the analysis of the law and society; and this scholarship works toward eliminating racial oppression as part of the broader goal of ending all forms of oppression.
>
> *(p. 448)*

Ultimately, CRT responds to post-racial society proponents who argue that race matters are concerns of a bygone era by highlighting the ways in which US workplaces remain sites of

Whiteness and unequal racialized privilege and power for Whites despite the fact that the law (1) opened the door for formal racial integration, and; (2) was supposed to legislate away such forms of discrimination and marginalization (Delgado & Stefancic, 2012).

The CRT framework is relevant to critical public relations scholarship for multiple reasons including, but not limited to: (1) everyone is raced; thus, public relations practitioners are employed in racialized work environments and have to navigate the challenges stemming from race that arise (see Edwards, 2010); (2) public relations is often the mouthpiece of organizations and is used as an agent of cultural production; thus, public relations has the ability to contribute to and shape metanarratives about race and/in society (see Edwards, 2013).

In short, a CRT research paradigm in public relations serves to further nuance, complement, and augment a small (in comparison to mainstream public relations research) yet growing line of critical public relations inquiry that has already questioned and dissected public relations and its ability to: (1) create culture – as a reflection of the interests of dominant powers – through the mechanism of identification, for example (German, 1995); (2) to deflect criticism and maintain power relations rather than foster an environment of collaboration and dialog – a critique of the Excellence Theory (Roper, 2005), and; (3) to manipulate symbols and images to the advantage of an organization and/or to the disadvantage of publics and society writ large (Mickey, 1997) to name a few. Scholars are also using the critical work of philosophers and sociologists to both challenge and extend public relations scholarship (Curtin & Gaither, 2005; Holtzhausen, 2012; Leeper, 1996; L'Etang, 2005; Motion & Leitch, 2007).

In sum, this chapter centers on the co-construction of race as a critical dimension in the tensions among organizations, groups, and individuals as publics, stakeholders, and organizational members as they seek to define the norms of enactment toward membership in a community. Central to such co-enactments and co-constructions, critical theory advises that both as scholars and practitioners, those interested in the power of public relations need to approach the relationships among the identifiable players as discursive tensions of power (empowerment) and marginalization (Heath, 2013).

Race: functions versus structures

In the discussion of public relations, race is more than a characteristic of a public; it is also more than a defining characteristic of members of a public. Race is a co-construction that shapes how the many voices see reality (mind/ideation), define identities (self), and the nature of identifications interwoven into community as normatively grounded meaning (relationships). As such, relationships are a discursive complex of others by which the tensions of privilege and marginalization are contested, co-created, and co-enacted as the norms of power (Motion & Leitch, 2007); hence, public relations can be viewed as an enterprise that "engages in battles for power through hegemonic definitions of legitimacy" (Heath, Motion & Leitch, 2010, p. 200).

One approach to such battles can be characterized as featuring the dynamics of structures and functions: "In functional approaches to PR, organizational goals are paramount and the PR system (of strategies, tactics, and evaluation) is aligned to work primarily in the interest of the organizational management" (Munshi & Edwards, 2011, p. 355). Another approach extended the critique of functionalism by stressing how

> the context of PR for functional scholars is the organization, and in organizational terms of engagement the focus on the strategy, process, and role of PR is both defined and evaluated within the bounds of the organization and its objectives. This paradigmatic way of thinking about PR may be pleasantly logical, but imposes blinkers on practitioners and scholars in

relation to race. In this rather limited worldview, the context of PR relates to environmental factors that affect the ability to communicate messages effectively, or the realization of organizational goals. The wider sociocultural processes in which organizations participate, remain invisible.

(Munshi & Edwards, 2011, p. 355)

Their emphasis of the sociocultural factors presses insightful public relations to delve deeply into the nature and norms of community with special sensitivities, one of which is for the dynamics of race.

Munshi and Edwards (2011) exposed, shed light upon, and challenged the functional view of public relations by demonstrating that: (1) race is better thought of as a process productive of, and inherent in, social systems – as opposed to being a category or rather a static characteristic that is clearly delineated and easily measured; (2) the role of race in public relations is more than tailoring better-designed messages to specialized public and market segments – for analyzing race as a variable associated with individuals does not and cannot capture "its fluidity, heterogeneity or its dispersed nature across groups in society" (p. 351). To view race solely in functionalist terms ignores the racialized historical context in which public relations as an industry emerged (Edwards, 2013), as well as masks contemporary roles public relations plays "as part of a system that racializes disadvantage by creating and circulating meanings that thrust a White worldview on to the reality of a racialized existence" (Munshi & Edwards, 2011, p. 354).

Presuming that critical theory is valuable for shedding light on the groundings by which people and organizations engage and negotiate space, the next section features racialization as grounding.

Racialization as grounding: a view of race in organizational and management communication

The criticism of racializing existence and advantage is not unique to public relations; rather, this criticism has also been occurring in other management communication-centered fields. In this chapter, however, the focus of critical approaches to race is the central rather than the peripheral concern. It is not viewed as a problematic in situational adjustments and communication by which organizations seek to connect strategically with publics. In fact, it can be viewed as a problematic strategically used to challenge organizations as they engage within communities. Thus, the analysis in this chapter does not presume that organizations can share information and provide corrective premises for decision-making that allow and encourage identifiable groups to extend goodwill to organizations. It suggests, rather, that discursive constructions become obstacles to organizational success by sufficing as inhibitors rather than facilitators to organizations' efforts to achieve their goals.

Contrary to the view that public relations helps organizations bend society to themselves, the approach featured here underscores how key constructions require that public relations lead organizational managements in adjusting to the dynamics of communities where they seek the license to operate and be rewarded. As such, many constructions, including race, are more than situational constraints to success, but rather the dynamics of community agency. Race, for that reason, becomes, as Kenneth Burke cautioned, a flaw in thinking. Centering this flaw in language, Burke (1934) warned that "if language is the fundamental instrument of human cooperation, and if there is an 'organic flaw' in the nature of language, we may well expect to find this organic flaw revealing itself through the texture of society" (p. 330).

Organizational communication scholars have noted the ways in which research concerning issues of race predominantly preserves Whiteness and organizational communication's disciplinary racial foundations (Ashcraft & Allen, 2003). In their analysis, they exposed five disciplined messages that disguise organization communication researchers' participation in preserving the normative power of organized Whiteness; they also provided suggestions for altering the landscape of preserving Whiteness in organizational communication research. Three of the five messages (myths) most relevant to critical race and the practice and study of public relations are:

> Message (myth) 4: Racial Discrimination Is a Function of Personal Bias, Interpersonal Misunderstanding, Organizational Failure to Manage Cultural Differences, and Disproportionate Demographics.
> Message (myth) 2: Race Is Relevant in So Far as It Involves Cultural Differences, Which Can Be Identified, Valued, and Managed to Improve Organizational Performance.
> Message (myth) 1: Race Is a Separate, Singular Concept That Is Relevant Only Under Certain Circumstances.
>
> *(Ashcraft & Allen, 2003)*

By this logic, race (as color-coded) masks normative assumptions – the implications of which not only misdirect attention and motive but also the co-construction of meaning. Such distortions subvert the assumptions regarding critical implications of biases that among other flaws lead communicators to focus incorrectly on how privileged perspectives are used to guide corrective approaches to meanings.

To unpack such observations about meaning, the analysis that immediately follows retains the messages in the original numbering as depicted in Ashcraft and Allen's 2003 work; however, we order them in terms of their prevalence and import (based on our perceptions) to the practice and study of public relations. To fully unpack these messages, we adopt the language of CRT theorists and ask: what would the discipline of public relations look like if race was placed at the center of research inquiry, design, and execution? In so asking, we present each of these messages (as logical) then problematize the message (myth), demonstrating how each message masks Whiteness norms in public relations. Examples are used to make our academic exercise of challenging the aforementioned messages more lucid. We continue by highlighting, then problematizing, Message 4.

Problematizing Message 4: the case of the National Football League

In the United States, the National Football League (NFL) – an American football sports league – made $9.5 billion in 2012, making it one of the top grossing professional sports leagues in the world (Isidore, 2013). In November 2013, the NFL in general and the Miami Dolphins (an NFL team) in particular made national headlines when a White player, Richie Incognito, was suspended from the team for "conduct detrimental to the team" (Walker, 2013). Incognito was under investigation by the Miami Dolphins, the NFL, and the NFL Players' Association for accusations of racially motivated harassment of teammate Jonathan Martin, a Black player (Walker, 2013). The Miami Dolphins released this statement in conjunction with Incognito's suspension:

> we believe in maintaining a culture of respect for one another and as a result we believe this decision is in the best interest of the organization at this time. As we noted earlier, we

reached out to the NFL to conduct an objective and thorough review. We will continue to work with the league on this matter.

(Walker, 2013, para. 3)

Subsequently, the NFL began an investigation which was conducted by Paul, Weiss, Rifkind, Wharton & Garrison LLP, a highly reputable corporate and entertainment law firm headquartered in New York City.

On February 14, 2014, in what has become known as the *Ted Wells Report*, the firm released a 148-page document. Key aspects of the report showed: (1) Martin was subjected to persistent harassing language; (2) the harassment humiliated Martin and contributed to his mental health issues; (3) the mistreatment of Martin is consistent with a case of workplace bullying; (4) the extent to which the abuse resulted from racial animus is unclear. Although a racial motivation on behalf of Incognito could not be explicitly derived from the *Wells Report*, it is clear that the mainstream US sports media outlets, as well as much of the US population that followed this story, saw it as a race-related issue. Immediately following the Wells Report, ESPN's *Outside the Lines* aired a one-hour special feature on the "N-Word" (a euphemism for "nigger") which was motivated in part by the Incognito case.

Taking the aforementioned Message 4 into account, the NFL might argue:

(1) That this case of harassment has everything to do with *"Racial Discrimination as Personal Bias"* on the part of Incognito and/or as *"Interpersonal Misunderstanding"* between Incognito and Martin, and as such the suspension, the subsequent investigation, and possible future NFL legislation will address the issues of "race" for the NFL.

(2) That in light of the investigation, the NFL needs to implement a policy to deal with the race issue. In this case, in particular, racial discrimination is the result of *"Organizational Failure to Manage Cultural Differences."* One such policy being discussed currently (as of February 25, 2014) among the NFL's competition committee is their consideration of a rule implementation that would penalize players for using the N-word on the field (ESPN.com news, 2014). The underlying thought with the implementation of this rule, but not directly stated, is that if racial epithets can be eliminated in the field of play (via penalties), this might help to address such language being used in locker rooms and other off-field venues. It might also demonstrate to external audiences and stakeholders that the NFL is being "proactive" in managing the "race issue"; therefore, such actions can help to safeguard the organization from being liable in subsequent race-based lawsuits that might emerge which could attribute blame to the organization for sustaining (or at the very least failing to challenge) racially hostile workplace environments.

(3) Relatedly, the NFL is not new to legislating race via race-related policies. In 2003, the NFL established the "Rooney Rule" which requires NFL teams to interview "minority" candidates for head coaching and senior football operation jobs (Reid, 2011). The rule emerged out of criticism that management ranks of the NFL lacked diversity, and this paucity of "diverse leaders" was problematic given that the vast majority of NFL players are Black (Reid, 2011). This rule in part is an inverted response to the message that *"Racial Discrimination is a Function of Failure to Manage Disproportionate Demographics"* insomuch as supporters of this message would argue that when persons are truly in the minority (fewer in number) there is the increased opportunity for discrimination against those minority voices. This Rooney Rule demonstrates the inverse: one would logically "expect" that predominantly White workplaces would have predominantly White leadership; however, when a predominantly Black workplace still has predominantly White leadership, what is being

communicated? Blacks are good enough to play the game/sport, but not good enough to manage and lead in this sports enterprise?

From a critical race theory perspective, the NFL is the perfect embodiment of the White Leader Prototype (Logan, 2011). Logan defined this prototype as "the notion that leaders…are (or should be) White, which reproduces Whites as actual leaders in a self-sustaining system that makes White leadership appear normal, neutral, and natural, rather than the result of racialized practices" (p. 443). The NFL was challenged and then implemented a policy (the Rooney Rule) after a flaw was highlighted in their organizational culture regarding the promotion of under-represented racial and ethnic persons (UREPs) – (see Waymer 2013 for a discussion of why "UREP" is used as opposed to "minority," a term under attack in various disciplines; or even the more politically correct "AHANA" – African American, Hispanic, Asian, Native American). Yet, the policy alone is just a bandage – for it does little to address the institutional and systemic racism that warrants the creation of the Rooney Rule in the first place. Moreover, former Black NFL coaches highlight that the Rooney Rule is broken:

> "We're at that stage where guys…who didn't get an opportunity, who had won and been very successful previously…obviously, there's some concern there…, and that's why I think the rule is going to be revisited.
>
> *(Associated Press, 2013, para. 14)*

The NFL, like many other organizations, takes the position that racial discrimination can be legislated away, and that persons exhibiting racial bias within the organization can and should be punished. It is the classic differentiation/dissociation strategy used in crisis communication based on image repair and/or apologia discourse (Brinson & Benoit, 1999; Hearit, 1994). Such actions, however, preserve and do not challenge the Whiteness status quo of the organization but merely serve as window dressing in the battle to address systemic racial discrimination in our organizations and society at large. This critique suggests that public relations responses in this case are not intended to foundationally address the flaws of race but merely enact messaging to manage the crisis of "Whiteness management." More than protecting "White" management, such strategies can be unpacked as being more foundationally the messaging to protect and even insulate the reward dependency of "Whiteness management" – an extension of Harris's (1993) Whiteness as property construct.

Such "crises" are tantalizing to scholars who seek to bring their insights to bear on the strategies of crisis management and communication. As such, we suspect several US public relations and crisis communication researchers will jump at the opportunity to analyze this case. They will likely make arguments such as given the racial and ethnic demographics of an NFL team, coupled with a hyper-masculine, macho culture, the NFL should have anticipated and been better prepared for such a crisis via diversity pre-crisis management (Waymer, 2012c). In fact, we expect such lines of analysis to proliferate. This sort of logic highlights the view that *"Racial Discrimination Is a Function of an Organizational Failure to Manage Cultural Differences"* yet does not critically analyze the role that communication and public relations play in creating and sustaining the racial ideologies that undergird this issue and other issues of race in organizations in the first place (Edwards, 2012, 2013). Rather than investigating the flaws of the language (and culture) of football, for instance, the analysis may merely look to explain how the "flaws" can be managed in ways that are less problematic. In fact, if "Whiteness" is the paramount dysfunction, there are likely to be voices that defend that paradigm and even criticize football managements for being "sensitive" or "worried" about looking bad.

Problematizing Message 2: the "business case" for the inclusion of race

> Those who perceive diversity as exclusively a moral imperative or societal goal are missing the larger point. Workforce diversity needs to be viewed as a competitive advantage and a business opportunity…If we are to form lasting business relationships with our customers and become a true global leader in the industry, we must understand our customers' diverse cultures and decisional processes, not merely their languages. To do so, we must begin with a diverse workplace.…To remain competitive for talent and for customers, it is imperative that we attract and value diverse talent and enable that talent to attract and value diverse customers.
>
> *(Chubb, n.d)*

This statement, which is highlighted on the webpage of one of the largest property and casualty insurers in the US, is the quintessential argument for requisite variety and "excellence" in public relations management – a theoretical position that argues that organizations cannot practice "excellence" in public relations if management is not tapping into the unique perspectives that diverse persons (including UREPs) can provide (Sha & Ford, 2007). This perspective, however, serves to highlight UREPs' status as a means of capital (human resources) and thus as a means by which organizations can be more effective in obtaining strategic objectives; yet, such a view masks the notion that UREPs might be targeted and employed for purposes of advancing strategic goals and objectives of the organization solely, and possibly not viewed as ends unto themselves (see the work of philosopher Immanuel Kant 1785 for a critical questioning of the ethics of using peoples as means to ends and not viewing them as ends unto themselves).

The business case for diversity and the aforementioned message (Message 2) – "*Race Is Relevant in So Far as It Involves Cultural Differences, Which Can Be Identified, Valued, and Managed to Improve Organizational Performance*" have become hegemonic insomuch as they overshadow the moral imperative of exposing, challenging, and neutralizing race. Simply look at the opening statement in this section from the Chubb Corporation. Then look at the majority of public relations research published on race to date: one would easily find studies that highlight strategies for recruiting more UREPs into the public relations major and thus the practice of public relations (Brown, White, & Waymer, 2011), strategies for how diversity management can be leveraged to augment corporate reputation (Waymer & VanSlette, 2013) or strategies designed to help organizations mitigate the escalation of crisis situations (Waymer, 2012c) among other scholarship that explicitly or implicitly serve the function of further entrenching the "business case hegemony."

Even when some scholars have taken a more critical approach to race in public relations (see Waymer, 2010), they still return to the functionalist language in their conclusions. For example, Waymer and Heath (2007) concluded in their naming and criticism of the managerial bias found in crisis communication research that organizations must be "reflective before and during the crisis…public relations can help organizations to be reflective, which, in turn, enhances their managerial abilities and perspectives. It enriches their planning and strategic options" (p. 106). This particular journal – the *Journal of Applied Communication Research* – requires that all contributors have a "pragmatic implications" section. In this critical-oriented work, why did the authors return to business-oriented, functionalistic conclusions? Possible explanations could be: (1) due to (legitimate) editorial demands, or (2) due to how the "requirements" emerge from or are possibly imposed on an editor insomuch as the publisher (Routledge) desires to keep content in an applied communication research journal as business- or functional-oriented as possible in order to hit more markets for profit-making reasons. The authors also could have returned to such positioning of race/diversity narratives (3) due to their personal ascription to and belief in the business case for race, or (4) due to possibly that these projects are just smaller representations of a larger cause that they are championing in both attempting to expose public relations and its hidden interest (Boyd & Waymer, 2011) as well as to leverage public relations, strategically, to help make society more fully functioning (Heath, 2006). Such unpacking, that is to call into the question our motives as authors for addressing matters of race, is highlighted to suggest the pervasiveness of the bias even when efforts are being made to correct the functionalist bias and its effects.

Despite the functionalist bias highlighted here, what is paramount from this discussion is the normative assumption of editorial demand/constraint. Who determines what types of race and public relations research gets published? Is there an academic space for purely race and critical public relations work? Do real or perceived barriers exist to the production and/or publication of these critical race public relations projects? And, do such projects either assume inherently a Whiteness bias or a presumption of color blindness or race neutrality?

Problematizing Message 1: the case of PR academic publishing trends on Critical Race

Although race research in public relations has its origins in the early works of Marilyn Kern-Foxworth (1989, 1991) and Debra A. Miller, who were concerned with the multicultural diversity in the practice of public relations and workplace environments, Pompper (2005) is credited as the first scholar to introduce a theoretical framework (CRT) to the discipline and practices of public relations via publication in a mainstream, refereed, public relations journal; this theoretical framework enabled scholars to problematize race, unpack the hegemonic power of this social construction, and avoid the instrumentalization of "raced" publics for the purposes of only message and audience segmentation. However, six years after Pompper's work, race as a domain of scholarly inquiry was still virtually invisible in public relations literature (Munshi & Edwards, 2011). Compelled to address this void, Munshi and Edwards served as special issue editors on race and/in public relations (see Curtin, 2011; Logan, 2011; Vardeman-Winter, 2011; Waymer & Dyson, 2011; Xifra & McKie, 2011 for contributions to this call). The following year, Waymer (2012d) edited a volume that also provided academic space for a critical discussion of race (see Carter, 2012; Edwards, 2012; Heath, 2012; Waymer, 2012b; Xifra & McKie, 2012). What is noteworthy here is that critical race in public relations scholarship is being covered almost exclusively in (or confined to?) special issues of journals, specialty journals (such as *Public Relations Inquiry*), and niche edited books or volumes (including this handbook of critical public relations). This form of control, whether it be editorial, reviewer, or disciplinary, serves to further ghettoize critical studies of race in public relations. This highlights the final message: "[Critical] *Race Is a Separate, Singular Concept That Is Relevant Only under Certain Circumstances.*" And in this case, arguments such as race is everywhere and that everyone is raced continue to exist on the margins and are not fully integrated into the studies we conduct.

So with our foundation established, we return to our opening question. What would the discipline of public relations look like if race were placed at the center of research inquiry, design, and execution? We are compelled to pose this question because as Munshi and Edwards (2011) argued, "PR is, consciously or otherwise, complicit in the privileging of Whiteness that is implicit in the way issues are framed" (p. 354). We pose this question because of the critical role public relations plays in constructing, delivering, and adapting messages "that contribute to ideological hierarchies of distinction among different objects, identities, attitudes, values, and behaviours" (Edwards, 2013, p. 243). Such observations rightly focus on the messaging and meaning implications for public relations scholarship and practice that go well beyond the capabilities of functional theory. Moreover, we must pose this question because as Edwards (2012) posited: society is inequitable; public relations operates on local, national, and global levels; marginalized persons, publics, and communities, including stigmatized racial groups, face greater disadvantage than other less or non-stigmatized groups; thus, public relations scholars and practitioners have an obligation to examine and address the different ways in which PR contributes to this inequity in terms of its internal structure and culture, its practices and effects.

In this chapter we continue in this vein of scholarly inquiry and critique about race and/ in public relations. In so doing, we consider the dialectical approach to understanding race as articulated by Munshi and Edwards (2011). Next, we turn our attention to environmental racism and risk-bearer agency to more concretely problematize the "racialized elite-racialized non-elite" dialectic, as well as to draw preliminary conclusions about what the practice and discipline of public relations would look like if race was made central to the work and subsequent analyses.

Agency, risk, and race

This section contains the presentation and analysis of a vignette that pits "scientific" objectivity and the social construction of race. More specifically, this example reveals the paradoxes that are fundamental, perhaps inherent, in racialized decision-making regarding public relations and risk communication. The question at hand is one of whether race should not, and perhaps does not, play a role in risk assessment.

Vignette: race and the unequal distribution of risks

A high school student – keen on advancing her photography skills – set out to take pictures along some, and then all streets named in honor of Martin Luther King, Jr. The idealism was soon dashed by a reality – as she realized (mind) that she (identity) was confronted by a community of risk inequity. This student soon realized that her "sociological" photography experience was able to document that wealthy White neighborhoods managed risks by assigning them to poor Black neighborhoods, thus exposing the Black neighborhoods exponentially to risk. Not only did residents of these neighborhoods endure the aesthetic risks of certain businesses such as junk dealers and auto parts/junk yards, these communities often also suffered health risks such as those presented by the presence of salvage, which can introduce harmful elements such as lead into their environments and drinking water. Waste management companies and city planners often presumed and then argued that such communities would benefit if garbage/trash dumps were located in Black neighborhoods because, so the argument goes, such facilities created jobs in the community. The unfair assignment of risk to these communities necessarily made subsequent assignments of risk to these communities more likely since government officials might say that "another commercial activity like a junkyard can do no more harm than what is already present in the community and might actually help the community and its residents if it generates jobs." Thus, the people of the community lacked control over the risks to which they were disproportionately exposed, and they also suffered from the hegemonic flaws present in the language of employment and job opportunities.

So what would the discipline of public relations look like if "race" was placed at the center of research inquiry, design, and execution? We turn to the Yates High School Collective Action to Mobilize Against Environmental Racism (CAMERA) Project (2014) as an illustrative example.

These Houston students, under the direction of Mr Ray Carrington, capture images of the inner city, Third Ward neighborhood environmental risks, and through various methods of community engagement they share these pictures to engage in a community conversation about environmental justice in the Third Ward:

> Since 1995, the students' work has been showcased in an annual exhibit at the Museum of Fine Arts-Houston. The project, called "Eye on Third Ward", is one of the museum's most acclaimed exhibits and is the only [one] of its kind among the nation's major metropolitan art museums. Each year, visitors are inspired by the profound wisdom and gravitas these young people convey through their photography.
>
> *(Yates CAMERA Project, 2014, para. 9)*

This is only one stage of these students' annual environmental justice campaign. Other steps include knowledge-sharing between students and their community members about the data the students find from public records about the sites chosen for photography, as well as sharing interpretations students draw from their sociological "walk" of their community. A final step is the culmination of the Yates CAMERA Project (2014) which concludes with a student-hosted exhibit of their work and the study findings:

> Third Ward residents as well as members of the news media, council members and others from local government, land use planners, developers, and other local decision-makers… [are] invited to see the finished product and to engage in a discussion on how to prevent and resolve environmental injustice going forward. The conversation will focus on the specific environmental threats encumbering the Third Ward and will be set against the backdrop of the neighborhood's ongoing gentrification.
>
> *(para. 19)*

For race to be central to public relations in this case, local government members, land use planners, and developers invited to this event would accept that racial and social class inequities exist. They would see this community and its residents as ends unto themselves, not as a blighted community that needs to be cleansed of a scourge. The members themselves would not be seen as the plague on the land (blight is an agricultural term used to describe a plant malady which often manifests itself in the form of dark spots and discoloration) in need of saving/revitalization (see Waymer 2012a for further discussion and critical interrogation of this blight/agricultural metaphor). They would not resort to the use of eminent domain laws to reclaim viable land in the inner city (see Waymer 2009) under auspices that the land is blighted and in need of restoration. Rather, they would see the residents as ends unto themselves, acknowledge racial and class disparities, and work with these communities as much as is reasonably possible to ensure that these areas are not disproportionately bearing society's risks. Additionally, they would work to ensure that "those environmental threats that present barriers to access of resources (massive highway projects and poor connectivity; lack of quality grocery stores and greenspaces) and that serve to marginalize and disenfranchise a community (infrastructure neglect and non-response to illegal dumping)" do not serve to further marginalize the community (Yates, 2014, para. 2). Given the fact that the Yates CAMERA Project has been ongoing for nearly 20 years, it appears as if the vision we are articulating of a race-centric approach to public relations efforts have not been fully realized. However, progress (a modernist term, but appropriate to use here) is being made. The Yates CAMERA project can serve as a model towards that end of a race-centric public relations approach. According to Yates (2014):

Sustainable solutions to environmental insecurity in a community must come from within the community itself. While scientists and academics may have capacity to generate datasets and establish correlations, it is at the grassroots level where the issues are identified and the real impacts are articulated. People from outside the community do not have an established sense of the history of a particular issue necessary to work toward a long-term solution.

(para. 15)

Thus, a community (broadly defined) is central to mobilizing persons, creating and developing, and then executing a sustained public relations program that keeps race at the center of its aim. The group then garners allies (in this case the Museum of Fine Art, Houston) as well as reaching out to other publics (government, developers, and planners in this case) to remind these groups that race matters, and is a central element to the plight these community residents are facing. While the issues this community faces have not been addressed completely, we like to believe that the community remains vital in Houston (Feldman, 2014), in part due to actions such as the Yates CAMERA project and those of the Wheeler Avenue Baptist Church – both cornerstones in the Third Ward community.

From a scholarship standpoint it is important to highlight that the term "risk racism" emerged one used to point out how communities where most of the residents were Black were systematically (and it was an historical artifact) being assigned the role of risk bearers. In the scholarship literature (and it's ironic that the battle took place in journals and not in the community), the battle over risk racism took on a unique dimension when some voices started, for various reasons, to call the phenomenon "risk equity." The point was that such societal assignments of risk were not only biased by race but also by income. Facetiously, we wonder: does such languaging/messaging (risk racism versus risk equity) make the conditions in which people live more or less palatable for the risk bearers? The real question, founded on ample flaws of language, may well be that "interest, interest, whose interest is at risk?" (Heath & McComas, 2015) better captures the spirit of our inquiry.

In sum, critical theory of public relations can and should reveal the biases and dysfunctions that guide messaging, decision-making, and management. That is an important role of public relations and one that calls for critical theorists to examine the turning points that are critical to some matter, the management of some issue, risk, crisis, identification, and image/reputation.

Conclusion

As a topic for discussion within public relations, this chapter has argued that the topic of race is dysfunctionally studied. Race is predominantly seen as an attribute of a public, as a culture, which can be instrumentalized for the benefit of an organization. Moreover, if we assume that empowerment is a key to public relations in general, and activism/social movement social justice public relations in particular (Holtzhausen, 2012), then a goal of public relations should be to end the instrumentalization and marginalization of publics. As a critical perspective, any theory of public relations and best practice that marginalizes and instrumentalizes people based on race violates the requirements for a fully functioning society (Heath, 2006). More specific, such actions weaken community, deny access to discourse (both infrastructure-ally and in forms of the arena in which discourse takes place), and colonizes people.

The term "race" is never neutral. It presumes a dialectic, often the polarity of more or less acceptable, powerful, and marginalized. As such the term and the literature that surrounds race and its normative role in discourse and management easily become simplified and reductive to avoid the "messiness" that accompanies the construct of race. Avoiding the "messiness," however, is unfortunate – for the greatest opportunity for the discipline of public relations to contribute to broader societal and philosophical discussions taking place in other disciplines is to wrangle in the messiness, not distance ourselves as objective, positivist/post-positivist researchers. But, if nothing else, the authors have aspired to emphasize the imperative of investigating race as a central theme for the critical inquiry of public relations. That objective is not only connected with the goal of making public relations a more constructive aspect of society, but more importantly one that supports the theory that a core function of public relations involves working to build humane and effective societies – that is, fully functioning societies (Heath, 2006). Scholars are beginning to take up the banner; they are problematizing the ways in which public relations, as an academic discipline and practice, can be viewed as a quest for (social) justice (Marsh, 2014). This chapter is another contribution of that ilk. Hopefully, it serves as a clarion call for critical scholars to get engaged, to address injustice both in writing and in practice, and to embody the principles of CRT that were, and still are, at the core of the CRT movement.

References

Ashcraft, K. & Allen, B. (2003). The racial foundation of organizational communication. *Communication Theory*, 13, pp. 5–38.

Associated Press. (2013, January 31). Ex-coaches: Rooney rule is broken. Retrieved on 20 April, 2015, from http://espn.go.com/nfl/story/_/id/8903044/black-former-nfl-coaches-say-rooney-rule-broken

Boyd, J., & Waymer, D. (2011). Organizational rhetoric: A subject of interest(s). *Management Communication Quarterly*, 25, pp. 474–93.

Brinson, S. L., & Benoit, W. L. (1999). The tarnished star: Restoring Texaco's damaged public image. *Management Communication Quarterly*, 12, pp. 483–510.

Brown, K., White, C., & Waymer, D. (2011). African-American students' perceptions of public relations education and practice: Implications for minority recruitment. *Public Relations Review*, 37, pp. 522–9.

Burke, K. (1934, May 2). The meaning of C. K. Ogden. *New Republic*, 78, pp. 328–31.

Carter, J. A. (2012). Two unreconciled strivings: Racial constructionism and racial eliminitivism in the critical philosophy of race. In D. Waymer (Ed.), *Culture, social class, and race in public relations*, pp. 79–95. Lanham, MD: Lexington Books.

Chubb. (n.d.). Business case for diversity. Retrieved on April 20, 2015, from http://www.chubb.com/diversity/chubb4450.html

Curtin, P. A. (2011). Discourses of American Indian racial identity in the public relations materials of the Fred Harvey Company: 1902–1936. *Journal of Public Relations Research*, 23, pp. 368–96.

Curtin, P. A., & Gaither, T. K. (2005). Privileging identity, difference, and power: The circuit of culture as a basis for public relations theory. *Journal of Public Relations Research*, 17, pp. 91–115.

Delgado, R., & Stefancic, J. (2012). *Critical Race Theory: An introduction*, 2nd edition. New York: New York University Press.

Edwards, L. (2010). "Race" in public relations. In R. L. Heath (Ed.), *The SAGE handbook of public relations*, pp. 205–22. Thousand Oaks, CA: Sage.

Edwards, L. (2012). Critical Race Theory and public relations. In D. Waymer (Ed.), *Culture, social class, and race in public relations: Perspectives and applications*. Lanham, MD: Lexington Books.

Edwards, L. (2013). Institutional racism in cultural production: The case of public relations. *Popular Communication*, 11, pp. 242–56.

ESPN.com news services. (2014, February 25). Ryan Clark: Tough to legislate rule. Retrieved on April 20, 2015, from http://espn.go.com/new-york/story/_/id/10509188/ryan-clark-pittsburgh-steelers-says-tough-police-use-n-word

Feldman, C. (2014, August 22). Third Ward: The epicenter of Houston's fight for racial equality. *The Houston Chronicle*. Retrieved on April 20, 2015, from http://www.houstonchronicle.com/life/article/Third-Ward-The-epicenter-of-Houston-s-fight-for-5706658.php#/0

German, K. M. (1995). Critical theory in public relations inquiry: Future directions for analysis in a public relations context. In W. N. Elwood (Ed.), *Public relations inquiry as rhetorical criticism*, pp. 279–94. Westport, CT: Praeger.

Harris, C. I. (1993). Whiteness as property. *Harvard Law Review*, 106, pp. 1707–91.

Heath, R. L. (2006). Onward into more fog: Thoughts on public relations' research directions. *Journal of Public Relations Research*, 18, pp. 93–114.

Heath, R. L. (2012). Was Black rhetoric ever anything but race in public relations? The challenge of identity. In D. Waymer (Ed.), *Culture, social class, and race in public relations: Perspectives and applications*, pp. 149–62. Lanham, MD: Lexington Books.

Heath, R. L. (2013). The journey to understand and champion OPR takes many roads, some not yet well traveled. *Public Relations Review*, 39, pp. 426–31.

Heath, R. L., & McComas, K. (2015). Interest, interest, whose interest is at risk? Risk governance, issues management, and the fully functioning society. In U. F. Paleo (Ed.), *Risk governance: The articulation of hazard, politics, and ecology*. London, UK: Peter Lang.

Heath, R. L., Motion, J., & Leitch, S. (2010). Power and public relations: Paradoxes and programmatic thoughts. In R. L. Heath (Ed.), *The SAGE handbook of public relations*, pp. 191–204. Thousand Oaks, CA: Sage Publications.

Hearit, K. M. (1994). Apologies and public relations crises at Chrysler, Toshiba, and Volvo. *Public Relations Review*, 20, pp. 113–26.

Holtzhausen, D. R. (2012). *Public relations as activism: Postmodern approaches to theory and practice*. New York, NY: Routledge.

Isidore, C. (2013, Feb. 1). Why football is still a money machine. CNNMoney. Retrieved on April 20, 2015, from http://money.cnn.com/2013/02/01/news/companies/nfl-money-super-bowl/

Kant, I. (1785). Groundwork for the metaphysics of morals. In A. W. Wood (Ed.) *Groundwork for the metaphysics of morals (1–79)*. London, UK: Yale University Press. (Original work published 1785).

Kern-Foxworth, M. (1989). Status and roles of minority review. *Public Relations Review*, 15(3), pp. 39–47.

Kern-Foxworth, M. (1991). Historical chronicle of people of color in public relations. *Public Relations Quarterly*, 36(1), pp. 28–30.

Leeper, R. V. (1996). Moral objectivity, Jurgen Habermas's discourse ethics, and public relations. *Public Relations Review*, 22, pp. 130–50.

L'Etang, J. (2005). Critical public relations. Some reflections. *Public Relations Review*, 31, pp. 521–6.

Logan, N. (2011). The White leader prototype: A critical analysis of race in public relations. *Journal of Public Relations Research*, 23, pp. 442–57.

Marsh, C. (2014). Public relations as a quest for justice: Resource dependency, reputation, and the philosophy of David Hume. *Journal of Mass Media Ethics*, 29, pp. 210–24.

Mickey, T. J. (1997). A postmodern view of public relations: Sign and reality. *Public Relations Review*, 23, pp. 271–84.

Motion, J., & Leitch, S. (2007). A toolbox of public relations: The *oeuvre* of Michel Foucault. *Public Relations Review*, 33, pp. 263–8.

Munshi, D., & Edwards, L. (2011). Understanding "race" in/and public relations: Where do we start and where should we go? *Journal of Public Relations Research*, 23, pp. 349–67.

Pompper, D. (2005). "Difference" in public relations research: A case for introducing critical race theory. *Journal of Public Relations Research*, 17, pp. 139–69.

Reid, J. (2011, February 19). NFL's Rooney Rule should be strengthened. *Washington Post*. Retrieved from http://www.washingtonpost.com/wpdyn/content/article/2011/02/19/AR2011021903268.html

Roper, J. (2005). Symmetrical communication: Excellent public relations or a strategy for hegemony? *Journal of Public Relations Research*, 17, pp. 69–86.

Sha, B.-L., & Ford, R. L. (2007). Redefining "requisite variety": The challenge of multiple diversities for the future of public relations excellence. In E. L. Toth (Ed.), *The future of excellence in public relations and communication management: Challenges for the next generation*, pp. 381–98. Mahwah, NJ: Lawrence Erlbaum.

Vardeman-Winter, J. (2011). Confronting Whiteness in public relations campaigns and research with women. *Journal of Public Relations Research*, 23, pp. 412–41.

Walker, J. (2013, November 4). Richie Incognito suspended by team. ESPN. Retrieved on April 20, 2015, from http://espn.go.com/nfl/story/_/id/9924206/miami-dolphins-suspend-richie-incognito-indefinitely-connection-jonathan-martin-incident

Waymer D. (2009). Liberty and justice for all? The paradox of governmental rhetoric. *Communication Quarterly*, 57, pp. 334–51.

Waymer, D. (2010). Does public relations scholarship have a place in race? In R. L. Heath (Ed.), *The SAGE handbook of public relations*, pp. 237–46. Thousand Oaks, CA: Sage Publications.

Waymer, D. (2012a). A city divided: Understanding "class issues" in government public relations. In D. Waymer (Ed.), *Culture, social class, and race in public relations: Perspectives and application*, pp. 31–44. Lanham, MD: Lexington Books.

Waymer, D. (2012b). Broaching an uncomfortable subject: Teaching race in an undergraduate U.S. public relations classroom. In D. Waymer (Ed.), *Culture, social class, and race in public relations: Perspectives and applications*, pp. 149–62. Lanham, MD: Lexington Books.

Waymer, D. (2012c). Crisis management and communication: Pre-crisis preparation that is sensitive to diverse populations. In B. Olaniran, D. Williams, & W. T. Coombs (Eds), *Pre-crisis management: Preparing for the inevitable*, pp. 281–98. New York: Peter Lang.

Waymer, D. (Ed.). (2012d). *Culture, social class, and race in public relations: Perspectives and applications*. Lanham, MD: Lexington Books.

Waymer, D. (2013). Minorities in public relations. In R. L. Heath (Ed.), *The SAGE handbook of public relations*, pp. 638–9). Thousand Oaks, CA: Sage.

Waymer, D., & Dyson, O. L. (2011). The journey into an unfamiliar and uncomfortable territory: Exploring the role and approaches of race in PR education. *Journal of Public Relations Research*, 23, pp. 458–77.

Waymer, D., & Heath, R. L.. (2007). Emergent agents: The forgotten publics in crisis communication and issues management research. *Journal of Applied Communication Research*, 35, pp. 88–108.

Waymer, D., & VanSlette, S. (2013). Corporate reputation management and issues of diversity. In C. Carroll (Ed.), *Handbook of communication and corporate reputation*, pp. 471–83. Malden, MA: Wiley-Blackwell.

Xifra, J., & McKie, D. (2011). Desolidifying culture: Bauman, liquid theory, and race concerns in public relations. *Journal of Public Relations Research*, 23, pp. 397–411.

Xifra, J., & McKie, D. (2012). Expanding the spectrum of PR and race: Lessons from European theorists, media critiques, and Catalan programming: In D. Waymer (Ed.), *Culture, social class, and race in public relations: Perspectives and applications*, pp. 149–62. Lanham, MD: Lexington Books.

Yates CAMERA Project. (2014). Retrieved on April 20, 2015, from www.camera.harc.edu

24

Critical management studies and the management of desire

Stephen Linstead

Publicity is essentially a matter of mass psychology. We must remember that people are guided more by sentiment than by mind....Mob psychology is one of the important factors that underlay this whole business.

(Lee, 1921, cited in Ewen, 1996, p. 132)

"Welcome to the dark side" was how financial journalist Tim Burt, newly appointed to "strategic corporate communications" consultants Brunswick, was welcomed by Reuters' finance director to a secret board-level discussion about an $18 billion bid for the company by its rival Bloomberg (Burt, 2012, p. vii). Since the 1980s, a new branch of financial and business PR had developed to manage corporate image and reputation, especially in the context of mergers and acquisitions, to influence the formation of opinion, and to manage relations with a range of media that since the digital revolution had become far more complex, more rapid in disseminating information (regardless of its accuracy), less easy to anticipate, and more three-dimensional (Burt, 2012, p. xi). Furthermore, crisis management was becoming more of a customary than an exceptional occurrence, with Goldman Sachs, Toyota, and BP at that time fresh in the public recollection in the wake of the 2008 financial crisis. The mishandling of the Deepwater Horizon oil well disaster in the Gulf of Mexico had raised anxiety levels far beyond the oil industry – no-one wanted to find themselves in BP's position when they experienced "reputational exposure". If a crisis befell them, they did not want their public communications to make it worse. But this required extensive and effective strategies for non-crisis, or "peace-time", PR.

There are significant continuities here with the origins of PR at the beginning of the last century. As I write this, it is 100 years since the Ludlow Massacre (1914), in which Colorado National Guardsmen and security officers from the Colorado Fuel and Iron Company fired on a tent community of striking trade unionist miners and their families, who had been evicted from their tied homes by the company, before invading the site and setting fire to the tents. The anxious miners had dug pits below the tents so their families could shelter from stray bullets: two women and 11 children suffocated or burned to death under one tent alone, with a total death toll of up to 26 people (accounts vary). The notoriously insensitive Rockefeller family owned the company, managing it from the Manhattan offices of John D. Rockefeller, Jr., but even they were compelled to respond to these events. They contracted Ivy Ledbetter Lee (quoted above), a PR counsel who had experience of handling previous strikes elsewhere, to handle their post-crisis reputational damage. This was perhaps the first example of what has now become a familiar role, and also provided dramatic evidence for the public to distrust corporate "spin". When Lee, who was one of the founding fathers of PR, attempted to spread the rumour that the fire had been started by strikers overturning a stove, rather than the company arsonists, and stated that 82-year-old union activist Mother Jones was a prostitute and keeper of a house of ill-repute, he was christened "Poison Ivy" by novelist and activist Upton Sinclair, a sobriquet that stuck (Ewen, 1996, pp. 78–9).

It would seem, then, that PR's connection with, or incorporation by, the "dark side" is a long-standing one, and that the recent emergence of scholarly research that focuses on shedding some light on the dark side of management and organization would share little common ground with it (Linstead, Maréchal & Griffin 2014). However, PR emerged in the same period that the social sciences of sociology, social anthropology and psychology were establishing themselves in the context of the extensive scientific, technological, economic, social, political, cultural and demographic changes that gave rise to a modernity that was both systemic and symbolic, functional and critical – and which challenged the traditional cultural "glue" that had given civil society its relative stability. Questions were raised about the relationship between the consciousness of the individual and the viability of democracy that to this day remain unresolved. PR and critical social thought travelled routes through this history that engaged energetically with advances in and problems of new knowledge, new discoveries and new technologies, and the roles of different sectors of society in responding to them. Sometimes their views converged – PR could display tendencies that were both cynical and idealistic, manipulative and altruistic, elitist and populist.

From its earliest days, PR has wrestled with those dimensions of its role that extend beyond those of the specific interests of its immediate clients; and despite the emergence to dominance on both sides of the Atlantic of a functionalist, instrumental, neo-scientific paradigm, there have remained those who take more critical, dialogical and relational approaches to communicative inquiry (L'Etang, 2008, pp. 254–5). L'Etang neatly summarizes contributions to the growth of critical PR of the past three decades that have paralleled a similar growth in what has been termed critical management studies (CMS), although there has been little dialogue between the two fields. In this chapter, I will attempt to encourage further cross-fertilization by first setting out some of the primary concerns of CMS, then by looking at how PR and critical thinking developed in relation to core debates that, I argue, centre on the concept of desire and its relation to power; and finally by identifying some common areas of concern over which the two fields might usefully collaborate.

Critical Management Studies (CMS)

CMS is a term first coined in the late 1980s to capture a range of heterodox approaches to the study of management that collectively contested the blind spots, silences and suppressions of classical management theory and dominant functionalist approaches. Mainstream management thought was dehistoricized, degendered, depoliticized, decontextualized and undersocialized – or at least where any of these issues emerged it was in a highly restricted and truncated form. Diversity in theory and practice was limited, global and cross-cultural issues were largely considered in terms of the challenges they presented for control and incorporation rather than as an encounter with the other, the environment was to be controlled and exploited before adaptation was considered as an option. Control and resistance were technical problems to be mastered or overcome, not political issues to be taken seriously and engaged. Emerging in Europe to challenge this orthodoxy, the movement encompassed a range of critical perspectives including Marxism, radical Weberianism, Frankfurt Critical Theory, critical psychology, critical realism, post-Freudian psychoanalysis, feminism, post-structuralism and postmodernism. It constituted a broad church that continued to embrace an increasing range of critical perspectives as they emerged onto the organization studies radar. As the diversity of the group might suggest, there is no specific counter-orthodoxy – perspectives often clash in acrimonious debate – between Derridean or Foucauldian post-structuralists and critical realists, for example. The emphasis may well be placed differently on philosophy, theory and practice as well. In the late 1990s the movement counter-colonized the ultra-orthodox US Academy of Management and generated a much-debated mission statement that attempted to contain the range of its thought and aspirations as being

> critical of unethical management practices and the exploitative social order. Our premise is that structural features of contemporary society, such as the profit imperative, patriarchy, racial inequality, and ecological irresponsibility often turn organizations into instruments of domination and exploitation. Driven by a shared desire to change this situation, we aim in our research, teaching, and practice to develop critical interpretations of management and society and to generate radical alternatives. Our critique seeks to connect the practical shortcomings in management and individual managers to the demands of a socially divisive and ecologically destructive system within which managers work.

Assembling the rainbow, or swarm, of perspectives within CMS is attempted by Alvesson, Bridgman and Willmott (2009) in the *Oxford Handbook of Critical Management Studies*. The task is daunting, and the choices, though broadly representative, are at times frustrating. Theoretical perspectives addressed specifically are Critical Theory (Frankfurt School), critical realism, post-structuralism and Labour Process Theory. Notable absentees might be considered to be critical institutional theory (Bourdieu, surprisingly, is indexed only once); actor network theory (Latour appears only three times); and although both Lacan and Žižek are indexed sparingly, psychoanalysis is not, nor are critical approaches to aesthetics and design. Further, although post-structuralism is discussed, postmodernism is treated *en passant* in little more than a paragraph, with Lyotard receiving only one citation (despite there being a chapter on "Information Systems"); Baudrillard, despite his massive contribution to the critical sociology of consumption alone, receives only three mentions, two of them in the methodology chapter; and Deleuze, with or without Guattari, a mere two, despite his undeniable status as a giant in the philosophical critique of capitalism and his massive influence on Hardt and Negri, who are also underrepresented if better treated.

To give the editors their due, they are constrained by the need to reflect the literature published, explicitly aligning itself or identified by other publications with CMS at the time. This content captures relevant publications since 2006 somewhat unevenly, and it certainly does not fully reflect trends since 2009. With regard to PR these omissions are unfortunate as they would offer significant leverage to critical approaches to PR. Whilst I can't set matters entirely to rights in this short chapter, I will take my cue from at least some of the critical absentees from the "hetero-orthodoxy" that the CMS *Handbook* provides. In doing this I will focus my attention on the concept of *desire*, and the way that it has been rethought throughout the twentieth century – from Freud, via critical theory, Lacan and Deleuze, and particularly in relation to ideology. I will make the connection here to early contributions to PR including those of Edward L. Bernays, Freud's nephew, who was often regarded as the most successful product of his own PR practice. Bernays is often dismissed as a mere layman "fan" and proselytizer of the work of his uncle, but reconsideration of his work alongside that of his contemporaries can be instructive in the light of more recent work on "ideology", identity, and how a deeper understanding of the dynamics of desire can illuminate work on image, discourse, rhetoric, motivation, wants and needs in PR (see Ewen, 1996; Tye, 1998). It also raises new questions of governance, ethics, emancipation and autonomy that resonate with recent work on critical PR.

The co-emergence of PR and the social sciences

Many CMS scholars unfamiliar with the history of PR on either side of the Atlantic would perhaps be surprised to discover the extent to which the pioneers of PR engaged with developments in contemporary social science. The curiosity was driven by the need to unpack the key relations between individuals, groups (particularly elites), and beyond that larger masses such as crowds (or herds) that might pose challenges for effective social democracy and the preservation of civic order in times of change and, indeed, conflicts of interest (Ewen, 1996; Tye, 1998). The enlightenment commitment to the capability of the individual for rational thought, and their freedom to exercise it, was coupled with a belief in the feasibility and desirability of the widest involvement of the people in the democratic process, with equal weight as individuals. By the turn of the twentieth century this had emerged in the need to educate and inform this public, to provide them with "the facts" upon which rationally to cogitate, and this was the commitment of early PR contributors, including the Georgia-born and Princeton-educated professional journalist Ivy Ledbetter Lee and Harvard-educated journalist-intellectual Walter Lippman. However by the 1920s a change had occurred – former socialist Lippmann was rapidly becoming an elitist advocate, and concerns were being shown regarding the divergence between the potentially educable and rational public and the emotion and image-swayed crowd or herd. Between the two, the question was whether the sentimental crowd could be dominated by a manipulative elite prepared to use the discoveries of science and social science for the preservation (or acquisition) of power and privilege, in new or restabilised systems of social order. The role of PR or propaganda in the First and Second World Wars was as significant in this debate as was the use of its techniques by the Nazis in their rise to power – reputedly including, with particularly savage irony, the work of Jewish Cornell graduate and nephew of Freud, Edward L. Bernays (to his shock) (Tye 1998, p. 111; Bernays, 1965, p. 652). The focus, and methods, of PR shifted in this period, but none of this was sudden, as the developing currents were grounded in ideas already familiar from the new sociology (Gabriel Tarde, Robert Ezra Park), psychology (Gustave Le Bon, Wilfred Trotter, Sigmund Freud), and political thought (Graham Wallas).

In Europe, key contributors to these debates were psychologist Le Bon, a favourite of Theodore Roosevelt, and sociologist Tarde (whose far-sighted work on the role of global media and virtuality has recently enjoyed a resurgence promoted by scholars such as Bruno Latour (Latour & Lepinay 2010), and within the CMS community, Barbara Czarniawska (2009)). Le Bon's (1895) work *The Crowd: A Study of the Popular Mind* demonstrated how much the experience of the Paris Commune in 1870 had affected the security of the liberal middle classes, who were increasingly fearful of the rise of socialism among the working hordes with their "herd" behaviour (Trotter 1916).

Le Bon argued that there was a difference between the (middle-class) public capable of rational thought, and the (working-class) crowd that was swayed by emotion rather than reason. While the rule of the mob threatened to overrun the rule of reason, Le Bon nevertheless argued that even among the reasonable "the part played by the unconscious in our acts is immense… the part played by reason is very small" (Le Bon, cited in Ewen, 1996, p. 133). What was worse, analysts had only scratched the surface of probing unconscious motives. Civilization, consisting of a rigorous and hierarchical social order devised and imposed by superior elites, had held the chaos of instinct in check; but the rise of democracy, the decline of religion and the awakening consciousness of the working classes threatened this stability. Le Bon argued that the crowd eradicated individual personality, and that it absorbed the individual into something beyond them, in which they jettisoned any reasonable or ethical capacities they had in favour of a popular or "collective mind". In a crowd they would think, feel and act differently from how they would as individuals – group psychology and individual psychology were distinct.

Le Bon was pessimistic about the effects of crowd behaviour on society. He did, however, think that these effects could be mediated, if not controlled, by leaders who understood the psychology of crowds. His friend Tarde, however, was more optimistic, but perhaps too far ahead of his time in seeing the social as being in the process of being superseded by the new public. This public was not connected by physical proximity and moved by emotional contagion, as was the crowd, but by a spiritual and mental connection that was sustained by the growing media and communication apparatus. The media even shaped and standardized the content of everyday conversation, as "one pen suffices to set off a million tongues" (Tarde, 1969, p. 313). The unruly crowd was the social group of the past, with the mass media developing the communicative work of conversation into a unified higher order of discourse, ultimately overcoming conflict. Tarde's vision of the evolving virtual community was perhaps rather too optimistic, but it certainly anticipated the effects of television, cinema and the Internet. Hardt and Negri (2000) similarly recognize the processes of informatization that they see as driving late twentieth century change, but argue that where globalizing socio-economic forces have created what they call "Empire", this does not standardize emotions and resolve conflict in the "public"; but rather generates a countervailing resistance to its own imperializing desire, not by the public, but by the virtually constituted "multitude".

Robert Ezra Park, who would later lead the development of sociology at the University of Chicago, argued in *The Crowd and the Public* (Park 1904) for a similar distinction between the "public mind" and the "crowd mind", the former critical and rational, the latter simple, brutish and impulsive. But Park was also concerned about the effects of the media that had excited Tarde. For Park, the media were making the distinction less and less discernible, rendering public opinion as a "naïve collective impulse…manipulated by catchwords" rather than a position arrived at by actual discussion of the facts (Ewen, 1996, p. 135). British political theorist Graham Wallas (1908) further underlined the fallacy of thinking that action was intellectually framed and formed by individuals who first think of a desired end, and then calculate the best means to achieve it (Ewen, 1996, p. 136). Subconscious non-rational inferences came first, and the art of politics was to discover how to exploit them.

In the post-war period, aided by the efforts of his nephew Bernays to publish his work in the USA, Sigmund Freud became more influential. His impact on PR was considerable as a result of his 1922 book, *Group Psychology and the Analysis of the Ego*, in which, whilst showing Le Bon great respect, he addressed his "brilliantly executed" work and showed point by point that the individual and the group were inseparable and mutually determining. One could influence the group via individual psychology, and the individual via group processes and mass suggestion. The predominance of fantasy and illusion emerging from unfulfilled wishes was noted by Freud, who agreed with Le Bon that crowds think in images rather than ideas, but added that this was also true of individuals encouraged to free associate. Images were the key to stimulating the imagination of crowds, promoting a state akin to mass hypnosis by feeding their hunger for illusion.

Walter Lippmann took the idea of understanding via the "pictures in our heads" even further in arguing for the creation of a pseudo-reality that would tame or predigest the "blooming, buzzing confusion" of the outer world. Symbolic pseudo-environments work via stereotypical associations to make the processes of interpreting complex events and relations easy by visualizing and dramatizing them. Images, photographs, and, increasingly, the output of Hollywood, had unrivalled power to engage individuals, displacing the need for conscious thought whilst activating the emotions. They could create in a dispersed public a "homogeneous will out of a heterogeneous mass of desires…an intensification of feeling [with] a degradation of significance" (Lippmann, 1925, pp. 37–38). By 1928 Lippmann was acknowledging that the public was entirely a virtual creation of media – a phantom. By the 1990s, Jean Baudrillard (1994) was taking this argument further in the context of richer media and more powerful communicative technologies to argue that the fantasy had now become more real than the real – it had become hyper-real. It was no longer possible to separate image from reality – an insight that Hollywood itself picked up and recycled in the feature film *The Matrix*. The public's appetite for illusion, and the easy way it offered of simulating the satisfaction of unfulfilled desires through fantasy, ensured that as long as Lippmann's elites kept on providing the blue pill of the hyper-real they would not seek out the painful red pill of reality.

Desire and critique

Beyond its importance to early contributions to the psychology of PR, the concept of desire is one of the most important in the philosophy of the twentieth century, although its presence is often implicit. Michel Foucault, for example, reserved the explicit use of the term for sexual desire, although much of his work rests on an understanding of desire as being discursively produced as a perceived lack by the subject of a specific element given value within a nexus of discursive relations by language, institutional recognition, access to knowledge and relations of power. Understandings of desire tend to fall into two broad orientations: one that we might call Hegelian, that sees desire as a transitive drive towards an object in order to resolve a perceived lack; and one that we might call Nietzschean, where desire is an intransitive drive, an autonomous movement lacking an object that may take many directions. For Hegel, desire is paradoxical, in that in desiring its own satisfaction, it desires its own death – a riddle that surfaces with relevance to PR in the desire of the subject to belong to a group, which necessitates a submerging of individuality. This produces a dynamic in which there is a dialectical movement between self and other. For Hegel, the subject first desires the other, in wanting to have knowledge of that which is not itself. In so recognizing the other *as* other, there emerges the reciprocal need in the subject to be recognized *by* the other – so desire for the other, which cannot ever be fully achieved, becomes desire for the recognition of the other, a validation of one's worth. In an interpretation developed by Alexander Kojève, the subject's desire does not stop at this point, but becomes a desire for reciprocity – that is, it is not sufficient to be recognized by the other, but the other's desire to be recognized by the subject also needs to be realized. Desire is not desire for the other, but the desire to be desired by the other.

Following from Kant, however, two additional understandings emerge: one is that there is always an element of the other that is radical, that we cannot understand because it is irreducibly other. The second is that in order to relate at all to the other, there must be elements that are not radical, that are not just assimilable but are already part of our own subjectivity. As a result there is an otherness, or alterity, within ourselves. But the consequence of this is that we cannot eradicate the possibility of a radical interior alterity, a part of ourselves that is other, that we cannot know unless, and until, it emerges dialectically. Alongside desire, then, is the ontological anxiety that results from this situation. Relations with others, and consequently relations in public, are animated by a combination of desire and anxiety. Control the means of stimulating desire and reducing anxiety and a more organic means of maintaining social order than repression and suppression, reward and punishment, is possible.

Within this scheme, desire emerges as a drive to resolve a perceived or experienced lack, and this basic understanding of desire as lack was carried into Freud's thinking. Freud developed through psychoanalysis an understanding of ego-defences, by which we protect ourselves from anxiety and cathexis, whereby the desire for an unattainable object is displaced onto a different object. The mechanisms can be complex and puzzling, but add up to the insight that as an analyst what you get is not usually what you should be looking for. What all these approaches emphasize is that the subject is insufficient…lacking something to complete its being.

An alternative non-dialectical route that sees desire as an overflowing of becoming, rather than an insufficiency of being, can be found in the work of Nietzsche and of Bergson, emerging powerfully in the multidisciplinary thought of Georges Bataille from the 1930s. For Bataille (1988), desire was a powerful driving force that was not initiated by a perceived lack – it was a flow of life that was exuberant, driven to excess, to explore and exceed its potential, emerging autonomously from within rather than intruding anxiously from without. This understanding also informs the thought of Gilles Deleuze and Felix Guattari, who displace the dialectical movement of history with that of the multidimensional rhizome. Desire is possibility rather than lack, potential rather than restriction. Freudian approaches steer us towards the underlying drives behind the masking mechanisms through which desire may be presented, and teach that objects may be presented that capture those underlying drives because they are unconscious and cathectic. Foucault, though not using these terms, put forward an argument that in effect saw desire not in terms of an ontological lack underlying its manifestations, but as created or manufactured by discursive formations (such as language) resulting from the operations of power on knowledge. Deleuze and Guattari (1984; 1987) reinstate desire ontologically, but not as lack needing to be fulfilled: for them language and other symbolic representations do not create the movement of desire, but catch its flow, temporarily diverting it.

Finally, in a crucial period that extended from the 1920s to the 1950s (and in the case of Habermas and Gadamer, beyond) what became known as Critical Theory connected the work of Freud with that of Marx, to resuscitate Marx's notion of ideology as the cornerstone of the critique of capitalism. For Marx, capitalism was imbricated with contradictions that produced ever-greater inequalities as value was extracted from the system, driving it ever-harder in terms of competition and growth. For those who benefited least from the system to continue to participate in it, coercion was always an option (as seen with the Ludlow Massacre) but what was preferable was a symbolic structure, such as a belief system, that blinded the workers to their own exploitation and commodification, and could even make them desire it. This function could be fulfilled by religion, famously condemned by Marx as the "opium of the masses", but more broadly was termed "ideology". Ideology was the more effective the more it was taken for granted, naturalized, and accepted as inevitably the way things were. Compliance and consent became unconscious, resistance was not considered relevant unless consciousness was raised.

Members of the Frankfurt School, notably Walther Benjamin, Theodore Adorno and Max Horkheimer, examined the societies of mass production and consumption that had arisen since Marx, alongside the relative decline of organized religion, and the growth of cultural media, and argued that ideology was no longer located in belief systems as readily identifiable as the Protestant Ethic. For them, ideology was at work in everything that stimulated desire for specific objects that could be consumed; specific social status symbols that indicated both recognition and belonging; and cultural products that produced sentiments (rather than emotions) that comforted human anxiety, reflecting back to us a pleasing image of who we were (even through tragedy). This Adorno (1980) called "kitsch", although the term had been in use since the mid-nineteenth century. The purpose of the mass media, channelling Freud, was to stimulate unconscious desire for products whilst generating sentimental kitsch, comforting our anxieties in reinforcing our sense of who and what we were. These were the workings of ideology. The purpose of Critical Theory, channelling Freud somewhat differently and a modernized version of Marx, was ideology-critique – the exposure of the cultural "doping" process and the raising of consciousness. This, of course, like psychoanalysis, was not necessarily straightforward.

Žižek (1989; 1997) notes Lacan's recognition of the common ground between Marx's treatment of commodity fetishism and Freud's analysis of the "symptom". Ideology rests upon a fantasy, and as it is articulated materially, reveals the tensions between its fantasy, reality (that occasions the need for articulation) and what Lacan calls "the Real" – that element or excess that cannot be represented, against which all forms of representational system inevitably fall short, and either occasion further attempts at representation or are foreclosed by some form of commitment to the fantasy (which kitsch, for example, does by an easy seduction). What lies behind the fantasy is the tension between what Lacan calls "Law", and its transgression. We could illustrate this by considering one of the most famous PR "events" ever staged – Edward Bernays' "Torches of Freedom" demonstration at New York's Fifth Avenue Easter Parade, on 31 March 1929, where debutantes stopped at a prearranged point of the route to light their own Lucky Strike cigarettes (Tye, 1998, pp. 28–35). Bernays' sponsor, whose identity was scrupulously concealed, was American Tobacco. Smoking for women was by this time accepted (Schudson, 1984, pp. 186–7, cited in Tye, 1998, p. 34), but not necessarily approved of, and there remained a taboo on women smoking outdoors in public places. Bernays consulted psychoanalyst A. A. Brill, and, encouraged by his advice, was able to persuade a group of young, stylish and independent-minded debutantes that this was an impingement on their freedom. They would, by lighting up in public, demonstrate their independence, both as consumers and individuals. Not only would Bernays stimulate a specific market for his tobacco sponsors' products, but the connection between consumption and identity that was becoming increasingly important in advertising would be taken another step further.

Brill's advice to Freud's nephew was that it was normal for women to want to smoke, as

> the emancipation of women has suppressed many of their feminine desires. Many women now do the same work as men do. Many women bear no children; those who do bear have fewer children. Feminine traits are masked. Cigarettes, which are equated with men, become torches of freedom.
>
> *(cited in Bernays, 1965, p. 38)*

Bernays was delighted to take up Brill's justification, and his metaphor, although Brill later qualified that women should not go so far as to offer men cigarettes, however, as "the cigarette is a phallic symbol, to be offered by a man to a woman. Every normal man or woman can identify with such a message" (Bernays, 1965, p. 395). This is more than simple social convention: in accepting the cigarette, the recipient accepts what Lacan would term the "phallic order".

In Lacan, the psychological terrain of the conscious and unconscious is understood in terms of the connections made between three domains: the Imaginary, the Symbolic, and the Real. The Imaginary is the sense of coherence and wholeness that makes the idea of self meaningful, and emerges from the early mirror stage when the infant sees the image of themselves reflected back to them. The Symbolic begins on the entry into language, a pre-given symbolic system but one that is also open and changing – here the child learns who it is within a system of others, distinct from the coherence of its own imaginary world. The Real is that which escapes adequate representation in language, those elements of meaning that remain external and elusive but necessary for experience to be understood. The symbolic can close off the route to coherence, or may provide a surrogate for it, or may open in the direction of the unarticulated real (as, for example, in art). Media, then, are a prime ground for influencing subject formation. Zizek (1997) is again helpful in that media provide not simply channels for desire, they shape desire itself.

> Fantasy mediates between the formal symbolic structure and the positivity of the objects we encounter in reality…it provides a schema according to which certain positive objects in reality can function as objects of desire…fantasy does not mean that when I desire a strawberry cake and cannot get it in reality, I fantasize about eating it; the problem is, rather: *how do I know that I desire a strawberry cake in the first place? This* is what fantasy tells me.
>
> (p. 7)

Reading Bernays' event from this perspective, we see that the simple sexual drive explanation is inadequate, and the connection to freedom is too easily made. For Lacan, the desire for coherence that stems from the fundamental lack in the feminine subject position is the imaginary at work – the desire for equality and freedom is the desire for balance and coherence. However, the symbolic system of law and order constrains the feminine into a subordinate position. Unable or unwilling to directly confront the Law, the unspoken Real of power, the feminine subject here seeks association with the symbols of those that possess or control the Law. The Law is phallic (understood in terms of power rather than sexuality) and the symbols of the phallic can be transgressively colonized – made especially easy where they are commodified into products – and the anxious feeling of lack is comfortably assuaged. Bernays' little tableau created the fantasy in which the desire for coherence and balance became the desire for a Lucky Strike cigarette rather than a strawberry cake. The taste, in either case, would have been neither the bitterness of tobacco nor the sweetness of strawberry – it was the freshness of freedom. Kitsch works similarly in providing pre-packaged and easily accessible solutions – establishing sentimental symbolic associations that temporarily appear to satisfy the desire for wholeness, emotional connectedness, significance, purpose and place in a community.

Taking a slightly different view of desire, Bernays' subjects, from his own accounts, were already well-formed, intelligent, energetic and imaginative, and their participation in the parade was a means of channelling their exuberance, although it was very much within a patriarchal mode of social entertainment. Bernays' crystalization of their aspirations for expression in a particular transgressive direction against the social grain did not create the drive, nor were they exclusively driven through a sense of lack. Indeed, their sense of themselves as fragmented subjects against an imposed sense of coherence was in tension with their participation in the event itself. Bernays, as was his habit, rationed the *commercial* information he released, and this move could be successful because the *social* movement already had its own momentum. Bernays briefly, and partially, captured the ladies' rhizomic potential.

Of course, Lacan would remind us that "freedom" remained untouched, except at the level of the symbolic, and although women smoking in public may well have increased cigarette sales, it did little for their social condition. Bernays was satisfied with that being his clients' objective, as his approach to PR always took the indirect route in appearing to address broader social purposes that often proved more successful for specific client goals in the long term (similar arguments are made by Chia and Holt, 2009, in relation to "the silent efficacy of indirect action" in corporate strategy). Yet the dark side here was that Bernays was amassing information about the negative effects of smoking on human health throughout the whole period of his work for the tobacco industry, and his employers were well-informed regarding these dangers – informed enough to suppress and even take action to discredit or raise doubt regarding research findings.

Regarding the relation between the symbolic and the inexpressible real, Bataille noted a difference between restricted economy (the field of production-based economics) and general economy (a symbolic and importantly moral field). Understanding the latter, which was the project of the humanities in particular, required recognition of the risks involved in addressing elements of experience and "knowledge" (he used the term "non-knowledge") that were felt or intuited but beyond representation, a regime that he called the "sacred". The fact that achieving states that allowed some seeing beyond, often cost artists and philosophers their health, their sanity and even their lives; the nature of the depressive cycles intensive work initiated, meant that a space was opened up for commodified and easily available forms of art – kitsch – to offer to fill the space of anxiety, anguish, jouissance and ecstasy, with comforting sentimentality. Hollywood recognized this from its early years, and as technology developed more and more rapidly – allowing more complex effects to be reproduced on a mass scale, as noted by Benjamin (1968) – the inexpressible "real" became displaced by the information-overloaded hyper-real, which is dissected by Baudrillard in his later work. At a more accessible level, Ritzer (2007) developed his somewhat anodyne reading of Weber into the McDonaldization thesis, regarding the spread of standardization of experience and modes of production from the fast food industry into all aspects of our everyday lives. Whilst this critical argument drew little on more radical sources, and even more radical readings of Weber, he also picked up on elements of Baudrillard's (1994, 1998) work on consumption, the symbolic and hyper-reality in examining processes of "enchantment" that conjoin the "experience economy" to the McDonaldization of production and services (Ritzer, 2010). Communication is of central importance here, and the processes critiqued are of central importance to media studies, advertising, PR and CMS more broadly. Whilst Baudrillard's work has featured in CMS, it has not been taken up as extensively as it perhaps merits (Grandy & Mills, 2004; Hancock, 1999).

Two authors whose work addresses the nature of the desiring symbolic space, without discussing it in terms of desire, have cast a long shadow over discussions of postmodernity in the past three decades in the form of the Habermas versus Foucault debate. Briefly, Habermas (1984) believes that the enlightenment project of emancipation is unfinished, and that systematically distorted communication, which works to legitimate ideology by manipulating rationality in the name of dominant interests, is its enemy. His solution is to identify and remove limiting conditions and establish equality between speakers, erasing misuse of power and domination in the "ideal speech situation". PR may itself find a place on either side of this trajectory, depending on the state of its conscience. For Foucault (2002), however, knowledge and power are inextricably bound together in the complex relations of what he calls "discourse". Discourse consists, of course, of speech, text and other signs, but for Foucault any specific discourse is also a matter of relations between sets of statements, ideas, institutional arrangements for communicating and qualifying these ideas, practical actions and the naturalizing "truth-effects" that ensue for lived reality as a result of the manipulation and monitoring of these processes. For him, the "ideal speech situation" is a warm fantasy that is yet another product of power/knowledge, and there is no sense that the truth is, or can be, "out there". He explicitly rejects the use of the terms "ideology", and "ideology critique", because they imply the possibility of a non-ideological position from which to launch such critique. PR's "truths" are accordingly better categorized as effects of its situated power/knowledge practices. The debate continues, but there are nevertheless considerable common areas of concern between the two. Both Foucault and Habermas have their advocates within CMS, yet although analyses have taken place of issues on the margins of PR (communication around the time of mergers and acquisitions, for example), PR as a field has not, surprisingly, been itself a core focus of attention.

Critical conclusions

In a pivotal contribution, Valerie Fournier and Chris Grey (2000) attempted to give some shape to the diverse and contested terrain of CMS, and argued that there were three discernible commonalities across the many strains and avenues of commitment constituting the emerging field. Much debate and argument ensued, and continues, and interested readers could profitably consult a variety of sources to complete the picture, including Alvesson (2011), Alvesson and Willmott (2011), Banerjee (2007), Cox, LeTrent-Jones, Voronov & Weir (2009), Fleming and Spicer (2007), Fournier and Grey (2000), Grey and Willmott (2005), Hancock and Tyler (2001), Jeanes and Huzzard (2014), Kelemen and Rumens (2008), Klikauer (2010), Linstead, Fulop & Lilley (2009), Parker (2002), Parker and Thomas (2011), Spicer, Alvesson & Kärreman (2009), and Tadajewski, Maclaren, Parsons & Parker (2011). By way of conclusion, I will use their framework of non-performative intent, denaturalization, and reflexivity to suggest ways in which CMS approaches might further inform PR thinking.

Non-performative intent

The performative intent of mainstream management studies is obvious, being aggressively committed to making organizations work better at whatever it is (they think) they do. For most of the organizations served by business schools, this equates to making money – but management also takes place in the field of public administration, and the voluntary sector, although all can mutually support a common system such as consumer or financial capitalism. The performative use of metrics to measure short-term activity rather than ethical processes produces a governmentality that seeks to align all sectors. Fournier and Grey (2000) see questioning what organizations do, rather than just the way they do it, as part of CMS – which entails understanding how things work; identifying their assumptions and the political systems in which they are embedded; assessing their human, social and environmental consequences, and exploring alternatives. It should be added, however, that performativity is not simply a matter of task performance, but also of how that very task performance also performs and instantiates identity: the more that business schools help business, the more they institutionalize and legitimate themselves within the business world, whilst helping to align the interests of society with those of business. CMS challenges this process.

Denaturalization

Inextricably bound up with performative mainstream work are the methods it uses to gather, establish and propagate its knowledge and "truths". Assumptions about ontology, epistemology and methods become unquestioned and self-sustaining, constituting a paradigm that reproduces a way of seeing reality as the natural order of things. Within mainstream management studies a functionalist approach remains the predominant mode of inquiry and analysis, which marginalizes other approaches and forces them to address the canonical orthodoxy in its own terms. CMS directly exposes and contests these often taken-for-granted assumptions.

Reflexivity

Mainstream research often pursues objectivity and seeks to eliminate "bias" on the model of natural science. Reflexivity, if it occurs, is superficial and concerned with eradicating technical error. This neglects the fact that social science inquiry can never be value-free, whether at the level of the researcher or the sponsoring research system. CMS approaches this not simply as a matter of personal subjectivity that requires correction, but as a matter of social and systemic subjectivity that positions researchers, research systems and the researched within specific power/knowledge-regimes and spheres of interest and influence – to the point of delineating what research is conceivable beyond how it may be conducted. For CMS, these issues are themselves part of the research process to be openly addressed.

Turning to PR, we may think that it is *performative* by definition, self-identifying as the business of "manufacturing" (Lippmann, 1922) or "engineering" (Bernays, 1947b) consent. But consideration of its history shows that this has not always been a simple matter. From its earliest days practitioners reflected on the nature of the discipline in different ways, at times seeing it as primarily educational and informative, a two-way process, a way of mitigating the damaging effects of rapid social progress, a way of manipulating the masses, a way of furthering democracy, or a way of facilitating a move beyond the traditional restrictions of the social. PR, or propaganda, mediated some of the great social initiatives of the twentieth century. Bernays (1944) advocated "welfare capitalism" in 1944, and was internally critical of the United Fruit Company's employment policies in Latin America, preparing a blueprint for reform in 1947 which they eventually adopted in 1956 (Tye, 1998, pp. 160–5). But Bernays also advocated some of capitalism's great evils as an aggressive publicist for the United Fruit Company's interests in the early 1950s, and by heavily influencing the US perception of the communist threat – leading to the CIA sponsoring an invasion of Guatemala that toppled its government (Tye, 1998, pp. 172–6).

From a CMS perspective we would need to ask what constitutes the "public" and the public good; what are the ethics of the "relations" with that public or specific sections of it, and to what extent are these exploitative; where does the professional understanding of PR as advice-giving and counselling position itself in terms of power/knowledge regimes of domination and democracy; and to what extent does PR as a practice orient itself to elements beyond the interests of its specific "client" and the ascribed desires of their perceived "publics"? The history of PR and the state has encompassed advocacy of the New Deal in the 1930s (Ewen, 1996, pp. 247–87); strategizing the "big business" backlash to Roosevelt's brand of populism in the late 1930s and 1940s (Ewen, 1996, pp. 306–36; Miller & Dinan, 2008, pp. 56–9); Ivy Lee and Carl Byoir separately advising Hitler, Goebbels and the Nazis in the 1930s (Miller & Dinan, 2008, pp. 18–20); selling Reaganomics and spinning Thatcherism in the 1980s (Ewen, 1996, pp. 394–7; Miller and Dinan, 2008, pp. 100–3); and a range of PR companies advising regimes involved in questionable activities including those in Zambia, Russia, pre-Arab Spring Egypt, Bahrain, Belarus and Sri Lanka on "reputation laundering" (Burt, 2012, pp. 106–8; Miller & Dinan, 2008, pp. 78–124). It is clear that however spectacular the rise of "spin" and its demonstrated ability to remake itself in the context of globalized "Empire" (Banerjee & Linstead 2001; Hardt & Negri, 2000), changes in information and media technology and the ability of social movements to access information (or be leaked it), communicate rapidly and organize digitally are having their effects. One of these is to motivate the idea of a public or "multitude" beyond the social that might directly contest the influence of "elites" – which throws into question the idea of performativity. Nevertheless, as Miller and Dinan (2008, pp. 78–98) demonstrate, the existence of "elites" is real and palpable, and neoliberalism has been entwined with PR since Lippmann influenced Hayek in the 1930s and the subsequent founding of the Mont Pelerin Society with its objective of undermining democracy in favour of corporate interests (Miller & Dinan, 2008, pp. 63–5). Another effect is increasingly to question the presentation of "responsibility" in corporate social *responsibility* (and representations of the "triple bottom- line"), which as Bobby Banerjee (2007) conjectures contains some good, some bad, and some downright ugly initiatives.

Denaturalization again might seem to run counter to PR's traditional thrust, which was to create narratives, or even participatory events in which narrative trajectories could be stage-managed and that made contestable actions or initiatives seem comfortable: reasonable, natural and even progressive developments. But again, PR can be at least partially redeemed from a critical point of view because of its openness to scientific discovery, whether in the social or natural sciences. There is, of course, much evidence of PR being used to suppress or distort the findings of science to mislead the public (as Bernays did when working for the tobacco industry), but Bernays kept the original reports in his archive and ultimately campaigned against the industry, successfully achieving a ban on cinema advertising of cigarettes and the inclusion of health warnings on cigarette packets (Tye, 1998, pp. 47–50). The potential critical role for PR here is huge, because since the 1990s concerns with climate change and damage to the natural environment have grown into genuine alarm over "greenwashing" efforts to divert, distract, delay, disinform and discredit environmentally responsible initiatives (Fineman, 2001; Laufer, 2003; ; Rampton & Stauber, 2001; Stauber & Rampton, 1995). A CMS influenced PR would explore how naturalizing processes are initiated and resisted, and how trust might be built through not taking things for granted – including the communication process itself. Much of PR has involved, and still does involve, Zelig-like characters who move around on the edge of history pulling the strings of events, creating impact that has its effects without going through tedious processes of rationalization and justification. Sometimes they have rationed information and access to it, and although some of that remains possible, in the Internet age it is more likely that the proliferation of both information and disinformation creates consumer bewilderment. A bewildered consumer – of ideas, ideologies, automobiles, political candidates or fast food – tends to revert to simple, often-subconscious routines for making sense and making choices, as Bernays and his colleagues were aware.

Reflexivity has traditionally been a phenomenon that PR has exploited in others in creating its hyper-realities and aspirational identities to which other subjects are seduced to aspire and conform. PR itself, though apparently reflecting on its own identity and principles, and in Bernays' case very carefully on its techniques, seems historically to have compromised itself from its very beginnings. What was espoused was not always practised, "professional neutrality" allowed practitioners to turn a blind eye to the state of moral turpitude of those they were advising and the effects of their advice on third parties. For CMS, such positions are no longer tenable: every position is imbricated with power relations, power and knowledge are inseparable, and manipulations of the representation of knowledge are political interventions. It is no longer acceptable nor possible to sidestep the ethical consequences of those positions and their responsibilities. Speaking truth to power must entail encouraging power to speak truth to the powerless. Humans may be caught in webs of signification they themselves have spun, but "they" are not all equal: the media vectors that constitute the communicative matrix are not the product of a democracy of spinarets, and behind the web several large spiders are invisibly lurking in the shadows. CMS would urge PR to be open about its position and its responsibilities in this multiplex crafting of meaning and leveraging of self and corporate interest.

Returning to our consideration of desire, CMS makes explicit the often-dark connection between psychological fantasy, knowledge and power that PR sometimes mediates and sometimes masks. Desire understood as lack can offer a means for control and manipulation on a mass scale, whether via the massive gatherings of crowds or the even larger assemblages reached by mass media and rendered complaisant by hyper-reality. Understood as an intransitive force of proliferative energy, desire can be seen to activate the collective creativity of the "multitude" made virtually interactive by the Internet. Tracing the history of PR through desire leads us to conclude that there is much common ground covered by CMS and PR, although the connections are rarely made; that CMS offers a useful set of conceptual tools to PR, whilst PR opens out a neglected set of narratives to CMS; and that as both CMS and PR find themselves questioning their future direction, they may well learn from each other to an extent that they have not so far achieved.

References

Adorno, T. (1980). Bloch's "Traces": The philosophy of kitsch. *New Left Review*, I/121. Retrieved on 15 November 2014 from http://newleftreview.org/I/121/theodor-adorno-bloch-s-traces-the-philosophy-of-kitsch

Alvesson, M. (2011). *Classics in critical management studies*. Cheltenham, UK: Edward Elgar.

Alvesson, M., & Willmott, H. (Eds.). (2011). *Critical management studies* (Four-volume set). London, UK: Sage.

Alvesson, M., Bridgman, T., & Willmott, H. (Eds.). (2009). *The Oxford handbook of critical management studies*. Oxford, UK: Oxford University Press.

Banerjee, S. B. (2007). *Corporate social responsibility: The good, the bad and the ugly*. Cheltenham, UK: Edward Elgar.

Banerjee, S., & Linstead, S. A. (2001). Globalization, multiculturalism and other fictions: The new colonization for the new millennium. *Organization*, 8(4), pp. 711–50.

Bataille, G. (1988). *The accursed share: An essay on general economy. Volume I: Consumption*. London, UK: Zone Books.

Baudrillard, J. (1994). *Simulacra and simulation*. Ann Arbor: University of Michigan Press.

Baudrillard, J. (1998). *The consumer society: Myths and structures*. London: Sage.

Benjamin, W. (1968). The work of art in the age of mechanical reproduction. In H. Arendt (Ed.), *Illuminations*, pp. 214–18). London, UK: Fontana

Bernays, E. L. (1923 [1961]). *Crystalizing public opinion*. New York, NY: IG Publishing.

Bernays, E. L. (1928 [2005]). *Propaganda*. New York, NY: IG Publishing.

Bernays, E. L. (1944–5). *Plain talk to liberals* – a series of full page advertisements placed in *The New Republic* and *The Nation* (see Tye, 1998, p. 105, and Ewen 1996, p. 374).

Bernays, E. L. (1947a). Bernays on fear. *TIDE*, 7 March, p. 56.

Bernays, E. L. (1947b). Engineering of Consent. *Annals of the American Academy of Political Science*, 250 (March), PP. 113–20.

Bernays, E. L. (1965). *Biography of an idea: Memoirs of public relations counsel Edward L. Bernays*. New York, NY: Simon and Schuster.

Borch, C. (2013). Gabriel Tarde (1843–1904). In J. Helin, T. Hernes, D. Hjorth & R. Holt (Eds), *The Oxford handbook of process philosophy*, pp. 185–201. Oxford, UK: Oxford University Press.

Burt, T. (2012). *The dark art: The changing face of public relations*. London, UK: Elliott and Thompson.

Chia, R., & Holt, R. (2009). *Strategy without design: The silent efficacy of indirect action*. Cambridge, UK: Cambridge University Press.

Cox, J. W., LeTrent-Jones, T. G., Voronov, M., & Weir, D. (Eds.) (2009). *Critical management studies at work*. Cheltenham, UK: Edward Elgar.

Czarniawska, B. (2009). Gabriel Tarde and organization theory. In P, S. Adler (Ed.), *The Oxford handbook of sociology and organization studies: Classical foundations*, pp. 246–67. Oxford, UK: Oxford University Press.

Deleuze, G., & Guattari, F. (1984). *Anti-Oedipus: Capitalism and schizophrenia*, vol. 1. London, UK: Athlone.

Deleuze, G., & Guattari, F. (1987). *A thousand plateaus: Capitalism and schizophrenia*, vol. 2. London, UK: Athlone.

Ewen, S. (1996). *PR! A social history of spin*. New York, NY: Basic Books.

Fineman, S. (2001). Fashioning the environment. *Organization*, 8(1), pp. 17–31.

Fleming, P., & Spicer, A. (2007). *Contesting the corporation: Struggle, power and resistance in organizations*. Cambridge, UK: Cambridge University Press.

Foucault, M. (2002). *The archaeology of knowledge*. London, UK: Routledge.

Fournier, V., & Grey, C. (2000). At the critical moment: Conditions and prospects for critical management studies. *Human Relations*, 53(1), pp. 7–32.

Freud, S. (2010 [1922]). *Group Psychology and the Analysis of the Ego*. New York: Boni and Liveright.

Grandy, G., & Mills, A. J. (2004). Strategy as simulacra? A radical reflexive look at the discipline and practice of strategy. *Journal of Management Studies*, 41(7), pp. 1153–70.

Grey, C., & Willmott, H. (2005). *Critical management studies: A reader*. Oxford, UK: Oxford University Press.

Habermas, J. (1984). *The theory of communicative action: Reason and the rationalization of society*. Boston, MA: Beacon Press.

Hancock, P. (1999). Baudrillard and the metaphysics of motivation: A reappraisal of corporate culturalism in the light of the work and ideas of Jean Baudrillard. *Journal of Management Studies*, 36(2), pp. 155–75.

Hancock, P., & Tyler, M. (2001). *Work, postmodernism and organization: A critical introduction*. London, UK: Sage.

Hardt, M., & Negri, A. (2000). *Empire*. Cambridge, MA: Harvard University Press.

Hobsbawm, J. (2010). *Where The truth lies: Trust and morality in the business of PR, journalism and communications*. London, UK: Atlantic Books.

Jeanes, E., & Huzzard, T. (Eds). (2014). *Critical management research*. London, UK: Sage.

Kelemen, M., & Rumens, N. (2008). *An introduction to critical management research*. London, UK: Sage.

Klikauer, T. (2010). *Critical management ethics*. Basingstoke, UK: Palgrave Macmillan.

Latour, B., & Lepinay, V. (2010). *The science of passionate interests: An introduction to Gabriel Tarde's economic anthropology*. Chicago, IL: University of Chicago Press.

Laufer, W. S. (2003). Social accountability and corporate greenwashing. *Journal of Business Ethics*, 43, pp. 253–61.

Le Bon, G. (2005 [1895]). *The crowd: A study of the popular mind*. Minneapolis, MN: Filiquarian Pulbishing.

L'Etang, J. (2008). *Public relations: Concepts, practice and critique*. London, UK: Sage.

Linstead, S. A., Fulop, L., & Lilley, S. (2009). *Management and organization: A critical text*. Basingstoke, UK: Palgrave Macmillan.

Linstead, S. A., Maréchal. G., & Griffin, R. W. (2014). Theorizing and researching the dark side of organization. *Organization Studies*, 35(2), pp. 165–88.

Lippmann, W. (1922 [2007]). *Public opinion*. Minnesota, MN: FQ Classics/Filiquarian Publishing.

Lippmann, W. (1925 [2011]). *The phantom public*. Piscataway, NJ: Transaction Publishers.

Miller, D., & Dinan, W. (2008). *A century of spin: How public relations became the cutting edge of corporate power*. London, UK: Pluto Press.

Park, R. E. (1972 [1904]). *The crowd and the public*. Chicago, IL: University of Chicago Press.

Parker, M. (2002). *Against management: Organisation in the age of managerialism*. Oxford, UK: Polity.

Parker, M., & Thomas, R. (2011). What is a critical journal? *Organization*, 18(4), pp. 419–27.

Rampton S., & Stauber, J. (2001). *Trust us, we're experts! How industry manipulates science and gambles with your future*. New York, NY: Tarcher/Putnam.

Ritzer, G. (2007). *The McDonaldization of society*, 5th edition. London, UK: Sage.

Ritzer, G. (2010). *Enchanting a disenchanted world: Continuity and change in the cathedrals of consumption*, 3rd edition. London, UK: Sage.

Spicer, A., Alvesson, M., & Kärreman, D. (2009). Critical performativity: The unfinished business of critical management studies. *Human Relations*, 62(4), pp. 537–556.

Stauber, J., & Rampton, S. (1995). *Toxic sludge is good for you! Lies, damn lies and the public relations industry*. Monroe, ME: Common Courage Press.

Tadajewski, M., Maclaran, P., Parsons, E., & Parker, M. (Eds). (2011). *Key concepts in critical management studies*. London, UK, Sage.

Tarde, G. (1890 [1903]). *The laws of imitation*. New York, NY: Henry Holt.

Tarde, G. (1969). *On communication and social influence*. In T. N. Clark (Ed.), *Gabriel Tarde on communication and social influence*. Chicago, IL: University of Chicago Press.

Trotter, W. (1916 [1985]). *The instincts of the herd in peace and war*. London, UK: Keynes Press/British Medical Association.

Tye, L. (1998). *The father of spin: Edward L Bernays and the birth of public relations*. New York, NY: Henry Holt.

Wallas, G. (1908). *Human nature in politics*. London, UK: A. Constable & Co.

Žižek, S. (1989). *The sublime object of ideology*. London, UK: Verso.

Žižek, S. (1997). *The plague of fantasies*. London, UK: Verso.

Part IV
Ways forward

25

Deconstructing Japan's PR

Where is the public?

Nancy Snow

"Japan is not necessarily the most interesting subject around the world."
(Masato Otaka, spokesman, Japanese embassy in Washington, DC)[1]

A quarter of a century ago, Karel van Wolferen, a 17-year veteran East Asian correspondent for the Dutch daily newspaper, *NRC Handelsblad*, published a critical assessment of Japan's political economy and parliamentary democracy system. *The Enigma of Japanese Power: People and Politics in a Stateless Nation* (1989) was well received internationally but not in Japan. This was at a time when most of the world's headlines were trumping the *wa* (harmony) of corporate and government relations known collectively as "Japan Inc." as well as the rise of Japan as an economic superpower to rival the US. In stark contrast, Karel Van Wolferen described a country still under the military-political protective thumb of the US, its former war nemesis and post-World War Two occupier, and without an active citizen public invested in how the nation was running. His concern then, as it is now, is a propensity in Japan to passivity in democratic government participation (Beeson and Stubbs, 2012). A paradox of Japan is a resilient populace with societal stability driven by *kizuna* (bonds in human relations), but with a weak political structure (Miura and Walker, 2012). A recent study of East Asian citizen participation by Doh Shin (2012) showed that deferential authoritarian types – those who go along with their political leaders and report living either in a full democracy or a democracy with just minor problems – were most numerous. Deferential authoritarians are over one-and-a-half times as prevalent as critical democrats (34 per cent versus 21 per cent) – citizens of democracies who report living either in a democracy with major problems or a non-democracy. Japan is of import since it is the oldest and most democratic East Asian nation state and has served as a model for democratization throughout the region (Beeson, 2009). Further, Japan's postwar occupation, allegiance, and bilateral alliance with the US in national security protection and constitutional heritage make this case study of the missing public in Japan's public relations (see Leitch & Neilson, 2001) a comparative bridge in the public relations literature from East Asia to a US-dominant core (L'Etang, 2005).

Karel van Wolferen's thesis still has applicability today: it lays out the incredulous real situation of a professed parliamentary democracy that is run by one dominant party, the CIA-created Liberal Democratic Party (Dubro and Kaplan, 1995; Mann, 1995), first hatched at the end of occupation in 1955, and which has, with few hiccups, occupied the Japanese political landscape ever since. As Jim Mann writes in the *Los Angeles Times*: "the CIA supported and subsidized top leaders of Japan's ruling Liberal Democratic Party while doing what it could to weaken and undermine its opposition, the Japanese Socialist Party." The LDP is responsible for the neoliberal policies of the second Shinzo Abe administration (2012–present), which include a three-arrow economic reform agenda as well as a US-championed state secrets law and Article 9 revision.

The subtext of Japan's enigmatic power holds a lesson for critical theory public relations scholars: you cannot question what does not exist. A state without a nation has little, if any, accountability or transparency to its domestic or global publics. Wolferen will not go so far as to call Japan a client state under the complete protectorate of the US – but he comes close. His analysis, along with an ex-insider's perspective, *Straitjacket Society: An Insider's Irreverent View of Bureaucratic Japan* (Masao Miyamoto, 1995) form a critical backdrop for Japan's public relations dilemma: it is in the world, but not of it. This invisible hand of information management manifests to this day.

In September 2014, the *New York Times* (Lipton, Williams & Confessore, 2014) ran an investigative story with a foreboding headline designed to draw eyeballs: "Foreign Powers Buy Influence at Think Tanks." Japan was singled out among a number of activist governments seeking to buy political influence at major think tanks in Washington, DC. When the Japanese embassy's minister for public affairs, Masato Otaka, was asked why the government of Japan spends so much money on political influence, his response was in keeping with common Japanese virtues of humility and reserve: "Japan is not necessarily the most interesting subject around the world. We've been experiencing some slower growth in the economy. I think our presence is less felt than before." No truer words were spoken about the need for Japan to invest more in its international public relations profile, but at the same time those words defy the numbers about this cultural and economic superpower. Otaka-san's choice of words illustrates a recognized lack of confidence that the Japanese nation has regarding its ability to persuade both generally and globally. This is reflected in an "in-house" rather than outside agency approach to public relations, coupled with a tradition of on-the-job training in persuasive communications. Japan has no professional accreditation system for public relations (Cooper-Chen & Tanaka, 2007). An academic study of public relations, critical or not, is missing at Japanese universities, driven in part by Japan's long tradition of lifetime employment that has led to in and out rotation in PR. One spends a career with a company, not with a rotation. Watson and Sallot (2001, p. 392) describe the "dearth" of recent public relations research in Japan; contrast this to a mountain of scholarly research on Japanese culture (Benedict, 1946; Gudykunst & Nishida, 1994). Even more troubling, there is a lack of understanding among Japanese people about how public relations relates to the public interest, promoted facts, and social truths that are separate from paid media advertising. International public relations is perhaps best known in a historical context to Cold War and Occupied Era Japanese scholars who recognize it in programs like the covert Panel "D" Japan, a postwar American propaganda program to change the mindset of the Japanese through measures such as pro-American themes in films, counterpropaganda campaigns against nuclear power and nuclear weapons in Japan, and payoffs to the LDP and Japan's main public broadcaster, NHK (Matsuda, 2007).

In this chapter Japan is considered a most interesting subject around the world as a case study to examine the paradoxical nature of public relations: a nation state that has one of the top economies in the world but with an internal and external reputation for a weak or "marginal" (Yamamura & Shimizu, 2009, p. 1) persuasive communications profile (Holmes Report, 2011; Batyko, 2012). For more than 40 years (1968–2011), Japan, a country whose geographic size is slightly smaller than its trans-Pacific neighbor state, California, was the world's second largest economy, with half the population size of its economic better: the US. Despite the rise of China, the world's largest developing economy in the twenty-first century, Japan remains a formidable economic giant in East Asia and worldwide, although, like the European Union, it has often been referred to as an economic giant and a political dwarf (Blaker, 1993; Bukh, 2014; Hellmann, 1988; Mahbubani, 1992). It is widely recognized as a cultural soft power superpower (Lam, 2007; McGray, 2002; Monji, 2010; Nye, 1990, 2004; Watanabe & McConnell, 2008), and its public diplomacy profile rests almost exclusively on promotion of a "Cool Japan" brand focused on mass consumer and creative industries (Christensen, 2011; Hayden, 2011; Snow, 2013b). It is led by the global popularity of *manga* (comic books), *anime* (animation), *cosplay* (costume play based on animation), J-Pop (such as the Akihabara-inspired girl group AKB48), modern J-Fashion (such as Harajuku and Lolita), as well as the traditional crafts and cuisine of Japan. Kenjiro Monji, the former director of public diplomacy at the Ministry of Foreign Affairs responsible for Cool Japan promotion, described it this way (Miller, 2011; Monji, 2010):

> We see many *cos-players* in various Japanese pop culture events. But I was also impressed that young girls in foreign countries were wearing Japanese young girls' fashion such as Lolita and high school uniform fashions. Therefore, I assigned three young fashion leaders as "*Kawaii*" or Cute Ambassadors. They were dispatched all over the world to promote Japan's pop culture and were received with many fans. In Recife, Brazil, 20,000 people gathered for *Kawaii* Ambassador's Fashion Show. One high school in Thailand that modified its school uniform after Japanese Anime characters drew eight fold applications for entrance.

Laura Miller (2011) describes the Cool Japan ideology as a cute masquerade and the pimping of Japan. It masks a global campaign of government exploitation of uncomplicated cuteness (*kawaii*) in which women and girls are one-dimensional passive objects and not active subjects that can shape, resist, create, or critique Japanese popular culture.

Japan's internal image is one of distinction. While it sees itself as nationally distinct rather than internationally common, it forges ahead paradoxically with seemingly safe versions of other countries' public diplomacy models, mainly those of its shadow superpower, the US, and those of shadow soft power theorist, Joseph Nye, Jr., but also from other countries that are seen as Japan's (almost) equal in high culture status – France for sophistication and luxury branding – or middle and geek class popular culture status (Cool Japan for Cool Britannia). For instance, the ministry of economy, trade and industry (METI) oversees the Cool Japan brand, which has raised eyebrows among some observers who question the viability of a notoriously uncool entity – a government bureaucracy – being used to promote creative culture. Manabu Kitawaki (Grunebaum, 2012), the director of a Meiji University summer English-language program on Cool Japan, even questioned the promotion campaign in the context of Japanese values:

> To call yourself cool is by definition uncool – and it defies Japanese modesty. Creativity doesn't spring from marketing. The Ministry of Economy, Trade, and Industry hired Dentsu for its Cool Japan campaign. It's become a way to funnel money to a big ad firm.

Despite its critics, METI raised the stakes in November 2013 (Snow, 2013b) with the creation of a $500 million dollar Cool Japan Fund to help Japanese industries become more globally competitive and expand their markets overseas. Japan sees itself playing "catch-up" with its regional rivals, China and Korea, and in anticipation of the global attention it will receive during the 2020 Summer Olympics it sees no other alternative in culture promotion (Snow, 2013a).

In a much broader politico-economic context, the phrase "Made in Japan" has come to signify advancements in high-tech (robotics, optical instruments, hybrid vehicles, high-speed rail), and the natural resource poor and earthquake prone country must rely on international trade to sustain this economy (Anholt, 2009). About one-third of Japan's 127 million population resides in the Kanto region on Honshu, Japan's largest island – which includes the Greater Tokyo area of 35 million inhabitants. The Greater Tokyo area is home to more than one-quarter of Japan's entire population and remains the most populous metropolitan area in the world. Tokyo is also the mega-city face that is home to Japan's postwar propaganda industries (public relations, public diplomacy), which intertwine in service to the interests of their primary clients – industry and government (Kerr, 2001; van Wolferen, 1989). The public sphere as promulgated by Habermas, Lennox & Lennox (1974) – and particularly a place and practice where the voices of everyday Japanese citizens who don't fill the corridors of the Diet or the executive suites of Toyota come together to form non-governmental opinion – is the weakest social institution in Japan, a result of historical tradition and culture that mandate social cohesion and stability and view too much public participation as chaotic and unstable. There are exceptions in Japanese history, with contests between labor and management, and, most recently, during national emergencies like post-3/11 (Avenell, 2009; Hasegawa, 2011; Slater, Nishimura & Kindstrand, 2012) when citizens were momentarily galvanized to protest against the Tokyo Electric and Power Company (Tepco), the agency responsible for exceedingly poor information management of the Fukushima-Daiichi nuclear power plant. But there exists no Ralph Naderesque Public Citizen or Common Cause public interest lobby to champion citizen rights on an ongoing basis. This is also a lack of education about the role and function of the citizen in a modern democratic open society, against the backdrop of the historical reality of a nation state replete with undemocratic structures. The concept of the "public" in Japan can itself be traced back to the Meiji era (1868–1912), known as Japan's Enlightenment period, that led to many modern economic reforms but without accompanying democratization (Yamamura & Shimizu, 2013). Japan's twentieth century interventionist foreign relations and authoritarian culture further stifled the rise of an autonomous public. In the postwar period, when Japanese citizens did "talk back" to their government, they were strongly influenced by a Marxist/socialist ideology, whether it was in opposition to atomic bombs in the 1950s or the Vietnam War and the Japan-US Security Treaty of the 1960s. This leftist orientation further radicalized in the 1970s and 1980s, thereby distancing dissenters from a mainstream that viewed peaceful protesters as more threatening to stability than weak political leaders. Shin (2012, p. 5) notes that East Asians are more supportive of hierarchism; they "understand fairness in terms of equality before the law and blame disruptions of peace on those who do not conform to rules and regulations. Critics of hierarchism say the immense trust placed in authority poses a serious risk." The memory of social movements in postwar Japan is one that is not a fond one for many Japanese. This further weakens a sphere for a public voice, or indeed any public opposition to political authority.

In the context of mass communications in support of corporate culture and government interests – from nationalist imperial regimes to military occupiers – public relations in Japan has a short, but predictable history. For a country that actively engaged in the two world wars of the twentith century, and established puppet regimes throughout Greater Asia, public relations became associated with the manipulation of international public opinion (wartime propaganda) in favor of Japan's push for imperial expansion and influence (Inoue, 2003). Public relations in this role and context was strictly a one-way controlled information campaign – to manage occupied territories and incite a nation to world expansion through armed force. It would take many years and total defeat in World War Two for Japan to begin to recognize public relations more along the lines of how modern industrialized democracies might use it as a form of information management practice, or to enhance an organization's relationship with its stakeholders.

This realization would come during the MacArthur democratization period of Occupied Japan after World War Two.

Not until the post-Occupation era decades of the economic miracle (1950s–1970s), when Japan emphasized mass consumption, did the public relations concept migrate to commercial marketing and consumer communications (Kelly, Masumoto & Gibson, 2002). It was then that public relations came to be associated interchangeably with advertising, an assumption that persists today with behemoth firms like Dentsu, the largest advertising and public relations company in Japan and the fifth largest paid media firm in the world (Yamamura, Ikarib & Kenmochic, 2013). Dentsu remains today the most influential Japanese firm in the domestic propaganda industry. Its longtime president, Hideo Yoshida, known as the "Demon of Advertising," viewed public relations in purely commercial and corporate terms, as was explained by his assistant, Kanjiro Tanaka:

> A corporation is allowed to exist when the society thinks its existence is desirable. For this, corporations need to widely inform the work they are doing. A corporation can exist when it informs and is accepted. This process is what public relations is.
>
> *(Yamamura et al., 2013, p. 150)*

Dentsu would play a key role in mass marketing promotion in the postwar period. Because of its large imprint in Japanese and global society at the time – Dentsu became the largest advertising company in the world in 1964, a position it retained until 1973 (Dentsu, 2014) – its model of corporate-style public relations was marketed to the Japanese people as the *ideal* model of public communication. This may explain the Japanese reaction to Vance Packard's *The Hidden Persuaders* (1957) and *The Waste Makers* (1960), which, when first released in the US, were presented as critical consumerism models of advertising and public relations. The Japanese language versions of both books became bestsellers and were not taken as critical models. They were presented as ideal models for Japan's postwar pro-growth economy (Yamamura et al., 2013, p. 150). An uncritical mass consumer mind was seen as essential to what would later be called "The Japanese Miracle."

Today, Japan's public relations expenditures are miniscule in comparison to paid media. For a country whose GDP and advertising budgets are about one-third that of the US, its public relations industries are only one-tenth the size of the US's (Batyko 2012). An environment of top-down control of information pervades. Access to information is limited, and community values of perseverance, self-control, restraint, and patience are stressed. After 3/11 struck, and food and water became scarce across wide areas of the country, global publics marveled in response to media reports of Japanese citizens standing quietly and orderly in long queues at stations and shops. This wasn't aberrant behavior but rather routine that was in keeping with Japanese traditional values (Sugimoto 2011). The picture of a well-behaved group of people responding to crisis is a positive image enhancer for Japan, but what about the picture of officials in industry or government not taking responsibility during that same crisis? In the immediate aftermath of 3/11, Tepco, the utility overseeing the second worst nuclear disaster in world history, displayed an inability (or an unwillingness) to communicate with its global audience. Perhaps it was an unwillingness masked as inability. When it did communicate, it was to offer an apology and to offer regret for the situation; but during multiple press briefings Tepco's CEO, Masataka Shimzu, offered little information about the gravity of the situation, which served only to frustrate the gathered press covering the crisis (Mie 2011). A year before 3/11, Toyota had made Japan subject to embarrassing international headlines when the longtime trusted brand had to recall more than 400,000 Prius and other hybrid vehicles as a result of the discovery of faulty brake systems. *Time* magazine's Bill Saporito (2011) described Toyota as "flat-footed by the spiraling public relations disaster as its global recall crisis worsened. Its chief waited weeks before giving his first full press conference." In 2014, another Japanese company, automotive parts company Takata Corporation, would suffer damning headlines when a *New York Times* investigation (Tabuchi, 2014) revealed that the company had not only failed to disclose the potential lethal consequences of its airbags deploying, but had covered up the tests and punished the whistleblowers who had brought the matter into the public arena. The company CEO, Shigehisa Takada, failed to address the press and sent his chief financial officer to an analyst briefing in Tokyo at the height of negative international media coverage.

A helpful, but not exactly determining, factor in explaining Japan's poor public relations strategy in these high profile cases is culture. There are cultural dimensions reflected in Japanese society that may apply to its public relations. Dutch social psychologist and former IBM executive Geert Hofstede (2009) explores Japan's culture in six dimensions: power distance, individualism, masculinity, uncertainty avoidance, pragmatism, and indulgence. Hofstede's work is open to criticism, most notably for its tendency to stereotype national cultures, but his extensive workplace datasets on culture and communication across more than 70 countries offer a useful insight in spite of this. Courtright, Wolfe and Baldwin (2011) champion the use of Hofstede's cultural dimensions in research and teaching, noting limitations that include conceptualizing dimensions in terms of dualities (masculinity, femininity) as opposed to continua; and also noting application limitations that assume individuals and groups act the same in national cultures. As Lisbeth Clausen (2006, p. 60) says about Hofstede's much-cited work, "While 'sophisticated' stereotyping is helpful as a starting point, it does not convey the complexity found in cultures or organizations." This author's dissertation on the cultural mediation roles of Fulbright exchange scholars (Snow, 1992) used Hofstede's cultural dimensions to create a Fulbright Intercultural Survey, and based a model of the cultural mediating scholar on the Hofstede-centric work of my faculty colleagues in the College of Communications at California State University, Fullerton – these colleagues included two of the leading intercultural communication scholars in the world: William B. Gudykunst (2005) and Stella Ting-Toomey (1988; 2005).

Asian cultures are known to be quite hierarchical in interpersonal relations (Zhang, Lin, Nonaka & Beom, 2005) and in this context power is distributed unequally. Hofstede views Japan as a borderline hierarchical society, but most outside observers tend to view it as extremely hierarchical due to the top-down management style of government and industry, both of which are largely centered in Tokyo. The paradox of power distance in Japan is that unlike high power distance societies where a top person can make all final decisions, in Japan there is often no single top executive in charge (almost always a man) who can make a final decision. This is where the *Ringi* system comes into play, a system that emphasizes the need for repeated consultation and input in order to reduce risk and reach consensus in the decision-making process (Clausen, 2006). Lazaridi writes (2012, p. 30):

> In the Ringi system no one has the right to make an individual decision; on the contrary, decisions are made by each group member on the principle of consensus. A decision is not made if unanimity is not reached. Correspondingly, the whole group is responsible for the failure or success of each particular decision. Everybody also therefore needs to be very diplomatic when expressing an opinion.

In such a system, it is hard to ask to see the manager in charge, thus relieving the system of individual responsibility.

Japan's educational system, in principle, is not unlike that in other modern industrialized democracies: it is based on meritocracy and hard work. Everyone is expected to have an equal outcome if they work hard enough, a modifying factor in power distance. McVeigh (2002, p. 14) challenges this assumption:

> The biggest myth of Japanese higher education is that…it is more meritocratic than others. Again, it depends how one defines one's terms, but there is considerable evidence that as in other places, education is geared toward a reproduction of elite/mass distinctions that hampers genuine meritocracy.

Relatedly, Asian cultures are known to be more collectivistic (in-group oriented) than individualistic societies, like many in the West where people are responsible mostly for themselves and their immediate families rather than social groups or society as a whole. Japan is collectivistic, but not as much so as its neighbors Korea and China where the extended family system and overseas diaspora are more extensive. Japan is more paternalistic than individualistic, and company loyalty is almost like a son's loyalty to a father. Certainly Japan is seen as more collectivistic than individualistic to Western eyes, but within Asia, Japan is viewed as more individualistic. The moderate collectivism mitigates an aggressive and assertive individual competitive nature. What manifests is high competition among groups – whether it is one company against another, a high school sports competition, a hotel competing with other hotels in an *ikebana* display, or even competition in presentation such as food presentation or Japan's famous gift-wrapping.

Hofstede (1980, 2001, 2009) notes that Japan is at the top of the masculine value scale and "is one of the most masculine societies in the world." Masculine societies are more competitive and stress economic growth as a priority over protecting the environment. Countries with "a more feminine value position will put higher priority on environmental conservation and a more masculine one on economic growth" (Hofstede, 1980, p. 297). Hofstede (1980, pp. 285–6) argues that countries with highly feminine values place more emphasis on life satisfaction and "work to live" activities, while countries with highly masculine values like Japan are more apt to "live to work" and place value on job satisfaction. The masculine values of endurance prevail in the excessively long hours in the Japanese workplace; this latter feature is creating challenges for Japan's efforts to re-employ women who have left the workplace to marry and have a family. Between six and seven out of ten married Japanese women will leave the workplace for good after having a child, with traditional thinking in Japan viewing childrearing as strictly a women's occupation (McKinsey & Company, 2012; Steinberg & Nakane, 2012).

In tandem with masculinity is Japan's high ranking in uncertainty avoidance. In a country that is one of the most susceptible to natural disaster, and in which earthquakes, tsunamis, typhoons and volcano eruptions are more norm than exception, it is no surprise that the Japanese are famous for planning for disaster. Planning for all contingencies is designed to minimize damage after disaster – which will always occur – and maximize the predictability of imminent disaster. The way people behave in a high uncertainty avoidance culture is quite ritualized and prescriptive. The high need for uncertainty avoidance makes people follow precedent and does not allow much room for change without lengthy feasibility studies or consensus-building measures. Japan displays a high need for pragmatism as is often heard in the phrase, *Shikata ga nai* (it can't be helped/nothing can be done about it.) Japanese *bitoku* (virtues) are practical and not driven by the notion of an omniscient, omnipotent God. Rather, one lives one's life as best one can, knowing that your life is a brief moment in a long history. This pragmatism applies to how Japanese workers are known to view investments or economically difficult times – like that of the early 1990s to the present day. Companies are not here to show profits every quarter, but rather to serve society over the long haul and over many generations. Related to pragmatism is Japan's low score in indulgence. Controlling one's impulses is strength, while giving in to indulgences like too much leisure time is weakness. Overly indulging oneself is restrained by social norms that favor controlling immediate gratification.

What all of these cultural values suggest about Japan's public relations industry is that a great deal of the workings of this persuasive communications sector is out of the sight and mind of the average Japanese citizen. The system as a whole, even the security of the nation's well-being, supersedes notions of the "public good" or "public interest" outside of how the public can support the status quo system. This explains why it is more often the case in Japan that even the highest levels of industry and government are able to get away with no public accountability statements. More often than not, public apologies are the norm if something goes awry, delaying, if not denying, the release of information that is so essential in a participatory democracy and which would shed light on the inner workings that led to the problem in the first place.

Japan's moral and cultural imperatives give up individual self-responsibility to the collective authority of the ministry-industrial complex. What dominates in Japanese society today is a cozy relationship – that is sometimes referred to as incestuous in nature – between the bureaucratic and corporate cultures. It is very common in this setting for political and corporate leaders to say that they have no information in response to any public demand for news during a crisis. As Batyko observes (2012, p. 10):

> The indications to the public relations practitioner are that this is a culture not well-adapted to unstructured situations, such as crisis. Power is held closely at the top of the hierarchy and response times are slow. Individualism is not valued, so it would be difficult to voice opinions that run counter to the chief executive. Female practitioners would find it most difficult to advance in this culture.

To compound the problem of the low budgets that are made available to it, public relations as a field of research inquiry is not widely recognized, studied, much less critiqued, in Japan. This means that public relations is not seen in a pejorative context as either "propaganda" or "spin" because it is almost invisible at the mass conscious level. There is a benign dismissal of the power that the public relations industry has in Japanese society and how government and business operate within that context. Many Japanese people are quick to downplay any prowess that the nation has in persuasive or promotional communications, thereby ending any opportunity to assess the topic. "We aren't good at promotion" is a common refrain. Further, foreign and domestic professionals in public relations acknowledge in unison the innocence and incompetence that the Japanese display toward international public relations, as this vivid example from Burson-Marsteller managing director and CEO, Shuri Fukunaga, shows:

> Japan has a weakness, and it is the country's naïveté in communications. Japan means well. It truly does. But it communicates its message to the world in undisciplined, staccato bursts. The messages are cast into the wide night sky like distant fireworks that disappear before making a strong impression on the viewers. Seen from the outside world, Japan fails to be convincing.
>
> (Branding Japan, 2014)

Ashton Consulting, Ltd. chief executive John Sunley adds that this lack of ability accentuates the negatives and downplays the positive aspects of Japan's society in the world. The main reason for this perception gap is "poor international communication by Japan and its industry." (FCCJ, 2014)

This raises the question of fame and infamy: Is it better for public relations to have a popular reputation for propaganda and spin, however "loose" such critical descriptions may be (Weaver, Motion & Roper, 2006), or is it better to be an almost unknown field of study and conversation? To put it another way, when it involves the public relations of public relations (L'Etang 1997), is it better to be feared than to never be feared at all? From my understanding as a professional who has worked in euphemistic areas of public relations such as public diplomacy and international public information, I consider the latter benign neglect to be the worst of two bad options. This explains the publicity purpose of this chapter – to shine a light on an industry that exists in Japan, but which has not reached any level of critical analysis.

In contrast to Japan, where public relations is either downplayed or viewed as ineffective, there is no country so awash in public relations propaganda as the USA, Japan's closest global ally. From the venture capital hub of Silicon Valley and the executive suites of the Creative Arts Agency (CAA) in Los Angeles, to the Office of the Assistant Secretary for Public Affairs at the Pentagon (Fulbright, 1970), to the Central Intelligence Agency in Langley, Virginia (Wilford, 2008) and finally, the magazine, fashion and television headquarters of Manhattan that make New York City the number one media market in the world, the US has no public relations equal. The British-based nation brand scholar Simon Anholt (Anholt & Hildreth, 2004) goes so far as to refer to the US as the most powerful brand in the world ("the mother of all brands"), in no small part due to its public relations and advertising industries that began to flourish in the early twentieth century. The entire foundation of international public relations industries originated in the US, and to this day non-US public relations scholars reference the work of Harold Lasswell, Edward Bernays, Ivy Lee or Walter Lippman when discussing the history of the profession. In contrast, living here as a half-time resident of Tokyo, Japan, one rarely hears the English or Japanese interchangeable pejoratives for public relations: "spin" (Stauber & Rampton, 1995) or "manufacturing consent."

As noted, the subject of public relations does not have the same breadth and depth of scholarly and public understanding within Japan as it does in the US or Europe. Japan has mass media and journalism departments and institutes – but just a handful of faculty with any public relations background to offer specialized courses, and no degree majors in public relations (Inoue, 2009). This is beginning to change with the rise of the digital economy and the social networked society, along with Japan's strong push for global education. Japan does have the "invisible hand" of influence of its post-World War Two market democracy sponsor, the USA, which covertly financed and propped up the anti-communist Liberal Democratic Party (LDP) during the Occupation period and beyond (Weiner 1994). Today, with few exceptions, the LDP has remained the ruling political party over the past 60 years; a comparable outcome would be if the Republican Party in the US had dominated the political landscape unopposed in the executive and legislative branches of government since 1955.

It is necessary to explore further the public relations situation in Japan with regard to the US, given the political-military history between the two countries. After Japan's defeat by the Allied Forces in 1945, the concept of public relations was widely introduced during the seven-year American Occupation and Reconstruction era. The Allied Occupation Army instructed local and national governments in the use of American-style public relations, which, in that context of a victorious power over a defeated nation, meant one-way communication from the American victors to the defeated Japanese (Inoue, 2003). The Japanese translation of "public" during that period was therefore associated with the publicity surrounding the American public administration of postwar Japan (Cooper-Chen, 1997; Inoue, 2009; Yamamura et al., 2013). PR meant marketing the occupying government's interests (government publicity), not the more common publicity agentry in the US that has come to be associated with sports, entertainment, and the celebrity culture. This paternalistic approach to understanding public relations, with the father figure General Douglas MacArthur at the helm as Supreme Commander for the Allied Powers (SCAP), operated as a combined form of political and sociological propaganda (Ellul, 1966), with the "political propaganda" serving to market the Occupation and Reconstruction of Japan to the Japanese public, and the "sociological propaganda" serving to promote a transformative market democracy model based on American ideals of democratization, liberalization, and disarmament. Even MacArthur's 1.83 meter height in comparison to the 1.65 meters tall Hirohito (Emperor Showa) served as a symbolic representation of what Ellul would later call "vertical propaganda," to underscore the leadership authority of the US in rebuilding Japan from its democratic postwar infancy to adult nation statehood. The corresponding "horizontal propaganda" associated with group socialization has been most often analyzed in the Japanese approach to education (including higher education) and corporate society, where consensus and risk-avoidance are paramount.

The long-serving post-war Japanese Constitution's disarmament feature, with its "Peace Clause" (or Article 9), renounced the sovereign right of war and banned Japan's ability to use the threat or use of force in resolving international disputes. Japan gave up its "war potential" and vowed to forgo anything but defensive forces. Article 9's acceptance by the people and by the political leadership in Japan was, paradoxically, a triumph of public relations, in that a militarized society that had widely accepted its war emperor as a divine figure and its military government as sacrosanct turned sharply against future war when facing the reality of total defeat and the first and only use of nuclear weapons by its former military enemy turned occupier. On July 1, 2014, the cabinet of Prime Minister Shinzo Abe reinterpreted Article 9 by fiat, and without reference to a vote in parliament, to allow Japan's Self-Defense Forces to be used in collective defensive operations and international interventions, and to defend allies if war were to be declared upon it. Though neighboring states like China and Korea denounced the move, the US supported it, a change that for French social theorist Jacques Ellul would be considered a modern continuation of the public relations propaganda foundation of the mid-twentieth century.

Procedurally, the Article 9 reinterpretation was a government public relations disaster in that thousands of Japanese took to the streets in protest, an image that had not been seen since the popular anti-nuclear protests following the Fukushima disaster. Further, international media and foreign intellectuals living in Japan were quick to criticize the action (Kingston, 2014; Ziegler, 2014). For a formal, "emperor-system" democracy (Dower 1999), the fact that the government felt comfortable with making such a drastic change by fiat is a triumph for conservatives and hawkish nationalists who had always resented the imposed Constitution. This is juxtaposed with the two-thirds majority citizen opposition to changing the 68-year pacifistic Constitution, which led to the Nobel Committee in Norway shortlisting "the Japanese people who conserve Article 9" for its peace prize. Nobel nominations notwithstanding, the 2014 update reinforces my conclusions that a Habermasian public interest and activist public opinion in Japan are weak in comparison to other comparable economically advanced societies. "Absent some adjustment in Japanese corporate culture, the public at large and, in particular, those in the practice of public relations, will see the results of the status quo whenever incidents like Tepco's and Toyota's transpire" (Batyko, 2012, p. 12).

Harold Lasswell (1937, p. 525) famously said that propaganda "as a mere tool is no more moral or immoral than a pump handle…the only effective weapon against propaganda on behalf of one policy seems to be propaganda on behalf of an alternative." In today's Japan, especially as it relates to man-made problems at Tepco and Toyota, it would seem that the pump handle of public relations is working effectively on behalf of policies that favor the government-industrial complex but ineffectively or not at all on behalf of the public's ability to offer any alternative policy formulations.

Notes

1   Quoted in Eric Lipton, Brooke Williams and Nicholas Confessore, "Foreign Powers Buy Influence at Think Tanks," *New York Times*, September 6, 2014. This was in response to a question about why the Japanese government gives money to Washington, DC research groups and think tanks. Mr Otaka added: "We've been experiencing some slower growth in the economy. I think our presence is less felt than before."

References

Anholt, S. (2009). *Places: Identity, image and reputation*. New York, NY: Palgrave Macmillan.

Anholt, S., & Hildreth, J. (2004). *Brand America: The mother of all brands*. London, UK: Cyan.

Avenell, S. A. (2009). Civil society and the new civic movements in contemporary Japan: Convergence, collaboration, and transformation. *The Journal of Japanese Studies*, 35(2), pp. 247–83.

Batyko, R. J. (2012). The impact of corporate culture on public relations in Japan: A case study examining Tokyo Electric Power and Toyota. *Public Relations Journal*, 6(3).

Beeson, M. (2009). Developmental states in East Asia: A comparison of the Japanese and Chinese experiences, *Asian Perspective*, 33(2), pp. 5–39.

Beeson, M., & Stubbs, R. (2012). *Routledge handbook of Asian regionalism*. New York, NY: Routledge.

Benedict, R. (1946). *The chrysanthemum and the sword*. New York, NY: Houghton Mifflin.

Blaker, M. (1993). Evaluating Japan's diplomatic performance. In G. L. Curtis (Ed.), *Japan's foreign policy after the Cold War: Coping with change*, pp. 1–42. Armonk, NY: M. E. Sharpe.

Branding Japan: PR gurus offer advice. (2014). *Shimbun*, 1, July 3. No author given. Retrieved on April 22, 2015, from http://www.fccj.or.jp/number-1-shimbun/item/405-branding-japan-pr-gurus-offer-advice/405-branding-japan-pr-gurus-offer-advice.html

Bukh, A. (2014). Revisiting Japan's cultural diplomacy: A critique of the agent-level approach to Japan's soft power. *Asian Perspective*, 38(3), pp. 461–85.

Christensen, A. R. (2011). Cool Japan, soft power. *Global Asia*, 6(1), Spring.

Clausen, L. (2006). *Intercultural organizational communication: Five corporate cases in Japan*. Copenhagen, Denmark: Copenhagen Business School Press.

Cooper-Chen, A. (1997). *Mass communication in Japan*. Ames: Iowa State University Press.

Cooper-Chen, A., & Tanaka, M. (2007). Public relations in Japan: The cultural roots of Kouhou. *Journal of Public Relations Research*, 20, p. 95.

Courtright, J., Wolfe, R., & Baldwin, J. (2011). Intercultural typologies and public relations research: A critique of Hofstede's dimensions. In N. Bardhan, & C. Kay Weaver (Eds.), *Public relations in global cultural contexts: Multi-paradigmatic perspectives*. New York, NY: Routledge.

Coy, P. (2014). Japan Inc. isn't a thing anymore, *Bloomberg Business Week*, May 1.

Dentsu (2014). The history of Dentsu. Retrieved on August 11, 2014, from http://www.dentsu.com/about/summary/history/index.html

Dinnie, K. (2004). Country-of-origin 1965–2004: A literature review. *Journal of Customer Behaviour*, 3(2), 165–213.

Dinnie, K. (2008). *Nation branding: Concepts, issues, practice*. Oxford, UK: Butterworth-Heinemann.

Dower, J. (1999). *The Showa emperor and Japan's postwar imperial democracy*. Japan Policy Research Institute Working Paper, 61(October).

Dubro, A., & Kaplan, D. (1995). A question of intelligence: Forty-five years of the CIA in Japan. *Tokyo Journal*, pp. 32–7.

Ellul, J. (1966). *Propaganda*. New York, NY: Knopf.

FCCJ (2014). "Branding" Japan: PR gurus offer advice. The Foreign Correspondents' Club of Japan, *1 Shimbun*, July 3. Retrieved on November 9, 2014, from http://www.fccj.or.jp/number-1-shimbun/item/405-branding-japan-pr-gurus-offer-advice/405-branding-japan-pr-gurus-offer-advice.html

Freeman, L. A. (2000). *Closing the shop: Information cartels and Japan's mass media*. Princeton, NJ: Princeton University Press.

Fulbright, J.W. (1970). *The Pentagon propaganda machine*. New York, NY: Liveright.

Gluck, C. (1998). Top ten things to know about Japan in the late 1990s. *Education about Asia*, 3(2). Retrieved on August 3, 2014, from https://www.asian-studies.org/eaa/gluck.htm

Grunebaum, D. (2012). Is Japan losing its cool? *The Christian Science Monitor*. December 12.

Gudykunst, W.B. (2005). An anxiety/uncertainty management (AUM) theory of effective communication. In W.B. Gudykunst (Ed.), *Theorizing about intercultural communication*. Thousand Oaks, CA: Sage.

Gudykunst, W.B., & Nishida. T. (1994). *Bridging Japanese-North American differences*. Thousand Oaks, CA: Sage.

Habermas, J., Lennox, S., & Lennox, F. (1974). The public sphere: An encyclopedia article (1964), *New German Critique*, 3 (Autumn), pp. 49–55.

Hasegawa, K. (2011). A comparative study of social movements for a post-nuclear energy era in Japan and the USA. In J. Broadbent, & V. Broadman (Eds), *East Asian social movements: Power, protest, and change in a dynamic region*, pp. 63–79. New York, NY: Springer.

Hayden, C. (2011). *The rhetoric of soft power: Public diplomacy in global contexts*. Lanham, MD: Lexington Books.

Hellmann, D. (1988). Japanese politics and foreign policy: Elitist democracy within an American green house. In T. Inoguchi, & D. I. Okimoto (Eds), *The political economy of Japan*, pp. 345–80. Stanford, CA: Stanford University Press.

Herman, E. S., & Chomsky, N. (2008). *Manufacturing consent: The political economy of the mass media*. New York, NY: Random House.

Hofstede, G. (1980). *Culture's consequences: International differences in work-related values*. Beverly Hills, CA: Sage.

Hofstede, G. (2001). *Culture's consequences: Comparing values, behaviors, institutions and organizations across nations*, 2nd edition. Thousand Oaks, CA: Sage.

Hofstede, G. (2009). Japan. Geert Hofstede cultural dimensions. Retrieved on October 5, 2014, from http://www.geert-hofstede.com/hofstede_japan.shtml

Hofstede, G., & Minkov, M. (2010). *Cultures and organizations: Software of the mind*, 3rd edition. New York, NY: McGraw-Hill.

Holmes Report. (2011). Does Japan have a PR problem? Retrieved on August 8, 2014, from http://www.holmesreport.com/featurestories-info/10420/Does-Japan-Have-A-PR-Problem.aspx

Inoue, T. (2003). An overview of public relations in Japan and the self-correction concept. In K. Sriramesh, & D. Verčič (Eds), *The global public relations handbook*, pp. 68–85. Mahwah, NJ: Lawrence Erlbaum Associates.

Inoue, T. (2009). An overview of public relations in Japan and the self-correction concept. In K. Sriramesh, & D. Verčič (Eds), *The global public relations handbook: Theory, research, and practice*, revised and expanded edition. New York, NY: Routledge.

Inoue, T. (2010). A culture of apologies: Communicating crises in Japan. Retrieved on August 8, 2014, from http://www.prsa.org/Intelligence/TheStrategist/Articles/view/8644/102/A_culture _of_apologies_Communicating_crises_in_Jap#.VA02cEhDuuU

Kelly, W., Masumoto, T., & Gibson, D. (2002). *Kisha kurabu* and *koho*: Japanese media relations and public relations, *Public Relations Review*, 28, pp. 265–281.

Kerr, A. (2001). *Dogs and demons: The fall of modern Japan*. New York: Penguin.

Kingston, J. (2014). Self-immolation protests PM Abe overturning Japan's pacifist postwar order. *The Asia-Pacific Journal: Japan Focus*, July 7.

Lam, P. (2007). Japan's quest for "soft power": Attraction and limitation. *East Asia*, 24(4), pp. 349–63.

Lasswell, H. D. (1937). Propaganda. In E. R. A. Seligman, & A. Johnson (Eds), *Encyclopedia of the Social Sciences*, vol. 12, pp. 521–8. New York, NY: Macmillan.

Lazaridi, K. (2012). Particularities of Japanese management, *Journal of Business*, 1(2), pp. 29–34.

Legewie, J. (2010). *Japan's media: Inside and outside powerbrokers*. Tokyo, Japan: CNC Japan K.K.

S. Leitch & D. Neilson (2001). Bringing publics into public relations: New theoretical frameworks for practice. In R. Heath (Ed.), *Handbook of public relations*, pp. 127–38. Thousand Oaks, CA: Sage.

L'Etang, J. (1997). Public relations and the rhetorical dilemma: Legitimate "perspectives", persuasion or pandering? *Australian Journal of Communication*, 24(2), pp. 33–53.

L'Etang, J. (2005). Critical public relations: some reflections, *Public Relations Review*, 31, pp. 521–6.

Lipton, E., Williams, B, & Confessore, N. (2014). Foreign powers buy influence at think tanks. *The New York Times*, September 6, A-1.

McGray, D. (2002). Japan's gross national cool. *Foreign Policy*, 130 (May/June), pp. 44–54.

Mahbubani, K. (1992). Japan adrift. *Foreign Policy*, 88, pp. 126–44.

McKinsey & Company (2012). *Women Matter: An Asian Perspective*. McKinsey and Company.

Mann, J. (1995). CIA keeping historians in the dark about its Cold War role in Japan, *Los Angeles Times*, March 20. Retrieved on November 17, 2014, from http://articles.latimes.com/1995-03-20/news/mn-45023_1_cold-war

Matsuda, T. (2007). *Soft Power and Its Perils: U.S. Cultural Policy in Early Postwar Japan and Permanent Dependency*. Palo Alto, CA: Stanford University Press.

McVeigh, B. (2002). *Japanese higher education as myth.* Armonk, New York: M.E. Sharpe.

Melissen, J., & Lee, S. J. (Eds). (2011). *Public diplomacy and soft power in East Asia*. Palgrave Macmillan.

Mie, A. (2011). Tepco apologizes, but too late? *Wall Street Journal*, March 15. Retrieved on November 10, 2014, from http://blogs.wsj.com/japanrealtime/2011/03/15/tepco-apologizes-but-too-late/

Miller, L. (2011). Cute masquerade and the pimping of Japan. *International Journal of Japanese Sociology*, 20(1), pp. 18–29, November.

Miura, L. & Walker, J.W. (2012). *The shifting tectonics of Japan one year after March 11, 2011.* The German Marshall Fund of the United States Policy Brief, March.

Miyamoto, M. (1995). *Straitjacket Society: An Insider's Irreverent View of Bureaucratic Japan*, 1st edition. Kodansha USA, Inc.

Monji, K. (2010). Japan's soft power and public diplomacy. Speech to the Japan-America Society. August. Retrieved on August 3, 2014, from http://www.ajstokyo.org/ajs_j/kenjiro_monji-j.html

Nye, J. S. (1990). Soft power. *Foreign policy*, 80, pp. 153–71.

Nye, J. S. (2004). *Soft power: The means to success in world politics*. New York: PublicAffairs.

Packard, V. (1957). *The hidden persuaders*. New York: Pocket Books (a division of Simon & Schuster).

Packard, V. (1960). *The waste makers*. New York: D. McKay Co.

Pharr, S., and Krauss, E. (1996). *Media and politics in Japan*. Honolulu, HI: University of Hawaii Press.

Saporito, B. (2011). Behind the troubles at Toyota. *Time*, February 10. Retrieved on November 10, 2014, from http://www.time.com/time/business/article/0,8599,1963595,00.html

Shin, D. (2008). *Confucianism and democratization in East Asia*. New York, NY: Cambridge University Press.

Shin, D. (2012). *Cultural origins of diffuse regime support among East Asians: Exploring an alternative to the theory of critical citizens.* Asian Barometer: A Comparative Survey of Democracy, Governance and Development, Working Paper Series 63, jointly published by Globalbarometer.

Sidorova, V. (2010). The culture of the image (the cultural determination of the image of consciousness by the example of Russian and Japanese cultures). *Cultural-Historical Psychology*, 2, pp. 34–44.

Slater, D. H., Nishimura, K., & Kindstrand, L. (2012). Social media, information, and political activism in Japan's 3.11 crisis. *The Asia-Pacific Journal*, 10(24), No. 1 (June). Retrieved on April 22, 2015, from http://japanfocus.org/-Nishimura-Keiko/3762/article.html

Smith, P. (2011). *Japan: A reinterpretation*. New York, NY: Random House.

Snow, N. E. (1992). *Fulbright scholars as cultural mediators: An exploratory study*. The American University. ProQuest, UMI Dissertations Publishing. 9312019.

Snow, N. (2013a). Branding Japan, *Foreign Policy in Focus*, November 13. Retrieved on April 20, 2015, from http://fpif.org/branding-japan/

Snow, N. (2013b). Uncool Japan. *Metropolis*, Issue 1024 (November 7). Retrieved on April 22, 2014 from http://metropolis.co.jp/features/the-last-word/uncool-japan/

Snow, N. (2015). Public diplomacy and public relations: Will the twain ever meet? In G. J. Golan, S-U. Yang, & D. F. Kinsey (Eds), *International public relations and public diplomacy: Communication and engagement*. New York, NY: Peter Lang.

Stauber, J., & Rampton, S. (1995). *Toxic sludge is good for you!: Lies, damn lies, and the public relations industry*. Monroe, Maine: Common Courage Press.

Steinberg, C., & Nakane, M. (2012). *Can women save Japan?* International Monetary Fund Working Paper 12/248.

Sugimoto, Y. (2011, April 7). Japan's contaminated corporate culture. *Business Spectator*. Retrieved on April 22, 2015, from http://www.businessspectator.com.au/bs.nsf/Article/Japan-nuclear-TEPCO-FukushimaDaiichi-pd20110406-FN44E?OpenDocument

Tabuchi, H. (2014). Takata warns of larger loss. *New York Times* (International Business section), November 6.

Ting-Toomey, S. (1988). Intercultural conflict styles: A face-negotiation theory. In Y.Y. Kim, & W. B. Gudykunst (Eds), *Theories in intercultural communication*. Newbury Park, CA: Sage.

Ting-Toomey, S. (2005). The matrix of face: An updated face-negotiation theory. In W.B. Gudykunst (Ed.), *Theorizing about intercultural communication*. Thousand Oaks, CA: Sage.

van Wolferen, K. (1989). *The enigma of Japanese power: People and politics in a stateless nation*. New York: Vintage Books.

Watanabe, Y., & McConnell, D. L. (Eds). (2008). *Soft power superpowers: Cultural and national assets of Japan and the United States.* Armonk, NY: M. E. Sharpe.

Watson, D. R., & Sallot, L. M. (2001). Public relations practice in Japan: An exploratory study. *Public Relations Review,* 27, pp. 389–402.

Weaver, C. K., Motion, J., & Roper, J. (2006). From propaganda to discourse: (and back again): Truth, power, the public interest and public relations. In J. L'Etang, & M. Pieczka (Eds), *Public relations: Critical debates and contemporary practice.* Mahwah, NJ: Lawrence Erlbaum Associates.

Weiner, Tim (1994). C.I.A. Spent millions to support Japanese right in 50s and 60s. *New York Times,* October 9.

Wilford, H. (2008). *The mighty Wurlitzer: How the CIA played America.* Cambridge, MA: Harvard University Press.

Yamamura, K., & Shimizu, M. (2009). Public relations in Japan: Expert opinion on its future. Institute for Public Relations. Retrieved on April 20, 2015, from http://www.instituteforpr.org/wp-content/uploads/Public_Relations_Japan.pdf

Yamamura, K., Ikarib, S., & Kenmochic, T. (2013). Historic evolution of public relations in Japan. Public Relations Review, 39(2), Jpp.147–55.

Zhang, Y. B., Lin, M., Nonaka, A., & Beom, K. (2005). Harmony, hierarchy and conservatism: A cross-cultural comparison of Confucian values in China, Korea, Japan, and Taiwan. *Communication Research Report,* 22, pp. 107–15.

Ziegler, D. (2014). Japan's pacific constitution: Keeping the peace. Banyan column on Asian affairs. *The Economist,* May 14.

26

Socially integrating PR and operationalizing an alternative approach

Jim Macnamara

This chapter contributes to critical thinking about public relations in two important ways. First, it reviews key literature and synthesizes the findings of several international research studies which reaffirm that claims made in the dominant paradigm of Excellence theory and other popular theories of PR and corporate communication for *two-way* interaction, *dialogue, co-orientation, relationships*, and even *symmetry* between organizations and their publics, are largely illusory and require rethinking. Research involving a range or organizations shows that PR and "strategic communication" are primarily implemented for dissemination of organization messages and persuasion, and these approaches are continuing even in social media which explicitly advocate interactivity and sociality. Drawing on recent research and critical studies, this chapter calls for PR to facilitate the integration of organizations into society for mutual organization–public benefit, rather than contribute to power relations that privilege organizational interests.

Second, in advocating a *social integration model of public relations*, this chapter takes an important step towards praxis, which Hegel, Marx and other founders of critical analysis advocated as part of criticism, by exploring how such an alternative model of PR might be operationalized. In doing so, it offers some answers to the critics' critics by advancing critical thinking towards practice, as well as contributing to critical PR theory.

Perennial problems with the dominant paradigm

Criticisms of the dominant paradigm of PR as espoused in Excellence theory, and particularly in the two-way symmetrical model as it has evolved, have been enunciated and discussed for more than two decades since the first Excellence Study text was published (Grunig, 1992). As these have been discussed in detail in a number of books and articles (e.g., Holtzhausen, 2000; Holtzhausen & Voto, 2002; Leitch & Neilson, 2001; L'Etang, 2008; L'Etang & Pieczka, 1996, 2006; McKie, 2008; McKie & Munshi, 2005, 2007; Motion & Leitch, 1996), the limitations, biases and inequities resulting from the dominant paradigm will be only briefly summarized here to set the scene for discussion of an alternative approach which is the focus of this chapter.

In summary, Excellence theory postulates that symmetry should be sought and can be achieved in communication and relationships between organizations and their publics by PR practitioners who, ideally positioned within the "dominant coalition" of senior organizational management, operate as "boundary spanners" representing both an organization's and its publics' interests, guided by their professional values, ethics and knowledge (Grunig, 2001; L. Grunig, J. Grunig & Dozier, 2006).

It needs to be recognized that Excellence theory has been "tweaked", "morphed" and revised considerably since its early iterations, as noted by Spicer (2007, p. 28). Ever since the criticisms of the two-way symmetrical model by Murphy (1991), Excellence theory has taken on and appropriated additional concepts and principles including Murphy's "mixed motive model" that lead, in turn, to the "new model of symmetry" (Dozier, J. Grunig & L. Grunig, 1995, p. 48; Grunig et al., 2002, p. 357), the "new contingency model" (Grunig et al., 2002, pp. 355, 358) and "the two-way contingency model" (p. 472). As well as this broadening and redefining of symmetry, Excellence theory also incorporated *situational* theory of publics (Grunig, 1966, 1968), *co-orientation* theory (Broom & Dozier, 1990; Verčič, 2008), *contingency* theory (Cameron, 1997; Wilcox & Cameron, 2010), *relationship* theory (Hon & Grunig, 1999; Ledingham, 2006; Ledingham & Bruning, 1998, 2000), and elements of *dialogic* theory (Kent & Taylor, 2002; Pearson, 1989), *rhetorical* theory (Heath, 2009), and even some aspects of *feminist* theory (Aldoory, 2007: Grunig, 2006; L'Etang, 2008, p. 253). Supporters say that this evolution addresses the criticisms made of Excellence theory and contemporizes it as a postmodern, socially responsible and responsive approach applicable to many if not most developed societies.

However, the "dominant paradigm" of PR remains grounded in *systems* theory (Broom, 2009; Grunig & Hunt, 1984), with its origins in scientific positivism (Holtzhausen, 2000, p. 96), particularly *behaviourism* (the belief that science can predict and manage human behaviour), and despite considerable evolution it continues to be seen as *functionalist*. While Jim Grunig strongly rejects associations with structural functionalism, PR theory predominantly focuses on consensus as an achievable goal, with inadequate recognition of conflict and human diversity; and its primary purpose is serving to maintain and perpetuate the system in which it operates (Lacey, 2006; Mooney, Knox & Schacht, 2013). Motion and Weaver note in a critical discourse analysis of PR literature that "even though functional theorists assert that public relations has to take into account notions of public interest, ultimately such perspectives privilege the interests of organizations, the elite or dominant coalition, and capital" (2005, p. 51). Media studies scholar Kevin Howley has critically observed that "the field of public relations purposively manages public opinion in order to serve the narrow interests of government and corporate power". Howley added:

> Key to the success of…elite interests is the skilful use of advertising, marketing and especially public relations in so-called "perception management" campaigns. Based on insights gleaned from behaviourism, psychoanalysis, and social psychology, the public relations industry has developed sophisticated techniques to manipulate public opinion in the service of elite interests.
>
> *(Howley, 2007, p. 348)*

Even in advocating relationships as the key outcome of public relations, and claiming that the objective of relationship management is "balancing the interests of organizations and publics", Ledingham stated that "the relationship perspective as a paradigm for public relations" was spurred by "reconceptualizing public relations as a management function", among other influences, and he acknowledged that relationship management is consistent with systems theory (Ledingham, 2006, pp. 465–6).

Drawing on Habermas (1984, 1989), cultural studies, and neo-Marxist critical theory, Demitrious (2013) notes that not only are "public relations' strategies, concepts and coherences…

steeped in the logic of early modernity, functionalism and pluralism" (p. 31), but that, despite the rhetoric of dialogue, relationships and symmetry, PR is positioned as "an offshoot of business" (p. 26) and as "the instrument of expansionist capitalism" (p. 45). As a result, she says an "antagonism between public relations and civil society exists in contemporary society" (p. 25).

The conceptual and theoretical framework of systems theory, behaviourism, and functionalism, combined with the practical positioning of public relations as a management function, gives inevitable shape to the dominant paradigm. Research consistently shows that, even in the age of Web 2.0-based interactive social media, which explicitly afford and advocate two-way interaction, PR and corporate communication are predominantly focused on dissemination of organization messages and persuasion (i.e., orientation rather than co-orientation). Some contemporary studies illustrating this continuing organization-centric and predominantly one-way nature of PR are discussed in following sections.

A particular problem with strategy and strategic communication

Before leaving the theoretical literature, a further significant factor to be noted is that US-originating Excellence theory, as well as European corporate communication and communication management theory, are informed by dominant understandings of *strategy* and *strategic management* theory (Dozier et al., 1995; J. Grunig, L. Grunig & Dozier, 2006; L. Grunig et al., 2002; Steyn, 2007; Verhoeven, Zerfass & Tench, 2011; Zerfass, 2008).

In the third and seminal text reporting on the Excellence Study, L. Grunig et al. (2002) list the first of 17 characteristics of excellent public relations as being "managed strategically" (p. 9). The focus on strategy and management is further emphasized in the updated summary of Excellence theory by J. Grunig et al. (2006) in which they state that PR must be a "strategic managerial function" and that "the senior public relations executive is involved with the *strategic management* processes of the organization (p. 38, emphasis added). In their seminal paper "Defining strategic communication", Hallahan, Holtzhausen, van Ruler, Verčič & Sriramesh (2007, p. 9) noted that "strategic communication has been used synonymously for public relations in much of the literature".

This focus in the dominant paradigm emanating from North America is not a geocultural bias that can be overcome simply by replacing it with European approaches. While departing from North American thinking in many respects, including rarely using the term "public relations" (Bentele, 2004; van Ruler & Verčič, 2004, p. 1), dominant European theories and models run into similar problems in relation to organization-centricity and power relations. In Europe, organization-public communication and relations are mainly conceptualized as *corporate communication* (Cornelissen, 2011; Van Riel, 1995; Van Riel & Fombrun, 2007, Zerfass, 2008), *strategic communication* (Aarts, 2009; Aarts & Van Woerkum, 2008), and *communication management* (van Ruler & Verčič, 2005).

Management and organizational communication theorists point out that "strategic" is related to power and decision-making (Mintzberg, 1979), organizational is related to survival and efficiency (Perrow, 1992) and being goal or "outcome focused" (Lukaszewski, 2001). This raises the question: whose goals and outcomes? In most cases, as Hallahan et al. (2007) acknowledged, strategic communication by an organization is defined as "purposeful use of communication to fulfil its [i.e., the organization's] mission" (p. 3).

Hallahan and colleagues mounted a concerted effort to redefine and rehabilitate the term "strategic" within PR and communication theory. They argued that "part of the problem with the term strategic is that it has been strongly associated with a modernist approach to management" in which strategic communication "privileges a management discourse and emphasizes upper management's goals for the organization as given and legitimate" (p. 11). However, they claimed that "alternative and more positive notions of strategy have...emerged since the 1950s" that "reject the use of strategic only in an asymmetrical context" (p. 13), and urged that "strategic must not be defined narrowly" (p. 27).

Instead, Hallahan and colleagues argued that contemporary models of public relations are based on two-way *transactional*, rather than one-way *transmissional* models of communication that recognize and engage audiences in an inclusive "win-win" process – as proposed in the "new model of symmetry" (Dozier et al., 1995, p. 48). In addition, they cited and supported Holtzhausen's (2005) view that strategic communication management includes recognition that organizational survival means that organizations must adhere to the dominant value systems of the environments in which they operate. In corporate communication literature, Cornelissen (2011) has stated that "strategy is about the organization and its environment" and that strategy involves "balancing the mission and vision of the organization...with what the environment will allow or encourage it to do. Strategy is therefore often adaptive" (p. 83).

Notwithstanding such defences of strategic communication, Murphy (2011, p. 3) notes that "control has long been a troublesome issue in strategic communication". Drawing on Deetz's (1992) identification of the twin purposes of communication – *participation* and *effectiveness* – Falkheimer and Heide (2011) called on scholars and practitioners to "break the dominant approach to strategic communication" – which has focused on control, persuasion and organizational effectiveness – and adopt instead a participatory approach (p. 14). In a pragmatic compromise, Torp (2011) called for what he termed "the strategic turn" to incorporate the duality that Deetz (1992) identified – openness to participation, while at the same time not abandoning the organizational imperative to represent and advocate its interests and seek to persuade. Murphy (2011) proposed that a network view of strategic communication provides a "holistic view of the opinion arena" and recognizes the interconnected, fluid and participatory nature of this environment (p. 14). This perspective is particularly relevant in examining organizational use of social media.

Within four main European conceptualizations of communication management, the *managerial* and *operational* roles are similar to the dominant US paradigm. However, European claims to a *reflective* role (e.g., van Ruler & Verčič, 2004, 2005; van Ruler, Verčič, Bütschi & Flodin, 2001; Verčič, van Ruler, Bütschi & Flodin, 2001) and an *educational* role (Verčič et al., 2001) offer promise for an alternative approach that better balances interests and power relations in organization-public relationships (OPR). The reflective role involves analysing standards and values in society and discussing these with organization management in order to adjust the standards and values of the organization to ensure social responsibility and maintain legitimacy. The educational role involves helping members of the organization become sensitive to social demands and expectations, and communicatively competent to respond appropriately to those social demands (Verčič et al., 2001).

The "sociocultural turn"

A "sociocultural turn" has emerged in public relations, according to Edwards and Hodges (2011). Pointing to the growing focus on postmodern, communitarian, rhetorical, feminist, cultural-economic, and other models of PR, they argue that increasing focus on sociological and cultural theories "constitutes a 'turn' in PR theory that shifts the ontological and epistemological focus of the field" (p. 3). Edwards (2012) notes that "much of the research presented in the 2010 *SAGE Handbook of Public Relations* (Heath, 2010) contests functional PR theory" and Edwards and Hodges (2011, p. 2) see the "sociocultural turn" comprising a shift from a focus on organizational interests to "the social world in which organizations operate". The first issue of *Public Relations Inquiry* in early 2012 celebrated this broadening and reconceptualizing of PR in critical scholarship. However, on a cautionary note, media scholar James Curran (2011, p. 203) warns that proclamations of a "turn" within any disciplinary field are often "accounts of ideas that make no attempt to relate intellectual development to a wider context" and, while drawing attention to a challenge to the status quo, can be premature.

Against this theoretical backdrop, it is informative to review research that puts such theories and models to the test. The following section briefly summarizes and synthesizes the findings of a number of contemporary studies of social media use in the context of PR, corporate communication and communication management. Research in relation to social media has been selected, as Web 2.0-based social media explicitly afford and advocate social interaction and participatory engagement. Van Dijck (2013, p. 11) says "the very word 'social' associated with media implies that platforms are user centred and that they facilitate communal activities". The key characteristics of social media have been identified as *interactivity, dialogue, participation* and *collaboration* (Boler, 2008; Bucy, 2004; Cover, 2004; Jenkins, 2006; Macnamara, 2014a). If two-way symmetrical communication exists, it should be evident in social media use by organizations.

The myths of two-way communication, dialogue, co-orientation and symmetry

More than 80 per cent of companies and organizations are now using social media (McKinsey, 2013) and social media use for PR is increasing (Wright & Hinson, 2012, 2014). PR and corporate communication practitioners rate "the social web" as the most important issue facing practitioners between 2012 and 2015 (Zerfass, Verčič, Verhoeven, Moreno & Tench, 2012, p. 52). However, a number of research studies show that practitioners are using social media predominantly for one-way transmission of messages and clinging to the "control paradigm" of communication.

One of the first multinational studies of organizational social media use was undertaken in 2011 in three European countries (Austria, Germany and Switzerland) and three Asia Pacific countries and one territory (Australia, New Zealand, Singapore and Hong Kong) to explore why and how companies, government departments and agencies, and non-government organizations (NGOs) use social media. The survey yielded 596 completed questionnaires in Europe and 221 responses in Asia Pacific, representing a total of 817 organizations. In addition, 14 in-depth interviews were conducted with heads of digital communication or social media in major organizations in order to gain qualitative insights.

Despite criticism of the "illusion of control" in PR and communication (Grunig & Grunig, 2010; Fawkes & Gregory, 2000, p. 122), "loss of control" over messages and image was cited as the concern in using social media in Asia Pacific (nominated by 58 per cent of practitioners), and as the second highest concern in Germany, Austria and Switzerland (nominated by 55 per cent of practitioners). The only concern rated higher in the European countries studied was the amount of effort and time required to use social media (Macnamara, 2014a, p. 176; Macnamara & Zerfass, 2012, p. 300).

Only 20 per cent of Asia Pacific organizations and 29 per cent of European organizations had tools or services to monitor all social media discussion of issues relevant to the organization and its stakeholders. A number of others were monitored selectively or in an ad hoc way, but in Asia Pacific, for instance, almost half of the 200-plus organizations studied either did not monitor social media mentions at all, or monitored only sporadically. This finding is supported by research conducted for the 2011 *European Communication Monitor*, which reported that only 33 per cent of organizations had tools or services for monitoring social media (Zerfass, Verhoeven, Tench, Moreno & Verčič, 2011); and by 2012 data from a longitudinal study carried out by Wright and Hinson (2012) of social media use by PR practitioners in the US, which reported that less than half (43 per cent) of organizations monitored what their publics said about them in social media. Given that monitoring is essential for listening to social media comments and conversations, this indicates that two-way communication and dialogue are not being practised by organizations online.

A comparative study of 78 websites of corporations and non-profit organizations in Singapore (51 per cent) and globally (49 per cent) conducted in 2004 (and again in 2009) similarly found that, despite rapid increases in the availability of communication channels that enable two-way interaction, "both corporations and non-profit organizations mostly utilized their Websites as information dissemination tools, where the information flow is one-way" (Sriramesh, Rivera-Sánchez & Soriano, 2011, p. 134). Sriramesh et al. reported that two-way symmetrical communication "increased slightly between 2004 and 2009", but "as of 2009 many for-profit and not-for-profit organizations were still a long way from fully utilizing the interactive features of social media" (p. 134).

A 2012 qualitative study of social media use by PR practitioners in Australia carried out by Robson and James (2013, p. 6) concluded:

> All participants understood the rules and ideals around social media (authenticity, inter-activity, two-way communication, etc.) but they are not necessarily adopting them in their practice. The interviewees primarily used social media platforms, or believed they are best for, one-way communication and message dissemination.

An international study undertaken by this author and colleagues to examine social media use by government agencies responsible for electoral enrolment and voting as a means to engage youth and disengaged citizens similarly found a lack of interactivity, dialogue and participation (Macnamara, 2012a; Macnamara, Sakinofsky & Beattie, 2012). All national and state electoral management bodies (EMBs) studied in Australia and New Zealand restricted interactivity on their social media sites so as only to allow citizens to 'like' Facebook pages or videos and 'follow' Twitter sites, with few opportunities to post comments or contribute additional content. UK organizations such as the Greater London Authority allowed a greater level of two-way inter-action on its website (www.londonelects.org.uk) and Facebook page during the period of the 2012 London mayoral election, including a facility to post comments – but most sites designed to engage youth were narrowly event-focused (i.e., centred around elections) and primarily involved dissemination of information. One EMB communication manager interviewed about the lack of social media use outside election periods said: "Between election periods, there's not really that much for us to say" (personal communication, 17 April 2012). This epitomized a focus on *speaking* and having something to *say*, rather than engaging in dialogue and symmetrical interaction.

Towards a social integration model of public relations

Research consistently shows that PR and communication management remain organization-centric and that practice remains predominantly focused on one-way dissemination of organizational messages (i.e., transmission rather than transactions and monologue rather than dialogue); and on attempts at persuasion (orientation rather than co-orientation) on behalf of and in the interest of power elites in society. This is found even in social media which offer extensive opportunities for *two-way* interaction, *dialogue, co-orientation* and *symmetry*. Symmetry, even in its mixed-motive contingent form, remains a myth, as Brown (2006) argued some years ago.

Such an approach is not conducive to building and maintaining relationships with publics, which are arguably the core of public relations (Center & Jackson, 1995; Hon & Grunig, 1999; Ledingham & Bruning, 1998, 2000). To the contrary, such an approach is likely to promote further alienation and dislocation between corporations, business, industry, governments, as well as other types of organizations and their publics. In short, PR and strategic communication management, as they are predominantly practised, are more anti-social than they are social. Moreover, they promote *disintegration* rather than integration of organizations within the societies and communities in which they operate.

Drawing on the concept of media literacy, Holladay and Coombs (2013) have proposed *public relations literacy* as a solution or antidote to the organization-centric persuasion-orientated approach of PR, which they note is often unseen by publics. While PR literacy, involving an ability to identify PR and recognize its selective and partisan representations, would provide a useful contribution to the critical interpretative frameworks available to citizens, it shifts responsibility for balance and social equity to publics and addresses the ontological, axiological and methodological flaws at the heart of PR *post-hoc* – i.e., it treats effects rather than causes.

A *social integration model of public relations* is proposed in place of organization-centric models. While being cautious in adding to the 472 definitions identified by Harlow (1976), and a number of others developed since, in a social integration model public relations could be described as follows:

> Public relations is the *counselling, communication*, and *relationship development and maintenance* functions of organizations (corporations, government departments and agencies, NGOs and non-profits) that help them integrate within the societies in which they operate. This requires ethical practices in all areas of organizational operations and a sensitive balancing of organizational and societal interests to produce greater equity and mutual benefits.

This conceptualization of PR does not vary greatly from Excellence theory in terms of high-level theory. Its approach also borrows and uses a number of middle-range theories such as Bernays' concept of *counsellor, two-way* interaction, *accommodation* (Grunig, 1992, p. 18; Grunig et al., 2002, p. 314) and *adaptation* as discussed in Kendall's (1997) RAISE model of PR planning. However, a social integration model of PR shifts the ontological, epistemological and methodological foundations of the field. Specifically, it requires abandoning the frameworks of functionalism and behaviourism that inform dominant models, grounded in the metanarratives of modernism and theories such as systems theory and cybernetics. Ontologically such a shift takes PR from being a function of management serving the singular reality and universalized truths of an organization, to being informed by pluralism and serving as a function *of* society and *for* society as well as organizations. Epistemologically it moves PR from a rationalist-scientific (and inevitably reductionist) approach, to a humanistic, subjectivist, social constructionist perspective of how knowledge, meaning and understanding are created. Methodologically it moves PR from quantitative generalizations with goals of prediction and control, to qualitative methods producing culturally and contextually specific findings with goals of understanding and social change (Creswell, 1994; Frey, Botan & Kreps, 2000). In disciplinary terms, it involves shifting PR out of management theory and places it in an entirely different environment of social theory, as described in the "sociocultural turn" (Edwards & Hodges, 2011). However, whereas Edwards and Hodges provide no tools for translating this theoretical "turn" into practice, the final section of this chapter attempts to put some flesh on the bones of a social integration model of PR for the reasons explained.

Operationalizing a social integration model – the next necessary step

Despite Marx's (1845, p. xi) observation that "philosophers have only interpreted the world in various ways; the point is to change it", and his exhortation for praxis to synthesize theory and practice, many if not most critical analyses of PR stop short of proposing how identified inequities might be redressed and change implemented. Jim Grunig (2001) threw down the gauntlet at the feet of critical scholars more than a decade ago, saying there is "a need for critical researchers and theorists to more clearly outline how their approaches contribute to advancing not only public relations theory, but also research and practice" – a challenge that has not been adequately met to date. Grunig added: "In a professional field such as public relations, I believe scholars must go beyond criticizing theories; they also have the obligation to replace theories with something better – an obligation that many critical scholars do not fulfil" (2001, p. 17). More recently, in *Public Relations Theory II*, Botan and Hazelton (2006, p. 9) stated:

> Critics of the symmetrical/excellence approach have spoken up, but either the field has failed to see enough merit in what they have said to develop their work into alternative paradigms, or they have limited their remarks to critiques and failed to conduct affirmative research, share their data, and sufficiently open their own theories to critical discourse.

One chapter cannot comprehensively outline an alternative model of public relations, but three key concepts are proposed as a contribution to theory development and operationalizing a new approach.

1. Challenging "dominant coalition" dogma

One starting point for change, informed by *standpoint theory* (Harding, 1987; Harstock, 1987), is challenging the prevailing PR dogma that the senior PR practitioner should be located in the "dominant coalition" of an organization to carry out her or his role effectively. The hypothesis that membership of the dominant coalition facilites the representation of stakeholders' and publics' views and concerns to management fails the tests of empirical evidence and experience. Interviews with senior PR and corporate communication practitioners confirm that membership of the senior organization management team requires philosophical alignment (described as "thinking the same way") and total loyalty to the organization (see Macnamara, 2014b, pp. 183–4). Autoethnographic observations from more than 20 years of experience in PR practice, including being a member of the senior executive team of several companies, also support this finding. Furthermore, senior PR practitioners working inside or even close to the senior management team are typically recruited because they already subscribe to, or become absorbed into, the thinking and culture of the organization. In such circumstances, "boundary spanning" becomes a fallacious claim by PR practitioners. Similarly, critical proposals to operate as an "organizational activist" (Holtzhausen, 2007) practising "professional activism and dissent" (Berger & Reber, 2006) are unrealistic at the top level of most organizations where such behaviour would inevitably lead to marginalization or even loss of employment.

Instead, a social integration model of PR, and implementation of a "sociocultural turn", suggests that the senior PR practitioner be located outside the dominant coalition. Precedents for an external advisor having influence but serving a "higher authority" include the role of external legal counsel and auditors who serve both organizations and society through a neutral – or at least a semi-independent – position, empowered by their knowledge and specialist expertise.

If the models of legal counsel or auditor are too lofty for PR practitioners to aspire to and achieve, the broader professional role of diplomacy is available as a model. Diplomacy is practised at a range of levels from operational roles in research and communication to senior policy advisors and ambassadors. Beyond informing structure, diplomacy also offers disciplinary insights for PR, as discussed in the following.

2. Embracing principles of public diplomacy

The field of public diplomacy, particularly the "new public diplomacy" with its focus on dialogue, cultivation of relationships and pluralism, as outlined by Joseph Nye (2010a, 2010b) and Nancy Snow (2009), has been discussed in PR literature for some years, but has not been embraced in mainstream PR theory or practice. L'Etang has stated that "PR practitioners are organizational diplomats" (2008, p. 239). But rather than simply claiming the mantle of diplomacy in a search for respectability, the social integration of organizations requires practitioners to apply key elements of public diplomacy. These include, first and foremost, being open to and accepting diverse views and conflict, rather than seeking consensus and symmetry, or alternatively "withdrawal from dialogue" (Grunig, 2001, p. 16) and "no deal" (Hon & Grunig, 1999), which constitute closure. Also, public diplomacy emphasizes negotiation and mechanisms for balancing disparities in power, such as turn-taking, "one vote one value", and appointment of ombuds. *Corporate* and *organizational diplomacy* are further discussed in Macnamara (2012b).

3. Incorporating the missing element of listening

Despite recognition of listening as a fundamental element of communication (Couldry, 2010), "listening" is not listed in the index or contents of most PR research monographs and textbooks – which include the main Excellence theory text (Grunig et al., 2002), as well as many other international texts (e.g., Botan & Hazelton, 2006; Cornelissen, 2011; Tench & Yeomans, 2009; Wilcox & Cameron, 2010). Heath and Coombs (2006) say: "Today's public relations practitioner gives voice to organisations", and add that "this process requires the ability to listen". But they go on to narrowly configure listening by saying "listening gives a foundation for knowing what to say and thinking strategically of the best ways to frame and present appealing messages" (p. 346). A search of leading PR journals over two decades also found only a few analyses of listening (Macnamara, 2014c). PR literature either ignores listening or frames it as *strategic action* designed to help an organization achieve its objectives, rather than take part in *communicative action* (Habermas, 1984).

At an applied level, a pilot study of organizational listening has revealed that PR and communication practitioners are overwhelmingly engaged in establishing an "architecture of speaking" in organizations and the one-way "work of speaking", with little infrastructure for, or commitment to, listening (Macnamara, 2013a, p. 9). This ongoing study provides clear evidence of the need for changes in PR and corporate communication, including an *architecture of listening* to truly engage with publics (Macnamara, 2013b, p. 168).

Critics of critical thinking may argue that the propositions advanced here are socialistic and even "pie in the sky", naïve and impractical. In a political and socio-economic environment of neoliberalism, current PR approaches may endure and even enjoy continuing growth for some time. But the widening "democratic deficit" is leaving citizens disengaged from their governments in many countries (Coleman, 2013; Couldry, 2010, p. 49; Curran, 2011, p. 86), has led to growing criticism of neoliberalism (Couldry, 2010, 2012), and resulted in social unrest caused by growing unemployment, collapsed health systems and environments that have been ravaged by industrialization. This will all place increasing pressure on governments and corporations to demonstrate their legitimacy, value and relevance to society – and not only to power elites. If public relations is not the function that helps integrate organizations within societies and their communities of stakeholders, then it is part of the problem rather than the solution.

Conclusion

As many critical scholars have noted, public relations is predominantly theorized and practised within a dominant paradigmatic framework grounded in behaviourism and functionalism, and nested within neoliberal capitalism. Kuhn (1996), who drew attention to the emergence and significance of unified communal worldviews in the natural sciences, regarded single paradigms as inappropriate for the social sciences – which deal with a "variety of problems" (p. 165) requiring a multi-paradigmatic approach (see Curtin, 2012). In the social sciences, Merton (1968) observed that "grand theories" become so broad and abstracted as to be empirically untestable. They also form a vortex into which many middle-range theories are drawn and colonized, thus losing their distinctness and purpose. This chapter concludes that public relations has to make space for new theories and models to continue the process of knowledge construction that is necessary for disciplinary progress, and offers "social integration" as one approach for the future, with some suggestions for praxis.

References

Aarts, N. (2009). *Een gesprek zonder einde* [A never-ending conversation]. Amsterdam: Vosspuspers.

Aarts, N., & Van Woerkum, C. (2008). *Strategische communicatie* [Strategic communication]. Assen, Holland: Van Gorcum.

Aldoory, L. (2007). Reconceiving gender for an "excellent" future in public relations scholarship. In Toth, E. (Ed.), *The future of excellence in public relations and communication management*, pp. 399–411. Mahwah, NJ: Lawrence Erlbaum.

Bentele, G. (2004). New perspectives of public relations in Europe. In B. van Ruler, & D. Verčič (Eds), *Public relations and communication management in Europe*, pp. 485–96. Berlin, Germany: Mouton de Gruyter.

Berger, P., & Reber, B. (2006). *Gaining influence in public relations: The role of resistance in practice*. Mahwah, NJ: Lawrence Erlbaum.

Bickford, S. (1996). *The dissonance of democracy: Listening, conflict and citizenship*. Ithaca, NY: Cornell University Press.

Boler, M. (Ed.). (2008). *Digital media and democracy: Tactics in hard times*. Cambridge, MA: MIT Press.

Botan, C., & Hazelton, V. (Eds.). (2006). *Public relations theory II*. Mahwah, NJ: Lawrence Erlbaum.

Broom, G. (2009). *Cutlip & Center's effective public relations*, 10th edition. Upper Saddle River, NJ: Pearson Education.

Broom G., & Dozier, D. (1990). *Using research in public relations: Applications to program management*. Englewood Cliffs, NJ: Prentice-Hall.

Brown, R. (2006). Myth of symmetry: Public relations as cultural styles. *Public Relations Review*, 32(3), pp. 206–12.

Bucy, E. (2004). Interactivity in society: Locating an elusive concept. *Information Society*, 20(5), pp. 373–83.

Cameron, G. (1997). *The contingency theory of conflict management in public relations*. Proceedings of the Norwegian Information Service, Oslo, Norway.

Center, A., & Jackson, P. (1995). *Public relations practices: Management case studies and problems*, 5th edition. Englewood Cliffs, NJ: Prentice Hall.

Coleman, S. (2013). *How voters feel*. New York, NY: Cambridge University Press.

Cornelissen, J. (2011). *Corporate communication: A guide to theory and practice*, 3rd edition. Thousand Oaks, CA: Sage.

Couldry, N. (2006). Transvaluing media studies: Or, beyond the myth of the mediated centre. In J. Curran, & D. Morley (Eds), *Media and cultural theory*, pp.177–94. Abingdon, UK: Routledge.

Couldry, N. (2010). *Why voice matters: Culture and politics after neoliberalism*. London, UK: Sage.

Couldry, N. (2012). *Media, society, world: Social theory and digital media practice*. Cambridge, UK: Polity.

Cover, R. (2004). New media theory: Electronic games, democracy and reconfiguring the author-audience relationship. *Social Semiotics*, 13(2), pp. 173–191.

Creswell, J. (1994). *Research design: Qualitative and quantitative approaches*. Thousand Oaks, CA: Sage.

Curran, J. (2011). *Media and democracy*. Abingdon, UK: Routledge.

Curtin, P. (2012). Public relations and philosophy: Parsing paradigms. *Public Relations Inquiry*, 1(1), pp. 31–47.

Deetz, S. (1992). *Democracy in an age of corporate colonization: Developments in communication and the politics of everyday life*. New York, NY: State University of New York.

Demetrious, K. (2013). *Public relations, activism, and social change*. Abingdon, UK: Routledge.

Dozier, D., Grunig, L., & Grunig, J. (1995). *Manager's guide to excellence in public relations and communication management*. Mahwah, NJ: Lawrence Erlbaum.

Edwards, L. (2012). Defining the "object" of public relations research: A new starting point. *Public Relations Inquiry*, 1(1), pp. 7–30.

Edwards, L., & Hodges, C. (Eds). (2011). *Public relations, society and culture: Theoretical and empirical explorations*. Abingdon, UK: Routledge.

Falkheimer, J., & Heide, M. (2011, May). *Participatory strategic communication: From one- and two-way communication to participatory communication through social media*. Paper presented at the International Communication Association 2011 pre-conference, "Strategic communication – A concept at the center of applied communications", Boston, MA.

Fawkes, J., & Gregory, A. (2000). Applying communication theories to the internet. *Journal of Communication Management*, 5(2), pp. 109–24.

Frey, L., Botan, C., & Kreps, G. (2000). *Investigating communication: An introduction to research methods*. Needham Heights, MA: Allyn & Bacon.

Grunig, J. (1966). The role of information processing in economic decision making. *Journalism Monographs*, 3.

Grunig, J. (1968). *Information, entrepreneurship, and economic development: A study of the decision making processes of Colombian Latifundistas*. Unpublished doctoral dissertation, University of Wisconsin.

Grunig, J. (Ed.). (1992). *Excellence in public relations and communication management*. Hillsdale, NJ: Lawrence Erlbaum Associates.

Grunig, J. (2001). Two-way symmetrical public relations: Past, present and future. In R. Heath (Ed.), *Handbook of public relations*, pp. 11–30. London, UK: Sage.

Grunig, J., & Grunig, L. (2010). Public relations excellence 2010. The third annual Grunig lecture series. *Journal of Professional Communication*, 1(1), pp. 41–54.

Grunig, J., & Hunt, T. (1984). *Managing public relations*. Orlando, FL: Holt, Rinehart & Winston.

Grunig, J., Grunig, L., & Dozier, D. (2006). The excellence theory. In C. Botan, & V. Hazelton (Eds), *Public relations theory II*, pp. 21–62. Mahwah, NJ: Lawrence Erlbaum.

Grunig, L. (2006). Feminist phase analysis in public relations: Where have we been? Where do we need to be? *Journal of Public Relations Research*, 18(2), pp. 115–40.

Grunig, L., Grunig J., & Dozier D. (2002). *Excellent organisations and effective organisations: A study of communication management in three countries*. Mahwah, NJ: Lawrence Erlbaum.

Habermas, J. (1984). *Theory of communicative action volume 1: Reason and the rationalization of society*, trans. T. McCarthy. Boston, MA: Beacon Press (originally published in German, 1981).

Habermas, J. (1989). *The structural transformation of the public sphere*. Cambridge, UK: Polity (original work published 1962).

Hallahan, K., Holtzhausen, D., van Ruler, B., Verčič, D., & Sriramesh, K. (2007). Defining strategic communication. *International Journal of Strategic Communication*, 1(1), pp. 3–35.

Harding, S. (Ed.). (1987). *Feminism and methodology*. Bloomington, IL: Indiana University Press.

Harlow, R. (1976). Building a public relations definition. *Public Relations Review*, 2(4), pp. 34–42.

Hartsock, N. (1987). The feminist standpoint: Developing the ground for a specifically feminist historical materialism. In S. Harding (Ed.), *Feminism and methodology*, pp. 157–80. Bloomington, IL: Indiana University Press.

Heath, R. (2009). The rhetorical tradition: Wrangle in the marketplace. In R. Heath, E. Toth, & D. Waymer (Eds.), *Rhetorical and critical approaches to public relations II*, pp. 17–47. New York, NY: Routledge.

Heath, R. (Ed.). (2010). *The SAGE handbook of public relations*. Thousand Oaks, CA: Sage.

Heath, R.., & Coombs, T. (2006). *Today's public relations: An introduction*. Thousand Oaks, CA: Sage.

Holladay, S., & Coombs, T. (2013). Public relations literacy: Developing critical consumers of public relations. *Public Relations Inquiry*, 2(2), pp. 125–46.

Holtzhausen, D. (2000). Postmodern values in PPR. *Journal of Public Relations Research*, 12(1), pp. 93–114.

Holtzhausen D. (2005). Public relations practice and political change in South Africa. *Public Relations Review*, 31(3), pp. 407–16.

Holtzhausen, D. (2007). Activism. In E. Toth (Ed.), *The future of excellence in public relations and communication management*, pp. 357–79. Mahwah, NJ: Lawrence Erlbaum.

Holtzhausen, D., & Voto, R. (2002). Resistance from the margins: The postmodern public relations practitioner as organisational activist. *Journal of Public Relations Research*, 14(1), pp. 57–84.

Hon, L., & Grunig, J. (1999). Guidelines for measuring relationships in public relations. Gainesville, FL: Institute for Public Relations. Retrieved on 23 April 2015 from http://www.instituteforpr.org/measuring-relationships

Howley, K. (2007). Community media and the public sphere. In E. Devereux (Ed.), *Media studies: Key issues and debates*, pp. 342–60. London, UK: Sage.

Jenkins, H. (2006). *Convergence culture: Where old and new media collide*. New York, NY: New York University Press.

Kendall, R. (1997). *Public relations campaign strategies: Planning for implementation*, 2nd edition. New York, NY: Addison-Wesley.

Kent, M., & Taylor, M. (2002). Toward a dialogic theory of public relations. *Public Relations Review*, 28(1), pp. 21–37.

Kuhn, T. (1996). *The structure of scientific revolutions*, 3rd edition. Chicago, IL: University of Chicago Press.

Lacey, A. (2006 [1976]). *A dictionary of philosophy*. London, UK: Routledge.

Ledingham, J. (2006). Relationship management: A general theory of public relations. In C. Botan, & V. Hazelton (Eds), *Public relations theory II*, pp. 465–83. Mahwah, NJ: Lawrence Erlbaum.

Ledingham, J., & Bruning, S. (1998). Relationship management and public relations: Dimensions of an organisation-public relationship. *Public Relations Review*, 24(1), pp. 55–65.

Ledingham, J., & Bruning, S. (Eds). (2000). *Public relations as relationship management: A relational approach to the study and practice of public relations*. Mahwah, NJ: Lawrence Erlbaum.

Leitch, S., & Neilson, D. (2001). Bringing publics into public relations: New theoretical frameworks for practice. In R. Heath (Ed.), *Handbook of public relations*, pp. 127–38. London: Sage.

L'Etang, J. (2008). *Public relations: Concepts, practice and critique*. Thousand Oaks, CA: Sage.

L'Etang, J., & Pieczka, M. (1996). *Critical perspectives in public relations*. London, UK: International Thomson Business Press.

L'Etang, J., & Pieczka, M. (2006). *Public relations: Critical debates and contemporary practice*. Mahwah, NJ: Lawrence Erlbaum.

Lukaszewski, J. (2001). How to develop the mind of a strategist. Part 3. *IABC Communication World*, 18(3), pp. 13–15.

McKie, D. (2008). Postmodernism and PR. In J. L'Etang, *Public relations concepts, practice and critique*, pp. 259–60. Thousand Oaks, CA: Sage.

McKie, D., & Munshi, D. (2005). Global public relations: A different perspective. *Public Relations Review*, 29(2), pp. 215–19.

McKie, D., & Munshi, D. (2007). *Reconfiguring public relations: Equity, ecology and enterprise*. London, UK: Routledge.

McKinsey. (2013). Evolution of the networked enterprise. McKinsey & Company. Retrieved on 23 April from http://www.mckinsey.com/insights/business_technology/evolution_of_the_networked_enterprise_mckinsey_global_survey_results

Macnamara, J. (2012a). Democracy 2.0: Can social media engage youth and disengaged citizens in the public sphere. *Australian Journal of Communication*, 39(3), pp. 65–86.

Macnamara J. (2012b). Corporate and organisational diplomacy: An alternative paradigm to PR. *Journal of Communication Management*, 16(3), pp. 312–25.

Macnamara, J. (2013a, November). *Organisational listening: A vital missing element in public communication and the public sphere*. Paper presented to the 2013 Public Relations Institute of Australia National Conference Research Colloquium, Adelaide, SA.

Macnamara, J. (2013b). Beyond voice: Audience-making and the work and architecture of listening as new media literacies. *Continuum: Journal of Media & Cultural Studies*, 27(1), pp. 160–75.

Macnamara, J. (2014a). *The 21st century media (r)evolution: Emergent communication practices*, 2nd edition. New York, NY: Peter Lang.

Macnamara, J. (2014b). *Journalism and PR: Unpacking "spin", stereotypes and media myths*. New York, NY: Peter Lang.

Macnamara, J. (2014c). Organisational listening: A vital missing element in public communication and the public sphere. *Asia Pacific Public Relations Journal*, 15(1), pp. 89–108.

Macnamara, J., & Zerfass, A. (2012). Social media communication in organizations: The challenges of balancing openness, strategy and management. *International Journal of Strategic Communication*, 6(4), pp. 287–308.

Macnamara, J., P. Sakinofsky, P., & Beattie, J. (2012). Democracy 2.0: Can social media engage youth and disengaged citizens in the public sphere. *Australian Journal of Communication*, 47(4), pp. 623–39.

Marx, K. (1845). Theses on Feuerbach. In *Marx/Engels Selected Works*, vol. I, part xi, trans. W. Lough, pp. 13–15. Moscow, Russia: Progress Publishers. Retrieved on 21 April 2015 from http://www.marxists.org/archive/marx/works/1845/theses/theses.htm

Merton, R. (1968). *Social theory and social structure*. New York, NY: Free Press.

Mintzberg, H. (1979). *The structure of organizations*. Englewood Cliffs, NJ: Prentice Hall.

Mooney, L., Knox, D., & Schacht, C. (2013). *Understanding social problems*, 8th edition. Belmont, CA: Cengage.

Motion, J., & Leitch, S. (1996). A discursive perspective from New Zealand: Another world view. *Public Relations Review*, 22, pp. 297–309.

Motion, J., & Weaver, C. (2005). A discourse perspective for critical public relations research: Life sciences network and the battle for truth. *Journal of Public Relations Research*, 17(1), pp. 49–67.

Murphy, P. (1991). Limits of symmetry. In J. Grunig, & L. Grunig (Eds), *Public relations research annual*, vol. 3, pp. 115–31. Hillsdale, NJ: Lawrence Erlbaum.

Murphy, P. (2011, May). *Contextual distortion: Strategic communication vs. the networked nature of everything*. Paper presented at the International Communication Association 2011 pre-conference, "Strategic communication – A concept at the center of applied communications", Boston, MA.

Nye, J. (2010a). Public diplomacy and soft power. In D. Thussu (Ed.), *International communication: A reader*, pp. 333–44. New York, NY: Routledge.

Nye, J. (2010b). The new public diplomacy. Project Syndicate. Retrieved on 21 April 2015 from http://www.project-syndicate.org/commentary/nye79/English

Pearson, R. (1989). Beyond ethical relativism in public relations: Co-orientation, rules, and the idea of communication symmetry. In J. Grunig, & L. Grunig (Eds), *Public Relations Research Annual*, vol. 1, pp. 67–86. Hillsdale, NJ: Lawrence Erlbaum.

Perrow, C. (1992). Organizational theorists in a society of organizations. *International Sociology*, 7(3), pp. 371–9.

Robson, P., & James, M. (2013). Not everyone's aboard the online public relations train: The use (and non-use) of social media by public relations practitioners. *PRism* 9(1), pp. 1–18. Retrieved on 23 April 2015 from http://www.prismjournal.org/fileadmin/9_1/Robson_James.pdf

Snow, N. (2009). Rethinking public diplomacy. In N. Snow, & P. Taylor (Eds), *Routledge handbook of public diplomacy*, pp. 3–11. London, UK.

Spicer, C. (2007). Collaborative advocacy and the creation of trust: Toward an understanding of stakeholder claims and risks. In E. Toth (Ed.), *The future of excellence in public relations and communication management: Challenges for the next generation*, pp. 27–40. Mahwah, NJ: Lawrence Erlbaum.

Sriramesh, K., Rivera-Sánchez, M., & Soriano, C. (2011). Websites for stakeholder relations by corporations and non-profits. *Journal of Communication Management*, 17(3), pp. 122–139.

Steyn, B. (2007). Contribution of public relations to organizational strategy formulation. In E. Toth (Ed.), *The future of excellence in public relations and communication management*, pp. 137–72. Mahwah, NJ: Lawrence Erlbaum.

Tench, R., & Yeomans, L. (2009). *Exploring public relations*, 2nd edition. Harlow, UK: Prentice Hall/Pearson Education.

Torp, S. (2011, May). *The strategic turn: On the history and broadening of the strategy concept in communication*. Paper presented at the International Communication Association 2011 pre-conference, "Strategic communication – A concept at the center of applied communications", Boston, MA.

Van Dijck, J. (2013). *The culture of connectivity: A critical history of social media*. Oxford, UK: Oxford University Press.

Van Riel, C. (1995). *Principles of corporate communication*. London, UK: Prentice Hall.

Van Riel, C., & Fombrun, C. (2007). *Essentials of corporate communications*. New York, NY: Routledge.

van Ruler, B., & Verčič, D. (2004). Overview of public relations and communication management in Europe. In B. van Ruler, & D. Verčič (Eds), *Public relations and communication management in Europe*, pp. 1–11. New York, NY: Mouton de Gruyter.

van Ruler, B., & Verčič, D. (2005). Reflective communication management, future ways for public relations research. In P. Kalbfleisch (Ed.), *Communication yearbook 29*, pp. 238–73. Mahwah, NJ: Lawrence Erlbaum.

van Ruler, B., Verčič, D., Bütschi, G., & Flodin, B. (2001). Public relations in Europe: A kaleidoscopic picture. *Journal of Communication Management*, 6(2), pp. 166–75.

Verčič, D. (2008). Co-orientation model of public relations. In W. Donsbach (Ed.), *International encyclopaedia of communication*. Retrieved on 23 April 2015 from http://www.blackwellreference.com/public/tocnode?id=g9781405131995_yr2013_chunk_g97814051319958_ss141-1

Verčič, D., van Ruler, B., Bütschi, G., & Flodin, B. (2001). On the definition of public relations: A European view. *Public Relations Review*, 27(4), pp. 373–387.

Verhoeven, P., Zerfass, A., & Tench, R. (2011). Strategic orientation of communication professionals in Europe. *International Journal Strategic Communication*, 5(2), pp. 96–117.

Wilcox, D., & Cameron, G. (2010). *Public relations: Strategies and tactics*, 9th edition. Boston, MA: Allyn & Bacon.

Wright, D., & Hinson, M. (2012). Examining how social and emerging media have been used in public relations between 2006 and 2012: A longitudinal analysis. *Public Relations Journal*, 6(4), pp. 1–40.

Wright, D., & Hinson, M. (2014). An updated examination of social and emerging media use in public relations practice: A longitudinal analysis between 2006 and 2014. *Public Relations Journal*, 8(2), pp. 1–35.

Zerfass, A. (2008). Corporate communication revisited: Integrating business strategies and strategic communication. In A. Zerfass, B. van Ruler, & K. Sriramesh (Eds), *Public relations research*, pp. 65–96. Wiesbaden, Germany: VS Verlag für Sozialwissenschaften.

Zerfass, A., Verčič, D., Verhoeven, P., Moreno, A., & Tench, R. (2012). *European Communication Monitor 2012: Challenges and competencies for strategic communication*. Results of an empirical survey in 42 countries. Brussels, Belgium: EACD/EUPRERA, Helios Media.

Zerfass, A., Verhoeven, P., Tench, R., Moreno, A., & Verčič, D. (2011). *European Communication Monitor 2011: Empirical insights into strategic communication in Europe*. Results of a survey in 43 countries. Brussels, Belgium: EACD/EUPRERA, Helios Media.

27

Expanding critical space

Public intellectuals, public relations, and an "outsider" contribution

David McKie and Jordi Xifra

Public relations, as with any academic and social practice worthy of respect, should contribute to the ideas of its time; critical public relations, as with any critical theory, should criticise, with a view to changing, social injustice. For the latter to be effective, someone with a substantial media presence – often acknowledged by the term "public intellectual" – can help significantly by expressing a justice agenda in the public sphere. So, let us start with a double-sided question on critical space: why are PR people not considered public intellectuals and why are public intellectuals not considered part of PR?

Etzioni (2006), as part of his work on "Public Intellectuals" (which he abbreviates to PIs), offers his specific answer to the first part:

> There is a group of people who have many of the attributes of PIs, who quack like PIs but do not qualify as PIs, precisely because their role is to form conceptions that support their employer, rather than to be critical. These people, sometimes referred to as "spin doctors," do address the public on a broad array of issues, in the vernacular rather than technical terms, but are a distinct species, because they are retained by the powers that be, or volunteered to serve them as their advocates.
>
> *(p. 4)*

In other words, although PR, in common with PIs, addresses the public on a wide range of issues in popularly accessible discourses and media, its practitioners are excluded because they opt for supporting the powerful rather than being "critical" of them. Etzioni (2006) explicitly refers to "propagandists or PR experts such as James Carville and Mary Matalin,…who, while in the advocacy role, clearly toe the line of those who employ them" (p. 4).

In this chapter, we begin by considering PIs in general. We dispute not only Etzioni's (2006) position that those in PR should always be excluded from being PIs, but also that PIs can sometimes be considered as doing PR. These contentions partially reject the view that PR only advocates for the powerful and that PIs are a distinct species without commitments to people with power, or people seeking power. To further illustrate the issues at stake, we present the resistance PR of Nobelist Albert Camus as an outstanding PI contribution to public thinking. We do so with regard to three themes – activism, non-violence and personal ethics – and situate all three as relevant to the ideas of our time. In addition, we illustrate how Camus used PR strategies and tactics to the extent that his contribution is not *despite* his committed PR activities but *because* of them.

Sources of expansion and spheres of influence

Etzioni (2006) is not alone in identifying the critical as being a central, socially desirable, and distinguishing feature of PIs. For Posner (2002) too, the PI has been a social asset for centuries and "exemplars include Machiavelli, Milton, Locke, Voltaire, and Montesquieu, and his [sic] ideologist is Kant, who linked philosophy to politics through the argument that the only morally defensible politics is one based on reason" (p. 26). This is a distinguished intellectual lineage, but not every exemplar – notably Machiavelli and Milton – is detached from communicating in the service of status quos although, even among prominent academic studies of PIs, there are conflicting views. Edward Said's (1994) ideal PI, for example, is definitely not someone serving the authority of a prince as Machiavelli did, or Puritan parliament power as Milton did, but someone "whose place it is publicly to raise embarrassing questions, to confront orthodoxy and dogma (rather than to produce them), [and] to be someone who cannot easily be coopted by governments or corporations" (p. 27).

Moreover, there are growing movements to expand the very notion of what counts as PR and reposition it outside the traditional idea of PR people as functionaries of government and management. Ironically, PR has also been slower to develop critical initiatives than other disciplines in the management field (see Linstead, this volume). Thus, as CPR grows, it can learn from similarly aligned projects in Critical Marketing (see Bourne, this volume) and Critical Management Studies (CMS) (see Alvesson, Bridgman and Willmott's (2009a) *The Oxford Handbook of Critical Management Studies*). This chapter practices what it preaches by drawing directly from Alvesson, Bridgman and Willmott's (2009b, p. 12) useful summary of three major critical concerns in CMS:

(1) the critical questioning of ideologies, institutions, interests, and identities (the 4 I's) that are assessed to be (i) dominant, (ii) harmful, and (iii) underchallenged
(2) through negotiations, deconstructions, revoicing or defamiliarizations;
(3) with the aim of inspiring social reform in the presumed interests of the majority and/or those non-privileged, as well as emancipation and/or resistance from ideologies, institutions, and identities that tend to fix people into unreflectively arrived at and reproduced ideas, intentions, and practices.

Our chapter's focus is partly organised around these three concerns. The first, the "dominant", "harmful" and "underchallenged" concern, is the assumption of boundaries for PR that essentially confine the field to the service of big business and governments and exclude activists and others (see McKie & Moloney, this volume). In line with the second of Alvesson et al.'s (2009b) CMS concerns – "negotiations, deconstructions, re-voicing or de-familiarizations" (p. 4) – we retrieve practices and practitioners excluded, ignored or marginalised outside the confines of "legitimate" PR (i.e., usually understood as the business PR that started in the US around 1900 and its corporate and government successors across the world). The delegitimisation of that inclusion-exclusion zone, although it is not yet embedded in mainstream textbooks, is under way on a number of different fronts.

In PR history, Lamme and Russell (2010) expanded by "re-voicing" pre-1900 PR not simply as antecedents to legitimate PR history but as a corrective to "misunderstandings... which have misinformed public relations theory for more than 20 years" (p. 282). Other extensions of the field's historical boundaries feature religious rehabilitations/resurrections such as Watson (2008) on the ninth century religious figure St Swithun; Brown (2003) on St Paul; Spaulding and Dodd (2014) on twelfth century St Hildegard of Bingen; and Carty (2014) on "State and Church as Public Relations History in Ireland, 1922–2011." Secular shifts include Rossler's (2014) imaginative claim for the existence of a Bauhaus PR and Martinelli's (2014) account of PR in suffrage movements. Holtzhausen (2012) illuminated South African PR by incorporating the actions of Boer campaigner and PI Emily Hobhouse into the field at the same time as the inclusion of activists in general as a vital category of PR was increasing (Coombs & Holladay, 2012).

In specifically "speaking up" for activists, Demetrious's (2013) book further interrogates and challenges the right of the term "public relations" to represent a unified field, "in part because it is ideologically invested to include some sectors and exclude others, in particular, activism" (Demetrious, 2013, p. 129) and in part because it "can also work to society's detriment by stifling important social change" (p. 129). She argues for replacing public relations by another, more inclusive, grouping under the name "public communication" (p. 129).

In even more expansive fashion *The Public Relations of Everything* (Brown, 2014) goes for an intervention closer to total inclusiveness at the outer edge of disciplinary expansion. Brown's (2014) book situates PR as encompassing nothing less than *The Ancient, Modern and Postmodern Dramatic History of an Idea*. The blurb – the book was not available at the time of writing – promotes "the radical position that public relations is a profoundly different creature than a generation of its scholars and teachers have portrayed it." It also claims that PR

> is clearly no longer limited, if it ever has been, to the management of communication in and between organizations [and] has become an activity engaged in by everyone, and for the most basic human reasons: as an act of self-creation, self-expression, and self-protection.
> *(http://www.routledge.com/books/search/)*

We welcome these expansions, see them as significant for the future of critical space, and seek to supplement them by arguing for PIs to be considered as part of PR. In doing this, it is necessary to distinguish our position from two others. The first is Antonio Gramsci's view of the organic intellectual, who can be a teacher or journalist and does not need to be prominent in the public eye. The second is University of Waikato researchers working to abolish distinctions between PIs and others by educating "ordinary" people on scientific discourse (Weaver, 2007). Both are valuable in democratising the PI space so that many more voices can become PI voices. The downside is that the voices occupy a smaller sphere of influence and is therefore the key point of difference with this chapter's concern with socially influential and highly visible PIs (examples from top 100 PI lists would include Noam Chomsky, Aung San Suu Kyi and Arundhati Roy). We choose this focus because they insert critical ideas into the larger public sphere. They have, above all, as Muller (2013) said of Camus, "real impact, measurable, to transform, even radically, institutions and relations between political actors and, in general, to guide the political reality a specific way" (p. 132).

A new role model? Albert Camus and differently aligned PR

As part of our retrieval project we consider the PI as also acting through PR. Camus is our exemplar because he also raises issues that continue to be relevant, especially in advocating principles and methods of non-violent political action (Muller, 2013; Sharp, 1998). And Camus did so in situations of war and injustice through tactics typical of PR "activist groups" (Demetrious, 2013).

Many of his actions seem designed to enact the aspirations in Alvesson et al.'s (2009b) third CMS concern, inspiring

> social reform in the presumed interests of the majority and/or those non-privileged, as well as emancipation and/or resistance from ideologies, institutions, and identities that tend to fix people into unreflectively arrived at and reproduced ideas, intentions, and practices.
>
> *(p. 12)*

Camus demonstrates both the principles and methods of non-violent political action and the tactics of PR activism. This contrasts sharply with traditional PR's integration into war-making from the Creel Committee to Hill & Knowlton's notorious contribution to the first Gulf War (see Miller, 1999); and later weapons of mass deception. Camus and other PIs play a role in promoting peace and other progressive causes and Moore's (2014) *Public Relations and the History of Ideas* imports the example of Gandhi as another PI who used many newspapers to publicise how non-violent civil disobedience could help eject the British from India.

Non-violent action is not a synonym for disobedience, and sometimes both help to enact PR strategies for activist groups. Non-violent action gathers force by taking activities and symbols, and knowledge and feelings, as ways of political non-violent action. In contrast to actions based on fear and terror, influential intellectuals use multiple nonviolent opportunities for individual and collective action in the political, economic and social fields. PR, as a process of creating symbols and meanings with social traction, can play a crucial role in implementing non-violent actions, and PR practitioners do not always have to align with the already-powerful (Xifra & McKie, 2011).

From this standpoint, the work of Camus uses non-violence as strategy and, in part, as philosophy. The distinction is that nonviolence as a philosophy is the search for a meaning to life and history, while non-violence as a strategy is the search for effective action (Muller, 2013). Camus shared some principles of the philosophy (rejection of war, finding non-violent alternatives to military confrontations) and his statements, writings and actions – that link with various political causes in France and beyond – align with non-violent strategies.

Albert Camus was born in 1913 in Algeria and came from a family of European settlers. In the 1940s he emerged as a significant figure in the French social landscape and then made his mark on the world scene in the spheres of philosophy and literature. During World War Two he participated in the Resistance through print media and as a journalist, become a political and cultural symbol for his fellow citizens, and won the Nobel Prize for Literature in 1957.

During his life, Camus maintained a political compromise that falls mainly within the left. But his independent positions on political issues brought him into conflicts with communists, radicals and socialists. Indeed, politically, he took divergent positions that, on several occasions, were opposed to the orthodoxies of both left and right. Camus did not preach non-violence, although he practised it through his principles of political action. In 1946 he published a series of opinion papers in *Combat* newspaper that were later compiled and published under the revealing title "Neither victims nor executioners". In these papers, Camus openly criticised the terror, the war and the murder legitimated by the nation state as well as by radical ideologies. He proposed the search for peace as a real alternative to a new global confrontation.

Clearly, the responsibility to speak truth to power, essential to PIs, was exercised by Camus during his public life. It included his expulsion from the Communist Party because of soft positions on the Arabs in Algeria, and it continued during World War Two with participation in the Resistance. It remained constant in public complaints against the authoritarianism of nation states and radical ideologues. Camus promoted solidarity with the demonstrations of students, workers and conscientious objectors. He took an active and controversial role during the colonial war in Algeria but stayed out of the two major camps, preferring to seek political alternatives (Todd, 2000).

Camus' commitment to different causes and people included: the defence of the Arabs in Algeria, resistance to the Nazi occupation of France, the solidarity with Hungarian workers, and opposition to the death penalty. Through the intensity and risk of his commitment, he made himself space as a kind of "unconditional cooperator" (Lichbach, 1996, p. 97), always ready to cooperate in collective action (reform, protest, revolution) without negotiations and cessions.

Camus' PR strategies and tactics

Camus showed the power of argument and persuasion as ways of non-violent opposition to the logic of terror and political injustice – as illustrated in the following five highlights from his speech "The artist as witness of freedom" (Camus, 2006):

(1) there is no life without dialogue, which is to persuade, not to insult or intimidate
(2) the dominant (from left to right) seek to make their opposites disappear (by silencing or killing them)
(3) where there is injustice, social disorder is warranted, and the antidote is to rule justly
(4) fraud, violence and blind sacrifice have failed as forms of politics; therefore, what remains is the obstinacy with human dignity and prudent loyalty
(5) after the atomic bomb we must choose to use science without causing destruction or opt for collective suicide.

These five serve as a playbook for a PI and a foundation for the critical PR of the future.

In terms of PR tactics, Camus used mass media, specifically French newspaper editorials, as well as plays and philosophical essays. For example, he vehemently opposed capital punishment, labelling it an act of revenge:

> Retaliation is related to nature and instinct, not to law. Law, by definition, cannot obey the same rules as nature if the crime is in the nature of man, the law is not made to imitate or reproduce this nature. It is made to correct it.
>
> *(Camus, 1960, p. 126)*

There are also larger aspects of Camus' work that are relevant to his PR activities. In fact, as Coombs and Holladay (2007) argue, activists can attempt, through PR, to build power and to persuade organizations, and sometimes governments, to alter their behaviours and policies. They have acted successfully in this way from Gandhi to Martin Luther King and Malala Yousafzai – with the first two figures recently being acknowledged for this by PR scholars (Kern-Foxworth, 1992; Moore, 2014).

PR strategies and practices are a critical part of an activist group's two general goals: to influence public opinion and behaviour, and to create and maintain "organized, structured, and coordinated efforts" (Smith, 2014, p. 7). The history of PR offers a lot of examples. Coombs and Holladay (2012) show how activists, through non-violent action, can be considered the hidden heroes of PR. That is another non-official, and still partly hidden, history of PR that remains to be written. In it, rather than the corporate advocates, the main characters will be activists, leaders of non-violent movements, and principled and prominent PIs.

Non-violent action, as a frank and political form of promoting insubordination (Sharp, 1998), is one of the pursued goals of activist groups. As Smith (2014) points out, activists use a variety of strategies and tactics to pursue their goals; some of them are confrontational but non-violent: boycotts, demonstrations and symbolic events that "are often designed to dramatize an issue or galvanize public attention" (p. 7).

Sharp (1998) systematised about 200 methods of non-violent political action into three subsets: (1) symbolic protest; (2) noncooperation (affective, social, economic and political); and (3) active intervention, which is subdivided into "non-violent coercion" and uncreative violence (e.g., fair trade, banking usury, clean and sincere human relationships). Although PR plays an obvious role in the symbolic protest, non-cooperation and active involvement are also PR tactics (Gorsevski, 2004).

Sharp's (1998) conceptualisations and classifications match with many of Camus' policy actions; his clandestine activity and his open actions within French society can be interpreted as non-violent strategies. According to Sharp (1998), the main objectives of nonviolent protest and persuasion are to show that a group is opposed to something, that forms of protest can be used for a particular purpose, and that they demonstrate a rejection of a social or political situation (Sharp, 1998). The different tactics and media that Camus used as activist include political speeches; letters of opposition (or support); signed public statements; assemblies of protest or support; leaflets, pamphlets, and books; newspapers and journals; and music and play performances.

Public speeches

Public speeches – spontaneous, formal or religious (e.g., a sermon in a church ceremony) – can become significant acts of non-violent protest (Sharp, 1998). Camus' trajectory as a successful writer, coupled with his political commitment, had him appear constantly in public settings. This situation bothered him deeply, but did not prevent him from setting out a credo for the writer that could also serve a PI or a critical and ethical PR practitioner:

> His talk in Turin, and in the three other cities, was entitled "L'Artiste et son temps"....In the Italian talk Camus attempted a definition of art, based on reality and revolt against reality. It was neither refusal nor total consent, and in consequence it represented a heartbreak perpetually renewed. The point was neither to flee reality nor to submit to it, but to know precisely how much reality to bestow on a work so that it did not disappear into vapidity. For over a period of a century and a half writers had been able to live in happy irresponsibility, but this was no longer possible; we must know that we cannot escape the common misery, and our only justification as artists is to speak for those who cannot. The free artist is not a man of comfort nor of interior disorder but of imposed order. Camus' plea was for freedom of the artist; art is the enemy of all oppressions, artists and intellectuals were the first victims of modern tyrannies of right and left, and when modern tyranny sees the artist as a public enemy, it is justified in its fears.
>
> *(Lottman, 1997, p. 652)*

In this extract the claim that the "only justification as artists is to speak for those who cannot" is akin to the role of the PI, the concern of CMS, and a goal for CPR. Another example came when Camus presented his ideas during the Cold War between the US and the USSR that characterised post-World War Two politics. Camus eschewed taking sides but "denounced threats to freedom in Western societies as well as Eastern ones, pleaded for freedom as the one good, the one heritage of the great revolutionary conquests of two centuries" (Lottman, 1997, p. 627).

Letters of opposition or support

Given the many possibilities and ways to make letters into a method of non-violent resistance, Sharp (1998) argues for addressing them to a person or group. He also notes that such expressions can become open and that their impact depends on the political situation in which they are used. He also stresses that letters are classified as a method of non-violence. The use of letters by Camus can be demonstrated at both the private and the public level. His letter-writing transcended national political circumstances. The letters became a frequent recourse to request, among other things, the freeing of political prisoners, support for strikers, the remission of capital punishment for activists, and the return of exiles. Camus also penned complaints about extreme poverty, expressed solidarity with the victims of totalitarianism, and called for accountability among writers.

Signed public statements

Such statements are addressed to both opponents and the general public, and the signatories may belong to an organisation or have some sort of occupation or profession (Sharp, 1998). In 1948 Camus composed, with René Char,

> a letter to *Combat* to protest the death sentences handed down by a French military court in Algeria against Moslem soldiers who had surrendered to the Germans in 1940, this in the face of the evidence that there had been two million French prisoners of war. Camus would later make the rounds of government offices to find out what had happened to the convicted soldiers, and learned that the sentences had not been carried out.
>
> *(Lottman, 1997, p. 566)*

In a paradoxical situation in the early 1950s, Camus signed a statement in favour of the return to France of the controversial writer Louis-Ferdinand Céline. Years later he continued showing solidarity through public pronouncements at meetings and conferences. The most well-known were meetings with students and Hungarian workers who rose against the communist government, and with Spanish exiles from Franco's dictatorship.

Assemblies of protest or support

Sharp (1998) considers an assembly as a meeting of a group of people wanting to express an opinion (of opposition or support) about issues they consider relevant – such as those relating to prisons, courts or government. From this standpoint, an assembly can be considered a method of protest and persuasion. The meetings can be legal or illegal, with stress on the role of civil disobedience in the latter. As a committed writer and PI, Camus was constantly appearing at meetings of protest or at meetings designed to garner political support. The former related more to international issues, while attendance at the latter type had more to do with internal French affairs.

International events, such as the execution of political prisoners, the repression of worker and student protests, or support for anti-Franco activists in Spain, called for Camus to assist different types of meetings. The Spanish theme was very close to the writer, not only for family reasons but also because of political events in commemoration of the Republican victory in the 1930s or in honour of Spanish exiles. Participation in social gatherings became more frequent with the outbreak of the war in Algeria. During a trip to the African country he sought to summon the moderates to appeal for a civil truce. Camus also participated in meetings with representatives of the Catholic Church, Protestants, Muslims, moderate nationalists and French liberals.

Leaflets, pamphlets and books

Leaflets, pamphlets and books are, together with journals and newspapers, one of the main methods used to communicate with a wider audience (Sharp, 1998). Sharp goes on to argue that the publication and distribution of such writings is relevant when the activist's goal is to hold a divergent approach to the regime, either by enacting a critical viewpoint or by supporting a group that can be considered "oppressed". Sharp (1998) also suggests that these practices are most commonly used by groups that may be subject to official censorship. That said, in situations of conflict, books and other methods for the expression of opinions and for generating actions in specific contexts can play a crucial role.

Newspapers and journals

The acquittal of Captain Alfred Dreyfus on treason charges, and particularly the effective intervention of novelist Émile Zola and his open letter *J'accuse* (I accuse) in the press, is a famous, and perhaps even a founding case in the history of PIs. Journalism occupied a similarly important place in the career and work of Camus. In *Alger Républicain* (where he started his career), Camus took a polemical stand, criticised the political system and society in the context of the rise of fascism before the war – sometimes in the Dreyfusian tradition.

At the newspaper *Combat*, which was born out of the Resistance, Camus tried to realise the noble aims of vigilance and objectivity, derived from the spirit of the struggle against the occupier and his collaborators. But it was in *L'Express* that Camus, most notably on matters concerning the Algerian war, fully expressed his journalistic talents – offering suggestions and also analysis of the situation at hand (Guérin, 2010). His own PI standing and literary prestige acted as a kind of moral guarantee of authenticity for the newspaper: "Camus the writer is aware that journalistic writing is transitory, is to contemporaries and only to them (while the writer writes for his contemporaries and posterity)" (Guérin, 2010, p. 22).

Newspapers and other media are the traditional channels via which to communicate opinions. Sharp (1998) acknowledges the legal and illegal existence of those media and stresses that the illegal and clandestine ones are related to civil disobedience and political non-cooperation. We can trace much of Camus' political thought through his various contributions to newspapers that included *Alger Républicaine, Le Soir, Paris Soir, Combat, Arts, Le Monde, L'Express, Caliban, La Gauche,* and *Franc-Tireur*.

Camus' contribution to the Resistance in France focused on publishing in the clandestine (and illegal) press. The writer lived the risks of an active member of the Resistance movement, and, writing for *Combat* in 1944, he chose words that invited direct action: "a thousand guns pointed towards him will not prevent a man who believes in the justice of a cause. And if he dies, others just say 'no' until the end of their force" (Camus, 2002, p. 331).

During the colonial conflict in Algeria, Camus also used print media and newspapers to send messages in defence of a multicultural Algeria. He proposed the coexistence of communities and argued the need for mobilisation for peace: "the simplifications of hatred and prejudice, which embitter and perpetuate the Algerian conflict, must be combated on a daily basis, and one man cannot do the job alone. What is required is a movement, a supportive press, and constant action" (Camus, 2006, p. 21).

Performances of plays and music

Under certain political circumstances, plays, operas and musical expressions can act as non-violent forms of political protest. The theatre was one of Camus' passions, and his credits include *Caligula* (1938), *The Misunderstanding* (*Le Malentendu*, 1944), *The State of Siege* (*État de Siège*, 1948) and *The Just Assassins* (*Les Justes*, 1959). During his youth Camus joined the Communist Party in Algeria and promoted the creation and adaptation of plays with "his friends in a theater group that would also constitute a form of political action. Calling it the Théâtre du Travail, their first performance was an adaptation of Camus' *Le Temps du Mépris*" (Lottman, 1997, p. 120). Camus remained committed to theatre work even after his expulsion from the Communist Party.

Paying tribute to the fallen is another category in the armoury of non-violent protest and persuasion (Sharp, 1998). The recognition and commemoration of "heroes" of the distant or recent past can be a method of civil resistance. Its roots are founded upon the feelings of guilt that are connected with the killing of political opponents. Camus' (1960) collection of articles, *Letters to a German Friend*, is dedicated to the memory of the French poet René Laynaud, who was killed by the Nazis. Camus also commemorates figures killed in the war to encourage their compatriots, to discourage collaborators, and to reproach the Nazis: "despite all the tortures inflicted on our people, despite our disfigured dead and our villages peopled with orphans, I can tell you that at the very moment when we are going to destroy you without pity, we still do not feel hatred for you" (Camus, 1960, p. 27).

Conclusion

There is no doubt that Albert Camus was a political reference point for his countrymen, and for many others around the world. His political commitment, which was far more than mere partisanship in the face of despotic ideologies, state bureaucracy, and violent methods, led him to defend various causes and people: including the repressed, the exiled, those sentenced to death, Muslim nationalists, left and right wing writers, striking workers, unions, students, and conscientious objectors. He was both a PI and an activist. As an activist Camus described his PR strategies and tactics of resistance: "[It is] in the small things and the big things…[and by] living life meaningfully, consciously, actively, honestly, responsibly, calling things the way you see them, being intolerant of practices that marginalize, dehumanize, and discriminate, speaking truth to power" (p. xv).

As an activist Camus is a figure deserving of a place in the new and evolving history of PR. In fact, as a journalist, he denounced the low newsworthiness of press releases. His work fits well with Holtzhausen's (2012) position that if PR as a practice doesn't resist "dominating power structures, public relations practitioners will become subjects serving the power needs of others, such as corporate managers and other powerful communicative entities who have a lot to gain from public relations practice" (p. 22). PR ethicists have long called for PR practitioners to act as the conscience of their organisations, to move to PI status in this era. Some will also need to act as the conscience of their nations and societies in relation to ecological degradation and social injustice (McKie & Munshi, 2007).

We end by emphasising one last ethical behaviour in Camus. Activism as PR, and the practice of activism through PR, may not always be possible but they do require ethical behaviours. Ethical PR is not an oxymoron and can become involved in specific issues such as denouncing violence (except as a last resort). Camus was an exemplar of effective non-violent rhetoric, a man who endorsed rebellion and resistance in his novels, essays, wartime journalism and political engagements, and in his range of effective PR work. He was an exemplary PI, as demonstrated by his personal (but socially responsible) denouncement of the FLN's (Front de Libération Nationale) violent terrorism during the Algerian War (1954–62): "At this moment bombs are being planted in the trams in Algiers. My mother could be on one of those trams. If that is justice, I prefer my mother" (cited in Todd, 2000, p. 379).

References

Alvesson, M., Bridgman, T., & Willmott, H. (Eds). (2009a). *The Oxford handbook of critical management studies*. Oxford, UK: Oxford University Press.

Alvesson, M., Bridgman, T., & Willmott, H. (2009b). Introduction. In M. Alvesson, T. Bridgman, & H. Willmott (Eds), *The Oxford handbook of critical management studies*, pp. 1–26. Oxford, UK: Oxford University Press.

Bowker, M. H. (2014). *Rethinking the politics of absurdity: Albert Camus, postmodernity, and the survival of innocence*. New York, NY: Routledge.

Brown, R. (2003). St. Paul as a public relations practitioner: A metatheoretical speculation on messianic communication and symmetry. *Public Relations Review*, 29(2), pp. 229–40.

Brown, R. E. (2014). *The public relations of everything: The ancient, modern and postmodern dramatic history of an idea*. Abingdon, UK: Routledge.

Camus, A. (1960). *Resistance, rebellion, and death*. New York, NY: Modern Library.

Camus, A. (2002). *À combat*. Paris, France: Gallimard.

Camus, A. (2006). *Oeuvres complètes*. Paris, France: Gallimard.

Carty, F. X. (2014). State and church as public relations history in Ireland, 1922–2011. In B. St John III, M. O. Lamme, & J. L'Etang, (Eds), *Pathways to public relations: Histories of practice and profession*, pp. 28–39. Abingdon, UK: Routledge.

Coombs, W. T., & Holladay, S. J. (2007). *It's not just PR: Public relations in society*. Malden, MA: Blackwell Publishing.

Coombs, W. T., & Holladay, S. J. (2012). Privileging an activist vs. a corporate view of public relations history in the U.S. *Public Relations Review*, 38(3), pp. 347–53.

Demetrious, K. (2013). *Public relations, activism and social change: Speaking up*. New York, NY: Routledge.

Etzioni, A. (2006). Are public intellectuals an endangered species? In A. Etzioni, & A. Bowditch (Eds), *Public intellectuals: An endangered species*, pp. 1–30. Lanham, MA: Rowman & Littlefield.

Gorsevski, E. W. (2004). *Peaceful persuasion: The geopolitics of nonviolent rhetoric*. Albany, NY: State University of New York Press.

Guérin, J. (2010). Camus, journaliste. *Synergies Inde*, 5, pp. 13–23.

Holtzhausen, D. (2012): *Public relations as activism: Postmodern approaches to theory and practice*. New York, NY: Routledge.

Kern-Foxworth, M. (1992). Martin Luther King Jr.: Minister, civil rights activist, and opinion leader. *Public Relations Review*, 18(3), pp. 287–96.

Khalidi, R. I. (2000). Edward W. Said and the American public sphere: Speaking truth to power. In P. A. Bové (Ed.), *Edward Said and the work of the critic: Speaking truth to power*, pp. 152–63. Durham, NC: Duke University Press.

Lamme, M. O., & Russell, K. M. (2010). Removing the spin: Toward a new theory of public relations history. *Journalism & Communication Monographs*, 11(4), pp. 281–362.

Lichbach, M. I. (1996). *The cooperator's dilemma*. Anna Arbor, MI: The University of Michigan Press.

Lottman, H. R. (1997). *Albert Camus: A biography*. Corte Madera, CA: Gingko Press.

McKie, D., & Munshi, D. (2007). *Reconfiguring public relations: Ecology, equity, and enterprise*. Abingdon, UK: Routledge.

Martinelli, D. K. (2014). The intersection of public relations and activism: A multinational look at suffrage movements. In B. St John III, M. O. Lamme, & J. L'Etang (Eds), *Pathways to public relations: Histories of practice and profession*, pp. 206–22. Abingdon, UK: Routledge.

Miller, K. S. (1999). *The voice of business: Hill & Knowlton and postwar public relations*. Chapel Hill, NC: The University of North Carolina Press.

Moore, S. (2014). *Public relations and the history of ideas*. Abingdon, UK: Routledge.

Muller, J. M. (2013). *Penser avec Albert Camus: Le meurtre est la question*. Paris, France: Chronique Sociale.

Posner, R. A. (2002). *Public intellectuals: A study in decline*. Boston, MA: Harvard University Press.

Rossler, P. (2014). *The Bauhaus and public relations: Communication in a permanent state of crisis*. Abingdon, UK: Routledge.

Said, E. W. (1994). *Representations of the intellectual: The 1993 Reith lectures*. New York, NY: Pantheon Books.

Sharp, G. (1998). *Politics of nonviolent action: Methods of nonviolent action*. Boston, MA; Porter Sargent Publishers.

Smith, M. F. (2014). Activism. In R. L. Heath (Ed.), *Encyclopedia of public relations*, pp. 6–8. Thousand Oaks, CA: Sage.

Spaulding, C., & Dodd, M. D. (2014). The public relations and artful devotion of Hildegard Von Bingen. In B. St John III, M. O. Lamme, & J. L'Etang (Eds), *Pathways to public relations: Histories of practice and profession*, pp. 41–54. Abingdon, UK: Routledge.

Todd, O. (2000). *Albert Camus: A life*. New York, NY: Carroll and Graf.

Watson, T. (2008). Creating the cult of a saint: Communication strategies in 10th century England. *Public Relations Review*, 34, 19–24.

Weaver, C. K. (2007). Reinventing the public intellectual through communication dialogue civic capacity building. *Management Communication Quarterly*, 21(1), pp. 92–104.

Xifra, J., & McKie, D. (2011). Desolidifying culture: Bauman, liquid theory, and race concerns in public relations. *Journal of Public Relations Research*, 23(4), pp. 397–411.

28

Algorithmic public relations

Materiality, technology and power in a post-hegemonic world

Simon Collister

The shift in scholarly analysis of public relations towards critical, cultural and sociological readings of the field is a welcome development in an academic canon traditionally dominated by functionalist, managerial perspectives. It can be argued, however, that current critical and cultural readings draw impetus and analytical rigour from theories rooted in phenomenological and socially constructed components such as language, symbols and identity. This chapter argues that as a result of such focus, analyses of public relations have not kept pace with developments in critical, cultural and social scholarship, in particular the re-emergence of a new, or neo, materialism (Coole & Frost, 2010, pp. 1–4).

This chapter will align public relations scholarship with neo-materialist theories, such as the Foucauldian "dispositif" (Foucault, 1980), Delueze and Guattari (1987) and DeLanda's (2006) semio-material assemblages and the "critical sociology" of Bruno Latour (2005). These approaches place a greater emphasis on the material – that is, philosophically realist – readings of the social and cultural realm in which public relations operates. The results of such analyses will identify and take account of the critical and cultural role played by hitherto overlooked material "objects", such as software, physical infrastructure as well as bodily and institutional interaction in shaping the purely phenomenological aspects of communication.

The chapter will offer an initial exploration of the field by focusing on the increasingly socio-technical digital environment within which an increasingly significant volume of public relations operates (Zerfass, Verčič, Verhoeven, Moreno & Tench, 2014; PRCA, 2014). Such a reading will develop and apply the concept of "algorithmic public relations" as a theoretical lens, and examples of where and how algorithmic public relations can be said to operate will be provided and a series of questions interrogating the implications of such a notion will be posed. These include: how might a renewed focus on non-human agency help us to understand the ways in which public relations power functions as a post-hegemonic force; and does the growth in computational aspects of communication reinvigorate political economic analyses of public relations?

The limits of social constructivism and the rise of neo-materialism

The first step in exploring the rise of materiality and its impact on public relations scholarship requires a brief, but pragmatic, assessment of some of the theories underpinning the recent "socio-cultural 'turn' in the field" (Edwards & Hodges, 2011, p. 1). This conceptual development has allowed scholars to ask pertinent questions about the power of public relations in constructing strategically favourable interpretations of the world and managing such interpretations to enable or prevent social change. In addressing such questions, attention is drawn to a range of concerns, such as individual agency, social structures, power, legitimacy and meaning-creation woven deeply into the fabric of broad sociological, critical and cultural theories (Cottle, 2003; Davis, 2000; Davis, 2002; Demetrious, 2013; Grunig, 2000; Heath, 2010; Holtzhausen & Voto, 2002; Ihlen, van Ruler & Fredriksson, 2009; McKie & Munshi, 2007).

Such theories depend on a socially constructed epistemology (Heide, 2009; Ihlen & van Ruler, 2009) whereby the phenomenological nature of communication – that is its symbolic and linguistic meaning – is foregrounded (Edwards & Hodges, 2011, p. 3) and even "privileged" (Ihlen & Verhoeven, 2012, p. 163). Heide (2009) asserts how Berger's social constructivism accounts for public relations' role in managing communicative interactions to "produce a common social reality" (Heide, 2009, p. 43) while Ihlen and van Ruler (2009) propose that in shaping the Habermasian public sphere public relations functions "as a social construction of mankind" (p. 10).

Exploring public relations from a neo-materialist perspective, however, requires a rethinking of such socially constructed approaches. Coole and Frost (2010), for instance, argue that from a neo-materialist perspective "the more textual approaches associated with the so-called cultural turn are increasingly being deemed inadequate for understanding contemporary society" (Coole & Frost, 2010, pp. 2–3).

Rather, by building on developments in science and philosophy, attention has turned to the material or physical elements constituting society and their interaction with the purely phenomenological. It is this resurgence in the centrality and validity of matter and the material – understood as "a commitment to the mind-independent existence of reality" (DeLanda, 2006, p. 1) – in contemporary society and its interrelation with the dominant analyses of language and representation, that has given rise to the term "neo-materialism". That is, neo-materialism is less about a reclaiming of positivist Durkheimian social science; nor is it a retreat into classical Marxist economic determinism. Rather it seeks to provide a theoretical framework to recognize the intricate and complex entanglements between physical and phenomenological objects.

Such a space is tentatively articulated in the neo-materialist work of Michel Callon (1986), which proposes a "generalized symmetry" between the materiality of the physical realm and the phenomenologically representative one. Such an account provides scholars with a "single repertoire" with which to undertake an analysis of the social space which leaves "no point of view…privileged and no interpretation…censored" (Callon, 1986, p. 200). Michel Foucault (1980), similarly, points us towards a fleeting account of the political and historical impact of such symmetry when he discusses the "dispositif" or apparatus. Defining the dispositif, Foucault states (1980, pp. 194–5) that it is a "thoroughly heterogenous ensemble consisting of discourses, institutions, architectural forms, regulatory decisions, laws, administrative measures…– in short, the said as much as the unsaid". The dispositif, then, can be understood as the interaction of a wide range of discursive and, importantly, *non-discursive* elements deployed to regulate society.

Although not adhering to a strict neo-materialist ontology, Foucault's work nonetheless plays a fundamental role in two distinct ways. First, the dispositif indicates a growing concern within Foucault's work of the role occupied by the physical, material elements and infrastructure of industrial society in establishing his general concept of governmentality (Dean, 2010). Second, the dispositif becomes a central influence for Gilles Deleuze and Felix Guattari's fully realized neo-materialist ontology of "assemblages"[1] (Deleuze & Guattari, 1987; Deleuze & Guattari, 1994; Deleuze & Parnet, 2002). Drawing together the diffuse work of Deleuze and Guattari into a cohesive theory, DeLanda (2006) uses the concept of the "assemblage" to put forward a comprehensive philosophy of society which asserts the world is continually reassembled through relational associations between material and semiotic elements. These semio-material assemblages continually work with and against each other in an attempt to either generate or undermine identity, cohesion and permanence in society.

Coole and Frost (2010, pp 1–2) highlight this persistent tension between the phenomenological and material by observing that

> there is an apparent paradox in thinking about matter: as soon as we do so, we seem to distance ourselves from it, and within the space that opens up, a host of immaterial things seems to emerge: language, consciousness, subjectivity, agency, mind, soul; also imagination, emotions, values, meaning, and so on. These have typically been presented as idealities fundamentally different from matter and valorized as superior to the baser desires of biological material or the inertia of physical stuff. It is such idealist assumptions and the values that flow from them that materialists have traditionally contested.

Focusing her attention specifically on communication, Terranova (2004) makes the case more directly: information, she asserts, has

> two sides....On the one hand, it involves a *physical* operation on metastable material processes that it captures as probabilistic and dynamic states; on the other hand, it mobilizes a *signifying* articulation that inserts such description into the networks of signification that make it meaningful.

(p. 70, italics in original)

Undertaking a neo-materialist analysis of public relations, then, requires a refocusing of the critical gaze on a broader – and hitherto largely unexamined – set of material components and actors present in the social and cultural domain, including, but not limited to, urban infrastructure, software code, physical space, economy and corporeality (Packer & Wiley, 2011; Gillespie, Boczkowski & Foot, 2014). Moreover, it calls attention to fresh considerations of established concerns within critical, cultural and sociological scholarship; namely, given the non-human nature of agency in a neo-materialist world how do we conceptualize power and where does it lie? What are the ethical and moral implications of communicating and acting from a quasi-subjective position? How can critical PR scholars study and understand such issues?

Neo-materialist readings of public relations: databases, datastreams and algorithms

Ontologically, neo-materialism extends across all domains with society. Given the chapter's space limitations, however, no attempt will be made to account for the entire impact it has on the micro, meso and macro[2] realms in which public relations operates.[3] Rather, the chapter will proceed by focusing attention on the specific ways in which neo-materialism can be operationalized through the socio-technical assemblages of contemporary digital communications.

Characterized popularly as the "digital revolution", the past decade has seen a dramatic multiplication of computing power, exponential growth in the adoption of technological hardware – such as personal computers, smartphones, tablets and "wearable tech" for everyday communication – and the almost inconceivably rapid transformation of digital media firms, such as Facebook and Twitter, into economically dominant global institutions.

The implications of such a seismic shift have led to calls for a fundamental reassessment of the ways in which we conceptualize contemporary society. Defined as either the "Network Society" (Castells, 2010) or the "Networked Information Economy" (Benkler, 2006), the globalized, post-industrial environment is conceived as being founded on decentralized and "socialized" networks of information production and consumption.

The public relations industry, while starting to adapt to these socio-cultural, technological and communicative shifts, has, on the whole, remained broadly concerned with maintaining efficacy in the changed communication landscape.[4] Yet few scholars have begun to explore the deeper ontological and theoretical challenges emerging from the growth in digital technology, and their impact on PR. Such issues urgently need addressing.

To achieve a reconceptualization of public relations in a digitally networked environment, we must first look to the underlying changes in communication wrought by technologically driven information production and processing. In a field-defining article, Manovich (1999) argues for a recognition that, with the advent of computationally driven communication, the dominant symbolic form of story-telling and "cultural expression" transitions from that of the narrative, typified by the novel and cinema, to that of the database. Databases, according to Manovich (1999), contain pieces of data as material objects which "appear as collections of items on which the user can perform various operations: view, navigate, search. The user experience of such computerized collections is therefore quite distinct from reading a narrative or watching a film" (p. 81).

This notion of the database as the contemporary symbolic form of media has been updated more recently owing to the growth of social media and mobile internet. As the adoption of these "always on" media formats, platforms and channels increasingly becomes the dominant form of media communication, Manovich (2012) argues we need to recognize a newer form of symbolic media: the "data stream". A direct descendent of the database, "[i]nstead of browsing or searching a collection of objects", within a data stream "a user experiences the continuous flow of events... typically presented as a single column".

In both cases, however, the crucial point to note is that these symbolic forms of media "do not tell stories; they don't have beginning or end; in fact, they don't have any development, thematically, formally or otherwise which would organize their elements into a sequence" (Manovich, 1999, p. 80). Rather, playing a central role in articulating and structuring these data streams as comprehensible and consumable media forms is the computational "logic" of algorithms. Algorithms are sets of rules that directly govern the behaviour and function of data (Lash, 2007, p. 70). Moreover, algorithms play a central part in determining the increasingly ubiquitous mediation of everyday life. As Manovich observes, algorithms operating within digital communication technologies, such as Facebook and Twitter, format "individual broadcasts from spatially distributed users...into a single constantly growing montage" (Manovich 2012) that enables users to communicate effectively.

Algorithms and the algorithmic processing of information, then, are functions central to communication in a digitally networked society. Moreover, it is possible to understand how they are entirely consistent with a neo-materialist reading of communication, and, ultimately, public relations. That is, it is only through the material processes of algorithmic computation that the rendering of representative, phenomenological information from the underlying databases or technological systems is possible.

Such a reading of contemporary communication, I believe, enables us to develop the notion of an "algorithmic public relations" that can adequately account for the socio-technical assemblages constituting contemporary communications practice. Having identified and set out some of the core features of such a concept it is now worth substantiating with some empirical examples.

Identifying algorithmic PR: three scenarios

1. Algorithms as disruptive forces for effective communication

In this first scenario, an activist group had started targeting the Facebook page of a high-profile global brand. In the research setting a meeting was convened between the agency's crisis management team, the client account team and the brand's corporate communication team. Together they sought to develop a strategy for responding to the crisis in order to address the activists' concerns, limit the reputational damage to the brand, and prevent an escalation of the situation.

At this point, activists' tactics had only impacted on the brand's Facebook presence and it was agreed that a response to their concerns would be developed and posted on the Facebook page. As the crisis was predominantly contained within Facebook, it was agreed that no further external crisis communications activity was required.

Before the brand's response could be issued, however, claims started to appear on its Facebook page that posts made there and comments added to existing posts were being censored. In an era of social media, where transparency and openness are paramount (and, moreover, publicly enshrined in the brand's own organizational policies for participating in social media), this was a serious development. An investigation was initiated rapidly on both the agency- and client-side to establish who was deleting users' comments.

While the investigation was under way, a high-profile blogger had picked up on the unfolding crisis and criticism of the brand's alleged "censorship" of debate on the Facebook page. As a direct consequence the blogger published a highly critical article criticizing the brand for adopting an undemocratic and "anti-social" approach to online debate. This post was subsequently picked up by other bloggers and traditional media and shared widely. As a result much greater attention and scrutiny was placed on the original issue and the brand's response to the situation, thus exacerbating the crisis.

After several hours of internal investigation it was confirmed that no individual employee of the brand or agency was responsible for deleting activists' posts and comments on Facebook. Rather, the content was being "censored" by Facebook's "auto-moderation" functionality (Constine, 2011) without any knowledge of the agency or brand.

Facebook's auto-moderation function is an algorithmic tool programmed to detect a number of "undesired" variables, such as profane language and other predetermined "keywords," and prevent them from appearing on a brand's pages by automatically "holding" the posts or comments unpublished for approval or deletion. While it can be argued that such a function is beneficial in helping brands and organizations from inadvertently publishing offensive content, it is notable here that Facebook's algorithm was responsible for exerting a non-human agency to "censor" online discourse. This unseen and material aspect of the communication process at work on the brand's Facebook page subsequently damaged the brand's reputation to a greater extent than the original crisis.

2. Algorithms as non-representational communications strategy

In this scenario a "digital reputation manager" from an international PR agency discussed a common approach adopted to help improve the perception of an organization with a poor public reputation by strategically targeting the search engine, Google's, results page. Google – and other search engines – are considered as being of central importance for online communication in general, and digital reputation in particular, since they can directly and indirectly shape public awareness and perceptions of an organization. Studies indicate, for instance, that the first page of Google results generate 94 per cent of clicks (Jensen, 2011) while the top result is responsible for a third of all clicks made by users (Goodwin, 2011).

Responding to this situation, the interviewee discussed how digital reputation management strategies would focus on generating positive – or often merely non-contentious – communicative content in order to populate search engine results pages (SERPS) and "push" reputation-damaging or undesirable results to much lower-ranked SERPs.

This is achieved by studying (and, to an extent, second guessing) Google's PageRank – the proprietary and commercially sensitive algorithm that determines where websites and content are displayed in Google's results based on a given search query (Levy, 2010). While the PageRank algorithm is a tightly guarded secret, a number of tactics can be deployed to "game" or "optimize" the results (Phillips & Young, 2009, p. 24).

These tactics represent what can be termed a "non-representational communication strategy": while the content or materials produced are representative at a surface level, the strategic aim of the activity is to produce a material effect on Google's algorithmic, computational function, rather than to exert a representational or phenomenological response by a human. That is, non-representational communication strategies primarily create and disseminate content that is designed solely to interact with and generate a positive outcome in search results – the "message" is created purely to trigger a positive (material) response by a search engine algorithm. This is in opposition to conventional, representational communication, which is designed to establish a mutual or communicative understanding based on textual or visual meaning.

3. Algorithms as sense-making processes

As more and more aspects of the strategic communication process become digitized, and the growth in everyday use of communication technologies produces increasingly vast quantities of data, an increasing number of activities and processes central to the public relations function require computational interaction. For example, in all research settings studied, software tools were used for activities such as monitoring online communications to identify and track client issues, measure brand performance, and identify and assess influential stakeholders. All of these activities – making use of the "big data" generated in the contemporary communications environment (Ampofo, Collister & O'Loughlin, 2015; Collister, 2013; Olsen, 2012) – rely on algorithmic or computational processes to gather, interpret and understand the wider social environment.

As a result, algorithms play a central role in the sense-making processes undertaken in public relations and communications settings (Heide, 2009; Walker, 2009). For example, the technologies regularly used by practitioners in the research settings to perform the strategic function of digital "horizon scanning", "social listening" or "social media monitoring" operate through identifying, categorizing and segmenting groups according to a wide range of social and cultural phenomena, including perceived influence in a given context, interests and lifestyles, gender, family status and even religion.

At a more granular level, the practitioners observed gauged the impact of their communication/public relations activity based on metrics derived from the algorithmic assessment of stakeholder behaviour. For example, the effectiveness of brand communication on platforms such as Facebook and Twitter rely on algorithmic quantification of metrics including "Likes," "Shares" and "Retweets". Here practitioners defer sense-making and interpretation to computational processes that in turn are used to plan – and in some cases attempt to predict – what types of message and content will be rendered successful, again privileging the material role played by algorithms in determining the effectiveness of their communication.

While it can be argued that PR practitioners have historically relied to some extent on third parties, or outsourced analysis of communications, it should be noted that the role of algorithms in these contemporary processes produces a set of arguably new problems. For instance, the non-human agency of computation highlights the indeterminability inherent in algorithmic PR; the reduced visibility – even invisibility – of algorithms in public relations planning, and the increasingly proprietary and commercially sensitive "black box" nature of their functionality. All of these reduce the opportunity for practitioner oversight of any bias or other consequential effect that may arise in managing strategic communication.

While this example offers a brief and specific instantiation of one way in which algorithmic public relations can present challenges for everyday practice, it also points to much broader and more significant theoretical questions for public relations. As human agency becomes reshaped (both negatively as well as positively) by contingent but non-human elements, fundamental questions arise. In a world where a quasi-subjectivity can be glimpsed as complex socio-technical assemblages comprising human and non-human actors, where does this leave issues of agency and structure? Such a question leads us to a central concern of critical and cultural analyses of public relations power.

Algorithmic PR, post-hegemonic power, ethics and future methodologies

Existing cultural and critical analyses of power within public relations scholarship tend to focus on the hegemonic or political economic implications of the discipline. For example, central to the power debate emerging from Edwards' and Hodges' (2011) "'radical' socio-cultural turn" in PR is the notion that it operates as a "locus of transactions that produce emergent social and cultural meanings" (p. 4). Public relations' ability to socially construct the world and society around us also forms a core tenet of recent sociological readings of the field (Ihlen et al., 2009).

These perspectives, rooted in the linguistic and semiotic phenomenological dimensions of power, are themselves not dissimilar to Foucauldian approaches whereby public relations creates discourses that generate "knowledge and identity positions which then influence the type of social relationships that are possible within and outside that discourse" (Weaver, Motion & Roper, 2006, pp. 18–19). Even postmodern analyses of power in public relations argue that the discipline is "*discursively constituted*" (italics in original) through "language and meaning creation" (Holtzhausen, 2010, p. 111).

As a corollary to such cultural accounts of public relations power, critical scholarship has focused on the deeper, structural forces underlying the creation and deployment of hegemonic representations. A range of media-sociological, political-economic and critical perspectives have confirmed that the power of public relations lies in the hands of dominant state and corporate institutions (Cottle, 2003; Davis, 2002; Herman & Chomsky, 1994; McChesney, 2013). Such institutional actors rely on their economic strength and structural position in society to deploy public relations as a means to control the flow of information in the public domain. This information and communication management, Habermas (1989) argues, devalues the civic good of society by creating a consensus based not on the "general interest" but biased towards dominant corporate and state interests (Habermas, 1989, pp. 193–5).

Assessing the impact algorithmic public relations has on power, however, requires us to go beyond socio-culturally constructed hegemonic representations. Algorithmic public relations functions at a material, non-representational level as computational processes embedded within the technological infrastructure of digital platforms. That is, algorithms are actively "producing and certifying knowledge" (Gillespie, 2014, p. 168) and exerting power as a computational function "enabling and assigning meaningfulness" (Langlois, 2013, p. 100) prior to interpretation. Interpreted as such, it can be argued that algorithmic public relations operationalizes power prior to and within the formation of conventional hegemonic representations, rather than as the hegemonic representations themselves.

This form of power emerging from computational and informational interaction is termed "post-hegemonic power" (Lash, 2007). Rather than exerting a hegemonic "dominance through ideology", post-hegemonic power has, instead, "moved out into the everyday and power operates from the inside rather than from above" (Beer, 2009, p. 991). That is, hegemonic power is conceived as a top-down force created through the strategic deployment of representational discourses built using language and cultural symbols. Conversely, post-hegemonic power is generated from within the everyday interactions between these representational *as well as* non-representational and material elements of the contemporary, technologically mediated social realm.

Recognizing the function of algorithmic public relations as post-hegemonic power, we can begin to recognize some of the questions and challenges it presents to public relations scholars. Given the ontological "general symmetry" (Callon, 1986) between the phenomenological and material domains of society, hitherto anthropocentric views of power and agency are increasingly undermined. This problematizes a range of existing assumptions predicated on socially constructed beliefs and the primacy of the individual in communicative processes. For example, scholars have argued for the recognition that digital communication can reinvigorate the "public sphere" by forcing institutional interests to adopt communication strategies that foster values such as transparency and openness, and connect citizens directly to institutional actors (Bertot, Jaeger & Grimes, 2010; Bimber, 2003; Castells, 2009; Grunig, 2009; Wright & Hinson, 2008).

However, algorithmic public relations' potential to exert a post-hegemonic power embedded in the material substrata of communication challenges this perceived "ethical turn". The Facebook crisis case study discussed above illustrates how, despite practitioners' aspirations to operate as openly and accurately as possible, their actions are undermined by unseen algorithms embedded within communication platforms. How can practitioners, tasked with applying and adhering to ethical values in communication – such as consciously "protect[ing] and advance[ing] the free flow of accurate and truthful information" and "foster[ing] informed decision making through open communication" (PRSA, n.d.) – ensure that this occurs when algorithms can play such a central role in (re)shaping communication.

Algorithmic public relations also requires us to reassess the role played by political-economic factors in shaping the contours of communicative power in light of the deprivileging of representational and cultural domains in post-hegemonic power. Economic-determinist approaches to public relations have been effectively challenged by studies drawing attention to the importance of public relations' cultural capital (Davis, 2000; Davis, 2002). Focusing on the fact that "PR does not necessarily rely on large capital expenditure", Davis (2000) demonstrates that "more organizations, not fewer, are likely to…set agendas and, on occasion, quite significantly disrupt their official and corporate counterparts" (p. 54).

From the perspective of algorithmic public relations the culturally symbolic dimensions of communication are downplayed and strategies focused on understanding and developing communications that can effectively interact with the material function of algorithms become more important. This *reintroduces* the notion of the political economy as a determining factor – albeit one that is problematically intertwined within socio-technical assemblages – as the resources required to plan and devise algorithmic communication strategies require a level of specialization afforded either by investment in training employees or outsourcing to specialist agencies, at least in the current market. Such expenditure is less available to civil society actors and thus reasserts the economic divide in public relations, which the affordance of cultural capital previously challenged.

As a corollary to the renewed economic influence in the computational communication environment, a number of dominant technology platforms, most notably Facebook, have identified a commercial opportunity in offering solutions to help "optimize" the performance of organizations' communications by allowing them to circumvent the potentially negative impact of their own algorithms operating on the platform, by paying to reach strategically targeted audiences (Delo, 2013). While more investigation needs to be conducted in this area, the detrimental impact on public relations activity for organizations with low budgets – often civil society groups and social movements – can't be overlooked.

Conclusions

The aim of this chapter has been twofold: first, it set out to identify some of the conceptual thinking that has arguably initiated a renewed interest in the significance of material properties in constructing and constituting the social realm; and to offer an overview of the key features of this neo-materialist ontology. Second, it assesses some of neo-materialism's implications for critical and cultural analyses of strategic communication. In order to build a bridge with public relations scholarship the chapter introduces the notion of algorithmic public relations – a theoretical framework that calls attention to the ways in which the materiality of contemporary communication technology changes our understanding of public relations.

Drawing on empirical examples of algorithmic public relations, the chapter then challenges dominant cultural and critical readings of public relations, which, traditionally, have been concerned with the representative and phenomenological dimensions of public relations power. In place of a socially constructed hegemony, rooted in linguistic and symbolic ideology, the chapter argues for a reading of algorithmic public relations through the lens of post-hegemonic power where, rather than imposed from above, power emerges from within the social realm through the symmetrical interactions occurring between the human and material apparatus constituting contemporary society.

While the notion of algorithmic public relations – underpinned by a neo-materialist ontology – has the potential to transform existing approaches to the field, the routes taken in this chapter are embryonic and key questions remain. As post-hegemonic power is neither rooted a priori in human or non-human agency, but rather is dispersed throughout complex and continual interactions of material and semiotic components, where does agency lie – if anywhere – in algorithmic public relations? Given its emergent and generative properties, how does post-hegemonic communicative power operate in any given scenario, and how or what actors can influence it?

Manovich (1999) argues that as human consciousness and behaviour increasingly interact with algorithms, both the algorithmic software and human "software" (that is, the brain's computational capacity) respond to each other and adapt their patterns of thinking and acting accordingly. It is into this rich, complex and multi-faceted realm that neo-materialist ontologies take us, and it is where public relations scholarship needs to extend its critical attention in order to remain consistent with the philosophical and theoretical developments occurring in contemporary critical and cultural thought. This chapter has provided one route into this landscape, but broader, more detailed exploration and assessment of the field is still required to fully comprehend the theoretical and applied implications of algorithmic public relations.

Notes

1 Legg (2011, 129) goes as far as to propose that the Foucauldian "dispositif/apparatus" functions dialectically with the Deleuzian "assemblage".
2 It should be noted, also, that within neo-materialism's "flat" ontology, hierarchical distinctions in any context – such as micro, meso and macro – are at least problematized and at most entirely rejected owing to the complex interrelations between and across all levels. See DeLanda (2006, chapter 1).
3 See DeLanda (2006) and Latour (2005) for more comprehensive accounts.
4 This has resulted in a slew of recent materials that address the practical changes required for strategic communication in a digitally mediated environment. See, for example: Scott, 2013; Solis & Breakenridge, 2009; Waddington & Earl, 2012.

References

Ampofo, L., Collister, S., & O'Loughlin, B. (2015). Text mining and social media: When quantitative meets qualitative, and software meets humans. In P. Halfpenny, & R. Procter (Eds), *Innovations in digital research methods*, pp. 161–93. London, UK: Sage.

Beer, D. (2009). Power through the algorithm? Participatory web cultures and the technological unconscious. *New Media Society*, 11, pp. 985–1002.

Benkler, Y. (2006). *The wealth of networks: How social production transforms freedoms and markets.* Newhaven, CT: Yale University Press

Bertot, J. C., Jaeger, P. T., & Grimes, J. M. (2010). Using ICTs to create a culture of transparency: E-government and social media as openness and anti-corruption tools for societies. *Government Information Quarterly*, 27, pp. 264–71.

Bimber, B. (2003). *Information and American democracy: Technology in the evolution of political power.* Cambridge, UK: Cambridge University Press.

Callon, M. (1986). Some elements of a sociology of translation: Domestication of the scallops and the fishermen of St Brieuc Bay. In J. Law (Ed.) *Power, action and belief: A new sociology of knowledge*, pp. 196–233. London, UK: Routledge & Kegan Paul.

Castells, M. (2009). *Communication power.* Oxford, UK: Oxford University Press.

Castells, M. (2010). *The information age: Economy, society and culture. Volume 1: The rise of the network society.* Oxford, UK: Wiley Blackwell.

Collister, S. (2013). The public relations power of big data In R. Brown, & S. Waddington (Eds), *Share this too: More social media solutions for PR professionals.* London, UK: John Wiley & Sons.

Constine, J. (2011). Facebook adds keyword moderation and profanity blocklists to pages. Inside Facebook website. Retrieved on 7 September from http://www.insidefacebook.com/2011/02/10/keyword-moderation-profanity-blocklist/

Coole, D., & Frost, S. (2010). *New materialisms: Ontology, agency and politics.* London, UK: Duke University Press.

Cottle, S. (2003). *News, public relations and power.* London, UK: Sage.

Davis, A. (2000). Public relations, business news and the reproduction of corporate elite power. *Journalism*, 1, pp. 282–304.

Davis, A. (2002). *Public relations democracy: Politics, public relations and the mass media in Britain.* Manchester, UK: Manchester University Press.

Dean, M. (2010). *Governmentality: Power and rule in modern society.* London, UK: Sage.

DeLanda, M. (2006). *A new philosophy of society: Assemblage theory and social complexity.* London, UK: Continuum.

Deleuze, G., & Guattari, F. (1987). *A thousand plateaus: Capitalism and schizophrenia*, Minneapolis, MN: University of Minnesota Press.

Deleuze, G., & Guattari, F. (1994). *What is philosophy?* New York, NY: Columbia University Press.

Deleuze, G., & Parnet, C. (2002). *Dialogues II*, New York, NY: Columbia University Press.

Delo, C. (2013). Facebook admits organic reach is falling short, urges marketers to buy ads. AdAge website. Retrieved on 12 September 2014 from http://adage.com/article/digital/facebook-admits-organic-reach-brand-posts-dipping/245530/

Demetrious, K. (2013). *Public relations, activism and social change*, New York, NY: Routledge.

Edwards, L., & Hodges, C. E. M. (2011). *Public relations, society & culture: Theoretical and empirical explorations.* Abingdon, UK: Routledge.

Foucault, M. (1980). The confession of the flesh. In C. Gordon, (Ed.), *Power/knowledge: Selected interviews and other writings*, pp. 194–228. New York, NY: Pantheon Books.

Gillespie, T. (2014). The relevance of algorithms. In T. Gillespie, P. J. Boczkowski, & K. A. Foot (Eds), *Media technologies: Essays on communication, materiality, and society*. Cambridge, MA: MIT Press.

Gillespie, T., Boczkowski, P. J., & Foot, K. A. (2014). *Media technologies: Essays on communication, materiality, and society*. Cambridge, MA and London, UK: The MIT Press.

Goodwin D. (2011). Top Google Result Gets 36.4% of Clicks [Study]. Search Engine Watch website. Retrieved on 7 September 2014 from http://searchenginewatch.com/article/2049695/Top-Google-Result-Gets-36.4-of-Clicks-Study

Grunig, J. E. (2000). Collectivism, collaboration, and societal corporatism as core professional values in public relations. *Journal of Public Relations Research*, 12, pp. 23–48.

Grunig, J. E. (2009). Paradigms of global public relations in an age of digitalisation *PRism*, 6.

Habermas, J. (1989). *The structural transformation of the public sphere: An inquiry into a category of bourgeois society*. Cambridge, MA: MIT Press.

Heath, R. L. (Ed.). (2010). *The SAGE handbook of public relations*. Thousands Oaks, CA: Sage.

Heide, M. (2009). On Berger: A social constructionist perspective on public relations and crisis communication. In Ø. Ihlen, B. van Ruler, & M. Fredriksson (Eds), *Public relations and social theory: Key figures and concepts*. London, UK: Routledge.

Herman, E. S., & Chomsky, N. (1994). *Manufacturing consent: The political economy of the mass media*, London, UK: Vintage.

Holtzhausen, D. R. (2010). *Public relations as activism: postmodern approaches to theory & practice*. New York, NY: Routledge.

Holtzhausen, D. R., & Voto, R. (2002). Resistance from the margins: The postmodern public relations practitioner as organizational activist. *Journal of Public Relations Research*, 14, pp. 57–84.

Ihlen, Ø., & van Ruler, B. (2009). Introduction: Applying social theory to public relations. In Ø. Ihlen, B. van Ruler, & M. Fredriksson (Eds), *Public relations and social theory: Key figures and concepts*. London, UK: Routledge.

Ihlen, Ø., & Verhoeven, P. (2012). A public relations identity for the 2010s. *Public Relations Inquiry*, 1(2), pp. 159–76.

Ihlen, Ø., van Ruler, B. & Fredriksson, M. (Eds). (2009). *Public relations and social theory: Key figures and concepts*. London, UK: Routledge.

Jensen, T. (2011). 2nd Page Rankings: You're the #1 Loser. Gravitate Online website. Retrieved on 7 September 2014 from http://www.gravitateonline.com/google-search/2nd-place-1st-place-loser-seriously

Langlois, G. (2013). Participatory culture and the new governance of communication: The paradox of participatory media. *Television and New Media*, 14, pp. 91–105.

Lash, S. (2007). Power after hegemony: Cultural Studies in mutation. *Theory, Culture & Society*, 24, pp. 55–78.

Latour, B. (2005). *Reassembling the social: An introduction to actor-network-theory*. Oxford, UK: Oxford University Press.

Legg, S. (2011). Assemblage/Apparatus: Using Deleuze and Foucault. *Area*, 43, pp. 128–33.

Levy, S. (2010). Exclusive: How Google's algorithm rules the web. Wired website. Retrieved on 7 September 2014 from http://www.wired.com/2010/02/ff_google_algorithm/all/

McChesney, R. (2013). *Digital disconnect: How capitalism is turning the internet against democracy*. New York, NY: New Press.

McKie, D., & Munshi, D. (2007). *Reconfiguring public relations: Ecology, equity and enterprise*. Abingdon, UK: Routledge.

Manovich, L. (1999). Database as symbolic form. *Convergence: The International Journal of Research Into New Media Technologies*. 5, pp. 80–99.

Manovich, L. (2012). Data stream, database, timeline: The forms of social media. Retrieved on 24 March 2014 from http://lab.softwarestudies.com/2012/10/data-stream-database-timeline-new.html

Olsen C. (2012). Big Data comes to the communications industry. Huffington Post website. Retrieved on 8 October from http://www.huffingtonpost.com/christian-olsen/big-data-comes-to-the-com_b_1343310.html

Packer, J., & Wiley, S. B. C. (2011). *Communication matters: Materialist approaches to media, mobility and networks*. New York, NY: Routledge.

Phillips, D., & Young, P. (2009). *Online public relations: A practical guide to developing an online strategy in the world of social media*. London, UK: Kogan Page.

PRCA. (2014). *Digital PR: Report 2014*. London, UK: Public Relations Consultants Association.

PRSA. (n.d.). Ethical guidance for public relations practitioners. PRSA website. Retrieved on 3 October 2014 from www.prsa.org/aboutprsa/ethics/

Scott, D. M. (2013). *The new rules of marketing & PR: How to use social media, online video, mobile applications, blogs, news releases, and viral marketing to reach buyers directly*. Hoboken, NJ: John Wiley & Sons.

Solis, B., & Breakenridge, D. (2009). *Putting the public back in public relations: How social media is reinventing the aging business of PR*. Upper Saddle River, NJ: Pearson Education.

Terranova, T. (2004). Communication beyond meaning: On the cultural politics of information. *Social Text*, 22, pp. 51–73.

Waddington, S., & Earl, S. (2012). *Brand anarchy: Managing corporate reputation*. London, UK: A & C Black.

Walker, G. (2009). Sense-making methodology: A theory of method for public relations. In C. H. Botan, & V. Hazleton, (Eds), *Public relations theory II*. Mahwah, NJ: Taylor & Francis.

Weaver, K., Motion, J., & Roper J. (2006). From propaganda to discourse (and back again): Truth, power and the public interest in public relations. In J. L'Etang, & M. Pieczka (Eds), *Public relations: Critical debates and contemporary practice*. Mahwah, NJ: Lawrence Erlbaum Associates.

Wright, D. K., & Hinson, M. (2008). *Examining the increasing impact of social media on the public relations practice*. Institute for Public Relations.

Zerfass, A., Verčič, D., Verhoeven, P., Moreno, A., & Tench, R. (2014). *European communication monitor 2014: Excellence in strategic communication – Key issues, leadership, gender and mobile media. Results of a Survey in 42 Countries*. Brussels, Belgium: EACD/EUPRERA.

29

Liberation public relations

Mark Sheehan and Jordi Xifra

Broadly speaking, critical theory – with its origins in Western Marxism – is a set of theoretical frameworks that consider injustice and oppression in society and suggest how to create possibilities for the freedom and equality of values and people. It analyses and criticises the way people are influenced to think by the capitalist culture, particularly by powerful players that either control the mass media or dominate other communication methods (McKie, 2005). Circumstances can coalesce to liberate the people from this condition. These circumstances can be due to major shifts in the dominant hegemony via a process of social reform and change. Such shifts may involve public relations playing a role in the liberating process since PR professionals "are members of a human community in which communication in all its forms plays a critical role in human inquiry and development" (Stoker & Stoker, 2012).

This chapter will focus on liberation in a societal and political sense, and its effects on public relations practice in two distinct countries: Spain and Australia. It will identify specific triggering events in the nation-building of these countries, including a historical perspective. These events will be analysed and critiqued to determine how they developed and liberated the practice of public relations. Although culturally distinct as nations, similarities can be drawn from a common public relations practice context. Specific events in Australia's timeline include the federation of the Commonwealth in 1901, when the six former colonies formed a new nation (Sheehan & Turnbull, 2012); the attempt by a progressive government to nationalise the finance industry in 1949 (Sheehan, 2011); and the efforts of welfare groups to improve public housing between 1950 and 1970. In Spain the events considered will include the transition to democracy from the mid-1970s to the early 1980s and the development of its political culture (Xifra, 2010). Heath (2005) would identify such triggering events as the "enormous, society defining debates" out of which public relations practice grew – or as this chapter will argue, was liberated under a set of particular national circumstances. In developing this argument the chapter will also seek to refute a claim made by many, and best summed up by Heath (2005), that public relations gained professional and academic status during the twentieth century in the United States and from there it spread to much of the rest of the world. This chapter will further critically argue for a liberation of public relations from such claims, and will discuss the circumstances in which Spain and Australia developed public relations free of US influence and as a reflection of their respective nation's growth.

The choice of the word "liberation" will also be considered. The connection to Liberation theology is not deliberate but does bring into the discussion certain principles expounded in this area to form a nexus with critical theory. Liberation theology, often branded as Marxist Christianity, shares some similarity with Gramscian thought – i.e., Liberation theology and Gramsci are both determined to persuade people to identify themselves according to their economic status. Expanding on this Liberation theory, public relations has the potential to become a tool of change, of liberation, just as Gramsci proposed in singling out the cultural unity of Christian Europeans. So long as the impoverished of many Western societies thought that their Christian identity was more important, they would readily join forces with Christian elites against atheistic revolutionaries. Changing the culture, for Gramsci, meant inducing people to alter their primary self-identification – i.e. you must consider yourself not as Christians but as poor.

Concepts of nationhood require different thinking by the populace – no longer a colony but a sovereign nation; no longer living under a dictatorship but in a nation in transition to democracy, and ultimately to a democratic state. Events and circumstances in a nation's development allowed a change in thinking and helped change these conceptions. Public relations played a role in this development.

Placing PR in a theoretical framework

For most of the latter part of the twentieth century, public relations theory development was based around the application of various models and paradigms of communication, organisational and management studies. From the 1980s academics began to look beyond these practice applied methods and sought links and recognition with psychology and sociology – but at this time "most studies developed from a largely US-centric literature with a focus on the structural or functionalist perspective" (Sison, 2012, p. 57). Sison arranges the influencing theories of public relations as four steps of a ladder that commences with systems theory, and follows with communication theories; public relations theory (Excellence theory); and then, logically, at the top of the ladder, rhetorical, interpretative, cultural, and critical perspectives. It is clear that Sison sees each step as providing support to a higher level of analysing public relations and understanding its role. She differentiates this final rung stating that "rhetorical approaches focus on how public relations practitioners create, interpret and shape messages", while critical theory examines power and influence, and finally postmodernism "questions the links between knowledge and power, dissensus and consensus, power and resistance, power and ideology and the representation of minorities and marginalised groups" (p. 58).

This chapter seeks to borrow and develop some of the tenets of Liberation theology as a starting point of discussion, and examine public relations from different perspectives. This perspective hopes to create a critical view of public relations and, as L'Etang (2008, p. 4) writes, to "unpick" the assumptions on which much public relations is based.

In creating Liberation public relations we have accepted the call of other academics to "provide the framework or 'lenses' for examining public relations in a critical way" (Macanamra, 2012, p. 420) and also in a postmodernist way that will "break up other theories in a process of continuous renewal" (Holthauzen, 2012, p. 23). In acknowledging the connection between postmodernism and critical theory, Sison (2012) also notes how Holtzhausen differentiates the two by noting the former's focus on "critiquing capitalist production and social systems from a Marxist perspective" and the latter's emphasis on "how power is discursively constituted through political and knowledge production processes" (p. 77).

The discussion of public relations as a liberating force must first take into account its role in society. Much has been written on defining public relations, with one author opining that "PR is caught up in a seemingly endless quest to define its identity through locating the essence of its practice" (Galloway, 2013, p. 147). This quest often follows a familiar path – through what are regarded as the ideas and key figures that have shaped public relations. Many academics have "mostly uncritically adopted" (Macnamara, 2012) this dominant view. But citing the works and practices of Bernays, Lippman and Ivy Lee as the definitive worldview of public relations, and using this as the basis for further argument, is flawed. Demetrious (2013) echoes Heath's earlier statement when she writes that concepts from Bernays' (1928) *Propaganda* "provide a valuable insight into the ideas, beliefs, and values to which public relations is anchored" (Demetrious, 2013, p. 14); and that consequently "from the outset public relations was conceptually weak and anchored to a flawed logic that affected its credibility and suitability in democratic society" (p. 14). Her attribution of these statements to how public relations was, and is, practised, ignores its devel-opment in different contexts. To maintain that Bernays himself "still retains high standing as the "father of modern PR"' (p. 13) is to once again fall prey to the dominance of the US-centric thinking on public relations and to become a captive of its prevailing PR theorists. L'Etang (2008, p. 328) wrote that "US scholars have always tended to assume the activities referred to as PR have been invented by Americans and then exported elsewhere" but in many cases Western PR academics have been guilty of swallowing this line of reasoning hook, line and sinker! It should be countered that Demetrious is not alone in presenting this pervasively negative view of Bernays' influence on public relations. In a more recent and deeper view of Bernays, US academics St John and Lamme (2011) present a re-evaluation of the ideology put forward in propaganda.

In focusing on Australia and Spain this chapter deliberately chooses two vastly different nations in terms of their culture and history. It examines the use of public relations as part of nation-building and how the practice of PR was initially employed and considered more as a Liberating activity in the theological understanding of the term.

Situating PR in a Liberation paradigm

At first it may seem incongruous to consider PR in a context usually associated with theology. However, this is not such a new approach and in the past decade it has not been uncommon for academics, when seeking to identify and recognise the function of public relations, to refer to the activities of Christian religions from previous centuries (Tilson, 2006, 2011; Lamme, 2014; Croft, Hartland & Skinner, 2008). Many of these articles seek to expand public relations provenance based on Watson's (2008) concept of public relations-like activities ("proto-PR") – such as positioning Eusebius's fourth-century biography of Constantine as polemical, hagiographic, and a means of promulgating an image of Christian development (Sheehan & Turnbull, 2012). In New Zealand, public relations has gone further, and academic Chris Galloway has recently applied theological concepts in an attempt to answer the question "What is public relations?" (Galloway, 2013).

As we observed in the introduction to this chapter, Liberation theology "attempts to use the insights of Marxist social criticism to forge a new vision of the Christian message" (Cohn-Sherbok, 1995, p. 1001). Also driving it is Gramsci's central thought which, through the theological lens, can be seen as "liberation [that] has been privatised at the expense of its social and, political and cultural dimensions" (Clements, 1995, p. 284). In addition to this concept of liberation to public relations, it is important to place it in the context of the devel-opment of Liberation theology as expounded by the Australian scriptural scholar Charles Hill (1989, p. 68): "Christian response in faith to Jesus takes a variety of forms because Christians live in a variety of times, places, cultures." For this chapter it is critical to see that not all publics are exposed to, or live in, a US public relations monoculture driven by the ideology of few individuals.

One of the founders of Liberation theology, Leonardo Boff, has written that it opts for a dialectical analysis that analyses "conflicts and imbalances affecting the impoverished and calls for a reformulation of the social system itself...in order to secure justice for all its members" (Berryman, 1987, p. 88). The concept of Liberation public relations does not propose that PR's role is to make society equal – rather, in some instances and in some nations it is used a tool of change not by corporations but by governments and those groups that seek social change not for commercial reasons but for the sake of social justice. Liberation public relations contends that the leaders and pioneers of public relations can also be found in social movements and providing counsel on their behalf.

An Australian perspective of Liberation PR

As we have discussed there is a common paradigm among some public relations academics, not just in the US, that public relations is practised in Australia as it is in the US. This assumption is supported by a view that public relations was easily transplanted to Australian society because of the similarity of the capitalist class structures of the two nations. From that perspective, public relations in Australia until the 1950s can be characterised as attempting to play a role in bringing about a better society. This section of the chapter will look at the attempts of PR in shaping society and giving the voiceless the opportunity to be heard – to be liberated. It will suggest how we can accept the pluralist (as opposed to a Marxist or elitist) role of the government within a liberation public relations context in Australia in the first half of the twentieth century.

Australia's colonial history and its role in the British Empire have shaped its national being. With one procedural act in 1901 the six colonies become a nation. Neither warfare, nor revolt, but a democratic ballot had decided the federation. A massive land with a sparse population of four million had already begun to form its character. It is noteworthy that the US railroad kings and oilmen had no equivalent match in Australia. In fact it was governments that, by the 1880s, ran rail transport in Australia. In 1920 the federal government established and built the Commonwealth Oil Refinery (COR), the only refinery in Australia. Sheehan (2014a) has observed that "many initiatives to build the new society fell to government", creating an environment in which the "cooperative approach of citizen and state came about in Australia" (p. 5).

Government departments saw the usefulness of public relations, and the key thrust in the early part of the twentieth century was to build the nation and encourage immigration. The commercial nature and use of public relations was negligible, and in a democracy with full enfranchisement it can be assumed that all parties were equally heard.

The key influencer for Australia at this time – culturally, socially, commercially and, as it happened, in PR – was still the United Kingdom. The Empire Marketing Board and its communications had an impact on all parts of the Empire, and its role was to make the British "Empire conscious consumers". But more than this it encouraged all members to see the "Empire as an ethical concern". Stephen Tallents influenced many Australians working in London at the time, including the future foreign minister and governor-general, Richard Casey. Tallents (1932) wrote and published, in effect, what was a public relations manifesto: *The Projection of England*. In it, he posited the view that "the new technologies of radio and film could promote a healthy national culture and act as the sextant and compass which would manoeuvre citizenship over the new democratic distances". In a recent biography of Tallents, academic Scott Anthony wrote:

> The 'Britishness' of public relations reflected the pioneers' roots in the public sector. Having worked alongside businessmen and trade unionists during the War, they contrasted the

lack of transparency and 'shoddy carelessness' of the private sector with the openness of government.

(Anthony, 2012, p. 13)

Anthony contrasts the patriotic Tallents' alignment of PR to public administration as an "ongoing infinite process of social development" (2012, p. 14) compared to the cynical Bernays "conscious and intelligent manipulation of the organised habits and opinions of the masses [and] the executive arm of the invisible government". It is this thinking that influenced the perception of the role of public relations in Australia at this time, and allows for a liberated approach for PR practitioners at this time, and one that is evidenced through their work.

In the first text to concentrate on Australian public relations campaigns (Sheehan and Xavier 2007) Sheehan outlined the significant campaigns of Australia up to the 1950s. All of them focused on government and social initiatives: immigration, construction of the Snowy Mountain hydro scheme, the building of Melbourne's Shrine of Remembrance. As was also the case with the Spanish comparisons, these campaigns of significance rarely had a commercial outcome. Macnamara and Crawford's (2013) work on the development of Australia Day as a national day of celebration adds further to this claim and shows that the historical record of Australian PR is different to that of the US, and that Australian PR was, in its infancy, liberated from the US paradigm. In this liberation it was formed in a different image – not as a reaction but as something that grew out of the character of a nation that was being newly formed, a nation that was referred to at home and abroad as "the working man's paradise".

A point of differentiation between the Spanish and Australian contexts is the early role of the individual practitioner and their own personal view of what public relations might achieve in a free society. This backdrop of freedom in Australia contrasts with Spain's totalitarian regime. Australia's first public relations consultant was George Fitzpatrick, and many academics (Harrison 2011; Tymson, Lazar & Lazar 2006; Tymson & Sherman, 1996) credit him with founding the first public relations consultancy in Australia in the early 1930s. However, as Gleeson (2013) has outlined in great detail and using forensic scholarship, Fitzpatrick had engaged in public relations activities since as early as 1918.

Gleeson (2013) documented Fitzpatrick's early involvement in charitable and community services and fundraising campaigns on behalf of a number of Sydney hospitals – including a major fundraising campaign for Sydney Hospital. Much of Fitzpatrick's work in this sector was done in an honorary capacity – he received no payment and one charitable organisation went to some lengths to point out that he received "no salary, bonus, honorarium or gratuity in any shape or form" and was himself a generous contributor to the charity.

Fitzpatrick's inclusion in this chapter is critical; if other writers insist that Bernays (or Lee for that matter) was the first counsel of public relations, that his early career and philosophies entitled him to the accolade of being the father of PR, it is reasonable to make this same claim for Fitzpatrick in Australia. However the contrast in their practice was stark.

A further example of the liberated development of Australian public relations is the extensive campaigns undertaken by social agencies in the 1950s. The Brotherhood of St Laurence (BSL), the charitable arm of the Anglican Church, employed public relations consultants John and Esta Handfield in a number of successful campaigns over a period spanning 30 years. The Handfields saw work in this sector as critical to their organisation, and to the growth of PR in Australia.

Following Tallents' and Grierson's use of film for their public relations work in the 1930s, BSL produced three films focusing on life in the slums around Melbourne. Sheehan has noted (2014b) that "as well as being promotional material for the Brotherhood of St Laurence and its work, these films also raised general awareness of inner-city housing conditions in Melbourne at the time". This campaign's focus was to pressure the state government to increase the supply of public housing.

Through astute presentation and media management, the Brotherhood brought back to prominence an issue that a jaded press no longer considered news. In early 1955 the campaign gained both government and opposition commitment to the demolition of a notorious slum suburb and the relocation of its tenants to public housing. This campaign signalled a growing sophistication in PR practice, evidenced by its use of research to monitor public reaction and media response to a single issue. Furthermore, the driving incentive behind this was not commercial but rather out of a desire to build a better society – the working man's paradise.

A Spanish perspective of Liberation PR

The term "liberation" is polysemic. From the perspective of contemporary history, its historical connotations are obvious. During the World War Two, the liberation movements against the Nazi occupation were numerous and ultimately effective. Liberation marked, therefore, the return to democracy in Europe, or rather, in most European countries. In Europe, some of the most eminent professionals and scholars of public relations were leaders of the Resistance and assisted in the liberation of their countries. This is the case of William Ugeux, leader of the Belgian Resistance and the main promoter of a European theory of public relations that was sketched out and led by Lucien Matrat (Xifra, 2012).

But in Spain there was neither liberation nor democracy until 1975. In 1945 Spain was still recovering from a punishing and destructive civil war. This war had brought about 40 years of dictatorship, and under this type of regime liberation movements had no chance of victory – although we can find examples of activism that led to public relations campaigns directly targeted at the totalitarian government of Franco.

Therefore, the history of Spain is an excellent framework for discussing Liberation public relations. Moreover – and even more interestingly – the history of Spain allows us to think about another kind of Liberation public relations that is different to the Australian one discussed previously. This liberation was born from the chains that linked public relations to propaganda – and the battle for the freedom to oppose and be separate from propaganda, a position expressed by the public relations founding fathers, most especially Edward Bernays. The history of public relations in Spain suggests that public relations can grow and develop under a totalitarian regime, regardless of propaganda. Nevertheless, we will not discuss here whether public relations is a (most sophisticated) form of propaganda, since this has been brilliantly argued by other scholars (e.g., Moloney, 2000). Instead, we want to emphasise how public relations can grow and develop under a dictatorship and coexist in different spheres: one of civil society and the other of the state.

Thus, in this liberation of public relations, we free it to exist outside exclusively democratic environments. However, in liberating it from those who consider it exclusively a democratic function, we do not remove this democratic function. We will first provide a brief overview of the history of Spanish public relations under Franco, using the investigations of Rodríguez-Salcedo (Rodríguez-Salcedo & Gutiérrez-García, 2007; Rodríguez-Salcedo, 2008, 2010) as our guide.

Spanish public relations, in the post-civil war era (1939–53), was shaped by public health and tourist campaigns that bore witness to the new political situation: the dictatorship of General Francisco Franco. In the following years, Francoist Spain saw the first PR campaigns, which were then called "prestige" campaigns and which were based on the personal genius of men working in advertising agencies or in the world of broadcasting. In 1953 a Spanish book about the theory of advertising first translated the English term "public relations" to "general relations with the public" (Rodríguez-Salcedo, 2008, p. 2009). Indeed, the theory and scant literature on the topic seemed to run parallel with practice. The first campaigns, which were developed in the late 1950s under the name of "prestige advertising", were known as "public relations" only after the pioneer Joaquin Maestre – who founded the first agency fully devoted to offering PR services in Spain in 1960 – met with Lucien Matrat, the father of European PR (Xifra, 2012), in Brussels. This meeting occurred at a time of national paradox for Spain: censorship of the media, yet social innovation and a period of economic openings. The private sector naturally became interested in establishing communicative links with their publics.

During the late 1950s, Western Europe experienced significant economic growth. At the same time, Spain was on the threshold of developing basic industries thanks to the "Plans for Stabilization and Development" [Planes de Estabilización y Desarrollo], which were beginning to bear fruit by early the 1960s. These plans set down the essentials for economic growth within an authoritarian system, and most importantly they relinquished some control thereby gently ushering in a period of liberation. As Rodríguez-Salcedo (2008) suggests, the origins of PR in Spain can be found precisely in this national development, between the mid-1950s and the early 1960s, a period which marked the changing-point for Spain's economic reality within the Franco regime. Nevertheless, she pointed out "the time conjunction makes the author of this article wonder whether it was industrial development that favored the dawn of PR, or vice versa" (Rodríguez-Salcedo, 2008, p. 289).

Following the creation of the first Spanish PR firm, the 1960s became a decade characterised by the search for professional PR associations. This was indeed a challenge in a post-civil war country where the right of assembly of any kind was neither socially acceptable nor politically permitted. As the profession grew in vitality during the 1970s, it searched in vain for social and official recognition from the fading and mortally wounded state system. The profession also brought about a certain acknowledgement and institutionalization for PR. It was then that the discipline was included, together with advertising, as a university degree course in the curricula of the three newly created Faculties of Communication Science: Barcelona, Madrid and Navarra (Xifra & Castillo, 2006; Xifra, 2007). In 1975 an Official Register of Public Relations Technicians [sic] was finally created. This register defined the profession and set out the conditions for qualifying to appear on the list – thus protecting against professional fraud.

We could make the contrary argument, as Rodríguez-Salcedo (2008) do, that while advertising and PR developed as different fields in other countries, the birth of PR in Spain was different. According to Rodríguez-Salcedo (2008, p. 290):

> It is difficult to separate the historical precursors of advertising and PR in the origins of the activity in the first half of the twentieth century. When, through historical research, PR campaigns were found, it turns out that they were created by advertising agencies or by advertising professionals, and were, at times, hidden under the designations of "social", "educational" and "prestige" advertising or "propaganda".

Perhaps this lack of clarity of its roles and content has, in turn, led to the notion that PR is merely a secondary tool of advertising, and that its application is limited to media relations – i.e., sending out press releases, setting up press conferences and keeping up good relations with journalists – and events planning. This may help to explain the profession's "present identity crisis" (Rodríguez-Salcedo, 2008, p. 290).

However, Franco used public relations for personal purposes. So, public relations can be seen as a government function of the authoritarian public administration. One of the most paradigmatic examples of this was the so-called Operation Catalonia. Franco and his government were based for a month in Barcelona (May–June 1960), and the cabinet meetings were held in the Palace of Pedralbes. During those days the government approved the Barcelona municipal charter and the transfer of Montjuïc Castle to the city council. This was among other measures "to try to improve its relations with the Catalan public opinion" (Polo, 2003, p. 77). Operation Catalonia was an attempt to repair the image affected by the so-called "Galinsoga Affair" that had occurred a month before the visit of Franco.

The incident involved Luis de Galinsoga, editor of *La Vanguardia*, then as now the most influential and widely circulated newspaper in Catalonia. Galinsoga was appointed to his position by the government (Franco personally selected the editors of the main Spanish newspapers) and was well-known for his strong anti-Catalan views.

The statement that unleashed the "affair" was the exclamation by Galinsoga, inside a church, that "all the Catalans are crap", a statement motivated by the fact that mass had been celebrated in Spanish *and* Catalan. In response, nationalist activists began a campaign to boycott *La Vanguardia* – publicly destroying copies, throwing stones at the windows of the newspaper's headquarters, and other actions. As one of the activists, Xavier Polo, remembers it, the most forceful action was to "put toilets filled with human crap on La Ramblas [one of the most famous streets in Barcelona] with the inscription: "Galinsoga, get out of the toilet" (Polo, 2005, p. 185). The affair ended with Galinsoga being dismissed, and the undertaking of an extensive tour and public relations campaign by Franco to repair the damage.

This case is, possibly, the most notable example of how a dictator had to deal with public relations campaigns (or image repair strategies) in order to manage the mood of the public. It is questionable whether this constitutes propaganda, because the aims were not those of the propagandist and because the strategy used was a reaction to a crisis of Franco's reputation among a *specific* public: Catalan civil society. The tactics used by Franco during his month in Barcelona were also public relations tactics: visits to Catalan symbolic places (e.g., Montserrat Abbey), visits to emblematic corporations (e.g., Seat [the motor company]), or attending events celebrated in places such as the Nou Camp, the stadium of Barcelona Football Club (a symbol of Catalan nationalism). In reflecting on these events it is difficult to imagine a society further removed from that of Bernays and his ilk in the US.

Conclusion

How much can we attribute these events to a liberated form of public relations? In comparing the birth and development of public relations based around the thinking of its widely cited founders – such as Bernays – we have attempted to identify a liberated approach for Spain and Australia. In Australia's case, this was not an approach consciously driven by commercial demands, but rather by enlightened government and social agencies; while in Spain the liberated approach was in reaction to a repressive autocracy. The practice as invented in these two nations was in fact free (or liberated) from the kinds of commercial constraints that imposed themselves on US practice – a practice that was long-accepted as the dominant paradigm of public relations and its role in societies.

We recommend a Gramscian approach to reconsider public relations not as a US invention developed for corporate propaganda, but rather as an indigenous organic activity responding to circumstances in the development of a nation. This chapter has sought to liberate thinking about why public relations is created. Who were the pioneers? And what were the circumstances of its inception? We have by no means attempted a comprehensive treatment of liberation in a PR context, but it has been our intention to start a discussion that focuses on the reasons for this way of thinking and the peculiar features that might characterise a different approach to the development of PR in a national context.

In this chapter we have seen how "liberation" has a sturdier political connotation. Through liberation the oppressed break the chains by which the oppressors have hitherto restricted their freedom. In Europe, the example of William Ugeux, leader of the Belgian Resistance and father of Belgian public relations, emphasises the democratic nature of the public relations function. But this is not always the case. In Spain, for example, public relations was not introduced by the Resistance. It was the fascists – in particular those who developed communication functions in the Franco government and did not oppose its methods – who introduced public relations to Spain. Thus, in this chapter's context public relations should also be liberated from the idea that it can only be developed within the framework of democracy. In fact, even those professionals from democratic countries, such as British PR pioneer Toby O'Brien, helped the Franco regime in its public relations efforts to generate public diplomacy and soft power (L'Etang, 2004). And so, it is time to liberate public relations from romantic visions. Public relations is a communicative weapon available to any nation state, from nascent ones and even to stateless nations (Xifra & McKie, 2012). Its techniques can serve propaganda purposes, but these can also generate reputation, attraction and sympathy for totalitarian regimes.

References

Anthony, S. (2012). *Public relations and the making of modern Britain: Stephen Tallents and the birth of a progressive media profession.* Manchester, UK: Manchester University Press.

Arceo, A. (2004). Public relations in Spain: An introduction, *Public Relations Review*, 30, pp. 293–302.

Bernays, Edward L. (1928). *Propaganda.* New York: Liveright.

Berryman, P. (1987). *Liberation theology: Essential facts about the revolutionary movement in Latin America and beyond.* Philadelphia, PA: Temple University Press.

Clements, K. (1995). Theology now. In P. Byrne, & L. Houlden (Eds), *Companion encyclopedia of theology*, pp. 272–90). London, UK: Routledge.

Cohn-Sherbok, D. (1995). Theology as praxis. In P. Byrne, & L. Houlden (Eds), *Companion encyclopedia of theology*, pp. 1001–16. London, UK: Routledge.

Crawford, R., & Macnamara, J. (2012). An "outside-in" PR history: Identifying the role of PR in history, culture and sociology. *Public Communication Review*, 2(1), pp. 45–59.

Croft, R., Hartland, D., & Skinner, H. (2008). And did those feet? Getting medieval England "on message". *Journal of Communication Management*, 12(4), pp. 294–304.

Demetrious, K. (2013). *Public relations, activism, and social change: Speaking up.* New York, NY: Routledge.

Dozier, D., & Lauzen, M. (2000). Liberating the intellectual domain from the practice: Public relations, activism, and the role of the scholar. *Journal of Public Relations Research*, 12(1), pp. 3–22.

Galloway, C. J. (2013). Deliver us from definitions: A fresh way of looking at public relations. *Public Relations Inquiry*, 2(2), pp. 147–59.

Gleeson, D. J. (2013). George William Sydney Fitzpatrick (1884–1948): An Australian public relations "pioneer". *Asia Pacific Public Relations Journal*, 13(2), pp. 1–11.

Harrison, K. (2011). Strategic public relations: A practical guide to success. South Yarra, Victoria: Palgrave Macmillan Publishers Australia.

Heath, R. L. (Ed.). (2005). *Encyclopedia of public relations.* Thousand Oaks, CA: Sage.

Hill, C. (1989). *Faith in search of understanding: Introduction to theology.* Blackburn, UK: Collins Dove.

Holthauzen, D. R. (2012). *Public relations as activism: Postmodern approaches to theory & practice.* New York, Routledge.

Lamme, M O. (2014). *Public relations and religion in American history: Evangelism, temperance, and business.* New York: Routledge.

L'Etang, J. (2004). *Public relations in Britain: A history of professional practice in the 20th century*. Mahwah, NJ: LEA.

L'Etang, J. (2008). Writing PR history: Issues, methods and politics. *Journal of Communication Management*, 12(4), pp. 319–35.

McKie, D. (2005). Critical theory. In R.L. Heath (Ed.), *Encyclopedia of Public Relations*, pp. 226–8. Thousand Oaks, CA: Sage.

Macnamara, J. (2012). *Public relations: theories, practices, critiques*. French's Forest, NSW: Pearson, Australia.

Macnamara, J., & Crawford, R. (2013) Reconceptualising public relations in Australia: A historical and social re-analysis. *Asia Pacific Public Relations Journal*, 11(2), pp. 17–34.

Moloney, K. (2000). *Rethinking public relations*. London: Routledge.

Polo, X. (2003). L'activisme polític i la persecució policial. In X. Bru, & C. Dropez (Eds), *Exili interior, represa I transició*, pp. 69–80. Barcelona, Spain: Proa.

Polo, X. (2005). *Todos los catalanes son una mierda*. Barcelona, Spain: Proa.

Rodríguez-Salcedo, N. (2008). Public relations before "public relations" in Spain: An early history (1881–1960). *Journal of Communication Management*, 12(4), pp. 279–93.

Rodríguez-Salcedo, N. (2010). Relaciones públicas en dictadura: el inicio de la profesión en España (1960–1975). In M. Montero (Ed.), *La edad de oro de la comunicación comercial: Desde 1960 hasta 2000*, pp. 61–131. Seville, Spain: Comunicación Social.

Rodríguez-Salcedo, N., & Gutiérrez-García, E. (2007). *50 years of public relations in Spain: From advertising and propaganda to public relations and reputation management*. Paper presented at Media, Communication, Information: Celebrating 50 Years of Theories and Practices, 50th anniversary conference, International Association for Media and Communication Research (IAMCR), Paris, 22–27 July.

Sheehan, M (2011). *Banking on victory: PR lessons from Australian government attempts at nationalization*. Paper presented at Barcelona Meeting COM: 2011 International Public Relations Conference, Barcelona, Spain, 28–29 June.

Sheehan, M. (2014a). Australia. *Asian perspectives on the development of public relations*, pp. 5–13. London: Palgrave.

Sheehan, M. (2014b). A brief history of public relations in Australia and New Zealand. In J. Johnston, & M. Sheehan (Eds), *Theory and practice: public relations*, 4th edition, .pp. 20–47. Crows Nest, Australia: Allen & Unwin.

Sheehan, M. & Turnbull, N. (2012). The impact of divergent historical and cultural factors on convergence in global communication practice. *Asia Pacific Public Relations Journal*, 14(1–2), pp. 33–50.

Sheehan, M., & Xavier, R. (2007). *Public relations campaigns*: Melbourne, Australia: Oxford University Press.

Sison, M. (2012). Theoretical contexts. In J. Chia, & G. Synott (Eds), *An introduction to public relations and communication management*, pp. 54–89, 2nd edition. Melbourne, Australia: Oxford University Press.

St John III, B., & Lamme, M. O. (2011). The evolution of an idea: Charting the early public relations ideology of Edward L. Bernays. *Journal of Communication Management*, 15(3), pp. 223–35.

Stoker, K., & Stoker, M. (2012). The paradox of public interest: How serving individual superior interests fulfill public relations' obligation to the public interest. *Journal of Mass Media Ethics*, 27(1), pp. 31–45.

Tallents S., (1932). The Projection of England. In S. Anthony (2012), *Public relations and the making of modern Britain: Stephen Tallents and the birth of a progressive media profession*. Manchester, UK: Manchester University Press.

Tilson, D. J. (2006). Devotional-promotional communication and Santiago: A thousand-year public relations campaign for Saint James and Spain. In J. L'Etang, & M. Pieczka (Eds), *Public relations: Critical debates and contemporary practice*, pp. 167–84. Mahwah, NJ: Lawrence Erlbaum.

Tilson, D. J. (2011). Public relations and religious diversity: A conceptual framework for fostering a spirit of communitas. *Global Media Journal: Canadian Edition*, 4(1), pp. 43-60.

Tilson, D. J., & Perez, P. S. (2003). Public relations and the new golden age of Spain: A confluence of democracy, economic development and the media. *Public Relations Review*, 29, pp. 125–43.

Tymson, C., & Sherman, B. (1996). *The Australian public relations manual*. Newtown, Australia: Millennium Books.

Tymson, C., Lazar, P., & Lazar, R. (2006). The new Australian and New Zealand public relations manual. Manly, NSW: Tymson Communications.

Watson, T. (2008). Creating the cult of a saint: Communication strategies in 10th century England. *Public Relations Review*, 34(1), pp. 19–24.

Weaver, C., Motion, J., & Roper, J. (2004). Truth, power and public interest: A critical theorising of propaganda and public relations. *Conference Papers – International Communication Association*, January 1, pp. 1–28.

Xifra, J. (2007). Undergraduate public relations education in Spain: Endangered species? *Public Relations Review*, 33(2), pp. 206–13.

Xifra, J. (2010). Linkages between public relations models and communication managers' roles in Spanish political parties, *Journal of Political Marketing*, 9(3), pp. 167–85.

Xifra, J. (2012). Public relations anthropologies: French theory, anthropology of morality and ethnographic practices. *Public Relations Review*, 38(4), pp. 565–73.

Xifra, J., & Castillo, A. (2006). Forty years of doctoral public relations research in Spain: A quantitative study of dissertation contribution to theory development. *Public Relations Review*, 32(3), pp. 302–8.

Xifra, J., & McKie, D. (2012). From realpolitik to noopolitik: The public relations of (stateless) nations in an information age. *Public Relations Review*, 38(5), pp. 819–24.

30

Being social

Creating a critical commons with public relations practice

Paul Willis

This handbook highlights the significant and diverse contributions made by critical scholars in the field of public relations. Their work has helped to change the way we think about PR and its impact on society. Although I'm not a critical scholar, insights from this rich seam of thinking inform my own research, teaching and consultancy in organisations. It has also made me behave differently (hopefully for the better) in other areas of my life. Just as critical public relations (CPR) scholarship has influenced my practice, this chapter is written in a spirit of reciprocity and driven by a desire to contribute to a wider discussion of what CPR might become. To contribute to this debate the chapter introduces the idea of a *critical commons*. This draws on insights from movements operating at the margins of academic discourse and makes the case for critical scholars to engage in more participatory forms of research. The emphasis is on research "with" practitioners and moves critical inquiry beyond something that is either done "for" or "to" them.

This focus on participation is put forward as an antidote to the regressive, largely conduit model that still underpins much academic practice and thinking (Willis & McKie, 2011). Critical scholarship may incorporate good theory but it is often knowledge that is "owned" and "transmitted" by researchers rather than developed through the act of collaboration. This discussion of the need for a more social epistemology therefore begins in a place where CPR has yet to venture. Confronting this issue is important if critical scholarship is to maintain its reputation as a progressive force in the field of public relations. Indeed, if PR as a practical discipline is to play its role in what Heath (2006) calls a "fully functioning society" (p. 93) it needs the support of a fully functioning academic community. To help achieve this, CPR (in common with other scholarly endeavours in the field) needs to guard against anti-social tendencies by embracing interdependence as well as action.

It is important to be clear at the outset that these arguments do not remove the right of critical scholars to be "anti-social", or indeed to generally disrupt and disturb as they see fit. Furthermore, L'Etang (2005) asserts correctly that CPR scholars should not be burdened by the need to justify their work with a functionalist concern to advance practice. Such an aspiration is, though, the purpose of this chapter – which explores aspects of CPR's character and its particular relationship with practice. Furthermore, it is argued that this orientation is crucial to the *overall health* of the critical project in public relations. This view is not positioned as "the" way forward but one of several futures that need to be considered if critical scholarship is to move from generating a better understanding of the world to changing things for the better. A diverse destiny for CPR is also important given that a key lesson drawn from the critical tradition is an inherent and healthy suspicion towards homogeneity.

Seeking to contribute positively to a culture of heterogeneity, the rest of this chapter is concerned with exploring the key ideas that underpin one of these possible futures. It begins with the claim that CPR needs to move in a new direction to maintain its relevance and makes the case for more social forms of research. It then introduces a series of multi-disciplinary and mutually reinforcing insights that underpin the notion of a *critical commons*. These are concerned with the nature of knowledge, productive areas of inquiry, the character of effective CPR-practice intersections, and the types of approaches required for achieving this. The chapter then engages with thinking from the fledgling information commons movement, debates about the contemporary focus of social science research, and the action modalities. Each engagement serves to highlight the potential for symbiosis between CPR and PR practice and to synthesise the insights into the preliminary characteristics of a *critical commons*. This "mental map" is designed to inform a wider reflection about the future development of CPR research. The chapter conclusion identifies an opportunity for the PR field to play a leadership role in the wider academy by forging new approaches to develop and promote this type of critical intervention in practice.

A case for change: bridging a divided discipline

There is a view that PR academics and practitioners inhabit different worlds. As van Ruler (2005) memorably put it in the title of her *Public Relations Review* commentary, "Professionals Are from Venus and Scholars Are from Mars". This way of viewing the relationship can lead to a simplistic debate centred on the idea that practitioners and academics exist for entirely different purposes (Moncur, 2006). Practitioners are portrayed as serving the needs of organisations. What interests they have in theory and research lies in applying these insights to improving organisational performance. In contrast, academics are seen to be motivated by different and higher objectives. These are driven by a desire to explore and understand more fundamental questions. How does PR affect the functioning and behaviour of organisations? What is the potential impact of PR on society or specific groups in society? The expectations generated by such scholarly perspectives then require public relations practitioners to perform a high wire act as they seek to walk a line between the needs of the organisation and those of society.

This links PR practitioners to what Meyerson (2003) calls "tempered radicals" (p. xi). That is, people committed to their organisation but also motivated by a cause, community or ideology that is different from, and possibly at odds with, the dominant culture of the place in which they work. For Meyerson (2003), tempered radicals "want to rock the boat, and they want to stay in it" (p. xi). This potentially puts them in a position of conflict in the organisation and swimming against a prevailing tide. At the same time, practitioners have their roles ascribed to them by their organisation as well as being subject to the constraining political and cultural processes that affect organisational life. They operate in what Whetton, Felin and King (2009) refer to as a complex "landscape of social entities and social actors" (p. 544).

Such an environment requires high levels of virtuosity from PR practitioners as it is where a range of competing interests collide. It also suggests that public relations scholarship needs to generate a better understanding of the points at which performative and emancipatory knowledge intersect. In generating that understanding, PR scholars can build on Lyotard's view that there are essentially three meta-narratives or purposes for knowledge. In Pedler and Burgoyne's

(2008) summary these are: speculative knowledge, which is theoretically rigorous but developed for its own sake and unconcerned with applications to practice; performative knowledge, which is associated with managerialism, problem-solving and the improvement of practice; and emancipatory knowledge which is concerned with the development of the person in the world and a particular desire to liberate them through knowledge. At the point of intersection a strong critical edge is required to apply "scepticism towards arguments, assumptions, practices, recognising the impact of social and political dynamics and the implications of the inequalities of power and control" (Antonacopoulou, 2010, p. S9).

CPR is well placed to engage with and inform such a process. Unfortunately, beyond the narrow confines of our academic community, critical scholarship does not have the influence and visibility it should. Indeed, how many CPR, as well as other public relations scholars, are content with the reach and impact of their work? To many of our key stakeholders (individual practitioners, professional bodies, policy-makers, citizens and community groups) we are invisible and our research goes unappreciated, if not unnoticed. This is one of the great ironies for a discipline concerned with communication and the engagement of others.

Avalanche warning

The lack of engagement and disconnection between theory and practice can be found in other examples. For instance, even though digital technologies such as social media have transformed our economy and culture, ways of thinking about research still reflect the analogue, pre-Internet world. McLoughlin and Lee (2008) note how Web 2.0 has facilitated a culture of participation in which "the line separating consumers and producers of content is becoming blurred" (p. 10). By adopting a learning paradigm they call Pedagogy 2.0, they bring to the fore strategies which focus on participation, personal voice and co-production. They argue for this emphasis on sociability because of the "increasing gap between the formalized interactions that occur in educational establishments and the modes of learning, socialization, and communication taking place in the everyday world" (p. 11).

Our ways of conducting research therefore need to change if we are to work effectively with practitioners to help them function in the complex world that is unfolding before them and us. It is also important for the wider sustainability of the higher education sector. Greater attention needs to be given to socially engaged research since much of the value that academics will add in the future will be around different forms of facilitated dialogue. In *An Avalanche is Coming*, Barber, Donnelly and Rizvi (2013) highlight why this orientation is imperative in a context where academic content becomes ubiquitous. They illustrate this point by noting the accelerating trend in which the latest scholarly knowledge can be downloaded for free from prestigious universities across the globe.

The need for new participatory approaches in research is also supported by the idea that academic fields are complex adaptive systems that require engagement, adaptation and diversity to survive. Zahra and Newey (2009) work with this thinking to situate academic entrepreneurship at the intersection of fields. In addition, Page (2011) notes that many contemporary challenges – from global economic inequalities to climate change – involve complex systems where "every challenge involves anticipating and harnessing diverse, adaptive entities, with interdependent actions" (p. 10). At the heart of such complexity-inspired perspectives is the premise that to confront these contexts – whether associated with the particular character of academic fields or the nature of the issues they face – requires the identification of trigger points or levers that can result in significant effects. With this last point in mind, the chapter now shifts from the case for change to the foundation for the *critical commons*.

Knowledge as a commons

The first insight underpinning the notion of a *critical commons* springs from an emerging area of scholarship associated not just with developing new ways of thinking about knowledge, but also action. Indeed, it has already resulted in a progressive global movement arising with "striking suddenness" driven by "a spontaneous explosion of 'ah ha' moments" amongst researchers, artists, activists and other citizens (Hess & Ostrom, 2011, p. 4). The movement argues that knowledge is best viewed as a resource shared by a group of people and as a complex ecosystem that can be characterised as a commons (Hess & Ostrom, 2011). It frames knowledge as being held in common ownership and as a community asset that is inclusive rather than exclusive. Nevertheless, thinking of knowledge in this way is different from natural resource commons such as water, fisheries and forests in one important aspect. The latter are subtractive resources in which one person's use "reduces the benefits available to another" while for the former (knowledge), the more people who share it "the greater the common good" (Hess & Ostrom, 2011, p. 5). Rather than being rivals for scarce resources, those involved in an information commons create greater value as more people use the resource and join the social community.

In a knowledge context, Bollier (2011) refers to this as "the cornucopia of the commons" (p. 34). This chapter agrees that combining insights from others and pooling knowledge is the most effective way to arrive at a deeper understanding of the sort of complex social phenomena that drive critical inquiry. It suggests that such issues cannot be tackled in isolation, but require collaboration; and the better the cross-fertilisation of ideas from different disciplines and higher levels of engagement between academia and a range of different stakeholders, the better the outcomes. This not only supports a democratic society and social wealth (Bollier, 2011) but also leads to better research outcomes through peer production and peer-to-peer knowledge-sharing.

Despite being based on a nascent area of research, an information commons movement has quickly developed and gained traction across both geographical and disciplinary boundaries. The Internet since the mid-1990s has been pivotal to this shift in thinking, particularly the development of what have been called global commons projects associated with the provision of free software, as well as the expansion of open source information resources such as Wikipedia. As this new virtual public sphere has developed, different ways of organising, communicating and creating knowledge have emerged. These set out to embody an open and democratic ethos (Willis, 2012).

In addition to suggesting progressive ways forward, the chapter argues that thinking of knowledge as commons also serves as an antidote to a regressive tendency that can blight academic fields. In this case, it is the potential for CPR to evolve into a form of anti-commons. First applied by Heller (1998) in relation to the knowledge sphere, the concept of the anti-commons in this context refers to the potential underuse of knowledge through practices such as intellectual property rights and patenting. This chapter suggests that CPR's potential to become an anti-commons is driven not by excessive regulation but by a lack of participation in, and engagement with, research by stakeholders such as PR practitioners. Indeed, Egan (2014) highlights how the notions of use and engagement are crucial to the commons concept. Drawing on another of the distinct intellectual traditions underpinning the commons movement, CPR needs to guard against creating a virtual form of enclosure. That is, a scholarly community characterised by separation rather than shared spaces, open social science and collective knowledge. In his historical overview of the movement, Wall (2014) concludes that such enclosure represents the true tragedy of the commons.

Exploring the ethically practical

A particular research orientation that can guard against the development of an anti-commons in CPR (and which also contains wider insights for the *critical commons*) is highlighted in contemporary debates about the future of social scientific inquiry in general. Flyvbjerg's (2001) influential polemic on the nature of social research draws on Nietzsche, Foucault and Bourdieu to develop a contemporary conceptualisation of social science based upon an interpretation of Aristotle's idea of phronesis. Flyvbjerg (2001) translates this as "prudence" or "practical common sense" (p. 56). Rather than being value-neutral, he positions the person who possesses phronesis as having knowledge on how to behave in particular circumstances "that can never be equated with or reduced to knowledge or general truths" (p. 57). For Flyvbjerg, phronesis is therefore about having a sense of the ethically practical. It focuses on the judgements people make in social contexts, and analyses the role of values and power.

Flyvbjerg's (2001) perspective suggests that one future for CPR lies in a focus on the fine grain of PR practice and the nature of the decisions people make in different circumstances. His focus on phronesis also recognises the inseparability of theory and practice. For Antonacopoulou (2010) it refers essentially to the knowledge that defines the way practitioners work through what they need to do and the course (or courses) of action they need to take to achieve their intentions. Understanding practice is therefore central to phronesis as part of an ongoing quest to exercise judgement "while being purposeful in defining and pursuing particular objectives" (p. S7). Antonacopoulou also notes that an integral aspect of phronetic knowledge is being critical.

Understanding what it is to be critical as part of a phronetic mode of knowing opens up two avenues. First, it helps practitioners to think more reflexively. This is important as an unquestioning tendency to adopt "best practice" is an enduring problem for the PR field. It is also a trait in the profession that is likely to intensify. The complex technical and strategic challenges of modern PR practice can encourage a form of xenomania in which new approaches and "solutions" are applied enthusiastically without consideration for their wider social implications. Second, a phronetic focus helps to bridge an artificial divide between practice and critical scholarship. Rather than portraying the preoccupations of these two communities as in opposition, the objective is to "understand the tensions as a useful foundation for broadening knowledge and action" (Antonacopoulou, 2010, p. S7). The final emphasis on "action" also moves our discussion from a consideration of the key area of inquiry in a *critical commons* to a wider exploration of the character of its research.

Shifting from critique to action: learning from the action modalities (1)

The next area we turn to for insight is what Raelin (2012) frames as the action modalities. This group of approaches, which includes action learning and action research, shares complementary epistemological assumptions concerned with expanding knowledge while simultaneously trying to improve practice. From this perspective knowledge arises not from the transfer from one mind to another "but as a contested inquiry among learners as they contribute to their own interpretations" and additionally provides tangible suggestions "for addressing the problem in hand" (Raelin, 2012, p. 369).

The action modalities' orientation serves as a counterweight to the development of more speculative knowledge. For example, Pedler (2005) suggests that "the critical view is at its best pointing out what is wrong, and less strong on the urgent concern with how best to go on" (p. 5). This leads him to conclude "what right do we have to criticise without the honest intention and heartfelt commitment to join in to make things better?" (p. 5). Pedler (2005) moves critical theory beyond a simple questioning of the system to a consideration of the specific steps required to actually improve it. The move concurs with the *critical commons* but with the caveat that delivering on such a promise is problematic. Action learning similarly aims explicitly to "do" better things in the world and is often similarly expected to focus on wicked social problems. Despite this intention action learning has always grappled against charges of managerialism and the accusation that much of its energy has moved from considering intractable problems towards "own job" issues (Pedler, 2005).

Another response to the accusation of a diminishing social impact has also emerged from within the action learning tradition itself. The aspiration for doing better things in the world has prompted Willmott (1997) to propose a form of "critical action learning" (CAL) to serve as an alternative to established practice in the field, as well as standing against what he regards as a positivist, compliant mainstream in management education. CAL itself remains on the margins of the action learning movement but the experiences of its advocates contain useful lessons for those in the PR field seeking to shift the emphasis of CPR discourse from critique to practical action. Reflecting on the emergence of critical action learning, Trehan and Pedler (2009) identify a key contribution in its promotion of a deepening of critical thinking on the daily realities of organisational life by emphasising the value of collective as well as individual reflection. Such a perspective reaffirms action learning's foundational trust in the wisdom of peers. In his earlier reflection on the implications of CAL, Pedler (2005) does note, however, that given the members of the average action learning set are likely to lack the ability to critique the organisational and social world from an independent standpoint, such a process requires knowledge and input from the "outside".

The need for outside intervention points to an active role for CPR scholars in a *critical commons*. Action learning does, though, have an ambivalent attitude towards the role of facilitators and Reg Revans, the discipline's founding father, preferred to avoid them (Dick, 1997). This scepticism draws us to another of the action modalities that is more comfortable with facilitation, and better demonstrates how this type of inquiry can be systematised in a research context.

Systematising participation for research: learning from the action modalities (2)

Action research shares action learning's focus on dialectic as opposed to didactic knowledge, as well as a preference for reflection-in-action rather than reflection-on-action (Raelin, 2012). As with action learning it also has an affinity with complex organisational contexts as "emphasis is placed on staying with the actual experience of what is, in focusing on the particularity of an actual, living situation and working with all the variation and all the uncertainty that is present" (Allen & Boulton, 2011, p. 169). As a living, emergent process, action research is therefore well suited to an investigation of issues around power, ethics and the conflicting "priorities" faced by PR professionals. The action research process is able to change and develop as participants deepen their understanding of the issues that need to be addressed, at the same time as developing their capacity as co-inquirers both individually and collectively. The ways that action research differs from action learning are important to the *critical commons* envisaged for public relations.

Zuber-Skerritt (2001) characterises the main difference between the two approaches as being the same as that between learning and research generally. That is, while each involves searching, learning, systematic inquiry and problem-solving, "action research is more systematic, rigorous, scrutinisable, verifiable and always made public (in publications, oral or written reports)" (p. 2). The veracity of such a process is important for the credibility of research outcomes and the quality of discourse in the *critical commons*, while the open character of action research fits more comfortably with the social spirit of a knowledge commons. In support of this last point, Dick (1997) highlights that while in action learning each participant draws different learning from different experience, in action research a team of people draw collective learning from a collective experience.

Action research essentially involves a series of cycles. Each cycle incorporates the diagnosis of a situation or problem, the development of a plan, data gathering, taking action, and then fact-finding about the results of what was done in order to plan again and take further action (Raelin, 2012). This chapter suggests that it provides a way forward for PR scholars and professionals looking to work together. Not only does it entail a certain degree of reflection, it augments this with the systematic and rigorous collection of data that a practitioner can call upon when seeking to address and resolve challenges. It is also common for scholars to act as facilitators in this process.

As with other key perspectives and influences discussed in this chapter, Reason and Bradbury (2008) position the origins of action research outside mainstream scholarly research. This family of practices continues to inhabit the margins of academia. Indeed, MacLean and MacIntosh (2011) note that, although action research has a long tradition in the social sciences, it does not feature regularly in most major international journals. This is because it comes from a different paradigm to conventional academic research, has different purposes, is based in different relationships, professes different ways of conceiving knowledge, and relates to practice differently (Reason & Bradbury, 2008).

From detachment to co-creation: learning from the action modalities (3)

The nature of action research changes the researcher from being a detached, unobtrusive observer into a role as a creative participant in an unfolding and essentially unpredictable dynamic. This movement aligns with the idea of research as an emergent, social process that requires ongoing reflection and action on the part of both academics and practitioners. Collaborative orientation is important because it rejects the positioning of one party "as the producer and the other as the consumer of knowledge" and prefers a form of co-creation that can lead to a situation where both sides can learn from the other and mutually "transform their practices" (Antonacopoulou, 2010, p. S22).

Co-creation is essential to the *critical commons* as it systematically assimilates the knowledge that practitioners (and others) can bring to CPR scholarship – not as the subjects of research but as co-researchers. This expands and enhances the pool of knowledge held traditionally by universities by transforming the research experience into something of extended value, impossible to replicate through more traditional modes of research (Reason & Bradbury, 2008). Co-creation also helps public relations scholars align their practice as academics with the principles they teach. Because it has dialogue at its core, co-creation generates the multiple perspectives that academics promote as part of the pedagogic discourse around stakeholder engagement. Co-creation thus generates different perspectives and ways of understanding, as well as iterative cycles of reflection and action that can involve practitioners and academics in a continuous process of collective sense-making and knowledge creation. Co-creation also helps to generate social capital and trust. This is important both for the quality of the research outcomes and the process of building (and maintaining) bridges between PR practice and the academic community.

These last two points are reinforced by my own experiences of co-creation "in the field" with my former colleague Anne Gregory. One case concerns the development of a co-created Masters programme in which the professionals who were enrolled as students shaped the curriculum, its core content, as well as taking responsibility for researching and teaching key aspects of the programme throughout its duration (see Willis & McKie, 2011). Asked to reflect on their experiences of co-creation the practitioners spoke of how the process created a strong sense of community which went beyond other programmes they had participated in. This was especially important for the learning, particularly in the context of critical reflections on their own practice. Students remarked how the trust built up within the group allowed them to talk about their own experiences of practice in an open manner. As one put it, "we could cut out the spin", allowing them to move beyond sanitised accounts of their practice and explore different contexts through a critical lens. The outcome was a willingness to share and learn from their experiences whether good, bad or indifferent.

In this context they also welcomed our role as academics in bringing a broader critical perspective to bear on the learning. We discussed critical thinking from the field and contextualised it around issues such as organisational power, values and ethics. The reflections from the students also added considerable value to our own thinking and research. Indeed, one of the benefits of co-creation is its blurring of the lines between tutor and student; academic and practitioner; researcher and subject. In such a context the question of who is teaching who becomes superfluous.

Synthesising perspectives: the key characteristics of a critical commons

The theme of communication being integral to, and constitutive of, knowledge is central to the action modalities. It also informs Jones and McKie's (2009) concept of "intelligent participation" (p. 181) that is based on the idea that "rather than simply being transmitted, project team knowledge is actually co-constructed and shared" (p. 181). By distilling the essence of the lessons drawn here from the action modalities, *intelligent participation* helps to capture the character and spirit of the research proposed for the *critical commons*. To reflect the need for investigations, which focus on power, values and ethics, this chapter expands Jones and McKie's concept to *critically intelligent participation*: a form of critical inquiry that seeks to integrate research and action within a systematic, cyclical and participatory process designed by co-creation to promote co-creation.

This is not to abandon structure. Bollier (2011) notes that what makes the idea of a commons so useful is its focus on social norms and rules. He also highlights how the expressive discourse of the commons is a way of establishing connections and building a sense of solidarity among people concerned with the sustainability of a particular resource – in our case knowledge. Discourse around a commons enables people to "develop more culturally satisfying mental maps for our time" (Bollier, 2011, p. 29). In keeping with this spirit five preliminary characteristics for a *critical commons* in public relations are presented to fill out our own "mental map":

1. It is underpinned by the idea that knowledge is a shared resource and a complex ecosystem best regarded as a commons: in this context collaboration drives social wealth.
2. Greater value is created as more people engage in a critical commons and join the research community: the more people that participate the greater the common good.
3. The focus of research is on the ethically practical: those involved in the critical commons explore issues such as how PR practitioners engage with tensions associated with power and values.
4. To enrich the process PR practitioners become active partners in the research process with academics: knowledge is co-created through *critically intelligent participation* which unfolds in cycles of dialogue and reflection.

5. The purpose of research is to generate strategies for action: those participating in the critical commons move beyond reflection to become catalysts for change.

Conclusion

Even when compared to other social sciences the study of public relations is still in its infancy as an academic discipline. This chapter contends that our journey to maturity as a field will depend on the further flowering of the critical community that has already added spice and richness to the field. It further contends that to keep moving progressively, CPR will need to engage in conversations and reflection about how it should develop. It suggests a key issue for CPR's future forward motion and sustainability is its relationship with the public relations profession and the improvement of practice. It introduces the idea of a *critical commons* to contribute to a wider debate about how CPR might become more open, inclusive and action-orientated in these interactions.

That said, the chapter acknowledges that the nature of CPR's relationship with practice is essentially contested territory and the practical fulfilment of more participatory research strategies is fraught with difficulty. Frisby, Reid, Millar and Hoebar (2005) note that although there has been a rise in calls for more participatory forms of research, there is little literature that addresses the specific challenges associated with bringing people together in such environments. So, in conclusion, the chapter calls for creativity, experimentation and small-scale pilot studies to help forge new approaches. It claims that such innovations will generate an opportunity for public relations not only to improve the health of its own field but also to take a lead on issues that cut across the social sciences.

References

Allen, P., & Boulton, J. (2011). Complexity and limits to knowledge: The importance of uncertainty. In P. Allen, S. Maguire, & B. McKelvey (Eds), *The SAGE handbook of complexity and management*, pp. 164–81. London, UK: Sage.

Antonacopoulou, E. P. (2010). Making the business school more "critical": Reflexive critique based on phronesis as a foundation for impact. *British Journal of Management*, 21, pp. S6–S25.

Barber, M., Donnelly, K., & Rizvi, S. (2013). *An avalanche is coming: Higher education and the revolution ahead*. London, UK: Institute for Public Policy Research.

Bollier, D. (2011). The growth of the commons paradigm. In C. Hess, & E. Ostrom (Eds), *Understanding knowledge as a commons*, pp. 27–40. Cambridge, MA: MIT Press.

Dick, B. (1997). *Action learning and action research*. Retrieved on 23 April 2015 from http://www.uq.net.au/action_research/arp/actlearn.html

Egan, M. (2014). Foreword. In D. Wall, *The Commons in history: Culture, conflict and ecology*, pp. xi–xv. Cambridge, MA: MIT Press.

Flyvbjerg, B. (2001). *Making social science matter: Why social inquiry fails and how it can succeed again*. Cambridge, UK: Cambridge University Press.

Frisby, W., Reid, C., Millar, S., & Hoebar, L. (2005). Putting "participatory" into participatory forms of action research. *Journal of Sport Management*, 19(4), pp. 367–86.

Heath, R. L. (2006). Onward into more fog: Thoughts on public relations' research directions. *Journal of Public Relations Research*, 18(2), pp. 93–114.

Heller, M. A. (1998). The tragedy of the anticommons: Property in the transition from Marx to markets. *Harvard Law Review*, 111(3), pp. 622–88.

Hess, C., & Ostrom, E. (2011). Introduction: An overview of the knowledge commons. In C. Hess, & E. Ostrom (Eds), *Understanding knowledge as a commons*, pp. 3–26. Cambridge, MA: MIT Press.

Jones, R., & McKie, D. (2009). Intelligent participation: Communicating knowledge in cross functional project teams. *International Journal of Knowledge Management Studies*, 3, pp. 180–94.

L'Etang, J. (2005). Critical public relations: Some reflections. *Public Relations Review*, 31(4), pp. 521–6.

MacLean, D., & MacIntosh, R. (2011). Organizing at the edge of chaos: Insights from action research. In P. Allen, S. Maguire & B. McKelvey (Eds), *The SAGE handbook of complexity and management*, pp. 235–53. London, UK: Sage.

McLoughlin, C., & Lee, M. J. W. (2008). The three P's of pedagogy for the networked society: Personalization, participation and productivity. *International Journal of Teaching and Learning in Higher Education*, 20(1), pp. 10–27.

Meyerson, D. (2003). *Tempered radicals: How everyday leaders inspire change at work*. Boston, MA: Harvard Business School Press.

Moncur, C. (2006). Embracing PR theory: An opportunity for practitioners. *Journal of Communication Management*, 10(1), pp. 95–9.

Page, S. E. (2011). *Diversity and complexity*. Princeton, NJ: Princeton University Press.

Pedler, M. (2005). Critical action learning. *Action Learning: Research and Practice*, 2(1), pp. 1–6.

Pedler, M., & Burgoyne, J. G. (2008). Action learning. In P. Reason, & H. Bradbury (Eds), *Handbook of action research: Participatory inquiry and practice*, pp. 319–32. London, UK: Sage.

Raelin, J. A. (2012). Action learning's good company: The action modalities. In M. Pedler (Ed.), *Action learning in practice*, pp. 369–80. Aldershot, UK: Gower Publishing.

Reason, P., & Bradbury, H. (2008). Introduction. In P. Reason, & H. Bradbury (Eds), *Handbook of action research: Participatory inquiry and practice*, pp. 1–10. London, UK: Sage.

Trehan, K., & Pedler, M. (2009). Critical action learning. In J. Gold, R. Thorpe, & R. Mumford (Eds), *Gower handbook of leadership and management development*, pp. 405–22. Aldershot, UK: Gower Publishing.

van Ruler, B. (2005). Commentary: Professionals are from Venus, scholars are from Mars. *Public Relations Review*, 31, pp. 159–73.

Wall, D. (2014). *The commons in history: Culture, conflict and ecology*. Cambridge, MA: MIT Press.

Whetton, D. A., Felin, T., & King, B. G. (2009). The practice of theory borrowing in organizational studies: Current issues and future directions. *Journal of Management*, 35, pp. 537–63.

Willis, P. (2012). Engaging communities: Ostrom's economic commons, social capital and public relations. *Public Relations Review*, 38(1), pp. 116–22.

Willis, P., & McKie, D. (2011). Outsourcing public relations pedagogy: Lessons from innovation, management futures and stakeholder participation. *Public Relations Review*, 37(5), pp. 466–9.

Willmott, H. (1997). Critical management learning. In J. Burgoyne, & M. Reynolds (Eds), *Management learning: Integrating perspectives in theory and practice*, pp. 161–76. London, UK: Sage.

Zahra, S. A., & Newey, L. R. (2009). Maximising the impact of organisational science: Theory-building at the intersection of disciplines and/or fields. *Journal of Management Studies*, 46(6), pp. 1059–75.

Zuber-Skerritt, O. (2001). Action learning and action research: Paradigm, praxis and programs. In S. Sankara, B. Dick, & R. Passfield (Eds), *Effective change management through action research and action learning: Concepts, perspectives, processes and applications*, pp. 1–20. Lismore, Australia: Southern Cross University Press.

31

Pushing boundaries

A critical cosmopolitan orientation to public relations

Anne Surma

I begin this chapter by briefly sketching two scenarios in the globalised environment of 2014:

> The world's largest global integrated security company, with a head office in Sussex, England, and offices in many locations around the world, employing over 600,000 staff, in Europe, North America, Africa and the Asia Pacific region. Global communications, including intranet and a range of social media platforms, are enabled by teams, located in various offices at home and in host countries and regions, dedicated to internal and external communications with specific stakeholder groups – employees, government and non-government clients, the community.
>
> A large body of stateless individuals, men and boys, accommodated in a makeshift detention facility in Manus Island, Papua New Guinea. They are living in limbo – literally, since there are no clocks on the wall. They lack the opportunity to make any coherent or long-term plans for their future lives, without ready or ongoing access to reliable communication media, or to exchanges with family and friends overseas, international non-government organisations, national governments or other agencies that might, in turn, recognise them, engage with them, and respond meaningfully to their plight.

Two different scenarios and two different worlds. And yet these worlds are also intimately interdependent. That is perhaps one of the key features of globalisation: that, because or in spite of the world's interconnectedness, the disjunction between wildly disparate experiences, between individual and group differences in status, relative power, voice and visibility is thrown into crude relief. I will return to comment on the ways in which these two scenarios – their cultural positioning, the situated relationships of those who inhabit them, and the language through which the experiences of those involved are mediated – intersect or collide in the world.

The chapter argues that a critically grounded version of cosmopolitanism provides a robust framework for reflecting on and responding to public relations practices in a context of globalisation. Predicated on ethical practices of care, embodied subjects' imaginative engagement with the other, and discursive and rhetorical sensitivity to worldviews and others' positions and perspectives, critical cosmopolitanism is presented as a radically disruptive and potentially transformative approach to (appraising practices of) communicating with and relating to others in the global public realm. Motivated by an understanding of both communication and critique as forms of social practice, the chapter also examines, through a critical cosmopolitan lens, some key features of recent government public relations communication relating to asylum seekers in Australia. An insistent refusal to respond to the asylum seeker as a feeling, thinking, situated subject to whom the powerful and relatively privileged are responsible, has urgent ethical and political implications, and serves to expose the pervasively dehumanising aspects of globalisation. Thus, more broadly, the chapter also aims to show how a critical cosmopolitan approach propels us to self-reflexivity: to interrogate and re-imagine the ways in which language in general and public communication in particular position us to view, understand, feel about and respond to marginalised, distant or unknown others.

Globalisation and cosmopolitanism[1]

The phenomenon of globalisation might be summarised as the accelerated movements and flows of people, finance, trade and services, and ideas and communications between and across state and continental boundaries. Globalisation is experienced and responded to differently by each of us, depending on our material situations, on the relationships which support and structure our lives and work, and on our relative capacity to exercise our agency and choices in terms of those movements and flows. In this sense, the boundaries transforming our lives are not only geographical, but also political, social and gendered, since patterns of human relationships in the family, at work, and in local, state and global communities affect and are affected by globalising forces. Thus, for privileged individuals and communities, borders and boundaries may be opening up in exciting and perhaps also confronting and challenging ways. Conversely, for people who are disadvantaged or marginalised, those borders and boundaries (both their existence and possible transgression) may be experienced by turns as either restrictive, protective or exclusionary.

The last few decades have seen a revival in popular, intellectual and practical interest in cosmopolitanism – in its many, and sometimes contradictory, variants. The term cosmopolitan derives from the Greek *kosmopolitês*, meaning "citizen of the world", and all cosmopolitan perspectives admit some sense of the people around the globe inhabiting a form of shared community, whether that is one understood from ethical, political, legal, social or cultural standpoints, or a combination of those. The cosmopolitan thinking and philosophical and religious leanings of ancient civilisations – Greek, Roman, Chinese and then Islamic and Christian – all motivated approaches that cultivated "an inclusive vision of human community" (Delanty, 2009, p. 20), and an awareness of – and sense of obligation to – those who live beyond one's own (familial, cultural. national) groupings. Later, the revitalisation of cosmopolitan thought emerged during the Enlightenment, with Immanuel Kant its best-known exponent, and evidenced in his work *Perpetual Peace* (1795). Here Kant argues that all rational beings are members of a single moral community, or "citizen[s] of a supersensible [moral] world" (Kant, cited in Kleingeld, 2003, p. 301).

In the nineteenth century, cosmopolitanism was derided by Marx and Engels as an "ideological reflection of capitalism", emanating from the influence of capitalist globalisation and achieved on the back of working classes across the world. However, in this sense, and inversely, Marx and Engels implied that the proletariat was the means of achieving the ideal cosmopolitan society beyond the state (Kleingeld & Brown, 2011). In the later twentieth and early twenty-first centuries, there has been an exponential resurgence of attention to cosmopolitanism, and we have witnessed the development of that interest through various disciplinary, ideological and philosophical dispositions and domains. The spectrum is indeed broad: from cosmopolitan political theorists who are interested in the development of global democracy (e.g., Held, 2002), to those who deliberate over ideas relating to universal norms of justice and/or the establishment of cosmopolitan legal institutions, regulatory frameworks and models of citizenship (e.g., Benhabib, 2006), to those who commend us to a universal moral vision (e.g., Nussbaum, 1994), to more local or situated ethical understandings (e.g., Appiah, 2006), to those who explore the social and cultural (e.g., Beck, 2006), communicative (e.g., Norris & Inglehart, 2009), and vernacular and visceral turns (e.g., Nava, 2007), to those who identify the cosmopolitan in literary (e.g., Walkowitz, 2006), visual (e.g., Szerszynski & Urry, 2006) and media (e.g., Silverstone, 2007) texts and practices.

Critical cosmopolitanism and caring in public relations

My interest in this chapter is in the specifically ethical and critical turn of cosmopolitanism, particularly in the way it can be mobilised to disrupt taken-for-granted ways of perceiving and interpreting our (communicative) relations with, obligations to, and responsibilities for others both within and beyond the borders of family, community and nation. Political sociologist Gerard Delanty uses the term critical cosmopolitanism to conceptualise the social world "as an open horizon in which new cultural models take shape" (2006, p. 27). He defines it specifically as a form of resistance to, or a "normative critique" of, the destructive aspects of globalisation; it constitutes a communicative, dialectical response to those aspects, as "embedded…in current societal developments" (Delanty, 2009, p. 250). It involves individuals, groups and communities interacting with each other within and across borders, territories, networks and temporalities and, in the process of doing so, undergoing "transformation in light of the encounter with the Other" (Delanty, 2009, p. 252).

In terms of public relations, such encounters may, at first glance, resonate with definitions of the practice that describe its *raison d'être*, particularly in liberal democracies, as having the potential for transformation – since the industry is purportedly committed to developing (some version of) "mutually beneficial relationships".[2] However, a closer look at most mainstream practice in the field reveals that the potential of a mutual or reciprocal relationship between an organisation and its public(s) cannot be assumed, and is often simply not possible, particularly as the avowed commitment to reciprocal response typically requires that both parties have a comparable capacity to engage and respond. Moreover, the mutuality referred to in the above definitions generally stops at a point determined by, and suited to, the interests of the more powerful player.[3]

A critical cosmopolitan perspective on public relations thus enables us to interrogate who falls inside and outside of the boundaries delimiting conventionally sanctioned relationships comprising mainstream public relations; and to interrogate why and how they do so. Other scholars have commented on public relations' often hand-in-glove relationship with capitalism (Holtzhausen, 2000; Miller & Dinan, 2003; Weaver, 2011) and, by extension, the neoliberal impetus of globalising forces (Dutta, Ban & Pal, 2012), and critical studies of global public relations provide significant insights into the unequal relations of power that obtain in such situations. Thus, at the risk of sounding glib, public relations might in many instances of its activity be regarded as *private relations*, and not only in terms of its explicitly commercial manifestations.[4] Neoliberalism has done its work so effectively that, as Bauman (2001, p. 107) observes, "it is the private that colonizes the public space, squeezing out and chasing away everything which cannot be fully, without residue, translated into the vocabulary of private interests and pursuits". A by-product of such colonisation is the tendency to reduce everything, including human lives and experiences, to rationalist accounting practices, thus risking their abstraction from the realm of responsible or caring relations.

In a capitalist environment, public relations initiatives are generally required to measure communicative success in empirical – and thus largely positivist, numerical, and amoral – terms.

Moreover, and in a bid to protect private interests and pursuits, the neoliberal and arguably anti-democratic thrust of a market-driven globalisation (see McKie & Munshi, 2007) might also be seen to translate matters of public (social) relations into those of security relations (see Robinson, 2011a, pp. 41–62).[5] As a result, according to Ulrich Beck (2006, p. 332), "the irony of the promise of security made by scientists, companies and governments…in wondrous fashion contributes to an increase in risks". If, as Beck also claims, "powerful actors…maximize risks for 'others' and minimize risks for 'themselves'" (p. 333), this will obviously influence the ways in which engaging with others through public relations is approached, practised and, ultimately, evaluated.

To counter such impulses, critical cosmopolitanism, as I develop it by combining threads from the work of scholars in a range of disciplines, has a specific focus on the ethical, relational, subjective and emotional dimensions of human experience and communicative practice in a context of globalisation – from material and situated perspectives. While the global inflection of recent work in public relations theory (e.g., Bardhan & Weaver, 2011; Curtin & Gaither, 2007; Sriramesh & Verčič, 2009) already treads comparable ground, the critical cosmopolitan approach I posit has a specifically ethical and critical insistence on exploring the complex social and political webs that connect us to one another, whether directly or indirectly, and, in particular, as I outline below, the ties of care – of interdependence and responsibility – embedded in those connections.

Feminist theorists have, for several decades, been reflecting in different ways on the ethics of care, founded on the understanding that people are always and everywhere "relational and…interdependent" (Held, 2006, p. 156), and that human subjectivity itself is constituted "through relations" (Robinson, 2011a, p. 54). Virginia Held, for example, argues that an ethics of care helps underscore connections between people as emotionally rich and mutually sustaining relations of interdependence, rather than exclusively rationally based or as centred on the needs and interests of the discrete individual. It is the emotions, Held claims (2006, p. 157), such as empathy, sensitivity and responsiveness, that are better guides to what we should or shouldn't do, in moral terms. In her study of care in a context of politics and international relations, Fiona Robinson (2009) argues that even in this domain, human beings are not "autonomous subjects, but…embedded in networks and relationships of care". Similarly, Held's (2006, p. 156) discussion of ethics of care in a global context argues that some of our responsibilities to care are not chosen but are nonetheless real and emerge from our social positioning and historical embeddedness. This means that caring relations

> are not limited to the personal contexts of family and friends. They can extend to fellow members of groups of various kinds, to fellow citizens, and beyond. We can, for instance, develop caring relations for persons who are suffering deprivation in distant parts of the globe.
>
> *(Held, 2006, p. 157)*

Here we see that relationality and the responsibility to care resonate with a critical cosmopolitan responsiveness to the ties of obligation that bind us, whether directly or indirectly, to unknown or distant others. In addition, they serve as a direct challenge to the idea of the "proper" province or limits of human responsibility and to the neoliberal promotion of individualism and self-sufficiency. They also push against the conventional meaning of "relations" found in mainstream public relations, unsettling its typically depersonalised, euphemistic currency as forging links with others in order to promote self-interested objectives. By contrast, from a critical cosmopolitan perspective in which notions of care are embedded, no subject is central: we are each, in a sense, off-centre, because we are always already in relation (to others).

The ethically driven critical cosmopolitan orientation and practice I outline above necessarily draws on the imagination *in order to* alert us to the complex relations of interdependence that obtain within and across local and global boundaries.[6] Communicating responsibly in public relations demands the use of imagination: the ethical capacity to think, feel and respond virtually, beyond our own time, situation and personal, professional and social networks, and into those of others. However, we may instead refuse our capacity for that expansive orientation to imagining, which in Delanty's terms entails "a view of society as an ongoing process of self-constitution through the continuous opening up of new perspectives in light of the encounter with the Other" (2009, p. 13). Like Delanty, who uses the term "translation" as a metaphor for describing the changes that might be effected through forging imaginative connections with others (p. 13), Appiah (2006, p. 85) uses the term "conversation", both literally as "talk" and metaphorically, "for engagement with the experience and the ideas of others". He refers to the role of imagination in the process of conversation and, although he does not elaborate, we can infer that he suggests the need for us to go beyond ourselves, beyond the conventional bounds of our social and temporal positions to be responsive to the other. In accounts such as these, the significance of the communicative dimension is clear and highlights the ways in which imagining and communicating may be combined to enrich (or indeed impoverish) our understandings of, and responsibility for, others. However, in communicating in the public domain our imaginative orientation – conceived as an emotional, empathetic and evaluative envisioning – will be situated by, and often find itself in tension with, instrumentally driven economic and political demands. Given the bias of the neoliberal impulse dominating globalisation processes, care is urgently required to redress the balance and to ensure that the human, the social and the relational are not displaced in our communicative interactions.

In other words, the ideological impetus of specific discourses (whether commercially, strategically, or risk-oriented, for example) mobilised in public relations activities can be interrogated, as we pay attention to the ways in which they make salient certain ways of understanding the world, rearticulate or re-present areas of social life differently, and simultaneously privilege and subordinate the different interests, values and temporalities of individuals and groups.[7] We can also explore the ways in which the alternative or competing discourses harnessed by some individuals, groups and communities will disrupt and reinterpret, complicate or differently inflect the meanings generated by those of the discourses preferred by their imagined or real interlocutors. By extension, our contextualised evaluation of rhetoric focuses attention on the constituent persuasive elements of public relations texts, and on the inscribed and interpretable impacts and effects (semiotic, practical, local and global) of those texts (constituted by discourses) produced, circulated and interpreted in specific contexts. It also involves reflecting on the ways language can variously position or modify individual, social and organisational relationships across different cultural and temporal contexts.

"Stop the boats": refusing to relate to asylum seekers

Let us now turn back to the two scenarios that opened this chapter. They motivate some specific questions about, and draw attention to, the blind spots in a particular instance of normalised and, for many, normative, public relations activity. In a globalised and interconnected world, they draw attention to the impossibility of the claim that public relations actors can speak unequivocally or with a singular voice – at least authentically – without exploiting or ignoring asymmetries and intricate networks of power, interdependent as those actors inevitably are with myriad others, close and far, to whom they are, in different ways and to different degrees, responsible.

The global organisation in the scenario opening this chapter is based on the integrated security and outsourcing company G4S, with a head office in England, which manages, on behalf of national and local governments worldwide, formerly state-run services as outsourced, privatised businesses.[8] One of this organisation's activities is the management and day-to-day running of detention centres – detaining asylum seekers and would-be refugees in various locations around the world. This is the location depicted in the second scenario, Manus Island, in northern Papua New Guinea, a detention centre commissioned and paid for by the Australian Government.[9] Until recently, local and international staff employed by G4S worked in the facility.[10] In both instances, and for reasons of "security", official G4S communication to the broader community from those responsible for managing and overseeing, or from those otherwise involved in the detention centres whether as employees or as asylum seekers, is either severely limited or, where it is available, often generic. So, for example, there is scant detail publicly available about what precisely G4S does on a day-to-day basis in managing the detention centre, how it does it, and with what impact.

Similarly, asylum seekers' opportunities to communicate with the world outside the detention centre are both very limited and heavily regulated, since their silencing is legitimised by the Australian government's construction of them as security risks – "illegals" or criminals (more of which below). Various non-government, activist organisations and media outlets, as well as the occasional whistleblower, are the alternative sources offering insight into the lived experiences and perspectives of asylum seekers in detention (Amnesty International, 2013; UNHCR, 2013; "Manus Island inquiry", 2014; "Manus Island whistleblower", 2014). In general, however, both groups involved in the scenarios above are mostly *spoken for* by the Australian government.

The government has attempted a return to a controlled-communication model of public relations, by means of a policy that severely restricts communication about asylum seeker-related activity. It has also adopted a reductively nationalist (and highly rationalist) discourse of border security. This is despite the fact that the government's responsibilities and obligations are manifestly and inextricably involved in complex international and global relations with individuals, private organisations and governments (e.g., Papua New Guinean and Indonesian) beyond Australian borders. Therefore, and as in the brief rendering through the pastiche of communicative styles in the scenarios above, it is unsurprising that the public communications from organisations such as G4S – concerning their management of detention centres and other services – is typically bland, depersonalised and abstract. For example, in relation to their provision of services to governments faced with "security challenges", the company announces the following: "G4S plays an important role in society by helping to ensure that governments are able to meet the expectations of their citizens, employees and legislative bodies – and by delivering tangible benefits within strict budgetary limits" (http://www.au.g4s.com/what-we-do/government.aspx). By contrast, the public communications from activists, such as Amnesty International, often focuses on the physical, psychological and emotionally fragile states of asylum seekers in detention (Amnesty International, 2013). In each case, versions of experience risk being essentialised – the corporate body as a dehumanised commercial system and the marginalised body as hapless victim. How did it come to this?

In what follows I offer a couple of instances of recent changes to the government's approach to the treatment of asylum seekers. In particular, I focus on the ways in which policy and legislative changes are discursively framed and rhetorically articulated in specific government public relations communications so that they actively fabricate the very contexts of (in)security and risk to which they claim to be responding. In other words, through a critical cosmopolitan lens, my aim is to highlight specific instances of government public relations communication that construct the tenor, and the untenability, of the asylum seeker "threat", and thereby limit the government's, Australians' and other people's potential for human and caring responses to these vulnerable people.

Since 2001, through successive Coalition (conservative), Labor and, once again, Coalition governments, the discursive and rhetorical practices of government public relations communications on asylum seekers arriving in Australia by boat (most often on the north-west coast) have become increasingly aggressive and militaristic (McAdam, 2013a; Refugee Council of Australia, 2014). With the number of people arriving by boat increasing significantly between 2011 and 2013, Labor and Coalition governments have run a series of public information campaigns whose running theme is self-evident – "No to people smuggling", "No advantage", "No way"– to apprehend people smugglers, "smash [their] business model" (Gillard in Jones, 2011), stop and (most recently) turn back the boats (usually to Indonesia). In each of these campaigns, the responsibility to care is deflected by transposing the culpability for the asylum seeker's plight onto the people smuggler (see Surma, 2013b).

Over the course of 2013, from Labor's implementation of the policy of offshore processing and resettlement of asylum seekers in Papua New Guinea and Nauru (asylum seekers will never be allowed to settle in Australia), to the Coalition government's establishment, in September 2013, of Operation Sovereign Borders,[11] to the renaming of the Department of Immigration as the Department of Immigration and Border Protection, the punitive and militaristic approach to a perceived threat is evident. The Operations Sovereign Borders' factsheet (Australian Government, 2014a), aimed at would-be asylum seekers, reinforces this position precisely by eliding a discourse of care: it effectively excommunicates these individuals, writes them out of the humanity of a caring relationship.[12] The key section in the factsheet reads as follows:

> If you come to Australia illegally by boat, there is no way you will ever make Australia home.
>
> Anyone seeking to illegally enter Australia by boat will be intercepted and safely removed from Australian waters (including children, families or unaccompanied minors).
>
> The rules apply to everyone: families, children, unaccompanied children, educated and skilled. There are no exceptions.
>
> You will be transferred within 48 hours to an offshore processing centre in Papua New Guinea or Nauru. Your claims will be assessed by the Government of Papua New Guinea or the Government of Nauru.
>
> If you are found not to be a refugee, you will be returned to your home country or a country where you have a right of residence.
>
> Even if you are found to be a refugee, you will not be resettled in Australia.
>
> (Australian Government, 2014a)

This is an unequivocal address to would-be asylum seekers (by turns, "you", "anyone" and "everyone"), whose identity is defined emphatically by the assumed illegality of their arrival, and without any acknowledgement of their narrative background as individuals or details of their relationships as members of families and communities.[13] Asserting that the new "rules" apply to everyone, including children, exposes the government's refusal of relational responsibility for, or the need to respond to, the needs of the most vulnerable individuals. Furthermore, the use of the conditional (if …) and the declarative statements in the simple future tense do the unashamed rhetorical work of dramatising the asymmetrical relations of power between the voice of government and the asylum seeker. The reference to the role of the Nauruan and Papua New Guinean governments in processing asylum seeker claims also shows that what might conventionally be undertaken under the jurisdiction of a national government can now be undertaken (although this remains a highly contentious move)[14] as it were by proxy, via political and commercial agreements, by other governments and corporate entities. In this way the lines of responsibility, the ethical, political and practical obligations to care, are deflected or blurred.

In the government's communication, the border of the nation is not treated as a space of engagement with difference, with the human, relational other but, rather, as a monological discourse of (in)security, repudiating (non-Australian) others' appeal for protection. Reinforcing such a move in a presentation to the Lowy Institute for International Policy, Sydney, entitled "The future of border protection", immigration minister Scott Morrison offers an imaginative evocation of the nation's borders as constituting a space

> within which, as sovereign nation states, we can apply the rule of law, operate our democracy, conduct our commerce, foster free markets, establish property rights, create the space for civil society, enable the expression of culture and provide for the freedom and liberty of all of our citizens. Our border creates the space for us to be who we are and to become everything we can be as a nation.
>
> *(Morrison, 2014)*[15]

Yet the impulse and impact of this rhetoric may be interpreted as heavily circumscribed, restricted as it is to a solipsistic understanding of the transformative possibilities of the border (and of democracy), given that the encounter in that space is only with "us", with ourselves. Morrison goes on to describe protection of the borders in predictably commercial terms, as Australia's "core business"; he further declares Australia's need to be "competitive at the border". He also announces that the success of no boats reaching Australian shores between late December 2013 and June 2014 "has delivered significant dividends in both humanitarian and economic terms"; that the money saved "following the collapse in illegal boat arrivals" is estimated as $2.5 billion; and that a further six detention centres (in addition to 4 others) are earmarked for closure (Morrison, 2014). Despite the defence of Operation Sovereign Borders as having yielded a humanitarian "dividend" in terms of asylum seeking individuals deterred from making the journey to Australia by sea, the immigration minister's emphasis is on the numerical and the statistical. His discursive frame serves to elide the human costs of privileging security and (apparently) commercially competitive measures, and recalls Vivian Sobchack's dictum that human responsibility requires "narrative not numeracy for its articulation" (Sobchack, 2004, p. 180).

Finally, as I finish drafting this chapter in late June 2014, the government has introduced to the House of Representatives the Migration Amendment (Protection and Other Measures) Bill 2014. Among other changes drafted is the requirement that asylum seekers seeking protection will now have to prove that it is "'more likely than not'" or "that there would be *a greater than fifty percent* chance that a person would suffer significant harm" if removed from Australia to a receiving country (Australian Government, 2014b; italics added). Thus, the burden of proof on asylum seekers to demonstrate their need for protection is now to be evaluated in percentage terms.

From the brief examples above, it is clear that the arrival of asylum seekers in Australia has been discursively and rhetorically constructed (and popularly understood) as a crisis of national security, a threat to the resilience and integrity of its national borders, and the protection of the interests of Australians.[16] Security discourses have thus also become a specific technique of the government (see Robinson, 2011a, p. 43), as it communicates in impoverished ethical and imaginative terms its strategic commitment to protecting the safety of its citizens. In addition, the discourses of accounting and economics shape announcements of the success of the country's border protection policies to date. Thus, such discourses and practices exacerbate conditions of insecurity, particularly for this most vulnerable of groups. Paradoxically, in its efforts to reassure the nation's people that it is honouring its responsibility to them, the government *simultaneously* disavows its obligations to care for the identities or the well-being of individuals seeking asylum.

Concluding reflections

In the broader community, the public relations slogan, "stop the boats", has now become part of the Australian vernacular. Thus, repetition, reductionism and resonance represent the three Rs for the government's public relations communication on asylum seekers in the national context. The same message is insistently repeated at the prime minister and immigration minister's joint or respective press conferences, during election campaigns, on departmental websites, and on the electronic and hard copy materials produced by government: "stop the boats". This approach – of reiterating the depersonalised imperative over and over again – is also highly reductive, as it aims to sever the potential for imaginative connection between the activity (abstractly conceived) of stopping the boats and the material, psychological and emotional impact of so doing on the lives of those people who have travelled a perilous journey on those boats, on their families, and on the lives they have left behind or are returned to.

Coming from the government of a liberal democracy, such approaches to public relations communication are particularly troubling and yet not unexpected in the contemporary market-driven, globalised environment, since the human freedoms, responsibilities, choices, and capacity to engage in civic life endorsed for the citizens of a nation state are assumed to be under competitive threat when non-citizen others seek access to them too. It might be countered that Australian government policy on asylum seekers is being led by public sentiment, and this is indeed borne out by the results from representative polling samples of the Australian population (Lowy Institute, 2014).[17] However, are democratic principles inevitably to be held hostage to populist sentiment, particularly when the "popular" view is one in large part developed and framed by hegemonic discourses that work to concentrate Australians' focus on depersonalised, instrumentalist accounts of relations with vulnerable, non-national others in terms of risk, competition and opposition, and that selectively confine understandings of care and interdependence to within the boundaries of the nation state?

A key task of a critical cosmopolitan approach as a reflexive endeavour is to examine and disrupt the relationship between centre and periphery, privilege and vulnerability: to identify the relative social and temporal positions of interlocutors and those muted or silenced in the globalised context of individual, social and political interdependence.[18] By means of this encounter with and acknowledgement of the other, we can better imagine the layered texture of and proper allocation of responsibility for communicative activity in a complex world. In the field of public relations, a critical cosmopolitan intervention that folds in an ethics of care provokes significant questions, with which I conclude this chapter.

To what extent are the responsibilities for practising and enabling caring relations between subjects articulated in specific public relations communications in a given context, within and across boundaries? In what ways are the background to, and the value of, relational identities invoked or elided in the discourses that construct, and in the rhetoric that communicates specific public relations activities and processes? Finally, in what ways does the language constructing the very identity of the profession of contemporary public relations itself reduce it to a rationalist, dehumanised enterprise, and how can that situation be addressed and redressed? It would be naive to believe that public relations actors in positions of power and privilege are eager to admit the fact of our interdependence in and responsibility for vulnerable others in a global world, and to adjust communications and other practices accordingly. Therefore, a critical cosmopolitan approach has the significant task of urging a self-reflexive, imaginative orientation, pushing at the conventional boundaries that delimit communications, and interrogating the rationale for the borders that public relations may collude in both constructing and perpetuating: those that separate "us" from "them", centre from margins, here from there, care from care-lessness.

Notes

1 Material in this and the following section draws on, and is adapted from, Surma (2013a).
2 This statement comes from the Public Relations Society of America (http://www.prsa.org/AboutPRSA/PublicRelationsDefined/#.U7InOTnsdSo). Similar statements, such as "establish[ing] and maintain[ing] goodwill and mutual understanding between an organisation and its publics", and "establish[ing] and maintain[ing] mutual understanding between an organisation…and its publics" are made by the Chartered Institute of Public Relations (http://www.cipr.co.uk/content/about-us/about-pr) and the Public Relations Institute of Australia (http://www.pria.com.au/aboutus/what-is-public-relations/) respectively.
3 See Lee Edwards (2011) for a comprehensive critique of the predominantly organisation-centric focus in public relations theory and practice.
4 Even activist organisations, such as Oxfam, are tailoring their rhetorical appeals to the donating (largely Western) public in the corporatised language of neoliberalism. Thus, in the "About us" statement on its home page, we find the following: "Oxfam is a world-wide development organisation that mobilises the power of people against poverty. We provide people with the skills and resources to help them create their own solutions to poverty" (https://www.oxfam.org.au/). Here, the rhetoric constructs individuals as atomised, and poverty as an objective (and delimited) problem.
5 McKie and Munshi point to the less benign configurations of globalisation, liberal democracy and the market economy, which public relations helps to shape and by which it is in turn shaped (2007, pp. 24–6).
6 Edwards (2011) articulates the role of imagination rather differently in her theorising of power in global public relations. She reflects on Appadurai's (1996) notion of the imagination, which foregrounds agency and is involved in formulating identities in a context of globally mediated events, networks and flows. She also highlights Appadurai's mobilising of imagination as a form of resistance.
7 Juliet Roper points out that communicative struggles over what is in "the public interest" or "the public good" are typically mobilised via the hegemonic discourses deployed by powerful (government or corporate) actors, and she questions whether such practices might be deemed either democratic or ethical (2005).
8 For details of G4S see http://www.g4s.uk.com/en-GB/. Slightly different details are provided on the company's Asia-Pacific-based site (http://www.au.g4s.com/)
9 The depiction of the centre is based on details gleaned from the report on Manus Island by Amnesty International (2013).
10 G4S lost the Manus Island contract in May 2014. Transfield Services (http://www.transfieldservices.com/) has now taken over.
11 Operation Sovereign Borders is headed by Lieutenant General Angus Campbell, who leads the activities involved in turning back boats and is the authoritative military voice and face of Australian border security.
12 This idea parallels Higginbottom's concept of "unpeople" – those in the southern hemisphere as constructed by transnational corporations (cited in Weaver, 2011, p. 258).
13 The status of asylum seekers as "illegal" according the Australian government is hotly contested, and disputed by legal experts (McAdam, 2013b). The issue of their labelling as "illegal" is actually implied as misleading in a Department of Parliamentary Services background note (Parliament of Australia, 2011, p. 3.)
14 For a discussion of who has responsibility for asylum seekers on Manus Island, from human rights, legal and Australian government perspectives, see ABC News Fact Check (http://www.abc.net.au/news/2014-02-27/who-is-responsible-for-asylum-seekers-detained-on-manus/5275598).
15 Feminist philosopher and professor of political science Joan C. Tronto (2013, p. 156) argues that when democracies "set the value of economic production higher than any other value", caring approaches and practices are marginalised.
16 The conflation of the asylum seeker and the terrorist identity is not uncommon in government rhetoric. Note, for example, immigration minister Scott Morrison's remark in concluding his speech on

restricting asylum seeker boat arrivals through increased border protection: he refers to the "increasing threat posed by those who would seek to do us harm, threaten our sovereignty and undermine our way of life" (Morrison, 2014).

17 The 2014 survey in Australia (based on 1,150 telephone interviews conducted with a representative sample of the adult population) found that 71 per cent of Australians favour "turning back the boats" of asylum seekers making for Australian shores (Lowy Institute, 2014).

18 See Robinson (2011b) for a discussion of the value of an ethics of care in participating in and evaluating dialogue when asymmetries of power inevitably obtain between interlocutors.

References

Amnesty International. (2013). This is breaking people: Human rights violations at Australia's asylum seeker processing centre on Manus Island, Papua New Guinea. Retrieved on 30 April 2015 from http://www.amnesty.org.au/images/uploads/about/Amnesty_International_Manus_Island_report.pdf

Appadurai, A. (1996). *Modernity at large: Cultural dimensions of globalization*. Minneapolis, MN: University of Minnesota Press.

Appiah, K. A. (2006). *Cosmopolitanism: Ethics in a world of strangers*. London, UK: Penguin.

Australian Government. (2014a). Operation Sovereign Borders Factsheet. Retrieved on 23 April 2015 from http://www.customs.gov.au/site/Translations/documents/Fact-Sheet-English.PDF

Australian Government. (2014b). 2014 Migration Amendment (Protection and Other Measures) Bill 2014. Explanatory memorandum. Retrieved on 23 April 2015 from http://www.comlaw.gov.au/Details/C2014B00154/Explanatory%20Memorandum/Text

Bardhan, N., & Weaver, C. K. (Eds). (2011). *Public relations in global cultural contexts: Multiparadigmatic perspectives*. New York, NY: Routledge.

Bauman, Z. (2001). *The individualized society*. Cambridge and Malden, MA: Polity Press.

Beck, U. (2006). *The cosmopolitan vision*, trans. C. Cronin, Cambridge, UK: Polity Press.

Benhabib, S. (2006). *Another cosmopolitanism*. Oxford and New York: Oxford University Press.

Curtin, P. A., & Gaither, T. K. (Eds). (2007). *International public relations: Negotiating culture, identity, and power*. Thousand Oaks, CA: Sage Publications.

Delanty, G. (2006). The cosmopolitan imagination: Critical cosmopolitanism and social theory. *The British Journal of Sociology*, 57(1), pp. 25–47.

Delanty, G. (2009). *The cosmopolitan imagination: The renewal of critical social theory*. Cambridge, UK: Cambridge University Press.

Dutta, M. J., Ban, Z., & Pal, M. (2012). Engaging worldviews, cultures, and structures through dialogue: The culture-centred approach to public relations. *Prism*, 9(2). Retrieved on 23 April 2015 from http://www.prismjournal.org/homepage.html

Edwards, L. (2011). Critical perspectives in global public relations: Theorizing power. In N. Bardhan, & C. K. Weaver (Eds), *Public relations in global cultural contexts: Multi-paradigmatic perspectives*, pp. 20–49. New York, NY: Routledge.

Held, D. (2002). Globalization, corporate practice and cosmopolitan social standards. *Contemporary Political Theory*, 1, pp. 59–78.

Held, V. (2006). *The ethics of care: Personal, political and global*. Oxford and New York: Oxford University Press.

Holtzhausen, D. H. (2000). Postmodern values in public relations. *Journal of Public Relations Research*, 12(1), pp. 93–114.

Jones, T. (Presenter). (2011, 4 August). Interview with Prime Minister Julia Gillard. Aired on ABC's *Lateline* programme [Television broadcast]. Sydney, Australia. Retrieved on 23 April 2015 from http://www.abc.net.au/lateline/content/2011/s3285862.htm

Kleingeld, P. (2003). Kant's cosmopolitan patriotism. *Kant-Studien*, 94, pp. 299–316. Retrieved on 23 April 2015 from http://www.rug.nl/staff/pauline.kleingeld/kleingeld-kant-cosmopolitan-patriotism.pdf

Kleingeld, P., & Brown, E. (2011). *Cosmopolitanism*. In E.N. Zalta (Ed.), *Stanford Encyclopedia of Philosophy*. Retrieved on 23 April 2015 from http://plato.stanford.edu/archives/spr2011/entries/cosmopolitanism

Lowy Institute. (2014). *The Lowy Institute poll 2014*. Lowy Institute for International Policy, Sydney. Retrieved on 23 April 2015 from http://www.lowyinstitute.org/files/2014_lowy_institute_poll.pdf

McAdam, J. (2013a). Australia and asylum seekers. *International Journal of Refugee Law*, 25(3), pp. 435–48.

McAdam, J. (2013b, 23 October). Are they illegals? No, and Scott Morrison should know better. *Sydney Morning Herald*. Retrieved on 23 April 2015 from http://www.smh.com.au/comment/are-they-illegals-no-and-scott-morrison-should-know-better-20131022-2vz6a.html

McKie, D. & Munshi, D. (2007). *Reconfiguring public relations: Ecology, equity and enterprise*. Abingdon, UK: Routledge.

Manus Island inquiry: Students tell of working in detention centres without job interviews, training. (2014, 13 June). ABC News. Retrieved on 23 April 2015 from http://www.abc.net.au/news/2014-06-12/manus-island-reza-barati-death-inquiry-cornall-report/5518262

Manus Island whistleblower speaks exclusively to *Guardian Australia*. (2014, 28 April). *Guardian Australia*. [Video file]. Retrieved on 23 April 2015 from http://www.theguardian.com/world/video/2014/apr/28/manus-island-whistleblower-speaks-video

Miller, D., & Dinan, W. (2003). Global public relations and global capitalism. In D. Demers (Ed.), *Terrorism, globalization and mass communication*, pp. 193–214. Spokane, WA: Marquette Books.

Morrison, S. (2014, 9 May). The future of border protection. Address to the Lowy Institute for International Policy, Sydney. Retrieved on 23 April 2015 from http://www.lowyinstitute.org/news-and-media/audio/podcast-future-border-protection-scott-morrison-mp

Nava, M. (2007). *Visceral cosmopolitanism: Gender, culture and the normalisation of difference*. Oxford and New York: Berg.

Norris, P., & Inglehart, R. (2009). *Cosmopolitan communications: Cultural diversity in a globalized world*. New York, NY: Cambridge University Press.

Nussbaum, Martha C. (1994). Patriotism and cosmopolitanism, *Boston Review*, 19(5). Retrieved on 23 April 2015 from http://bostonreview.net/martha-nussbaum-patriotism-and-cosmopolitanism

Parliament of Australia. (2011). Asylum seekers and refugees: What are the facts? Department of Parliamentary Services. Canberra: Commonwealth of Australia. Retrieved on 23 April 2015 from http://www.aph.gov.au/binaries/library/pubs/bn/sp/asylumfacts.pdf

Refugee Council of Australia. (2014). Timeline of major events in the history of Australia's refugee and humanitarian program. Retrieved on 30 April 2015 from http://www.refugeecouncil.org.au/fact-sheets/australias-refugee-and-humanitarian-program/timeline/

Robinson, F. (2009). EIA interview: Fiona Robinson on the ethics of care. Carnegie Council for Ethics in International Affairs. Retrieved on 30 April 2015 from http://www.carnegiecouncil.org/studio/multimedia/20090305/index.html

Robinson, F. (2011a). *The ethics of care: A feminist approach to human security*. Philadelphia, PA: Temple University Press.

Robinson, F. (2011b). Stop talking and listen: Discourse ethics and feminist care ethics in international political theory. *Millennium – Journal of International Studies*, 39(3), pp. 845–60.

Roper, J. (2005). Symmetrical communication: Excellent public relations or a strategy for hegemony? *Journal of Public Relations Research*, 17, pp. 69–86.

Silverstone, R. (2007). *Media and morality: On the rise of the mediapolis*. Cambridge and Malden, MA: Polity Press.

Sobchack, V. (2004). *Carnal thoughts: Embodiment and moving image culture*. Berkeley, Los Angeles and London: University of California Press.

Sriramesh, K., & Verčič, D. (Eds). 2009. *The global public relations handbook: Theory research and practice*. Revised and expanded edition. Abingdon, UK: Routledge.

Surma A. (2013a). *Imagining the cosmopolitan in public and professional writing*. Basingstoke, UK: Palgrave Macmillan.

Surma, A. (2013b). Writing otherwise: A critical cosmopolitan approach to reflecting on writing and reading practices in fiction and non-fiction. *TEXT*, 17(1). Retrieved on 23 April from http://www.textjournal.com.au/april13/surma.htm

Szerszynski, B., & Urry, J. (2006). Visuality, mobility and the cosmopolitan: Inhabiting the world from afar. *The British Journal of Sociology*, 57(1), pp. 113–31.

Tronto, J. C. (2013). *Caring democracy: Markets, equality and justice*. New York, NY: New York University Press.

UNHCR. (2013). UNHCR monitoring visit to Manus Island, Papua New Guinea, 23–25 October 2013. Retrieved on 30 April 2015 from http://unhcr.org.au/unhcr/images/2013-11-26%20Report%20of%20UNHCR%20Visit%20to%20Manus%20Island%20PNG%2023–25%20October%202013.pdf

Walkowitz, R. L. (2006). *Modernism beyond the nation*. New York, NY: Columbia University Press.

Weaver, C. K. (2011). Public relations, globalization, and culture: Framing methodological debates and future directions. In N. Bardhan, & K. Weaver (Eds), *Public relations in global cultural contexts: Multi-paradigmatic perspectives*, pp. 250–74. New York: Routledge.

32

Public relations and sustainable citizenship

Towards a goal of representing the unrepresented

Debashish Munshi and Priya Kurian

Is the "public" in "public relations" really "public"? In taking a critical look at the discourses of mainstream PR, we have consistently found a hierarchy of publics ranging from dominant elite ones which are vociferously represented, to many that are not represented at all (Munshi & Kurian, 2005; 2007). If indeed, as we argue, PR does not engage with a multitude of publics, can it ever play a role in grappling with the pressing issues facing global citizenry – climate change and disparities in the sharing of planetary resources and seemingly intractable socio-political conflicts?

To truly live up to the "public" in public relations, PR needs to situate itself in the larger context of citizenship, the values and ethics that inform it, and the attitudes and behaviours that characterize it. In this essay, we look at how public relations might re-imagine itself as an instrument of not merely citizenship but of what we call "sustainable citizenship" (Kurian, Munshi & Bartlett, 2014). We first outline a framework of sustainable citizenship for public relations built on a platform of resisting dominant narratives and fostering a transnational public sphere of resistance. We then look at alternative models of representing and building relationships with marginalized publics that disrupt hegemonic discourses of public relations. We engage with post-colonial theory and subaltern historiography for theoretical sustenance and look for inspiration to activists and their acts of resistance. To illustrate our argument that the resistance of activists is not merely activism but public relations of social justice and sustainable citizenship, we focus on two specific case studies – one on the networks and alliances being built by those working to push back the ravages of climate change and another on those trying to move the voice of Palestinians into the global consciousness. These are two current examples of alternative communicative action resisting a dominant narrative that has held sway for a long time.

Sustainable citizenship and empowering the subaltern

As both a concept and a process, sustainable citizenship "is an idea of active citizenship with an ethical commitment to long-term holistic sustainability grounded in social justice that explicitly recognises and addresses power differentials and marginality" (Munshi & Kurian, 2015). From the point of view of critical PR, this notion of sustainable citizenship encompasess building active relationships among a variety of publics to empower those without power. At one level, such a notion stands in opposition to the discourse of what Whitman (2008, p. 178) calls "corporate citizenship" which is geared towards "supplanting broad community-based democratic participation with narrow and specialized forms of participation based on corporate values". At another level, sustainable citizenship broadens the idea of public participation to include those whose voices are muted or silenced by the high decibel levels of the carefully crafted rhetoric of powerful lobby groups.

Infusing a notion of sustainable citizenship into PR scholarship and practice is a significant challenge. The field has historically been ideologically obsessed with the idea of being a part of the "dominant coalition" (Broom & Dozier, 1986; Grunig, 1992; Grunig & Hunt, 1984). It is this obsession that has aligned public relations with elite publics, often to suppress those that stand up to corporate logic (Dutta-Bergman, 2005; Munshi & Kurian, 2005). The dominant coalition is not just a group of people with decision-making powers in organizations; it represents the neo-colonial agenda of Western market-based lobby groups. In mainstream PR, therefore, "those marginalized sectors of society who don't matter" to neo-colonial agendas "are left out of the discursive space" (Dutta & Pal, 2010, p. 214).

Following subaltern historiography offers us a way out of the clutches of mainstream PR theorizing. In the field of history, a group of South Asian scholars led by Ranajit Guha (1982) have been compiling an impressive and influential collection of historical accounts from the perspective of the "subaltern" – a term first used by Antonio Gramsci (1971) to denote groups subjected to the hegemony of the ruling classes – and to challenge the dominant histories written from the point of view of the elites. This initiative has also been successfully replicated by Latin American scholars who, as Beverley (1994, p. 271) says, have been "writing in reverse".

Our idea of sustainable citizenship revolves around a notion of democracy that resists hegemonic power. This idea calls for subaltern publics to build relationships with each other and to craft alternative narratives that can challenge structures of power wielded by dominant coalitions. As Dutta and Pal (2010) point out, it is in the "spaces of resistive practices that alternative imaginations of public relations as a field of engagement that imagines the possibilities of structural transformation…can become possible" (p. 205). Creating the space for subaltern perspectives could also open up possibilities for PR scholars to "look at the processes and practices involved in participation of marginalized subjects in countercultural movements that exist outside the realm of the very public sphere conceptualized by the civil society projects" (Dutta-Bergman, 2005, p. 286). However, to create such a space entails reframing what constitutes PR.

Scanning popular textbooks on PR (e.g., Lattimore, Baskin, Heiman, & Toth, 2011; Seitel, 2013; Wilcox, Cameron, & Reber, 2014) reveals how overwhelmingly US-centric the history of PR is. This tendency is often justified because PR is seen to flourish in the democratic political system of the US and "because the democratic model is more closely identified with the United States than with any other country" (Sharpe & Pritchard, 2004, p. 15). Such a claim is obviously spurious since the identification of democracy as being primarily residing in the US is surely propagandist – or based on ignorance at best – given the ancient and historic traditions of democracy elsewhere in the world. Keane (2009) traces the origins of democracy back to ancient Mesopotamia around 2500 BC, from where it travelled eastwards to India in about the fifth century BC (see also Muhlberger, 2012), and westwards to the city states of Byblos and Sidon and then on to Athens. If we were to *provincialize* US PR along the lines of the postcolonial scholar Dipesh Chakrabarty (2008), we could show how the inflated status accorded to a unidimensional history limits a broader understanding of PR. In his landmark book, *Provincializing Europe: Postcolonial Thought and Historical Difference*, Chakrabarty (2008) challenges the classic liberal theorists' idea that history belonged to Europe and that Europe was intellectually ahead of other regions. Chakrabarty (2008, p. 8) argues that this kind of ideological superiority is what allowed John Stuart Mill to write foundational essays which "proclaimed self-rule as the highest form of government and yet argued against giving Indians or Africans self-rule on grounds that were indeed historicist – Indians or Africans were not yet civilized enough to rule themselves." The history of the twentieth century too, "for most people in Europe and America", is "still largely defined by the two world wars and the long nuclear standoff with Soviet Communism" (Mishra, 2013, p. 8). But, as Mishra (2013, p. 8) argues, "it is now clearer that the central event of the last century for the majority of the world's population was the intellectual and political awakening of Asia and its emergence from the ruins of both Asian and European empires.

In recent years, PR historians have productively spread out to regions away from the US (see e.g., L'Etang, 2004; Sriramesh & Verčič, 2009; St John III, Lamme, & L'Etang, 2014; Watson, 2012), and there is increasing work being done in the realm of nation-building and PR (Taylor & Kent, 2006). There have also been significant advances in tracking what Edwards and Hodges (2011) call the "socio-cultural turn" in public relations, marked, for example, by work on critical perspectives on PR (L'Etang & Pieczka, 2006), postmodern and postcolonial perspectives on PR (McKie & Munshi, 2007), social theory and PR (Ihlen, van Ruler & Frederiksson, 2009), PR and social construction (Mickey, 2003), PR and democracy (Moloney, 2006), and race and PR (Edwards, 2010; Munshi & Edwards, 2011). Yet, there is still a way to go in looking at PR as resistance. Some insights into PR as resistance can be found in alternative histories of communicative action that remain largely undocumented in the West. Mishra (2013), for instance, looks at world history through the eyes of (lesser known) intellectuals, journalists and poets in the non-Western world. He implicitly points to public relations as a tool of resistance via a biographical sketch of three intellectuals of the nineteenth and twentieth centuries who lifted Asia from the "ruins of empire" by building relationships with a variety of transnational publics and spreading the message of their core ideas. The first was Jamal al-Din al-Afghani, an Iran-born activist who lobbied leaders and built networks around the world from India, Afghanistan, Egypt and Turkey to Germany, Russia and Britain – with the aim of resisting the advance of Western colonialism (see also, Keddie, 1983); Liang Qichao, a Qing-era, journalist-cum-radical reformer who used his *New Citizen* journal to spread the word of republicanism and democracy in China and beyond (see also, Levenson, 1970); and Rabindranath Tagore, an Indian poet, philosopher and anti-colonial activist with the unique distinction of writing and composing the national anthems of India and Bangladesh, and significantly influencing the composition of that of Sri Lanka as well. Rabindranath Tagore proved to have the ability to rally support for his ideas of resisting imperialism across Asia (see also, Habib, 2011). In the spirit of what we would term sustainable citizenship, all three men built and nurtured relationships across the East and the West to take their message of anti-imperialism to the world through powerful writings that straddled prose and poetry. All of them connected with subaltern publics as an act of resistance.

Two exemplars of resistance as PR

Leapfrogging into the contemporary era, we can see several ongoing struggles against dominant and hegemonic structures in the world, all of which deserve the attention of scholars interested in critical PR. In the interests of space, however, we have chosen to focus on two movements reflecting alternative models of PR imbued with a sense of sustainable citizenship. Each of these movements – one environmental and one socio-political – are led by subaltern publics and resist dominant frames. These include the attempts by local and global activists to break the stranglehold of rich and powerful governments backed by corporate interests that are endangering the future of the planet by refusing to act decisively on climate change; and the networks of solidarity for Palestinian sovereignty against the mediatized narrative of Zionism fuelled by the US PR machinery.

Combating climate change

Anthropogenic climate change is widely acknowledged as the most serious existential threat facing the planet. Unchecked, it will trigger rising sea levels and extreme weather conditions, spread disease, destroy agricultural systems, threaten the lives and livelihoods of millions of people, and render the Earth uninhabitable. Despite this stark scientific and ecological reality, an unholy squad of fossil fuel industries, mass media, conservative think-tanks primarily in the US, and a handful of contrarian scientists have come together to thwart any kind of meaningful action on climate change. The enormous wealth of the profiteers of global neoliberal capitalism who fund climate denialism, and the resulting political and economic clout they wield, has resulted in their extraordinary success in both controlling the message about climate change and paralyzing the possibilities for meaningful action by states.

The story of climate change, then, is at least in part the story of public relations as propaganda shaped by often unseen dominant actors. As L'Etang (2006) points out, "one of the major features of propaganda is that the source or sender of the message is not always identified" (p. 27; see L'Etang, 2006, for a nuanced discussion on propaganda and public relations). According to Urry (2011, p. 95), corporations have taken advantage of "public relations techniques" and set into motion processes of "building coalitions, manipulating public opinion, and lobbying politicians", often by setting up front organizations such as the Global Climate Coalition. Oreskes and Conway (2010) illustrate how some prominent scientists have even led industry-funded misinformation campaigns to "mislead the public and deny well-established scientific knowledge over four decades on issues ranging from tobacco, acid rain, the ozone hole, global warming, DDT, and now climate change". Also critical to the manufacture of doubt have been the English language news media, especially in the US, Australia and the UK, where a commitment to the principle of "balance" has translated into a practice of giving equal space and credibility to "both sides" of the issue – even when there is no scientific dispute that climate change is occurring (Boykoff & Boykoff, 2004). As Hoggan and Littlemore (2010, p. 21) point out, the media, as a measure of self-protection, "frequently fall back on the notion of balance: they interview one person on one side of an issue and one person on the other". Such a strategy, entirely reasonable on social and political issues where diverse viewpoints have potentially equal standing, is less appropriate for coverage of issues such as climate change that, although marked by contentious social, political, economic and cultural aspects, are also grounded in science – a science that has unequivocally established the reality of climate change. The authors go on to uncover memos and plans to swamp newspapers with letters and articles from "scientific sceptics", many of them the same people who have previously worked for the tobacco lobby. The seeming "debate" about climate change was in effect an "entire strategy bent on making doubt…'conventional wisdom'", funded by the fossil fuel industry, and carried out by "think tanks and junk scientists" (Hoggan & Littlemore, 2010, p. 43). As they point out, "Denier scientists were being paid well, not for doing climate research, but for practicing public relations" (p. 3).

The consequences of such cynical manipulation of public opinion have been felt on many fronts. The domination of the public sphere by the elite minority voices of the fossil fuel industry through the deployment of tools such as an often-pliant news media, and "scientists" who were prepared to sow the seeds of confusion, has led to the paralysis of global and domestic climate policy-making. Even as consensus among scientists on the human-driven climate change grew, political leaders – particularly among the greatest polluters per capita, including the US, Canada, Australia and New Zealand – walked away from their commitments to reduce greenhouse gas emissions as part of the Kyoto Protocol. Domestically, countries such as New Zealand witnessed a concerted and extraordinarily successful effort by lobby groups representing the farming sector, as well as industry, to thwart attempts at regulating greenhouse gas (GHG) emissions even when the government made a serious effort to address climate change (Barry & King-Jones, 2014).

It is in the face of such political paralysis, and in the toxic commitment to continued destructive economic policies and practices, that we find a powerful new voice in the form of the diversely constituted global justice movement. The climate justice movement is growing in leaps and bounds, and now comprises thousands of local, regional, national and global organizations. It "has the potential to influence future negotiating outcomes by arming developing countries with concrete proposals, 'shaming' wealthy, industrialized countries (i.e. moral suasion) into taking more aggressive action, and subjecting alternative policy proposals to public scrutiny" (Roberts & Parks, 2009, p. 396).

The movement straddles both the First and Third Worlds. It combines the work of environmental, human rights and developmental non-governmental organizations such as 350.org started by author Bill McKibben; Generation Zero, a New Zealand youth-led climate change organization; Avaaz, the global activist group; the Third World Network and Focus on the Global South; alongside climate change workshops run by the likes of Al Gore and other forms of localized activism such as awareness-raising work in the Pacific Islands and Maldives – among the most vulnerable areas to climate change. The involvement of people such as McKibben, scientist James Hansen, Jeanette Fitzsimons (former leader of the Green Party of New Zealand) and Sunita Narain, the influential director of the Centre for Science and Environment in Delhi, have given climate change activism some much-needed heft. Another feature of the climate justice movement has been the involvement of young people in sharply questioning the priorities and agendas of the establishment. The huge scale of the mass protests against governmental inaction over climate change – which on 21 September 2014 involved more than 600,000 people across 2,500 locations around the world (United Nations Framework Convention on Climate Change Newsroom, 2014), and the coverage given to the Rockefeller family's withdrawal of funds from fossil fuel investments (Goldenberg, 2014), for example – are all signs of an alternative public relations movement that is beginning to counter the hegemonic influence of elite lobby groups funded by powerful business interests.

Many of those who champion the cause of addressing climate change argue for a public relations based on "truth", not falsehood; of commitment to the public good, including the well-being of the most marginalized; and one that is principled, not manipulative (Hoggan & Littlemore, 2010). How successful such marginalized discourses will be in successfully bringing about change remains to be seen.

Claiming an other history in the Middle East

The story of the Middle East (or more accurately West Asia) is dominated by the conflict in Israel-Palestine. The rival claims to the Holy Land notwithstanding, the state of Israel was created on the platform of a strategically planned and executed public relations campaign by Zionist activists. In their insightful work, Toledano and McKie (2013) outline how Zionists achieved their objective "to persuade world public opinion to support Zionist goals" and "to raise resources for the implementation of the Zionist ideology and political plan" (p. 42). In keeping with the hierarchies of mainstream PR, the Zionist public relations machinery strategically neglected the major public of the Arab population living in Ottoman Palestine – a strategy that "Israeli leaders still believe in" (p. 44). It is hardly surprising, therefore, that Israel has been relentlessly occupying more and more of the UN-mandated Palestinian land through unauthorized settlements in the West Bank, the cornering of the bulk of resources (including water), erecting walls to separate the people, blockading the Gaza strip, and inflicting disproportionate aggression against Palestinians in the name of security (Fisk, 2005; Peled, 2013; Said, 2003; Veracini, 2006) The most influential sponsor of this ongoing PR offensive has been the US, which has consistently provided financial and military aid to Israel and has steadfastly blocked UN resolutions against the state (Chomsky, 2010; Mearsheimer & Walt, 2007). Mearsheimer and Walt (2007) describe in detail the PR strategies used by the "Israel lobby" in the US, a group whose "political power is important not because it affects what presidential candidates say during a campaign but because it has a significant influence on American foreign policy" (pp. 5–6). According to Mearsheimer and Walt (2007, p. 9), "it is difficult to talk about the lobby's influence on American foreign policy", or indeed on shaping a dominant pro-Israel narrative "without being accused of anti-Semitism or labeled a self-hating Jew". The latter labelling is particularly pervasive as some of the leading critics of the state are either Israeli or Jewish. The prominent feminist scholar Judith Butler (2012, para. 4), who is both Jewish and critical of Israel's policies, says:

> For me, given the history from which I emerge, it is most important as a Jew to speak out against injustice and to struggle against all forms of racism. This does not make me into a self-hating Jew. It makes me someone who wishes to affirm a Judaism that is not identified with state violence, and that is identified with a broad-based struggle for social justice.

The Holocaust and the genocide of the Jews by Nazi Germany remains one of the most horrific examples of human brutality ever, and the vulnerability felt by the Jewish population to threats to its security and identity are well documented. But public relations, from a human rights point of view, needs to spread the message of learning from the traumatic history of the Holocaust to ensure that vulnerable populations *anywhere* in the world are protected. Such PR would need to resist the position of dominant forces. One act of resistance is to challenge the label of anti-Semitism levelled against any attempt to criticize Israel (Butler, 2003). Indeed, this kind of labelling is an example of what the postcolonial communication scholar Mohan Dutta (2014) calls "communicative inversions" which deploy "the rhetoric of open communication to accomplish objectives that in reality reflect closed communication". To open up the debate, there is a need for a narrative of resistance, something that peace activist Miko Peled (2013), son of a former Israeli general and a Zionist, builds so eloquently in *The General's Son: Journey of an Israeli in Palestine*: "Mine is the tale of an Israeli boy, a Zionist, who realized that his side of the story was not the only side" (p. 4). The other side of the story, according to Peled, has not been adequately told. In a blog post, Peled (n.d., para. 3) describes his homeland as one where

> half the population is governed by a radical Zionist regime that sees the struggle for control over the land as a zero sum game, and the other half of the population is governed by the security forces of this Zionist regime; one nation ruling over another while controlling the land and its resources.

The Palestinians have not had the gift of a successful PR campaign to get their side of the story out. Yet the links between grassroots activists, Jewish Israeli champions of the Palestinian cause, and human rights groups in different parts of the world are beginning to slowly but steadily make a visible imprint of their version of history and their narratives of persecution. This, to our minds, is the kind of public relations as sustainable citizenship that we envision. Although the US government remains a strong ally of Israel, and although the governments in Europe are wary of openly challenging Israel – especially in the light of the tragedy of the Holocaust – public opinion is now more accepting of the Palestinian narrative than before.

An example of public relations as resistance has been the growing influence of the Boycott, Divestment and Sanctions (BDS) global movement, which campaigns for an economic and cultural boycott of institutions and businesses complicit in the Israeli occupation of Palestinian land (Barghouti, 2011; Bullimore, 2012). The movement was "initiated by Palestinian civil society in 2005, and is coordinated by the Palestinian BDS National Committee (BNC), established in 2007. BDS is a strategy that allows people of conscience to play an effective role in the Palestinian struggle for justice" (BDS Movement, n.d.). The BDS Movement has three primary demands, which require that Israel: (1) should end "its occupation and colonization of all Arab lands occupied in June 1967" and dismantle the illegal wall; (2) recognize the "fundamental rights of the Arab-Palestinian citizens of Israel to full equality", and; (3) uphold the rights of "Palestinian refugees to return to their homes and properties as stipulated in UN Resolution 194" (BDS Movement, n.d.).

In writing about Barghouti's (2011) book on the BDS, Nobel laureate and South African peace activist, Archbishop Desmond Tutu (2011) says:

> I have been to Palestine where I've witnessed the racially segregated housing and the humiliation of Palestinians at military roadblocks. I can't help but remember the conditions we experienced in South Africa under apartheid. We could not have achieved our freedom without the help of people around the world using the nonviolent means of boycotts and divestment to compel governments and institutions to withdraw their support for the apartheid regime.

The endorsement of Tutu and several other influential peace leaders has galvanized an alternative public relations campaign which has led to networks of BDS proponents that "are diverse, multicultural, and concerned with a variety of social justice issues" (Hallward, 2013, p. 34). This campaign has a long way to go yet, but is pushing against the far more entrenched Zionist narrative. It thus succeeds in reaching out to a global citizenry, educating many about the brutal realities of Palestinians while providing an avenue to express solidarity with them. Munnayer (2014), for example, points out that the BDS "is actually shifting attention *toward* the Palestinian plight. It is doing so before new audiences, and in ways and places that were not imagined a mere five years ago." Similarly, student-led initiatives, such as Students for Justice in Palestine, which has a presence especially in the universities of the US and Canada, and Students for Justice in the Middle East in New Zealand, are examples of local initiatives for education and awareness-raising about the situation in Palestine, while also promoting the BDS Movement.

Perhaps the most recent expression of the challenge to the dominant Zionist discourse has been the protests by academic staff and students in the US against the decision by the University of Illinois Urbana-Champaign to revoke the appointment of Professor Steven Salaita, a Palestinian American, after he had accepted a tenured position there. The decision by the university, widely alleged to have been triggered by pressures from major funders, was based on his criticisms of Israel's bombardment of Gaza in July–August 2014 (Guarino, 2014; Abunimah, 2014). The case has not only caused an uproar in the US over what is seen as a blatant attack on academic freedom, it has also provoked more than 2,700 scholars to sign up to an academic boycott of the university (Robin, 2014).

Conclusion

The movement to counter the long-established public relations strategies of the pro-Israel lobby, especially in the US, and the one to get states to act decisively and quickly against the ravages of climate change in the face of firmly entrenched narratives of fossil fuel-driven lifestyles, serve as exemplars of a kind of critical public relations that challenge and disrupt traditional, hegemonic discourses of public relations. By engaging with publics in a non-hierarchical manner, such alternative models of public relations can live up to the idea of sustainable citizenship – which strives for equality through an active resistance of dominant narratives.

References

Abunimah, A. (2014) Univ. of Illinois admits pre-emptive firing of Israel critic Steven Salaita. Electronic Intifada. Retrieved on 23 April 2015 from http://electronicintifada.net/blogs/ali-abunimah/univ-illinois-admits-pre-emptive-firing-israel-critic-steven-salaita

Agarwal, A., & Narain, S. (1991) *Global warming in an unequal world: A case of environmental colonialism.* New Delhi, India: Centre for Science and Environment.

Barghouti, O. (2011). *Boycott, divestment, sanctions: The global struggle for Palestinian rights.* Chicago, IL: Haymarket Books.

Barry, A., & King-Jones, A. (2014). *Hot air* [DVD]. Wellington, New Zealand.

BDS Movement. (n.d.). An introduction to BDS. Retrieved on 23 April 2015 from http://www.bdsmovement.net/bdsintro

Beverley, J. (1994). Writing in reverse: On the project of the Latin American subaltern studies group. *Disposition,* XIX(46), pp. 271–88.

Boykoff, M. T., & Boykoff, J. M. (2004). Balance as bias: Global warming and the US prestige press. *Global Environmental Change,* 14, pp. 125–36.

Broom, G. M., & Dozier, D. M. (1986). Advancement for public relations role models. *Public Relations Review,* 12, pp. 37–56.

Bullimore, K. (2012). BDS and the struggle for a free Palestine. In A. Lowenstein, & J. Sparrow (Eds), *Left turn: Political essays for the new left,* pp. 196–210. Melbourne, Australia: Melbourne University Press.

Butler, J. (2003). No, it's not anti-semitic. *London Review of Books,* 25(16), pp. 19–21.

Butler, J. (2012). Judith Butler responds to attack: "I affirm a Judaism that is not associated with state violence". The war of ideas in the Middle East, Mondoweiss, 27 August. Retrieved on 23 April 2015 from http://mondoweiss.net/2012/08/judith-butler-responds-to-attack-i-affirm-a-judaism-that-is-not-associated-with-state-violence

Chakrabarty, D. (2008). *Provincializing Europe: Postcolonial thought and historical difference.* Princeton, NJ: Princeton University Press.

Chomsky, N. (2010). The real reasons the U.S. enables Israeli crimes and atrocities. Interview with Kathleen Wells in Race-Talk, AlterNet, 16 August. Retrieved on 23 April 2014 from http://www.alternet.org/story/147865/noam_chomsky%3A_the_real_reasons_the_u.s._enables_israeli_crimes_and_atrocities

Dutta, M. (2014). (In)Civility and Phyllis Wise: When claims to academic freedom ring hollow. Culture-centred approach blog, 24 August. Retrieved on 23 April 2015 from http://culture-centered.blogspot.co.nz/2014/08/pincivility-and-phyllis-wise-when.html

Dutta, M., & Pal, M. (2010). Public relations and marginalization in a global context: A postcolonial critique. In N. Bardhan, & C. K. Weaver (Eds), *Public relations in global cultural contexts: Multiparadigmatic perspectives,* pp. 195–225. New York, NY: Routledge.

Dutta-Bergman, M. (2005). Civil society and public relations: Not so civil after all. *Journal of Public Relations Research,* 17(3), pp. 267–89.

Edwards, L. (2010). "Race" in public relations. In R. L. Heath (Ed.), *The SAGE handbook of public relations,* pp. 205–21. Thousand Oaks, CA: Sage.

Edwards, L. (2011). Critical perspectives in global public relations: Theorizing power. In N. Bardhan, & C. K. Weaver (Eds), *Public relations in global cultural contexts,* pp. 29–49. New York, NY: Routledge.

Edwards, L., & Hodges, C. (2011). Introduction: Implications of a (radical) socio-cultural "turn" in public relations scholarship. In L. Edwards, & C. Hodges (Eds), *Public relations, society and culture: Theoretical and empirical explorations,* pp. 1–14. New York, NY: Routledge.

Fisk, R. (2005). *The great war of civilization: The conquest of the Middle East.* New York, NY: Harper Collins.

Food and Agriculture Organization. (2014) Agriculture's greenhouse gas emissions on the rise. 11 April. Retrieved on 23 April 2015 from http://www.fao.org/news/story/en/item/216137/icode/

Goldenberg, S. (2014). Heirs to Rockefeller oil fortune divest from fossil fuels over climate change. The *Guardian.* 22 September. Rerieved on 23 April from http://www.theguardian.com/environment/2014/sep/22/rockefeller-heirs-divest-fossil-fuels-climate-change

Gramsci, A. (1971). *Selections from the prison notebooks*. New York, NY: International Publishers.

Grunig, J. (Ed.) (1992). *Excellence in public relations and communication management*. Hillsdale, NJ: Lawrence Erlbaum.

Grunig, J., & Hunt, T. (1984). *Managing public relations*. New York, NY: Holt, Rinehart and Winston.

Guarino, M. (2014). Professor fired for Israel criticism urges University of Illinois to reinstate him. The *Guardian*. 9 September. Retrieved on 23 April 2015 from http://www.theguardian.com/education/2014/sep/09/professor-israel-criticism-twitter-university-illinois

Guha, R. (1982). *Subaltern Studies I*. Delhi, India: Oxford University Press.

Habib, (H. (2011). Celebrating Rabindranath Tagore's legacy. *The Hindu*, 17 May. Retrieved on 24 April from http://www.thehindu.com/opinion/lead/celebrating-rabindranath-tagores-legacy/article2026880.ece

Hallward, M.C. (2013). *Transnational activism and the Israeli-Palestinian conflict*. New York, NY: Palgrave Macmillan.

Hoggan, J., & Littlemore, R. (2010). *Climate cover-up: The crusade to deny global warming*. Berkeley, CA: Greystone Books.

Holtzhausen, D. R. (2002). Towards a postmodern research agenda for public relations. *Public Relations Review*, 28, pp. 251–64.

Ihlen, O., van Ruler, B., & Frederiksson, M. (Eds) (2009). *Public relations and social theory*. New York, NY: Routledge.

Keane, J. (2009). *Life and death of democracy*. London, UK: Simon & Schuster.

Keddie, N. R. (1983). *An Islamic response to imperialism*. Berkley, CA: University of California Press.

Kurian, P., Munshi, D., & Bartlett, R.V. (2014). Sustainable citizenship for a technological world: Negotiating deliberative dialectics, *Citizenship Studies*, 18(3–4), pp. 393–409.

Lattimore, D., Baskin, O., Heiman, S., & Toth, E. (2011). *Public relations: The profession and the practice*, 4th edition. Boston, MA: McGraw Hill.

L'Etang, J. (2004). *Public relations in Britain: A history of professional practice in the 20th century*. Mahwah, NJ: Lawrence Erlbaum Associates.

L'Etang, J. (2006). Public relations and propaganda: Conceptual issues, methodological problems, and public relations discourse. In J. L'Etang, & M. Pieczka (Eds), *Public relations: Critical debates and contemporary practice*, pp. 23–40. Mahwah, NJ: Lawrence Erlbaum Associates.

L'Etang, J., & Pieczka, M. (Eds.) (2006). *Public relations: Critical debates and contemporary practice*. Mahwah, NJ: Lawrence Erlbaum Associates.

Levenson, J. (1970). *Liang Ch'i-Ch'ao and the mind of modern China*. Los Angeles, CA: University of California Press.

McKie, D., & Munshi, D. (2007). *Reconfiguring public relations: Ecology, equity and enterprise*. London, UK: Routledge.

Mearsheimer, J. J., & Walt, S. M. (2007). *The Israel lobby and U.S. foreign policy*. New York, NY: Farrar, Strauss, and Giroux.

Mickey, T. J. (2003). *Deconstructing public relations: Public relations criticism*. Mahwah, NJ: Lawrence Erlbaum.

Mishra, P. (2013). *From the ruins of empire: The revolt against the West and the remaking of Asia*. London, UK: Allen Lane.

Moloney, K. (2006). *Rethinking public relations: propaganda and democracy*. London, UK: Routledge.

Muhlberger, S. (2012). Ancient India. In B. Isakhan, & S. Stockwell (Eds), *The Edinburgh companion to the history of democracy*, pp. 50–9. Edinburgh, UK: Edinburgh University Press.

Munnayer, Y. (2014). How BDS is educating the public about Israel's brutal policies. *The Nation*. 10 July. Retrieved on 23 April 2015 from http://www.thenation.com/article/180590/responses-noam-chomsky-israel-palestine-and-bds

Munshi, D., & Edwards, L. (2011). Understanding "race" in/and public relations: Where do we start and where should we go? *Journal of Public Relations Research*, 23(4), pp. 349–67.

Munshi, D., & Kurian, P. (2005). Imperializing spin cycles: A postcolonial look at public relations, greenwashing, and the separation of publics. *Public Relations Review*, 31(4), pp. 513–20.

Munshi, D., & Kurian, P. (2007). The case of the subaltern public: A postcolonial investigation of CSR's (o) missions. In S. May, G. Cheney, & J. Roper (Eds), *The debate over corporate social responsibility*, pp. 438–47, New York, NY: Oxford University Press.

Munshi, D., & Kurian, P. (2015). Imagining organizational communication as sustainable citizenship. *Management Communication Quarterly*, 29(1), pp. 153–9.

Munshi, D., Kurian, P., Foran, J., & Bhavnani, K-K. (2014). Making just climate futures: A proposal to the Rockefeller Foundation. Retrieved on 23 April 2015 from https://sites.google.com/a/waikato.ac.nz/climate-futures/links

Oreskes, N., & Conway, E. (2010). *Merchants of doubt*. New York, NY: Bloomsbury Press.

Peled, M. (2013). *The general's son: Journey of an Israeli in Palestine*. Charlottesville,VA: Just World Books.

Peled, M. (n.d). Tear down the wall. Miko Peled's blog. Retrieved on 23 April from http://mikopeled.com/

Roberts, J. T., & Parks, B. (2009). Ecologically unequal exchange, ecological debt, and climate justice: The history and implications of three related ideas for a new social movement. *International Journal of Comparative Sociology*, 50(3–4), pp. 385–409.

Robin, C. (2014). 2700 scholars boycott UI. 21 August. Retrieved on 23 April 2015 from http://coreyrobin.com/2014/08/21/2700-scholars-boycott-ui-philosopher-cancels-prestigious-lecture-salaita-deemed-excellent-teacher-and-ui-trustees-meet-again/

Said, E. (2003). *Culture and resistance: Conversations with Edward Said* (David Barsamian, Ed.). Boston, MA: South End Press.

Seitel, F. (2013). *The practice of public relations*, 12th edition. Upper Saddle River, NJ: Prentice Hall.

Sharpe, M., & Pritchard, B. (2004). The historical empowerment of public opinion and its relationship to the emergence of public relations as a profession. In D. Tilson, & E. Alozie (Eds), *Toward the common good: Perspectives in international public relations*, pp. 13–36. Boston, MA: Pearson Education.

Sriramesh, K., & Verčič, D. (Eds) (2009). *The global public relations handbook: Theory, research and practice*. New York, NY: Routledge.

St John III, B., Lamme, M. O., & L'Etang, J. (Eds) (2014). *Pathways to public relations: Histories of practice and profession*. London, UK: Routledge.

Taylor, M., & Kent, M. (2006). Public relations theory and practice in nation building. In C. Botan, & V. Hazleton (Eds), *Public relations theory II*, pp. 299–315. Mahwah, NJ: Lawrence Erlbaum.

Toledano, M., & McKie, D. (2013). *Public relations and nation building: Influencing Israel*. London, UK: Routledge.

Tutu, D. (2011). Review of Barghouti, O. (2011). *Boycott, divestment, sanctions: The global struggle for Palestinian rights*. Chicago, IL: Haymarket Books. Publisher's webpage, http://www.haymarketbooks.org/pb/boycott-divestment-sanctions

United Nations Framework Convention on Climate Change Newsroom. (2014). 600,000 people march for climate action. 22 September. Retrieved on 23 April 2015 from http://newsroom.unfccc.int/unfccc-newsroom/600-000-people-march-for-climate-action/

Urry, J. (2011). *Climate change & society*. Cambridge, UK: Polity Press.

Veracini, L. (2006). *Israel and settler society*. London, UK: Pluto Press.

Watson, T. (2012). Editor's introduction: Bournemouth University's 2011 history conference. *Public Relations Review*, 38(3), pp. 339–40.

Whitman, D. (2008). "Stakeholders" and the politics of environmental policymaking. In J. Park, K. Conca, & M. Finger (Eds), *The crisis of global environmental governance: Towards a new political economy of sustainability*, pp. 163–92. New York, NY: Routledge.

Wilcox, D. L., Cameron, G. T., & Reber, B. H. (2014). *Public relations: Strategies and tactics*, 11th edition. Boston, MA: Pearson Education.

Index